THE OXFORD
LITERARY HISTORY
OF AUSTRALIA

THE OXFORD
LITERARY HISTORY
OF AUSTRALIA

Editors: Bruce Bennett and Jennifer Strauss
Associate Editor: Chris Wallace-Crabbe

Melbourne
OXFORD UNIVERSITY PRESS
Oxford   Auckland   New York

OXFORD UNIVERSITY PRESS AUSTRALIA

Oxford   New York
Athens   Auckland   Bangkok   Bogota
Bombay   Buenos Aires   Calcutta
Cape Town   Dar es Salaam   Delhi
Florence   Hong Kong   Istanbul   Karachi
Kuala Lumpur   Madras   Madrid   Melbourne
Mexico City   Nairobi   Paris   Port Moresby
Singapore   Taipei   Tokyo   Toronto   Warsaw

and associated companies in
Berlin   Ibadan

OXFORD is a trade mark of Oxford University Press

© Bruce Bennett, Jennifer Strauss and Chris Wallace-Crabbe
1998
First published 1998
Authors retain copyright for their contributions to this volume

National Library of Australia
Cataloguing-in-Publication data:

The Oxford literary history of Australia.

   Bibliography.
   Includes index.
   ISBN 0 19 553737 8.

   1. Australian literature—History and criticism.
   I. Bennett, Bruce, 1941–.   II. Strauss, Jennifer, 1933–.
   III. Wallace-Crabbe, Chris, 1934–.   IV. Title: Literary
   history of Australia.

A820.9

Text design by Steve Randles
Cover design by Steve Randles
Typeset by Syarikat Seng Teik Sdn. Bhd., Malaysia
Printed by Kyodo Printing Co. Pty Ltd, Singapore
Published by Oxford University Press,
253 Normanby Road, South Melbourne, Australia

CONTENTS

ACKNOWLEDGMENTS

The editors wish to thank their respective university institutions, where much of the research and editing for this book occurred: University College, University of New South Wales at the Australian Defence Force Academy in Canberra and Monash University in Melbourne. On behalf of ourselves and our contributors, we wish to acknowledge the resources made available, in many parts of Australia, by that threatened species, the library; and Australian Research Council grants greatly facilitated the research efforts which went into this book. We also wish to thank research assistants, Susan Cowan (Australian Defence Force Academy) and Kate Chadwick (Monash University). With Associate Editor, Chris Wallace-Crabbe, we have reason to express sincere gratitude to Peter Rose at Oxford University Press, who has been a source of encouragement and sensible advice throughout. As editors and writers for this book we wish to acknowledge also the hard work of our fellow contributors in what has been a learning experience for all of us.

MAKING LITERARY HISTORY

An Introduction

When Australian athletes at an Olympic Games triumph in one way or another, many commentators automatically proclaim that they are 'making history'. Literary success is sometimes assumed to be similar: prizes are awarded, for example, to books in national or international competitions. Their authors might expect to 'make history', though only some will be chosen for this purpose. This analogy between sporting and literary achievements might be extended a little further. Both are dependent on widespread notions of the 'nation' as a primary context and framework of significance. 'Representing the nation', and enhancing its reputation in the international arena, are seen to be crucial. The analogy also draws attention to aspects of a late twentieth-century preoccupation in Australia (as in many other countries) with competition, success, and rewards.

Although this book gives significant attention to our literary 'champions', it is not principally about winners and losers. (We are reminded of Henry Handel Richardson's remark that Australian literature was dominated by tales of successful adventure, but that she found greater literary interest in the stories of 'the failures, to whose lot neither fortunes nor stirring adventures fell'.) This *History* shows that literary fortunes, like others, wax and wane, both during and after a writer's lifetime. Our interest in the generally recognised 'major' works of writers therefore includes both their artistic qualities and the genesis of these achievements in the lives, social institutions and geography which have shaped them. Because of the existence of *The Oxford Companion to Australian Literature* (2nd ed, 1994), we have not attempted to give a comprehensive coverage of individual writers and their works. Nor do individual major writers or texts engage all our attention; we have sometimes discussed groups and constellations of writers, or texts, which can be seen to comprise literary movements, or tendencies (towards, say, modernism, or a preoccupation with gender issues, or national or regional concerns). Limited as we have been by the constraints of space in this single-volume *History*, we have tried to show that literary history is not restricted to a formalist analysis of individual texts but that it grows from, and contributes to, a network of social and political conditions, local and international.

No history of this kind springs entirely newborn. By the latter decades of the twentieth century, a relatively sophisticated literary culture had developed in Australia, thanks in part to a widespread recognition since the 1970s of the value of Australian literature and its subsequent inclusion in many school and university curricula. The literary histories of H.M. Green, Cecil Hadgraft, Geoffrey Dutton, G.A. Wilkes, Leonie Kramer, Ken Goodwin, Laurie Hergenhan, and Bob Hodge and Vijay Mishra, together with other research and publications in the field, have provided frameworks and a background of references for the work presented here. (Bibliographical details of these and other major reference works are given in the Guide to Reference Material.) With these and other resources at our disposal, we have attempted to re-examine the field of Australian literature and culture, as we see it at the close of the twentieth century.

Australia is not alone in its need for reference works of this kind, which 'place' literary texts in the context of a nation's history. The histories of Indian literature in English by Meenakshi Mukherjee, or of Canadian literature by W.H. New, provide examples from other countries, as does Sacvan Bercovitch's massive project of an eight-volume *Cambridge History of American Literature*. Although restricted to a single volume ourselves, we have tried, by choosing expert researchers and writers from many parts of Australia, to avoid the charge laid against an early history of American literature, that it was narrowly conceived and should therefore have been called *A Literary History of Harvard University, with Incidental Glimpses of the Minor Writers*. The sixteen contributors to this *History* work at ten universities in different parts of Australia and come from a wide variety of educational backgrounds and international experience. Most pertinently, they are all scholars of distinction in the broad field of Australian literary and cultural studies.

A literary history can be expected to take 'literature' as its principal focus. But what is this beast, with its sometimes magnified capital L status? The term has broadened and multiplied its usages in the Australian context, as it has elsewhere in the English-speaking world. The critical and theoretical lenses have changed. A shift can be observed from a *belles-lettres* tradition in which written works were valued chiefly for their beauty of language, and their emotional effects or uplifting moral sentiments, through New Critical engagement with autonomous linguistic structures, to more recent conventions which value literature mainly for the ideas, images or stories it contributes to a wider set of political conversations, or discourses. In this process, aesthetic concerns ('beauty', 'taste', etc.) have given way to issues, themes or ideology. The once firm distinctions between 'high' and 'low' cultures and their corresponding literatures have been interrogated and the constructedness of canons has been exposed. From talk-back radio to school lessons and even university research, literature in the 1980s and 1990s has been treated often as a source of themes and issues which bear on matters of urgent contemporary relevance. If this book reveals some of these tendencies, it might therefore be seen, historically, as a partial response to the 'nervous nineties' during which it was conceived and produced. But commentary and analysis will also be found which resist this tendency by drawing attention to the fact that literary texts are never simply 'given'—that artistic and shaping qualities have gone into their making, which can and should be appreciated. Where there is history, there is also human agency, and the writers of this book have been encouraged, in a spirit of pluralism, to develop their own perspectives on the material under discussion.

The period during which this *History* was thought about, planned and written (1995–97) seemed to offer a pause, after apparently contrary tendencies in the 1980s towards a democratised notion of literature as merely any 'writing' or 'discourse', and those post-structuralist theories which encouraged philosophical speculation and seemed to push literary study towards forms of esotericism. This pause may have enabled us to survey the field of the literary with a relatively open view, using where appropriate the perspectives of contemporary theory. What we found in that field, and our authors have brought into this literary history of Australia, included a variety of texts ranging from letters, diaries, reports, petitions, journals and essays to the more traditionally recognised genres of the novel, short story, poem and play. We have tried to keep a kind of running watch on the major genres in every period. At a time when oral language usage was strenuously investigated, and its value emphasised, it was appropriate that this study should also take within its purview of the literary such seemingly paradoxical forms as 'Aboriginal oral literature' and other performative uses of language in film, video and drama. Nor have we shrunk from discussion of the social institutions and market forces within which a 'literature industry' has been seen to emerge.

If 'literature' has been a contentious term for us, so has 'history'. History may be thought of most broadly as a narrative of past events. Given this, readers may be surprised to find that our story in this volume offers no firm date of commencement. Instead, Adam Shoemaker's opening chapter shows how problematic are notions of 'a beginning' in relation to an 'Aboriginal Australia' tens of thousands of years before either of those words were used or their modern meanings imagined. We would like our first chapter, in the words of its author, to 'cycle backwards into the past and forwards into the future'. Authors of other chapters in the book, while principally focusing on the literary activity of a particular time period, also exercise the freedom to use flashbacks or flash-forwards to indicate continuities or differences across time. And we have used sub-headings within chapters to indicate shifts of focus. As a whole, however, the book is designed to provide reference points to Australian literature in a roughly chronological order, and this framework is buttressed by an annals-like Chronology, which is presented after the main text and which invites readers to link literary activity and achievement to a context of Australian or world events.

In the construction of our sections and chapters in this book, we located a number of major turning points, or crises, in the general history of Australia, which have impacted on literature as on other aspects of the personal and social lives of Australians.

These moments of trauma and change include the settlement, or invasion, of this country marked by the landing of Governor Phillip at Sydney Cove in 1788; the beginning of the gold rushes in 1851; the beginning of the First World War in 1914; the Second World War in 1939; and Australia's involvement in the Vietnam War from 1965. What these moments have in common is that they are all international events with enormous consequences for Australians' views of themselves; and they provide convenient apertures through which others may view Australian culture. While European settlement had great and traumatic consequences for black Australians, the discovery of gold led to large-scale white (and Chinese) immigration to Australia, and a reassessment of concepts like 'luck', 'favour' and the 'fortunes' of individuals. The First and Second World Wars, on the other hand, required many Australians to leave their country for foreign theatres of war which, in turn, became 'Australianised' for those on the home front in the pages of newspaper reports, journals, and books. More recently, the trauma of the Vietnam War became a rallying point for counter-cultural, anti-authoritarian forces in Australian society, which sometimes unwittingly imitated American protests.

We do not wish to suggest that the crises mentioned above were the only events of major significance in Australian history, but rather that each of them had immediate and long-term influences on Australians' thinking and writing about themselves; and at each of these points Australians asked themselves difficult questions about hope and despair, power and marginality, love and death. The human imagination works in mysterious ways, however, and it would be a mistake to seek unique intensity only at these, or other points of historical trauma. As this *History* recurrently shows, artistic expression often ripens gradually in the memory. Thus a novel about the gold rushes, the First World War or Vietnam, for example, may not appear until twenty, or thirty, years after the event; and there are some notable examples of historical novels, poems or stories being written fifty, or even one hundred, years after the events they depict. With its long gestation, and its sometimes gradual impact on a society, literature can, in its way, both make history and outlast it. Our usual approach in this *History* is to locate a literary text in the period of its composition and publication, and in relation to other writings by the same author. In this way we build a cumulative picture of literary creativity and concerns at different points on the historical map.

How 'Australian' is the literary history of Australia? The literary representations of this country by its writers are discussed frequently in this 'national story', which has its moments of awe, indifference, delight, and, occasionally, fervour. Images of the country range from those of an Aboriginal Dreaming to pre-discovery European imaginings of *Terra Australis Incognita*; from the paradisiacal to purgatorial experiences recorded by early settlers; from the sense of a 'white Australia' to the more recent notion of Australia as 'part of Asia'. We have been concerned not to present these 'Australias' as determined by historical circumstances but as written by human agents who are inevitably affected by the geography and history of their circumstances. The creative spirit is alive and well in these renditions of Australia, whether they are presented in a spirit of reconstruction or deconstruction; and it operates at times well beyond the confines of the 'national'.

Technological advances in transport and communications systems have led to such increases in actual and virtual travel that Marshall McLuhan's talk in the 1960s of a 'global village' now seems a mere preview to our 'postmodern' age. One paradoxical effect of these changes, however, has been to increase interest in the local and particular, demonstrated in contemporary Australian culture by regional literary anthologies and 'national' films and plays. At a social and political level, the High Court's Mabo decision in 1992 has revived interest in notions of belonging to, or owning, the land. This *History* reveals, at many points, a complex and shifting interplay between local, national and international concerns in the lives of writers and in their literary works.

In this *Literary History of Australia* we hope to provide a springboard to knowledge and appreciation of the literature of a nation. The development of a shared memory among Australians of the way our writers have thought and felt will increase a national sense of community; and it also has the potential to increase our capacity to think and imagine ourselves into new situations. Readers in other countries may discover an enhanced, comparative appreciation of literature and history. For it is clear that an in-depth understanding of global culture depends on a comparative understanding of the literature of many nations, including Australia. This *History* is designed to provide a readable and enjoyable entry into the creative spirit of Australia, expressed through the skill and vision of its writers.

BRUCE BENNETT AND JENNIFER STRAUSS
CANBERRA AND MELBOURNE, 1998

PART ONE

TO 1850

I

WHITE ON BLACK/BLACK ON BLACK

Adam Shoemaker

'A BEGINNING . . .'

The historical dates which constitute what is known as 'chronological time' have often been used to imprison Australia's indigenous people. Terms such as 'prehistory' and 'pre-literacy' carry with them the strongest possible sense of a time before—and a time after. Of course, these dividing lines have been imposed retrospectively upon Black Australians by those who are not members of that culture. Such arbitrary demarcations also imply that the past begins when it is recorded in legible script, not when human beings began to commit stories to memory.

What cannot be ignored is the fact that scores of Aboriginal verbal artists have told and re-told tales which defy datable chronology. Indigenous Australian storytellers lay down tracks in their narratives: tracks which are typically circular; which journey for-wards and backwards; which involve transformations, metamorphoses, changes. Above all, these are stories in which journeys take place, in which journeys themselves *are* the story.

This chapter begins a different narrative: the genesis of Black Australian writing in English. In some ways, the end-point defines the process: the presence of oral narratives on tape and in print leads us back from the present to the past. As Marjorie Bil Bil puts it in her 1995 collection of narratives and poems:

> Art is learnt by telling stories . . .
> It just lies there from the beginning.[1]

But this search for 'the beginning' can also become obsessive; it can become a tyrannical quest for 'the earliest poem' or 'the first letter in English'. What I want to propose in this chapter, and in its companion later in this volume, is that such a process is ultimately self-defeating and fruitless. It is less important to be able to date with precision the first writing by a Black Australian than to explore the signposts of *all* indigenous Australian literature, and our appreciation of Aboriginal verbal art will constantly expand as our exposure to it increases: what does it still say about contemporary Australia? What can we learn from it about the land called the 'Island Continent'? How does this writing cycle backwards into the past and forwards into the future—teaching, warning, entertaining and inspiring the reader?

In this sense, I am assuming that the search for points of inception will always be partial and incomplete and—as in the case of indigenous rock art—our sense of what constitutes 'beginnings' will continually change. Above all, it depends upon what we are searching for in the first place. Are we seeking, as Penny van Toorn has recently termed it, 'Literature–with–a–capital–L';[2] that is, examples of poetry, drama and verse? Or is the definition far broader? Can we consider Black Australian writings to encompass any meaningful inscriptions: petitions (in any medium), diaries, letters, song lyrics, transcribed oral narratives, message sticks, sermons, carvings, rock art, body markings, drawings, speeches, articles and submissions?

While it is far more challenging to adopt this eclectic definition, I believe it is the only one which begins to do justice to the complexity of Australian indigenous cultures. As Stephen Muecke has proposed, once literature becomes 'iterature' (literally *de*capitalised as 'a minor version of the majority term . . . in a language which shakes the edifice of Correct Standard English words and sentences') our understanding of Black Australian culture's innovativeness, flexibility and resistance expands dramatically.[3]

This chapter embarks on a journey to discover Aboriginal writing in the largest possible sense. No brief essay can cover all aspects of indigenous literature in depth, but it can signal the richness of such work and the value of seeing it from plural perspectives. Of course, even the choice of the term 'literature' implies the adoption of certain theoretical perspectives; ones which can differ quite dramatically from those which are typically brought to bear upon collections of 'writings'. Nevertheless, I propose to use these two terms interchangeably.

FROM ORAL LITERATURE TO VERBAL ART

If, as I am arguing, linear chronology is not the prime determinant, what is the most helpful starting point for this journey through indigenous communication? One way in is through a concentration upon words themselves, whether they are sung, recited, declaimed or transcribed. In this connection it is inevitable that oral literature in translation has to be considered, since it presents powerful religious concepts (such as the Dreaming) as well as specific points of cross-cultural contact. The key here is that every song and every song cycle has a specific status and an implied audience. Some of these are highly sacred and would never be performed for non-initiated (let alone non-Aboriginal) people. Most sacred song cycles are also restricted on the basis of sex: some are explicitly 'men's business' while others can only be viewed and heard by women. It is clear, then, that when we try to understand and appreciate such verbal art we are experiencing only a small sample of it: that which lies in the public domain.

Public song cycles—which involve all members of a community—have an intrinsic relationship with travelling and journeying (both in the geographic and the mythical sense); they showcase music, dance, mime and storytelling skills in a way to which no English transcript on the page can do justice. By virtue of the fact that the transmitters of such song cycles have most frequently been anthropologists, they come to the reader initially through such works as T.G.H. Strehlow's *Aranda Traditions* (1947) and *Songs of Central Australia* (1971) or via the collaborations of Catherine and Ronald Berndt, such as *Djanggawul* (1952), as well as the latter's *Love Songs of Arnhem Land* and *Three Faces of Love* (1976). A second level of exposure for the English-language reader has been through the reprinting of song cycles by editors of specific anthologies of Australian literature; for example, Rodney Hall's inclusion of the Wonguri-Mandijigai 'Moon-Bone Song' in the *Collins Book of Australian Poetry* (1981).

The excerpting of fragments of song cycles in such collections as the first (and some-times the only) reference to so-called traditional Aboriginal culture carries with it many drawbacks: not only does it represent Black Australian culture as being prior and other-worldly (rather than everpresent and relevant) but it also segregates these texts at the beginning of such publications. Rather than being entire and continuous, these excerpts become fragmentary; they are typically relegated to the first few pages of the anthology, almost as if they are a preface to the contemporary world of Australian writing, mired in the past. Thus, the positioning as well as the genre of these song cycle extracts often mili-tates against their receiving the respect they deserve.

A third and very different level of reflection of traditional song cycles appears in the work of Black Australian authors themselves. Here, in an attempt to recapture the on-going power of these texts, writers such as Mudrooroo (1938–) have explored their rhythms and connections in intriguing ways. Not only has he produced an interlinked suite of thirty-five poems in his *The Song Circle of Jacky* (1986) but they embrace issues which are at once historical and immediately present:

> On Nadoc day a youthman strangled in a cell:
> Who killed him; who were his murderers?
> 'Not I,' said the cop, 'I only took him in.'
> 'Not I,' said the town, 'I never spoke his name,
> It's no fault of mine that he had to die—
> We treat them as we would our own,
> There's no racism in our town.'[4]

Mudrooroo also invokes the potency of such verbal art in the midst of his fiction. His 1983 novel *Doctor Wooreddy's Prescription for Enduring the Ending of the World* is punctuated by a pivotal scene in which the indigenous Tasmanians dance a corroboree to solidify their resistance to the incursions of the Europeans:

> The eyelashes flutter together—
> Breast to breast together—
> Heart to heart together—
> Fluttering, seeking, finding—
> Dance, men, dance you to me—
> Sing women, sing me to you:
> We come, we are coming—
> You come, you are coming—
> Hallahoo, hallahoo, ho ho:
> Hallahoo, hallahoo ho ho![5]

The implied eroticism of this verse is no accident: it also underlies much of the traditional song poetry from Central Australia—the explicit model for Mudrooroo's verse.

Verbal art thus stems from a source which is thousands of years old, yet is fresh and pertinent to the reader today. This is as true of individual public songs, frequently known as *tabu djabi*, as it is of song cycles. Often far shorter and more distilled, they closely resemble Japanese *haiku* or minimalist verse, enhanced with a lyricism and sense of playfulness. A classic example from the Pilbara district of Western Australia mixes philosophy with wittiness in a unique way:

> Sit with dignity and talk with composure!
> No small talk! Elaborate on this:
> What means more to you: The silly splinter that went in?
> Or the spirit from heaven—which you really are—
> To wait in the waterhole?[6]

Yet another form of writing is found in dual-text material, published in an Aboriginal language as well as in English. Although this process gathered pace in the 1970s and 1980s, with the publication of texts such as *Stories of Obed Raggett* (1980) in Pintupi/Luritja and English, this was by no means a contemporary phenomenon. As early as the 1860s corroboree songs were being gathered in Queensland by Tom Petrie, who spent many years observing the local Aboriginal people of the Brisbane area. In her *Tom Petrie's Reminiscences of Early Queensland* (1904), Petrie's daughter Constance Campbell Petrie recorded his findings, even arranging the music with the assistance of a local conductor. The lyrics—both in English and in the language of the Moreton Island people—tell the story of the mysterious disappearance of a young man while turtle-hunting:

> My oar is bad, my oar is bad;
> Send me my boat,
> I'm sitting here waiting . . .
> *Dulpai-i-la ngari kimmo-man*
> ['Jump over for me friends'].[7]

The potential cross-over from oral transcription to poetry implies that there is an innate lyricism in Aboriginal and Islander languages which is given free rein in the verse format. It is for this reason that questions of genre divisions between poetry and prose become difficult to maintain—and often meaningless—when one is examining indigenous verbal art. Billy Marshall-Stoneking has been intimately involved in the latter process, as one of the first non-Aboriginal authors to act as a Literature Production Supervisor in a remote Aboriginal community. Working with Pintupi/Luritja elders in Papunya from 1979 until 1983, Marshall-Stoneking played a significant role in positioning and punctuating the words of Aboriginal speakers, producing a fascinating blend of English and traditional language in the process. The impact of a piece like Tutama Tjapangarti's 'Wangka Tjukutjuk' is crucially linked to its bilingualism, as well as to the way in which the words leap out from the page:

> Ohhh,
> too much/
>> little bitta cheeky bug/
> kapi purlka/ walpa purlka/ ohhh! ebbrywhere!
> jitapayin WHOOF! gone. Pinished!
> /kapi kapi kapi/cough'a cough'a cough'a
> ohhh, too much.[8]

The cadences of Pintupi speech obviously imprinted themselves heavily upon Marshall-Stoneking, so much so that some of his own work, published under the title *Singing the Snake* (1990), is virtually indistinguishable from that of his Aboriginal mentors. For example, in 'Dreamin Mine' he writes:

> porkupine properly
> kuka palya!
> little bitty talka mine
> porkupine
>> dreamin
> ooohh too much
> olden times
> ebbrywhere ebbrywhere
> cook em   cook em   cook em
> cook em
>
> porkupine mine
>> too much![9]

Admittedly, Marshall-Stoneking does subtitle the poem 'After Tutama Tjapangarti', yet it is almost impossible to determine where the voice of Tjapangarti ceases and Marshall-Stoneking's begins. As this observation applies to a significant proportion of the poems in this collection, it marks *Singing the Snake* as a publication in which the tightrope walk between collaboration and appropriation is a particularly fine one. At other times, in works such as Paddy Roe and Stephen Muecke's *Gularabulu* (1983) the reader is always aware of who is speaking and in whose language the text is printed.[10] Similarly, in Bill Neidjie's seminal collection of oral stories, *Story About Feeling* (1989),[11] there is no uncertainty of authorial voice, although the book has quite openly been edited (as was *Gularabulu*) by a non-Aboriginal writer. In terms of the theme of this chapter, *Singing the Snake* is a troublesome and worrying text by virtue of the fact that any distinction between 'black' and 'white' speaking positions is, at times, totally erased. In the context of verbal art, its position is a unique one.

One of the issues foregrounded by Marshall-Stoneking's collection is the extent to which historical texts can also be imbricated with this uncertainty of voice. Since English was always a second language for indigenous Australians and since literacy was extremely low among members of the Aboriginal community in the eighteenth and nineteenth centuries, is it true that nearly all publications by black writers were 'ghost-written' during that period of time? It is very difficult to adjudicate between the different realms and influences of transcription from oral sources (when the speaker is an Aboriginal person) and dictation from oral sources (when the speaker is a European and the actual transcriber of the words is a Black Australian). The further back one examines the record, the more one finds that various agendas were being served when indigenous people were being encouraged to write in English. A Protector of Aborigines, for instance, could make his program of imposed culture appear incredibly successful if he could demonstrate that one of his charges on a mission station had been able to master written English —under his instruction—and had been able to extol the Protector's virtues (in writing) at the same time.

BLACK AUSTRALIAN JOURNALISM

It is for this reason that in his ground-breaking study of Aboriginal print journalism, *For the Record* (1996) Michael Rose is suitably circumspect about the external influences upon the fascinating publication, variously called *The Aboriginal* or *Flinders Island Chronicle*. The *Chronicle* was produced between September 1836 and December 1837 in Tasmania, under the tutelage of George Augustus Robinson, the Commandant of the Flinders Island Aboriginal Settlement. As Rose puts it:

> This extraordinarily interesting publication—handwritten and handcopied in English, and to be sold for two pence—was, without doubt, the work of three Aboriginal clerks in the employ of Robinson. There is some debate however, over what influence Robinson had on the content of the newspaper, and whether anyone other than a few Aboriginal people on Flinders Island at the time were capable of reading it.[12]

What cannot be questioned is the significance of this publication. *The Flinders Island Chronicle* is not only the 'first Aboriginal newspaper in the Australian colony';[13] it also demonstrates that Black Australian writing in this form pre-dated the journalism of David Unaipon by nearly a century.[14] In other words, any claims that Aboriginal publication began in the 1920s have to be seen as false; even more, the fixation of some scholars upon a single individual as the driving force behind Aboriginal literature has to be questioned very seriously. As Penny Van Toorn put it in her excellent 1996 article in *Meanjin*, the presence of so much pre-twentieth-century indigenous Australian writing and 'the silence of literary studies on the matter . . . says a great deal about the conditions under which decisions were and are made as to what counts as "writing", what counts as "literature", what counts as "authorship" and who counts as "Aboriginal" '.[15] On all four counts, *The Flinders Island Chronicle* is a crucial text.

Published three years after the forced removal to the island of many of the 'The Native People of Van Diemen's Land' (including Truganini and her husband Wooreddy), the articles in the *Chronicle* are suffused with two emotions: self-congratulation and sorrow. Concerning the first, the concept of order and regulation is uppermost: the 'Aboriginal Youth Editor', Thomas Brune, writes that 'they behave themselves under the Directions of the Commandant'[16] and that 'The people which is now on the settlement is well behaved themselves under the directions of the Commandant'.[17] In brief, Robinson established a benign dictatorship, which even extended to injunctions against carrying wood on Sundays and included exhortations to use soap at least daily. At the same time, the pages of the paper are saturated with images of death: coffins, graves and funerals are mentioned quite explicitly in issue after issue, an eloquent testimony to the phenomenally high mortality rate which the Flinders Island Aborigines were suffering at the time.

One of the most moving editions of the paper was published on 17 November 1837, when the atmosphere of being cursed is inescapable and plaintive:

> The brig Tamar arrived this morning at green Island. I cannot tell perhaps we might hear about it by and by when the ship boat comes to the Settlement we will hear news from Hobartown. Let us hope it will be good news and that something may be done for us poor people they are dying away the Bible says some of all shall be saved but I am much afraid none of us will be live by and by as then as nothing but sickness among us. Why dont the black fellows pray to the king to get us away from this place.[18]

This is powerful prose, a heartfelt plea for salvation in the midst of damnation. It is even more sobering to recall that the final issue of the paper was only one month later, when its editor was struck down by the same diseases which he had lamented were ravaging his community.

PETITIONS OF THE PEOPLE

If there is any dominant theme in the Aboriginal writings of this earlier period it is one of entreaty. Again and again—and this is in large measure because of the Christian context in which so many of these works were written—the authors are on figuratively bent knees, beseeching the powers which control them to recognise and to alleviate their suffering. So it is no wonder that one of the most significant and durable forms of Black Australian writing has been the letter or petition, enabling people who have always resisted their mistreatment to press their claims to a higher authority.

Even though indigenous people were often thrust into powerless positions, they did not accept their lot unquestioningly. Since the earliest days—and this extends back to Bennelong's letter to Lord Sydney's steward on 29 August 1796[19]—Aboriginal Australians have not been prepared to be the passive recipients of injustice. Again and again they have forced the issue, pressed the point and lobbied far and wide. At times this approach has been a purely personal one. For example, in *North of the Ten Commandments* (1991) David Headon includes a letter written on 2 January 1874 to the editor of the *Northern Territory Times* which displays Black Australian resourcefulness and assertiveness, as well as a very good grasp of written English:

> Mister—My father go up tree 'long my country to get 'em stick. Him fall down; very much hurt; foot very bad. Me, Duncan, him son, carry him long camp; put stick on leg; but no get better.
>
> You say now, Mister, that big corroboree Parliament give blackfellow plenty physic, plenty good things; so now you make Doctor come long camp and see my father; then him get better, and me, Duncan, sit long printing paper, be what whitefellow call printer's berrowa.
>
> Very good,
>
> DUNCAN[20]

Although specific individual examples like this exist, it is the *community petition* which is by far the dominant mode of such communication. In almost every case, these depositions represent a collective movement towards the assertion of strength as well as progress towards freedom. There are numerous examples: one of the most prominent is the 15 May 1841 'Testimony to Gawler', which eight Aboriginal children from the Kaurna people of South Australia wrote to Governor Colin George Gawler, commending his fairness, protection and justice and seeking its continuation.[21] Another high-profile South Australian petition concerned the *Aborigines (Training of Children) Act*, introduced to the South Australian Parliament on 20 September 1923. In response, three representatives of the Point McLeay Community Council submitted a deposition to the Governor, written by Mrs E.N. Kropinyeri on behalf of all of the people of the mission, urging the repeal of the legislation.

On the same theme, Michael Rose notes the importance of *Australian Abo Call: the Voice of the Aborigines* (1938) as a further development of the strategy of petitioning— this time in the journalistic area. 'A professional quality, tabloid newspaper',[22] *Abo Call* was founded by the Aborigines Progressive Association (APA) in New South Wales, the driving force behind the 1938 'Day of Mourning' protests in Sydney, led by William

Ferguson and Jack Patten. Yet again, pride and assertiveness were the key features of the publication; as Patten wrote:

> This paper has nothing to do with missionaries, or anthropologists, or with anybody who looks down on Aborigines as an 'inferior' race.
>
> We are NOT an inferior race, we have merely been refused the chance of education the whites receive. 'The Abo Call' will show that we do not want to go back to the Stone Age.[23]

However, in the history of Australian petitions, none is more significant than the bark petition submitted to the federal parliament by the *Yirrkala* people of Arnhem Land. Received in Canberra on 14 August 1963 and designed to oppose mining in sacred areas on their tribal land, the bark petition created a sensation, both domestically and overseas. Media coverage combined with international pressure to force this most innovative example of Black Australian writing to the top of the political agenda: a House of Representatives Select Committee was formed and began deliberations immediately.

And, although its recommendations for compensation were not acted upon and mining did go ahead on the *Yirrkala* people's traditional lands, the bark petition became a potent symbol for Aboriginal rights, leading to the referendum of 1967 and, eventually, to the passage of the Northern Territory's land rights legislation in 1976. Most importantly, although the petition was a harbinger of change in Aboriginal affairs, it drew upon a venerable literate tradition of Black Australian protest—a thrust towards freedom and independence via the power of the word.

LETTERS, DIARIES AND JOURNALS OF EUROPEAN EXPLORATION

If Aboriginal and Islander writing is remarkable for its treatment of non-linear time and its concentration upon the resonant symbol of land, European observations of indigenous Australians have always been characterised by their fascination with the chronology of history and the capture of territory—and language. As many commentators have noted, the naming of the continent has always been only a heartbeat away from its claiming; therefore, the journals, diaries and letters of invasion are highly significant documents.[24]

Taken together with diaries and journal entries, the epistolary form of Australian writing was—especially in the eighteenth and nineteenth centuries—a key reflection of attitudes towards race, towards England and towards conquering the continent. But long before the British set sail for the southern ocean, the arrival of the Dutch set a pattern for this form of intercultural contact. Though it is little known, the Aborigines of Cape York were—through the words of the Dutch sailor Jan Carstensz—the first Black Australians to be described in writing to the outside world. As John Mulvaney has related in his 1989 study *Encounters in Place*, Carstensz and his crew arrived in the region between April and May 1623. They attempted to land on seventeen occasions and encountered Aboriginal people on nine of those.[25]

According to the Dutch sailor's journal, the Black Australians were both numerous and inquisitive; as he wrote, they 'showed no fear and were so bold as to touch the muskets of our men . . . while they wanted to have whatever they could make use of'.[26] After the Dutch kidnapped one of the blacks, the relationship soured dramatically: several weeks later the Dutch sailors were opposed at the Wenloch River (near Mapoon) by about two hundred armed Aborigines. Carstensz lamented in his journal that 'in spite of all our kindness and our fair semblance the blacks received us as enemies everywhere' —hardly an accurate reflection of his own people's aggressive actions![27]

As Mulvaney summarises, 'The prompt departure of the Dutch, their adverse reports on this and other expeditions, and a failure to penetrate the coastal fringe, must have been assisted by a fear of Aboriginal attack'. What is noteworthy too is that Black Australian oral tradition keeps these events alive to this day; as one Aurukun elder put it in 1975: 'They had defeated the Dutch before at Cape Keerweer' . . . 'and they could do it again'.[28]

This episode is both fascinating in its own right and as a precursor to Aboriginal/ English contact over a century later, because it establishes a paradigm of the power of words on both sides of the racial divide. While Carstensz no doubt believed that, as a literate European, he was 'telling the story' of the encounter, Aboriginal people had then, as they do now, their own codes of communication and of cross-cultural contact. Those codes involved elaborate preparations for first meetings with outsiders (including the use of symbolic, ceremonial body-painting, itself another form of inscription). Although they may not have been wielding the quill, Black Australians were by no means shut out of the communicative equation at the time, even if the journals of the European explorers frequently misunderstood the forms of this literate and sophisticated black response.

The following century, when British officers became the observers and recorders of their first contacts with Aboriginal Australians, several surprising revelations were made. On the one hand, commentators ascribed a series of highly negative characteristics to the blacks; on the other, they immediately recognised that Aborigines possessed certain quite particular and noteworthy skills. For example, writing in 1793, Thomas Watling observed that 'Irascibility, ferocity, cunning, treachery, revenge, filth and immodesty, are strikingly their dark characteristics' yet, at the same time, he noted that 'In imitation they are extremely apt, particularly in mimicry; and they seem also in many other respects to be capable of much improvement'.[29] If this inconsistency is not telling enough, consider the response of the explorer Charles Sturt who, in 1833, penned the following diary entry entitled 'Providential Deliverance from Danger': 'As we neared the sand-bank, I stood up and made signs to the natives to desist; but without success'[30]—as if there were a universal sign-language which all but the most benighted races could comprehend! Yet, minutes later (if we are to believe Sturt) the 'natives' on the banks of the Murray River responded most dramatically to the unfurling of the Union Jack:

The eye of every native had been fixed upon that noble flag, at all times a beautiful object, and to them a novel one, as it waved over us in the heart of a desert. They had, until that moment been particularly loquacious, but the sight of that flag and the sound of our voices hushed the tumult.[31]

Clearly, the journals of exploration are as much fictional constructs as they are factual ones: the hyperbole, the embroidery, the exaggerated emphases tell us as much about the authors themselves as they reveal about the people whom they encountered. This excessive style of observation reached its zenith in the work of Thomas Mitchell who, in 1839, described Black Australians in the most amazing terms:

[They] repeated their gesticulations of defiance with tenfold fury, and accompanied the action with demoniac looks, hideous shouts and a war-song—crouching, jumping, spitting, springing up with the spear, and throwing dust at us, as they slowly retired. In short, their hideous crouching postures, measured gestures, and nasty jumps, all to the tune of a wild song, with the fiendish glare of their countenances, at all times black, but now all eyes and teeth, seemed a fitter spectacle for Pandemonium, than the light of the bounteous sun.[32]

Aside from the obvious predilection for self-aggrandisement which one notes in these extracts, there is also a serious theme. It is one of genuine fear: of the unknown; of the Australian environment; of Aboriginal people. As historians like Henry Reynolds have demonstrated quite conclusively in books such as *Frontier* (1987), the sense of being at war with Black Australians which took root almost immediately after the settlement of Sydney was widespread, heartfelt and inescapable. Once their land had been invaded— and, as Reynolds notes, the editor of the *Northern Territory Times* used this precise term in 1875—most of the British believed that warlike retaliation would be inevitable.[33] In every corner of the colony, Europeans reported abiding feelings of dread, bordering upon paranoia. The nineteenth-century perception that Aboriginal Australians were devils, that they were highly dangerous despite their primitive nature, was extremely widespread.

In this sense, what was written was an accurate barometer of fear even if it also pointed to an immense level of ignorance. Then, as now, the two often went together, feeding the desire for an ever-increasing, violent response: one of massacres, of dispossession, of forced removal. The European fixation upon peace and security led, paradoxically, to a redoubled level of aggression.

SCHIZOPHRENIC ATTITUDES

Yet perhaps this is not so paradoxical. If there is any lesson which we can learn from what has been written, it is that European attitudes to Aboriginal people were quite contradictory: compassion was tinged with malice; terror was leavened by pity; the desire for control was tempered by the desire for distance from Black Australians. This was no more obvious than on certain Christian missions where, in order to 'elevate' indigenous people, their depraved natures had to be highlighted—and then excoriated. One of the most evocative pieces of Aboriginal literature of the nineteenth century is an untitled poem written by a young Aboriginal man living on the Poonindie Mission of South Australia in the mid-1850s. It concerns the distancing of Aboriginal people outside the mission from their brethren interned in it. The anonymous author writes:

> Whenever I take my walks abroad,
> How my poor I see.
> What shall I render to my God
> for all his gifts to me?
>> Not more than others I deserve,
>> Yet God hath given me more;
>> for I have food while others starve,
>> or beg from door to door.
> The poor wild natives whom I meet,
> Half-naked I behold,
> While I am clothed from head to feet
> And covered from the cold.[34]

The ambivalence of this extract is striking, and it is a feature which characterises the written expressions of so many Aboriginal people living under the mission system. It is as true of Poonindie as of Point McLeay, the mission station where David Unaipon was raised, worked and died, that what is alluded to is intense suffering on a psychic level. Overall, no matter what genre is being utilised, Black Australian writing cannot avoid an exploration of this theme, whether it is through articles, speeches, paintings, poems, stories, plays, letters, songs or novels. As Marjorie Bil Bil has written, like the body, like the land, like the word—'It just lies there from the beginning'.

2

THE 'SETTLING' OF ENGLISH

Delys Bird

'I am a B-b-british object.' David Malouf, *Remembering Babylon*

In all of its modes, from the most formal and official of its discourses to the least, English in the Australian colonies was engaged in a process of self-definition. More accurately, perhaps, the process was one of the redefinition of the self in its individual and social aspects, in relation to the radically changed social, historical and natural circumstances that colonists confronted in their new world exile. This preoccupation is expressed in the stumbling words that are the first spoken in David Malouf's contemporary novel of Australian colonial life, *Remembering Babylon* (1993, p. 5). The man who utters them is barely recognisable as such by the children to whom he announces himself in this way. He has been living outside colonial society for most of his life and is now entering it. His words indicate a problem central to colonisation, one that I will call the subject/object problem. The man can identify himself only as other, as object. His sole point of reference is his cultural heritage, which is his remembered Britishness. Emigration—especially colonial emigration—entails a loss of the sense of self and of history. That loss is represented in a shift, both for individuals and for social groups, from the condition of being subject (which we must occupy in order to speak and write, and to act) to the condition of being object (in which we lack agency, of speaking or any other kind). It is signified by an analogous shift in the referential property of language, so that meaning itself becomes provisional. The space that was the new world was unnamed in English, without history, lacking the necessary cultural markers to enable the colonisers to re-inscribe themselves as colonial subjects. Still legally British subjects, bound to the imperial centre not just by law but by language and cultural ties, the transportees and colonial travellers, wives and mothers, officials and soldiers and later the emigrants who peopled the early Australian settlements, could identify themselves initially only as British objects. The colonial world and the place of these colonisers in it had to be written into being in English in order for those rupturings of self, place and history to be overcome. This process of textualisation took place with some texts remaining 'British', using the conventions and structures that shaped the discourses of the original social world. In others the tendency is towards hybridity, as old world literary conventions are transformed to a greater or lesser extent through the struggle to create discursive practices capable of translating that new world.

MAPPING A CONTINENT

The existence of a Great South Land had long figured in the imaginations and the calculations of European and Asian geographers. The great exploratory sea voyages of the Portuguese, the Spaniards and the Dutch through the sixteenth and seventeenth centuries 'discovered' land masses in the South Seas. But those explorers found nothing in their sightings to confirm what had been expressed either in arcadian images of a fertile land, often imagined as supporting a white race living in paradisal harmony, or in material hope of lands rich in spices or precious metals; nothing to rouse the colonising or the plundering ambitions of their nation states. It took the coincidence of Britain's seventeenth-century colonial expansion, and the landings of English voyagers—first Dampier on the west coast, known as New Holland, where he found himself almost accidentally in 1688, and to which he returned in 1689; then Cook towards the end of the eighteenth century on the east coast—to awaken British imperial interest in the South Land.

Dampier's journals, published as *A New Voyage Round the World* (1689), became an immediate best-seller, a forerunner to the immensely popular publications of Australian colonial life. To Dampier the land appeared unproductive: sandy, waterless and generally uninviting to European habitation. Its inhabitants, whom he described infamously as 'the miserablest People in the world', without clothes, houses or religion (those material and moral markers of late seventeenth-century European civilisation), were equally disappointing to the acquisitive European voyager seeking trade. But by the time Cook reached the eastern shores of the southern continent (still thought of as separate from Dampier's New Holland coastline) nearly a century later, a scientific model of learning informed English intellectual life. The South Pacific, as Bernard Smith demonstrates in *European Vision and the South Pacific* (1960, 1985), captured the attention of that European scientific imagination from the beginning of the eighteenth century. Voyages of discovery were now expected to benefit science as well as commerce and imperial expansion. Cook's was undertaken at the request of the then influential Royal Society. Its major purpose was to observe the transit of the planet Venus from Tahiti; a secondary purpose was strategic and imperialist, to establish whether a continent existed in the South Seas and annex it. Cook did not claim to have discovered a southern continent, but he did claim the east coast of Australia for England, and the voyage had important effects on scientific knowledge in Europe. For example, observations of the distinctive botany of what was to the European voyagers a new world upset the symmetry of the eighteenth-century Linnaean system, which depended on the concept of a transcendent order. Unlike Dampier, Cook thought the land eminently suitable for European settlement, and its people free from the corruptions of European civilisation. Although their apparently wandering life and lack of possessions meant that 'they may appear to some [Europeans] to be the most wretched people upon Earth . . . in reality they are far more happier than we Europeans'.[1] Dampier's version of the land as degraded and barren, and Cook's as offering a fertile future, establish the terms of a dialectical paradigm, variously described by critical commentators as moving between, for example, prison and paradise, gloom and optimism, that shapes much colonial writing.

The British Government's 1786 decision to establish a penal colony at Botany Bay was the outcome of an ongoing debate about how to deal with extreme overcrowding in English gaols. That situation had been exacerbated by the loss of the American colonies as a dumping ground for the English 'criminal' class after Independence. The decision was bolstered by imperial objectives: a desire to thwart French colonial advancement, the need to establish a southern trading post, and the recognition of the advantages of having access to New Zealand flax and Norfolk Island pine for ships' ropes and masts. Settlement of the South Land was represented in English according to a range of discourses—of discovery, economic interest, defence, natural history and science, law and punishment and so on—and justified by Enlightenment and religious imperatives. Late eighteenth-century colonisers believed their God-given duty was to improve the natural landscape of the new world by making it productive; in addition, its indigenous inhabitants would be Christianised and civilised. The contemporary moral philosophies upholding these colonising ideologies may be traced in the small selection of books that accompanied educated first settlers on the First Fleet, which included Adam Ferguson's *An Essay on the History of Civil Society* (1767).[2] From such a perspective, the settling-in of English seems a benign phrase, assuming a process of assimilation and transformation of the colonised world. This, however, is a misrepresentation.[3] English colonisation was an often violent intervention, not a simple process of accommodation. Imperial superiority and whiteness were naturalised as normative standards in English, while the language of the colonisers had often destructive effects on the environment it classified and brought under its control: an environment considered to include its original inhabitants who were made indistinguishable from it. At the same time, English was an awkward tool for the colonisers, as ill-fitted as their other tools to reshape that environment. Homi Bhabha refers to colonial writing as an 'act of translation',[4] and it was the process of rendering intelligible the colonial space their European culture was so ill suited to translate that produced the beginnings of an Australian literary culture.

The coincidence of the beginnings of European settlement in Australia and the beginnings of the print revolution in Europe is significant for a narrative of Australian colonisation. A large and varied written record of both its official and unofficial aspects was made possible by the new and rapidly improving print technology. A printing press arrived with the First Fleet, but there was no one to operate it until George Howe, a convict printer, set it up, and used it to print the first colonial newspaper, the *Sydney Gazette*, in 1803. Colonial writings, made exotic by distance and novelty, were in demand from the metropolitan centre, where the rise of literacy and the growth of a mass reading public guaranteed a readership.[5] Thus educated colonisers, occupying a position on the edge of the empire from which they could add to the intellectual questions and issues of their age as well as carry out its imperial ambitions, immediately began writing themselves into a place in their own English colonial history.

The volume of that imaginative written record of colonisation is out of proportion to the tiny size of the colonial population. Around one thousand people, about three-quarters of them convicts, arrived with the First Fleet, and in 1850 the entire white population of all the colonies was only just over four hundred thousand. The extent of their writing indicates the colonists' urgent need to record their experience, and to respond to the swift social changes that marked the period. By 1850 the coastline and much of the interior of the continent had been mapped. Sydney and Melbourne were cities of fifty thousand and thirty-nine thousand people respectively; banks, courthouses and libraries were established in the eastern colonial centres, and an education system, including both secular and denominational schools, a network of Mechanics' Institutes, and Sydney University (1849), was established. All the colonies had achieved a degree of legislative independence from Britain. The Eastern colonies had a flourishing pastoral industry. Swan River Colony and South Australia had different colonial histories, since neither was originally a convict settlement, although Swan River Colony became one in 1850. Both relied on land sales to attract settlers and raise colonial revenue. South Australian settlement was based on Edward Gibbon Wakefield's theories of colonisation, as was the settlement at Australind in the West. The Western and Southern colonies, as well as Moreton Bay in the North, were still economically vulnerable and culturally tentative by 1850.

Definitions of the literary depend on the context and culture that constructs them. In the late eighteenth century the literary genres were constituted by epic poetry, history and biography. Elizabeth Webby points out that at that time the category of literature would have excluded 'comic and satiric verse, popular drama, all types of fiction and of course letters and diaries'.[6] Yet these are precisely the kinds of writing that mark the beginnings of an Australian literature. This survey of those beginnings thus uses the term 'literary' to include any writing that undertakes a self-conscious engagement with aspects of the new world and the complex processes of colonisation, in an attempt to construct an imaginative, linguistic response to the diversity of that colonial world. Such writing has been described as a way of making sense through language of the new world. So-called 'serious literature', with its relatively rigid conventions and elaborated metaphoric and symbolic systems, attuned to the traditions of European culture, was ill suited to undertake that process. Discussing Thomas Watling's *Letters from an Exile at Botany-Bay* (1794), Ross Gibson argues that the mode of metaphor, constructed through selection and combination, depends on an intelligible linguistic (or visual) system to convey its meanings. Such a system was no longer available to the colonial writer or artist. Like many others, Watling recognises the incapacity of English to express his situation: 'never did I find language so imperfect as at present . . .'.[7] Caught in the position of colonial object and struggling to find a linguistic subject position adequate to 'make sense' of the colonial world, Watling's remark indicates that the work of 'making sense' would require new linguistic and symbolic tools.

Developing the Colonial Genres: Public and Political Writing

The earliest literary works produced from the new colony were the First Fleet annals: official and semi-official accounts of the settlement. Formally, they were part of a trend towards prose realism in Europe, one that included the new genres of journalism, the literary essay, and the novel, which gained literary status through its claim to verisimilitude. The increasing importance of the natural sciences affected literary forms too, in that the kinds of writing that used empirically exact observation and description were valued. Metonymic or descriptive prose, not surprisingly, became the most successful mode in early colonial writing, reflecting both new European literary preferences and the incapacity of those 'serious' or traditional literary forms, which were subject to the restraints of their tradition, to tell the story of colonisation, locate a colonial history and give a voice to the colonial experience. Realism has thus been a dominant influence in Australian literature since its beginnings. Governor Arthur Phillip's first despatches, published in England as *The Voyage of Governor Phillip to Botany Bay* in 1789, reflect these trends, as well as ways the British publishing industry shaped the production of colonial writing. The cost of publishing in the colonies, when all the materials had to be imported, was exorbitant, and less than half the items listed up to 1849 in Ferguson's *Bibliography of Australia* (1941–86) had an Australian imprint. Habitual rewriting by English editors, and what H.M. Green calls 'improvement', was common. Using examples from Phillip's original journals and the changes made by Stockdale, his editor, Green illustrates how Stockdale made Phillip a character in the drama of first settlement, diminishing the strength of the original.[8] The exercise of power by the metropolitan centre over the colonial outpost is thus evident not only in its legal and economic aspects, but in its cultural domination. It was able to control colonial literary production, through choosing what should be published as well as by determining its final form. With diminishing effect, Australian writers were subject to these forms of cultural hegemony, which affected the whole literary culture, until at least the 1950s.

Many of the officers of the First Fleet wrote, self-consciously, about their experiences of the process of settlement. Marine Captain Watkin Tench's *A Narrative of the Expedition to Botany Bay* (1789) has attracted a great deal of commentary, in relation to his fresh and independent response to the new world, and his refusal of the limitations of the position of observer and recorder adopted by the majority of early colonial writers. Instead, Tench uses his narrative perspective to analyse as well as describe. Setting down the activities of the first days of settlement, Tench suggests this doubled perspective: 'the scene to an indifferent spectator, at leisure to contemplate it, would have been highly picturesque and amusing' (pp. 59–64). Natural history played an important role in the composition of the colonising empire. John White, Surgeon-General to the First Fleet, had no formal scientific training, yet in his *Journal of a Voyage to New South Wales* (1790) he uses empirical observation and taxonomic description, the techniques of natural science, to represent a female kangaroo, who 'has a pouch or pocket, like the Opossum, in which she carries her young. Some have been shot with a young one, not larger than a walnut, sticking to a teat in this pocket . . .' (pp. 146–7). Tench's description of an emu is even more exact: 'On dissection many anatomical singularities were observed: the gall-bladder was remarkably large, the liver not bigger than that of a barn-door fowl, and after the strictest search no gizzard could be found' (p. 32).

That some discourses are more suitable than others for colonial conditions is confirmed by the extent and importance in early writing of descriptive prose of different kinds and the failure of most of the poetry to achieve a new response to colonial circumstances. Highly conventionalised with a weighty tradition, poetic discourse lacked the flexibility and hence the range of expressiveness of the newer prose discourses. Colonial poetry has typically been read as feeble or attenuated, pretentious or somehow broken-spirited, while the prose is habitually described as vigorous and vital. Elizabeth Perkins develops H.M. Green's characterisation of colonial poetry as always 'looking over its shoulder, in the vain attempt to find a capable medium', which was to be found in 'action in its various fields, or in literature that was a by-product of action', to suggest an illustrative difference in Charles Tompson's writing between his 'confined meditative verse' and his 'urgent, strenuous prose'; the difference indicating the effects of 'new conditions [which] compelled colonists to evolve new voices'.[9] In the late eighteenth century, 'civilisation' represented the culmination of a long historical process towards a social condition of refinement and order, and included both the earlier sense of culture as the proper cultivation of the land in all its aspects, and its extension to include the cultivation of the human mind. Poetry was the literary mode through which that cultivated mind best expressed itself, yet in the absence of civilisation, poetry in its classical mode was unable to engage in the acts of translation necessary to construct a new culture.

Colonisation was justified in its civilising purpose by the 'lack of culture—agricultural, civil and intellectual'[10] of the South Land and its inhabitants. Civilisation meant the possibility of a moral future for the Australian colonies; even the practice of transportation was informed by an Enlightenment belief in the regenerative effects on human beings of industrious occupation in a rural setting. This imperial narrative depended on the belief in an evolutionary movement from barbarity to civilisation, and was complicated, as Elizabeth Perkins has pointed out, by the dual meanings English culture gave to the category of the barbarous or the primitive. It represented not only 'chaos in need of order, and original sin in need of redemption' but also 'innocence and a source of imaginative creation' (p. 140). In colonial writings, these oppositional meanings are held in an apparent tension between optimism—the hope of the promised land—and pessimism—the actuality of its degraded present—a tension Perkins refers to as the colonial dilemma. Such tensions are often evident, too, in what Homi Bhabha calls the ambivalence that lies at the heart of colonial discourses, an ambivalence accentuated by the use of those colonial discourses in a non-European, so-called primitive context, in which their power and authority may be decentred.

Many of these tendencies are apparent in both the formal and popular verse of colonial Australia. The 'high', formal poetry does no more than attempt to incorporate the colonial experience into an established literary tradition; while the 'low', informal modes of poetry, less reliant on tradition, convention and civilising expectations, are freer to convey the colonial condition directly. Poetry in both modes using Australia as a topic was published in England and written by those with no firsthand knowledge of the colonies. The best known examples of this secondhand form of colonial representation in formal poetry are Erasmus Darwin's 'Visit of Hope to Sydney-Cove, near Botany-Bay', written as a frontispiece for Stockdale's publication of Phillip's journals (1789), and Robert Southey's 'Botany Bay Eclogues' (1794). Each poet's work illustrates the literary ease, and resulting hollowness, of traditional poetic translations of the colonial situation, made from the security and ignorance of the metropolis. Darwin's neoclassical ode anthropomorphises Hope, who visits Sydney Cove, bringing the blessings of civilisation. Aided by Time and Truth, she reveals the gloriously Europeanised future aspect of the colony, with 'broad streets', '[E]mbellish'd villas', 'tall spires' and so forth, to the 'tumultuous . . . Joy', presumably of the colonists, who were at that time in danger of starvation. Southey on the other hand adopts the perspective of the transportees, but uses a typically elevated, moralising diction to present a view of the savage colonies. 'Elinor' is a morally degraded exile, a 'wretch' who welcomes 'ye savage lands, ye barbarous climes' as fit punishment for her sins. She finally looks to 'the saving hand of Grace' to 'fit the faithful penitent for Heaven'. Each of these poems reproduces an aspect of the paradise/hell dichotomy which had structured colonial representations since Dampier declared the southern continent 'wretched', while Cook pronounced it 'promising'.

Popular verse, usually in the form of ballads, was also imported into the colony. An Australian literary tradition is often thought of as having its beginnings in the ballad, perhaps because of the *Bulletin*'s publication of numerous bush ballads—the so-called 'literary' ballads—in the 1890s. Yet in his history of the Australian ballad, Cliff Hanna points out that there are almost no indigenous Australian broadside ballads and that '[o]f the few indigenous convict songs that survive, none derives from the first forty years of the colony'.[11] It is significant that Australian ballads had their beginnings in broadside, or street song, and the new print technologies, not the older tradition of oral, or 'folk' ballad. Relatively simple in their language and structure as well as in their stories, ballads provide immediate access to dominant attitudes of their time, which they uphold or contest; sometimes one work does both. Most early ballads, from Britain and Ireland, deal with transportation; a few with political persecution; many lament the separation from home and loved ones; a high proportion are exemplary. In 'The Female Transport' (date unknown—from broadside), 'Sarah Collins' ends the tale of her enticement into bad company with a warning: 'Young girls I pray be ruled by me, your wicked ways give o'er./For fear like us you spend your days upon Van Dieman's shore', upholding the British legal ideology that harsh punishment of crime acts as a salutary lesson. Other ballads opposed that ideology through humour and sarcasm: convicts are 'True patriots all, . . . [who] left our country, for our country's good'; or pathos: 'Tho' crime is bad, yet poverty makes many a man to be/A transport from his native land across the raging sea'.[12]

The first book (or pamphlet) of poetry published in the colonies was Barron Field's *First Fruits of Australian Poetry* (1819). Field was a judge of the Supreme Court of New South Wales, and his poems testify to the expectation of the age that educated gentlemen, 'men of letters', would take part in literary activities. Much colonial poetry is occasional and amateur in this sense and was self-published. British publishers were not interested in colonial poetry, yet the expense of publishing in the colonies put it out of reach of most writers. Field's poetry laments the lack of either classical or familiar poetic associations in the alien environment, a lament that was mocked at the time and has been since for its pretension, but which has also been read as a witty parody of colonial literary pretentiousness.

Lachlan Macquarie's term as governor of the colony of New South Wales (1809–21) is significant for his encouragement of colonial culture. He supported the convict poet Michael Massey Robinson, who wrote a series of odes to mark public occasions between 1810 and 1826. Despite stilted language and banal sentiments, this public poetry exists as an early example of a colonial literary genre that celebrated the achievements which would contribute to a glorious continental future. Charles Harpur, Australian-born son of emancipist parents, is, however, the only poet of this period who achieves an original 'Australian voice'. Harpur successfully adapted English poetic forms as well as classical cultural traditions to the conditions of Australian colonial life, and his poetry conveys his delight in the Hawkesbury River countryside in which he grew up; his passionate republican beliefs and political reformism; his religious mysticism; and his condemnation of tyranny. His work was often radical in tone and he was an accomplished satirist. Harpur's ambition was to achieve recognition as the first authentic Australian poet; the lack of such recognition frustrated him. During his lifetime he published a great deal of poetry as well as prose on political, social and literary issues in a range of journals, but his only book publications were minor in relation to the scope of his writing: prior to 1850 only *Thoughts: A Series of Sonnets* (1845) was published.

SUBVERSIVE, POLEMICAL AND DRAMATIC WRITING

Unpublished, anonymous and usually very bad verse circulated in the colonies in the form of screws of paper, referred to as pamphlets, or pipes. Containing often scurrilous information about individuals and challenges to authority of all kinds, such writing testifies to the tenor of colonial life. The editor of the *Australian Quarterly Journal* described the colony of New South Wales in 1828 as 'a very centre of jealousies and fears—squabble and contention—libel and litigation' (p. 246, quoted in Green, p. 49). Energetic argument, often carried out through the independent colonial newspapers, was a feature of the literary and social life of all the colonies and is evident in much colonial literature. Native-born and emigrant settlers, squatters and pastoralists, often expressed vigorous, oppositional interests, while colonial personalities engaged in fierce verbal and written debate. There were major protests against continuation of the convict system; autocratic military governments and governors were subject to virulent public criticism; regulations relating to the sale and ownership of land were a topic of violent contention; and the refusal of the imperial authorities to grant self-government to the colonies was a constant source of publicly expressed conflict. Widespread use was made of poetry as a vehicle for political and social comment, and anonymously published poetry carried often vicious satirical attacks on politicians and their policies. Colonial politicians like Lang, Wentworth, and William à Beckett used poetry as a means of political expression in order to evade the constraints of political rhetoric. It gave them an alternative political voice and enhanced their political reputations as they engaged in what was regarded as a suitable occasional activity for gentlemen.

Independent colonial newspapers were important in the literary and the socio-political life of the colonies. They not only published a great deal of original poetry, much of it topical and ephemeral, but also encouraged the development of other genres. Writers benefited from increased print outlets, and papers with an interest in the local scene gave the embryonic colonial communities a focus. Early papers were the *Australian* (1824–48), established by W.C. Wentworth, and the *Sydney Monitor* (1826–41) in Sydney, and Andrew Bent's paper in Hobart, originally called the *Hobart Town Gazette*, which Bent had to change to the *Colonial Times* (1825–57) when Governor Arthur set up a rival, government-backed newspaper, also called the *Hobart Town Gazette*. Papers were followed by local magazines, often published monthly, which had more concentration on literary publishing. Some, like the earliest, the *Australian Magazine* (1821–22), published in Sydney by a group of Wesleyan missionaries, used mainly material culled from overseas sources: others were self-consciously parochial and used original local writing. Most colonial newspapers and journals were short-lived. This was due to their cost as well as the small size of their potential audiences, but it also indicates the strong preference of many colonial readers for imported rather than local publications.

Debate concerning the standard and proper source of the work published in these journals and newspapers, and their relationship to the construction of an Australian literary culture, reproduces the divided and often ambivalent nature of that process. This debate, which has been long-lasting, is represented in a commentary on the presence of colonial Australian literature in the *Colonial Literary Journal*, published in Sydney as a 'weekly miscellany of Useful Information' over about a year from June 1844. In the first issue, an essay, 'Periodical Literature', establishes the role of literature as a moralising and civilising agent. These properties are best exemplified by the eighteenth-century English essayists Steele and Addison, published in English periodicals like the *Tatler* and *Spectator*.

By analogy, the *Colonial Literary Journal*, and essays like 'Periodical Literature', are essential to dispel ignorance and promote a civilised colonial society, since '[K]nowledge ... strikes at the root of all evil—religious, moral and political'.[13] The question of whether the colonies can produce the kind of writing that would achieve this ideal of a virtuous society is taken up in an essay in a later edition, presented as a conversation between two friends overheard arguing the existence of an Australian literature. While one contends 'we have no colonial literature, nor do I see any materials from which a literature purely colonial could be raised', the other says he should 'abolish the use of the word "Colonial"' and adopts a nationalist position: 'Depend upon it that Australia will never be more than a cipher among the nations, until her sons assume to themselves national characteristics, and proudly stamp them by the pen to be acknowledged and admired by the world!'[14] The defender of a national literary culture has the better of the debate, citing American literature as a colonial example, and quoting at length from Charles Tompson, Charles Harpur, and prose writer 'Martin'.

Conflict between those who held to the 'colonial mentality',[15] which remained tied to Britain and European cultural values, and the neo-nationalists who looked forward to a truly independent Australian future, was focused in mid-century by W.C. Wentworth's proposals for a colonial peerage. Wentworth was a significant figure in colonial cultural and political life: the member for Sydney in the government of New South Wales from 1843, a political rhetorician, poet and prose writer. In his important and very widely read early prose work, the *Statistical, Historical and Political Description of the Colony of New South Wales and its Dependent Settlements in Van Diemen's Land* (1819), Wentworth proposes radical reforms to the colonial political system and states his aim, which is 'to promote the welfare and prosperity of the country which gave him birth' (Preface, p. vii). His vision of Australia's future is based on his belief in its rural potential, which will be realised by the influx of migrants attracted by his work. In his much anthologised long poem 'Australasia' (1823), Wentworth again adopts a nationalist vision. The poet proclaims himself a 'native bard', and predicts the glorious potential of Australasia, 'last-born infant' of the empire, to take up its natural inheritance as 'a new Britannia in another world' if that great power should weaken. An increasingly conservative, neo-patrician elder statesman by 1854, when he introduced his Constitution Bill for an upper house in the New South Wales parliament, Wentworth modelled that proposal on the English House of Lords. The Bill brought violent protests from democratic republican leaders like J.D. Lang, D.H. Deniehy and Henry Parkes, who addressed meetings and wrote against Wentworth's scheme. The division between the two positions is conveyed in their rhetoric; Wentworth's high-flown and aristocratic, Lang's and Deniehy's energetic and colloquial. In a written report of a speech addressing 'Fellow Colonists of New South Wales', Lang urges them to throw off their status as a 'mere colony' and embrace that of a 'Sovereign and Independent State [in which] our noble city would be the flourishing capital of a great and powerful confederation'. Deniehy's famous address to Parliament in response to Wentworth's Constitution Bill, known as the 'bunyip aristocracy' speech, contrasts Wentworth's Australia, with its 'new-fangled Brummagem aristocracy swarming and darkening these fair, free shores' with his: 'a land where man is bountifully rewarded for his labour, and where a just law no more recognises the supremacy of a class than it does the predominance of a creed'.[16]

These live dramas were matched by the importance of colonial theatre and performance during the early decades, especially in the south-eastern colonies. George Farquhar's *The Recruiting Officer* (1706) was the first play performed in the colony of New South Wales, by a group of convicts and officers to celebrate the birthday of George III on 4 June 1789. Thomas Keneally's novel *The Playmaker* (1987) is based on this event. A history of colonial drama is one of government control and censorship that imposed severe limitations on the use of local topics and themes. The first theatre built in Sydney (1796) used convict actors until it was closed by the authorities in 1798 because of rowdy audiences. Another opened in 1800; after it was closed, 'Sydney had no official theatre for over three decades'.[17] The Theatre Royal opened in 1833, after its owner, Barnett Levey, a 'stage-struck merchant', had lobbied for years to obtain a licence. It allowed him to present only 'such Plays and Entertainments . . . as have been performed at one of His Majesty's Licensed Theatres in London'.[18] During these decades all plays performed in the colonies had to be approved by the government censor, the colonial secretary. Such forms of regulation ensured that colonial theatre remained provincial; no indigenous drama dealing with current social issues or colonial maladministration could pass the censor. The status of drama as potentially the most publicly inflammatory of the literary modes, and the vulnerability of the colonial representatives of British discourses of imperial law and order, are both represented in this history of colonial theatre.

The first play set in Australia, *The Bushrangers*, was written by David Burn, a radical journalist and playwright. Performed in Edinburgh in 1829, it was not staged in Australia until 1971. Burn's outlaw hero was based on Tasmanian bushranger Matthew Brady, who had recently been hanged; his life of crime is shown as motivated by a deep sense of the injustice of the penal system; and Burn included leading colonial figures in the play. Henry Melville's *The Bushrangers: or Norwood Vale*, on the other hand, using fictional characters and stock melodramatic situations, was produced in Hobart and Launceston in 1834, and published in the *Hobart Town Magazine*, making it the first local play written, performed and published in Australia. Charles Harpur also wrote a play based on the life of a bushranger, John Donohue, published (but not staged) in 1853 as *The Bushrangers: A Play in Five Acts and Other Poems*. Extracts had been published in 1835 by the *Sydney Monitor* as 'The Tragedy of Donohue'. Harpur's final revision of the play in 1867 was called *Stalwart the Bushranger*; it remained unpublished until 1987. The subtitle of Samuel Prout (nicknamed 'Sprout') Hill's *Tarquin the Proud, or the Downfall of Tyranny* (1843) indicates the theme of much of the colonial drama of this period. Playwrights like Burn, Harpur and Prout Hill found, in the then popular European genres of melodrama, romance and gothic tragedy, appropriate dramatic vehicles for their dramatisations of the colonial experience, with its potential for brutal oppression and corruption as well as for individual liberty and heroism. Other local dramatists avoided censorship by using remote historical or exotic settings, or by turning to comedy and farce. Among the ten plays attributed to Edward Geoghegan, who was writing for the stage in Sydney in the 1840s while still under sentence, *The Currency Lass* (1844) is a slight but entertaining comic operetta that illustrates the kind of theatre preferred by the authorities. *Arabin, or the Adventures of a Settler*, a play adapted from a colonial novel published in London in 1845, was produced in Melbourne—where censorship seems to have been less strict than in Sydney—in 1849. Combining 'stock elements of early nineteenth century melodrama' and 'observable realities of the settler's life', it was advertised on its opening night as an 'entirely COLONIAL PRODUCTION'. Margaret Williams uses it as an example of the 'direction early Australian writing for the theatre might have taken had not both the exotic settings of romantic drama and the colonial secretary's licensing helped turn it from local subjects'.[19]

Writings about convict life, by convicts or ex-convicts, are important in a culture that developed from penal beginnings. Henry Savery, transported for forgery to Hobart Town, wrote a series of essays and sketches observing social life in colonial Tasmania, published as *The Hermit in Van Diemen's Land* in the *Colonial Times* in 1829 and in book form the following year. In addition to publishing the first book of colonial essays, Savery is author of the first novel both written and published in the colonies. *Quintus Servinton: A Tale Founded Upon Incidents of Real Occurrence* (1831) is a transportation novel with a happy ending, disguised as a fictional autobiography. It combines the modes of convict memoir and autobiography, and its tone of self-justification, typical for such works, is tolerable. The self-justifying narrator of *The Memoirs of the First Thirty-two Years of the Life of James Hardy Vaux* (1819) is intolerable. Important as the first published account of the colony from a convict's point of view, *The Memoirs* included Vaux's *Dictionary of Flash Language*, the first work of its kind. The notoriety of the colourful pickpocket George Barrington, transported from London to New South Wales in 1790, about whom numerous newspaper articles, broadsides, chapbooks and pamphlets were written, and the success of those 'Barrington' books, none self-authored, seem to have prompted Vaux to write his *Memoirs*, which went into several editions. The author announces himself as 'A swindler and thief, now transported to New South Wales for the second time, and for life. Written by himself'.

A work of a very different kind, *The Victims of Whiggery, A statement of the Persecutions experienced by the Dorsetshire Labourers . . . and Reflections upon the System of Transportation* (1837) is the autobiographical account of George Loveless, telling of the wrongs perpetrated against the six Dorsetshire labourers, of whom he was one, who became known on their transportation as the 'Tolpuddle Martyrs'. James Tucker (also the author of two plays) wrote *Ralph Rashleigh* in 1844–45 while on reconviction from ticket of leave in Port Macquarie. In manuscript until 1929 (1952), it is the most significant literary work in this field. A long, fictional autobiography that posed as a memoir, *Ralph Rashleigh* is a convincing contemporary depiction of convict life which insists on the brutality and inhumanity of those within the system as well as that of the system. The novel traces Tucker's despairing search for a spiritual home, which is nowhere to be found in the colonies.

EXPLORATION, MIGRATION, TRAVEL AND ADVENTURE

By the 1820s the colony of New South Wales had expanded across the Blue Mountains and consolidated on the Cumberland Plain, and a new colony had been established in Van Diemen's Land. Especially in England, the colonies now appeared to offer illimitable opportunities, and a period of major pastoral expansion brought increased colonial wealth, reinforcing this perception. A new era of growth for the south-eastern colonies, together with the founding of free enterprise settlements in Western and South Australia, produced a more optimistic narrative of colonisation, with freedom and openness contending as dominant modes of representation against exile and incarceration which had been predominant. Literary imaginations were stimulated by new conditions, responding enthusiastically, Robert Dixon argues, 'both to the settled pastoral regions and to the newly discovered unsettled interior of the continent. Bush travel, bivouacking, kangaroo hunting and other masculine themes suggest the beginnings of a frontier mythology based partly on a comparison with the American experience, but also emerging directly from life in Australia'.[20] Women also wrote of their travel, and some of their pleasure in the increased freedom that colonial life offered, although this was complicated for most genteel women by an unaccustomed burden of domestic work. Miles Franklin's *All That Swagger* (1936) presents a view of the character-forming nature of such work for women.

The records of the great inland explorations in the explorers' journals constitute a major area of colonial literature, telling a heroic story of imperial expansion and land acquisition. Explorers' journals and that more domestic mode, travel writings, were enormously popular in the metropolis at the time they were published, and have recently provided the basis for major reconstructions of colonisation as a linguistic process, through the work of commentators like Ross Gibson and Paul Carter, while Simon Ryan has recently analysed modes of imperial annexation through the explorers' visual as well as linguistic textualisation of the land.[21] Such journals fulfilled the period's expectations of the private and public roles of educated people. Keeping a journal was part of their private role; in addition, an explorer's journal was expected to be a public, scientific record of the expedition. John Oxley carried a 'Memorandum' from the Colonial Office when he set out on the first journey into the interior in 1817. It instructed him to: 'keep a detailed Journal ... [in which] all observations and occurrences of every kind with all their circumstances, however minute, and however familiar they may have been rendered by custom, should be carefully noted down; ... he should be as circumstantial as possible in describing the general appearance of the country, ...'.[22] Sturt in 1829 and Mitchell in 1836 carried similar instructions.

Some explorers' accounts, such as Sturt's, Mitchell's and later Eyre's, move beyond the demand for precise documentation to become compelling chronicles that have much in common with nineteenth-century realist novels. George Grey's *Journals of Two Expeditions of Discovery in North-West and Western Australia During the Years 1837, 38 and 39* are divided into sections like those of serialised fiction. Grey speaks directly to his readers, including them in his dilemmas and dreams and drawing them through the sections that shift from despair to hope, or the reverse. At the end of the first volume, a series of mishaps and natural accidents has left the expedition with almost no food. Having to decide whether to try to reach Perth by sea or by land, Grey has chosen the sea, which is proving treacherous; the party is ill and exhausted and its boats are almost unseaworthy. Its final sentence in the tradition of the nineteenth-century serialised novel or the contemporary soap opera, compels the reader to continue:

> For one second the boat hung upon the top of the wave; in the next, I felt the sensation of falling rapidly, then a tremendous shock and crash, which jerked me away amongst rocks and breakers, and for the few following seconds I heard nothing but the din of waves, whilst I was rolling about amongst men, and a torn boat, oars, and water-kegs, in such a manner that I could not collect my senses (p. 412).

The discourses of the colonial explorations of Australia are driven by similar compulsions. Explorers always seek to read on, into the body of the land to discover its secrets: an inland sea, or great rivers or fertile pastures. Strongly shaped by desire, the rhetoric of exploration is characteristically sexualised. Grey approaches the north-west coast of the continent like an ardent lover: 'At the first streak of dawn, I leant over the vessel's side, to gaze upon those shores I had so longed to see' (p. 67). Invocation of the unknown land as other is a common motif in explorers' journals. Appropriated first through Grey's sight, the land will be made familiar and colonised as he maps it. Unlike Sturt's, Grey's journeys are not plotted in a tragic mode. Structured as an adventure narrative, without the heights of neoclassical (and self-important) heroism of Mitchell's, Grey's *Journals* are threaded with accounts of overcoming physical privations. They chart the process of exploration as an education in the land and its people, one emphasised by the trope of self-reflection. An encounter with an Aboriginal group leaves Grey badly wounded and alone, his companions having gone for help. His meditations 'arise[ing] naturally from my present circumstances. I sat upon the rocky ledge of a cool clear brook, . . .—in such scenery I had loved to meditate when a boy, but now how changed I was;— wounded, fatigued, and wandering in an unknown land'. Grey's use of the familiar literary motif of the poignant comparison of an earlier with a present self is particularly striking in the difference it marks between the former securely situated self and the present dislocated colonial self. That difference represents the constant threat to the colonial subject of losing, quite literally, the sense of self, even when that self is authoring the narrative of discovery. Grey attempts to resolve his wavering self by projecting a generalised heroic explorers' fate: 'And in this way very many explorers regularly die' (p. 154).

Like all contemporary travellers, Grey uses the literary and visual trope of the prospect, since it is only from a prospect that the land can be surveyed and incorporated into the viewer's experience. Gaining a prospect, Grey can visualise the triumph of civilisation as the aim of his explorations: 'I painted in fancy the rapid progress that this country would ere long make in commerce and civilisation' (p. 163).

In the 1820s free emigrants were being sought by the colonies to enable expansion and by the 1830s both government and private schemes existed to encourage migration. Economic and political instability in Britain after the Napoleonic wars meant that, for those with some capital, Australia's pastoral potential looked extremely attractive. At the same time, women were being induced to migrate to the colonies through schemes aimed at reducing the colonial gender imbalance and civilising what was considered a degraded and disordered colonial society. New social circumstances produced new writings; both migrants' own experiential records and emigrants' manuals. The latter were often written in England by those who had never been to the colonies, and offered typically misleading advice and inflated views of what the colonies had to offer. The best-known, Sidney Smith's *Sidney's Australian Handbook* (1848), was published when emigration to the colonies was revived after the depression, and became a publishing phenomenon in England. Better informed, Wentworth's *Statistical Description* explains its purpose in its subtitle: *'with particular enumeration of the advantages these colonies offer for emigration; and their superiority in many respects over those possessed by the United States of America'.* One of the most interesting works in this genre, Peter Cunningham's *Two Years in New South Wales* (1827), combines memoirs, an account of the writer's colonial experiences and advice for potential emigrants. Cunningham had been surgeon-superintendent on five convict transports to New South Wales before he settled in the Hunter River district in 1825. Fictional accounts of emigration, like Charles Rowcroft's *Tales of the Colonies; or Adventures of an Emigrant* (1843), were also very popular. Although *Tales* pretends to be the journal of a long-term settler, Rowcroft spent only four years in the colonies, much of that time in Hobart.

Migration has been a significant feature of Australia's European history (indeed, it is a history of migration) and has marked its literature. Louisa Anne Meredith (formerly Twamley), an English artist and poet, wrote *Notes and Sketches of New South Wales: During a Residency in that Colony from 1839 to 1844* for publication after her arrival in the colony, newly married to Charles Meredith. She draws on travellers' tales, emigrant narratives and natural history writing, as well as the new, masculine genre of the literary sketch, popularised by Washington Irving.[23] A confident observer and social commentator who subjects the natural and the social worlds she encounters to minute observation, Meredith displays little of the doubt that marks so much colonial writing. Although she makes early reference to 'this little work' (p. vii), and modestly disclaims scientific knowledge, these are not signs of colonial disaffection, but conventional feminine allusions that place her work in the female, moralising domestic sphere. She has 'sketched every-day things with a faithful and homely pencil' (p. viii). Meredith's embryonic plot is typical of a range of emigrant narratives. It includes the decision to migrate and the voyage; the arrival in Sydney; the emigrant's experiences and adventures in the colony; and the achievement of success; but the traditional return is transformed, as the couple leaves New South Wales happily for Tasmania. Meredith frames her sketches with the by then familiar aesthetic principle of the picturesque, drawing on its descriptive categories of the beautiful or the sublime—the Blue Mountains are admirably sublime.

Alexander Harris's migrant fictions made him one of the major prose writers of this era. His first Australian work, *Settlers and Convicts, or Recollections of Sixteen Years' Labour in the Australian Backwoods* (1847) was signed by 'an emigrant mechanic'. It was followed by the much longer and more ambitious three-part novel, *The Emigrant Family or The Story of an Australian Settler* (1849). Typically of early nineteenth-century colonial narratives, and in the tradition of Defoe and other eighteenth-century prose writers, Harris insists on the realism of his works. An 'Advertisement' precedes *Settlers and Convicts*, stating that 'though published anonymously, the truth of the accounts given in this little work may be fully depended upon' (p. xxxi), while *The Emigrant Family* follows 'the delineation of the actual life' (p. 5) of that family. Harris's perspective as he writes of everyday life is both moralising and didactic. The alleged realism of these novels and the use in *Settlers and Convicts* of the narrative perspective of an ordinary working man are both signs of what would become a dominant strain of social realism in Australian literature. The mechanic's democratic ideology would also become familiar in the political orientation of later writing, such as Joseph Furphy's *Such is Life*, Henry Lawson's fiction and poetry and Miles Franklin's novels.

Settlers and Convicts depicts the Australian character as honest, manly and hospitable. The ideal emigrant is a yeoman farmer, and the narrative is always engaged with social issues. The narrator argues, as did many social commentators and colonial administrators, that the ability to purchase small holdings would keep the labouring classes out of the pubs, create a strong economy and resolve current dissatisfaction with land laws. Harris writes from a sense of the injustice that exists at all levels of the system, and in the service of all those who are at the mercy of employers or overseers. Books and self-education through reading are presented as a central value; the Bible is a powerful, humanising influence. Proposing the ideal of a social mean, the narrator compares the 'primitive simplicity of the scene' of an Aboriginal camp at evening with '"the busy hum" of "crowded cities"'. It prompts him to ask whether two such opposite states are both God's creation and to conclude that either of the two extremes of 'barbarism' and 'luxury' must be dangerous (pp. 134–5).

The Emigrant Family, with its overdrawn romance plot and melodramatic sub-plots, has more in common with the exaggerations of much colonial drama than with the emerging form of realist Australian fiction. Characters, especially females, are stereotyped and the often conservative didactic narrative is irritating. During a long-drawn-out process in which young and formerly wilful Marianna Bracton learns her proper feminine behaviour and role, the narrator comments on Marianna's changed appearance after an illness: 'they who delight to study the secret paths along which human spirits are led to their goal of perfection, . . . would have consoled themselves as they observed how faithfully the feminine journey was being taken, and that redundance of determination got rid of which would have endangered Marianna's future happiness'.[24] Schooled into conventional femininity, Marianna will now fulfil the colonial woman's ideological role as a civilising influence, making her representative of many women in much later nineteenth-century fiction. Miles Franklin's refusal of just such a schooling for Sybylla in *My Brilliant Career* (1901) appears perhaps more original by comparison than contemporary readers might allow. While the gender, race and class ideologies that structure colonial society are very apparent in Harris's work, only class issues are subject to any significant questioning.

RELIGION, MORALITY AND DOMESTICITY

Many of the colonies' leading figures were clerics, while religious discourses informed much colonial writing and sustained many colonists in their new lives, just as religious conviction justified colonising ideologies and structured conflicts in colonial politics and political writing. English class structures had long been defined by religious difference. Until early in the nineteenth century an education at Oxford or Cambridge, public office and a seat in Parliament were available only to Anglicans. The vast majority of landowners, those who were in positions of power and authority in England, were Anglican, as were professional men. Urban businessmen and tradespeople, on the other hand, were more often members of Nonconformist denominations. Catholicism was by then largely the religion of farm labourers and the urban poor. Colonial establishment figures were predominantly Anglican and political and economic struggles for power were often based in the conflict between Anglican authority and the challenge of Nonconformism. In New South Wales political life, for example, John Dunmore Lang's democratic republicanism, based on his Presbyterian faith, contested William Charles Wentworth's Anglican Australian form of neo-imperial power.

Journals, letters and chronicles written by colonial clerics illuminate the ways in which religious belief intersected with the conditions of colonial life.[25] That familiar social and literary tension between the chaos (human and natural) of the new world environment and the order English colonisation sought would be resolved, according to the authority of the Anglican Church, by its civilising influence, which would regulate colonial society according to God's will. That will ordained a social structure within which people were expected to resign themselves to their class position; it also endorsed what was seen as the natural rule of husband over wife. Religious observance in established churches was the mark of civilisation. The Reverend John Wollaston, who arrived with his family in Swan River Colony in 1841, displays such attitudes in his journals. His paternalistic offer to 'civilise' Aboriginal peoples—'I shd not mind [preaching under a Tree] —but they must first be taught the English language, for theirs is quite an unmanageable tongue . . . incapable of being reduced to any rules of grammar'[26]—demonstrates the destructive exercise of Anglicanism. The reference to 'preaching under a Tree' parodies the Nonconformist belief that neither clergy nor church was necessary for worship, and its corollary, that Christianity can best be practised in the deeds and expressed in the feelings of everyday life; that is, in Harris's kind of 'practical Christianity'. The assumption that Anglican English is the true measure of a civil society is a doubly exploitative form of colonialism which seeks to impose Christianity by removing the indigenous languages.

Peopled in the beginning by convicts, the colonies were understood as places of potential (or actual) social—hence moral—disorder, a state that was anathema to the English ruling class. It had been haunted since the French Revolution by the potential anarchy of the lower classes, a terror which was exacerbated by increases in poverty, crime, social unrest, and the activities of the Chartists. Throughout the 1830s, debates took place about the kinds of free settler who should be encouraged to emigrate. When transportation ended in New South Wales in 1840, these debates were focused on an increase in the number of Irish emigrants, who were seen as a threat to the Anglican ideal of a morally righteous and industrious society. Mary Teresa Vidal's *Tales for the Bush* (1845; 1995) translate Australian colonial life in the tradition of the moral tale, an enormously popular genre in the early nineteenth century. Vidal, whose husband was a clergyman, presents the colonies as places of moral temptation where Irish ignorance and Catholicism might flourish. Such tales acted as a didactic form of religious teaching to confirm their intended audience among the labouring and servant classes in their position in a sober, thrifty and dutiful population of workers. 'Ruth' tells the story of Mrs Walsh and her two children, modest, humble Ruth and unsteady Dick, who emigrate to New South Wales. Ruth is horrified by the apparent classlessness of colonial life: 'The blunt manners of every one she saw in New South Wales struck her very much' (p. 26). Colonial egalitarianism is not valued, but presented as emblematic of a breakdown in social structures, indicating a loss of moral values and spiritual beliefs. In her dress and manner, Ruth provides a much needed reminder to others—Mary White, a nursemaid, is recalled by Ruth's appearance to her former, better self—that the English class system is far preferable to the colonial class muddle.

Access to authorising colonial discourses like Anglicanism gave writers a secure position as colonial subjects, although, even in such powerful discursive positions, there are moments when the vulnerability of the colonial ego and the ambivalent meanings that produce the colonial space brought about shifts in that subjectivity. In the less public discursive practices of letter, diary and journal writing, the subject/object split suffered by the colonial self becomes most evident. These forms of writing were regulated and governed by strict literary and social conventions at that time, just as were the more public forms. Keeping a journal was not an idle or purely personal occupation for Australian colonists; it was considered the duty of every educated young person. To be able to write well was one of the measures of the cultivated person, and letter writers or diarists were expected to provide a careful record of the events and experiences of their lives, and to

reflect on those events. Letters were the most extensively produced literary form throughout the first decades of settlement, reflecting the desire of colonists to 'write home' and
those 'at home' to receive news of colonial life. Sections of diaries and journals were often
reproduced in letters, or written to be circulated among family and friends in Britain,
and some letter and journal writers expected that their work might be published.

At a time when the distinctions between the public, masculine world of industry
and commerce and the private, feminine world of home and family were becoming more
rigid in England, the less stable social structures of the colonies made it more difficult
to enforce such distinctions. Colonial diary writing reproduces the blurring of social and
literary boundaries between the public and private spheres, indicating the ideological
structuring and the artificiality of such boundaries. George Fletcher Moore's *Diary of Ten
Years of an Early Settler in Western Australia* (1884), published retrospectively in London,
partakes of both these worlds. He wrote, as many did, to inform family and friends in
England of colonial life, to console himself, and to identify his narration with a romantic, fortunate history of colonisation. Moore emigrated to Swan River Colony in 1830
and was a colonial official as well as a farmer; acquired extensive property; gained positions of colonial power on the Bench and in government, and made explorations that
were recognised by a river being named after him. Yet Moore's writing is often expressive
of his feelings, which are tied to his former family life. Here, he writes to his brother: 'I
lose all spirit when writing to you, . . . for where is the overflowing of affection, the out-
pouring of unrestrained communication?' (p. 107). Moore also describes the political
world of the colony. Like many colonial writers, he reflects on Aboriginal life and culture.
He welcomed as well as 'employed' Aboriginal people, and compiled and published *A
Descriptive Vocabulary of the Language in Common Use Amongst the Aborigines of Western
Australia* (1842). Nevertheless, Moore supported the contradictory official policy
towards Aboriginal people, which on the one hand presented the need for 'protection', on
the other for harsh control.

In one dramatic incident, Moore describes an encounter with an Aboriginal group
that includes Yagan, who with his father Midgegoroo was reputed to have caused the
recent deaths of several white men:

> Have had a long, angry, and wholly unexpected conference to-day with the very spirit of evil
> himself, I mean the notorious Ya-gan. . . . [After much discussion between the two men, to
> which the Aboriginal group listens attentively] Ya-gan again stepped forward, and leaning
> familiarly with his left hand on my shoulder, while he gesticulated with his right, delivered a
> sort of recitative, . . . I regret that I could not understand him, but I conjectured, from the
> tone and manner, that the purport was this:—'You came to our country; you have driven us
> from our haunts, and disturbed us in our occupations: as we walk in our own country, we are
> fired upon by the white men; why should the white men treat us so?'
>
> This reminded me of a chorus in a Greek tragedy; . . . [and] There is something in his
> daring which one is forced to admire (p. 192).

This confrontation between men of influence from the colonising and colonised cultures, by then in a situation of guerrilla warfare in south-western Australia, dramatises the silencing power of English over Aboriginal cultural discourses. The narrative shift in the stereotyped characterisation of Yagan from devilish to heroic, and Moore's poignant rendition of Yagan's supposed statement about the dispossession and death English colonisation has brought to Aboriginal groups, appear to place the two men in a position of equal recognition and knowledge. However, Moore's unselfconscious self-positioning as translator of Yagan's words makes him both interpreter and recorder of the scene, and his appropriation of the incident into English through his use of the literary conventions of the 'recitative' and 'Greek tragedy', disempowers Yagan as an independent cultural presence.

It has been suggested that the conventional constraints that shape the discursive practices available to those in positions of authority are ones women are free of; she has 'only to respond'[27] to her colonial situation. Yet seeing and writing are always culturally prescribed activities and the conventions of 'feminine' discourses are surely as regulatory as are those of so-called masculine discourses. Nevertheless, the idea that women's experience of the colonial world might be less mediated than men's is suggestive. It acknowledges that women's imaginative responses to their new landscapes were shaped through a set of historical and social circumstances different in subtle but significant ways from those of their male peers. It is significant that women colonists, many of whom migrated only because the decision to do so was made by men in their families, wrote sometimes of their increased sense of energy and freedom in colonial environments where social expectations about what women could and should do were often more relaxed than in the old world. This is especially so in the writings of women who travelled and settled beyond urban colonial centres. Despite the often very hard and unaccustomed work many women had to do, and despite the absence of the social structures on which such women were accustomed to rely, their writing may convey a sense of colonial agency in contrast to the confinement of their former lives.

Women's role in the colonies, however, remained defined in domestic terms—they were expected to give birth, raise families and provide a moral, civilising influence. Their position thus remained ambiguous, at once essential to the imperial enterprise of building a stable, pious and obedient society, and at the same time partial to it, since that enterprise was necessarily structured through masculine activities. Male colonists, on the other hand, had an often increased scope for such activities—they had a position to take up and a purpose to fulfil, as administrators, explorers, pastoralists, labourers, poets and so on. The nostalgia and confusion that is so typically an outcome of migration to the colonies, and which is referred to in colonial writings as a lack of association with all that was known and familiar, is suffered by both female and male colonists, but is differently inflected for women, who are distanced from the politically active centre of colonial life as well as from their former lives. The habit of endowing known objects and scenes with a particular quality through the feelings and memories associated with them had acquired the status of an aesthetic cult in the early 1800s, and its place in literary colonial writing is significant.[28] The longing of the colonial subject for such associations and the nostalgia connected with their loss and remembering is striking in much colonial writing. A recovery of a coherent, subjective self in the colonial situation became possible if the strangeness of the new environment was made familiar by bringing to it associations from the past. Such a strategy is particularly evident in many of the so-called 'feminine' writings of domestic life, or the private sphere.

Louisa Clifton's journal represents with striking clarity, if rather self-consciously, the effect of colonial migration, which is disaffection from the known self. She claims indeed that she is rendered inarticulate by the experience. Clifton was a reluctant emigrant, who travelled out of a sense of duty with her family to the new, Wakefield-inspired settlement at Australind, south of Perth, where her father was appointed Administrator. Before the journey she repressed any feelings about her future: 'I do not allow myself to think or speak of it'[29] and on arrival she writes of her experience as an emigrant self split between the way she feels and her inability to speak that feeling: 'I never before experienced such an entire incapability of mental exertion; the sense of distance imposes a barrier to communication not as far as feelings are concerned, only in the verbal expression of them. My heart is just as warm as ever, but my pen is frigid and powerless' (pp. 60–1). However, Clifton goes on to place herself in the position of a cultivated and enlightened observer of the new landscape and begins to inscribe a colonial self. Her delight in the encampment on shore, described in a letter to her brother Waller, perhaps represents the new freedoms available for women in colonial life, and she employs the trope of the picturesque to bring the unfamiliar into the realm of the familiar: 'I cannot describe half of the amusing and curious incidents of the day nor convey to your mind an adequate idea of the picturesque appearance of a bush encampment in such a climate and with such scenery on all sides' (pp. 55–6). Perhaps a more complex negotiation of the split between the security of the old world and the desolation of the new one is conveyed in Georgiana Molloy's writing of her first baby's death to her friend Helen Story. The baby's grave, 'though sodded with British clover, looks so singular and solitary in this wilderness, of which I can scarcely give you an idea'.[30] Molloy, who was to become in her new environment a talented Australian botanist, initially through her involvement in gardening, here uses that environment to represent what she then saw as an unintelligible conjunction of the familiar, the British clover, and the unfamiliar, the wilderness.

Eliza Brown's letters to her father are rendered particularly poignant by her unusually clear representation of the gendered differences that the nineteenth century constructed between female and male sensibilities, as well as of the power of the parent culture to reduce and trivialise colonial literary productions. Eliza Brown's husband had borrowed from her father to bring his family to Swan River Colony in 1841. He was not always able to repay the debt, so that she continually mediated the economic relationship between husband and father. During her correspondence with her father, he requests that she confine her letters to only one a year; a request that appears not to be directly related to this conflicted relationship. In her reply, she

promise[s] only a single letter. If a parent cannot bear with my infirmity how can I expect any one less bound by kindred ties to listen with interest to the outpourings of my heart in its search for sympathy, tedious descriptions and labours in vain for that is the light in which I now regard these unfortunate productions.[31]

As Brown asks her father to return her letters: 'Pray dearest Papa send me those unworthy annals, they . . . will be useful to me as documents from which to cull reminiscences of a settler's life . . .' (p. 134), her letter writing may be seen as emblematic of the colonial condition and of the ambiguous subjective positioning of middle-class women in the colonies. While her correspondence is always properly feminine, using polite epistolary conventions and aware of the proprieties of her status as daughter and wife—she is always conciliatory, apologising and humbly thanking—it has offended her father. Freed from the immediate restraints of her father's will, Brown is judged by him to be overly discursive, expansive, and demandingly emotive in her writing self. She has become a disorderly colonial subject and her letters are thus unacceptable to the authorising father. Ordered to reduce both the length and frequency of her writing, Eliza Brown is contrite. But in her request that her letters be returned, she claims a new, colonial women's story, one that she had sought to verify in the communication with her father, but which would now be self-authorising. She characterises 'the private letter' as 'a woman's weapon' (p. 134), a mode of self-expression that she will not give up.

The capacity of women's writing to challenge patriarchal prescriptions and limitations on women's lives has been an ongoing feature of much Australian women's literary writing; in the same way much colonial writing challenged the cultural control imposed from the metropolis. Charles Harpur exemplifies this challenge in his writing. Although he acquired no poetic status outside the narrow scope of his colonial world, and little within it, the range and originality of his work was located in and derived from its colonial environments, social and natural, in a way that had not been available to previous writers. Harpur's 'Discourse on Poetry', published in part in the *Empire* (1849), illustrates his belief that poetry had a clear social as well as an aesthetic function, and that the foundations of a new society must include, indeed be based in, its own poetic voices. The writings of these colonial selves are marked by their isolating experiences of defamiliarisation and disorientation; their imperial and neo-national imperatives; within gender relations as well as those of race and class; above all through the consequences of the confrontation of the invading culture with its new environment.

FICTION FIELDS AND FUTURES

Frederick Sinnett migrated from England to the colony of South Australia in 1849. Like many emigrants, Sinnett led a peripatetic colonial life that often included work as a journalist on newspapers and magazines. He was one of the founders of *Melbourne Punch* (begun 1855, one of Australia's longest running magazines) and of other journals. Sinnett has a place in the beginnings of Australian literary culture, not just for his writing and editorial work, but for his critical essay, 'The Fiction Fields of Australia', published in two parts in 1856 in the *Journal of Australasia*.[32] His was the first attempt to define critically the nature of Australian literature and 'Fiction Fields' established the terms of a debate that was ongoing over at least the next century. Sinnett's enquiry was not into the 'feasibility of writing novels in Australia', but the 'feasibility of writing Australian novels'. He argued that its universal nature distinguishes the truly literary work; that great Australian novels could be written according to this criterion, since human nature is everywhere the same; that Australia had advantages for the writer in the novelty of its scenery and customs; yet that those few Australian novels that had been written were 'too apt to be books of travel in disguise' (p. 31). Sinnett's implied denigration of such writing is not ours today. It is precisely because colonial writing is the writing of all kinds of travellers in their particular contexts that it begins to acquire those qualities that differentiated it from the universalism Sinnett valued. By 1853 Sydney had five bookshops; and several major Australian publications in the 1850s, including Catherine Helen Spence's *Clara Morison: A Tale of South Australia during the Gold Fever* (1854), and Henry Kingsley's *The Recollections of Geoffry Hamlyn* (1859) begin the consolidation of the conflicted history of the settling-in of English in Australia.

PART TWO

1851–1914

3

LITERARY CULTURE 1851–1914:
FOUNDING A CANON

Elizabeth Perkins

The definition of a literary tradition—whether national or regional—can be in the nature of the case only a kind of majority report. It stresses only those elements in the older literature which at a particular time are felt to have value, to constitute a usable past. The literature of earlier centuries—except for the omnivorous literary historian—exists only in the minds of those who actually read it and find it significant.

Jay B. Hubbell, Who Are the Major American Writers? (1972)

The Canon, once we view it as the relation of an individual reader and writer to what has been preserved out of what has been written, and forget the canon as a list of books for required study, will be seen as identical with the literary Art of Memory.

Harold Bloom, The Western Canon (1994)

Australian Literature degree courses introduced by universities in the middle of the twentieth century selected their nineteenth-century texts from a 'canon' established some fifty years before by readers, critics and publishers. The period under review saw a deliberate effort by writers and critics to establish a literary culture independent of and supplementary to the British heritage. The foundation of this putative canon, which retains some authority and is supported by publishing agendas, was more complex than the following account has space to suggest. Although its makers endorsed universal aesthetic excellence, they may not have been completely unaware of some of the contemporary social forces determining the criteria they adopted when admitting work to the national tradition. The conquest of the canon by popular writers like Henry Lawson and A.B. Paterson, and the claims of short fiction to canonical recognition, are significant stages in the development of Australian literature. Popular appeal was also emphasised by the most vigorous nineteenth-century Australian drama which promoted two of the major themes engaging both the general public and the serious reader—convict and outlaw figures, and bush life, and the ambivalent values attached to them.

Canonical texts demonstrate their contemporary cultural usefulness by illuminating their own epochs and the present, and are usually those which, as Howard Felperin suggests, have a history of critical attention as well as a wide general readership.[1] Despite the efforts of the early proponents of an Australian canon, a history of critical attention needed some time to take root. Three years before the first Chair of Australian Literature was established in 1962 at Sydney, the oldest Australian university, the Melbourne poet and academic Vincent Buckley doubted there was sufficient Australian writing to constitute a separate university course of study. Buckley felt there was no 'convincing canon of books, or a habit of critical discussion capable of dealing with the issues which the existence of this body of work presents us with.'[2] The academy, however, including Buckley himself, already taught some Australian texts as elements in undergraduate literature courses, and Australian writing attracted serious critical attention in earlier programs of public lectures at universities, in the annual round of Commonwealth Literary Fund lectures given in universities since 1940, and in newspapers and literary journals.

Because poets command a smaller and presumably especially discriminating readership, poetry, in the past at least, tended to represent the clearest register of cultural taste. This chapter on the establishment of literary tradition emphasises the poets whose reputations developed between the beginning of the gold rushes and the outbreak of the First World War, making them part of the canon later accepted by lecturers and teachers. Central to literary culture, however, were distinctively Australian prose writers like Marcus Clarke (1846–81), Rolf Boldrewood (Thomas Alexander Browne, 1826–1915), Henry Lawson (1867–1922) and Steele Rudd (Arthur Hoey Davis, 1868–1935) whose reputations were firmly established within this period, and whose work, unlike that of Catherine Spence, Tasma (Jessie Couvreur), Ada Cambridge, Rosa Praed, Barbara Baynton, Louis Becke (George Lewis), Price Warung (William Astley) and Ernest Favenc, for example, has never been out of print.

When Tom Inglis Moore drew up the first full-length undergraduate course in Australian Literature for Canberra University College in 1955, no one questioned his selection of poets, or his emphasis on Clarke, Boldrewood and Lawson as representative prose writers of the late nineteenth century. The earliest New South Wales poets, Michael Massey Robinson, Barron Field and Charles Tompson were noted—with William Charles Wentworth's 'Australasia' ode as the precursor of nationalism—but of the poets writing chiefly before 1914 those emphasised in Moore's course were Charles Harpur, Henry Kendall, Adam Lindsay Gordon, George Gordon McCrae, James Brunton Stephens, Ada Cambridge, A.B. Paterson, Henry Lawson, Bernard O'Dowd and Christopher Brennan.[3] These represent the poets of 'major' and 'minor' status found on most nineteenth-century poetry courses now. Fear of over-evaluation and irresponsible comparisons between Australian and English writers underlay A.D. Hope's warning to students at Sydney University in 1953 that Australian criticism was 'provincial in its outlook' and that now '[i]t must approach its task of judging the merits of Australian writing in the same spirit and with the same standards as it has when it approaches English literature'.[4] Earlier makers of the Australian canon were concerned with the same problem. Thomas Heney in 1888 saw dangers in provincial criticism and wanted colonial literature evaluated by a slowly matured critical judgment, and H.G. Turner and Alexander Sutherland in 1898 warned Australian reviewers against meaningless laudation and the deadening effect on quality when local products were injudiciously praised merely because they were local.[5]

THE CANON BEFORE 1860

A canon develops where there is a society with readers and an adequate literary culture. When workable gold was discovered in 1851, the six colonies centred on Sydney, Hobart, Melbourne, Brisbane, Adelaide and Perth had already established the beginnings of an Australian literary culture. Inland towns like Goulburn in New South Wales or Bendigo in Victoria, thriving on the pastoral industry or nearby goldfields, also had their Mechanics' or Arts' Institutes where occasional lectures were given on Australian literature, while a number of regional newspapers published the work of colonial poets.[6] Turner and Sutherland in 1898 claimed that between 1835 and 1885 Victoria 'contributed to the world's libraries hundreds of books worthy to live', an achievement due to a period of 'quickening intellectual development, of widely-spreading education, of enterprising journalism, of facilities of travel that brightened the intellect and widened the sympathies, and, above all, of peace and material progress'.[7] By the mid-century, literary activity and the consciousness of a cultural life were under surveillance by the arbiters who shape, but do not wholly control, the developments of literary canons.

The development of a canon of literature depended not only on the production of literature but also on the existence of what was called 'a periodical literature' to disseminate and assess this production. As a reviewer in the *Sydney Chronicle* on 12 June 1847 wrote, when commenting on a mediocre collection of poems celebrating the end of transportation to New South Wales in 1843, 'So long, however, as we are destitute of periodical publications, devoted solely to literature and science, so long will New South Wales remain at the very bottom of the literary ladder, unable to ascend a single step'. This survey cannot cover the many essays and reviews in newspapers and periodicals that influenced the critical accounts and anthologies through which the development of the tradition is traced. Poetry was especially dependent on periodical publication, if less dependent than novels on the forces that drove the Australian and overseas publishing industry, although serialisation of novels and publication of short stories in newspapers and journals widened the readership for prose fiction.

Self-conscious shaping of the Australian canon is obvious. The earliest writers, especially those born in the colony, like the poet Charles Harpur (1813–68), began to construct a canon of national literature and their criteria were nothing less than classical excellence and Australian uniqueness. For Harpur and his literary compatriots, classical excellence lay in those qualities which Bloom, the American defender of the Western Canon, recognises as spiritual power, spiritual authority and aesthetic dignity, dependent upon a work's mastery of figurative language, originality, cognitive power, knowledge and exuberance of diction.[8] In a note to a poem, later called 'The "Nevers" of Poetry,' published in the *Sydney Empire* in March 1858, Harpur rejected critical interference in Australian literature by outsiders like Frank Fowler who came with this express purpose 'all the way from Fatherland'. Harpur wanted a finger-tip in the pie of establishing a critical basis for 'a national literature' and this poem he drily claimed was his 'contribution to the canonical foundation of it'.[9] The poets in Harpur's early canon include William Charles Wentworth, Henry Parkes, Henry Halloran, Daniel Deniehy and John Dunmore Lang. Harpur regarded Parkes as a political antagonist and James Martin, named as an essayist, as a personal enemy and each had commented scathingly about the other's writing. Harpur's parody of Wentworth's celebratory 'Australasia' is famous. In asserting the integrity of national literature, however, he sank his personal animosity and political difference in a stand against imperial patronage. Twelve years before, in the last of three lectures on modern poetry given at the School of Arts in June 1846, R.K. Ewing listed, with some severe criticism, Halloran, Wentworth, Parkes and Harpur among the colonial poets. Ewing included Charles Tompson whose delicate pastoral poetry Harpur apparently overlooked. Tompson (1807–83) was the first Australian-born poet to publish a collection in Australia, and the sentiments and technique would have given Tompson's *Wild Notes, from the Lyre of a Native Minstrel* (1826) a place in Harpur's canon.

The early canon-makers knew what they wanted: a literature which was national but not narrowly nationalistic. The *Sydney University Magazine* in 1852 called for a 'National Literature' which should comprise work of beauty and of the imagination, clearly stamped with a unique identity, free from servile imitation, self-dependent and written by poets whose intellect and sensibility were shaped by the Australian environment and culture. Deniehy may have had this in mind when, in the *Empire*, 22 April 1853, he wrote that Harpur's *The Bushrangers: A Play, and Other Poems* (1853) contained 'the most satisfactory proof of the existence of native genius of a high order, that has yet been offered to the public'. Harpur was a national poet who produced exquisite poetry of a 'rare and delicate imaginative loveliness', with the stamp of a 'free, self-dependent, and self-moulded intellect', which could be taken as a type of the growing native mind and encourage 'hope for the grandeur of our national destinies'.

Frederick Sinnett's 'The Fiction Fields of Australia', published over two issues of the Melbourne *Journal of Australasia* in 1856, deserves the importance accorded it by scholars like C.H. Hadgraft, who edited the essay as a monograph in 1966. Acknowledging Australia's lack of 'archaeological accessories', apart from Aboriginal associations, Sinnett asserts that Australia nevertheless possesses all the attributes of human society and an abundance of scenery to provide material for the creative genius.[10] In her natural and external circumstances she has 'more of what we used to call romance' than England, perhaps a reference to the convict and pioneering history soon to be exploited in fiction and drama. Sinnett foresees writers like Lawson, Baynton, Praed and Furphy who would convince readers that the conversations of squatters, bullock-drivers and diggers could make literary material. In arguing at length that the right conditions exist for the development of Australian literary genius, Sinnett indirectly supports the notion of a canon, and his detailed discussion of Catherine Spence's *Clara Morison* (1854) suggests that he would have given this novel a place in it. He is less enthusiastic about Alexander Harris's *Martin Beck* (1849, 1852) and Charles Rowcroft's *Tales of the Colonies* (1843) and *The Emigrant in Search of a Colony* (1851) but does not dismiss their achievements.

EARLY CRITICAL ACCOUNTS: WALKER AND BARTON

The first critical account of literature in New South Wales published in book form was a lecture on 'Australian Literature' by the Windsor solicitor William Walker in 1864. The Sydney audience for literary addresses like this included the coterie of men with cultivated taste, centred on the solicitor Nicol Drysdale Stenhouse (1806–73). 'The Stenhouse Circle' had considerable influence on the literary culture of Sydney, providing a critical audience which was sympathetic to the intentions of colonial writers but not injudiciously extravagant in commending their work. Walker singles out Wentworth, Harpur and Kendall and cites approvingly 'the animated and highly patriotic apostrophe [from Wentworth's 'Australasia' ode] which is often quoted', that is, the fourteen lines parodied by Harpur.[11] Writing by Joseph Sheridan Moore, the satirist William Forster, Halloran, James Lionel Michael and Deniehy is considered important, but Walker mentions only two novels, Louisa Atkinson's *Gertrude the Immigrant* (1857) and Harris's *Martin Beck*. 'The two best known and most popular poets' are Harpur and Kendall. Harpur, Walker believes, is to some extent entitled to the honour of poet laureateship.[12] His poetry is 'dreamy and philosophical—often obscure, but betraying true poetic fire and inspiration'. Kendall is placed above Harpur, a position which he was to maintain for the next hundred years. The smoothness and tenderness of Kendall's poetry are noted, and his characteristic grief, gloom and sadness are regretted. 'The Muse of Australia', 'The Curlew Song' and 'The Maid of Gerringong' are praised, and Kendall is commended as 'a true child of nature' and a young man Australia may well be proud of.

Edmund Barton's *The Literature of New South Wales* and *The Poets and Prose Writers of New South Wales* both appeared in 1866. *The Literature of New South Wales* was an annotated bibliography of newspapers and journals, and the work of the poets and prose writers who had published monographs since the beginning of the colony. The second volume comprised short commentaries to illustrate extracts from the work of fourteen of the writers Barton considered most important, including Harpur and Kendall. Barton doubts the status of Harpur's work partly because of its narrowness of culture, although Harpur produces some fine landscape painting and local colouring, and possesses 'a certain amount of genius'.[13] Barton acknowledges that Harpur always gives an impression of power and that he 'laid the foundation stone of our national poetry'. Kendall's work seems more promising to Barton, who finds it distinctively Australian and original: 'He has an artist's eye for landscape, and if his shading is rather too dark, his outlines are none the less true'. As an example of colonial satire, Barton prints excerpts from William Forster's 'The Devil and the Governor', an attack on Governor Gipps. Forster is represented in later anthologies, but has not achieved prominence. Henry Halloran (1811–93), hailed by Barton as the 'Poet Laureate of the Colony', is an interesting case of a poet who has not made it even into a minor canon. Barton serves Halloran well by reprinting his long, semi-serious, gently satiric poem, 'The Bards' Colloquy', in which Harpur, Kendall and Halloran meditate on the aspirations of their poetic practice while enjoying a peaceful smoke. Halloran's copious output, from the 1830s to 1890, should perhaps remain a footnote because his verse is usually bland and noticeably lacks the sometimes eccentric and sometimes compelling originality of Harpur's; but he contributed to a tradition and influenced Kendall and Harpur, for whom he was also a rival to be emulated and surpassed.

DOUGLAS SLADEN: THE FIRST ANTHOLOGIST/CRITIC

Douglas Sladen, an editor, poet and novelist, is remembered now chiefly for three influential anthologies of 'Australian'—that is, Australian and New Zealand—poetry published in London in 1888.[14] His Introduction to *A Century of Australian Song* (1888), effectively a synopsis of the development of Australian and New Zealand poetry, is still quoted by literary historians. Colonial and London critics were concerned that Sladen, then based in England, intended to offer a definitive canon of Australian and New Zealand poetry to an international readership. The intention of *A Century of Australian Song*, however, was promotional rather than canonical in that it was 'a selection of poems inspired by life and scenery in Australia'. Sladen points out that the character of Australian poetry was now largely determined by the editorial taste of the great weekly papers, and commends the editors who 'patriotically, have shown a desire to encourage an Australian School of Poetry'.

Largely through Sladen's efforts, Adam Lindsay Gordon's bust was placed in Westminster Abbey in 1934, and in his Introduction Sladen foregrounds Gordon and Kendall, with the apparent intention of later questioning Gordon's eminence as an Australian poet. Sladen begins with Wentworth's 'Australasia' ode as the first noteworthy Australian poem, but asserts that Australia's poetic literature dates from Harpur who is 'generally' regarded as 'the grey forefather of Australian poets'. Sladen was unsurprised by the paucity of blank verse poems by Australian poets as 'to a great extent it is the offspring of a classical education', a suggestion that might have pleased Harpur whose blank verse poem, 'The Creek of the Four Graves', is printed in Sladen's anthology. Sladen resurrects Lang and Parkes as under-rated poets, and in fact Parkes's verse retained some reputation until his death as a famous elder statesman in 1896.

A substantial discussion of Kendall and Gordon distinguishes carefully the kinds of poetry in which Gordon was superior, that is, bush life and action poetry: 'Kendall wrote like a poet who had been to the races; Gordon like a poet who had raced'. Sladen nevertheless thinks Kendall the better poet, and makes one of those judgments deplored by later Australian critics, equating stanzas and lines by Kendall with others by Keats and Shelley. Gordon's faults are 'want of culture and knowledge, narrowness of scope and sympathy', and Sladen prefers Harpur's long poem, 'The Witch of Hebron', at that time little known, to Gordon's 'Ashtaroth', although 'Harpur has written very few other poems that could be mentioned with Gordon's'. Sladen concludes that Gordon 'has had very much the start of Kendall in England; and so far as the semi-cultivated portion of poetry-readers are concerned, we doubt not will continue to have', but Kendall would eventually become the supreme favourite with 'that cultivated class of intellect that delights to be made the confidante of Nature'.

Discriminating in most respects, Sladen occasionally over-estimates writing now considered minor. 'Orion' Horne (Richard Hengist Horne), 'the little warden of the Australian gold-fields', is praised for his popular *Orion* (1854) which ran into ten editions by 1888, and which 'almost rivalled' Keats's 'Endymion'. Horne remains a historical figure. The contemporaries Arthur Patchett Martin and Garnet Walch, remembered now for essays and stage drama respectively, are said to show 'brilliant capacity' and their poetry, though small in quantity, has 'put them in the front rank of Australian poets'. James Lionel Michael (1824–68), the 'literary father' to Henry Kendall, is cited for his verse novel *John Cumberland* (1860) which Sladen, like Barton twenty years earlier, compares to Coventry Patmore's *The Angel in the House*. Sladen believes Michael suffered undeserved neglect, but his work rarely appears now outside period anthologies. James Brunton Stephens (1835–1902), commended for his verse novel *Convict Once* (1871) which is placed above Gordon's 'Ashtaroth', still retains a place in anthologies and literary criticism. *Convict Once*, a monodrama of passion, guilt and remorse, is narrated by a beautiful ex-convict, Magdalen Power, now a Queensland governess, who seduces the lover of one of her pupils. Written in graceful hexameters, the poem has the energy of serious melodrama and contains some memorable lines which express Magdalen Power's struggle with her proud emotional nature and self-imposed discipline and humility. Brian Elliott sees Magdalen as an epitome of 'the hovering malaise of the colonial world', but the poem now could be placed beside both the convict/outlaw literature of the period and the novels of women writers like Rosa Praed.[15] Another poet whose work is still valued is George Gordon McCrae (1833–1927), whom Sladen calls a poet 'of first-class reputation and achievements'. *The Story of Balladeàdro* and *Màmba, 'the Bright-eyed': An Aboriginal Romance*, both published as monographs in 1867, are not great poetry or accurate depictions of Aboriginal life and culture. McCrae, however, was inspired by direct contact with Aboriginal people, and apart from some well-meant efforts by Eliza Dunlop and Harpur to write Aboriginal elegies, McCrae was the first to attempt to give serious representation in a conventional literary genre to the voice of indigenous Australian people. Francis Adams (1862–93) was making a name as a poet and essayist in 1888 when his *Songs of the Army of the Night* was published. Sladen reprints only from the earlier *Poetical Works* (1887) but in critically assessing Adams's 'new methods of versification' he may have the later volume, influenced by Walt Whitman, in mind. Adams's importance is suggested by Inglis Moore's focus on him, along with Henry Lawson and Creeve Roe (Victor Daley), as an exponent of social criticism in ballad form. Of the other balladists, Sladen regrets he has no examples of the work of John Farrell or Victor Dale[y], who were 'spoken of so highly by the Australian Press', and both these *Bulletin* poets with democratic sympathies appear in later twentieth-century anthologies. Women poets (some with male pseudonyms) are reasonably well represented in *A Century of Australian Song* but of those included only Caroline Leakey and Australie (Emily Manning) are presently found in late twentieth-century anthologies of women writers. Sladen regrets Mary Hannay Foott's absence but although he offers comments on many women writers, Ada Cambridge is not mentioned.

Sladen's *Australian Poets 1788–1888* (1888) includes many of the same poets, but the anthology is not confined to Australian landscape themes. Additions include poems by several women, such as Harriet Martin, and by Robert Sealy, whose verse, published in newspapers and in the collection *Scraps by Menippus* in Sydney in 1859, is a respectable contribution to early Australian satire. The Introduction comprises Patchett Martin's 'Concerning Australian Poets', in which he praises Brunton Stephens as 'the most gifted of all the writers of verse in Australia'. Martin admits that Australian literature cannot develop until there is also 'an Australian school of criticism', but warns that we should not forget our great English heritage in the 'petty endeavour to establish an "Australian literature"'.[16]

A largely critical review of *A Century of Australian Song* appeared in the *Sydney Quarterly Magazine* in September 1888. The writer was Thomas Heney, a minor but respected literary figure, and editor of a number of colonial newspapers, including the *Sydney Morning Herald*. Heney summarises the objections of those who were unconsciously or consciously aware that canons were being created, arguing that compendious anthologies like Sladen's put at risk the reputations of Australian writers, critics and readers. Like later academics, he deplored the notion that 'much ought to be forgiven a man or woman who writes upon Australian subjects from Australian standpoints on the ground of their local appeal'. Rejecting provincial criticism as dangerous, Heney advocated 'severe canons of art, the laborious discipline of learning', and the 'final arbitrament' of 'the slow and matured judgement which all work must experience, but only genius can abide'.

BYRNE, PATCHETT MARTIN, AND TURNER AND SUTHERLAND: IMPERIAL PATRONAGE AND JUDICIOUS PATRIOTISM

Gordon was the only poet discussed in Desmond Byrne's highly-regarded *Australian Writers* (1896), but essays on Clarke, Henry Kingsley, Ada Cambridge, Boldrewood, Mrs Campbell Praed and Tasma indicate their international status. Byrne may never have visited Australia and his judgments, although occasionally patronising, are free from provincialism. Byrne's Introduction, ignoring efforts by the *Melbourne Review*, the *Argus*, the *Colonial Monthly* and the *Sydney Quarterly Magazine* among others, claims that Australians 'make no special effort to encourage the growth of a literature of their own', although the young, highly civilised country is 'self-governing to the extent of being a republic in all but name'.[17] Commending Gordon's rare vigour and melody, his delicate ear for the music of words, Byrne denies that there is much uniquely Australian in his work, and questions Clarke's famous 1867 correlation of Gordon's melancholy tone with the influence of the Weird Melancholy of Australian landscape, suggesting that '[t]his explanation, if not wholly erroneous, is at least much exaggerated'. Byrne attributes the character of Gordon's poetry to the character of the poet himself. Although he does not quite remove Gordon from the canon of Australian poets to give him a minor place among the English, he believes that Gordon's poems are admired 'for the human interest in them; for what they tell of tastes and personal qualities dear to the pleasure-loving and fighting Briton in whatever land he may be'. English readers do not 'ask for' the poems of Harpur, Kendall or Brunton Stephens; nevertheless Byrne comments on Kendall, who 'almost deserves to be called the Australian Shelley', but whose 'thoughts are too remote from the common interests of life', and who has recorded only what is sad and painful in his own character.

The brief but influential *The Beginnings of an Australian Literature* (1898) was delivered in London as a lecture by Arthur Patchett Martin, who had lived in Australia for thirty years, and edited the *Melbourne Review* and several anthologies which included Australian verse and prose. Martin describes himself as 'the publicist' who first introduced Gordon to English readers, and his account of Australian prose and verse is dominated by a discussion of Gordon's life and work.[18] Martin's account begins by doubting that any literature written in English should be designated by its colonial origin, but concedes that there is convenience in using the terms American or Australian literature. He offers some faint praise to a few Australian writers such as Harpur, Kendall (beside whose lyrics Harpur's lines 'read like so much disjointed prose'), Brunton Stephens, and Martin's 'old Melbourne friend', G.G. McCrae. Martin's comment on the subject of McCrae's Aboriginal lays is too crass to warrant repetition. The women novelists Mrs Campbell Praed, Ada Cambridge and Tasma fare better than any of the poets other than Gordon. Martin endorses Clarke's claim that Gordon's work might be seen as 'something very like the beginnings of a national school of Australian poetry'. Martin assures his English audience that the younger generation of Australia had achieved nothing in literature since the death of the 'two remarkable young Englishmen', Clarke and Gordon: 'I fear that the youthful vigour and ability of the colonies have been displayed on the cricket-field and the mining market rather than in the poorly remunerated services of the Muses'. An echo is heard of the conflict between the imperial Fowler and colonial Harpur when Martin attacks Turner and Sutherland's recently published *Development of Australian Literature,* and deplores their reservations about any of the Australian writers who had won approval in London. Misreading contempt in Turner and Sutherland's assessment of the *Bulletin* school, Martin, from the vantage point of London, weighs up its strengths and weaknesses. He recognises 'a certain native vigour and originality', and he praises the thoroughly Australian beauty and pathos of Paterson's 'On Kiley's Run'. Deflating the expectation that, at the end of the nineteenth century, Australia possessed anything worth calling a literary tradition, Martin concludes that the 'literary output' of Australia comprises 'a couple of novels written forty years ago by a half-forgotten English novelist [Henry Kingsley's *The Recollections of Geoffry Hamlyn*, 1859]; some half-dozen other stories, including Marcus Clarke's *For the Term of His Natural Life*; and Adam Lindsay Gordon's collected poems'. Martin finds nothing distinctively Australian, apart from a few selections from Kendall and the best of Paterson's racy ballads, but in these 'strangely assorted volumes and scattered selections' he faintly discerns 'The Beginnings of an Australian Literature'.

Not a skerrick of imperial patronage appears in *The Development of Australian Literature* (1898) by Henry Gyles Turner and Alexander Sutherland. The former, a Melbourne bank manager, founded and then co-edited the *Melbourne Review* (1876–85) with Sutherland, Professor of English Literature at Melbourne University. Of the earliest poets, only Harpur's achievement is seen as considerable, although James Lionel Michael is given more attention than he had received for many years. The biographies of Gordon and Kendall which enraged Martin were reprinted from the *Melbourne Review* and the *Australasian*, and the strengths and deficiencies of the work of both poets are fairly assessed. Both are seen as leaders of the twenty-five poets discussed, often at length and with extensive quotation, in Turner's overview of Australian poetry. In Brisbane, Turner explains, 'it would be flat blasphemy' to place Brunton Stephens behind Gordon. Brunton Stephens's work, including *Convict Once*, is praised for its power, insight, and glowing imagination. A few writers discussed have hardly if ever been heard of again, but there are thoughtful assessments of the work of Australie and Jennings Carmichael (Mrs Francis Mullins). Ada Cambridge's work is given one of the most perceptive reviews it was to receive for some decades. Turner believed that of its class it was 'poetry of most perfect form', but exclusively introspective and predominantly sad, although it was also '[a]dmirable in rhythm, intense in expression, lofty in thought, and musical in a minor key'. 'Strong conviction, and the solemn earnestness of tone' saved her denunciatory poems from being classed with the 'Literature of Revolt' of which Turner apparently disapproved. Contrary to Martin's suggestion, the *Bulletin* balladists, Paterson, Lawson, Farrell and Dyson, are not slighted and although Turner places Paterson's verse above Lawson's for robustness and vigour of expression, he also notes that Lawson's 'The Star of Australasia' rises higher into the region of poetry than anything written by the other three balladists. The Preface and the 'Introductory' offer an explanatory account of the position of Australian literature at the end of the century. Contriving to be positive and balanced where Martin seemed dismissive and sneering, Turner and Sutherland nevertheless endorse his conclusion: their account is 'the story of a childhood that may yet be valued as the preliminary to a strong and robust manhood'.

THE MULTIPLE ROLES OF THE SYDNEY *BULLETIN*

The Sydney *Bulletin* (established in 1880) fostered the robust manhood of Australian poetry, especially after A.G. Stephens introduced the Red Page literary columns in 1896, and encouraged the growth of Australian short fiction at a time when the genre also gained strength in Europe and America. If the *Bulletin* through the editorial policies of J.F. Archibald and Stephens somewhat forcibly shaped the Australian short story and the ballad, it encouraged a greatly diverse range of other poetic forms. Possibly its best effect on writing of all kinds was to curb diffuseness and value crisp, clear language, a 'modernising' impulse which drew Australian writing further from the formal language and periodic sentence found in much Victorian literature. The 'nationalistic' element fostered overtly at times by Stephens and the *Bulletin* is indicated in Stephens's review on 15 February 1896, in which he joined Lawson with Paterson as two writers who, 'with all their imperfections' mark 'something like the beginnings of a national school of poetry. In them, for the first time, Australia has found audible voice and characteristic expression'. Gordon is dismissed with the New Zealander Alfred Dommett as 'aliens in birth and thought', and Kendall's poetry is too individualistic: 'not Australia, but Kendall, strikes the dominant note in Kendall's verses'. The *Bulletin* was also responsible for facilitating the work of the unorthodox Tom Collins (Joseph Furphy, 1843–1912), whose novel *Such is Life: Being Certain Extracts from the Life of Tom Collins* was edited by Stephens and published by the *Bulletin* in 1903.

When Paterson's *The Man from Snowy River, and Other Verses* (1895) and Lawson's *In The Days When the World Was Wide and Other Verses* (1896) appeared, their reputations as balladists were so well matched that they were both enhanced by the factitious rivalry set up by the *Bulletin* between Paterson's relaxed ironic celebration and Lawson's tense and darker scrutiny of the bush and life in general. Paterson's verse became more popular and more widely read, and he remains the leading exponent of the typical Australian ballad. Lawson's reputation as a poet has wavered, but although he published some poor verse, critical opinion tends to agree with Dennis Douglas's assessment in the Melbourne *Age*, 21 October 1967: 'Lawson, without recourse to unthinking loyalties or complacent truisms, was the first poet to re-create bush attitudes seen from within, and to successfully adapt the ballad to portray realities of urban life'. Apart from Lawson and Paterson, whose works were popularly held to be synonymous with Australian Literature, *Bulletin* contributors to the Australian ballad included Mary Hannay Foott, Will Ogilvie, Edward Dyson, E.J. Brady, Victor Daley and George Essex Evans. Their verses were diverse in subject and style, and augmented rather than displaced the more lyrical and reflective poetry. That balladists made poetry popular does not imply readers' poor taste or an upsurge of narrow nationalism. A study of the *Bulletin* well into this century suggests that the light focused on balladists also helped to illuminate very different types of poetry, like that of Bernard O'Dowd, Mary Gilmore, Christopher Brennan and Shaw Neilson. It is difficult to find poets during this period who did not publish in the *Bulletin* or its associates the *Lone Hand* (1907–21) and the *Bookfellow* (1899–25). By 1914 realistic verse—in what ways the typical *Bulletin* prose or verse piece was realistic is a matter for discussion elsewhere—was rivalled by *Bulletin* encouragement of lyrical, philosophical, reflective, mystical and whimsical poetry. The *Bulletin* also published Roderic Quinn, David McKee Wright, Victor Daley and others, like the Queenslander Lala Fisher, who responded to the 'Irish Renascence' of the Celtic Twilight group.

Although Brennan was almost immediately recognised as an important poet, many found his poetry obscure and un-Australian, and his *XXI Poems (1893–1897): Towards the Source* sold poorly compared with O'Dowd's *Dawnward?* (1903) and Gilmore's *Marri'd and Other Verses* (1910). Gilmore's reputation, like that of John Shaw Neilson, whose first collection was *Heart of Spring* (1919), and E (Mary Fullerton), who published *Moods and Melodies* in 1908, lies outside this period. Debate continues about the poetic merit of the prolific William Baylebridge, who published privately seven volumes between 1908 and 1914. The reputation of Bernard O'Dowd (1866–1953), however, was established early. His verse has much of the magisterial power and originality found in Harpur's poetry, and in *Poetry Militant* (1909) O'Dowd also attempted to frame an aesthetic. His most popular work is found in *Dawnward?*, including the famous sonnet 'Australasia', and *The Bush* (1912), but the influence of his 'beloved master', Walt Whitman, sometimes turned his tough lyricism to strident polemics, and his compassionate humanity to aggressive politics. His passionate rhetoric has impressed some later critics but displeased others, including James McAuley, who deplored his bardic afflatus and gnostic humanism.[19] During O'Dowd's lifetime, however, his work was highly regarded as a poetry of ideas and the often critical voice of Australian nationalism, and it remains important minor poetry.

HARPUR AND THE CANON

The poetry of Charles Harpur, over seven hundred poems ranging from epigrams to extended narratives, has been rediscovered in the later twentieth century and attracts serious critical attention but no popular readership. Lacking university education, this son of convict parents read as widely as any graduate, and assimilated his learning within a consciousness perhaps too sharply aware of his social restrictions as an individual and national responsibilities as a poet to allow the free play of his obvious intellectual power. Hampered by an often severely limited income, Harpur dedicated all his intellectual wealth and sensitivity to recording and celebrating the landscape of Australia and the infant nation, and acclaiming and chastising its people and its short history.

By 1860 Harpur had published a verse drama and major poems like 'The Kangaroo Hunt', 'The Creek of the Four Graves', 'A Storm in the Mountains', 'A Poet's Home', 'A Coast View', 'The Dream by the Fountain', and a collection of sonnets, although he revised all this work over the next ten years. In everything he wrote he was consciously adding to the tradition of Australian literature and intellectual culture. In 1883 Harpur's widow authorised the publication of a collection of his *Poems* edited by H.M. Martin, but *Poems by Charles Harpur* seldom represents the strongest versions of his poems, nor does it suggest his range of poetry and the ideas embodied in it or emphasise his unique voice. Nevertheless the edition must be credited with contributing to Harpur's place in the canon before 1914 and it occasioned several substantial articles on his work in literary journals. An unsigned review by Brunton Stephens in the *Brisbane Courier*, 5 October 1883, praises Harpur's originality, his lyrical achievement and his acute observation and 'mastery of nature in all her moods', his intensity of insight, and the 'sheer force of earnestness', and 'communicative vividness of imagination that compels the reader to feel that he is under the sway of a genuine master'. Harpur's work, as the preceding survey shows, always had a respected place in Australian literature. His reputation has grown steadily, supported by a body of analytical criticism fostered by many scholars including C.W. Salier, Judith Wright, A.G. Mitchell, Elizabeth Perkins and Michael Ackland.[20]

KENDALL AND THE CANON

The greater accessibility of the poetry of Henry Kendall (1839–82), in terms of publication of collections and immediate appeal to the reader, gave him a much higher reputation in his lifetime and well into this century than his mentor Harpur. Kendall also left criticism and journalism which widened his readership. After the publication of *Poems and Songs* (1862), *Leaves from the Australian Forests* (1869) and *Songs from the Mountains* (1880) his position as the foremost Australian lyricist was established. Kendall was conscious of his role in forming a tradition of Australian Literature, as he intimated in his letter to the London *Athenaeum* which the journal printed in February 1866. To Barton, who quoted from the *Athenaeum* letter, Kendall's *Poems and Songs* represented 'the highest point to which the poetic genius of our country has yet attained'. Critics tended to place Kendall above Harpur especially as a poet of Australian landscape, and while some drew comparisons with English poets, others like Barton considered that his work bore not 'the slightest resemblance' to any other. Kendall's satire, as in 'The Song of Ninian Melville', has more wit and dexterity than Harpur's, and pieces like 'Black Kate' and 'Black Lizzie' ridicule not the Aboriginal women, but the unadaptable minds and poor conduct of Europeans. While Kendall's 'forest' songs tend to emphasise his lyrical strength, his 'mountain' songs, like 'Dedication—To a Mountain', 'Beyond Kerguelen' and 'Mount Erebus' have a more dramatic energy. 'The Hut by the Black Swamp' and 'Ghost Glen' powerfully evoke the corruption of natural landscape by human evil, a recurring motif of nineteenth-century writing. Barton doubted that Kendall would become a popular writer because he required a cultivated reader, but several poems by Kendall, like the celebratory 'Bell Birds' and 'September in Australia' and the elegiac 'Mooni', are well known to the public, and an inexpensive facsimile edition of *Leaves from the Australian Forests* is available in supermarkets. Kendall's work has had substantial critical support from scholars like Tom Inglis Moore, T.T. Reed, Judith Wright, A.D. Hope, Ken Stewart and Michael Ackland.[21]

GORDON AND THE CANON

Gordon's reputation continues to fluctuate but he remains today an even more popular poet than Kendall and also a focus of critical attention, although his status as an 'authentic' recorder of Australian bush life was eventually usurped by Lawson and Paterson. The romance and tragedy of Gordon's life in Australia, which began when his English family sent the troublesome twenty-year-old to South Australia in 1853, included two years in the mounted constabulary, horse-breaking and steeplechase riding, and, with an inheritance from his parents, land investment and two years as a member of the South Australian parliament. Financial losses and an unsuccessful claim to the Scottish barony of Esslemont contributed to Gordon's suicide at dawn on a Melbourne beach on 24 June 1870. Gordon's poetry was enhanced by the context of his biography, which was public knowledge before Sutherland's detailed account appeared in *The Development of Australian Literature* in 1898. The first Australian poet published in an Oxford edition, Gordon sometimes seems now, as Sladen and Byrne suggested, to be an English rather than Australian poet. Whatever is said about his essentially English inspiration, his poetry does respond at first hand to his Australian experiences, and he will never fail to attract readers stimulated by the depiction of manly tragedy and heroic effort against hopeless odds. 'The Sick Stockrider', 'From the Wreck' and 'How We Beat the Favourite' subtitled 'A Lay of the Loamshire Hunt Cup', catch popular attention in *Bush Ballads and Galloping Rhymes* (1870), also available in a facsimile edition in supermarkets. Gordon also appeals to more serious readers, because, as Frank Maldon Robb wrote in the 1912 edition, Gordon's work as a whole embodies 'the drama [which] is that of processes going on in the soul itself, not in its environment or deeds merely'.[22]

BRENNAN AND THE CANON

When Christopher Brennan (1870–1932) completed his best work with the conclusion of the Wanderer sequence in *Poems 1913* (1914) his status was confirmed as a serious poet with recognisable international affiliations. Although Brennan may not have been influenced directly by any earlier Australian poetry, it provided him with a literary environment as important as the European spirit and aesthetics of Baudelaire and Mallarmé, and the varieties of German and other mysticism that interested him. There is, despite all their differences, some connection between Brennan and Harpur, who might have longed for the kind of poetic career open to Brennan. Both articulated an aesthetic with moral overtones on which they attempted to base their work; both, allowing for Brennan's greater mastery, wrote delicate lyrics and sonorous blank verse; both, as Brennan shows in The Burden of Tyre (MS 1903), did not hesitate to express hatred in verse; both responded to and drew upon the heritage of English poetry, especially seventeenth-century mystics and the Romantics; both engaged with German philosophy and mysticism, although Harpur's engagement was unorganised and tentative. Where Brennan's assimilation of the landscape took symbolist form, Harpur's poetry also frequently used landscape as symbol. Social and political engagement was open and pervasive in Harpur's work, whereas it was covert and diffused throughout the best of Brennan's, and Harpur sometimes wrote trenchantly pointed satire, a genre that did not greatly interest Brennan.

Changing perspectives on Brennan's poems and critical prose have not shaken his status, and the many commentators contributing to criticism of his work from different positions and with varying degrees of enthusiasm confirm its importance.[23] Although he is not both the focus of academic attention and a loved popular writer, as are Clarke, Gordon and Lawson, Brennan's restless search for the Other, and failing in that, his search for a home or a pathway in the universe, are the hidden themes of much Australian poetry. His poetry assimilates, refines and re-presents specific relationships, situations, cityscapes and landscapes in resonant metaphors and symbols. Although many images in the Wanderer poems arise from physical journeys made by Brennan across Sydney city and landscapes, the true landscape of the poems is a metaphysical landscape of the emotions, the spirit and the soul. Brennan's work epitomises much of what the first poets struggled to accomplish. Among the many ways in which the balladists may be read, attention has been given to the sadness that underlies their humour, irony and resilience. Paterson's vision splendid of the sunlit plains extended and the wondrous glory of the everlasting stars becomes a vision of loneliness and isolation, a metaphor for the loneliness of a soul lost in an indifferent universe; the awe at finding oneself an atom adrift in limitless space. Lawson's cloud of dust on the long white road and the teams with their weary load creeping on, inch by inch, was an Australian reality, but it is also a metaphor for the dreary struggle with life beneath Brennan's 'sky of uncreated mud'.

CLARKE, BOLDREWOOD AND THE EARLY CANON

The reputations of Clarke and Boldrewood were established by 1914, and have not been shaken. Although Clarke is acknowledged as a more substantial writer, Boldrewood's work remains important, partly because it embodies the tensions between British and Australian class structures and society which took a subtler and more problematic form towards the end of the century. Both wrote prolifically but their popular reputations rest on their two major novels. Clarke's *His Natural Life* (1870–72) and Boldrewood's *Robbery Under Arms* (1882–83) were enthusiastically received by the wide readership of the newspaper serials. In book form they won overseas fame by their sheer narrative interest, and in the case of Clarke's novel, by its emotional power. Neither novel is concerned with naturalistic realism, although actual landscape and places are often depicted with dramatic clarity.

There is symbolic force as well as narrative intensity in Clarke's story of Richard Devine. Although innocent, Devine becomes the convict Rufus Dawes and suffers under the vindictiveness of the convict transportation system, the malice of his cousin, Maurice Frere, an officer on the transport and John Rex, a brutal convict. The hopeful future of the colonies despite a convict past emerges in the longer serial version, in which Devine is transported for murder in the context of the commercial manufacture of artificial gems. Dawes survives and achieves ultimate prosperity and reinstatement together with the child Dorcas, whose mother, Dora, since her own childhood, has been an image of purity and innocence in the midst of the brutality and corruption of the penal system. *For the Term of His Natural Life*, the revised book version, first published in 1882, heightens the representation of the convict system as a violation of the social family, by entwining numerous strands of the plot with Devine's English family and depicting Rex as Devine's half-brother. *For the Term of His Natural Life* questions the easy transition from penal colony to respectable free society with the death of Dawes and Dora (now Sylvia) in a shipwreck. The women, notably Sylvia, are feebly drawn compared with the men, but the resourceful Sarah Purfoy, Rex's lover, is a memorable and even credible character.

Boldrewood's *Robbery Under Arms* reinforces rather than questions the legal system. Dick Marston, Australian son of the soil and nature's gentleman, upholds both class distinction and justice by narrating from gaol, where he is rightfully imprisoned, the story of his misdemeanours and repentance. Led astray by his ex-convict father, who converts from poaching in England to cattle-duffing in New South Wales with the aristocratic Captain Starlight, Dick is eventually captured, and his brother Jim and Starlight are killed in a battle with the police. Dick's exploits include initial capture and escape, prospecting on the Turon goldfields, romance with the pure Grace Storefield, betrayal by the spiteful Kate and the part-Aboriginal Warrigal, and bushranging episodes with an enlarged band of desperadoes based on several real-life bushrangers. The moral is emphasised by contrasting Dick's decline with the growing prosperity of George Storefield, Grace's brother. Eventually gaining his freedom, Dick marries Grace and moves to Queensland, confident of fair-dealing from country people who will always lend a chap a helping hand when he shows that he means to go straight for the future.

The reputations of Clarke and Boldrewood grew in their own time, fostered by republication of their work. Byrne's thoughtful chapters on Clarke and Boldrewood in *Australian Writers* (1896), one of the earliest assessments of their writing, emphasised the importance of their fictional chronicling of historical events. Later scholars like Laurie Hergenhan, Alan Brissenden and Michael Wilding consider the psychological implications of heroes like Clarke's Rufus Dawes and Boldrewood's Dick Marston. The perennial relevance of the best convict and bushranger narratives is indicated by recent revisions in criticism like the post-colonial and Marxist approaches of Bob Hodge and Vijay Mishra, and Robert Dixon's analysis of the ethical and political implications of the colonies as sites for late nineteenth-century adventure tales.[24]

SHORT FICTION

The seventeen prose collections and reprints Lawson published between *Short Stories in Prose and Verse* (1894) and *Triangles of Life and Other Stories* (1913), together with his appearance in the *Bulletin* and anthologies, confirmed his reputation, at home and in England, as the most popular representative Australian writer, or as Stephens said in 1905, the most original and characteristic writer. Lawson's fiction met with some reservations, even from Stephens, and some later academic neglect and references to a period of decline beginning with *The Romance of the Swag* (1907). Nevertheless the many popular and scholarly selections of his work before and after Colin Roderick's comprehensive and critical editions (1967–85) demonstrate a sustained public and academic interest. From the first analytical accounts, like that of H.M. Green, Lawson criticism flourished, with earlier accounts now extended by others including psychological, feminist, sociological, and neo-socialist approaches by Xavier Pons, Michael Wilding, Kay Schaffer and others.[25]

The sketches of Steele Rudd, beginning with *On Our Selection* (1899), had fourteen publications or reprintings before 1914. Together they comprise a burlesque tragicomedy of the lives of small selectors battling an environment that seems almost beyond their comprehension. The popular appeal of the struggles of the Rudd family emphasises that the literary tradition inherited from the nineteenth century only rarely communicates a sense of kinship with the soil.[26] Metaphysical alienation is added to *Bush Studies* (1902) of Barbara Baynton (1857–1929) which awaited proper recognition until reprinted in the later twentieth century. A.G. Stephens, who published 'The Tramp' (later 'The Chosen Vessel') in *The Bulletin Story Book* (1901), praised Baynton's truthful glimpses of Australian life and suggested that Australian journals found their graphic psychological realism unpalatable. Critics now argue that Baynton's ironic nihilism and unflattering depiction of the Australian male contributed to her early neglect.[27]

A SECOND ROUND OF ANTHOLOGIES

Anthologies were important in the process by which authors became available to the public and academies. The American lecturer Bruce Sutherland, teaching Australian literature at Pennsylvania State College, convinced that Australian literature was beginning to count in the world, commented in *Meanjin* in Autumn 1950 on the lack of anthologies like those used to teach the outline of canonical American literature. The reading public for poets, including many now forgotten, was widened in the later nineteenth century by the availability of anthologies like William Yarrington's *Prince Alfred's Wreath: A Collection of Australian Poems* by various authors (1868), *Sydney Punch Staff*

Papers (1872), Christmas annuals in 1875, 1877 and 1881, Patchett Martin's *An Easter Omelette in Prose and Verse* (1879) and *Our Exhibition Annual* (1878). These collections, and the post-Federation anthologies, indicate a ground swell of public acceptance of Australian poetry without which the emergence of any kind of canon is an esoteric phenomenon with little cultural significance. This publishing activity expanded immediately after Federation, with Bertram Stevens's seven separate anthologies running into twenty-one new editions or reprintings between 1906 and 1932.

Stevens's *The Golden Treasury of Australian Verse* (1909, 1912, 1913) is typical of these anthologies, which usually concentrate on shorter and lyrical poems. *The Golden Treasury* includes some New Zealand poets, but also poets who by the mid-century were firmly part of the Australian canon. Stevens's informative Introduction, conservative and untouched by nationalism, offers sound appraisal of writers, journals and literary movements. The first *Oxford Book of Australasian Verse*, edited by Walter Murdoch, a significant landmark, appeared outside this period in 1918, but covers much the same poets as *The Golden Treasury* although it includes work by several more recent writers like Zora Cross. Short fiction reprinted in the *Bulletin's A Golden Shanty: Australian Stories and Sketches: Prose and Verses by Bulletin Writers* (1890) and *The Bulletin Story Book* (1901) enlarged the readership and reputation of prose writers like Lawson, Becke, Favenc, Louise Mack, Baynton and Steele Rudd, most of whom had already published individual titles. Building on the English tradition, titles like 'The Golden Treasury' of Australian verse and 'A Golden Shanty' of Australian prose indicate awareness of accumulated cultural capital owned by the nation. Late twentieth-century anthologies now recover writing from the nineteenth-century heritage in response to changing ideological interest in different facets of our national literature.

Public awareness of literature, even if comparatively few people read very widely or deeply, made it easier for Prime Minister Alfred Deakin to establish the Commonwealth Literary Fund in 1908. Inspired by the British Royal Literary Fund, the CLF represented financial assistance and an assurance of the cultural value of the writer's vocation that most nineteenth-century poets received only from a limited circle of supporters. To the lack of such assurance, critics like Byrne, Patchett Martin and Turner and Sutherland attributed much of the melancholy of Australian poetry and the absence of the great, calm, healthful type of genius.

Although the canon is fostered by the academy, there is collusion, often inadvertent, between teaching institutions, the body of criticism they generate, popular readership and publishers' agendas. C.J. Dennis's *The Songs of a Sentimental Bloke* (1915), which sold over 60 000 copies within eighteen months, may claim both popular success and academic respectability, in that it satisfies the criterion of canonical excellence described by Bloom as strong literary originality emerging from an agonistic relationship of anxiety with earlier great works. Dennis's street dialect romance between the Melbourne larrikin Bill and his sweetheart Doreen who works in a pickle factory, is distinguished by the fluent (and stylised) voice given to the larrikin culture, and by the way the working-class *Songs of a Sentimental Bloke* engages with Shakespeare's aristocratic *Romeo and Juliet.*

By the 1950s the academy began to accept a canon from which the majority of verse published in the nineteenth century was missing, and in which formerly acclaimed poets held a very minor place. It is not easy for writers to acquire canonical status even when literature is in its infancy. Some poets, especially women, omitted here, but republished generations later for academic and general readers, have waited for an appropriate milieu to demonstrate the qualities of their work. Partly because women tended to publish critical essays anonymously in literary journals, the role of women as critics is almost invisible before 1914, although as influential readers their contributions to the tradition were significant. Critical reviews and articles by and about women like Ada Cambridge and Catherine Martin are now being rediscovered. Once the value of the work is acknowledged, writers and critics are not easily displaced, although their fortunes fluctuate according to the fashions of the academy, which is itself responding to changes in the socio-political climate.

4

LITERATURE AND MELODRAMA

Robert Dixon

MELODRAMA: A DIRTY WORD

For much of the twentieth century the terms 'melodrama' and 'melodramatic' have been used in a pejorative way. As Christine Gledhill observes, 'melodrama was . . . constituted as the anti-value for a critical field in which tragedy and realism became cornerstones of "high" cultural value, needing protection from mass, "melodramatic" entertainment'.[1] In the 1960s, however, melodrama began to receive serious critical attention, particularly within areas of theatre studies such as the history of theatricality and performance. In more recent debates, Peter Brooks's *The Melodramatic Imagination* (1976) has stimulated both revisionist literary criticism and a rich field of interdisciplinary work in cinema, theatre and cultural studies. The logic of the present chapter is at once historical and conceptual, extending to late nineteenth- and early twentieth-century Australian culture current debates about a 'melodramatic field' constituted by a number of issues, including the formal properties of melodrama as an aesthetic category; the history of the form; its relation to the class structure of colonial society; its role as a mediator of social change; its representation of and reception by women; and its use in the demarcation of 'high' and 'low' culture.

In *English Melodrama* (1965), an early attempt to define melodrama as an aesthetic form, Michael Booth stresses its concentration on plot at the expense of characterisation, its reliance on sensation, the recurrence of character stereotypes, and the rewarding of virtue and the punishment of vice according to a moral scheme of stark simplicity.[2] In melodrama's 'dream world', 'virtue and vice coexist in pure whiteness and pure blackness; . . . after immense struggles and torment, good triumphs over and punishes evil, and virtue receives tangible reward' (p. 14). The moving force of melodrama is not the hero, who tends to be passive, but a villain, motivated by revenge or the desire to possess money, property, or the heroine (p. 18). The sequence of events set in train by the villain's threat to the heroine may include 'shootings, stranglings, hangings, poisonings, drownings, stabbings, suicides, explosions, conflagrations, avalanches, earthquakes, eruptions, ship-wrecks, train wrecks, apparitions' and torture (p. 14). From around 1860, such spec-tacular episodes, involving increasingly elaborate stage machinery, became known as 'sensation scenes', from Dion Boucicault's pronouncement: 'sensation is what the public wants, and you cannot given them too much of it' (cited, p. 165).

Nineteenth-century melodrama has been described as playing a 'key role in mod-ernity as a mediator of social and political change'.[3] Yet the term's 'semantic sprawl'[4] defies any definitive categorisations grounded in particular generic features, originary historical moments, or attachment to class interests. Peter Brooks's influential historiography iden-tifies melodrama's originary moment in the final decades of the eighteenth century, when its use by the bourgeoisie as a vehicle for contesting the power of the aristocracy fore-shadowed its availability as a framework of values for a post-sacred world that could no longer be underwritten by church, state, or monarchy.[5] Yet in nineteenth-century England the increasing emphasis on spectacle meant that this bourgeois heritage was fused with earlier, more 'popular' cultural traditions such as dumb show, harlequinade and acrobatics which, together with music, formed a complex *mise-en-scène* of non-verbal signs that allowed melodrama to become a readily consumable form of mass entertain-ment. Focusing on these developments rather than its bourgeois heritage, Booth argues, contrary to Brooks, that in nineteenth-century Britain, melodrama was 'essentially enter-tainment for the industrial working class . . . its basic energy was proletarian' (p. 52).

Melodrama's relation to the vexed category of 'the popular' has drawn different responses from historians of nineteenth-century Australian culture. Essentialised and ahistorical notions of 'the popular' associate a fixed body of genres or texts with a class fraction and a subversive relation to official culture, an approach found in John Docker's influential, though problematic, fusion of Brooks and Bakhtin in a series of articles on carnivalisation and popular cultural forms.[6] The objection that this is to endow the popular with a political essence, so that it is always already associated with liberation, is voiced by critics such as John Frow, who follows Stuart Hall in arguing against notions of an expressive relation between class structure and a 'fixed inventory of forms', and for the 'inherent ambivalence of popular cultural forms'.[7]

Melodrama is exemplary in this model. Despite persistent attempts to read it as the expression of a particular social class, it became a central cultural paradigm precisely be-cause it emerged at a meeting point of class interests whose differences it was able to per-form and mediate. As Veronica Kelly observes, 'melodrama can . . . serve a political and Utopian function as well as an ideological and regressive one'.[8] The convergence of bour-geois and popular traditions was reflected in the heterogeneous programming and mixed audiences that characterised mid-nineteenth-century English melodrama. At Covent Garden, for example, scenes from Shakespeare's plays, often chosen for their capacity for melodramatic performance, rubbed shoulders on the same program with pantomimes like *Puss in Boots* and melodramas like Isaac Pocock's *The Miller and His Men* (1813). As Christine Gledhill argues, 'Melodrama arose to exploit these new conditions of production, becoming itself a site of generic transmutation and "intertextuality". Based on commerce rather than cultural monopoly, melodrama multiplied through translation, adaptation, and, in the absence of copyright laws, piracy' (p. 18). Melodrama, then, was not *essentially* a popular mode, but a site of cultural mediation whose protean form allowed it to negotiate conflicts between popular and bourgeois, metropolitan and regional, masculine and feminine identities.

MELODRAMA AND CULTURAL BIFURCATION

It is important to remember that the emergence of categories of 'high' and 'low' or 'popular' culture is in fact a feature of a nineteenth-century cultural argument epitomised in England in Matthew Arnold's *Culture and Anarchy* (1869) and in America in the conceptualisations of 'Order, Hierarchy and Culture' discussed by Lawrence W. Levine.[9] Particular manifestations of such general distinctions can be seen in the regulatory practices beginning to affect nineteenth-century drama. Certain kinds of plays were marked as more 'legitimate' than others and audiences became segregated along class lines. Critics and theatre managers also sought to define behaviour appropriate to different performance contexts, rowdy intervention being tolerated in vaudeville but not in the concert hall or art gallery. If the terms 'high' and 'low' culture have no empirical validity as a way of labelling melodrama as a class form, they had none the less a powerful valency in the aesthetic debates of the period.

In Australia, as elsewhere, the process of cultural bifurcation belongs to the second half of the century. Before the gold rushes, both the fare offered by colonial theatres and the social composition of their audiences were extremely mixed. Mr Theodore Wopples, for example, whose company is on tour in Ballarat in Fergus Hume's novel *Madame Midas* (1888), realises that by varying his program he can lure both the 'upper' and 'lower' classes: 'One night they would play farcical comedy; then Hamlet, reduced to four acts . . .; the next night burlesque would reign supreme; and [then] . . . melodrama'.[10] Yet by mid-century there were signs of the beginnings of divergence in popular entertainments. From the gold rushes of the 1850s to the depression of the 1890s Australian cities expanded rapidly, and the cultural differentiation increasingly evident in cultural practices was echoed in the material fabric of the cities, urban segregation along class lines becoming more common from about 1860. The period after 1851 also brought a decline in the traditional forms of pre-industrial popular pastimes, as middle-class attitudes to leisure became more influential. According to Richard Waterhouse, 'the new wave of immigrants . . . brought with them the cultural baggage of industrial rather than pre-industrial Britain . . . The tavern, the turf and the prize ring were to be abandoned for mechanics' institutes and debating societies, while theatre was to be given a high moral purpose'.[11] Melodrama, Waterhouse observes, 'was probably the theatrical medium which continued to bring all classes together in more or less even proportions' (p. 266).

The legitimising of the theatre was achieved in numerous ways, including the regulation of performance spaces, audience behaviour, theatrical repertoire and acting styles. While early nineteenth-century theatres housed a social microcosm under one roof, by the end of the century there tended to be a separation of 'legitimate' theatres from the vast buildings of the late-Victorian era, such as Melbourne's Alexandra Theatre, specialising in 'lower' forms like spectacle melodrama. At the beginning of the period, theatre audiences felt free to come and go as they pleased, to interrupt a performance, to throw things, and to request changes to the program. As the actor Richard Fullerton remarked of American theatre, 'The egg as a vehicle of dramatic criticism came into early use in this Continent'.[12] Later in the century, however, rowdy behaviour became increasingly unacceptable. A report in the Melbourne *Argus* of 1 July 1878 commented on the behaviour of the gallery boys during a performance of George Darrell's melodrama *Back from the Grave*, 'It is just a question . . . whether the theatre is to be given up to these young savages, and all decent people driven away'.[13] Critics also moved to quarantine 'low' forms such as melodrama and pantomime from 'serious' content—notably the plays of Shakespeare—and this was reflected, in turn, in different styles of acting. The Shakespeare plays most performed in mid-century—*Richard III, Hamlet, King Lear, Othello*, and *Macbeth*—lent themselves to a melodramatic performance style Harold Love describes as 'semaphore acting'.[14] Later in the century fashions in performance changed, and the melodramatic style fell into critical disfavour. In Australia this important change in taste took place during Walter Montgomery's controversial *Hamlet* in Melbourne in 1867. The theatre critic James Neild, writing in the *Australasian*, approved Montgomery's acting as it accorded with his own modern preference for dramatic realism above melodrama. Rival critic James Smith, on the other hand, whose tastes were more traditional, complained that Mr Montgomery's performance was 'essentially lymphatic . . . [and] exhibits none of the "stern effects" . . . which actors of greater vigour have been accustomed to display'.[15] Critical commentary on the theatre therefore played a crucial role in discriminating a 'legitimate' culture for the post-gold-rush generation, with theatre critics acting as the self-appointed 'cultural missionaries' for an educated, cultivated colonial democracy.[16]

An Australian Melodrama?

Studies of melodrama in nineteenth-century America demonstrate the transformative effects of America's unique socio-political conditions on melodramatic conventions and their meanings.[17] In dealing with the adaptation of melodrama to Australian conditions, we need similarly to be sensitive to the processes of transformation that negotiate and express metropolitan/colonial tensions. As Margaret Williams observes, the distinctive qualities of Australian melodrama 'are to be found as much in the relation of its colonial characters and situations to the stock characters and situations of traditional melodrama as in the caricatured bush world it portrays'.[18]

The first half of the nineteenth century produced a number of melodramas adapting the genre to colonial subject matter, including David Burn's *The Bushrangers* (performed in Edinburgh in 1829, though not professionally staged in Australia), Henry Melville's *The Bushrangers; or, Norwood Vale* (1834) and Charles Harpur's *The Tragedy of Donohoe* (1835). Melville's play succinctly illustrates the conventional plot: an English country gentleman, Mr Norwood, emigrates to Van Diemen's Land in search of financial security; his daughter Marian and her sweetheart, a young emigrant, are the traditional heroine and hero; the low characters are an Irish servant and an Aboriginal; the villains are the bushrangers, who threaten Mr Norwood's property and his daughter's virtue. In contrast to Burn's play, which celebrates the bushranger as the oppressed victim of an unjust social system, Melville's moral scheme endorses the dominant social order. Its plot, character groupings and social point of view anticipate, in a simple way, a good deal of emigrant fiction written during and about the pre-gold-rush era, including Alexander Harris's *The Emigrant Family; Or, the Story of an Australian Settler* (1849); Louisa Atkinson's *Gertrude the Emigrant: A Tale of Colonial Life* (1857) and *Cowanda, the Veteran's Grant* (1859); Henry Kingsley's *The Recollections of Geoffry Hamlyn* (1859); and Mary Theresa Vidal's *Bengala; Or, Some Time Ago* (1860). Thomas McCombie's novel *Arabin; Or, the Adventures of a Colonist in New South Wales* (1845) was one such novel actually to be produced as a stage melodrama under the title *Arabin; or, the Adventures of a Settler* (1849).

Melodrama's heyday from the 1860s to the 1890s was a direct response to the tastes of the new mass audiences created by the gold rushes and was facilitated by the larger theatres built to accommodate them. Melbourne in the 1850s was reputed to be the richest city in the world, its vast wealth reflected in its grand public buildings, parks, private homes and places of entertainment. Katharine Brisbane notes that 'entrepreneurs built theatres and hippodromes the size of our present arts complexes', equipping them with the latest advances in technology to reproduce on stage the increasingly elaborate sensation scenes.[19] One of the most successful Australian melodramas of the period was George Darrell's *The Sunny South*, which opened at Melbourne's Opera House in 1883. Born in England in 1850, Darrell emigrated to Australia in the early 1860s, and went on to become the pre-eminent playwright of the post-gold-rush immigrant generation. In 1877 he formed Darrell's Dramatic Company for the Production of Australian Plays, his early work including *Transported For Life* (1877), *Back from the Grave* (1878) and *The Forlorn Hope* (1879). It was during a benefit performance of *The Forlorn Hope*, under the patronage of the Australian Natives' Association, that Darrell first styled himself a 'Native Australian Playwright'. Yet, as Margaret Williams observes, these melodramas were really Anglo-Australian, perfectly judged to appeal to a generation of expatriates whose allegiance was still ambivalent. Like many Anglo-Australian novels of the period, such as Henry Kingsley's *The Recollections of Geoffry Hamlyn* and Rolf Boldrewood's *The Miner's Right* (serialised in 1880), Darrell's Anglo-Australian dramas invariably begin in England, often with the need to redeem an ancestral estate, the characters emigrating *en masse* in Acts Two or Three before returning Home in Act Five.[20]

The Sunny South begins at Chester House in England, where Worthy Chester has squandered his inheritance. The family estate is about to be possessed by a villainous creditor, Eli Grup, when Worthy's elder brother Morley Chester (Matt Morley)— supposed dead in the colonies—returns to claim his birthright. Learning that the estate is in debt, Matt Morley goes back to Australia to make a pile on the goldfields. When the action shifts to the mining camp in Act Three, the colonies are seen to have a desirable levelling effect on the British class system, as Boldrewood also shows in The Miner's Right. Like Hereward Pole, Darrell's English characters must cross-dress as diggers to enter this democratic society. But the massive nugget they find on the Queen's Birthday indicates the essentially imperial nature of the play's patriotism: it is wrapped symbolically in the Old Flag and will be used to redeem the estate in England. Eli Grup now employs bushrangers, led by Dick Duggan, to kidnap Matt Morley's sweetheart, the Australian-born heroine Bubs Berkley, and the play culminates in some spectacular 'business' on the Zig Zag Railway, with the entrance on stage of Matt Morley's train and its ambush by bushrangers, followed by the arrival of the police train and a pitched battle between police, diggers and bushrangers. The fact that the bushrangers are villains suggests the lack of a clear fit between melodrama and 'the popular'. As Geoffrey Serle observes, 'Bushrangers clearly were not heroes . . . to patrons of the popular theatre [at this time]'.[21] The name Dick Duggan alludes to Jack Duggan, hero of 'The Wild Colonial Boy', yet Morley declares, 'We want no red-handed assassins lurking round in this fair country' (p. 68). In the end the Chester estate is redeemed by colonial wealth, Matt Morley regains his true identity as Morley Chester Esquire and returns with Bubs to England.

The expatriate quality which helped to make The Sunny South such a success in the early 1880s eventually spelled the end of Darrell's reign. The immigrants of the 1850s demanded the style of theatre they had known in England, but as they aged and went less to the theatre, the theatres were filled by their locally born children, whose tastes and loyalties would initiate the transition to a new era. The new 'King of Melodrama' was Alfred Dampier. Dampier and his family came to Australia in 1873, initially to manage the Melbourne Theatre Royal, and soon established a pattern of successfully adapting colonial novels for the popular stage. Yet Dampier sought to reconcile the commercial appeal of sensation melodrama with the high moral purpose that was increasingly claimed for the serious theatre. Speaking in 1889 of his performance in Valjean, a dramatisation of Hugo's Les Misérables, he reflected, 'If by your artifice you can teach [people] . . . to distinguish between the false and the true, the good and the evil, you are doing something . . . towards moulding the future of Young Australia; and in my opinion, the stage, in time should be . . . as great a moral teacher as the pulpit'.[22] Richard Fotheringham observes that Dampier was something of an 'uneasy populariser' who 'sought, and for many years achieved, a kind of cross-class identity which won him the respect of all' (xvi).

Dampier's first adaptation of a major Australian novel was from the revised and re-titled 1882 version of For the Term of His Natural Life. Dampier's play opened at the Royal Standard in Sydney in 1886. Clarke himself was an experienced playwright and both versions of his novel have strong affinities with stage melodrama, including the wrongly accused and essentially passive hero Rufus Dawes and the heroine, Sylvia, whose purity and innocence are cynically exploited by the villain, Maurice Frere. Yet there was considerable discussion about Clarke's revised ending, the *Age* of 19 May 1890 noting that *For the Term of His Natural Life* presents problems of adaptation to the stage, since 'the *dénouement* [in which Dawes and Sylvia drown in a shipwreck] is utterly opposed to popular predilections of the exigencies of dramatic effect'—in other words, audiences of melodrama required a happy ending. Dampier accordingly followed the ending of the serial, in which the heroine's recovery of her memory saves the condemned Rufus Dawes from the gallows. The *Bulletin* of 12 June 1886 noted that 'a happy termination is . . . tacked on which proves that the wicked man does not always flourish like the verdant eucalyptus'.[23]

The climax of Dampier's career was the seasons of 1888 to 1892 at Melbourne's Alexandra Theatre. His first great success there was the melodrama *Marvellous Melbourne* (1889), whose complicated plot and sensation scenes in Melbourne's China Town were ideally suited to the large theatre. In 1889 the company was joined by Tasmanian-born writer and journalist Garnet Walch, and it was their collaborative adaptation of Rolf Boldrewood's novels *Robbery Under Arms* and *The Miner's Right* in 1890 and 1891 that made the Alexandra seasons into celebrated national occasions. Richard Fotheringham notes in his introduction to *Robbery Under Arms* that it was a moment when a wave of nationalist sentiment flowed through the theatre world. In October 1889 Henry Parkes had given his Tenterfield oration, in which he called for a national parliament, and the first meeting of the Premiers took place in Melbourne in February 1890, as *Robbery Under Arms* was being rehearsed only a few hundred yards away (p. xxxi). The review in the *Argus* on 3 March noted that the audience found it 'racy of the soil, full of those associations around which most of the romance of a young country must gather'. Reviewers again discussed the adaptation, *Table Talk* of 7 March 1890 noting that '*Robbery Under Arms*, although a vividly dramatic work of fiction, is difficult to dramatise'. One reason was that Boldrewood's novel has no true villain. Dampier and Walch solved this problem by making one out of the policeman, Inspector Goring, who identifies himself as a cad by menacing Aileen Marston.[24] But the main difference is in the morality of the two texts. Fotheringham argues that in his novel Boldrewood worked against the melodramatic imagination, while 'the stage version returns the story to melodramatic orthodoxy' (p. lxvii). For Boldrewood, the former Police Magistrate, individuals are responsible for their own actions; they must recognise right and wrong and act appropriately or be punished by law. For Dampier, on the other hand, the drama embodies a theme of human regeneration, and a recognition that social institutions themselves are flawed. The different morality is reflected in the altered ending, which allows the bushrangers not only to survive their last battle with the police, but to get off scot free. The *Bulletin* of 8 March 1890 suggested, tongue in cheek, that the new ending showed 'the triumph of virtuous bushranging over a despicable police system'. This complex relationship between the novel and stage versions of *Robbery Under Arms* exemplifies melodrama's capacity to mediate social tensions, and confirms the view taken in recent theories of scholarly editing that a text is a process rather than fixed object, a field of cultural contestation rather than a single and consistent work of art.[25]

Dampier's Alexandra seasons appear to mark the birth of a nationalist theatre in the 1880s analogous to the rise of a nationalist school of writers and painters in the next decade. In support of such a reading, Margaret Williams cites the *Bulletin* review of *Robbery Under Arms* as the motto for her chapter on the rise of a national theatre: 'A vast multitude rocked the cradle of Australian national drama with their feet, and the gallery-boys whistled and howled like the wind amongst the gums of the primeval forest'.[26] Yet such a reading is now being subject to cautious revision by theatre historians. Richard Waterhouse is one who warns against viewing the period retrospectively through a nationalist paradigm, arguing instead that the colonial stage was a local inflection of international trends.[27] The vast majority of melodramas produced in Australia were of English and American origin. For example, no locally written melodrama enjoyed such sustained support as *East Lynne* and *Uncle Tom's Cabin*. Dampier was not an enthusiastic promoter of other Australian playwrights, and of the new plays only *Robbery Under Arms* remained for any length of time in his repertoire. When *The Miner's Right* closed after 26 performances it was followed by a resumption of Dampier's 'Shakespearean Friday' and then by the wild-west spectaculars *The Scout* and *The Trapper*. Richard Fotheringham concludes that while historians have selectively read from the Alexandra seasons a nationalistic message and depicted Walch as a nationalist forced to work in an expatriate-dominated theatre, the reality was more complex (p. xli). As Veronica Kelly argues, what made a play significant was not its provenance—whether foreign or locally written—but the kinds of meanings local audiences might pull from it in the actual reception.[28]

Patriotic melodrama reached its apotheosis in the genre of invasion-scare literature that was common in the first decade of the new century. In Federation Australia, as in Edwardian England, mounting fears of war spawned a crop of lurid novels and plays featuring Japanese, Chinese, Germans and Russians as imagined invaders. These include Ambrose Pratt's *The Big Five* and *The Commonwealth Crisis* by Charles Kirmess, serialised in the *Lone Hand* in 1907 and 1908–9 respectively, and Randolph Bedford's melodrama *White Australia: or, the Empty North* (1909).[29] These texts represent what might be termed the melodrama of politics, in which world-historical events are allegorised according to the Manichaean scheme of melodrama. Again, in defiance of any clear connection between melodrama and popular opinion, contributors to this literature tended to occupy privileged social positions despite their use of 'popular' narrative forms. Bedford's *White Australia* is a local adaptation of Guy du Maurier's popular play *An Englishman's Home*, which was then running in Melbourne, and uses the conventions of melodrama in an allegory about Australia's invasion by Japan. It begins on the pastoral station of Geoffrey Pearse near Katherine in the Northern Territory. Pearse has employed an engineer, Macquarie, to build a modern airship to defend Australia in the event of a Japanese invasion, believing it will be the 'saviour of the Commonwealth'. Cedric, Pearse's nephew, has been to Oxford, and Kate Pearse describes him as a 'sneering Englishman'. The fact that he has a Japanese servant, Yamamoto, alludes to the recent alliance between Britain and Japan after the defeat of the Russians in 1905. Yamamoto is a spy whose assignment is to neutralise the airship in preparation for a Japanese naval invasion, and then to steal the Australian technology: 'Japan sucks the white man's brains'. The story echoes speculations in the *Lone Hand* that same year that, with Britain facing its traditional foes in Europe, only 'the new science of aeronautics' could protect Australia from its 'insolent' Oriental enemies. In Act III the airship leaves the North just as Japanese troops arrive in large numbers, while Act IV uses the airship in a sensation scene. In mid-flight Yamamoto threatens to blow up the ship's explosives but at the last minute Cedric repents, struggles with Yamamoto, and the two villains fall to their deaths. The Australians continue their journey to Sydney, where they attack the Japanese fleet in another sensation scene: 'Jap fleet in Sydney harbour, the city by night—bombardment and partial destruction of the city . . . The airship appears above and drops explosive shells on the Jap fleet'. The play closes with a patriotic tableau in which Macquarie and Victoria Pearse receive the thanks of the population of Sydney (or Melbourne, for the directions indicate that the scene may be set either in Macquarie Street or Swanston Street): 'The buildings show effects of the bombardment, and the southern cross flag is shown on almost every building'.

The closing scene of *White Australia*, in which the urban population of Sydney or Melbourne looks to country folk for national redemption, tends to confirm the arguments of Graeme Davison and Leigh Astbury that the popular bush nationalism of the Federation period was in fact a consequence of urban myth making, the creation of an emerging urban intelligentsia rather than a rural folk culture.[30] The problem with Davison's thesis, as Ken Stewart argues, is in the opposition he sets up between bush workers and an urban intelligentsia, for many were both well educated *and* profoundly conditioned by provincial experience.[31] Steele Rudd, whose Dad and Dave stories inspired the last great example of nineteenth-century stage melodrama, was a case in point. In his biography of Arthur Hoey Davis, Richard Fotheringham demonstrates that, while his upbringing on the Darling Downs fitted the bush legend, as a successful public servant in Brisbane he had no personal desire to promulgate it except as Steele Rudd. Davis was an educated bureaucrat and writing was part of his gentleman status. Steele Rudd could fulfil readers' fantasies of 'the ragged-trousered rural reporter' in a way that Davis could not, and A.G. Stephens's linking of the fictional characters to the authorial persona via the name Rudd brilliantly grounded Davis's texts in the myth of the bush.[32] First produced in Sydney in May 1912, the stage version of *On Our Selection*, scripted by Ned Duggan and Bert Bailey, can be seen as an urban revival of one of the oldest forms of Victorian melodrama, the village melodrama, whose mythologised bush setting mediates class conflict and provides a buffer of nostalgia against Australia's increasingly complex international relations in the years before the First World War. In Bailey's original production the screens depicted enormous gum trees and eucalyptus oil was sprayed in the auditorium before performances. The acts end with traditional curtain tableaux, such as the 'picture' of Dad and Mum seated on a log at the end of Act One as he delivers the famous speech, '[I can do] Wot the men of this country with health, strength and determination are always doin'. I can start again'.[33] The transformation of the Steele Rudd sketches, which first appeared in the *Bulletin* in 1895, into the play in 1912, and then into Ken G. Hall's film of 1932, also exemplifies the successful transmission of melodrama from stage to cinema in the twentieth century.

MELODRAMA AND THE NOVEL

Peter Brooks's argument that the melodramatic mode is reworked in the 'novelistic representations' of the late nineteenth century allows it to be used as a category for exploring relations between the stage melodramas and romance novels of the period. Brooks's aim was to recapture the connection between the novel and other forms of entertainment: 'The novel . . . still maintained an unembarrassed relation to popular entertainment . . . And . . . among the most vital of these popular forms is melodrama' (pp. ix–xi). The improvements in printing technology, particularly the larger steam-driven press, meant that it was possible by mid-century to produce fiction cheaply for a mass audience who now, thanks to improvements in education, were increasingly able to read. By then it was probably cheaper to buy a novel, certainly to buy a popular periodical in which fiction was serialised, such as the *Australian Journal* or the *Sydney Mail*, than it was to go to the theatre. Noting the importance of serial fiction, Elizabeth Morrison argues that 'locally produced newspapers were . . . the most widespread . . . form of print culture available in the Australian colonies'. As the visiting journalist Richard Twopeny put it in 1883, Australia 'is essentially the land of newspapers'.[34] As there was virtually no publishing industry in Australia, however, authors who wished to be really successful had to go overseas. The increasing emphasis on free trade offered British publishers such as Macmillan, Bentley, and Chapman and Hall spectacular opportunities to exploit colonial markets, which, between 1875 and 1914, were flooded with imported books. As Morrison observes, it was perfectly consistent with the ethos of the New Imperialism that Australian readers could purchase British shilling novels or cheap 2s 6d paper-covered colonial editions.[35] As a consequence, local writers like Mary Fortune and Price Warung (William Astley) died penniless after attempting to earn a living from writing in Australia, while expatriates like Guy Boothby and Rosa Praed, who lived and published in London, enjoyed considerable financial rewards.

While there are clear formal differences between the novel and the multi-media stage spectaculars of Victorian melodrama, they also have a number of features in common. These include scenes and situations in which virtuous and vicious characters are locked in a relentless struggle; characterisation which replicates stage stereotypes; dialogue that is copiously rhetorical; narrative commentary which invokes a Manichaean moral scheme; and melodramatic imagery, a prose equivalent to the spectacular excess and visual language of the stage. Above all, these familiar formal conventions meant that, like stage melodrama, the popular fiction of the period was easily consumable, not only in the drawing room, but also in the trams and railway carriages where reading was increasingly enjoyed. Readers schooled in the formulaic plots and roller-coaster emotions of the stage could re-create those effects in the relatively private act of reading, deriving pleasure and satisfaction from their competence in the rhetoric of melodramatic forms.

One of the most important subjects continuing to link the novel to stage melodrama in the last quarter of the nineteenth century was the burgeoning field of crime and detection, a subject still of poignant relevance to many colonials. The ongoing research of Lucy Sussex and Elizabeth Webby has uncovered the identity of one of the first women writers of detective fiction, Waif Wander (Mary Fortune) (?1833–?).[36] From 1868 for over forty years she contributed crime stories to the Melbourne periodical the *Australian Journal*, publishing under the heading, 'The Detective's Album'. The title refers to detective Mark Sinclair's photographic record of the crimes he has solved and provides a link between the stories, which exploit the generic conventions of romance and melodrama, including foundling children, wicked relatives, occult happenings, disguised villains and 'ruined' young women.

One of the world's first best-selling detective novels, Fergus Hume's *The Mystery of a Hansom Cab* (1886), was written to attract the eye of theatre managers, and was produced on the stage in London in 1888. Its lesser-known sequel *Madame Midas* (1888) also has strong connections with melodrama, and was performed by Dampier at the Alexandra in the 1888–89 season.[37] Gaston Vandeloup, the alias of Octave Braulard, is a Frenchman who escapes from New Caledonia to Australia after being convicted of poisoning his mistress. In Ballarat he attaches himself to Madame Midas, who has made her fortune on the goldfields, and seduces the ingenue Kitty Marchurst. Hume's splendidly stereotypical characterisation is helped by numerous references to stage melodrama made possible by the presence in the story of Theodore Wopples and his touring theatre company, in which Kitty works for a time after Vandeloup abandons her. The climax of the plot is the attempted poisoning of Madame Midas in the bedroom of her rented home in St Kilda, the setting of *The Mystery of a Hansom Cab*. During the inquest, Kitty's evidence is dismissed by the lawyer, who is able to prove that her testimony resembles an episode in the melodrama 'The Hidden Hand', in which she acted while touring with the Wopples. Kitty is exonerated, but as a fallen woman is obliged to attempt suicide on the banks of the Yarra. She there meets Vandeloup, now a fugitive from the Melbourne police, who falls to his own death in the river. Such stock melodramatic types are the very stuff of Hume's social critique, personifying the dark underside of the city that had recently been dubbed 'Marvellous Smellbourne': 'People are passing to and fro on the bridge . . . and the dead body [of Vandeloup] drifts slowly down the red stream far into the shadows of the coming night . . . past the tall warehouses where rich merchants are counting their gains' (p. 282). In Hume's self-reflexive melodrama, the melodramatic imagination thus acquires the status of moral realism.

Guy Boothby enjoyed a brief career in the theatre in Adelaide before moving to London around 1894. He began publishing in the *Windsor Magazine*, where the first of his Doctor Nikola novels, *A Bid for Fortune*, was serialised in 1895, and he went on to become one of the most famous crime writers of the day. *A Bid for Fortune* was followed by *Dr Nikola* (1896), *The Lust of Hate* (1898), *Doctor Nikola's Experiment* (1899) and *Farewell Nikola* (1901). Part international criminal, part mad scientist, Dr Nikola has similarities with both Sir Arthur Conan Doyle's Sherlock Holmes and Moriarty, and with H.G. Wells's Doctor Moreau. With its oriental villains and its complex story of disguise, kidnapping and detection, *A Bid for Fortune*[38] had much in common with the recent stage melodrama *Marvellous Melbourne*, particularly in its original form, which was set in Sydney. Doctor Nikola is seeking a mysterious Chinese talisman which has found its way into the hands of the Colonial Secretary of New South Wales. Nikola's plan to secure it involves a double kidnapping. In Port Said his associates abduct an English lord and replace him on his tour of Australia with an impostor. In Sydney the impostor proposes marriage to Phyllis Wetherell, the daughter of the Colonial Secretary, who is also kidnapped and held to ransom in exchange for the talisman. Both kidnappings are interrupted by the hero, Richard Hatteras, who becomes Phyllis Wetherell's lover. A goldminer and pearl trader from Thursday Island, he is the heir to an English country house and title. The novel's confusing plot, rapid changes of scene and proliferating identity crises enact anxieties about Australia's place both within the Empire and in Asia, and an uncertain response to changing roles for men and women.

Another genre that remained important in the final quarter of the nineteenth century was the pastoral romance, which also retained strong links with melodrama. N. Walter Swan's *Luke Mivers' Harvest*, for example, won first place in the *Sydney Mail* competition for the best original work of fiction in 1879.[39] The selection, made by William Bede Dalley for the influential Fairfax Press, suggests that Swan's novel spoke for and to the prevailing literary taste of the Australian colonies in the late 1870s more strongly than Catherine Helen Spence's unsuccessful entry, the radical utopian novel, *Handfasted*. Swan's melodramatic tale of moral temptation, entrapment and revenge is the vehicle for his critique of the rampant materialism of Victorian society after the gold rushes. Luke Mivers senior is a wealthy squatter in the Western District who believes that money solves all social problems. One of the men he has ruined, John Slater, uses his daughter Margaret's beauty to entrap Luke Mivers junior by encouraging him to raise money against a forged note. Slater is the archetypal villain of village melodrama, using his daughter's beauty 'to decoy Mivers into excess and extravagance' (p. 245), while his 'lean fingers' gather money at interest like 'iron talons' (p. 9). The countervailing value of goodness is expressed in Swan's lyrical descriptions of the sunlit natural landscape as yet untouched by human hands. As in the fiction of Swan's model, Dickens, the ground of his satire of 'the autocracy of the purse' (p. 73) is conventional middle-class values. In the end, Margaret repents of her part in her father's scheme and confesses that she has really come to love Luke, but as a morally fallen couple they die at the hands of Aborigines on the Palmer River in Far North Queensland. Luke Mivers senior and Slater also die in a repudiation of the motive forces of revenge and greed, and the mantle is passed to Mivers's innocent niece, Helen, and his illegitimate son, Bryan Fitzgerald.

VERSE MELODRAMA

Similar conservative attitudes to romantic love, marriage and the proper role of women in society are found in the verse melodramas of George Essex Evans, which enjoyed a favourable response in their day, though they are now little read. They include 'The Repentance of Magdalene Despar' and 'John Raeburn' (1891), and 'Loraine' and 'The Revenge of Amos Mostyn' (1898).[40] Drawing heavily on melodramatic conventions, they involve stories of treachery and loss in love, often centring on the figure of the *femme fatale* and illustrating Evans's 'exalted principles' (ix), which are essentially the traditional late Victorian roles of men and women writ large as conflict between 'Good' and 'Evil'. An obvious influence is James Brunton Stephens's verse melodrama *Convict Once* (1871), much admired in the 1880s and 1890s, whose central female character conceals a convict past. In 'The Repentance of Magdalene Despar' the principles of Good and Evil are personified in a classic Victorian opposition between the good woman and the fallen woman. The poem is narrated by Magdalene Despar in the autumn of life, her recollections beginning with her ominous marriage to an older man. While the husband 'grows cold', she remains 'a wife, with woman's longings' (p. 163), but they are held together by duty to their child, who dies suddenly at the end of Part One. Haunted by memories, they sell their station by the sea and move to the city, traditional seat of vice in melodrama, where her beauty provides the opportunity for sexual adventure: 'I plunged into the vortex of a wild and reckless set,/ . . . Till in all the pride and splendour of my vanity —I fell' (p. 166). This is followed by long passages of moralising and retrospective regret: 'O frailty of woman! . . . / canst thou cleanse the soiled lily?' (p. 168). Like the hero of Kipling's *The Light that Failed* (1891), her husband displaces his anger against women on to the battlefields of Africa, where he dies with his comrades-in-arms. Years later, Magdalene returns to the old station to see the grave of their child and hears its voice calling from beyond death. In the end the setting becomes increasingly allegorical, as she travels 'From the shores beyond the Dawning to the verge of Death's dark portal' (p. 177), becoming a penitent 'Bride of Death', a type of the Victorian Magdalene. Evans's verse melodramas were less popular than his ballads, such as 'The Women of the West', but they have a number of connections with the ballad tradition: their pastoral settings and characters, their plots, and the moral scheme that informs their action. For this reason they have links with more popular forms like the stories and poems of Henry Lawson, where the melodramatic machinery is often just below the surface. Lawson's verse melodrama 'Ruth', for example, was originally written as a short story, 'The Hero of Redclay', which he tried to have Bland Holt perform in the late 1880s.[41] The melodramatic imagination is the link between these forms that critics have claimed for divergent cultural purposes.

The popularity of verse melodramas in the 1880s and 1890s also provides a local context for Christopher Brennan's ambitious *Poems (1913)*, normally considered in the context of European thought.[42] Brennan's symbolist theory of the *livre composé* conceived it as a poetic drama figuring forth the essential dualisms of late romantic thought. 'The true thinker', Brennan argued, 'perceives in the world a continued drama' between matter and spirit; life consists 'not merely of high movements and hours in insight, such as give birth to poetry, it consists also of days, weeks and calendar months of dullness and mediocrity'.[43] The task of poetry as Brennan understood it is to enact the dramatic relationship between these two levels of being, which finds expression partly in the Manichaean symbolism of light and dark; partly in the autobiographical circumstances of his marriage to Anna Elisabeth Werth; and partly in myths such as the Hebraic story of Lilith, Adam's first wife. Mapped over Brennan's attempt to reconcile the two levels of being is also the historical dilemma of the colonial intellectual who fails to achieve adequate recognition in his own society. Brennan's conception of this poetic drama is Manichaean, and his symbolic language has much in common with recent fashions in verse melodrama. But melodrama proper seeks to resolve its Manichaean oppositions hierarchically, imposing good over evil, masculine over feminine. Brennan's quest in *Poems (1913)*, by contrast, is for a union of oppositions, summed up in his theory of the symbol as that which 'transcends our broken, imperfect life, or divided, discursive consciousness'. Throughout 'Towards the Source', Brennan's protagonist anticipates that through 'nuptial' ceremony, body and spirit, light and dark, male and female, will be united, overcoming the Manichaean dilemma. But instead of woman being a 'passage' to a higher reality she remains separate, resolutely physical; instead of being a means of transcendence, sex becomes a 'baffled hope', a 'miasm of flesh', a 'tomb'. The emergence of Lilith in 'The Forest of Night' personifies this failure to unite the subject and object of desire, and the drama ends in solipsistic despair, the original hope for a reconciliation of opposites now recognised as an egotistical illusion. While the Manichaean scheme of *Poems (1913)* draws on the tradition of verse melodrama, the manner of its resolution suggests that Brennan's poem is best understood as enacting the failure of the (male) romantic quest.

FEMALE POINT-OF-VIEW MELODRAMA

The recurring association of melodrama with the domestic, and therefore with women's sphere, has led to Laura Mulvey's distinction, influential in cinema criticism, between male and female point-of-view melodrama. 'Roughly', Mulvey argues, there are two different initial standpoints for melodrama. One is coloured by a female protagonist's dominating point of view which acts as a source of identification. The other examines tension in the family, and between sex and generations; here, although women play a central part, their point of view is not analysed and does not initiate the drama.[44]

Mulvey's argument suggests the desirability of making similar distinctions among examples of late nineteenth-century melodrama. Swan's *Luke Mivers' Harvest* clearly depicts its women characters and the domestic sphere from a masculine point of view, while its critique of materialism supports a Dickensian ending which celebrates the honest and pure couple with lower-middle-class values, and the redeeming power of romantic love. Similarly conservative attitudes to gender inform the verse melodramas of George Essex Evans and Brennan's *Poems (1913)*. By contrast, the work of women novelists like Rosa Praed, Barbara Baynton and Tasma produces a woman's point-of-view melodrama characterised by moral ambivalence and self-reflexivity.

This is not to imply that all nineteenth-century Australian women writers were attracted to melodrama. On the contrary, the tradition that can loosely be termed domestic realism was in some respects opposed to melodrama. Mary Theresa Vidal's last novel, *Bengala: or, Some Time Ago* (1860), is a rural domestic comedy inspired by the works of Jane Austen. In her dedication, Vidal pointedly contrasts her novel with 'more recent and highly-coloured pictures of the same subject'—presumably Kingsley's *The Recollections of Geoffry Hamlyn* (1859). While an Austenesque comic realism dominates the earlier parts of the novel, which deal with the lives of the gentry at Langville, a country house, later episodes dealing with outdoor aspects of colonial life are rendered in a more exaggerated style. Yet, as Susan McKernan observes, Vidal's commitment to domestic realism even undercuts the sensational and melodramatic potential of episodes such as the visit to Langville by bushrangers.[45] Catherine Helen Spence was another admirer of Austen who developed a mode of domestic realism in her early novels, including *Clara Morison* (1854), *Tender and True* (1856) and *Mr Hogarth's Will* (1865). Clara Morison is a young Scot who emigrates to Adelaide, where she spends most of her time in kitchens, parlours and bedrooms, and receives accounts of the better-known (male) colonial world, such as the goldfields, through letters and visitors' reports. In such novels it is as if the mode of domestic realism resists the excesses of melodrama, holding it at a distance, both spatially and stylistically. After 1870 the revival of romance in the works of Robert Louis Stevenson, Henry Rider Haggard, Andrew Lang and Rolf Boldrewood brought a renewed interest in melodramatic conventions. While some Australian women writers, particularly those who continued to get local serial publication, such as Ada Cambridge in *The Three Miss Kings* (serialised 1883, book 1891) and *A Woman's Friendship* (serialised 1889, book 1988), continued to favour domestic realism, others who published directly in book form in England, such as Rosa Praed and Tasma, found themselves encouraged to write adventure/romance and melodrama, though they did so from a specifically female point of view. In their works the melodramatic themes of imprisonment and loss of love enable a critique of late Victorian marriage.

Fiona Giles's anthology of short fiction, *From the Verandah* (1987), usefully represents the period to 1909, including work by Tasma, Ellen Augusta Chads, Ellen Liston, Waif Wander, Ethel Turner, Flora Beatrice, Ada Cambridge, Rosa Praed, Louise Mack, Barbara Baynton, Mary Gaunt and Mary Hannay Foott.[46] Most of these women were professional writers whose work enjoyed wide circulation in literary journals and anthologies, and some were successful enough to publish their own collections, such as Tasma's *A Sydney Sovereign* (1890) and Barbara Baynton's *Bush Studies* (1902). Many of their stories use conventional situations from melodrama to explore contemporary sexual politics. Ellen Liston's 'Cousin Lucy's Story', for example, has a two-part structure in which a respectable married woman recalls for her male relatives an episode that took place before her marriage, when she assisted an escaped convict to evade police custody. This nested tale is pure Victorian domestic melodrama. Mary Miles is a pretty girl, 'pure and good', who is seduced by a cad while working as a servant. When her brother Harry accidentally kills her lover he is sentenced to life imprisonment. Just before her own marriage, Lucy risks her reputation by helping Harry Miles escape to America, and arranging for Mary to begin a new life with him there. Lucy's intervention in the lives of Harry and Mary Miles can be read as a female commentary on the morality of domestic melodrama which resists the stereotyping of the fallen woman. The re-telling of her action constitutes, in turn, a recurring resistance to conventional morality, the law, and her own identity as the wife of a respectable man. The frame, in which she tells the story to her male relatives, shows the potential for women's re-telling even of stereotypical tales to effect an unsettling of conventional values.

Tasma's story 'Monsieur Caloche', first published in the *Australasian* in 1878, draws upon the melodramatic situation of the villain beating the heroine, not only to expose the sexual contract, but also to critique the materialism of late nineteenth-century Victoria and its suppression of culture and sensibility, here associated with the older and more refined culture of Europe. Sir Matthew Bogg is an ignorant bully who persecutes Monsieur Caloche, a French youth of 'unmanly susceptibilities' (p. 95), whom he tries to toughen up on one of his pastoral properties. Their encounter has complex resonances— sexual, homophobic, misogynistic, xenophobic—expressed through the rhetoric of melodrama. Bogg's aggression erupts into action when he strikes Caloche across the chest with his coach whip and Caloche runs away to die in the bush. When the body is found, Bogg learns that 'Monsieur' Caloche is in fact a young French woman cross-dressed as a man. Her sex is discovered when Bogg and his manager find and strip the body, revealing marks of the whip on her breasts: it was 'a girl with breast of marble, bared in its cold whiteness to the open daylight, and to his ardent gaze . . . A virgin breast, spotless of hue, save for a narrow purple streak, marking it in a dark line from the collar-bone downwards' (p. 114). In Sir Matthew Bogg's whipping of Henriette Caloche, a stock situation of contemporary melodrama is charged with unusual thematic complexity and emotional force, combining her role as woman, effeminate 'man', innocent child, and cultured foreigner in a brash, masculine and materialistic society.

In her novels of the 1890s Tasma was increasingly drawn to melodrama as a vehicle for exploring contemporary sexual politics.[47] The heroine of *The Penance of Portia James* (1891), for example, is a young Australian girl living in London who has promised to marry her brother's mining partner, John Morrison, when she comes of age.[48] Despite her reservations, Portia goes through with the wedding only to have another woman, Mary Willett, reveal that she and Morrison have a child. Portia is now like a 'prisoner' seeking to escape from a 'dungeon' (p. 145), and fears she may become 'what is called an hysterical subject' (pp. 37–8). She flees to the home of her 'emancipated' friend Anna Ross, an artist living in the Latin Quarter of Paris, but when Mary Willett is fatally injured in a road accident Portia returns to her husband. In an ending reminiscent of Henry James's *The Portrait of a Lady* (1881), she promises the dying woman that she will stay with the child's father and bring up his son. Tasma's deployment of melodramatic language and situations is complicated, however, by the fact that she attributes the heroine's entrapment in marriage to her own inability to make decisions and assert herself: 'Her action in marrying a man she did not love simply because she had no power to resist surrounding influences . . . seemed to prove . . . that she was without the moral support known as backbone' (p. 267). It is left to the stronger New Woman to express Tasma's critique of marriage, yet in the account of Anna's bohemian existence Tasma turns upon the very character who would help her heroine to escape from bondage. Anna smokes, wears masculine clothes and initiates liaisons with numerous men. She believes that if Portia were to follow her example she would gain 'a sense of independence and power you have never known before' (p. 207). But like the Edwardian feminist Rose Scott, Tasma implies that as another male invention 'the free love doctrine' (p. 272) can operate to women's disadvantage and that women must find their own forms of emancipation. Her sympathies seem divided between the weak heroine and the 'emancipated' bohemian, opting for a woman who is self-responsible and decisive. As the tragic ending of Portia's return to her marriage indicates, no such woman character exists in the novel.

Rosa Praed is another novelist in whose work the theme of female entrapment recurs. Of the novels with Australian settings, *Outlaw and Lawmaker* (1893) and *Fugitive Anne* (1902) employ the conventions of the bushranging and captivity genres to develop Praed's distinctive critique of women's deference to 'respectable' men. Less well known are her domestic melodramas and occult novels set in England. *The Bond of Wedlock* (1887), for example, is a self-styled 'domestic melodrama' which uses the theme of imprisonment to question melodramatic morality, suggesting that in women's lives nothing is straightforwardly good or evil, and that the deceptive clarity of such moral alternatives may well be part of what entraps them in marriage.[49] Ariana Lomax is a beautiful but dissatisfied young woman whose 'provincial puritanism' and 'bourgeois rectitude' leave her caught indecisively between her tiresome husband, Harvey, and her lover, Sir Leopold

D'Acosta. She refuses her husband's demands that she ask D'Acosta for money, and the chapter 'A Foul Stroke' ends with Harvey beating her in the prose equivalent of a curtain tableau. Harvey's violence stirs Sir Leopold into plotting against him, D'Acosta paying his former mistress, Babette Steinbock, to seduce Lomax, so providing Ariana with grounds for divorce. In the two women characters, Praed exploits the moral binarism of melodrama while complicating its stereotypical effects. Babette Steinbock is a prostitute by choice, in contrast to the respectable Ariana, who is made miserable by her adherence to conventional roles. As Babette explains, 'in this country, a woman can only be really free when she is immoral; and so I mean to take up with immorality again for the sake of my freedom' (p. 45). Praed questions the traditional melodramatic opposition between virtuous and fallen women, deploying the two characters not as polar opposites, but as aspects of a more complete female subjectivity fragmented and dispersed by patriarchy. Ariana, the good woman, admits, 'There's another woman in me which might have come out under different conditions. If I were to let that woman have play, I'm afraid that I might lose myself' (p. 64). *The Bond of Wedlock* therefore begins by gesturing self-reflexively towards the moral universe of melodrama, which it exploits as its formal vehicle, only to render its clear-cut morality problematic. In the closing lines of the novel the displacement of Ariana's own 'bourgeois' romanticism by her second husband's 'cynical philosophy' is expressed precisely in terms of a rejection of the simplicities of melodramatic morality. 'Why need we be melodramatic?' D'Acosta asks; 'Ideal morality, love, sentiment, and so forth, is the monopoly of the bourgeoisie nowadays' (p. 131). *The Bond of Wedlock* was dramatised as *Ariane* at the Opera Comique in 1888. It is perhaps a measure of its success in establishing a woman's point-of-view melodrama that, two months after the play opened, the *Illustrated Sporting and Dramatic News* was pleased to announce that the 'end of the run of "Ariane" is sanitary and not unwelcome'.[50]

Praed's most sustained use of melodrama to explore issues affecting women was in her occult novels, one of the major genres of her fiction, though still little studied.[51] These include *Affinities: A Romance of Today* (1885), *The Brother of the Shadow* (1886) and *The Soul of Countess Adrian* (1891). *The Brother of the Shadow*[52] is the story of a psychic researcher's treatment of a young English woman possessed by a malign spirit from ancient Egypt, and has many similarities with Rider Haggard's *She* and Bram Stoker's *Dracula*, both published in the following year. With its theme of female captivity by the personification of evil, the vampire novel has many associations with melodrama and its prose relation, the gothic novel. In Praed's novella, however, the moral identity of the characters is blurred. Instead of the psychic researcher opposing the demonic force in a bid to re-inscribe conventional womanhood, as happens in both *She* and *Dracula*, he is made literally the instrument of that evil force and, symbolically, its source. Colonel Julian Vascher has married in India, and his wife, Antonia, suffers from a mysterious nervous illness that can only be relieved by morphine. Advised that mesmerism may help, Vascher places her under the care of Dr Lemuel Lloyd, a Harley Street specialist who has 'come a cropper' over his experiments with occult practices. Antonia becomes possessed by a malign spirit, 'the brother of the shadow', which can be read as a projection of the male psychic researcher's lust for his female patient. Lloyd's 'instrument', the syringe of morphia, causes Antonia to droop 'like a bruised flower . . . The prick of the needle drew blood. He felt himself brutal' (p. 33). Praed's concern is with professional malpractice, the problem of a doctor or psychic researcher's vampire-like desire to possess his women patients. At the end of the tale, when the evil spirit is exorcised, it is appropriate that the good doctor is destroyed with it. Praed therefore used occult themes to critique the contemporary institutions of marriage and romantic love, and their underwriting by medical and psychiatric discourse. As historian Alex Owen argues, the occult allowed Victorian women to speak in different ways about the social construction of femininity.[53]

MELODRAMA AND MODERNITY

The increasing moral ambivalence of women's point-of-view melodrama is quite distinct from the modes of farce and parody with which nineteenth-century melodrama always happily co-existed, and suggests that it might be useful to review Peter Brooks's argument that melodrama's function was to reinforce moral pieties in a de-sacralised society. In an important extension of Brooks's notion of the 'moral occult', Tom Gunning has questioned Brooks's historiography, which assumes that melodrama declined at the end of the nineteenth century as its spectacular apparatus began to separate from its role in signifying the moral occult. In his reading of the horror plays of Andre de Lorde, Gunning finds that their 'dark endings . . . not only do not reveal a moral occult, but actually display a vertiginous image of order destroyed and discourse rendered meaningless'. In these plays the modern discourses of medicine and psychiatry become problematic, the final revelations uncovering not moral truth but, literally, 'a corpse, madness and speechlessness'. Instead of representing a decline from an earlier golden age, late melodrama's obsession with sensation, particularly its staging of the new urban milieu and its technology, shows that 'the entertainment based in sensation both portrayed and helped to mediate the new abrasive experience of modernity'.[54] This is suggestive for my reading of the melodramatic novels of Praed and Tasma, which similarly question the value of modern discourses of truth—patriarchal marriage, romantic love, law, medicine and psychiatry. It might be argued, then, that in late Victorian melodrama, the women's point of view registers most acutely the 'abrasive disorder of modernity'.

Of course this vertiginous collapse of values was not confined to women's writing, but reflected the increasing sense of uncertainty that we associate with the culture of the *fin de siècle*. The 1870s were a watershed, marking a qualitative turn from the confidence of the high Victorian period to a time of growing doubts about the fate of the British Empire, worries about national efficiency, and fears of racial and cultural decline. The invasion of Egypt in 1882 and the death of Gordon at Khartoum in 1885 fuelled imperial anxieties. By 1902 the protracted campaigns of the Boer War had revealed glaring deficiencies in the Empire's military capability. To these anxieties were added other, more

tangible threats both at home and abroad. In the early years of the new century, industrial conflict erupted throughout Britain on an unprecedented scale, while suffragettes
conducted an increasingly militant campaign for votes for women. There were also foreign threats, most immediately from Germany, but also from Russia and, after Japan's
victory at the battle of Tushima in 1905, from the 'coloured' races. As these crises unfolded, it was increasingly apparent that British and colonial interests were on divergent
courses, opening a fracture in imperial ideology around the difficult relation between
empire and nation.

The moral ambivalence of the *fin-de-siècle* period is expressed in the tales about the
convict system written by Price Warung (William Astley). These originally appeared in
the *Bulletin* and *Truth* between 1890 and 1894, and selections were published subsequently, including *Tales of the Convict System* (1892), *Tales of the Early Days* (1894) and
Tales of the Old Regime and the Bullet of the Fatal Ten (1897).[55] Although often praised for
their realism, these stories draw heavily on the vocabulary of stage melodrama and the
gothic novel but work, through their themes of entrapment, persecution and torture, to
problematise melodrama's moral scheme by a process of inversion that is a function of
'the System'. A note to the tale 'The Secret Society of the Ring' explains, 'At Norfolk
Island it was the awful custom among the more hardened convicts to invert the meaning
of "good" and "bad". A "good" man was a notorious criminal; a "bad" one was a man who
sought to act honestly and purely' (p. 126). Captain Maconochie, the new Commandant
of Norfolk Island, tries to break the Ring by instigating liberal policies, allowing the convict Henry Reynell to work outside the prison as an independent farmer. In making himself the Commandant's man—in being a 'true man to an Establishment officer' (p. 158)
—Reynell wins back his personal humanity but incurs the punishment of the Ring,
which sentences him to death for becoming a 'bad' man. The Ring is 'an empire of evil
within an empire of horror' (p. 139). Its ceremonies are blasphemous inversions of the
Anglican liturgy and 'the benignity of British Justice', the narrator remarking that
'parody was the richest fruit of the System' (p. 159). Yet for all its appearance of conventional evil, the Ring claims a moral authority through its resistance to the System: 'There
was the might of England behind the System—the majesty of her law, the sanctity of her
State religion, the wisdom of her administrators' (p. 140). In such passages, melodrama's
terms of value are inverted, becoming signs of corruption and evil. The opposition
between the System and the Ring makes the Ring into a subversive other 'empire' that
resists the values of the British Empire, or 'the Establishment' (p. 139).

Price Warung's inversion of traditional values lent itself to appropriation by the
anti-imperialist, anti-British, and pro-republican voice of the Sydney *Bulletin* under the
editorship of J.F. Archibald. But his lurid, gothic tales also represent, indirectly, a humani-
tarian ethic that was shared by other *Bulletin* writers of the 1890s and 1910s, including
Barbara Baynton and Louis Becke, who were also drawn to the melodramatic situations
of captivity and persecution. The physical and psychological entrapment of women by
men is a recurring trope in Barbara Baynton's short stories, and in her novel, *Human Toll*

(1907). In 'Squeaker's Mate' a woman crippled by a falling tree is held prisoner in a hut when her partner, Squeaker, brings home a new 'mate', whispering threats to her through the cracks in the slab hut that he will set fire to it if she is not quiet. The story climaxes in Squeaker's vicious beating of his old mate with a stick. Similar images of entrapment and torture in 'The Chosen Vessel' suggest that the woman's ideological entrapment by an ideal of femininity controls her as surely as any physical restraint. The swagman's imagined entry into the hut has all the trappings of melodrama: the presence of her innocent child, the swagman's 'cruel eyes, lascivious mouth, and gleaming knife', and the answering cry of the curlews.[56] But the simple moral scheme associated with those devices is complicated by the implication that her feminine self-image is as much a threat to her as the gleaming knife. The woman is simultaneously an object of the rapist's desire and of Peter Hennessey's religious veneration. Baynton's complex interrogation of the ideal of the good woman—the 'chosen vessel'—uses, but goes far beyond, the basic melodramatic situation, not in any sense rehearsing a 'moral occult' but interrogating moral pieties and leaving them hollowed with doubt. In so far as 'The Chosen Vessel' is melodramatic, it is that distinctly modern form in which the reader finds uncertainty rather than the moral pieties of nineteenth-century stage melodrama.

Louis Becke's stories also invert 'normal' values through the devices of melodrama to complicate the idea of the white Australians' superiority to the people of the Pacific, over whom they assume a sub-imperial sway through commerce. Macy O'Shea, one of the traders in *By Reef and Palm* (1894), already has a Polynesian wife when he purchases a second one, Malia, the half-caste daughter of a fellow trader. Such is the effect of white culture on the islands that 'the transaction was a perfectly legitimate one'.[57] As so often in Becke's stories, one exchange leads to another. O'Shea's first wife sinks a knife into Malia's breast, destroying her value as a sexual and financial investment. In retaliation, O'Shea has his first wife flayed, making good his loss by cutting off her right hand and keeping her as an agricultural labourer. But when she dies from her wounds her death is the final exchange, since it cheats him of that last investment in the body of the native woman. Becke's relation to Australia's sub-imperialism in the Pacific was ambivalent, and there is no doubt that he was often complicit with Orientalist views. Yet, like Barbara Baynton, he uses the theme of captivity and torture to reflect critically upon the pieties of White Australia, particularly the connection between sexuality and colonial power.

The decline of moral certainty that finds expression in the darkly cynical stories of Price Warung, Barbara Baynton and Louis Becke is also reflected in Norman Lindsay's children's story, *The Magic Pudding* (1918), which mocks the very idea of heroes and villains.[58] The 'pudding thieves', who constantly dress in disguise to abduct the pudding, are apparently recognisable as melodramatic villains: 'One was a Possum, with one of those sharp, snooting, snouting sort of faces, and the other was a bulbous, boozy-looking Wombat in . . . a hat that marked him down as a man you couldn't trust in a fowl-yard' (p. 28). Yet the 'pudding owners' are themselves illegitimate, since Bill Barnacle and Sam Sawnoff stole the pudding from the Chinese cook Curry and Rice, whom they 'shoved' off an iceberg in a shipwreck; so that the two groups are effectively indistinguishable from each other on moral grounds. Nor is there any relief from vice in the traditional pastoral setting of village melodrama, for the Mayor and Constable, and the Judge and Court Usher in the little country town of Tooraloo are equally greedy 'pudding thieves'. Lindsay's beguiling children's story can therefore be read as a parody of the tendency to allegorise contemporary events along melodramatic lines, which requires transparently good and wicked sides, heroes and villains. Not the least of such events was the First World War itself, during which Lindsay wrote the tale in his eyrie at Springwood.

By the beginning of the twentieth century the combined populations of Sydney and Melbourne had reached one million, providing a lucrative market for a wide range of new popular entertainments, of which film was to emerge as the dominant form. Melodrama was never far from the origins of cinema, the earliest cinematograph exhibitions competing for audiences with other visually-oriented media such as magic and vaudeville, while many early 'story' films derived from stage material. Among the first narrative films, made for the purposes of moral instruction by the Limelight Department of the Melbourne Salvation Army in 1898, was the story of 'a young girl saved from the clutches of a villain by one [Salvation Army] lassie, while another was seen "dealing it out" to the rogue'.[59] *Soldiers of the Cross* (1900), one of the first Australian feature films, was directly inspired by religious melodramas such as *The Sign of the Cross*, which played to packed houses in Melbourne during 1897. The film exploits for evangelistic purposes the spectacular effects and emotional extremes to which audiences of stage melodrama were accustomed. The premiere was held on 13 September 1900 at the Melbourne Town Hall. The visual displays, consisting of both lantern slides and short reels of film, featured stonings, crucifixions, beheadings, burnings at the stake and other tribulations of the early Christians, accompanied by an original musical score, the crowd of four thousand people reacting with 'involuntary interjections, moans of pity, sighs of relief'.[60] *Soldiers of the Cross* was therefore a religious melodrama in the sense that it exploited for religious purposes the emotional response of the crowd to music and visual sensation. As the Salvation Army's Brigadier Philip Kyle wrote, 'It is a great assault upon the conscience through eye and ear gates'.[61]

Among the first locally produced features to appear in the cinemas that began to spring up from around 1905 was *The Story of the Kelly Gang* (1906), which had its origins in the stage melodrama still running in Melbourne. Film audiences schooled in melodramatic response sympathised with the threatened virtue of Kate Kelly, cheered the Kelly boys, and hissed the schoolmaster. The *Bulletin* complained, 'there is a deal too much racket about the show', but conceded it was 'the sort of bellowdrama that the lower orders crave for'.[62]

The most prolific director of the pre-war silent film era was Raymond Longford, whose early features, made between 1911 and 1918, show the strong influence of stage melodrama in their plots and acting style. These include *The Fatal Wedding* (1911), *The Romantic Story of Margaret Catchpole* (1911), *The Tide of Death* (1912), *The Midnight*

Wedding (1912) and *Australia Calls* (1913). The screenplay for *Australia Calls*, which deals with the subject of Asiatic invasion, was adapted from Randolph Bedford's earlier stage melodrama *White Australia*:

> the rejected suitor turns traitor, and in return for the girl, £5000 cash and a passage out of the country, he undertakes to guide the Mongolian forces. The girl is captured and brought into the Chinese camp, but the Australian aeroplane, manipulated by [Capt. W.E.] Hart, happens through the air, rescues her, and carries her off amid storms of bullets and a typhoon of applause.[63]

It was not until *The Sentimental Bloke* (1919) and *On Our Selection* (1920) that Longford effectively shed melodramatic conventions to pursue the more naturalistic style of acting and *mise-en-scène* for which he is now remembered. On the acting in *The Sentimental Bloke* he commented that, 'The true art of acting is not to act . . . That's what I have drummed into the ears of my characters and I think it has its effect in the naturalness of my pictures'.[64] In *On Our Selection*, Longford pursued this same vision of naturalness, preferring 'the starkly true Australian characters of the book to the puppets of the play, with all its old trappings of mortgages, flinty-hearted moneylenders, black-moustached heavies in polo suits, and the various other borrowed stage traditions'.[65] But the taste for melodrama remained in other films of the silent era, such as Franklyn Barrett's *The Breaking of the Drought* (1920). In 1932, when Ken G. Hall's relatively theatrical version of *On Our Selection* was released, Raymond Longford invoked the pejorative sense of the term that we now associate with the modern era. 'I have little doubt', he wrote, 'the talkie now on the slips will be a faithful reproduction of the old melodramatic tripe that was originally served up as the Steele Rudd story [on the stage]'.[66] Despite Longford's disapproval, the 'old melodramatic tripe' was indeed to survive with a vengeance not just into the new age of the talkie, but beyond that into our own age of television.

5

NATIONAL DRESS OR NATIONAL TROUSERS?

Susan K. Martin

'It is not in our cities or townships, it is not in our agricultural or mining areas, that the Australian attains full consciousness of his own nationality . . .'[1] Joseph Furphy, *Such is Life* (1903)

In Ellen Augusta Chads's 1891 story 'The Ghost of Wanganilla' the Australian landscape is apparently haunted by the ghost of a 'defiant' white woman.[2] This figure appears each full moon to terrorise white settlers on their way to the local ball. The narrator of the story, Mr Meredith, recounts the events around his confrontation with this hilltop apparition, which he claims must be 'either an insane woman or some . . . [man] playing an ill-timed jest' (p. 39). Meredith's investigative excursion is intended to impress his sweetheart, referred to as his 'bright particular star', but this backfires. His stallion baulks as he approaches, 'the white figure apparently watching and waiting our coming' and the narrator is thrown from his horse, receives a broken arm, a 'threatened brain fever', and wakes up two weeks later, in the house and care of the sweetheart (pp. 40–1). His account of the rest of the events is a secondhand description of his own rescue. Some of the young men mount the hill after him, but before they can reach the threatening white figure it is struck by lightning and disappears, just as one of the party sees that it is an illusion caused by an oddly-formed dead gum tree.

This story raises a number of the concerns around nation and nature in nineteenth-century Australian literature. In the initial part of the story the reader is faced with a landscape which is threatening, and apparently explicitly female. The haunting apparition, linked to the feminine cycles of the moon, threatens to prevent the easy passage of the white squatters across the landscape, and to interrupt their cultured pursuits with its inexplicable natural defiance. It is possible to read the story as showing a successful confrontation with threatening feminine nature, which is proven harmless, and subdued so that the civilised progress of masculine, Anglo-Saxon settlement is assured.

However, one might suggest that this story makes fun of a masculine perception of the landscape as an unreasoning and hostile feminine force. The story shows that it is the restricted angle of vision of the male narrator and his companions that produces an incorrect and distorted understanding of the place—there is no haunting and no feminine in the landscape not projected by a masculinist and confrontational white settler viewpoint.

Nevertheless the white madwoman in the moonlight is rather disturbingly connected to the white woman who is Meredith's 'star'. His guiding light, the object of his affections, watches silently from below while he attempts to mount the hill and subdue a white female beacon, the object of his quest, who is apparently watching silently from above. The 'star' remains firmly seated on her skittish horse, while Meredith's stallion appears emasculated by fear. Instead of succeeding in his quest Meredith is knocked senseless and finds himself delivered up to the more truly feminine domestic space presided over by his beloved 'Ellie', who is named only at this point. So subdued is he by the blow to his head, and perhaps to his perceptions, that he must go 'home' for two years, back to the reassuring centre of European culture, under the supervision of the 'star', whom he marries, and of God. Meredith's account of the story closes with the display of a 'prettily-carved papercutter' made from the remains of the gum tree. This might be seen as the final civilising of that threatening feminine uncontrollably natural figure—turned into the letters of the story and a letter opener. But it is Mrs Meredith (Ellie, the 'star') who displays the object, so that the final image of the story is of a woman in possession of access to letters—a woman with a knife in her hand.

There are further implications to the story beyond the complications of the feminine investment in the Australian landscape, and the taming, Anglicising and Christianising of the nation (the recounting of the tale takes place around Christmas time, 'the Master's birthday') (p. 36). The white female ghost and the bleached gum tree serve to displace the fact that the landscape is indeed occupied by others—haunted not by a white woman, but by the dispossessed people of the region, who are absent from the story, but present in the apparently Aboriginal name of the district in which the ghost appears, and in the title of the tale. Nineteenth-century notions of Australian nationhood are entirely founded on just such fantasies of absence and invisibility, and yet, as in this story, are haunted by them.

The idea that the Australian nation is an entity fully imagined some time in the 1890s has been a commonplace of Australian cultural understandings. It has become self-fulfilling. The nationalist possibilities and explorations of the Australian 1890s have been filled out and most thoroughly explored even by those who might wish to claim earlier, or later, different, or even no, inceptions of national consciousness. The result of this has been that modern understandings of nation in Australia circulate around the 1890s whether this was *the* critical moment or not. If, as Homi Bhabha argues, nations are realised or invented retrospectively, the 1890s have been ineradicably installed in Australian discourses as the moment the Australian nation emerges from the 'myths of time', and the period and its texts must be dealt with in the light of this.[3]

THE 1990S RE-READ THE 1890S

Australian nationalism, of the nineteenth century and in its present form, has recently become an object of intensified criticism. Some have suggested that what are now seen as moments of national formation, such as the Heidelberg School's depiction of 'distinctively Australian' light, landscape and character, never existed in the ways we now think of them.[4] Other discussions have focused on the ways in which the concentration of national identifications around figures like the lone bush worker are both anachronistic and somewhat ridiculous for the urban Australia of the twentieth century, and have critiqued the way they work to exclude much of the geographical nation's population— most women, all Aborigines and Torres Strait Islanders and other Australians of non-Anglo-Celtic background.[5] Internationally, the usefulness and continuance of the idea of the nation itself has been questioned.[6]

In this light it could seem easier to dismiss—as outmoded, Anglocentric and masculinist—literary figurations of national identity in Australia in the 1880s and 1890s and after. But the 'Australian Legend' continues to circulate in popular culture.[7] The images surrounding such national types are still invoked to 'mean' or represent the nation in many contexts.[8] The sources usually drawn upon, and the forms still in circulation, are those derived from nineteenth-century Australian writing, painting, song, and forms of media such as newspapers and journals. Certainly attention needs to be paid to the continued sales and familiarity of literary figures like Henry Lawson (1867–1922) and A.B. (Banjo) Paterson (1864–1941), as well as the resurrection of writers such as Miles Franklin (1879–1954) and Barbara Baynton (1857–1929) as 'alternatives' to these, who nevertheless seem to offer some of the same understandings of national type and landscape.

In the 1880s, the story goes, national fervour began to foment and to be expressed or consolidated, particularly in the popular presses. New journals such as the *Bulletin*, *Bull-Ant*, *Worker* and later the *Lone Hand*[9] provided an outlet for rising national sentiment. This arose among working men and the lower and struggling classes, in conflict with the pastoral and professional interests which dominated state politics and were voiced in established papers like the *Australasian* and *Age*, and largely also in the published monograph fiction of the period. In this version of history new national understandings were invested in aspects of the rural and the wilderness—the itinerant workers on the land, and the landscape itself—in opposition to an urban population and scene understood to be tainted by European beliefs and aesthetics not compatible with the original, 'indigenous' Australia—by which no reference to the Aboriginal population was intended.

It can be argued that the modern nation has mainly been imagined through the rise of literacy and modern media, that the very act of reading a vernacular newspaper instils in its reader a particular understanding of simultaneous time which allows 'him' to see himself as part of a (national) community.[10] Feminist re-readings of this model have questioned the masculinity of this national subject. Postcolonial criticism has contested the notion that all forms of 'imagined community' have a European origin, so that any anti-colonial or postcolonial nation can only represent itself in reference to these models.[11] For the white Australian community, however, national imagining was undoubtedly conducted primarily through British understandings of nation.

THE 1890S IN THE INTERNATIONAL CONTEXT

It is not only in Australia that the end of the nineteenth century, the *fin de siècle*, is seen as a period of heightened anxiety and unrest, fragmentation and disruption. The 'sense of an ending' in a temporally obsessed age heightens already circulating concerns.[12] Although such Western anxieties were geographically and historically specific a number of critics have noted rising concern about the permeability of boundaries—geographic boundaries as well as those defining gender, sexuality and the boundaries of the self.[13]

In Australia such anxieties were partly negotiated in narratives about state and national boundaries.[14] *Such is Life* by Joseph Furphy (1843–1912) was written in the 1890s, first submitted for publication in 1897, and finally published as a novel under the name 'Tom Collins' by the Bulletin Co. in 1903. In it Collins's loss of geographical orientation forms a pivotal episode, and state rivalries anchor identities and colour the conversations. At times the men in *Such is Life* seem infinitely comfortable in the landscape, true Australians in their proper place, the bush, outwitting women and capitalists and easily occupying all spaces. However, with Collins as the ultimate representative of this, such confidence is shaken when this supposedly skilled navigator finds himself so lost that he does not know which state, apart from the state of nature, he is in. Losing his clothes in the Murray River, and disoriented because, '[i]t never occurred to my mind that Victoria could be on the north side of New South Wales' (p. 100), Collins embarks on a series of adventures which seem to confirm arguments about gender anxiety at the turn of the century. A woman in trousers called Jim, moustachioed like most of Furphy's women, and the man who screams like a woman when Tom attempts to take his trousers (p. 109), are only heightened examples of the gender confusions and inversions which permeate the entire novel.

In the last decades of the nineteenth century Australia was moving toward Federation. It was an increasingly urbanised society in the east, though still carrying overtones of the 'frontier' in the west. The country experienced economic boom in the 1880s but a drastic drought and its share of the international economic depression at the end of the century. This was an era which saw the rise of workers' movements and unions, a popular temperance movement and successful Australian women's suffrage organisations. Concepts of nation and national identification, and hence the struggle over the meaning and constitution of nation were heightened toward the end of the century.

Since the 1980s it has been argued that the conception of 1890s culture and nation was grounded in a 'masculinism' requiring analysis.[15] Previous invocations of national type and character had ignored gender and erased the fact that, in the words of Marilyn Lake, there was 'a contest between men and women at the end of the nineteenth century for the control of the national culture'.[16] In this battle the new national values being produced around the itinerant bush worker were conceived and figured in opposition to notions of character and lifestyle harnessed to the feminine. The bush worker was a rural, unmarried, independent, drinking, smoking, nomadic anti-authoritarian. The bush heroes of Henry Lawson, 'Banjo' Paterson and Joseph Furphy, Price Warung's convicts and Edward Dyson's men superficially fit these patterns.

In opposition to these fantasies were the domestic values established across the nineteenth century in Anglocentric cultures, and associated with women. These were based on belief in a domestic haven maintained by the wife and honoured by the husband. This ideology favoured stability and reliability, temperance and religion, an established and urban or semi-urban environment—home and family. So masculinity in Australia came to be defined as in opposition to the domestic, while the domestic was depicted as a site of conservatism and a threat to national values. The radical nature of early temperance and sexual 'purity' movements was masked in arguments which depicted them as aimed at spoiling masculine fun and curtailing (male) freedom, rather than protecting women and children from neglect, poverty and violence. Arguably the women's movement in Australia was brought into being by the rise of this masculinist culture (p. 11).

Lake sees a coincidence at the turn of the century between the aims of women and the state, and even some parts of the labour movement, leading to a 'feminisation' of the national culture—a triumph of domestic ideology marked by the installation of the 'family wage' in 1907 (p. 14). However, some elements of the national culture—such as the literary canon—might be seen to have gone in the opposite direction.

Much of the masculinist rhetoric of the 1880s and 1890s appeared in the fiction, poetry, journalism and cartoons of journals like the *Bulletin*, though of course these arguments were by no means homogeneous.[17] As well as representations *within* writing, the same unequal dichotomy was being set up in the valuing and understanding of Australian literature at the time. Thus women's writing, particularly popular women's romance fiction, was resituated on the negative side of a dichotomy which grouped Realism, the rural, egalitarianism, originality, action and male bonding against Romance,[18] the home and the urban, conservatism, unoriginality, feeling and heterosexual love or female bonds.[19]

One controversial psychoanalytic reading of Australian culture suggests that in fact the Australian self has been defined since the beginning of white settlement as a masculine self, in opposition to women, but also to a feminised landscape, a devouring or rejecting mother.[20] Thus the national identity depends upon the 'othering'—that is both rejection and incorporation-through-definition—of the feminine in all its forms.

Neither the supposed 'masculine' nor the 'feminine' forms of writing conform to these retrospectively perceived patterns in full. For instance, William Lane (1861–1917) was propounding feminist ideas in conjunction with his socialist approach to the labour question in his writing for the *Worker*, which he edited, and in his novel, *The Workingman's*

Paradise (1892), first serialised in the journal in 1891. The work of nineteenth-century writers like Ada Cambridge (1844–1926) and Rosa Praed (1851–1935) was middle class in audience, ideology and aspirations, but was nevertheless often set in the bush and espoused some 'masculinist' values identified with the working classes. Even the claimed sources of the iconic national type, such as Lawson's fiction and poetry, do not uniformly praise this type any more than they consistently produce negative images of the domestic, or denunciations of the bush.[21]

While the popular women writers published in book form, and were frequently published by British companies with European circulation, they were also published in local newspapers and journals, if mostly those like the *Australasian* or the *Sydney Mail*, which might be seen to serve the 'conservative squattocracy'.[22] It is an over-simplification to identify the sympathies of such groups as purely 'British', and as somehow detached from nationalist movements and sympathies. As one historian points out: 'native and imperial loyalties mingled happily [only] so long as Australian interests did not suffer'.[23]

Despite this diversity, there *has* until quite recently been a dichotomy, however artificial, which has worked to erase much nineteenth-century Australian women's writing (along with much men's writing which reflected urban, feminist or 'imperialist' causes) from the literary record. There has also been a prolonged devaluation of its form and content. The canon of Australian writing has been formed around texts which exhibited features consistent with the perceived values of the 1890s, so that as well as the ballads of Paterson, Edward Dyson, Barcroft Boake, and the writing of Lawson and Furphy, earlier work was retrospectively considered in terms of its unique 'Australianness'. By these criteria the 'mateship' of Rolf Boldrewood's *Robbery Under Arms* (1882–83/1888) and the specificities of a masculine convict system in Marcus Clarke's *For the Term of his Natural Life* (1870–72/1874) meant that these early fictions were privileged over works like Catherine Helen Spence's domestically-based exploration of the gold rushes, *Clara Morison* (1854), or Caroline Leakey's female-centred, less racy novel about the convict system, *The Broad Arrow* (1859).[24] Rediscoveries of nineteenth- and early twentieth-century women's writing concentrated on work such as Miles Franklin's and Barbara Baynton's which exhibited some of the valued features of the masculinist tradition.

SOME BEGINNINGS OF A NATIONAL SUBJECTIVITY

Obviously the nation as object and affiliation was being produced before the 1890s in fiction, as elsewhere. Even in early 'guidebook' novels like Thomas McCombie's *Arabin* (1845), Alexander Harris's *The Emigrant Family* (1849) or Henry Kingsley's *The Recollections of Geoffry Hamlyn* (1859) there are attempts to locate national 'types' and invest national identification in the natural environment.[25] In *Robbery Under Arms* by Rolf Boldrewood (squatter Thomas E. Browne, 1826–1915),[26] the tedious moralising about the naughty behaviour of the dashing bushrangers becomes a schizophrenic gesturing toward ideal national character through negatives. That is, everything the heroes are not is registered by the tendentious narrative voice as everything which could make the country great. This is highlighted through the character of the aptly named George Storefield and his sister Grace, whose honest and saving ways render them prosperous landholders in contrast to the reprobate itinerant cattle-duffer Dick. The latter, redeemed by Grace, is poised to reform at the close of the novel, though his future ideal behaviour, like most of the notions of national character, is beyond the boundaries of the adventure narrative.

Women writers also posited ideal white citizens for a half-imagined nation. Mary Vidal's perfect servants in *Tales for the Bush* (1845), and flawed masters with potential in *Bengala* (1860), have values in common with Maud Jean Franc's Christian domestic fictions published from the 1860s to the 1880s. These depict emerging national character —but along Protestant and feminine lines.

Novels, like other national texts, invoke nations of readers to the extent that they assume or address common national values and a set of national readers. Thus a significant occurrence across the latter third of the nineteenth century in Australia is the increasing local publication of Australian writing, and the serialisation of local fiction in national and regional papers and magazines. This would suggest a shift in the context of these fictions, from addressing and describing a British outpost to Britain toward addressing and invoking a national identity to itself.[27] At the same time, as in other colonies, there was a proliferation of national forms and ideas in other arts and sciences.[28]

As with many colonised countries, the constitution of the nation in the imagination was partly effected through setting up an oppositional relationship to the coloniser; in Australia's case, to Britain. The choice of the Australian landscape and its inhabitants as distinctively 'Australian' is expressed in the closing lines of Lawson's 'The Bush Undertaker': 'And the sun sank on the grand Australian bush—the nurse and tutor of eccentric minds, the home of the weird, and of much that is different from things in other lands'.[29] There is some tension in Australian writing across this period between an idea of nation constituted through its people, and an idea of nation understood through place and distinctive environment. This division does not necessarily align with the masculinist/ feminist division.

MASCULINE AND FEMININE NATIONS AND THE NATIONAL LANDSCAPE

One of the dominant ways in which Australian space has been conceptualised in fiction has been as a hostile environment against which it is necessary to battle, as in Chads's story discussed earlier. This idea has always appeared alongside more positive, utopian and Arcadian images.[30] Depicting the environment as hostile has generally worked well for fictional developments of national place and character. It has served to highlight and make heroic an individual, often masculine concept of struggle, and the definition of distinct characteristics invoked by a supposedly distinctive place. It facilitates the development of bonds between men, and occasionally even between men and women, united against a hostile bush. Typical of many such representations is Henry Lawson's 'Settling on the Land', from *While the Billy Boils* (1896), in which the trials of a selector are chronicled.[31] After spending weeks attempting to grub impossible stumps, and being harassed and sabotaged by the squatter,

> Tom ploughed and sowed wheat, but nothing came up to speak of—the ground was too poor; so he carted stable manure six miles from the nearest town, manured the land, sowed another crop, and prayed for rain. It came. It raised a flood which washed the crop clean off the selection, together with several acres of manure, and a considerable portion of the original surface soil; and the water brought down enough sand to make a beach and spread it over the field to a depth of six inches. The flood also took half a mile of fencing from along the creek-bank, and landed it in a bend, three miles down, on a dummy selection, where it was confiscated (p. 7).

Every other venture—into sheep, fruit growing and vines—is similarly ruined by the environment or men, including a fight with an entire dummy selector family in which, '[t]he woman was the worst' (p. 8). Tom ends up in a 'lunatic asylum', soon joined by the squatter, who has 'been ruined by the drought, the rabbits, the banks, and a wool ring' (p. 9).[32] In Simpson Newland's *Paving the Way* (1893), there are invocations of national type, and some attempt to legitimise ownership of 'available' landscape through a dubious recasting of Aboriginal dispossession as righteous battling for territory against a noble but inferior foe. Price Warung's 1890s 'convict' stories, many of them first published in the *Bulletin*, help mythologise a historic past for the nation, and position in heroic light a formerly shameful convict inheritance by offering convicts as progenitors and source for later nineteenth-century 'national' characteristics of faithfulness and hardiness, bonded horizontally against a corrupt and exploitative upper class.[33] Steele Rudd's *On Our Selection* series (1895–1903), while offering a view of selection life and the rural environment almost as negative as Lawson's in 'Settling on the Land', valorises as it ridicules the endurance and dreams of the small selector's family. The sentimentality of these stories has often been overlooked in concentration on their satire of the harsh Australian landscape and the clumsy and ill-fated small landholders. In 'The Night We Watched for Wallabies' (1899) Dad drags his sons out in the freezing night, ostensibly to guard the already denuded wheat field from marauding wallabies, but actually to remove the boys from the scene while their mother gives birth.[34]

While there is the usual clumsiness and destruction of property involved in the story (Dad walks into one of the draught horses which falls over and takes a fence with it), and the usual black portrait of the bush and hopeless rural poverty, there is also a mystification of birth and even of femininity in this story. The fertility and ubiquity of marauding vermin are complexly linked to the cycle of life silently proceeding in the house, even while the cold and depressed masculine sphere around the wallaby fires is explicitly segregated from the feminine domestic interior and the cryptic (to the boys) presence and occupation of midwife Mrs Brown.

Barbara Baynton has been seen to highlight the maternal as the redemptive in her otherwise bleak fiction.[35] However a comparison of Rudd's story with Baynton's 'Bush Church' (from *Bush Studies*, 1902) suggests a level of sentimentality in the former's depiction of selectors' families, and bush birth, which Jyne the local 'Rabbit Ketcher' [midwife] and the ghastly collection of ignorant brutish selectors in the latter story belie. Some of this might be a form of class bias, but the squatters come off only a little better than the selectors, the major difference between the grazier's wife and the local women being that the former 'thought so much of herself that she always brought a nurse from town' instead of calling on Jyne's expertise (p. 69).

While the debate over national subjectivity did have gender as one of its main points of contestation, the common adoption of Baynton as representative of the 'feminine' or 'feminist' side of this debate, usually against Lawson, is misleading.[36] Baynton is one of few women writers of the period who was published in that supposed bastion of the new masculinist national consciousness, the *Bulletin*. 'The Chosen Vessel', although heavily edited and under another title, appeared in 1896, and Baynton had a number of poems published there in the late 1890s and early 1900s.[37] Though too much weight can be put on such publication, and on Baynton's correspondence with and 'assistance' from the editor, A.G. Stephens, this token publication still suggests that Baynton's writing accorded with masculinist ideology in ways that the work of female contemporaries like Ada Cambridge or Mary Gaunt (1861–1942) did not.

'The Chosen Vessel', for instance, affirms a number of the accepted features of masculinist tradition. In this story of a woman raped and murdered by a 'tramp', the bush is no place for women or families and the environment is unforgiving and isolating. On the other hand, Baynton castigates some aspects of bush mythology in this story, and others such as 'Squeaker's Mate'. Usually the danger in the bush is not the bush itself, but the men *in* the bush—in both these stories, one of those celebrated itinerant workers. Like Chads and other women writers of the period, Baynton critiques and even ridicules some of the myths imposed on the bush—the vision of the Virgin Mary in 'The Chosen Vessel' is a hysterical delusion of religious bigotry which costs the real maternal figure of the story her life. As in 'The Ghost of Wanganilla', supernatural white female figures in the landscape turn out to be projections of masculine fantasy and desire. Baynton's story, 'The Dreamer', however, tries to convert those delusions of a maternal landscape to more 'feminine' usage, as a pregnant woman makes her way through the alternately nurturing and hostile bush towards a longed-for mother who turns out to be dead. Baynton is not a representative nineteenth-century female writer, but one divided, like Miles Franklin, by the split between traditions no longer particularly compatible. She depicts a place frozen and divided by religious, class and national affiliations that, in 'The Chosen Vessel', sacrifice female subjectivity to understandings of nationalism based on the removal of the feminine from the political sphere.

For middle-class women in the nineteenth century the making of the national subject was necessarily connected to the constitution of a middle-class female subject in

Australia embedded in, but different from, its source of definition, the internationally recognisable British Lady. The problem was faced in works by women including Mary Vidal, Maud Jean Franc, and Ellen Liston, and developed in the works of slightly later writers such as Ada Cambridge, Rosa Praed, Tasma, and Mary Gaunt: how to appropriate or continue the status and power available to the British Lady, but re-situate that Lady in Australia?[38] The solution usually consisted of an argument for a particular, hybrid, Australian Lady, equal or even superior to the British version—but likewise transferable, carrying recognisable international cultural capital. This led to fiction which did consider distinctive Australian environments, and specific social conditions, but generally in terms of the ways they enhanced or threatened middle-class female Australian subjects.

Men's fiction was usually more centrally engaged in distinguishing an Australian man *from* British identifications, especially class-based British understandings of masculinity, through series of oppositions. A hostile or difficult environment formed a better background for exploring or inventing the distinct qualities of this Australian subject, though of course each sex was also engaged in the representation of the ideal national subject of 'each' gender. These gender divisions are not mutually exclusive.

It can be useful to compare a seminal figure like Henry Lawson with a writer like Ada Cambridge in order to consider in a different light the supposed division between popular romance and bush realism; to rethink both the national subject and the nation as place. Ada Cambridge was a well-known and prolific writer of popular romance fiction from the 1870s into the early twentieth century. Her stories, mostly set in Australia, were frequently serialised in Australian newspapers, before being published in Britain.[39]

If you consider Lawson's 'Joe Wilson' stories alongside Cambridge's newspaper serials it is possible to read Cambridge as representing those alternative and muted, interrupted visions of 'the' nation which don't win the prize. Titles like 'A Girl's Ideal', *Sisters, The Three Miss Kings* and *A Woman's Friendship* (all by Ada Cambridge) register differences of concern in terms of class, social issues and gender to 'The Bush Undertaker', 'The Drover's Wife' or 'The Union Buries Its Dead'.[40] Typically, Cambridge's fiction, like that of most of her female contemporaries, is concerned with female protagonists whose social status is threatened middle class, and whose marital status requires resolution. The two are integrally related, and not just because a woman's uncertain class position can be resolved through a felicitous marriage. It is also because of the national affiliations and identifications which affect female class status and influence marital choice. In these fictions the Australian-ness of the heroines both imperils their social standing and facilitates a certain amount of freedom, independence and initiative. By contrast Lawson's central character is generally the mobile male but the resolution of this protagonist's social status, which is often still the focus, is enacted in a very different context.

In 'A Girl's Ideal', a Cambridge story first serialised in the *Age* 1881–82, the heroine Mary is returning to Australia with her widowed mother, and sister Nina, after struggling to live in genteel poverty in Britain. Unsuccessful attempts to maintain class through association with the father's clerical relative—'He said nasty things of mother behind her back—he called Nina "colonial"—he snubbed us and sneered at us . . .'—have been substituted for the uncertain prospect of living with the mother's less dignified relative, a bank manager in a country town (p. 176). The family's descent in the world is marked by their loss of the station Wattlebank. Furphy, with his interest in river banks and borders, might have appreciated the punning shift from pastoral riverbank to commercial savings bank. Mary, like many of Cambridge's heroines, longs to work for her living, but is thwarted by her mother's belief that 'it is unladylike, and . . . it would somehow disgrace us' (p. 177). The narrative explores the options for young women of genteel background, positing a core gentility which is based less on birth than on intrinsic features:

> She looked, to the eyes of the multitude of men crowding the platform of the railway station, on their way citywards to business, the picture and pattern of a modest and noble woman . . . She took her place amongst these men in a well-filled carriage—an unprotected maiden lady, singularly becoming that undignified position—serene in her majestic consciousness of being perfectly able to take care of herself . . . (p. 258).

The bonus is that an intrinsic 'lady' can get away with quite a lot, as is evident in this passage, without truly imperilling her social status, for anyone refined enough will recognise her social place. Only the vulgar are unable to recognise the lady—a convenient way to doubly distinguish her. In *A Humble Enterprise* Cambridge goes so far as to have her perfect lady run a tea room, and in the short story 'A Sweet Day' the genteel heroine is first noticed by the hero tending bees and packing honey. In each case one of the elements that guarantees her status is the recognition of it by a suitor of suitable class and wealth.[41] 'A Sweet Day' is used to imply the superiority of the Australian lady, when she is acknowledged, and ultimately married, by an English nobleman who whisks her back to Britain to exert her ample talents in taking charge of his household and raising young dukes.

In 'A Girl's Ideal', as in a number of the fictions of Rosa Praed, Catherine Martin and others, the heroine decides her national affiliation through a choice between an Australian and a European suitor.[42] In this case the opposition is between a British officer, who has been serving in India, and an Australian squatter. The sample of true, noble manhood is the Australian, fortuitously in possession of a suitable rural haven, 'one of the prettiest, as it was one of the oldest, residences in the district' (p. 266). In this way particular notions of Australian subjectivity, even down to hints of superior genetic type, are produced through romance, rather than realism, and the affiliation of people with land and nation is enacted through marriages which combine all the ideal local ingredients, but also assert an international affirmation which would be rejected by much of the men's nationalist fiction.

Indicative of the different orientation of Cambridge's understanding of the national subject is her repeated use of the Melbourne Great Exhibition of 1888 in novels and stories as a site for romantic frisson and various forms of sorting—of romantic partners, sheep from goats, the aesthetically gifted from the hopelessly vulgar and so on. Great Exhibitions of the nineteenth century were moments of Imperial display and national identification, and this particular one marked for Australians the centenary of white settlement in Australia. In Cambridge it seems to stand for a sort of cultural coming of age, in which Australian products stand side by side with the best Europe has to offer, and Australian subjects demonstrate their refined national taste in an international forum. It is a very different site for national identifications to the vaguer, anti-urban concentration on the bush and its associated personalities and skills, though these too are privileged by authors like Cambridge and Praed. The difference is that a Cambridge story— for example *A Woman's Friendship*—offers the Great Exhibition *and* a bush excursion, *and* notions of egalitarian values and female suffrage as loci for investigations of national subjectivities through the responses of the main two female protagonists, and their disappointing squatter friend.

By comparison, Lawson's Joe Wilson stories, written 1899–1901, and published in England in 1901 and Australia in 1902, might seem the epitome of the Australian legend.[43] 'Joe Wilson's Courtship', for instance, is set in the bush and centres on a hard drinking, rough living, soft-hearted itinerant bush worker and his mate. Ostensibly about male–female relations—romance even—the plot in fact chronicles male–male negotiations around and over the body of a woman aptly named Mary.[44] Joe's mate sets up Joe for romance, and arranges the target and trajectory of that romance, even to the extent of organising Joe's work so that Joe can watch the reflection of himself being watched in the window he is working on. Feminine, domestic interventions in Joe's personal arrangements (the tidying of his room and washing of his handkerchiefs and collars (pp. 264–5)) offer signs of returned affection, but they are strangely removed compared to the masculine dealings between Joe and his mate, and the physical battle over Mary's honour fought with a threatening foreigner, Romany.

Most of the 'courtship', and indeed the marriage described in subsequent stories, revolves around misunderstanding and failed communication. The window episode is a fascinating instance of this. Joe becomes a man, and a love object, through being the subject of Mary's gaze, but her look at him must be returned and resisted as soon as it is received in order for him to retain that identity. In the ongoing relationship chronicled in the Joe Wilson stories it is the failure to look, to sustain and reaffirm the particular identity as husband, citizen, property owner, and even the failure to provide the window, literally or metaphorically, which causes so much friction between the couple.

Actual domestic space is central. The window in 'Joe Wilson's Courtship' is in 'a rotten old place that might have been the original hut in the Bush' (p. 255) which Joe is pulling down in order to build a new buggy house for Mary's employer, the squatter, Black. She watches him from the laundry in what was once the old homestead, now behind the current 'two-storey brick house'. This series of dwellings reflects an upward mobility which could be Mary's (her employer's son is courting her). Joe's dismantling of the old building on the other hand, could be read as rebuilding based on the original pioneering foundations. Mary and Joe could be the new Australian inhabitants of a national future which turns its back on the direction taken by the hierarchical squattocracy and builds anew; but this is dubious in the light of the subsequent stories in which Joe mostly agonises about his ability to provide or maintain a proper home.

Here the masculine Australian subject remains intact, or is verified exactly through a narrative which shows him to be almost incapable of negotiating directly with the feminine, despite his affirmation through effective dealing and fighting *for* her. Womanish articulateness appears as a weakness compared to physical action—in 'A Double Buggy at Lahey's Creek' the purchase of a long-desired buggy for Mary after several years of marriage is represented as making up for years of failed communication, and indeed seen to facilitate fresh communication, though mostly through a sort of negative reversion to 'Do you remember . . .' (p. 342). Parts of the romantic exchange in 'Joe Wilson's Courtship' threaten to emasculate the man, in terms of Lake's arguments about the domestic, as when Joe helps Mary peg clothes on the line (p. 260), or, believing Mary is washing his handkerchiefs, washes them himself first, and tidies his own room. This story almost seems to posit a fundamental natural incompatibility between men and women in the rather obscure image of the ivy, rose bush and grape vine on the verandah where Joe first sees Mary in a 'frame of vines': 'More than once since then I've had a fancy to wonder whether the rose-bush killed the grape-vine or the ivy smothered 'em both in the end' (p. 255).

However, the complete hostility to the domestic perceived by some critics is perhaps over-simplistic. 'Brighten's Sister-in-Law' chronicles Joe's desperate dash through the bush to get aid for his convulsive son. It is sentimental, though it can certainly be read in terms of the loss of masculine freedom to domestic and family concerns. The child, Jim, is another imperilled, intelligent, uncanny 'coming Australian' of uncertain future like Furphy's Mary O'Halloran. Nevertheless, here as elsewhere, the bushman is blamed and blames himself for his own failures in the role of husband and father, roles which are *not* represented as without value. Stories such as this, and 'Water them Geraniums' are radically ambivalent in their representation of bushwomen and men. Men's drinking and neglect is blamed on women's nagging: 'Most bushwomen get the nagging habit . . .' (p. 319), but at the same time women's nagging and loss of hope and femininity is blamed on the dehumanising bush environment which men are condemned for bringing them to. The uses of romance in these stories are sometimes comparable to those in stories by women writers, but the concentration is on masculine identity and subjectivity, so of course there is no notion of national affiliation defined through marriage. It is possible to argue that domesticity is a threat to the freedom and happiness of *married* males and all females, because the bush is antithetical to domesticity, but the values of domesticity are not necessarily denied by Lawson.[45]

The widening gap between the gendered understandings of Australia as place and identity leads up to Franklin's *My Brilliant Career*. This is a novel which brings the two possibilities—nation as people and nation as place—together but simultaneously pulls them apart—combining romance with bush nationalism-realism; attempting to find a position for a female subject in an increasingly masculine country, and producing an individual, Sybylla Melvyn, whose middle-class status is threatened, defining herself through the appropriation of 'working-class' ideals. As fragmented and contradictory as the narrative is in some ways, it is more coherent in its narration of a homogenised 'Anglo-Celtic Australian self' versus threatening others. Even more than Baynton's work it is neither with nor fully against the preceding 'female' tradition in Australia, and the increasingly powerful, 'nationalist' authentic masculin(ist) tradition.

The dismissal of women's fiction as romance, and its devaluation in the 'Australian Tradition', is evident in Henry Lawson's preface to *My Brilliant Career*. This dismisses the 'girlishly emotional parts of the book—I leave that to girl readers to judge; [but] the descriptions of bush life and scenery came startlingly, painfully real to me . . . as far as they are concerned, the book is true to Australia . . .'[46] The 'girl' reader gets about as much credence as an urban reader in Lawson's formulation here, and is removed from the constructed sphere of the 'Australian' along with him, or worse, her.[47]

The 'girlishly emotional' parts of *My Brilliant Career*, alongside Baynton's occasional privileging of the maternal and the domestic, and her contradictory representations of the bush, may reveal these writers' strategic attempts to parody, excavate or avoid the unavoidable popular and prolific women writers of nineteenth-century Australia. Some contemporary women writers never easily fitted this model. It certainly starts to break down at the end of the century, when writers like Franklin and Baynton—burdened with the limitations of the genteel female subject in a friendly environment produced by many of their female predecessors—subscribed to alternative versions of the male and female Australian identity in efforts to locate a national identification that might be accessible to both.[48]

There were other narratives being produced across the nineteenth century and into the twentieth which do not fit either paradigm. Writers such as Rolf Boldrewood echo Kingsley's notion that an exodus back to the home country is the ultimate goal and guarantee of colonial hybrids. This sort of fiction is parodied by Joseph Furphy in *Such is Life*, and countered by William Lane's fictional exodus in search of a new and untainted great south land. Urban community and its Australian identity is abused and celebrated in various fictions by men and women—for example, in Francis Adams's *The Melbournians* (1892) and Mrs Russell's *Joyce Martindale* (1893).

The sorting process of the late 1880s and 1890s lends weight to some of these versions of the national narrative and devalues others, as Federation approaches and 'nationalism' is an increasingly useful political concept. Geographical struggles may have given more weight to the landscape—and helped define the masculine subject—at the same time as rising, or changing, feminist movements began to cast doubts on the usefulness and effectiveness of the international Lady, and even of the individualist model of ideal subject,[49] thereby weakening the romantic narratives produced around her.

Joseph Furphy, like Lawson, reveals concerns about the irruptions of a feminine understanding of the state into the masculine sphere, but Furphy's work is more aware, or productive, of the fragmentary nature of this 'nation', even, like Franklin, reproducing this stylistically. *Such is Life* is both a celebration and a satire of the bush hero, showing class, gender and boundary anxieties. Another angle on national type is offered by

Furphy's extended joke in *Such is Life* on *The Recollections of Geoffry Hamlyn* by Henry Kingsley (1830–76). The decline of the family, whose good fortunes in Kingsley are the just deserts of genteel blood and behaviour and hard work in the colony of which they are the new 'patriarchs' (p. 151), ridicules the 'Anglo-Australian' fictional model of an aristocratic pastoral class and happy peasantry transplanted bodily to the new world, and in most cases transplanted back once their fortune is made. Furphy recasts the plot to have the noble patriarch die of apoplexy in debt, the fine son take to forgery, and the daughter marry for money.

It is interesting that this critique of the Anglo-Australian novel takes as its representative *Geoffry Hamlyn* rather than more threatening popular Australian women's fiction. Furphy picks on men's writing, through Kingsley, or English women's popular writing—through Ouida—in a way that implicitly critiques 'Anglo-Australian' women's romance as well, though without acknowledging the popularity, or indeed the presence, of that form in the published version of *Such is Life*.[50] Like Miles Franklin, Furphy disavows plot and romance, in favour of the more nationalistic values of 'truth' and egalitarianism, but neither acknowledges one of the key sources of such negatively defined values by naming it.

Such is Life exhibits some of the 'classic' features of what has come to be seen as stereotyped masculinist, Anglo-Celtic nationalism. At various points the novel proposes the landscape as virgin and available to the active settler, merely awaiting defloration: 'Our virgin continent! how long has she tarried her bridal day! . . .' (p. 65). The narrator, Collins, speculates on the 'coming Australian' and the National type, and flirts with the active debate occurring at the end of the nineteenth century concerning the proposed unique features arising from the specificities of climate and gene pool in the Australian situation (p. 144, and note). The ideal Australian in *Such is Life* appears to be a man; and the ideal values are exhibited by the itinerant workers who populate Tom's picaresque narrative—bullock-drivers whose rough exteriors generally conceal hearts of gold and deep-seated fellow feeling, so that they help one another out in situations ranging from impounded bullocks, and shortness of rations, work, tobacco and good grass for the livestock to the search for lost children.

The obverse of this is of course that not even this single narrative (to the extent that *Such is Life* can be described as a single narrative) fits the ideal paradigm propounded for the masculinist texts of the 1890s. The coming Australian most forcefully proposed is Mary O'Halloran, a six-year-old girl whose name and religion are uncertain—she is unbaptised because of the schism between her Irish Catholic father and Protestant Scottish mother. She shows great promise but dies, lost in the bush, with that promise unfulfilled. 'Nature's precious link between a squalid Past and a nobler Future, broken, snatched away from her allotted place in the long chain of the ages! Heiress of infinite hope, and dowered with latent fitness to fulfil her part, now so suddenly fallen by the wayside' (p. 198).

The sincerity of speculations such as that in the famous virgin bride passage need to be considered carefully in the light of Collins's marriage metaphor alone—*Such is Life* is a text which suggests love is an impossible dream, and shows marriage as an unmitigated disaster, or unrealisable ideal, as Mary's unfulfilled 'dowry' suggests. The fact that the speculations arise from the musings, or pipe, of an unreliable and unobservant narrator must also be taken into account.

The proposals of a coming race are made problematic by the incidents surrounding Mary's loss, in which Thompson points out that those individuals most suited to engage with the delusively promising landscape are in fact the least 'civilised' (p. 186), illustrating his point with the story of the search for Mary, where the 'uncivilised' Bob is better than a dog, but not as good as 'an old, grey-haired lubra, blind of one eye . . .' (p. 191) who finds the child. The very embedding of lost child narratives in the heart of *Such is Life* disrupts the lines of promise and fulfilment present elsewhere. Once again, even more deeply encoded is the present absence of an Aboriginal population who, alone, can read and traverse the landscape correctly, including following the doomed footsteps of white hope across that landscape.

The chapter of the novel in which Tom loses his sense of direction (discussed on p. 92) is also the source of some of Tom's most profound speculations on nationality, most of them centred around the unmentionable but precious signifier of manhood, his missing trousers:

> A lifelong education, directing the inherent loyalty of human nature, invests anything in the shape of national or associational bunting with a sacredness difficult to express in words. Loyalty to something is an ingredient in our moral constitution; and the more vague the object, the more rabid will be our devotion to the symbol . . .
>
> Now with insignia, as with everything else, it is deprivation only that gives a true sense of value; and speaking from experience, I maintain that even the British Flag, which covers fabulous millions of our fellow-worms, dwindles into parochial insignificance beside that forky pennon on the farmer's clothes-line, which latter covers, in a far more essential manner, one half of civilised humanity. (p. 117)

Again, the association of trousers with national insignia seems to inscribe the national subject firmly as a male subject. But in fact there are so many women in the novel literally or metaphorically wearing the trousers that even this does not follow. At the same time, Collins's pondering on the superficiality of such insignia—masculine or national—makes both gender and national identification appear largely a matter of circumstance and borrowed colours. This cannot be reconciled with the earlier ruminations on the emergence of a biological national type. Typically none of the famous writing of turn of the century nationalism really stands up to any sustained search for the united production of national type, character or even style attributed to them. They represent, in fact, the nation as it stands in all its incoherence and multiplicity—more a collection of small-scale signifiers like Furphy's trousers than one single solid symbol.

PART THREE

1914–1939

6

LITERARY CULTURE 1914–1939: BATTLERS ALL

Jennifer Strauss

ABSORBING THE SHOCK OF WAR

Given the entrenched image of Australia's national identity as baptised in the blood shed at Gallipoli and confirmed in the mud of French trenches, it is surprising to find how little of this mythology originated in memorable contemporary works of poetry and fiction. If the period 1914–18 has a canonical candidate it must surely be C.J. Dennis's *Songs of a Sentimental Bloke* (1915), which chronicle the Bloke's conversion, through love and marriage, from gang membership and cheerful larrikinism to culture (attending performances of Shakespeare) and cultivation (of a rural berry farm). The *Bloke's* immense popularity was rivalled initially by its 1916 sequel, *The Moods of Ginger Mick*, in which the Bloke's best mate enlists, drawn to the 'flamin' war' as a paramount 'Stoush'; but it is the Bloke, not the soldier, who has retained a hold on the public imagination. He was translated into film by Raymond Longford in 1919 and F.W. Thring in 1932, while Dennis's centenary in 1976 generated a television musical (1976), stage performances, and, ultimately, a ballet (1985). On the evidence of such adaptations, *The Sentimental Bloke* cannot appeal solely through its stylisation of Australian folk idiom (occasionally indeed a source of critical devaluation); rather, a considerable part of its attractiveness probably lies (especially in times of social uneasiness) in its representation of social and sexual conflicts as locally manageable, capable even of blissful resolution.

Dismissals of contemporary literary responses to the First World War as inadequate have perhaps depended on too narrow a demand for 'creative' or high-culture texts. Broader definitions of 'literature' have allowed recent revisiting of the position, held by many of the reading public at the time, that the war had in fact produced a roughly contemporaneous classic in C.E.W. Bean's *The Story of Anzac* (1921, 1924). Since this text is central to the argument of Chapter 8, I will limit my discussion to the treatment of war in the more traditional 'literary' genres.

There are undoubtedly early examples of war's valorisation: resurgent imperial patriotism produced popular images in fiction and poetry of Mother England, calling her freedom-loving offspring into battle against the rogue male warrior bent on civilisation's destruction. The denunciation of Germany in C.J. Brennan's 'A Chant of Doom' (the title poem of his 1918 collection) is politically consistent with his 1903 attack on Britain's Boer War imperialism, circulated only in manuscript until published as *The Burden of Tyre: Fifteen Poems by C.J. Brennan* (1953). 'A Chant of Doom' cannot, however, be seen as aesthetically consistent with the earlier work; it shows only too well how war's emotional charge can derail into bombast even the most intellectual, the least apparently nationalistic, of poets.

As the war progressed (or, more accurately, stagnated), moral confusion and disillusionment tended to displace enthusiasm. Peter Weir's 1981 film *Gallipoli* has drawn criticism for the naivety displayed by his two protagonists in believing that war promised manly adventure and access to a wider world. But the rhetoric of the First World War recruitment can be shown to have played on such prospects, and the consequent expectations, along with their disabusing, are charted in Kylie Tennant's *Foveaux* (1938):

> At first the war in Europe was just exciting. The only other chance people from Foveaux had had of being killed on a large scale was when some Dutch farmers in Africa had refused to play the game according to British rules. The prospects of the teams in this new war were discussed with all the serious consideration that might be given to a Test match . . . The young men, falling over themselves to enlist, were only afraid the war might be declared off before they had their innings . . . Patriotism . . . was almost universal in those early months. It was a grim contrast to the bewilderment and despair of the later years when the bereaved found out that they had sent their men to a game that had no rules.[1]

Tennant is, of course, writing retrospectively and after experience of the prolonged economic depression that followed the First World War and was often seen as its consequence. The view that warfare had proved a costly mistake is not, however, merely a post-Depression phenomenon; the voicing of such judgments during the event is evident in the war-weariness, the scepticism about exclusive claims to righteousness, expressed in 'To God: From the Weary Nations', published in 1916 by Furnley Maurice (Frank Wilmot).[2]

Pro-war patriots objected that such works were a particular betrayal of those soldier-writers who exhibited in patriotic ballads and anecdotal, often humorous, prose writing a proper will to fight. Time has, however, tended to consign these to oblivion, preserving as more characteristic a disillusioned stoicism which sees itself as obliged to soldier on, accepting the cards dealt out by an indifferent chance. In *Flesh in Armour*, Leonard Mann's 1932 novel of the campaigns in France, the heroic Sergeant Blount and the suicidal Frank Jeffreys (equally inept as soldier and lover) represent extremes. Between these, the troops as a group endure—much as the early settlers had slogged on against rural hardship, and as the characters of the Great Depression were to face poverty and unemployment in plays and novels such as Louis Esson's *The Battler* (1922) or Tennant's *The Battlers* (1941). Hardened into a national stereotype, as distinct from an immediate survival mechanism in intolerable circumstances, such an attitude can be seen as exasperatingly limited, a possibility articulated in A.D. Hope's protest against Australians as a race 'whose boast is not: "we live" but "we survive"'.[3]

Possibly the novel required a period of gestation for the aesthetic comprehension and shaping of wartime experiences, a result eventually achieved in works as different as Roger McDonald's *1915* (1979), Patrick White's *The Twyborn Affair* (1979), or David Malouf's *Fly Away Peter* (1982).[4] Such an argument overlooks two interesting novels, both closer in time to the events of the First World War, but largely unknown to the Australian public until considerably later: Frederic Manning's *The Middle Parts of Fortune* and Lesbia Harford's *The Invaluable Mystery*.

The nature of Manning's novel, and the obscuring of his reputation by his expatriate status and the anonymity of the book's early editions (1929, 1930) is discussed in Chapter 8. *The Invaluable Mystery* has a different history. Harford (1891–1927) was always known as an Australian writer, if only through a toehold in poetry anthologies. In 1985 Drusilla Modjeska's 'Introduction' to *The Poems of Lesbia Harford* revived interest in this exemplary 1920s feminist and socialist figure.[5] It also reminded people that Harford had worked in the later part of her life on a novel never published and apparently lost. Its manuscript retrieved, *The Invaluable Mystery* finally appeared in 1987.[6] One can see why 1920s publishers might have been unenthusiastic about a novel which dealt with an episode that Australians averse to 'black armband' views of history preferred to forget: the internment, under the 1914 War Precautions Act, of Germans resident in Australia. The story is, however, focused less on the father and son who must suffer this fate or evade it by enlistment, than on Sally, whose femaleness excludes her from classification as a public threat but condemns her to social displacement in a private sphere deprived of a 'proper' household head. The implications of this are explored through the eyes of various characters. Her father is so anxious to see her respectably married that even the radical free-thinker with whom she shares a tentative sexual attraction is an acceptable suitor. This character, Stepanoff, is probably based on Guido Baracchi, an early lover of Harford's who was one of several 'Wobblies' (Industrial Workers of the World) imprisoned in 1917 for expressing anti-war opinions during the second conscription campaign. Through Stepanoff and his associates, discussions of pacifism and of capitalism's instigative role in the war are introduced, but are atypically interwoven with concerns about how women can achieve autonomous political and sexual identity. The argument that sex, whether as marriage or 'free love', will interfere with such a development in Sally is powerfully put by the experienced Fanya and is apparently heeded by Stepanoff, since the novel closes with his decision not to wake the sleeping Sally with the princely kiss of a conventional romance ending. That this leaves her as freed potential rather than forsaken maiden is no small part of the radically discomforting nature of Harford's novel.

The Invaluable Mystery is a novel of the Home Front, where those not on Active Service had to define their general positions with regard to war as well as having, in many cases, to cope with the personal anguish of loved ones endangered, maimed or killed in battle. The ambivalent, even flatly contradictory, responses that could be generated are visible in the poetry of Mary Gilmore (1865–1962). Her socialist principles predisposed her to see 'the bloody hands of war' as manipulated by capitalist greed,[7] while her maternalism made her particularly sensitive to the painfulness of the situation of women like the one in 'The Mother' (1917), who struggles to maintain belief in the rhetoric of heroic death, when experience speaks to her of the dog lying dead in the street, 'Blood in his mouth/ Dust in his eyes'. The stance of the resolutely sacrificial mother in 'The Woman of Five Fields' is more characteristic, for Gilmore's personal admiration for active courage predisposed her to hero-worship, while her nationalism predisposed her to accept the ANZAC as the true modern warrior-hero.[8] In effect, she opposed war, but gave unqualified support to the Australian soldiers conducting it. Tennant attributes a similar development of attitude to the originally enthusiastic citizens of Foveaux. During an Eight-Hour Day march, spectators embittered by the imprisonment (under the War Precautions Act) of striking workers, are confronted with a Victoria Cross winner bearing a banner proclaiming 'Join the One Big Union—the Khaki': 'the crowd gave the banner a warm reception for the sake of the man carrying it. That was all' (p. 101).

BETWEEN WARS: MORE THAN A MERE HIATUS

The whole interwar period, compared with those which preceded and followed it, was an uncertain, cautious and shabby era. (Russel Ward, *Australia Since the Coming of Man* (1982))

T.S. Eliot's description of 1919 to 1939 as 'Twenty years largely wasted, the years of *l'entre deux guerres*' encapsulates views of the period as one psychically as well as economically destitute, entirely overshadowed by the worldwide Great Depression.[9] Though not without basis, such unifying generality is over-simplified. As Ian Reid argues in *Fiction and the Great Depression* (1979), the common economic factors of the phenomenon produced different consequences in different specific contexts. While he concludes that the Depression in Australia was indeed a profoundly disturbing social trauma, influencing all significant fiction within its period and for some time thereafter, he by no means endorses Ward's dismissive generalisation of between-wars literary culture as self-consciously 'barren'. Like Reid, I would argue that this period was an important phase in the conceptualisation of what it might mean to be an Australian writer, adding that it also saw considerable consolidation of the processes of literary production.

While there were certainly ideological cross-currents and conflicts among the writers of the 1920s and 1930s, there was also a considerable conviction that they shared in the task defined in Louis Esson's play *Australia Felix* (1926) when a character declares, 'In my opinion, Australia hasn't been discovered yet. That's a job in store for our writers and artists. Captain Cook discovered only the outline'.[10] In their copious literary correspondence the writers of the period show much more sense of shared productive effort than of barrenness. They may sometimes disparage fellow writers, but are more often supportive, even lavishly celebratory, of new works, new writers.[11] If M. Barnard Eldershaw's *Plaque with Laurel* (1937) recognises comical aspects in the hunger of contemporary writers to be convinced that one of their number is capable of greatness (and that Australian society is capable of recognising this), it also reflects the emotional depths of such ambitions.

Any such loosely enveloping camaraderie was, however, to prove unsustainable. This was not only a result of the chilly and divisive political climate of the Cold War, but also, and ironically, of the intellectual climate generated by the very event that writers of the 1920s and 1930s had struggled to bring about: the raising of Australian literature to the status of official culture. An early swallow to a full-blown summer of Australian literary criticism appeared in 1930, when H.M. Green published *An Outline of Australian Literature*. Regarded as a preliminary sketch for the full-scale portrait of the two-volume *A History of Australian Literature* (1961, revised by Dorothy Green 1985), the *Outline* nevertheless aimed at being the first comprehensive critical survey to 1928. But any claim to comprehensiveness, in stressing inclusiveness, necessarily summons up its Janus twin of exclusion. Even in 1928 Inglis Moore had received, in the midst of Mary Gilmore's encomiums for a survey of contemporary poetry, a reproach for failing to notice Ada Cambridge.[12] As Australian literary production increased, and as scholarly surveys and academic syllabuses joined with anthologies to establish the boundaries of inclusion, individual and partisan anxieties about exclusion would become more urgent and more divisive to any idea of a literary community.

During the 1950s many of the writers who, in the 1920s and 1930s, might justly have considered themselves as constituting Australian literature tended to be pushed aside. In the academic arena, schools of 'close reading' (whether Leavisite or New Critical) tended to be impatient with the provinciality of nationalist concerns and with the content-oriented, even doctrinal, nature of much social realist writing. And when the defence of a national literature as worthy of attention was mounted, it was along lines that tended to exclude or depreciate a large part of the work of the 1930s and 1940s: writing by women. Defiance of what A.A. Phillips would define as 'The Cultural Cringe' (*Meanjin*, 1950) stimulated a desire for an Australian tradition more definite—and more clearly value-laden—than could be provided by any all-inclusive broad survey. The foundation stones of such a construction, set in place as they were by Vance Palmer's *The Legend of the Nineties* (1954) and Phillips's *The Australian Tradition* (1958), ensured that it would be a peculiarly masculine one. And as this version of Australian literature began to gain some purchase in the academies, its orientation seemed no more than natural to establishments so much more exclusively male than the readership which had, by their purchasing and reading patterns in previous decades, accepted women writers as central to their experience of Australian literature.[13]

When feminist voices began to insist that neither the supposedly universal literary canon nor the local nationalist one reflected an adequate picture of the literary past, the recuperation of marginalised Australian women writers was taken up with particular energy in two areas—the over-emphasised 1890s (see Chapter 5) and the neglected 1930s and 1940s. Between Drusilla Modjeska's seminal *Exiles at Home: Australian Women Writers 1925–45* (1981) and Maryanne Dever's *Wallflowers and Witches: Women and Culture in Australia 1910–1945* (1994) there were numerous critical discussions of the network of women writers identified by Modjeska: Marjorie Barnard, Eleanor Dark, Jean Devanny, Flora Eldershaw, Miles Franklin, Nettie Palmer, Katharine Susannah Prichard. Quite as importantly, this activity has made available out-of-print or unpublished texts, as in Carole Ferrier's editing of both the 1982 re-issue of Jean Devanny's *Sugar Heaven* (1936) and Devanny's unpublished autobiography, *Point of Departure* (1986). Like the autobiography of fellow Communist Party member Katharine Susannah Prichard, *Child of the Hurricane* (1963), this reveals the gaps operative between avowed principles of equality and unexamined practices governed by gender stereotypes about the nature of women's work and sexuality.[14]

NOT A VINTAGE PERIOD FOR POETRY

It is noticeable that the writing of the women listed above reflects the dominance of fiction, especially of social realist fiction. This is sometimes thought to have created an unfavourable environment for poetry, and—despite the fact that it clearly commanded a readership in journals and magazines as well as individual volumes—the poetry of the 1920s and 1930s has commonly been judged as stylistically unadventurous, ignoring, if not actively resisting, avant-garde literary developments in Europe and America because of its engrossment with problems of Australian identity and Australian idiom.

It is true that social realism's claim to be the correct literary mode for writers with a social conscience could create problems for poets who combined left-wing political sympathies with an appetite for what was going on in avant-garde poetry. Australian poets of the between-wars period were not universally ignorant of, or hostile to, modernism; but some of those who knew and admired it also doubted its appropriateness to what they believed should be written in Australia. Furnley Maurice, otherwise Frank Wilmot, manager of Melbourne University Press, did consciously attempt to introduce principles of · modern European and American poetry into his *Melbourne Odes* (1934). A large-scale evocation in loosely-structured free verse of the beauty and squalor of city life during the Depression years, the sequence's impressionistic effects have some striking affinities with Christina Stead's treatment of 1920s Sydney in *Seven Poor Men of Sydney*, also published in 1934. The most striking of the series is 'Upon a Row of Old Boots and Shoes in a Pawn Broker's Window'. Its combination of social indignation and macabre imagery has, however, made it less popular with anthologists than his affectionate depiction of the meeting of country and city in 'The Agricultural Show, Flemington, Victoria'. Maurice's friend and political ally, Lesbia Harford, on the other hand, despite showing a taste for modernist complexity in some early poems, made a politicised decision to write 'little fresh songs' for the proletariat. It is difficult to say that her judgment was entirely wrong, since some of the most engaging poems of this period are certain short lyrics which compress considerable suggestiveness and resonance into a simple frame.

Mastery of such an effect distinguishes one of the most astonishing of Australia's lyric poets, John Shaw Neilson (1872–1942). Life as an impoverished and itinerant rural labourer afflicted, from 1905, with an inability to read any but large print, seems hardly an ideal precondition for the production of delicately formal poems that pierce as much by their lyric joy as by their pain. Few could have claimed more justification for writing with gritty realism of bush hardship, but Shaw Neilson has another story to tell in 'The Poor, Poor Country':

> My riches all went into dreams that never yet came home,
> They touched upon the wild cherries and the slabs of honeycomb,
> They were not of the desolate brood that men can sell or buy,
> Down in that poor country no pauper was I.[15]

There is little doubt that Neilson's poetic survival depended on the lifeline of recognition cast by A.G. Stephens after 'Polly and Dad and the Spring Cart' appeared in the *Bulletin* in 1896, and Neilson remained for some time something of a poet's poet.[16] His increasingly secure reputation has led to the publication of Cliff Hanna's *John Shaw Neilson* (1991), the first, but undoubtedly not the last, attempt to establish a critical textual edition of his poems from the maze of manuscript and published versions, many of the latter having been affected by editorial intervention.

Of these poets, only Furnley Maurice can be seen as connected to a movement consciously dedicated to shifting Australian poetry from a perceived stylistic stagnation, since his advocacy of modernism foreshadowed the brief but ebullient 1940s flowering in *Angry Penguins* (see Chapter 9). There were, however, other attempts within the period to renovate poetry's diction and symbolic repertoire by forms of cultural grafting, and although these had more immediate local success than modernism, they have failed notably to convince posterity of their lasting value. The 1920s saw images of Bacchus in the Bush, Pan at Paddington, Sirens in Sydney generated by European-oriented enthusiasts for acculturating a neo-Hellenistic strain in the Antipodes. These are often called the Vision group, from the name of the short-lived but influential journal largely inspired by Norman Lindsay (1879–1969). Their major claim to virtue is probably the nurturing of Kenneth Slessor, who co-edited *Vision*'s four issues (1923–24), but in the event his poetry (discussed in Chapter 8) soon ceased to be typical of a style seen at its best in some gracefully accomplished lyrics from Hugh McCrae (1876–1958). The very titles of McCrae's popular collections (*Satyrs and Sunlight*, 1909 and 1928; *Colombine*, 1922; and *The Mimshi Maiden*, 1938) suggest that the Victorian trustees of the National Gallery were by no means out of step with public taste in pursuing a 1920s purchasing policy which favoured Burne-Jones over Cézanne.

A very different kind of poetry, although one also in search of a mythology, was produced by the Jindyworobaks (further discussed in Chapter 8). The 'Jindies' were a late

1930s movement originating in South Australia. Often dismissed as no more than a tin-eared manifestation of aggressive nationalism, they can be seen more charitably as expressing an early environmentalism which, perceiving Aboriginal culture as having achieved an identity with the 'primal essence' of the land, imagined that it could be appropriated and improved upon.[17] If post-colonialists are offended by the ahistoricity of the Jindyworobaks' assumption that it was both proper and possible to appropriate Aboriginal culture, many Jindyworobak contemporaries were deeply offended by the notion that white Australia should base its modern culture on that of a people still almost universally referred to as Stone Age. The obtrusive flourishing of Aboriginal words within some Jindyworobak texts provided a convenient ground for the kind of ridicule forthcoming in phrases such as R.H. Morison's 'Jindyworobakwardness' or James McAuley's 'Jindyworobaksheesh' (*The Blue Horses*, 1946). The issue may not, however, be dead: as Chapter 1 shows, recent Aboriginal writing has revived interest in the possibilities of the mixed language text.

Influential critical opinion in the 1950s—notably that of poet-critics James McAuley and Vincent Buckley—attacked both these groups: the Jindyworobaks for their didactic nationalism and their diction, the Vision group for the libertarian and Nietzschean elements of their vitalism. But this did not entail endorsement for social realism. McAuley, a convert to Catholicism and neo-classicism after an initial flirtation with modernism and loss of faith, became a formidable Cold War warrior for whom there was little distinction between socialism and communism. This was not the philosophical case with Buckley, but his aesthetic distaste for much social realist writing was not very different from that of Patrick White, who declared himself appalled, on his return to Australia in 1948, by realism's prevailing 'dun-coloured' dreariness.[18]

QUESTIONS OF VITALITY: STAGE AND PAGE

One area of White's rebellion against realism was drama, although it was not until the beginnings of the dramatic renaissance of the 1960s that his 1947 play *The Ham Funeral* would be staged in Australia. And it seems unlikely that he would have approved the plays that resulted from 1920s attempts to revivify the Australian practice of a genre even more subject to fluctuating vitality than poetry. Whatever the reason, the 1920s and 1930s were a lean time for drama. From the relative isolation of Western Australia, Henrietta Drake-Brockman (1901–68) won the 1938 New South Wales sesquicentenary competition with her entry *Men Without Wives* (see p. 120), but the most determined effort to mount a repertoire of specifically Australian plays was that of Louis Esson (1879–1943). Influenced by the nationalist agenda of Ireland's Abbey Theatre, Esson's version of a socialist mission was to write about ordinary people with a realism infused with poetic feeling. The Pioneer Players, set up in Melbourne in 1921 with the involvement of Vance Palmer and Furnley Maurice, failed to establish an audience although it struggled through two seasons, during which three of Esson's plays were performed. These (like most of the Australian plays written during the period) were one-acters, the best-known being *The Drovers* (written in 1920).[19]

Esson reminds us that writers often cross category boundaries to appear in a supposedly oppositional camp, for he also wrote poetry, short fiction and articles, and not all of these conformed to the principles guiding the Pioneer Players. Hugh Anderson's chosen title for his 1980 anthology of Esson's writing, *Ballades of Old Bohemia*, indicates aspects of Esson's writing as a witty man about town. Such aspects link him to those usually thought of as opponents of realism and, if rather erratically, of nationalism: that is, to the Vision group, who might well have been called the Bohemians rather than vitalists. Vitalism was after all not incompatible with some aspects of early socialism, for instance in its Nietzschean opposition to institutional regulation of morality; and William Baylebridge showed in *This Vital Flesh* (1939) that he at least believed that nationalism could be re-shaped according to vitalism's tenets. Indeed, the vitalists published quite regularly in the *Bulletin*, where Norman Lindsay, who thought of himself primarily as an artist, frequently appeared as a cartoonist, both art-forms being manifest in his first novel, *A Curate in Bohemia* (1913). His literary capacities had matured considerably by 1930, the date of *Redheap*, first in a trilogy satirising the adult hypocrisies and pretensions of a country town Victorian in both its geography and its official morality. In its anti-provincialism, its depreciation of country towns as places to be expeditiously escaped from, *Redheap* merely exaggerates a stance common in Australian literature. What was uncommon, indeed outrageous, was its sexual libertarianism; its celebration of adolescent sexuality; and especially its representation of young girls as sexually forward sirens rather than pathetically seduced victims. Banned in Australia until 1958, *Redheap* was published in America under the title *Every Mother's Son*.

Lindsay's classic contribution to Australian literature has nothing to do with sex, but a great deal to do with its rival in importance—food. *The Magic Pudding* (1918) is a rumbustious variant on the ever popular horn-of-plenty motif. The battle to possess this self-replenishing, multi-flavoured object is fought between characters with suitably Australian names like Bunyip Bluegum and Watkin Wombat, and enlivened by the vociferous participation of the pudding itself. In the prevailing realist climate, fantasy remained in demand in children's literature, although many adults relished not only *The Magic Pudding* but also the more decorous adventures of May Gibbs's engaging gumnut babies Snugglepot and Cuddlepie and their tormentors, the Big Bad Banksia Men. In contrast to the fairy world of Ida Rentoul Outhwaite, whose charm lay almost entirely in the illustrations, the appeal of both Lindsay and Gibbs was very much textual, and nationalist in the sense that their work satisfied the feeling, already demonstrated in Ethel Pedley's *Dot and the Kangaroo* (1899), that Australian children's literature should have a specifically Australian context.[20]

THE GROWTH OF PUBLISHING ACTIVITY

From a distance greater than that of their immediate successors, and with a longer prospect on the context of literary culture, we can regard this period as one of consolidation, marked by substantial growth in the number and scope of texts published, and by anxious (sometimes combative) attempts to define the proper nature of Australian writing and to secure social support for its production. *The Annals of Australian Literature* (2nd edn, 1992) give a crude measure of increased output: 59 pages cover 1789 to 1913, the following 25 years (to 1938) require 35.[21] But absence of publication details in the *Annals* obscures the fact that local publishing was less active than local writing: a recent study shows that overseas publication constituted 66 per cent of all Australian titles between 1920 and 1940.[22]

Apart from self-publishing, the initial experience of publication for most writers was in a journal or newspaper. These were not only the major outlet for poetry and short stories, they also sometimes published novels in serialised form, although this was more likely to happen in an established journal such as the *Bulletin*. If the *Bulletin* of this period was not the literary powerhouse it had been under Archibald and Stephens, its very continuity must have made it something of a Rock of Ages for writers in a period when literary journals led lives of butterfly brevity, and not even the formidable A.G. Stephens could maintain for longer than 1911–25 his revived monthly version of *The Bookfellow*, with its ambitions for literary comment and reviewing as well as poetry and fiction.[23] In such circumstances, the *Bulletin* Red Page, under the 1925–40 editorship of Cecil Mann, provided space, as well as a reading public, for a surprisingly eclectic range of poetry and fiction.

Of particular importance for novelists was the *Bulletin* prize run by its editor S.H. Prior 1928–29, and resumed from 1935–46 as a commemorative award in his name. Even more attractive than its monetary value (one hundred pounds) was the likelihood of subsequent publication. Published prize-winners include M. Barnard Eldershaw's *A House is Built*, joint winner with Katharine Susannah Prichard's *Coonardoo* in 1928, Vance Palmer's *The Passage* in 1929, Miles Franklin's *All That Swagger* in 1936, and Kylie Tennant's *Tiburon* (1935) and *The Battlers* (1941). An impressive roll-call, it is also one that indicates a strong preference in the judges for realist writing and national themes.

Australian publishing houses did not always concur with the judges: both *A House is Built* and *Coonardoo* were initially published in 1929 in London (the former by Harrap, the latter by Jonathan Cape), after rejection by Angus and Robertson. Indeed, the fact that most Australian library holdings of works initially published overseas tend to be of subsequent Angus and Robertson editions contributes to a somewhat exaggerated view of its role as the Grand Old Firm of Australian publishing. Nonetheless, as Nile and Walker show, it did become the major local publisher of 1930s Australian titles, outstripping rivals such as Melbourne's George Robertson and Co. (Robertson and Mullen after 1922), and the New South Wales Bookstall company, highly successful popular publishers in the 1920s.

Angus and Robertson's publishing activities illustrate some of the ways of avoiding financial risk in a notoriously chancy business. Before the advent of institutional subsidies, the author was frequently required either to guarantee publishers against loss, or to pay all production costs, with the publisher acting essentially as a distributor.[24] The risk of initial publication might be left to overseas publishers or, especially in the case of unknown authors and/or controversial texts, to a small local enterprise. The publication history of Xavier Herbert's *Capricornia* is a case in point. By Herbert's account, the novel began in 1930 as *Black Velvet*, a work dealing with inter-racial sexual relations in the north of Australia. Several years of revision broadened the scope considerably by introducing the profound attachment to the land which would become the driving force of Herbert's monumental late work *Poor Fellow My Country* (1975). Shown the now-renamed *Capricornia* in 1933, P.R. Stephensen (1901–65) not only encouraged Herbert to complete it and took part in its editing, but, after at least one abortive attempt, achieved its publication through the Publicist Press. This enabled *Capricornia* to win the 1938 Commonwealth Prize for 'the best Australian novel published or accepted for publication during the year 1937'. Angus and Robertson, who had twice rejected Herbert's manuscript, now became his publishers, rushing through their own 1938 printing and obscuring there and in all subsequent re-printings Stephensen's role as the original publisher.

RADICAL NATIONALISM'S 'WILD MAN OF LETTERS'[25]

Among those who wrote, produced and promoted Australian literature in the period 1920–50, Stephensen, also discussed in Chapter 8, is particularly interesting because his career shows so clearly both the power of the idea of nationalism over the literary imagination and the power of the pressures of world history to fragment the Australian writing community.

Neither of Stephensen's earlier personae—as a Communist-sympathising Rhodes Scholar of 1924, or as a member of London's publishing world, a past translator of Nietzsche (1922) and a newly-recruited enthusiast for D.H. Lawrence—obviously foreshadowed the Stephensen who in 1936 issued one of the most polemical documents of cultural nationalism: *The Foundations of Culture in Australia: An Essay towards National Self-respect*. There was, though, a portent in *The Bushwhackers* (1929), a collection of short stories informed by nostalgia for the bush of his childhood. This might make it less surprising that, returning to Australia somewhat disillusioned with English culture, Stephensen should have been anxious to reassert the value of Australian-ness and that he should have gravitated towards so longstanding a bastion of bush-based nationalism as the *Bulletin* or looked with approval on the Jindyworobaks.[26] Stephensen was perhaps unlucky in his historical context, although it is hard to say whether it was his disposition towards ideologies in general that led him down the road of contemporary Fascism, or whether this was intensified by the patronage of W.J. Miles, who funded *The Publicist* to push ideas which increasingly became those of Stephensen himself: Anglophobia; anti-Semitism; anti-Communism; isolationism. Stephensen's defiant assertion of such ideas, and of a consequent degree of sympathy for Germany and Japan even after the outbreak of the Second World War, led to his establishment of the Australia First movement in 1941, and thence to his arrest and internment from March 1942 until the end of the war, an action later criticised by an official inquiry of 1944–45 as an infringement of civil liberties.[27] It is indicative of the bitterness of the ideological breach between Stephensen and even those writers whom he had published in the past, such as Eleanor Dark and Xavier Herbert, that there was no outcry from Australian writers over his prolonged internment. Herbert was in fact to satirise both the Australia First Movement and Stephensen in *Poor Fellow My Country*.

MILDER NURTURERS OF AUSTRALIAN WRITING

The Jindyworobaks can be seen as an extreme instance of the impulse to form alliances to foster a national literature; the same motive inspired the formation of what was to be, for forty-five years, Australia's mainstream literary association. The Fellowship of Australian Writers (FAW) was formally inaugurated at Sydney's Lyceum Club on 23 November 1928.[28] The first President was John le Gay Brereton, Professor of English at Sydney University, a fact that challenges the notion that Australian universities were, until very recently, consistently indifferent, even hostile, to Australian literature. One of the most significant FAW activities was the revivifying and refocusing of the Commonwealth Literary Fund (CLF). Established by the Deakin government in 1908, the CLF's function had been to provide pensions and grants-in-aid to impoverished writers and their dependants. A campaign during the 1930s resulted in the greatly extended charter of functions described in Chapter 10. The role of the FAW in this development was recognised by representation on the advisory board of the CLF; Vance Palmer and Flora Eldershaw served in this capacity for over a decade.

Mention of these names is a reminder of the system of informal networks which, in addition to formal structures such as the FAW, were of great importance in building a sense of literary community. The most celebrated of such networkers were undoubtedly Vance and Nettie Palmer, who cultivated the role after their return to Melbourne from England in 1915, seeing it as part of their commitment to the development of Australian literature.[29] Recent work by Modjeska and Ferrier (see p. 112) has highlighted the role of Nettie (1885–1964) as a central point of communication for a whole group of women writers, supplementing the attention already drawn to her role as an early local promoter of the work of Henry Handel Richardson.[30] At the time, however, it was Vance (1885–1959) who was seen (if, on the evidence of Chapter 7, not always gratefully) as the embodiment of 'the man of letters', with a public profile that placed him at the centre of literary activity through his novels, his literary journalism, and his tireless use of the medium of radio through the Australian Broadcasting Commission (ABC) to further the cause of writers by reviewing their books and discussing literary issues. With fine even-handedness, the initial Victorian Premier's Literary Awards (1985) named a prize for each: fiction for Vance and non-fiction for Nettie.

WRITING THE 'REAL' AUSTRALIA

If there was considerable consensus among writers and readers of the 1920s and 1930s that Australian literature was to be valued for its capacity to represent Australian reality, this did not mean universal agreement as to just what should be selected for represen-tation or how representation should be effected. If realism was the dominant approved mode, it was also a mode loosely conceived. Its practice was often explicitly value-laden in ways that did not accord with the more precise aesthetic prescription that realism should be based on an observation both meticulously detailed and magisterially detached. Notions of writing the real Australia often proved to have less to do with modes of representation than with granting certain aspects of Australian life a privileged place as more essentially, in effect more metaphysically, real than others.

Notions of the Bush as Australia's true reality had gained a flying start in the ex-perience of the first settlers. Given the strangeness of its actual and imminent presence, to become 'at home' in the bush might very well have seemed, in the early stages of settle-ment, an essential step towards entering Australian reality. But for the Australian popu-lation of the 1920s and 1930s literal bush-living was increasingly a minority experience: in terms of demography, the bush was retreating further and further into the outback, and the spate of childhood reminiscences of bush life seemed to suggest not only that the indi-vidual reminiscer had been removed in both time and space from the bush, but that bush life in general constituted a lost childhood of Australia.[31] Nonetheless, the project of privileging the bush as Australia's definitive reality was not yet to be relegated to mere nos-talgia. There remained an audience with an appetite for accessing, if only through litera-ture, a kind of life still perceived as actively present at the heart of Australian experience.

It was here that non-fiction had an important role. In travel writing, biography, autobiography and history the sobriety of reportage offered a guarantee of authenticity. This was one factor making such writing viable in the British market, which was less interested in yet another urban culture than in one which offered, through its very dif-ference, potent testimony to the far-flung reach of Empire. It might be the voice of the expatriate Australian, as in the 1931 English republication of Mary Fullerton's 1921 *Bark House Days*, or that of the immigrant or visiting Englishman offering the benign versions of the Pommy in the Bush found in William Hatfield's *Sheepmates* (1931) or Thomas Wood's *Cobbers* (1934). In either case, bush-centred nationalism contributed to imperial narratives as well as to the thrust for distinctive identity.

In either case, also, the 'documentary' stamp upon content tended to obscure the fact that the narrative practices of bush realism were often indistinguishable from those of fiction. Nowhere is this better illustrated than in the case of the very popular Ion L. Idriess (1889–1979). In stories like *Lasseter's Last Ride* (1931), *Flynn of the Inland* (1932), or *The Cattle King* (1936), Idriess peopled the Australian outback landscape with Australian heroic actors. That the underlying narrative structures were the familiar ones of romantic adventure increased his appeal, offering the comfort of a familiar vehicle for transportation to this other world, remote yet claimable as the reader's true ground of Australian-ness.

It was, of course, a very masculine world. A rare woman like Ernestine Hill might spend five years wandering the Birdsville Track and Arnhem Land in order to write *The Great Australian Loneliness* (1937), but in general white women came to the outback in the wake of their husbands: 'The Head of the Family decided that the bush was the place for us, and so, of course, to the bush we went. The Head of the Family had a roving spirit': so begins *No Roads Go By* (1932), Myrtle Rose White's account of life on a South Australian cattle station. Like Mrs Aeneas Gunn before her, White writes with a certain insouciance, drawing on the comedy of the misadventures of the new chum who manages to 'come good' in a crisis. Female persistence in exceptional competence, on the other hand, especially if linked to independence of matrimony, was likely to render a woman unplaceable in the social system of the bush.[32] Bush-given freedom from some of the more restrictive stereotypes of femininity is largely pre-pubertal. Girl children like Littl'un in *No Roads Go By* or Norah Linton in Mary Grant Bruce's *A Little Bush Maid* (1910, but serialised in *The Leader* 1905–07) must surrender much of it as they approach their socially approved apotheosis into wives and mothers.

The common iconography of the bush wife is as a descendant of Lawson's 'Drover's Wife', a stoical victim of such hardship and loneliness that a man of true nobility and/or rationality must hesitate to ask her to assume the role. In *Flynn of the Inland*, the founder of the Flying Doctor service reflects: 'One of the tragedies of the life is that many of the men of the Centre never marry. They dare not ask a white woman to share the loneliness —especially in these days when city life holds so much'.[33] Henrietta Drake-Brockman's 'Men Without Wives' (1938) was a West Australian drama designed to fortify city girls against the selfish frivolity of such decamping wives as Mollie in *Coonardoo* (1929). Its implications were clear: unless white women accepted their duty to become pioneer wives, pioneering white men would enter into transgressive sexual relationships with Aboriginal women.

The outback of Australian literature of this period is not only a man's world; it is a *white* man's domain. And yet one disconcerting consequence of the retreat of the bush from Harpur and Kendall's coastal forests through Lawson and Baynton's struggling farmlands to the desert outback, was that the figure of the Aborigine re-emerged as a presence, no longer able to be comfortingly, if sorrowfully, cast as a member of the lost tribes. It could be argued that such restored visibility was a pre-condition not only of a succeeding struggle of white Australians to come to terms with the history of their relationship with the country's indigenous population but also of the demands of Aborigines to be audible as well as visible within Australian literary culture. It must nonetheless be said that the attitudes expressed in this non-fictional writing of the Outback were still ones which justified dispossessing Aborigines of their land by denying their full humanity. Subsumed under the concept of the Primitive, they could be protected with kindly condescension (*The Little Black Princess*, 1905) or firmly suppressed if the 'savagery' of the primitive should erupt into violence. The latter position was unquestioned, even when, as in Idriess's *Man Tracks* (1937), a degree of grudging admiration was accorded to a display of manliness which challenged the more common representation within this period of an Aboriginal passivity simultaneously valued and despised.

Inconsistency often marked even those voices that were beginning to challenge simplistic divisions between black primitivism and white progress, or to insist that white occupation of Australia had involved behaviour less than civilised. At times, the building of national identity seemed to require a softening of certain realities of past black–white encounters. In an interesting revelation of the lack of genre purity in bush realism, Mary Gilmore says of her revisions to *Old Days, Old Ways* (1934):

> I have taken out two chapters. One on scalping the blacks and the bonuses paid to the scalpers, as I thought it too horrible for this book: whose aim is to suggest romance in Australian historical associations, to excite wonder at what was done and endured, and to awaken pity for both black and white (*Letters*, 103).

There is no such sparing of sensibilities in the opening chapter of Herbert's *Capricornia*, and his devastatingly ironic narrative of the 'permanent' planting of 'Civilisation' contains no compensatory representation of 'Nature'. The civilisation which establishes its territory by offering flour spiced with arsenic to the inconvenient previous incumbents is, for Herbert, an extension of nature rather than its dualistic opponent. Consequently, we find the narrative outcome to the offering of arsenical flour implied in the reflection 'Nature is cruel. When dingoes come to a waterhole, the ancient kangaroos, not having teeth or ferocity sharp enough to defend their heritage, must relinquish it or die'.[34]

Non-fiction clearly had an important contribution to make in the project of writing Australian identity, and here one should note that there was now felt to be sufficient substance in Australian experience to justify the writing of its history. The fact that W.K. (Keith) Hancock's *Australia* (1930) initiated this enterprise at a time when history was still part of *belles lettres* has had an important effect on subsequent historical studies. As Herbert should remind us, however, it was in 1920s and 1930s fiction that the most fundamental attempts were made to identify the particular realities of Australian life, and to construct, as well as challenge, mythologies of reality.

THE SEVERAL FACES OF REALISM

Most of the fiction writers of the 1920s and 1930s shared a rather loosely formulated notion that realism required a sober depiction of Australian experience as it could be historically documented or presently observed within the compass of reasonably quotidian life. They were also for the most part either actively socialist or sympathetic to socialist principles, and this made them inclined to be critical of much of what they observed, although they rarely suggested wholesale remedial programs. It is true that, as the world's political climate grew ever more stormy in the 1930s, and as literature was seen to be a target for both political suppression and political manipulation in the rising fascist regimes, questions of the relevance of literature took on new urgency.

Such questions might arise abstractly in debates over the ideas of left-wing American and European writers—especially those of Maxim Gorky and the Russian Social Realist school.[35] But a practical test of unity came with the government's attempts, both farcical and sinister, to prevent the 1934 entry into Australia of Czech socialist writer Egon Kisch as a delegate to the Congress against War and Fascism.[36] Dissatisfaction with the strength of the FAW's response to this attack on the free circulation of ideas led to the formation of the Writers' League, specifically anti-fascist and internationally oriented, under the presidency of Katharine Susannah Prichard, but the groups were reunited when the FAW became more actively anti-fascist with the outbreak of the Spanish Civil War.

It is not till the postwar period that we find sustained theoretical attempts to draw a sharp distinction between true 'socialist realism' and liberal social realism. Members of the Communist Party of Australia (CPA), who worked especially through the Australasian Book Society, saw much of social realism as trammelled in bourgeois sensibility and prone to unproductive low-spiritedness because of its lack of a proper grasp of necessary programs of change.[37] Such theories were anticipated by Jean Devanny, who, in a 1942 ABC broadcast on 'The Workers' Contribution to Australian Literature', declared *Sugar Heaven* (1936) to have been 'the first really proletarian novel of Australia'. Devanny (1894–1962) was well-qualified to meet her own prescription that workers' literature must predominantly feature 'the problems and the true—as against the imagined—characteristics of working people'.[38] A miner's daughter, she had migrated from New Zealand to Australia in 1929 with an established career as a novelist and a firm commitment to working-class interests. For her, writers *were* workers: *Sugar Heaven* (1936) was writer's work developed out of her political work as an organiser of Queensland women affected by the 1935 cane-cutters' strike in protest against cost-cutting methods which increased the exposure of workers to Weil's disease. Woven into the story is the conversion of one young wife from conventionally feminine apoliticism into enthusiastic activism and the recalling to duty of another, who is at risk of allowing sexual passion to distract both herself and her lover from the central cause. What is striking is that Eileen is neither *femme fatale* nor fallen woman. Sexuality is acknowledged as an urgent reality of human experience, and stereotyped responses to Eileen's adultery, permitted into the novel through Dulcie's initial response of prudish disapproval, are subverted by the latter's developing understanding and sympathy.

Apart from her general outspokenness, Devanny's views on female sexuality, especially her attacks on the sexual double standard, made for an uneasy relationship with a CPA hierarchy increasingly determined to make sexual respectability a distinguishing mark between itself and left-wing liberalism. Having endured a period of expulsion (1940–44), she finally left the Party in 1950, differing in this from Katharine Susannah Prichard (1883–1969), the most stalwart of writer members of the CPA, although otherwise their careers have significant similarities.

Like Devanny, Prichard found that the Party was anxious to use writers' talents to advance Communist ideology, but also determined that they should do their share of political drudgery, to the extent that Prichard complains to Vance Palmer, among others, of being too tired to write. Moreover, writing that struck non-party friends as excessively ideological might very well be insufficiently so for the Party—and some work might please neither. One of Prichard's most neglected works is *Haxby's Circus* (1930). It is also one of her most scathing depictions of the exploitation of women, and of their own collaboration in that exploitation. Through its heroine it develops an extremely tough-minded stance on sexuality. Partially crippled as a result of her father's carelessness, Gina finds a soul-mate in the dwarf clown Roca, but sexual fulfilment comes from another source, and although she welcomes it, it is not her whole existence. It is her lion-tamer lover who dies for love, driven to suicide by the mere sight of the object of a past passion. Gina, while she has work to do in running the circus, survives.

The idea of hard plebeian work as the truly heroic activity is not exclusive to Marxist ideology: work as salvation is an ideological element in the social democracy of novels such as Vance Palmer's account of a Queensland fishing village, *The Passage* (1930). One suspects, however, that the circus may have been a dubious area of acceptable work to the CPA hierarchy, while other readers might be disconcerted, not only by the novel's refusal of conventional romance values and their determination of narrative outcome, but also by its sympathetic treatment of sex between the less than physically perfect.

Prichard had avoided such pitfalls in the more highly regarded *Working Bullocks* (1926, 1991), set in the serious milieu of the karri timber industry of Western Australia. Nationalists, romantics, and CPA members alike might approve an outcome in which the thoroughly masculine, physically powerful Red Burke, the bullock-team driver, rejects the distractions of both frivolous females and horse racing in favour of a union not only with his true sexual mate, Deb, but also with the forest which is, by birthright and nature, their proper habitat. Yet Prichard does not really offer anything as reductively simple as this, and her title, as well as the sombre reflections of Mrs Colburn as the lovers drive off, suggests that Red and Deb are as much under the sway of natural time and enforced labour as the animals they drive. Yet if the novel does not satisfy one criterion of socialist realism—an outcome indicative of positive systemic change—not many readers will consider it thereby inferior to the more ideological conclusion of *Intimate Strangers* (1937). There, in a resolution described by Prichard herself as a failure of her 'literary conscience',[39] the marriage difficulties of Greg and Elodie Blackwood are dissipated by their joint commitment to work for a new social order—a union again achieved within the context of a mediating and unifying force of nature, in this case the ocean.

No such solution is available in the world of colonial pastoralism that is not merely the setting, but the subject, of *Coonardoo* (1929). The natural environment here is perceived by white settlers as an adversary to be mastered by the colonising will; but, as in *Capricornia*, any such mastery is ephemeral. The settlers' achievements are doomed to failure—natural forces are uncontrollable; their pastoral practices destroy the natural ecological balances that make the land viable; and isolation intensifies the distortions of human nature, especially human sexuality, intrinsic to their society. In this context, natural sexual attraction, which Prichard saw as the necessary (if not sufficient) basis for any serious union of female and male, can only be acted on if it does not transgress the rigidly enforced boundaries of racial division. For the white Hugh Watt and the Aboriginal Coonardoo such an attraction must be a source of mutual incomprehension and destruction. Significantly, the most 'successful' settlers in the novel are the post-sexual Bessie Watt (benevolent but paternalistic) and the brutal, casually lustful Sam Geary.

Coonardoo itself was received as transgressive. There were those who sympathised with its proto-environmentalism and its attack on the brutalities of rural colonisation, but jibbed at sympathy for miscegenation in a period when theories of eugenics and racial purity, not yet tainted by their adoption into Fascism, could still be espoused by liberal socialists. There was also undoubtedly a disturbing unfamiliarity in Prichard's choice of an Aboriginal woman as the experiential centre of her novel. While there may be some justice in later feminist and postcolonial criticism which finds Prichard guilty of a double essentialism in her representation of Coonardoo as passionate woman and primitive Aborigine, the work should not be denied radical status within its own time.

The re-casting of white Australians from heroic or dogged pioneers to destructive intruders involved a considerable and controversial revision of their reality status. Unresolved to the present day, the conflict, or uneasy cohabitation, of these representations begins visibly within the 1930s to fracture any coherent view of the historical relationship between white Australians and the natural environment. From such a perspective, one may re-read as indicative those apparently innocent by-products of bush realism, the animal-centred narratives of Frank Dalby Davison's *Man-Shy* (1931) and *Dusty* (1946). Their implicit view of rural white Australians as intrusive and destructive emerges more explicitly in the non-fictional *Blue Coast Caravan* (1935) and *Children of the Dark People* (1936), early examples of conservationist social protest, provoked by observing the destruction wreaked on the natural environment by Queensland developers. Davison (1893–1970) also had a strong interest in social and sexual mores, translated into his FAW activities on issues of civil liberties and censorship. A number of his short stories, such as 'The Woman at the Mill', the title story of his 1940 collection, present sexuality as a force both fulfilling and destructive, working in a manner corresponding to the strict definition of social (rather than socialist) realism: non-lyrical, non-judgmental, concerned with the lives of 'ordinary' people.

Positive readings of pioneer Australia were by no means abandoned by fiction, but their major advocate has proved to be as perplexing to criticism after her life as she was elusive to identification within it. Stella Miles Franklin (1879–1954), apart from such major publications under part of her own name as *My Brilliant Career* (1901) and *All That Swagger* (1936), was responsible—under the pseudonym Brent of Bin Bin—for a family chronicle of rural life in six novels, from *Up the Country* (1928) to *Gentlemen at Gyang Gyang*, published posthumously in 1956. Stylistically, Franklin cannot be classed as a social realist. Her lifelong admiration for Furphy is reflected in her spurning of the neatness of well-wrought structures in favour of picaresque and digressive flow, and her style combines, often disconcertingly, the florid (for visions of nationhood) and the brusquely detached (for human foibles, especially sexual ones). She certainly believed, however, that she knew and wrote the reality of Australia.

All That Swagger reveals the curiously patchwork nature of her nationalist mantle. Anxious to assert that 'the national idiom had been democratically fixed, its spirit a fresh attempt at egalitarianism', she is nonetheless ideologically committed to defining an élite of hard workers and visionaries, against whom she can measure and reject the class differences that common sense obliges her to recognise. Conceding an Australian squattocracy, she emphasises its environmentally-imposed distinctiveness from an English squirearchy, and her choice of an Irishman, Dan Delacy, to demonstrate model pioneer behaviour in contrast to some dubious English representatives, reminds us that the generalising of white Australia as Anglo-Celtic glosses over major sectarian stresses operative within Australia before the Second World War. For Franklin, Delacy,

> in attacking, with single-handed hardihood, the wilderness beyond the fringe of the transplanted squirearchy, was a portent of an Australia which still pecks at its shell a hundred years after his arrival. His practice of equality with all men was part of a continent-wide experiment which was to flower in measures of political freedom and protection for the ordinary man which raised the personnel of the Australian working class to an unprecedented level and then left it shoaled for lack of continuing inspired leadership (p. 99).[40]

It is difficult to agree that Delacy practices *equality* with all men, given the paternalistic nature of his relationship with the Aboriginal Doogoolooh or the Chinese Wong Foo. 'I'll have to keep him as a pet', he says of Doogoolooh after saving his life (p. 35), and while the fellow musterers who find Wong Foo occupying Dan's bed are amused that 'Delacy had acquired another picturesque associate' (p. 88), Wong Foo's later status in the Delacy household is hardly that of an 'associate'. On Aborigines more generally, Delacy's atypical acknowledgment 'Sure we've taken their ground' (p. 27) does not lead him to abandon his own efforts to satisfy the land hunger bred by poverty-stricken Irish origins. And Franklin herself obliterates Delacy's earlier perception of Aboriginal ownership at the end of the novel. It is a vision of Australia as 'gorgeously empty', free from 'the accumulations of centuries of human occupation' that inspires Dan's descendant and spiritual heir as he ascends the empyrean, both figuratively and literally, the romance of aeroplanes having supplanted that of horses.

'Family saga' as a catch-all term does little to convey the differences that exist between Franklin and two of its other exponents: Brian Penton and M. Barnard Eldershaw. Penton (1904–51) is unusual among writers of the period, not in being a journalist and editor (of the *Daily Telegraph*), but in being aggressively anti-Labor. In the two volumes of his uncompleted trilogy—*Landtakers* (1934) and *Inheritors* (1936)—he returned uncompromisingly to the convict period of colonisation which Franklin had written off as superseded by the free settlers of Delacy's generation. Penton's early Australia is a land 'taken' in the worst sense of the word: a dumping ground for convicts about whose brutal and brutalised lives Penton refuses to be sentimental, or a resource to be plundered by those anxious only to make from it enough money to let them return to the comforts of civilisation. And in his sense that the country is capable of exacting a penalty for its exploitation, Penton's affiliations are more with *Capricornia* or the early pages of Richardson's *Fortunes of Richard Mahony* than with Franklin.

Setting and tone are very different in the best known of the pre-war novels jointly written by Marjorie Barnard (1897–1987) and Flora Eldershaw (1897–1956). *A House is Built*, published in London after serialisation in the *Bulletin*, is a novel of urban Australia, tracing the fortunes of a Sydney merchant family from the 1830s to the 1880s. Within this framework it offers a critique of gender roles in capitalism's distribution of work. Fanny's disappointment in love makes her a 'failure' as a woman, but she proves a success at business when given the opportunity through her brother's absence on the goldfields. His return means reassertion of masculine control of the public world and Fanny must dwindle to dabbling in genteel works of charity. The irrationality of this is emphasised by the fate of the 'natural' heirs to the family enterprise, her two nephews. The elder suicides after surrendering business secrets to his Delilah-like lover; the younger must then sacrifice his natural artistic inclinations to take over the business. If neither its narrative nor its characters seem able to rupture the confines of bourgeois society, *A House is Built* makes only partial accommodation to the pattern that critics such as Edward Said posit as paradigmatic of the novel as bourgeois social re-enforcer: that is, that it should end with the protagonist's accession to stability (usually through marriage) or with the destruction of those protagonists who, through an excess of intellectual or emotional energy, cannot conform to social order.[41] There is no happy accommodation to society; in fact it is through their accommodation to society that Fanny and Lionel, who are not so much excessively as inappropriately endowed, are destroyed.

The realism of *A House is Built* did not consist solely in its analysis of the emotional cost of erecting an enterprise vulnerable not only to human frailty but also to the boom and bust pattern of Australia's entrepreneurial history (a central element of *The Fortunes of Richard Mahony*). At a more mundane level, the novel was built on careful historical research. And among their other contributions to general literary life, Barnard and Eldershaw played a significant role in the development of historical writing with *Phillip of Australia* (1938), *The Life and Times of Captain John Piper* (1939), and *My Australia* (1939).

Such works also laid the ground for the substantial developments in the historical novel which were to take place in the next decade, one of the most outstanding being the trilogy of Eleanor Dark (see Chapter 10). In the 1930s, however, Dark's novels dealt with contemporary issues in a way that placed her as one of the most intellectual of the social realists, and, apart from Henry Handel Richardson, one of the most concerned with psychological states and the representation of inner reality. Influenced by modern European writers, she was among the earliest Australians to use what are now commonplaces of fictional technique: notably interior monologues to represent the flow of consciousness and compressed and interrupted time sequences to reflect more accurately the way in which time is experienced always as a present moment, but one in which the present carries with it layers and intertwinings of both past and future. This temporal intersection is central to the issue of hereditary madness in *Prelude to Christopher* (1934). Interest in madness, especially in hereditary madness associated with tertiary syphilis, was a worldwide phenomenon and powerful inspirer of literary work in the first half of the twentieth century. Apart from the fact that the novel's emphasis on heredity caused it to be associated with eugenic theories which became anathema through their adaptation to Nazi social theory, Dark's rather melodramatic treatment of Linda necessarily suffers by comparison with Richardson's devastating study of the decline and death of Richard Mahony, already published in 1929 in *Ultima Thule*, third in the trilogy of *The Fortunes of Richard Mahony*.

The characters of Dark's 1930s novels are predominantly artists, professionals, and intellectuals. This sets her apart from the prescriptions of strict socialist realism, as her preference for urban settings sets her apart from the more common nationalist privileging of the reality of the rural. While she pays her dues to the latter in *Return to Coolami* (1936), the novel is equally concerned with the problematic consequences of exercising the theoretical sexual freedom of the New Woman. More complex and psychologically convincing, *Waterway* (1938) combines themes of economic and emotional entrapment and confusion in the story of a single day in the life of a group of Sydney harbourside dwellers. The *deus ex machina* of a sinking ferry effects a resolution to the condition of several of the characters, this being a generally optimistic novel, in striking contrast to the bleakness of the personal and political lives in Dark's last study of the contemporary life of ideas. Not published until 1945, *The Little Company* is an epitomal account of the final collapse of the hopes invested in international socialism during the 1930s. General discouragement at the onset of the Second World War becomes specifically Australian dismay with the 1941 entry of Japan as a combatant, while family structures and individual lives reflect the stress of social change. In such circumstances, it is something of a gamble with public sympathy to suggest that what matters most for the sibling authors, Gilbert and Marty, is that they should be able to break the writer's block that has afflicted them as the war takes hold and as Gilbert's wife (horrible example of God's police as she may be) approaches a nervous breakdown. For Dark, their recovery of the will to write is an affirmation of the life of the mind in the face of historical darkness: for the reader, one of the ironies of the plot is that Dark herself is not to take the route chosen by Marty, the strong feminist who decides to write the lives of ordinary working women; instead she will follow the path chosen by Gilbert, that of writing the history of the past in order to understand the present.

Characters in the novels of Kylie Tennant (1912–88) come from further down the social scale and have less psychological depth than those of Dark or Barnard Eldershaw. Her accounts of the Depression years cover groups in a small-town setting in *Tiburon* (1935), an urban one in the imaginary Sydney suburb of *Foveaux* (1938) and a rural one in *The Battlers* (1941). Tennant's partisanship for society's outcasts goes with a strong contempt for its more hypocritical ideologues of every sect and party, a theme at the heart of *Ride on Stranger* (1943), also discussed in Chapter 10. In her final condition, Tennant's Shannon—pragmatic, capable, and kind—is akin to a better-known character: Mary Mahony, inhabitant of a novel so far referred to only in passing.

OUT OF BOUNDS

It may seem strange to have deferred for so long consideration of *The Fortunes of Richard Mahony*, a work ranked by many as pre-eminent not only in the 1920s, but in Australian literature generally; a work the scale of which was not fully appreciated until its 1930 publication drew together the earlier *Australia Felix* (1917), *The Way Home* (1925), and *Ultima Thule* (1929). The fact is that Henry Handel Richardson (Ethel Florence Lindesay Robertson, née Richardson, 1870–1946) does not fit comfortably into this chapter—which has a certain appropriateness, since each of her works is concerned with a character who experiences difficulties in fitting in to the context in which they find themselves. If Maurice Guest is too ordinary to cope with Leipzig's world of high art and complex passions in the 1908 novel that bears his name, Richardson's other protagonists are too extraordinary for their worlds, whether this is the small boarding-school stage on which the incipient artist Laura must learn (*The Getting of Wisdom* (1910)) or the wider fields of nineteenth-century colonial Australia and imperial England, which afford no abiding place (except in death) for the restless spirit and unstable fortunes of Richard Mahony.

Richardson herself was barely known as a member of the Australian writing community. All her work was written and published in England, under a pseudonymous identity so closely guarded that, as late as 1924, Nettie Palmer had no idea that Richardson should be included in her *Modern Australian Literature 1900–1923*. Palmer records the results of her enlightenment by Mary Kernot in a 1928 journal entry that tells us a great deal about Richardson's contemporaneous reception:

A re-reading of 'The Way Home' has sent me back to the first volume, and I'm surprised at the way I missed so many of its implications . . . I don't think I was so mistaken about it as Arthur Adams, who passed it by contemptuously as a dull chronicle written by a 'retired grocer', but . . . I certainly didn't see its significance for this country . . . My impression was that Mahony's life on Ballarat would be a mere 'colonial' episode in a long saga . . . It is plain from the second volume that Richard, for all his reactions, is definitely tied to this soil. 'The Way Home' is a bitterly ironic title, surely; where is home to Richard? Not here; not in that England he dreamed about sentimentally in his grocery-store at Ballarat, but hated when he savoured it again. The third volume, due this year, may provide a home for his proud spirit somewhere.[42]

Not everyone was so receptive; in 1935 Richardson declared, 'What these critics don't see is . . . that I dropped a European book into a struggling literature, which will go its own way, in days to come, almost uninfluenced by it'.[43] It was a shrewd analysis. Despite its painstaking accumulation of factual detail, Richardson's novel, with its primary fascination with psychology and philosophy, and its aesthetic allegiance to European naturalism, was as much outside the bounds of social realism as was Herbert's *Capricornia* with its markedly different qualities of satirical polemic and sprawling narrative. This very breaking of the bounds of social realism would, however, be instrumental in keeping these two novels prominent in the criticism of following decades, along with the work of Christina Stead and Patrick White, whose early novels were already suggesting, late in the period, new directions for fiction.[44]

7

LITERARY DEMOCRACY AND
THE POLITICS OF REPUTATION

Richard Nile

A delineation between 'high' and 'low' culture is commonly noted in industrial societies but it is perhaps the distinction drawn between 'serious' and 'commercial' culture which is more readily apparent in first world settler societies like Australia. In a perceptive comment made in 1964, Australian historian Ian Turner noted: 'As in all industrial societies, expanded leisure created a demand for entertainment rather than self culture, and the satisfaction of this demand soon became commercial enterprise'.[1] This development linked two important trends: a segregated workforce and the mass market. Under conditions of industrialisation, an Australian working class became the basis of the mass market and its primary consumers.

By the beginning of the twentieth century Australia was a highly developed industrial democracy with one of the best standards of living in the world. Never quite the 'working man's paradise' of its collective imagining, Australian democracy nevertheless favoured a version of able-bodied manliness in which myths of egalitarianism and classlessness abounded. After 1907, for instance, the basic wage specified the minimum amount which should be paid to male workers. The minimum wage covered the cost of living on the bare essentials required to sustain a man, in full-time employment, and his family, and no employer could legally pay less than this amount.

Australia's social democracy was underpinned by four main features: the taking of Aboriginal lands, the unpaid or lowly paid labour of women, the 'White Australia' policy, and foreign relations determined by the British Empire. Between the 1870s and the 1940s the average work week decreased, if erratically, by about one third from more than sixty hours to a standard forty-hour week, creating conditions for the mass market to develop. Based on this reduction we might suppose a proportionate increase in working-class leisure time. In the 1920s and 1930s, not only were Australian workers likely to work fewer hours than had previously been the case, they were likely to spend more time under-employed or out of work. From an average of 10 per cent unemployment throughout the 1920s, rates jumped to one in three out of work during the worst years of the

Depression in the early 1930s. Participation rates in the paid workforce remained low until the 1940s, when the 'all in' effort of war brought about full employment.

While the Depression severely restricted the buying power of the unemployed, culture became significantly cheaper for those in paid employment. Entrance prices for the movies, sports, dance and theatre generally came down and the number of radio licences actually increased. Australian literature received a significant boost by a 25 per cent devaluation on the currency which encouraged Australian publishers to increase production of Australian books. Importers of second-hand books also increased their turnover. More generally, throughout the interwar decades, new industrial technologies created the goods and new advertising techniques (refined during the First World War) combined to create industrial consumerism. By the interwar years Australia had entered a classic phase of industrialisation which began symbolically with the opening of BHP's steel smelter in Newcastle in 1915. With industrialisation came commercial culture. Something of a mass culture 'rush' began to develop at this time when unprecedented numbers of Australians began leaving the bush for the cities and the expanded suburbs which were made possible by revolutions in transport technology, specifically the cheap motorised vehicle.

Literature and National Life

In 1930 W.K. Hancock argued that Australia, as a young settler society born out of the industrial and democratic revolutions in Europe, one which had proclaimed its nationhood in 1901, was especially prone to material acquisitiveness. Hancock had studied de Tocqueville's writings on North America and concluded that Australia was cursed by the dead-levelling influences of democracy. Australia, he concluded, is 'merciful to the average'.[2] Hancock also observed that Australians were equally at home declaring a loyalty to Britain or to Australia. He used Alfred Deakin's phrase 'independent Australian Britons' to describe this particular neo-colonial frame of mind. Visiting American anthropologist, Hartley Grattan, similarly observed Australia as a neo-colonial democracy heavily influenced by commercialism. 'As in all young countries the culture of Australia is to a very small extent an integral part of national life', he wrote in a prefiguration of Robin Boyd's 'Australian ugliness': 'Such a cultural life as does exist is almost as insubstantial as those idealised houses painted on billboards'.[3]

In these circumstances, the effort to create a national literature was a noble undertaking by small groups of middle-class writers who proposed more discerning cultural insights than the industrialising masses. Their literary objectives involved the building of defensive walls against the peculiar mix of colonialism and commercialism which characterised Australia at the time. Paradoxically, those writers who identified with the nationalist cause tended to publish in London, in many instances finding that they were unable to be published in their own country. They entered the ken of colonialism in the name of nationalism in order to hold up a torch to the false values of commercialism. The conditions in which they worked, many felt, stacked the odds against the creation of serious literature. The single largest Australian publisher of the interwar years, Angus and Robertson, for instance, promoted best-selling commercial writers while rejecting overtures by many of those who proposed a higher national purpose by writing serious fictions. An attitude quickly developed among the latter that to publish in Australia was to be marked as a populariser and writer of inferior books. While many of them noted the contradiction implied by this literary condition others, including H.M. Green, viewed London imprints on Australian books as a natural product of ongoing colonialism. In keeping with the observations of Hartley Grattan and Hancock, in 1928 and again in 1930 Green used the image of Australian literature as a branch of English literature which he retained in his two-volume history published a generation later.[4]

The maintenance of the London connection may have prolonged a form of vernacular colonialism in Australian literature. In this regard, interwar writers seemed to lack the cheeky confidence of the locally published writers of the 1890s. Verse, ballads and short fiction had been encouraged in this decade by the *Bulletin* and other magazines, newspapers and journals of the period. According to Chris Wallace-Crabbe, the quarter century to 1935, however, represented perhaps the 'saddest phase of Australian culture'. With the decline of the *Bulletin*, Australian literature lost a centre, a focus and a nationally inspired literary agenda. Under conditions dominated by British publishers, once confident writing gave way to an 'uneasy over-the-shoulder squinting towards England'. Even the most 'ambitious' creative writing 'showed a tendency to waver towards clichés and stereotypes of the lending library'.[5]

By the 1920s literary production had shifted emphatically in favour of the novel, which became the preferred literary form of a new generation of writers. These writers tended to possess more formal education than their predecessors, they relied heavily on the patronage resulting from their middle-class circumstances, and they attended to the task of creating a national literature as part of a full-time professional and aesthetic commitment. They were conscious of their differences from the writers of the 1890s and their role in the development of an Australian intelligentsia. Novel production and distribution, on the other hand, required a concentrated industry such as that which clustered around Paternoster Row in London. Australia possessed neither the infrastructure nor the capital which could support such an industry. The few local publishers, Angus and Robertson, for instance, were principally booksellers with a publishing arm. They had to compete against British publishers who could produce books more economically because of larger print runs which reduced the unit cost. Distribution was dominated by Gordon and Gotch whose rates were very often beyond the capacity of small publishing companies. The paradox thus emerged that while the novel became the vehicle for the expression of national culture, only one or two Australian publishers had the capacity to publish and market Australian books. In a very real sense, Australian publishers published those books which they felt had a good chance of appealing to the Australian market in sufficient volume to make the title commercially viable. Generally speaking this meant a book which could command a print run of 5000 in order to return a profit to the publisher. A print run of 3000 was just enough to break even.[6] Such figures almost immediately knocked out serious writers from consideration by the few Australian publishers which possessed sufficient resources to publish and market books in Australia.

The effects of British publishers on serious writing are difficult to measure with any accuracy but for those writing 'nationally', the temper seemed to be hardly ever offensive, the mood was rarely democratic, as novel writing developed within a neo-colonial context. Visiting Australia in 1920, Somerset Maugham commented that cultural endeavour was 'strangely timid' for such a young country. Lacking 'originality', creative effort, he said, appeared hamstrung by an almost slavish adherence to convention.[7] Yet such conformity was seen by some nationalists, including Vance and Nettie Palmer, as an antidote to the slickness of commercial culture. Nettie encouraged Vance to maintain a steady course based on his preferred imagined community of artisans and craftsmen rather than the worlds of labour, capital and suburban living, a topic he only approached—and then awkwardly—in *The Swayne Family* (1934), when he finally secured a place in the lists of Angus and Robertson. The 'most heartening thing that can happen now', Nettie reminded him in 1919, 'is for anyone to do progressive, constructive work'.[8] Between 1920 and 1924 Vance attempted writing popular fictions under the self-deriding pseudonym, Rann Daly, but he gave up the experiment in favour of more weighty literary undertakings just as the first phase of cheap soft-cover books ended. 'A little while ago the publication of a novel was not a very serious undertaking', he observed in 1922, 'and a characteristic Australian book might have hoped to slip through'.[9] As more and more books were published as hardbacks at a greater price than the soft covers, Vance Palmer, along with many of his contemporaries, worked towards writing thought-provoking and critical fictions with a 'national' message. He subsequently removed from his list of publications those books he had written during what he called his 'pot-boiling' phase.

At the time when Vance gave up his attempt to write commercial fiction, Nettie identified the major publication challenge facing writers who saw a more significant cultural role for themselves. 'We are dependent', she wrote in *Modern Australian Literature* (1924), 'on the taste of English publishing houses that apply their own tests to an Australian book, and select what they want'.[10] London publishers were at this time the centre of a global English language trade which took in more than seventy countries. The emerging nationalist aesthetic, 'serious' writers rationalised, stood a better chance of being accepted from within the presumed heterogeneity of an international trade rather than the narrower limits of antipodean commercialism. Australian writing could then be considered alongside the best English-language literature in the world. The blandness of a good deal of interwar fiction may be related to writers' attempts to write with an imagined British audience in mind. It may have been a remarkable achievement on the part of so many Australians that they found London imprints for their books. Yet Australian books published in London, far from the imagined heterogeneity, were published according to a standard commercial formula in print runs of 3000 copies, on the basis that 1000 would be made available to the British retail trade, 1000 went to the lending libraries, while 1000 were sold in what were called 'colonial editions'. The guaranteed sales to lending libraries were an inducement which encouraged British publishers to consider so many Australian titles. The thought that British lending libraries were a key economic consideration behind the decision to publish Australian titles in London would have been devastating to the small and insecure groups of writers who had avoided the apparent commercialism of local production and dedicated themselves to producing a serious national literature. Seeing their books marketed in colonial editions in Australia must also have hurt their nationalist pride. Circumstances were about as tough as they would ever be in Australia.

BENCHMARK BOOKS AND THEIR PUBLISHERS

An equivocal review of Katharine Susannah Prichard's *Working Bullocks* (1926) in the *Times Literary Supplement* might suggest that while it was the intention of British publishers to secure lending library sales as a condition of signing a contract with an Australian author, the empire could write back in unsuspected ways and some of the much hoped-for nationalism could break through. 'There is something courageous, surely, in calling a book *Working Bullocks*', the reviewer commented:

> such a title being likely to put off nine women out of ten—and that is a large proportion of novel readers. In a way it suits this vigorous, uncompromising story of life on the land in Western Australia, but it does seem as if a more attractive name would have been even more expressive; 'the working bullocks' are not dumb, driven cattle nor primitive, inarticulate people. They are the strugglers and pioneers in the bush and the townships.[11]

Apparently a story dealing with 'strugglers' and 'pioneers' suited lending library preferences—they certainly suited the colonial book trade—but an uncompromising story about Australian workers and their conditions pushed the novel into a different category. It is little wonder, then, that the book so excited Australian contemporaries.

In only a few instances did serious Australian books exceed the 3000 limit set by British publishers, and reprints were rare. In terms of the Australian audience, very few Australians who were not directly involved in creating a national literature had any notion at all that the best creative talents in the country were working to establish a national literature for their benefit. Writers might have suspected the importance of the British market by the royalty rates that applied to their books. For Australian authors who published in London, British sales were worth three times the royalty rate of Australian sales. *Working Bullocks* was, however, a lending library failure, as was *Intimate Strangers* (1937), and Prichard received less back in British royalties than she had paid to type the original manuscript.[12] Resurrected by an Australian re-printing in 1944, the book has long been considered one of the best from the period.

According to Nettie Palmer, Australian publishers considered a 'serious novel' a 'contradiction in terms'.[13] M. Barnard Eldershaw's *A House is Built* (1929) and Prichard's

Coonardoo (1929), joint winners of the inaugural *Bulletin* novel competition, were but two of many significant literary undertakings rejected by Australia's best known and biggest publisher, Angus and Robertson. According to Nettie Palmer, *A House is Built* was returned with a simple note from George Robertson, the firm's founding owner: 'In the opinion of our reader, the book would not have a large sale'.[14] *Coonardoo* was rejected because it was considered too controversial. 'The story is a powerful one, and sales of ten thousand copies doubtless awaits it', Robertson sarcastically brushed off an inquiry from Louis Esson, 'but A&R have done their fair share of presenting to the world pictures of hardships and "sordidity" of Australian life, and another publisher must father it'.[15] In fact, Angus and Robertson was more a publisher of adventures and romances than hardships and sordidness and on the eve of renewed censorship in Australia, the company was the very model of conservatism as far as subject matter was concerned. 'A&R's books', wrote Nettie Palmer, 'must above all be innocuous'.[16]

George Robertson considered himself to be a bookseller first and foremost and a publisher second. He sometimes made a point of reminding Australian writers that he had built his empire out of the retail trade. In addition to Prichard and Barnard Eldershaw, Angus and Robertson's list of rejected authors included Miles Franklin (arguably the only novelist Robertson regretted never publishing), Leonard Mann, Vance Palmer and Kylie Tennant, all of whom identified with the nationalist cause. Once these authors were established with London imprints on their books, Angus and Robertson secured the rights to publish reprints and new titles. Reprints have flourished since the 1960s in particular, conveying an impression of Angus and Robertson as the original publisher.

If Robertson took advice it was likely to come from the ringing of his cash register rather than the complaints of literary aesthetes that they were being ignored. Robertson's successor, Walter Cousins, 'really was not interested in what you would call literature', according to Beatrice Davis who began as an editor in 1937 and who was joined by Colin Roderick in 1945 in attempts to gradually overturn this attitude: 'He had a marvellous way of rejecting manuscripts: he wrote a very short report which said "Unsaleable"'.[17] Arguably, it was gifted professionals like Davis and Roderick who turned around the relationship between serious writers and local publishing.

Angus and Robertson's inauspicious start as a publisher had been a slim volume of verse, H. Peden Steel's *Crown of Wattle*, published in 1888, but in the 1890s the company capitalised on the popularity of A.B. (Banjo) Paterson and Henry Lawson in the *Bulletin* and published *The Man from Snowy River* in 1895 and *While the Billy Boils* and *In the Days When the World was Wide* in 1896. Into the twentieth century, titles which became closely associated with the company included works by C.J. Dennis, Norman Lindsay's *The Magic Pudding*, Dorothy Wall's *Blinky Bill* series and May Gibbs's *Gumnut Tales*. In non-fiction Angus and Robertson was responsible for *The Australian Encyclopaedia* (1925) and the *Official History of Australia in the War of 1914–1918*. In their different ways each of these made a significant contribution to the articulation of Australian nationalism as did books by Ion L. Idriess, William Hatfield, Neville W. Cayley, Lennie Lower, Walter Murdoch, Frank Dalby Davison, Ernestine Hill and Frank Clune.

Far from being a danger to national cultural values, it might be argued that commercially successful literature in the twentieth century had strong lines of continuity reaching back into the working-class literatures of the 1890s, at least in as much as local books took a local setting for granted, were locally produced and reached a local audience. Serious writers of the 1920s and 1930s very likely found it difficult to accept this proposition but instead claimed that they were the guardians of culture and the rightful inheritors of what they called the Lawson–Furphy tradition. *Working Bullocks* became the accepted literary benchmark of the period. According to Vance Palmer, Prichard was a 'writer's writer' who had only been read by a handful of readers but who had given confidence to the nationalist project.[18] By the common agreement of literary élites, *Working Bullocks* was the novel which broke the long literary drought which set in soon after Furphy's *Such is Life* was published in 1903.

This view has been sustained in critical discourse up to the present. In fact, there may have been plenty in the midst of drought. More than 1200 novels were published in between those two literary landmarks. Between 1904 and 1922 A.C. Rowlandson's New South Wales Bookstall Company produced and sold an estimated six million books in the price range of sixpence to one shilling for paperbacks to two shillings and sixpence and three shillings and sixpence for hard covers. Bookstall competed directly with the British crown novel which Rowlandson believed was too expensive for everyday Australians. His authors included Steele Rudd, Arthur H. Adams, Louis Becke, Randolph Bedford, Edward Dyson, Beatrice Grimshaw, Norman Lindsay, Sumner Locke and A.G. Stephens. In an early example of vertical integration Bookstall books were marketed through a network of eight shops and fifty railway stands; but they were also retailed through the regular trade which included bookshops, department stores and newsagencies. Rowlandson worked off an established infrastructure—like Angus and Robertson, he was a bookseller who became a publisher.

The 'shilling magnate', as Rowlandson became known around Sydney, gambled in 1904 with a record advance of £500 paid to Steele Rudd to kickstart Bookstall with *On Sandy's Selection*. Rowlandson needed to sell 20 000 copies to break even. Within a month he had sold twice as many copies and *On Sandy's Selection* went to several reprints, securing the future of Bookstall as a publisher of commercial fiction. By 1927 Bookstall held copyright over all of Steele Rudd's books, apart from *On Our Selection*. Rudd lived well on an average annual income of £700 while his books contributed an estimated 1.2 million copies of the six million copies sold by Bookstall in this period. Rudd was perhaps Australia's first bankable author, though he later found the going tough when his attempts to return to farming failed, as did investments he made in film.[19] Rowlandson died in 1922 and, while his company continued to produce books, its days as a publisher were over.

Under the influence of a middle-class sensibility, the novel predominated in the interwar years, but serious Australian writing also included poetry, short fiction, novels and drama, as opposed to the ballads, yarns and sketches of the 1890s. In this phase, the term 'literature' seemed to assume a different connotation, in a more general movement away from a condition of vernacular culture towards an aesthetic nationalism. Although novel writing still identified with aspects of working-class challenges, the sensibility was overwhelmingly of the class above it (even among Communists such as Katharine Susannah Prichard and J.M. Harcourt).[20] Where writers from the 1890s assumed an organic relationship with their audience, writers in the 1920s and 1930s tended to individualise and essentialise the (unrecognised) talent of the artist. 'I want people to realise about *Coonardoo*', Prichard wrote in 1929, 'it hardly exists as a book in my mind'.[21] It was better to 'forget the gentle reader', she said, 'I always say, "Oh, after all, I write to please myself . . ." The worst part of it is, I don't please myself—often'.[22] Middle-class writers assumed the responsibility of preserving culture against the false consciousness of the masses.

Under these circumstances of class differentiation, serious literary debate tended to focus on the development of the novel but in other areas of creative endeavour the new class aesthetic is also discernible. Kenneth Slessor, for instance, criticised the rhymes of C.J. Dennis: 'An unfortunate philosophy seems to be afoot amongst local writers with regard to being Australian. The idea is that to be intensely and typically so you must sing in the perverted variety of Billingsgate'.[23] In a satirical verse imitation he wrote: 'The said CONTRACTOR shall in every case/Pen bilious lyrics to the Populace/ and preach to the (copyright) Doctrine of Smile/On each dial'.[24] As the influence of the *Bulletin* declined in the postwar years, new groups of poets such as Slessor, R.D. FitzGerald, Jack Lindsay and Adrian Lawlor, among others, concentrated on new forms of aesthetic poetry. In this they were aided considerably by personal patronage and by the development of small privately owned presses. Their intention, unlike the novelists, was never to be read by a wide audience but by a discerning smaller one.

As publishing opportunities for verse and ballads in book form dried up in the 1920s, so too did opportunities for short fiction. Editorial policies also changed markedly in this period and freelance writers who had proliferated before the war were squeezed out with the professionalisation of journalism. Freelancers had been a rich source of contribution to Australian literature through their contributions to newspapers and magazines. Very few now had an opportunity by maintaining an association with journalism and most drifted off into other fields of endeavour. Some made their way into radio, which was expanding opportunities for writers, but many potential creators of literature may have been lost by the new arrangements inside the newspaper and magazine offices which now favoured the full-time professional journalist. The shift in emphasis also meant that newspapers and magazines now made available less space for creative works.

At the same time, syndicated offshore stories created new editorial and reader expectations. In 1919 the editor of the New York *Independent* wrote that, although Australians produced 'poems, cartoons, editorials and book reviews' which were above the American average, short fiction fell below the standard.[25] In an Australian response, Harry Douglas argued that short fiction had been overly influenced by the *Bulletin*'s formula for yarns and sketches, 'that the whole art of short story making is knowing what to reject—as the be-all and end-all of the business'. Short fiction published in papers and magazines gave the impression of being an 'episode, storiette, a sketch, a precis of a novel or novelette—anything but a story'.[26] John Hetherington argued that the popularised yarn restricted opportunities for writers of serious short fiction. Meanwhile commercial writers had 'chucked . . . artistic integrity to seek the crock of gold at the foot of the magazine rainbow'.[27] Although Vance Palmer in the 1930s published two volumes of short fiction which represented a substantial shift in the genre, it was not until the 1940s that short fiction in volume form was published in any significant way. A related development was the inauguration in 1941 of the annual anthology series, *Coast to Coast*, edited by Beatrice Davis.

THEATRE, RADIO AND FILM

The problems confronting serious theatre were also put down to commercialism: 'Now that the Australian theatre—what there was of it—has gone west, chased by the dime novel, melodrama film and Cockney pantomimes called plays, a requiem falls due . . . Vanished are the dreams of an Australian theatre, local in-writers, producers and actors'.[28] Musical comedies dominated live theatre in the interwar years and an audience preference for shows such as *Spangles* and *Galley Girls*[29] did little to help the socially conscious efforts of Louis Esson and his co-founders of the short-lived Pioneer Players. 'Audiences nurtured for so long on a diet of musical comedy mainly eked out with light comedies, farces and detective thrillers', wrote Beatrice Tildesley in 1926, 'do not readily enjoy a play which requires mental digestion'.[30] J.C. Williamson continued to import overseas acts in decades when local talent found the going tough. The most written about and, therefore, most conspicuous 'could have been' of the interwar period was Louis Esson. Those who achieved success were popularisers such as Roy Rene who scripted and played the character Mo, a vaudeville and radio performer. In 1934 Ken Hall, who made his name in Australian cinema with his several films drawn from the writing of Steele Rudd, worked with Rene to make *Strike Me Lucky*.

Out of a population of around seven million people in the 1930s, more than two million Australians regularly listened to the 'wireless'. Although the Australian Broadcasting Commission, founded in 1932, developed radio plays which kept Max Afford and Edmund Barclay particularly busy, by 1938 Tom Inglis Moore lamented that dramatists, such as Esson, were financially the poorest of a poor lot who were attempting to create a durable Australian literary culture.[31] Writers who contributed materials to the ABC included Dymphna Cusack, Mary Durack, Dulcie Deamer, Ruth Park, Katharine Susannah Prichard, Betty Roland and Sumner Locke Elliott.[32] One of the major objectives of the ABC was cultural improvement, and Vance Palmer made a substantial contribution over several years with his literary talks. The inaugural board of the ABC said that it was the obligation of the national broadcaster to 'realise the state of taste and improve the culture of the community, encourage education and foster the best ideals of the Christian civilisation'.[33] Its major contribution was arguably in the area of the development of Australian music but many Australian writers got their start with 'Aunty'.

Licensing for radio reflected the split between serious and commercial culture: A-class licences allowed listeners to tune into the non-commercial broadcasting while B-class licences provided access to commercial networks. Gordon Massey, a successful advertising executive, spoke of writing for commercial radio as 'probably the most lucrative form of authorship in Australia today . . . the most profitable line of creative effort that has so far existed in this country'. A successful radio dramatist, he estimated, could make 'considerably more than £1000 a year' out of 'perseverance, study—and of course luck' but if 'fame is your desire', if authors cared about their names at all, then, Massey advised, 'commercial radio is not for you'. Radio listeners, he went on to say, 'care little who writes the plays . . . they are unlikely to remember it . . . So if you desire to make a name that will ring down the ages, write novels, stage plays or what you will—anything but commercial radio'.[34]

Film also presented potential opportunities and Australian authors often signed film options which accompanied their literary contracts. Yet few realised this potential, aside from Rudd, *On Our Selection* (1920 and 1932), *Rudd's New Selection* (1921), *Grandad Rudd* (1935), *Dad and Dave Come to Town* (1938); C.J. Dennis, *Sentimental Bloke* (1919 and 1932), *Ginger Mick* (1920); and F.J. Thwaites, *Broken Melody* (1932). Australian films of the interwar years tended to draw their literary inspiration from earlier periods: *The Man from Snowy River* (1920), *Robbery Under Arms* (1920), *While the Billy Boils* (1921), *Joe Wilson's Mates* (1921), *The Mystery of a Hansom Cab* (1925), *For the Term of His Natural Life* (1927), *The Romance of Runnibede* (1928) and *Seven Little Australians* (1939). A few actors like Errol Flynn and Louise Lovely moved to Hollywood, but only Helen Simpson's *Under Capricorn* (1937), directed by Alfred Hitchcock in 1949, seems to have had its film option realised internationally. Graeme Turner has pointed out in *National Fictions* that the renaissance of Australian film in the 1970s and 1980s drew heavily on historical themes with period pieces drawn from literature: *Picnic at Hanging Rock* (1975), *The Getting of Wisdom* (1977), *My Brilliant Career* (1979), *The Man from Snowy River* (1982), *We of the Never Never* (1982). However, very few drew on those books published in the interwar period, though versions were made of the comic strip characters *Fatty Finn* (1980) and *Ginger Meggs* (1984).

A FALSE BINARY? LITERATURE
VERSUS COMMERCIAL WRITING

The making of the binary—literature/commercial writing—helped define for national-ist writers not only the nature of their task but also helped to explain the reasons for their commercial failure. Increasingly, their roles became those of public intellectuals engaged in the very gradual process of educating a community about its deeper realities. While commercial fictions might be popular now, 'proper' writing, it was hoped, would be read and understood by succeeding generations. The worry of it all was that the success of commercial writing with Australian book-buyers might lead to a muddle-headed view that this was the extent of Australian literature. The popularity of Ion Idriess, wrote Frederick Macartney in 1936, 'causes his name to be frequently joined with the names of our really important writers which is not fair to the reputation of our literature'.[35]

J.K. Ewers, in his critical study, *Creative Writing in Australia* (1945), identified Idriess and William Hatfield as the two writers who opened up new possibilities for Australian literature, though apparently for reasons more sociological than aesthetic. 'The year 1931 was one of the gloomiest in Australian history', he wrote. 'The economic depression, coming like a nemesis after the false prosperity of the post-war decade, reached its nadir in that year.' In terms of reading publics, *Lasseter's Last Ride* and *Sheepmates* were arguably the most important Australian literary events of the interwar decades. 'Neither was in itself a classic', Ewers maintained; but neither was it often men-tioned subsequently that 'both books were published in Australia'.[36]

The Palmers referred to writers such as Idriess and Hatfield as slapdash. Idriess in particular seems to have been loathed by his serious-minded contemporaries:

> You know—Idriess' sentimental distortion of some genuine experiences and impressions in the jungle of North Queensland or in islands of the Torres Straits: or reminiscences of a mis-sionary to New Britain telling how his wife gave a present of six yards of navy-blue print to their first Christian bride: or an account of Queensland's air-mail. All very well, but making them want no novels except of the frothiest order.[37]

This critique could be read as a mixture of envy for the big sales and sour grapes at the ease with which Idriess appeared to be able to put together a good selling book. Along with Mary Gilmore, who was a driving force behind the establishment of the Fellowship of Australian Writers in 1928, Miles Franklin was one of the few to see that potential for serious writing might reside in the success of commercial writers. 'For years I used to wish that the wonderful yarns heard around Australia could be garnered in book form and now you have achieved a splendid success in the field led by Mr Idriess', she wrote encouragingly to Walter Cousins at Angus and Robertson. 'Now you must discover and produce the great and truly Australian novel as the prize bloom in Australian national literature.'[38] The mooching up made little impression on the bookman and publishing practices in Australia remained unchanged. Franklin died in 1954 and left her small estate in the hope that the annual prize that now bears her name would give encouragement to the very kind of writing Australian publishers had so conspicuously failed in the 1920s and 1930s.

According to his biographer, Idriess did not 'pontificate on the creation of Australian culture through literature', but rather maintained that serious writers like Vance Palmer 'were out of touch with reality, and he thought that they were far more uncertain of their own identity' than the average Australian. 'As the brilliant doyens of culture put forth an almost unbroken diatribe lamenting the lack of understanding of the Australian character', Idriess was 'showing Australians who they were'.[39] If the biographer's words idealise the subject too much and are too harsh on his critics, the Palmers could paint their own word pictures situating themselves in relation to the more robust world of the popularisers. 'The chairs must be in the right place, the fire going properly, the glasses ready', Nettie said of the many weekend meetings she and Vance enjoyed with the Essons:

> What is to be expected of Brent of Bin? Hasn't the achievement of Henry Handel Richardson and Katharine Prichard given new fillip to our prose? Is Chester Cobb a real writer, or just a clever journalist exploiting the stream of consciousness? Has the Barnard Eldershaw couple got the staying power, or is their novel likely to be all they'll do?[40]

Covering the years 1925 to 1939, Nettie's diary contains no mention of Idriess, nor Hatfield, nor many of the other writers who were achieving commercial success at this time. That Nettie's notebooks were very likely revised, at least in part, well after the circumstances they describe had passed, tends to support the proposition that serious writers, who had their backs to the wall as far as publishing was concerned, worked to shut out commercial writers from consideration.

His commercial success provided Idriess with a desk in Angus and Robertson's building where he would go to do 'some scribbling', as he called it. This arrangement shares some similarities with Henry Lawson's early association with the publisher, though Lawson's presence at A&R, as time went by, was commonly regarded as little more than a nuisance.[41] At work, Idriess seemed to like stub pencils more than stubbies of beer. Such sober and frugal work habits may well have pleased the old bookman. Hundreds of used pencils were collected specifically for the writer's use. Idriess's diminished pencil is difficult to explain in terms of the economies of writing alone but success can have a transforming effect and his hand writing, unlike Vance Palmer's which grew smaller with the years, elaborated into big loose patterns, 'perhaps best described as square and easy to read'.[42] In other respects also unlike Palmer, Idriess maintained that literature was primarily a saleable commodity. Averaging more than a book a year between 1927, when his first title appeared, and 1939, Idriess published thirteen books in 190 Australian print runs amounting to almost half a million copies. In contrast the combined life works of Vance Palmer sold around 5 per cent of this figure.[43]

Writers of the Palmer acquaintance found it difficult to accept that while they spent time planning, styling, writing and re-writing, commercial writers seemed to be able to dash off stories with apparent ease—and make money. Tom Inglis Moore sided with Palmer and said that it was quite unfair that the man with the small pencil and the big hand was the only Australian writer of the interwar years able to make a living out of his craft.[44] In habit and temperament serious writers were probably very different from commercial writers. It would be difficult to imagine Vance Palmer, a man of letters, who dressed almost invariably in brown suits, blue shirts and bow ties, rolling up his sleeves and leading the knockabout life of Idriess.

In terms of work practices, Palmer probably shared more with Marjorie Barnard, who believed that writing should be done slowly, with care and consideration. Barnard felt that she had little alternative but to 'stick to novels, a few short stories, if I can find a way to raise these delicate plants, occasional critical articles (that no one will want to pay for) and lead an ascetic life'.[45] Certainly, commercial writers tended to publish much more than those who saw a higher role for the writer, but the attitude towards the former overlooks the very real complexities involved in writing popular fiction which, contrary to perceptions, was rarely made successful by stringybark methods. Katharine Susannah Prichard seemed to acknowledge as much when, in 1932, she wrote to William Hatfield who, like Idriess, had a close working relationship with Angus and Robertson. She found Hatfield's *Ginger Murdoch* (1932) 'delightful' and said that she 'should have loved to have written him myself—which is an oblique compliment, I suppose, but the highest from one writer to another'.[46] But perhaps the compliment resides in the fact that it comes from a generally recognised serious writer to a commercial writer.

Idriess, it might be argued, was successful not because he was slapdash but because he worked diligently at his craft. The major pressure on him was to keep up the pace of production. Where serious writers might write with an eye to posterity, commercial writers were only as good as their next contracted book. It was precisely because many people thought they could dash off their own Idriess and make a fortune that there were so many failures in this line of writing, including moonlighting by serious novelists. 'Let nobody suppose that all you need to do is to shut your eyes and write with tongue in cheek', advised 'Grant Doyle Cooper'; commercial writing was a 'professional job'.[47]

COMMERCIAL SUCCESSES AND FAILURES

There were also risks involved and sacrifices. E.V. Timms, for instance, sold the family farm on the promise of his early success with *The Cripple in Black* (1930).[48] His next novel, 'The Honeymoon Inn', was rejected by Angus and Robertson with the curt report: 'Only a very gifted writer could make a seller out of such a theme and plot. Mr Timms has badly failed. He hasn't the humour or the turn for sparkling dialogue; and yet nine tenths of the extravaganza are attempts at both'. The reader concluded: 'Mr Timms thinks it a better laugh than *James Don't be a Fool!* Candidly, any laughter it may provoke would probably be more cynical than appreciative'.[49] Declining the manuscript, Angus and Robertson suggested Timms try London, possibly to keep in the good books with an author who showed some promise of being able to turn in a good yarn every now and then. He did so, but felt he had been diddled when his London literary agent forwarded a cheque for *The Cripple in Black* which was far less than the author had expected. The agent dropped the author, suggesting perhaps that he should go back to the farm: 'I had high hopes but I have no time to waste on an author who flurries around like an old hen with one chick'.[50] Eventually Timms's gamble paid off and his books did achieve good sales figures when he caught the tide of interest with his historical saga, beginning with *Forever to Remain* (1948).

Frank Clune claimed to have held down more than fifty different jobs before he turned his hand to writing in the early 1930s. At the time he was self-employed as an accountant, a business he clung to even after he became one of the best-selling authors in the country, such were the exigencies of a writing life. With a head for figures and an eye for success, he wrote 29 titles and sold more than half a million copies of his books over thirteen years to become a 'competitor with F.J. Thwaites for the title of best-selling Australian author'. Along the way, he 'acquired a newspaper column, and gathered a one million listening audience for his weekly *Roaming Around Australia* broadcast over a network of eight stations'. Branded as the 'the man who makes the cliché pay',[51] Clune employed ghost writers and published books at a rate of more than two a year for thirty years.

Frederick Thwaites invested his money back into his career and established himself as a successful writer and self-publisher. His first novel, *The Broken Melody* (1930) sold in excess of 125 000 copies and went through over 40 editions to 1950. He self-published 24 of his 31 romance and adventure novels with an average circulation of 10 000 copies each. Author of 30 detective novels by the age of 35, J.M. Walsh was for a time more prolific until he burnt out. Lennie Lower made his name as a journalist. His book *Here's Luck* became a best-seller in 1930. It was followed soon after by *Here's Another* (1932), *Life and Things* (1936), *Loweritis* (1940) and *The Bachelor's Guide to the Care of the Young* (1941). He was, arguably, Australia's first celebrity writer. According to Cyril Pearl, Lower was

> an integral part of Sydney life. In clubs and pubs, in lolly shops and luna parks, in the towering clinker-brick *chateau* of the millionaire pork-packer and the underground tiled *chalet-de-nécessité* of the troubled pedestrian, in the streets and on the beaches, he was a man of infinite laughs, a much-loved man. Even the Sydney taxi-driver hunched ape-like over the frayed cigarette, would emit an approving, almost human grunt if you asked him to deposit you at the newspaper where Lower worked.[52]

Yet for all the celebrity and success, the derision of fellow writers was often a high price to pay. Jealousies sometimes ran high and the as yet unwritten and unpublished 'great' novel commanded more respect than the successful seller. Under these conditions, market-place failure registered commitment to national ideals and martyrdom to the cause of serious writing. Commercial success risked the charge of philistinism. Nettie Palmer admonished Dorothy Cottrell not to waste her considerable literary skills writing commercial fiction. Cottrell, apparently, had more to offer than *Earth Battle* (1930):

'Anxious onlookers can only hope she will some day write a careful sound book. We ask merely of her, something different and better'.[53] Literary talent squandered on commercial writing irritated Nettie Palmer and in 1930 she wrote to Esther Levy criticising Roy Bridges's *Negrohead*. 'I can't, honestly, find anything but the commercial costume novel', she said. 'When he digresses into realistic character drawing for a short time, he never sustains his work and never shows development'.[54] Alice Grant Rosman's successful novels were critically ignored, as were the books of Dale Collins, Kathleen Tynan and Joanna Cannon. In 1932, after Rosman's *Benefits Received* became a best-seller in Australia and America, a small review in the trade journal *All About Books* commented that the success should 'effectively dispel any lingering doubts that Australian readers fight shy of Australian authors'.[55]

Far from being a fight shy population, Australians made books more popular than Australia's legendary boxing hero, Les Darcy. The most lucrative per capita book market in the English-speaking world, Australians seemed possessed by an insatiable 'demand for sheik stories, Foreign Legion and Wild West Adventure fiction and "happy ending" love romances'.[56] By the 1920s the Australian market was consuming an annual average of 3.5 million imported books, worth over a million pounds. A further one million secondhand books were annually imported in a flourishing US trade. In 1921 the largest British publisher of Australian books, Hodder and Stoughton, despatched its first full-time overseas representative to be located at Sydney. Only one British company to this time, Butterworths, publisher of scholarly and text books, with a manager and secretary, had set up offices in Australia—at Elizabeth Street, Sydney. Hodder and Stoughton's specially selected representative was Bill Smart, a former rugby second row whose literary credentials included a liking for Zane Grey heroes. In keeping with his inclination for stories featuring chivalrous cowboy heroes, innocent heroines and ruthless villains, or perhaps just as a measure employed to keep the readers at bay, the man from Hodder and Stoughton was rumoured to carry a revolver wherever he travelled in the Antipodes with his hampers of offerings in the yellow label series. With Bill Smart in Australia, Hodder and Stoughton's confidence grew steadily while the company's close links with leading distributors and bookstall companies increased visibility in the market. In 1928 the publisher achieved its best result in Australia and posted a record company profit.[57] Among their best-sellers in Australia were Grey, Arthur Conan Doyle, J.M. Barrie and Baroness Orczy.

READERS, BUYERS AND LITERARY REPUTATIONS

Book-buying and reading habits are quite different entities and the relationship between the two is far from straightforward. It is notoriously difficult to ascertain how readers read, but Lyons and Taksa have tentatively suggested that Australia's reading public developed highly differentiated ideas on what constituted serious reading and what made reading for fun or escape.[58] Book-buying evidence seems to suggest that Australians preferred the latter but the popularity of reading matter generally suggests that the public would read just about anything they could get their hands on. They were, arguably, the most broadly literate English-language community in the world.

Between 1929 and 1937, *All About Books* recommended 1500 titles to Australian and New Zealand readers. Almost 11 per cent of the titles were Australian novels, of which only thirteen were listed in the category 'Novels of Literary Merit'. In the category 'Novels for Popular Reading', the section suggested by the Australian and New Zealand Booksellers Association to contain best-sellers, the Australian tally rose to 149 titles. That is, according to these figures, Australians were over ten times more likely to produce a novel for popular reading than they were to produce books of literary merit. This summary of book-buying preferences seems to be borne out by newspaper polls and surveys of library usage. In 1928, for instance, the Sydney Municipal Library reported it had made almost 400 000 loans over the previous twelve months. Almost half of the books taken out were in the general fiction category while just over one quarter came from the section featuring geography, travel, history, biography, literature and drama.[59]

Given that Australian reading habits were highly developed, it is perhaps understandable why Frank Dalby Davison was disappointed that Angus and Robertson marketed his novel *Man-Shy* like a 'wild-wester',[60] but it was one of the best-read books of the interwar period, selling an estimated 500 000 copies in Australia and overseas. Serious authors (in the sense used in this chapter) tended to resist the label of popular writer but among those who appeared in the category 'Novels for Popular Reading' were Vance Palmer (1930, 1935), Katharine Susannah Prichard (1930), Miles Franklin (1930, 1932, 1933), G.B. Lancaster (1933, 1934), Martin Boyd (1934), Eleanor Dark (1934, 1936) and Brian Penton (1934). Surprisingly, Roy Bridges scored a place with Prichard and Henry Handel Richardson in the 'Novels of Literary Merit' category.

The largest selling novel by an Australian author to 1935 seems to have been Fergus Hume's *The Mystery of a Hansom Cab*. A story set in Melbourne and first published in 1886, it had allegedly sold more than 25 000 copies in its first print run. Another copy published by the Hansom Cab Company in 1887 was credited with more than 100 000 sales, and a later undated edition published by Jarrods of London with 559 000 copies.[61] In 1927 the Melbourne *Argus* held a literary competition in an attempt to discover which Australian books were most highly regarded by Australian readers. Adam Lindsay Gordon (459 votes), Henry Lawson (421) and Henry Kendall (412) headed the poetry section while in prose Marcus Clarke (393), Rolf Boldrewood (315) and Mrs Aeneas Gunn (292) were the most highly regarded novelists.

The results of the *Argus* poll irritated both Vance and Nettie Palmer who said it was little more than a popularity contest. A year later Arthur Upfield published his first novel, a thriller, *The House of Cain*. Upfield was soon labelled a commercial writer and was excluded from the company of serious writers on the basis that he was not a proper author but one who wrote for the market. Upfield maintained that popular fiction was the 'backbone' of Australian culture because it possessed 'no pretensions'. 'Better a good story with plenty of errors', he wrote, 'than a piece of prose perfectly done and having no story'.[62] Bald claims that typified his attitudes, such as there were only 'two subjects to write about—crime and sex'[63] must have confirmed the Palmers' negative view of him.

Yet Vance Palmer seemed to call also for a literature that rumbled with the crude vigour of an Upfield novel. Vance and Nettie's stated visions for a democratic Australian literature should have been well suited to the kind of books produced by commercial writers. 'We can take for granted, then', Nettie Palmer wrote in 1924, 'that qualities of the Australian novel, after 1900, are mostly those of the short story, with vigorous and pointed ways and its lack of roundness and suavity'. In this spirit Vance Palmer, a generation later, wrote in *The Legend of the Nineties* (1954):

> A tradition of democratic writing was thus established, and it has not been lost, for it is strongly marked in the Australian novel ... It is not too much to say that this body of writing, deriving from the literary pioneers of the nineties, has given Australians a clearer conception of their qualities and limitations, and brought some coherence into their social life. More than any political movement towards unity it has made them a people, able to respond to things that touch the national being ... Creative impulses were liberated that achieved something definite in the arts but also in the social and industrial field, laying the basis for future development and providing a tradition.[64]

At the end of the 1930s serious writers, through the Fellowship of Australian Writers, were able to convince the federal government to support their efforts through a restructuring of the Commonwealth Literary Fund and support for lectures in Australian literature at Australian universities. By the 1960s and 1970s Australian literature was being studied in universities and at schools and the CLF became the Literature Board of the Australia Council. Commercial literature continued to be written and continued to be popular with the Australian reading public (see Chapter 12). But with the backing of formidable institutions such as their own writers' organisations, prizes, libraries, universities and schools, serious writing also had its public. With more Australian publishers expressing confidence in such writing and with British publishers setting up branches in Australia, a few of its practitioners also broke through to sell their manuscripts in large numbers. The strange antipathy between the two types of writing continued in some quarters (for example, in criticism of commercially successful writers such as Thomas Keneally and David Williamson) but with a larger and more diverse body of writers, the insecurity which once dogged literary politics seemed to diminish.

8

NATIONAL MYTHS OF MANHOOD:
ANZACS AND OTHERS

Adrian Caesar

Myths operate in society to foster beliefs which in turn make it 'natural' to look at things, events, people in specific, ideologically freighted ways. These systems are neither static nor monolithic; they constantly evolve, responding to changes and pressures within the society they codify. This chapter deals with the development of cultural myths in the period 1914–39, that is with an agglomeration of words and images which, through being often repeated and carrying meanings significant but not necessarily inherent, may come to have the appearance of truth.

The 'bush myth' and the 'Anzac legend' are two such intimately related systems of language and image. Both are about character traits and nationality. The Anzac myth postulates the idea that the Australian 'character' was tried, tested, and not found wanting in the crucible of war, so that Australian nationhood was confirmed on the heights of Gallipoli in 1915. A critical analysis of the Anzac myth, however, may demonstrate that it encapsulates tensions and contradictions which relate to divisions within Australian society and to Australia's complex relationship with the British Empire. Developments in literary portrayals of the bush in the same period show similar tensions and contradictions. Just as the Anzac myth uses the bush myth to confirm the idea of the nation's 'blooding', so their symbiosis continues after the First World War.

Before an Australian soldier set foot upon the Gallipoli peninsula a series of images and ideas were already in place which could be drawn upon, repeated, and elaborated into what became the 'myth' of 'Anzac'. It is tempting to think that whatever had happened once the troops were landed on 25 April, the myth would have irresistibly come to fruition. As early as 1883 a newspaper article in Melbourne had proclaimed that 'our men are splendid material for an army; very much above the average of the line in physique and intelligence'.[1] Two years later, Henry Lawson in 'Sons of the South' imagined a day of nationalistic apotheosis when 'the Star of the South shall rise—in the lurid clouds of war . . .' Less specifically, but no less influentially, from the 1880s to the outbreak of the war there was a popular tradition of adventure fiction in which the characteristics of embryo 'Anzacs' can also be discerned. The idea of the 'bushman', the explorer, the adventurer, independent, egalitarian, anti-authoritarian, a good shot and horseman, full of mateship, initiative, and courage did not take a great deal of re-modelling to be transformed into an ideal soldier and in turn into a representative type of the nation.

Australia's involvement in the Boer War, whilst too limited and controversial to impinge widely upon the nation's imagination, nevertheless was the occasion for further developments of prototype 'diggers'. As Shirley Walker has argued, 'Banjo' Paterson's newspaper despatches from South Africa found and celebrated the virtues of the bushman in the Australian soldier.[2] Another war correspondent, the South Australian A.G. ('Smiler') Hales, made a similar celebratory contribution to the idea of the bushman soldier in his *Campaign Pictures of the War in South Africa* (1901) and *Camp Fire Sketches* (1902). In J.H.M. Abbott's personal memoir of his service in South Africa, *Tommy Cornstalk* (1902), we find a portrait of a 'long-limbed fellow with a drawling twang' who loves sport, comes from the bush, lacks reverence, and knows only the 'discipline of enthusiasm'; he bears a very close resemblance to some versions of the 'Anzac' who made his debut in 1915.[3]

Having said so much, it is important to emphasise that, as recent critics have made clear, the paradigms of masculinity which prefigured the Anzac myth are fraught with potential tensions and contradictions.[4] In this discussion of Australian war literature I am concerned with society's need to generate and believe in a myth of soldierly prowess, the internal contradictions within the myth, and the political implications of these rather than with any corrective interpretation of military-historical or political facts: E.M. Andrews in his recent and admirable study, *The Anzac Illusion*,[5] has already provided such a service.

The initial response to the performance of Australian troops at Gallipoli came from journalists, both British[6] and Australian, who were obviously aware of the propaganda value of exciting phraseology and hyperbolic praise. The journalists were also, of course, working within the constraints of a censorship which prevented any depiction of pain, mutilation, horror, excessive fear, or sickness. The most famous of these reports was written by an Englishman, Ellis Ashmead-Bartlett, who under a headline which proclaimed, 'AUSTRALIANS AT DARDANELLES; THRILLING DEEDS OF HEROISM'[7] spoke of the Australians as 'a magnificent body of men' who before the landing were 'cheerful, quiet and confident' and who, without waiting for orders, enthusiastically sprang ashore and 'went in with cold steel'. Later we are told of 'this race of athletes' scaling the cliffs heedless of Turkish fire—of their gallantry and endurance, and of the 'happy' wounded.[8] C.E.W. Bean, the official Australian correspondent, though less lurid than Ashmead-Bartlett, also contributed to the impression of heroic dash when he spoke of the Australians ascending the heights 'like a whirlwind with wild cheers and flashing bayonets'.[9] As Robin Gerster has noted, the Education Department of New South Wales printed both of these despatches in a pamphlet for distribution to senior schoolchildren in that state.[10] These boastful accounts of the prowess of Australian manhood were immediately appropriated as propaganda for the pursuit of the Empire's war.

It did not take long for others to take up what Gerster has called the 'heroic theme in Australian war-writing'—the 'Big-noting' of his title. The *Anzac Book* edited by C.E.W. Bean, John Masefield's *Gallipoli*, E.C. Buley's *Glorious Deeds of Australasians in the Great War* and *A Child's History of Anzac*, Oliver Hogue's *Trooper Bluegum at the Dardanelles* and *Love Letters of an Anzac*, and C.J. Dennis's *The Moods of Ginger Mick* all appeared in 1915–16 and played a part in establishing 'Anzac' and 'the Anzac' in the nation's imagination. The immensely popular writers for children, Mary Grant Bruce and Ethel Turner, each turned out a trilogy dealing with the war and contributing to the Anzac myth.[11] Ethel Turner's *The Cub, Captain Cub*, and *Brigid and the Cub* appeared in 1915, 1917 and 1919 respectively while Bruce's contributions were *From Billabong to London* (1915), *Jim and Wally* (1916), and *Captain Jim* (1919). Other pre-1918 books celebrating Australian soldiery included *The Coo-ee Contingent* (1917) by Gladys Hain, Hugh Knyvett's *Over There with the Australians* (1918), and *Saints and Soldiers* (1918) by Harley Matthews.

All these celebrate the achievement of the Australian soldier, finding in him qualities said to be distinctive of his nationality. But what is interesting is that this nationalism is not in opposition to British imperialism but rather contributes to, and is contained by, that imperialism. And the 'digger' who emerges from these books, though physically homogeneous (he is tall, lean, bronzed) and a very good fighter, nevertheless has disconcerting characteristics which are contradictory and threaten to fracture any unified idea of a 'national type'. Robert Dixon in his recent study of Anglo-Australian popular fiction 1875–1914 locates in adventure stories and masculine romances 'fissured, radically inconsistent texts', in which the discourses of empire, gender and nation are in dynamic tension.[12] The same might be said of popular literature arising from the First World War; within the burgeoning myth of Anzac there are manifest contradictions identifiable both within and between individual texts.

The Anzac Book has been credited with first revealing the 'characteristic forms of behaviour and attitude which became the mainspring of the Anzac legend',[13] and furthermore with representing a 'radical shift in literary tastes, martially speaking, from the meekly colonial to the stridently nationalistic'.[14] The book is a compilation of stories, poems, skits, cartoons and sketches garnered from soldiers in the last weeks of the Gallipoli campaign. What is elided in the claims for the book quoted above is the heterogeneity of the contents and their political implications. It might be easier in some respects to read the book as propaganda for the British Empire than as a statement of idealistic nationalism.

The prominent place of the British flag on the cover is an apt clue to the ideological orientation of the contents. For the contributions are by no means a univocal expression of Australian nationalism, and the soldiers presented are not uniformly Australian diggers. On the contrary, New Zealanders and Englishmen have prose and poetry included, and the feats of English, Irish, Scots and Indian troops are celebrated. The only allied troops who fought at Gallipoli who fail to attract such praise are the French, and the reason for this is obvious—they were troops of a different Empire.

Much has been made of the way that the portrait of the Australian soldier emerging from *The Anzac Book* has been sanitised by the editor. What has received less attention is the fact that there is no such unitary figure in the book at all. Two 'Anzac Types' are explicitly identified. One is 'the typical bushman, tall and lean, but strong as a piece of hickory'. This fellow has 'laconic' speech, and is usually 'sentimental as a steam roller', but has 'endless amounts of initiative' and is extremely efficient. He is a great horseman, and a dead shot. The other is a 'Dag' from the city, a speaker of working-class argot whose 'initiative' expresses itself in petty thievery, who mistakes an Indian donkey for a Turk, and who jibs at authority.[15] These two are radically different figures whose literary forebears may be traced back respectively to Adam Lindsay Gordon's 'Sick Stockrider' and the eponymous hero of Louis Stone's novel *Jonah* (1911).

In order to make 'Anzac' into a synonym for 'Australian', New Zealand has to be silently deleted from the acronym; and to produce a unified 'Anzac' soldier, the different masculinities implicit in the images above have to be either ignored or forcibly brought together. But if we choose instead to recognise and investigate these ideological and stylistic tensions, they not only reveal something of the pressures and rifts at work within Australian society at the time, but also the relationship of these to British imperialism.

In the work of E.C. Buley, Mary Grant Bruce, Oliver Hogue, Hugh Knyvett and Ethel Turner we find various versions of the noble and wholesome Australian soldier who is a servant of the Empire and who is either middle-class or a 'natural' aristocrat. Buley was an Englishman whose *Glorious Deeds of Australasians in the Great War* (1915)[16] and *A Child's History of Anzac* (1916) are blatantly propagandist. In the former the physique, dash, bravery and bush background of the 'Australasian' soldiers are dwelt upon as is their imperial allegiance. In the latter the 'Anzac spirit' is the 'spirit of self-sacrifice' which is said to be a 'priceless treasure not only to the Australian and New Zealanders, but to the whole great Empire to which they belong'.[17] 'Anzac' and 'Anzacs' are owned by the Empire.

In *Captain Jim* Mary Grant Bruce's fictional Linton family show that their first allegiance is to Empire rather than nation by moving from their 'Big station in Northern Victoria' to England for the duration. The son of the family and his friend are too young to join the Australian forces, so they repair to England where, prepared by their boarding school education with its cadet training, they find no difficulty in becoming officers in a 'famous British Regiment'. They are, however, 'immensely tall', 'lean', and 'deep-bronze, with a look of resolute keenness' and so conform to the Anzac type. While they are away fighting, the rest of the family run a nursing home which is described in a chapter entitled 'Australia in England'.[18] The Australian men are contained by the British army just as Australia is symbolically contained by England.

Barbara Baynton, like Mary Grant Bruce, was living in England during the war and wrote at least two idealised portraits of the Australian soldier which were published in the significantly titled *British Australasian*. In 'The Australian Soldier: An Appreciation and a Tribute', Baynton defends her compatriots against charges of 'lawlessness'. The Australian soldiers, she argues, have no equal 'for bravery, initiative, endurance, and great tenderness'. They have 'placed the welfare of the Empire, and its necessity, above their own'. In London these 'shy wayfarers' are said to be as lonely as Christ in his 'bitter Gethsemane'. In dramatic contrast to the brutal masculinity portrayed in her earlier *Bush Studies*, Baynton writes as if all Australian soldiers are innocent 'bush-born boys shy and untamed as the wild birds of their own country'. In offering them hospitality, 'not one of these boys ever abused [her] shelter, nor did an offensive action, nor said an offensive word'. Their officers are promoted from the ranks, they own 'no master on earth'.[19]

Despite this implicit egalitarianism, Baynton's soldier here is a paragon of bourgeois rectitude, if not a 'natural' aristocrat. Elsewhere, the issue of class threatens to bifurcate the image of the Anzac, creating anxiety in authors who want to cling to the idea that Australians are egalitarian and democratic. In *The Coo-ee Contingent*, for instance, Gladys Hain has her narrator imply that Australians are less class-bound than their English counterparts, yet class-relations are implicit in several stories where officers and their servants are featured.[20] The last chapter, 'The Old School', clearly speaks of a private education not available to the Australian working classes.[21] Oliver Hogue's Trooper Bluegum sets himself up as Every Australian Man, willing to put allegiance to King and Empire before his love-life. Yet his overt enthusiasm about his various promotions bespeaks middle-class ambition, as does his penchant for Chablis and cigars, and, most tellingly, his analogy likening Germany to the 'bushranger' of Europe threatening the 'Home Station' of England.[22]

Harley Matthews's *Saints and Soldiers* and C.J. Dennis's *The Moods of Ginger Mick* (1916) present us with Anzacs who do not conform to these polite and polished heroes. 'Ginger Mick' is neither a bushman nor middle-class, and his name and hair colour declare Catholic Irish descent rather than Protestant Anglo-Saxon. He is also a petty criminal, but is transformed into a 'real man' by putting on the Anzac uniform. Dennis explicitly argues in this vernacular poem that the shared uniform erases class differences, a notion which neatly side-steps the way that the hierarchical organisation of the military institutionalises its own class system. Moreover, at the close of the poem, Mick's epitaph is provided by an Englishman who describes the deceased as a 'gallant gentleman'. To be killed for the cause confers recognition by the Empire, which includes honorary membership of the upper-middle-class.

The protagonists of Matthews's short stories are fierce fighters, but as a corollary of this they are rough, tough and ready, great boozers and gamblers who think nothing of breaking petty regulations. This focuses another important tension in many portrayals of the 'Dinkum digger'; that is, the difficulty of reconciling duty, obedience and discipline with initiative, daring, and anti-authoritarianism. Interestingly, this is a conflict that Joseph Bristow has identified in images of imperial masculinity in the second half of the nineteenth century.[23] Like the issue of class, it threatens to shatter the integrity of the nationalistic 'Anzac' image.

In the 1920s the most important addition to the literature of Anzac was C.E.W. Bean's *The Official History of Australia in the War of 1914–1918*. Of the twelve volumes that comprise this work, Bean edited six and wrote six, which were published in 1921, 1924, 1929, 1933, 1937 and 1942 respectively. Although he described the work as 'a repository of factual information',[24] it is much more than this, and its importance for this chapter lies in its repetition of certain ideas about Australian nationality and national traits which serve to dignify popular myth by giving it the imprimatur of 'official history'. Despite being widely praised for its depiction of front-line action, its evocation of atmosphere, and its wide sympathies for the fighting man, it did not sell as well as *The Anzac Book* or *The Moods of Ginger Mick*.[25] Doubtless its length and cost were contributing factors. Nevertheless, Bean's history gave to the Anzac myth a patina of academic respectability that perhaps it had lacked hitherto.

Bean's predisposition to see the Australian soldier in a particular, heroic light is suggested by his pre-war life. Born in Bathurst, New South Wales, in 1879, he was educated in England at Clifton College and Oxford University. He was called to the bar in 1903 and returned to Australia in 1904 where he worked on the country legal circuit (1905–7). His experiences of country Australia inspired a series of newspaper articles published in the *Sydney Morning Herald* (June–July 1907). Later he became a reporter for the same paper and was sent to western New South Wales to gather material for a series of articles about the wool industry. This was followed by a trip by steamer down the Darling River in search of copy. From these experiences came *On the Wool Track* (1910) and *The Dreadnought of the Darling* (1911), wherein we can perceive Bean's enthusiasm for the idea that the 'real Australia' is located in the outback. It is here that he also finds masculine characteristics parallel to those used to describe the Australian soldier in the *Official History*.

The characteristics of *the* 'Australian' which Bean quickly establishes in the opening volume of the *Official History*, *The Story of Anzac*, will have a very familiar ring to any reader of *On the Wool Track*. 'He' possesses a 'peculiar independence of character', 'vigorous and unfettered initiative', any restraints being self-imposed rather than the product of external authority. His 'reputation for indiscipline' is off-set by 'self-control' in 'critical moments'. The Australian's 'prevailing creed' is said to be 'inherited from gold-miner and bushman' and is that 'a man should at all times and at any cost stand by his mate'. The bush is also located as the place where the Australian has learnt to be at least 'half a soldier' before the war breaks out. In order to cover the inconvenient fact that most of the AIF were city bred,[26] Bean adds that 'the bush still sets the standard of personal efficiency even in the Australian cities'. The Australian is viewed as a great soldier, but 'off parade [he] is a civilian', and has a 'sort of suppressed resentfulness, never very serious, but yet noticeable, of the whole system of officers'. Physically the Australian is 'large-framed', 'wiry and lean'. At the close of the book, the Australian's motivation is inspired by an ideal which, Bean argues, transcends love of fighting, hatred of the enemy, attachment to country or empire. Rather, he says, they were 'true to their idea of Australian manhood'.[27]

But like other writers' attempts to produce a homogeneous image of 'the Anzac' or 'the Australian', Bean's is threatened with internal contradictions. His historiographical method has been aptly praised for its leavening of the abstract movements of platoons, companies, battalions and brigades with selected narratives of individual dramas. Although some NCOs and private soldiers are mentioned in these, junior officers are by far the most represented. In describing the relationship between subalterns and the ranks at Gallipoli, Bean's perceptions in *On the Wool Track* are clearly influential: 'They conversed with [their men] as freely as a manager with the old hands on an Australian sheep-station . . .' As Jane Ross remarks, Bean's metaphor casts 'doubt on his whole egalitarian model'.[28]

Furthermore, Bean's footnotes tell us about the multiplicity of origins of his protagonists, including the fact that a significant number of the AIF were English born. The very idea of 'manhood' that Bean was using to glorify the Australian troops was itself a development of the late Victorian English ideal of the 'soldier hero'.[29] Australia and Australians proved themselves, excelling not principally in their own terms but in militaristic ideas of manhood inherited from the Empire. Perhaps the most interesting 'return of the repressed' in Bean's description of the Australian soldier is his insistence that this paragon of ideal masculinity has 'an almost feminine sensitiveness about laying open his feelings to another's gaze', and again is 'as sensitive as a girl' concerning those 'feelings which he did profoundly possess'.[30]

If not always 'girlish', Bean's 'Anzac' in the *Official History* is certainly a figure of some politeness and nobility. Harley Matthews's 'Band of Boisterous Boozers' from *Saints and Soldiers* are conspicuous by their absence. This is not entirely the case with another eccentric production of 1921, William Baylebridge's *An Anzac Muster*. Like Matthews, Baylebridge disrupts the image of the wholesome digger, and goes further than Matthews in presenting salacious and misogynist accounts of the Anzac's sexual activities. But unlike Matthews, Baylebridge's prose style is mannered and elevated; his tales are shaped according to Chaucer and Boccaccio. The result is to aggrandise the Australian soldier into an aristocratic Nietzschean superman.[31]

An Anzac Muster was published in London in a limited edition of only 100 copies. It was not reprinted until 1962 when a new edition appeared edited by P.R. Stephensen. Despite this extremely modest public airing, the book was positively received by early literary historians, and more recently Robin Gerster, despite various reservations, has suggested that the work deserves the status of an 'underground' classic. My own view coincides with Brian Elliott's remark that *An Anzac Muster* strikes one as 'bogus, bogus and bogus'.[32] Thankfully the opposite may be said of the efflorescence of 'personal memoirs' that appeared in the 1930s. This is not to say that such books were artless, 'truthful' or 'realistic' in any uncomplicated way, but rather to assert that they convey to the reader more convincing accounts of battle experience than Baylebridge, or for that matter any of the earlier propagandists we have mentioned.

Red Dust (1931) by J.L. Gray, Leonard Mann's novel *Flesh in Armour* (1932), Ion L. Idriess's *The Desert Column* (1932), J.M. Maxwell's *Hell's Bells and Mademoiselles* (1932), *The Grey Battalion* by May Tilton (1933) and G.D. Mitchell's *Backs to the Wall* (1937) all contribute to the Anzac myth in various ways, but also enrich the Australian literature of war by the complexity and diversity of their various accounts. As we might expect from writers who had served, and had ten years to assimilate that service, the ambivalences in these texts are very marked indeed—there is a need to justify and celebrate their participation in war, but also an impulse to register the fear, filth, discomfort, degradation, horror and loss consequent upon their experience.

J.L. Gray's/Donald Black's[33] *Red Dust* is a clearly written and impassioned account of the author's service with the Light Horse in the Jordan Valley. In the early parts of the book there are denunciations of the war, the politicians waging it, and the Christian ideology underwriting it. Black speaks of 'The pity of it all, the infinite pity'. He feels 'nauseated and sick at heart' at the thought of the soldier's 'sacrifice' to the 'greed of nations, the greed of power, the greed for wealth'. The creed 'For God, King and Country' is described as 'a mockery' and a 'hypocritical sham'.[34] But in a fascinating reversal of the usual pattern of war memoirs which conventionally move from innocence to experience and disillusion, Black's trajectory is towards 'acceptance', and the book ends rejecting the 'glory' of war, but nevertheless finding value in it. The war as a site of adventure on behalf of the British 'breed' has conferred upon the author his 'manhood'.[35]

In Maxwell's memoirs and in Mann's novel drawing upon his experiences in the AIF, pre-war adventure fiction is specifically identified as inspiration, frame and model for participation in the 'great adventure' of war.[36] In Maxwell as in Black the excitements of war are favourably compared with the 'prosaic life of a city' in peacetime. Yet both *Hell's Bells and Mademoiselles* and *Flesh in Armour* also express their share of horrors and brutality. Both struggle to unite divided images of the Anzac soldier and the war. Maxwell, for example, can refer to the soldiers as 'crusaders', and speak of 'self-sacrifice' yet, contrary to the august connotations conjured by such images and ideas, he delights in recounting the boozing, brawling and womanising he was involved in during the war. He repeats other tenets of the Anzac myth—the Australian dislike of saluting officers, their fighting capability, their physique, and their anti-authoritarianism—which is implied by the digger's 'immortalization of Ned Kelly'; yet he records men breaking down through nerve strain, arguing that this cannot be called cowardice, and he is proud of being promoted through the ranks, describing the man whom he accepts as his servant as possessing 'dog-like fidelity' and 'servility'. In England he notes that he rides in a first-class carriage, and, most extraordinarily, he proclaims that he is 'British and proud of it'. 'The educated Englishman', he avers, is 'the finest gentleman to be found in the whole world'.[37]

The ambivalence in Mann's fiction is, if anything, even stronger than Maxwell's. Here, in a story which re-creates the appalling conditions and multiple confusions of the Western Front and spares us little of its horrors, we are also treated to several celebrations of the Australians' prowess. The achievements of Australian troops are glorified, yet one of the central characters in the book, suffering from repeated nerve strain, and finding that his beloved English girlfriend has previously slept with another member of his platoon, commits suicide. Terror, loneliness and despair are placed against Mann's defensive need to boast about the Australians' martial prowess. The creed of mateship is destructively disrupted by two soldiers' involvement with the same woman. Mann's character makes the fatal error of loving a woman more than his fellow soldiers.

This is a rare occurrence in Australian war writing which, as a direct corollary of the violence being expressed, more typically legitimates the direct expression of love and tenderness between men, as well as promoting effusions about the splendour of the male physique. Black speaks of his 'love' for his fellow trooper, Smith, in *Red Dust*,[38] while Maxwell feels 'elation' at the physique of his colleagues,[39] and Mitchell weeps as he tends a mate dying of wounds.[40] What is taboo in civilian life becomes a commonplace of war literature, helping to explain, perhaps, the enduring popularity of the genre in Australian culture.

The finest book by an Australian to emerge from the First World War was described by E.M. Forster as a 'love story'.[41] This is Frederic Manning's classic *The Middle Parts of Fortune* or *Her Privates We* (1929).[42] Although Manning left Australia as a young man and served as a private in an English regiment during the Battle of the Somme, his literary treatment of this experience has interesting features in common with some of the other texts discussed earlier. *The Middle Parts of Fortune* cannot properly be said to contribute to the Anzac myth or to be concerned with nationalism. Yet its 'Australian-ness' is of great interest.

Unlike the famous English novels and memoirs which also appeared in the late 1920s and early 1930s,[43] Manning's book seeks to ennoble the experience of the private soldier rather than dealing with the officer class. Set entirely in France, the book provides an intimate and detailed study of the soldiers' lives, in and out of the line, as they prepare for the major offensive which serves as the dramatic climax of the book. Such description is juxtaposed with philosophical reflection upon the meaning of the experience. The vehicle for this intellectual speculation is the major character, Bourne, through whose sensibilities we experience the world of the estaminets no less than the trenches. As critics have previously remarked, Bourne has much in common with Manning himself. With the Tommies, but not of them, it is never explicitly stated that Bourne is Australian, yet he boasts of the Australian's ability to swear, and feels that the English regiment he serves in could do with a leavening of Australians. Bourne also shares the typical Anzac's impatience with petty differences between officers and men. This and his friendship with the Tommies seem to mark him as a democrat. Yet, like Maxwell and Mitchell in their war memoirs, there is also something of the natural aristocrat about Bourne. He is the leader of his group of friends; he is a good scrounger and can speak French fluently. He is asked to apply for a commission, and mixes with officers, NCOs and men with equal ease. His philosophical reflections, and even his speech, are in stark contrast to the working-class argot of the soldiers, which is reproduced with high fidelity in all its profane colour.

Manning's book is more profound in its philosophical contemplation of war than others discussed here, but shares with the works of other Australian memoirists a conservative valorisation of war. Despite its grim portrayal of the discomfort, fear, brutality and sadness of war, *The Middle Parts of Fortune* sets out a thesis that the tragedy of war constitutes a triumph because it represents the assertion of choice and will against massive odds, and the finding of 'freedom' in such action. In this way it has rightly been seen as prefiguring existential philosophy.[44]

War, in Manning's text, is presented not only as a constant of the human condition, but also as metaphor for that condition. The problem with this is that it erases any political considerations about the causes of the war, implies that any 'protest' against war is futile, and, most importantly, misrepresents the situation of the English Tommies in the trenches. For when they went over the top they did so in the full knowledge that to refuse amounted to desertion for which they could be shot. What Manning views as an act of choice and will was in fact made in response to powerful coercion. But Manning's purpose is to glorify the English Tommy, and by extension the British cause. The Shakespearian epigraphs to each chapter serve this dual purpose; the working-class Tommy of 1916 is brought into a martial and literary tradition in which he is an expendable yet dignified player in a tragedy which redeems British polity.

BACK TO THE BUSH: THE INTERWAR YEARS

The establishment and perpetuation of the Anzac myth in Australia and Britain contributed to the broader context of Australian politics and culture during the 1920s and 1930s. Whether he was a bushman, a 'dag', a natural aristocrat, or working-class hero, whether he was a private school chum or a crusader sporting the cross of St George, a Homeric warrior or laconic humorist, these various images of the Australian soldier collapsed into the single signifier 'Anzac' which in turn became part of the nation's idea of itself. The very power of the Anzac myth was that it could mean so much to so many different sections of the Australian populace whilst almost invariably representing a nationalism that was inseparable from its imperial sources. As Peter Kirkpatrick has perspicaciously remarked, after the war we were 'ourselves, but we were also somehow other than ourselves, part of an Imperial culture which the blood of almost 60 000 Australians had helped re-define'.[45] The conservatism of the Anzac myth was then in concert with dominant ideologies of the 1920s and 1930s. These were years governed by conservatives in Federal parliament, and although Labor was represented in some States, as Manning

Clark has remarked, 'there was little to distinguish a Labor from a non-Labor administration'.[46] Alistair Thomson, in *Anzac Memories*, has demonstrated the way in which the Anzac myth was appropriated and used by Empire loyalists in the postwar years, particularly through the auspices of the Returned Sailors' and Soldiers' Imperial League of Australia.[47] Popular journalism also played a part. *Smith's Weekly*, for instance, styled itself the 'Digger's paper', and had a page of each issue devoted to readers' contributions which unfolded the 'Unofficial History of the AIF'. As a present-day reading of George Blaikie's history of *Smith's Weekly* will suggest, the paper was in this and other ways a purveyor of dominant middle-class values.[48]

Given the close relationship between aspects of the Anzac myth and a nationalism that would seek to define a distinctive Australian-ness in the bush, it is perhaps not surprising to find that the interwar years also witnessed an intense literary interest in outback Australia. The First World War followed by the Depression of the 1930s may also have encouraged urban and suburban readers to turn away from the city and all its attendant manifestations of modernity and to foster a nostalgia for 'bush values'. As Beverley Eley has suggested in her biography of Ion Idriess, tales of adventure in the bush may have provided 'an opiate of escapism to thousands of people suffering under the depression'.[49]

This outback literature was of two kinds. On the one hand there was a large popular literature, both fiction and non-fiction, which catered for what Craig Munro has called 'one of the central obsessions of the 1930s: the "Vast-Open Spaces"',[50] and on the other there were a few texts which emanated from the more radical intelligentsia which had distinctly literary as well as political pretensions. What all these contributions to the Bush myth have in common, however, is that they embody similar tensions to those found in the texts extolling the Australian soldiery. An ideal of democratic egalitarianism is professed in books which are replete with discriminations of race, class and gender.

The popular writers included Roy Bridges, William Hatfield, J.H.M. Abbott, Jack McLaren, A.G. Hales, Ion L. Idriess and Frank Clune. Several of these authors were also purveyors of the Anzac myth who in the interwar years not only perpetuated the idea of the bushman as a quintessentially Australian hero, but also continued the traditional interest in convicts and bushrangers within Australian folk and literary culture.

The years between the wars also witnessed an ongoing interest in the figure of the explorer as hero. As Tim Bonyhady's study demonstrates, Burke and Wills 'retained a central place in Australian culture' until the outbreak of the First World War. Bonyhady further suggests that the more 'recent form of exploration—the race for the South Pole' had 'provided new English heroes who eclipsed the Victorian explorers'.[51] Scott's journals provided a heroic ideal of masculine self-sacrifice which was exploited to inspire British troops in the First World War, and performed a similar function in Australia. What is striking about this is the eclipse of Australia's own Antarctic hero, Douglas Mawson, by his British colleagues. Mawson's *Home of the Blizzard* which tells the story of the Australian Antarctic Expedition 1911–14, including an account of Mawson's extraordinary lone journey back to base following the death of his two companions due to accident and illness, was published in 1915 when the country had its attention firmly focused upon the heroism and sacrifice at Anzac Cove. It was not until Mawson led a second expedition to Antarctica in 1929 that interest in *Home of the Blizzard* was revived and the book was made widely available in abridged versions suitable for use in schools.

Frank Clune, a veteran of Gallipoli, brought exploration back closer to home with the publication of his *Dig* in 1937. Written, as many of his books were, in collaboration with P.R. Stephensen, this popular account of the Burke and Wills expedition was criticised by some reviewers for its melodrama, levity, and mixing of fact and fiction, but nevertheless it struck the right heroic note with others who found in the story 'an epic that should be in the possession of every Australian'. One of the most interesting responses demonstrates clearly the way in which it was possible to re-cast the Burke and Wills story in the light (or darkness) of Scott's Antarctic expedition. The reviewer opined that Wills's death was 'as splendid a vindication of the human interest as Captain Oates's great sacrifice in the blizzard'.[52] Certainly the public found something to their taste in the book as it was reprinted within ten days of its publication and again two months later. By 1948 it had sold 60 000 copies and by 1957 had topped the 100 000 mark.

Despite Clune's success with this and other books, Ion Idriess remains the best known of the popularist writers of the 1930s. Having made his contribution to the Anzac myth with *The Desert Column* (1932), Idriess, 'a frustrated explorer', went on to write over forty books, a number of which appeared in the 1930s: *Lasseter's Last Ride* (1931), *Flynn of the Inland* (1932), *Gold Dust and Ashes* (1933), *Drums of Mer* (1933), *The Cattle King* (1936) and *Forty Fathoms Deep* (1937). As the titles of these books imply, Idriess had a romantic and sentimental attachment to the bush and its masculine heroes which made for great success. In 1933 alone Idriess sold approximately 34 000 books. The book which has outsold all his others, however, is *Flynn of the Inland* which by June 1945 had been through twenty-four editions and had sold 56 924 copies. As Eley remarks, 'accurate records have not been kept since but the book is still in print and sells well today'.[53] Idriess is reputed to have sold over three million books by 1979 and in 1980, as Adam Shoemaker has pointed out, he was still the highest selling author published by Angus and Robertson.[54]

REBEL INTELLECTUALS

In 1936 P.R. Stephensen published in book form his tripartite essay *The Foundations of Culture in Australia*, a fascinating piece of cultural criticism and a cry from the heart of an energetic radical. Born in 1901 and thus too young to have served in the First World War, Stephensen was one of a number of Australian writers and intellectuals who flirted with extreme and dangerous ideas in the 1920s and 1930s. Almost inevitably he had been hailed early in his career by that doyen of the Australian artistic intelligentsia, Norman

Lindsay, as another aristocratic 'voyager from Olympus to earth'. Stephensen was also involved with Norman's son Jack and John Kirtley in the London publishing venture, the Fanfrolico Press, of which Norman Lindsay was the 'spiritual and financial patron'.[55]

Stephensen, always drawn to extremes, was a member of the Communist Party in the early 1920s, but from 1925 to 1930 he moved gradually away from communism, becoming increasingly interested in the profoundly undemocratic ideas of Nietzsche. D.H. Lawrence, particularly his novel *Kangaroo* (1923), also played a significant part in Stephensen's intellectual development. And *The Foundations of Culture in Australia* takes as its starting point Lawrence's perception of the 'Spirit of the place' in which he discerned 'a spiritual quality of ancient loveliness' and 'an element of terror'.[56]

The Foundations of Culture in Australia is ostensibly an argument for an indigenous culture based on the idea of place, and a separatist and isolationist politics severing Australia from Empire. But in the pursuit of these arguments we find in a more exaggerated form many of the contradictions which we have perceived within the Anzac myth. Indeed Stephensen invokes the Anzac experience to argue against militarism on the grounds that 'The AIF was the outstanding, non-conscript, civilian, *democratic*, army of the Great War' which gave us a history from which 'we suddenly perceived that we are indeed a Nation, with our own permanent quality'. The Australian soldier, according to Stephensen, however, has a curiously aristocratic and Nietzschean character; he represents *the superior value of the individual man*. It will come as little surprise to remark in this context that Stephensen was an admirer of Baylebridge's *An Anzac Muster*. The democratic 'common man' of Australia, according to Stephensen, is a 'free thinker, an individualist to his core' who will follow 'the intellectuals whenever these decide to give a strong and unwavering lead in the matter of proclaiming "Australia First" as the only constructive national Idea' (pp. 130–3). Here in embryo is the Fascism that Stephensen was to espouse in the later years of the 1930s and early 1940s.

In 1936, however, Stephensen was still trying to reconcile aristocratic idealism and aggressive denunciations of the middle classes with democracy. His attitude to Britain was also deeply ambiguous. On the one hand he argues for an 'autonomous culture' in Australia, but on the other insists that British history is Australian history until the nineteenth century. He deplores the massacre of the Aborigines and the despoliation of the land by early pioneers, while simultaneously arguing that Australia has only one race and is entirely homogeneous. In concert with this proclamation of white supremacy, he articulates the idea that Australia should become the 'permanent domicile of the white race . . . *A New Britannia in Another World*' (p. 189). Australia, according to Stephensen, was going to become itself by becoming a bigger and better Britain.

Another contradiction in Stephensen's position was that he despised some aspects of Australian literary culture. He championed Lawson and Paterson, presumably because he could find therein versions of the Australian bushman as a 'natural' aristocrat, but he could not 'accept the carefully fostered legend that Australians are of the naturally uncouth, "rough digger", "Dad and Dave" or "Bloke" type'. Furthermore, he deprecated the tradition of convictism, arguing that this was 'the prerogative of English-minded writers' (pp. 28, 59–63).

Two novelists, Xavier Herbert and Brian Penton, both acquaintances and associates of Stephensen, produced books in the 1930s that were set in the outback yet went well beyond the usual properties of the bush legend. Stephensen admired Herbert's *Capricornia* (1938) but was dismissive of Penton's *Landtakers* (1934).[57] Both books take an exceedingly tough and unsentimental look at different areas of 'settlement' of the bush, and seek to find something quintessentially Australian in this experience.

Penton's book is set in Queensland between 1842 and 1864. It tells the story of Cabell, a young British immigrant, and his horrific experiences as he establishes himself as a squatter. The novel shows the brutality of this process as Cabell is involved in a massacre of Aborigines and in difficult and violent relationships with ex-convicts. Throughout the narrative Cabell dreams of going 'home' to Britain but in the end forfeits this idea. The book is replete with ambivalence. On the one hand Penton demonstrates the way in which this harsh outback experience changes Cabell into an 'Australian', but there is always the feeling that 'home', 'culture', 'comfort' and the warmth of loving relationships lie in England. Pride at his achievement and shame at its cost are inextricably mingled. This is why Stephensen objected to the book; it was too allied to the 'convict' tradition for his tastes. Yet in its refusal to sentimentalise, its imaginative confrontation with the awful rigours of the pioneer experience, *Landtakers* remains a highly impressive and important work.

Herbert's *Capricornia*, completed by 1932 but not published until six years later, was more to Stephensen's taste. So much so that in these six years Stephensen substantially 'edited' the book, giving rise to a controversy about the extent of his responsibility for the published text which finally appeared under the imprimatur of his own Publicist Publishing Company. In the discussion which follows, however, I have adopted the conventional attribution and written as if Herbert were the sole 'author'.

Herbert was an Anglophobe, and there is no yearning for England here. 'Capricornia' is Herbert's sobriquet for the Northern Territory, and this vast sprawl of a novel attempts to give a portrait of life there from about 1885 to 1930, with all its violent machismo. Central to this endeavour is a confrontation with white racism as it is expressed against Aborigines, half-castes and Chinese. Much has been made of Herbert's outrage at white treatment of Aborigines, and his apparent sympathy for the half-caste in the figure of Nawnim/Norman, portrayed, as his names suggest, as caught between two cultures. But the tonal uncertainty of the narrative renders these issues complex; the tragic is often dealt with in a comic tone. It is true that passages of loud indignation against racism are put into the mouths of some characters, and the narrator also levels irony in the same direction. Yet in the first few pages a metaphor suggests that the conquest of the Aborigines by whites was part of a 'natural' process, and elsewhere the narrator seems to be condescending towards Aborigines. From the perspective of the late 1990s there is also the further worry that Herbert sees Aborigines as 'victims', and that in portraying his central half-caste character as belonging happily to neither Aboriginal nor white society, he is implicitly suggesting that racial 'purity' might be a good.

Not in doubt, however, is Herbert's interest in what Stephensen calls 'race and place' (p. 14). Just as D.H. Lawrence identified the land as 'aboriginal'[58] so in Capricornia Herbert has his half-caste character, Norman, discover his 'Aboriginal heritage' alone in the bush, and another character, Andy, remarks that the 'Spirit of this Southern land' wants 'to keep a bit of the place in its aboriginal glorious wild state and has chosen this here Capricornia for it'.[59]

Another group of Nationalist poets emerged in the 1930s who also wished to investigate the relationship between Australia, the land, and Aboriginality: the Jindyworobaks. Although the movement did not formally come into being until 1938, the three young men who initiated the movement were all writing and publishing earlier in the 1930s. The leading proponent was Rex Ingamells and his first supporters were Flexmore Hudson and Ian Mudie. All three came from South Australia, and, significantly, as Robert Sellick has recently pointed out, all three spent most of their lives in Adelaide. Their contact with Aboriginal people and the bush can therefore legitimately be called into question. Like the city writers creating the bush myth of the 1890s, it is possible to view the Jindyworobaks project as 'the product of an urban need'.[60]

Ingamells had a predilection towards poetry which dealt with Australian landscape, flora and fauna. Reading the first instalment of Stephensen's *The Foundations of Culture in Australia* in 1933 led him back to Lawrence's *Kangaroo* and these formative influences, together with anthropological works like Spencer and Gillen's *The Arunta* (1927)[61] and James Devaney's *The Vanished Tribes* (1929), culminated in Ingamells's statement of Jindyworobak aims in a pamphlet entitled *Conditional Culture* (1938).[62] Like Stephensen, Ingamells stresses the need for a distinctively Australian culture, separated from Europe and based on an acknowledgment of the 'spirit of place' or as he termed it 'environmental values'. Intimately connected with such values was a recognition of the distinctive spiritual quality of the land which was expressed by and through its Aboriginal inhabitants.

The word 'Jindyworobak', lifted by Ingamells from *The Vanished Tribes*, was taken to mean 'to annex, to join' which in turn signified for Ingamells an attempt to come to an 'understanding of Australia's history and traditions, primaeval, colonial and modern' while at the same time 'endeavouring to free Australian art from whatever alien influences trammel it'.[63] This represents an extension and intensification of the nationalism implicit in the work of novelists in the 1920s and 1930s who attempted in their work, however inadequately, to come to terms with Aborigines.

Looked at in the most benevolent light, it is possible to view the Jindyworobak ambition to incorporate Aboriginal words into their poems as an attempt to displace or de-centre the language of the colonising power and produce a distinctively Australian language.[64] Similarly, through their ambition to learn by listening to the land, and notionally at least to the land's original inhabitants, they might even be seen as distant precursors to the political impetus that has resulted in the Mabo legislation.

On the other hand the Jindyworobaks' use of *The Vanished Tribes* as a source book points to several weaknesses in their program. As Sellick argues, the title of this book tellingly reveals the Social Darwinist orientation of Devaney, and by implication his followers. Furthermore, the lack of precise linguistic attribution to the 'Aboriginal' language used by Devaney, and adopted by the Jindyworobaks, threatens to disarticulate the reality of Aboriginal language and experience: 'The language itself was "annexed" and an artificial one created. It is for this reason that the "Aboriginality" that they [the Jindyworobaks] created is a fragile one with only a contingent relationship to the reality of both past and present Aboriginality . . .'[65]

Ingamells and Mudie both joined Stephensen's Australia First party. As its name implies, this was a party ostensibly dedicated to ridding Australia of British influence. Unfortunately, as Craig Munro has shown, it tended towards attitudes more in keeping with European fascism. Flexmore Hudson was more circumspect about this and the use of Aboriginal language. His poetry is often dull and prosaic but is more democratic, and for its time, has some startlingly overt expressions of homo-eroticism. Mudie, whom Xavier Herbert regarded as a 'blood brother' and who from 1934 was a close friend and disciple of Stephensen, is altogether more problematic. He is the most politically strident of the Jindyworobaks, and his poems often have undertones of violence, and what A.D. Hope described as 'traces of the fanaticism of the Hitler Youth Movement'.[66] In this his work encapsulates an irony that Stephensen was also prey to: namely that while denigrating everything not Australian, both of them looked to European fascism for a model. And Mudie's poetry has an odd relationship to European modernism. T.S. Eliot, dismissive of the bourgeoisie and modern democracy, looked back in *The Waste Land* to locate value in the aristocratic culture of the past. Mudie, equally dismissive of twentieth-century realities, invents a pure and primitive past in which to locate his aristocratic values. The difference is in tonality. Mudie replaces Eliot's ennui with a Nietzschean vitalism.

Another strand of inward-looking, anti-democratic intellectual élitism in the 1920s and 1930s was provided by Norman Lindsay. He differed from Stephensen, Herbert and the Jindyworobaks because he was not interested in the Australian bush or its Aboriginal inhabitants. What he had in common with these writers, however, was an ostensible turning away from European modernism because of its decadence, and a celebration of Australian vitalism. That the latter philosophy was in fact derived from Europe was an unacknowledged contradiction in his position. Lindsay's nationalism was similarly contradictory. He insisted that he was not a nationalist, yet sought to isolate Australian creative endeavour from that of other countries.

His major aesthetic principles were articulated in *Creative Effort* (1920, 1924) and provided the platform for the four issues of the magazine *Vision* (1923–24) edited by Norman's son, Jack, and the poet, Kenneth Slessor. The elder Lindsay's philosophy was derived from Plato and Nietzsche, and insisted upon a division between Life and Existence, the former being spiritual, the latter material. Political, commercial and scientific endeavours were said to serve the body—art served the mind. It did so by transmuting the world of the senses into that of 'Beauty, Gaiety and Uprightness'. Rather like D.H. Lawrence, Lindsay converted the Wesleyan Methodism of his childhood into a sexual religiosity which attacked bourgeois morality while at the same time paradoxically insisting upon the spiritual dimensions of the flesh.

The artist, unlike 'the mob' with its 'mob mind', had to do with Life rather than existence. Added to this aristocratic disdain for popular experience was a thoroughgoing sexism, homophobia and racism. Ironically, for all his hankering after the aristocratic, Lindsay could not separate himself from widespread conservative attitudes of the 1920s and 1930s: Lindsay like Stephensen was an anti-Semite.

Apart from his book for children, *The Magic Pudding*, which is dealt with in Chapters 4 and 6, Lindsay's importance to literary history resides in the number of writers, particularly poets, whom he directly influenced. The most significant of these were Kenneth Slessor, R.D. FitzGerald and Douglas Stewart. Slessor and FitzGerald were involved in the genesis of *Vision* and both had early poems published in that magazine. Stewart was a New Zealander who spent some time in Australia in 1933–34, but did not settle in his adopted land until 1938. Thus the bulk of Stewart's 'Australian' output lies beyond the scope of this chapter. Yet, like FitzGerald and Slessor, he plays his part in the perpetuation of the myths of masculinity that are my subject.

Taking his lead from Lindsay, Stewart declared that poetry should be an art that 'presents a heroic image of the life of man'. He also advocated 'arrogant vitality' and 'joyous gusto'. Not surprisingly, then, he is drawn to the outback, to the soldiers, ex-plorers and bushrangers of the popular tradition to find his subject matter. His verse plays *Fire on the Snow* (1939)[67] and *Ned Kelly* (1943)[68] remain his best-known work. The former is based on the story of Scott of the Antarctic. It dramatises the final stages of the journey to the South Pole and the attempted return in which Scott with his four com-panions died. The death of Scott and his men is portrayed as an image of heroic sacrifice rather than an indulgence in needless suffering and self-punishment. The explorers are the type of the soldier, saint and martyr. *Ned Kelly* is a more complex play, in which Stewart is caught between a celebration of heroic action and vitality in the figure of the naturally aristocratic hero, and a conservative morality which sees the Kelly gang as inevitably doomed. What is clear, however, is an unmitigated scorn for any masculinity which allies itself to domestic, bourgeois aspirations.

R.D. FitzGerald's work is less populist than Stewart's, and although it may be allied with the 'vitalist' tradition associated with Norman Lindsay, it is so in a much more thoughtful way. Although the tendency of the work is always towards the affirmation of Life, the poetry itself in its plainness, its abstractions, its tendencies towards prose often has knotty and lugubrious qualities that militate against the 'gaiety' and 'gusto' recom-mended by Lindsay. FitzGerald's work takes on the major themes of Romanticism—the dialectic between flux and stasis, dream and reality, nature and the creative power of memory and imagination are all assayed in verse which shows great technical skill, yet reads as rather old-fashioned and stolid today. The syntactic inversions to maintain patterns of metre and rhyme seem particularly archaic and infelicitous. Nevertheless FitzGerald still has his admirers, most recently Julian Croft, and he undoubtedly plays an important part in the postwar burgeoning of Australian poetry. FitzGerald was also interested in adventure and exploration as templates for heroic masculine endeavour and achievement, as his narrative-dramatic poems 'Heemskerk Shoals' and 'Between Two Tides' amply testify.

The most significant of Lindsay's acolytes, however, was Kenneth Slessor. Born in 1901, Slessor's first published poems were schoolboy effusions about the First World War which expressed aspects of the Anzac myth. Later he served as a war correspondent in the Second War and here, as in his later journalism, he continued to laud the figure of the Australian soldier as the repository of a national ideal.

The popularist and democratic direction of such writing was in conflict with much of Slessor's serious poetry which developed in the 1920s under Lindsay's influence. The early work published in *Thief of the Moon* (1924) and *Earth Visitors* (1926) is characterised by an extravagance of verbal decoration which suggests Slessor's desire to escape the humdrum confines of existence into the immortality of Lindsayan Life. Some of these poems have a tangential relationship to the more aristocratic versions of Anzac masculinity. Just as Baylebridge and others sometimes likened the Australian soldier to the gods and heroes of ancient Greece, so Slessor has Greek gods and other Immortals visiting earth and pleasuring 'serving girls'.

Slessor, however, is at his best when resisting such impulses, and poems like 'The Night Ride', 'A City Nightfall' and 'Winter Dawn', all published in the 1920s, prefigure his later work. Here diction is refined and there is some mild experimentation with form. What is always eschewed is anything remotely connected with the powerful bush myth. Rather, Slessor views both city and bush pessimistically. Following T.S. Eliot, Slessor's city and suburbs are inhabited by the living dead, while the bush is the purveyor of mysterious but potentially annihilating forces.

Like the Jindyworobaks, and so many of the other writers dealt with here, Slessor turns away from contemporary urban and suburban society with disgust, but instead of looking to the bush and 'environmental values' to find an arena of exotic escapism, he turns instead to the eighteenth and nineteenth centuries, especially in Europe, its aristocratic artists and its men of action and adventure. His is a determinedly 'masculine' poetry. 'Five Visions of Captain Cook' and 'Captain Dobbin' are illustrative of his best work. The first of these seeks to mythologise Cook and the 'origin' of Australia. Slessor's poem, though by no means solemn, positively re-enacts the colonial moment and its attitudes; because Cook 'sailed Westabout', Slessor argues, 'men' now 'write poems in Australia'. 'Captain Dobbin' is even more swashbuckling in its relation of the despoliation of the Pacific Islands by men such as Dobbin and his cronies. There is a nostalgia in these poems for masculine adventure and camaraderie. Reading them it comes as little surprise that Slessor supported the Anzac myth so wholeheartedly. And we are reminded of the popular tradition in Australian adventure fiction which has often located its action in the South Seas.

Slessor's greatest poem is 'Five Bells', an elegy for Joe Lynch in which the poet's habitual themes concerning the powers of memory and imagination to combat the passage of time and mortality are given consummate expression. This most successful of poems paradoxically is about failure; the failure of language to adequately re-create Joe, the failure of memory and art to grant immortality or to stay the passage of time. Beyond these ideas Slessor's art met an impasse. Apart from three further lyric poems, two of them arising from his experiences during the Second World War which can be read as footnotes to 'Five Bells', he published no further poetry. Nevertheless, he continued a career as a journalist and 'man of letters' in which his pronouncements about poetry continued to reflect the influence of Norman Lindsay.

Slessor's life and art embody in interesting ways some of the tensions implicit in the ideas and images of nationalism that have been discussed in this chapter. He worked all his life for popular magazines and newspapers—*Smith's Weekly*, the *Sun*, the *Daily Telegraph*—and there is little to suggest that his views differed from their conservative nationalism which was part of, and contained by, the British Empire. He was a 'man's man', enjoying a drink and a punt on the horses; he was chronically ambivalent about women. In all of this he came close to the 'democratic' ideal of one side of the 'Anzac myth'. But in his art he was an aristocrat, hankering after masculine heroes who rose above the ordinary to inscribe themselves in history through the force of their power of imagination. In this he steered close to another aspect of the Anzac myth: the soldier as natural aristocrat.

Nationalism and 'national types' are about the need to create an imaginary community which has defined boundaries. In the texts we have looked at here, various writers have tried to define Australia and Australian-ness, but have been constantly thwarted as their models keep defying boundaries and implicating them in England or Europe or class distinctions or femininity or Aboriginality. The white, male hegemony is seen to be riven with its own internal contradictions. Perhaps the most striking of these is that in attempting to define 'Australia' and 'Australianness' the writers discussed here all travel away from urban, suburban, and even rural domestic life where the majority of Australians live and work to locate an essence elsewhere in the geography of the imagination.

PART FOUR

1940–1965

9

CLEARING A SPACE FOR
AUSTRALIAN LITERATURE 1940–1965

Patrick Buckridge

This chapter is about the development of Australian literature as an institution between 1940 and 1965. It will have less to do with individual writers, readers and works than with political pressures and strategies, administrative structures and processes, group identities and professional associations. But an institution functions, effectively or otherwise, by recruiting individuals, enabling them to act according to its institutional norms, and mediating their relationship to the wider society; thus the experiences of individual writers and readers are likely to provide insights into the workings of the institution as a whole at particular moments in its history.

WRITERS AND READERS: A NEW RELATIONSHIP

In November 1942 a twelve-year-old Sydney schoolboy named Gavin Greenlees won an ABC poetry competition for a poem called 'Rumors', evoking the anxieties of city life in the wake of the invasion scare. It was published in several places, and reviewed favourably and at some length by Edgar Holt, himself a former poet, later the editor of *Smith's Weekly*, and at this stage the literary editor of the *Daily Telegraph*. 'From a twelve-year-old mind', Holt enthused, 'the poem is bafflingly assured, mature, sardonic'.[1] We can judge for ourselves:

> Rumors are going round. Someone saw
> That man sign a paper—
> Absorbing these towns in his signature
> Till, battered and destroyed,
> They are thrown up on some pitted earth
> With sisters of charity moving between the ruins
> And scarred walls making faces at us.
> Someone thought
> That a periscope poked its way through a pile

Of official documents until it reached
The brains of those in high places.
Someone thought that in the bay
The water reddened, and the storm put out
A sword of lightning to warn us.
Someone thought they saw the fingers of a hand
Come out and write upon a wall
A warning in an unknown tongue.
Yesterday the cat was restless,
Staring with his fiery eyes
Into a certain corner of the room.
She was the same way when your mother died.
All these warnings and more have we seen
But because of our good sense we refuse to heed them.

In certain ways the Greenlees poem—its authorship, publication and reception—seems to epitomise its historical moment with some precision. Not just in its congruity of mood with the worst days of the war, but also in the sense that the whole event conveys of literary activities happening in a cultural space lacking anything much in the way of a permanent and dedicated infrastructure, but nonetheless crowded with temporary and provisional forms of support and encouragement. The ABC, the metropolitan dailies, the new literary and cultural journals (some within the armed forces)—all combined to form a peculiarly open and volatile environment for writing and reading that was very different from that before the war, but different too from the situation that began to develop in the 1950s and 1960s, which will be our main concern in this chapter.

An institution may be thought of as 'a more or less coherent set of relationships, beliefs, and practices, usually organised around a specific social function or functions'.[2] The key terms in that definition are 'relationships', 'beliefs', 'practices' and 'functions'. Each term helps to bring into focus a particular dimension of the complex process of change that occurred in Australia's literary culture during and after the war; and each of these dimensions is itself quite complex. 'Relationships', for example, must include those between writers themselves, between writers and readers, between writers and the market, and between writers and the state. How did these various relationships change?

The most important single factor in initiating new patterns of mutual association, mentoring and influence between writers—though it was hardly a 'single factor'!—was the war itself. Depression at home and the contested rise of fascism abroad had politicised many literary intellectuals in the years preceding the outbreak of hostilities, and this had led to the formation of new, more politically engaged writers' organisations such as the Writers' League, and to increased membership and a more militant agenda for established organisations such as the Fellowship of Australian Writers (FAW).[3] But these changes were limited in their nature and scope, and wartime conditions—despite the straitened circumstances they brought to most of the population—provided more motives and opportunities than ever before for individuals to try their hands as writers, and to seek out support and encouragement from others.

Even life in the armed forces provided a fertile environment. The memoirs of writers who joined up, like Donald Horne and Geoffrey Dutton[4]—and the reported activities of others such as the famous hoaxers Harold Stewart and James McAuley, with their accomplice Alec Hope[5]—evoke a range of training and even combat milieux in which literary discussion and experimentation was endemic, stimulated by extended exposure to the company of like-minded people, and invigorated by the presence in Australia of American writers, such as the poets Karl Shapiro and Harry Roskolenko, both of whom (together with the Welsh poet Dylan Thomas) were published by the quarterly arts journal *Angry Penguins* (1940–46).

Up to a point—and for its own morale-building purposes—the army supported and encouraged literary endeavours by the publication (from September 1941) of *Salt*, the Army Education Service's monthly magazine of fiction, reflection and poetry, distributed free to Australian troops. The army also published a series of large-format cloth-bound annuals for sale to the troops and their families at home and abroad, containing a mix of news and photographs from the front, together with—in increasing quantity as the war proceeded—selections of anonymous short fiction, sketches and poetry about combat and non-combat experience.[6] Perhaps the writers' very experience of collective anonymity, combined with the intense emotions and wider cultural awareness war service brought with it, contributed to the surprising breadth and vigour of literary life in the services in the early 1940s.

Outside the services, patterns were also changing for writers. Actual collaboration remained, as it had been before the war, a viable but unusual option for fiction writing, with Dymphna Cusack and Florence James, joint authors of *Come In Spinner* (1951), emulating M. Barnard Eldershaw (Marjorie Barnard and Flora Eldershaw), the best-known of the interwar collaborators. More significant, perhaps, than formal collaboration was the ethos of collective and co-operative endeavour that surrounded the practice of writing in many quarters both during and after the war.

This ethos reached a kind of apotheosis in 1942, in the impassioned calls by Vance Palmer and others for a 'united front' of writers against the invasion threat. Even without that edge of desperation, organised writers dedicated themselves to the task of helping to win the war. In the collection of ABC radio talks, *Australian Writers Speak* (1942), published by the FAW, the reigning spirit is one of group solidarity based less on class-consciousness than on a shared national identity. A typical manifestation was the 'School of Writing' lecture series (1940), organised by the Sydney branch of the FAW, and delivered by a dozen or so more or less prominent writers to teach members of the general public the 'craft of writing' across a range of genres. Literature, it was implied, did not have to be produced by a special 'artistic' class of people; anyone who was willing to learn could produce it.

Not everyone agreed. When Brian Penton, editor of the Sydney *Daily Telegraph* (1941–51), and the novelist Eleanor Dark, were approached to participate in the School of Writing both declined, declaring their belief that literature of any value came from long and solitary self-exploration, and was not teachable by precept and example. It was appropriate, given Penton's opposition to 'collectivising' the literary imagination, that his newspaper should have been responsible for one of the wealthiest (and shortest-lived) individual literary prizes, the *Daily Telegraph* Novel Competition (1946), worth ten times the *Bulletin*'s S.H. Prior prize (1935–46). The *Telegraph* prize was won, in its first and only offering—and even then only after endless unexplained delays—by *Come In Spinner*.[7]

Writers' relationships were further shaped by the emergence, at about the same time, of two literary quarterlies, both of which which have now survived for well over half a century: *Southerly* (1939–), the quarterly journal of the Sydney branch of the English Association, edited by R.G. Howarth, and *Meanjin Papers* (1940–), edited by Clem Christesen, first from Brisbane then, from 1945, from Melbourne, in a sometimes vexed relationship with the University of Melbourne. In their earliest incarnations both journals served as important forums for contemporary Australian fiction and poetry, with literary criticism added in *Southerly*, social and political commentary in *Meanjin*. In the latter journal especially, notwithstanding its regional location in the early years, new and unknown Australian writers were sometimes able to rub shoulders in the same issue with leading contemporary writers and intellectuals from all over the world.

There were thus opposing currents in wartime literary culture as far as writers' relationships with one another were concerned; but a new sense of democratic co-operation and collectivity in writing does seem to have been the dominant note of the period. Relations between writers and readers reflect a similar diversity, but again a dominant form of this relationship does begin to emerge, and is characterised by a high degree of interactive equality.

The most striking manifestations of this occurred in the popular media: in the daily newspapers, for example, where writers such as Katharine Susannah Prichard, Eleanor Dark and Dora Birtles were given space beside other public intellectuals to express their views on political and cultural questions, and where readers were encouraged to reply and to disagree with them. In the newer medium of radio the pattern was even clearer; the famous ABC 'listening groups', formed in 1943 by the Director of Talks, Gabriel Parry, as a way of entertaining services personnel in their barracks in the evening, became very popular with the general public. Throughout 1943–44 the newspapers and the radio joined forces, and Sydney people in large numbers participated in a regular 'hookup' between the two ABC stations and the *Daily Telegraph* in which the big issues of the day were debated across the media.[8]

In fact, the war witnessed a transformation in the relation between writers and readers that might fairly be described as a surge of 'reader-power'. Several factors combined to bring it about: one was the new technological possibilities for interaction and dialogue between writers and their audience, together with new social and political reasons to try them out; another was the change in the dominant image of the writer of literature during the war from that of a 'creative artist', a poet, a gifted shaper of words, to that of a public intellectual, somebody whose responsibility it was—together with other informed individuals and groups—to engage in intelligent discussion and debate on urgent national issues. As the public entered the debates by all the avenues newly available to them, whether by radio, the daily newspapers, the new quarterlies, or the freshly re-animated clubs and societies, readers could imagine themselves writers—and even become them in reality—more easily than at any time since the old days of the *Bulletin* and its 'great print circus'. But the added respect and social relevance writers undoubtedly gained in this process came at a cost, namely the loss of their 'special' status as literary artists, and of their assumed entitlement to recognition and support for the special functions they performed. In other words, writers gained respect, but lost caste.

One measure of the shift in the reader/writer relationship is the distance that separates Vance and Nettie Palmer's assessments of Henry Lawson in the 1942 collection *Australian Writers Speak*: Vance speaks of the 'national values' his work embodies, whereas Nettie's focus is on the subtle intimacy of his bond with the reader, an emphasis A.A. Phillips would echo in his 1948 essay on Lawson's 'craftsmanship'.[9]

Another indication of that same power shift is contained in the famous attack on artistic modernism, the 'Ern Malley' hoax of 1944. In early October 1943 James McAuley and Harold Stewart, two young Sydney poets of classical and scholarly inclinations, spent an idle afternoon in Army Intelligence cobbling together a set of sixteen short, opaquely allusive poems, invented a deceased young poet, Ern Malley, to go with them, and sent them off with a covering letter from Ern's equally non-existent sister Ethel, to *Angry Penguins*, the most self-consciously 'modernist' literary journal in Australia at the time. The youthful editor, Max Harris, flamboyant *enfant terrible* of Australian literary Surrealism, was completely taken in, trumpeted their brilliance, and published them without delay in a special 'Ern Malley' issue.

The hoaxers' intention, which they explained to the newspapers soon after the 'Ern Malley' special issue appeared, had been to expose to public ridicule the lapsed literary standards of *Angry Penguins* and its editor; and in the exposing at least, they were highly successful. Debate about the literary value of the poems themselves, and about the validity of the 'exposure' they achieved, continues to this day, but what is certain is that the hoax marshalled Australian popular sentiment against literary modernism as never before. In doing so it further weakened the autonomy of the literary sphere itself in Australia, in so far as that autonomy rested on the ascendancy of the writer's 'high art' prerogatives over the tastes and expectations of a general readership. The fact that Stewart and McAuley were hardly 'general readers' themselves is ironic, but strictly irrelevant to the institutional effect of their actions. There is a further irony in the fact that McAuley, and an apparent co-conspirator, the poet A.D. Hope, both played crucial roles in re-establishing a different form of institutional autonomy for Australian literature in the following decade.

The Ern Malley affair might be viewed as no more than an unusually lively instance of the perennial Ancients vs Moderns debate, with Stewart, McAuley and Hope scoring a victory for the classical literary values of precision and lucidity against the looser expressivism of the modern movement. What makes it clear, in retrospect, that larger, more directly political forces were also engaged is the almost immediate involvement of the state in the attack on Harris. For the affair did not end with mere laughter and personal discomfiture but with the successful prosecution of Max Harris for obscenity by the South Australian police, a personally and politically motivated charge based on some lines of doubtful meaning in some of the poems.[10] In that sense the affair and its legal consequences were a key moment in the translation of popular philistinism into repressive state power.

THE WRITER AND THE LAW

The most visible attacks on the autonomy of literature after the war occurred in court cases, involving the prosecutions of publishers, or writers, or both, for either obscenity or libel. In one case, that of Robert Close's *Love Me, Sailor* (see p. 176), the two avenues of attack coincided in the obscure charge of 'obscene libel'; but the two were usually distinct, and in practice addressed somewhat different aspects of the question of literary autonomy: how far the writer could be permitted the liberty of 'obscene' language in the interests of 'truth' or 'literary merit'; and whether the writer could be held responsible for fictional resemblances to the real world.

The history of Australian censorship is a long and depressing one. To an observer like Peter Coleman, writing in the early 1960s (on the eve, unknown to him, of a late resurgence), it was a story of progressive emancipation from the shackles of prudery and prejudice, a triumph for the tradition of cultural liberalism.[11] To Judith Brett, writing on the near side of the censorship struggles of the late 1960s, it seems rather that the shackles remained firmly padlocked—certainly in law and often enough in practice—until the development of offset printing gave effect to the determination of younger writers like Frank Moorhouse to bypass the moral 'gatekeepers' in the printing and publishing industries.[12]

During the 1930s matters had reached an extraordinary pass with up to five thousand overseas publications prohibited as illegal imports, including well over four hundred works of world literature (featuring, notoriously, works by Boccaccio, Shakespeare and Daniel Defoe), and a handful of Australian novels, including *Redheap* (1930) and *The Cautious Amorist* (1934) by Norman Lindsay, and *Upsurge* (1934) by J.M. Harcourt. By the end of that decade, though, the struggles of various organisations against the rigid 'moral' censorship of literature had made real headway. Between 1937 and 1939, on the advice of the newly established Literature Censorship Board (1937), the Minister for Customs lifted the bans on about a hundred books, including *Moll Flanders* (1722), *Ulysses* (1922), *The Well of Loneliness* (1928), *A Farewell to Arms* (1929), and *Brave New World* (1932). With the wartime liberalisation of sexual mores, the stage seemed set for literature to assume a more respected and privileged status than it had enjoyed for many years, perhaps since the nineteenth century. In fact, as the intensified assaults of the postwar period show, the institution became more vulnerable to outside pressures than it had been for generations.

The first taste of the legal battles that would follow the *Angry Penguins* prosecution of 1944 came a little over a year later, with the case of Lawson Glassop's novel about Australian soldiers in Tobruk, *We Were the Rats* (1944). Described by Peter Coleman as 'the first case in which an Australian publisher was prosecuted for publishing a serious novel', the Glassop case seems remarkable chiefly for the intransigence of the appeal judge in upholding the magistrate's finding of obscenity in the face of the prosecuting barrister's explicit reluctance to press the matter, of agreement on both sides as to the literary merits of the book, and of protests from bodies as diverse as the Rats of Tobruk Association, the FAW, the Australian Journalists' Association (AJA), the Australasian Book Society, the Newcastle Housewives' Association, and the Acting President of the New South Wales branch of the Returned Servicemen's League (RSL) (pp. 47–9).

Two other features of the Glassop case are worth noting as indicators of the institutional state of affairs for literature in postwar Australia. The first is the defence tactic of 'high cultural' ridicule against the police witness. The following exchange is typical:

'Have you ever heard of Byron?' 'No.'
'He was a Lord.' 'Yes, I've heard of him.'

. . .

'Do you know whether he was a war correspondent?'
'I know he was a writer, but I'm not sure if he was a war correspondent.'
'Have you ever heard of Shelley?' 'I know a man in Sydney named Shelley, but I take it you refer to an author or something.'
'Have you heard of Chaucer?' 'No.'
'Never met him in the Vice Squad?' 'No.' (p. 48)

Similar exchanges had occurred in the *Angry Penguins* case, and they occur in most of the high-profile obscenity prosecutions of the 1950s and 1960s. The legal intention is usually clear enough, and the liberal press has great fun reporting it; but as a defence tactic it has almost invariably failed to impress either magistrates, judges or jurors. It is as if in the very act of invoking, on behalf of writers, the power and authority of 'cultural capital' the law demonstrated that in the courtroom no such power or authority existed. Neither the cultural deficits of the police, nor the acknowledged literary merits of the work, were able to protect literature from the regulatory incursions of state power.

The other interesting feature of the Glassop case has to do with the attention given to single *words*, specifically 'swear-words', in the finding of obscenity. Descriptions of actions and bodies also played a part in the judgment, though in the case of *Rats* such material is restricted to 'extracts from some of the salacious magazines read by the troops in Tobruk' (p. 48). But the police case rested mainly on the use of the word 'bloody', said to be offensive, and on the appearance of two stanzas from one of the more profane recensions of 'The Bastard from the Bush'. To which the appeal judge added, in something of a freewheeling spirit, that 'the dialogue from beginning to end teems with the irreverent use of the name of the Founder of Christianity'.

The focus on the obscene or blasphemous expletive is an oddly recurrent feature of postwar prohibitions and prosecutions, particularly in the censorship of drama—oddly, not just because of the evident hypocrisy, so blatant as to be barely worth noting, of the policemen and judges who professed to be offended by it, but also because it seems so unconnected with the usual rationales for censorship, which speak of the tendency to 'deprave or corrupt' public morality. Max Harris fulminated in 1970, towards the end of a second wave of postwar censorship, that the Australian censors' 'terror of words' was unique, and uniquely embarrassing, in the world.[13] But the phenomenon invites more local perspectives, at least in its early phase.

In October 1948 Sumner Locke Elliott's *Rusty Bugles*, a play depicting the monotony of life in a Northern Territory army camp in 1944, was first performed by the Sydney Independent Theatre. Following complaints about its 'blasphemous language', the play was banned from further production by the New South Wales government. Within a month the expletives were deleted, the ban was lifted, and the play went on to successful seasons in all the capital cities (except Brisbane).

Older members of the Brisbane audience of Alex Buzo's *Norm and Ahmed* in 1969 might thus have felt a touch of *déjà vu* when the police closed down the performance, and laid prosecutions, on the basis of the word 'fucking' (though not the word 'boongs') in the last line of the play. Informing both plays is the working-class 'radical nationalism', the mateship and the larrikinism of armed services culture, so much of which was embodied in the popular lexicon of swear-words, including the Great Australian Adjective 'bloody' (so-called since the nineteenth century). The targeting of such words, at least in the earlier period, can be read as a move to limit the authority of that radical nationalist tradition as a source of mainstream cultural ideals, seeking to replace it with a more staid and proper tradition of civility, a middle-class suburban 'way of life', marked 'not to be disturbed' by profane expletives or by the (sometimes disruptive) nationalist myths they could signify.

But drama, it seems, was not the most dangerous instrument of social subversion; the novel was. And for novelists in the immediate postwar years, the cultural politics turned very nasty. In 1946 Robert Close was tried and convicted in the Victorian Supreme Court on a charge of 'obscene libel' arising out of the publication by Georgian House the previous year of his novel *Love Me, Sailor*. This case too hinged in part on the meaning of a single word ('rutting'), but the unprecedented severity of the sentences—three months gaol and a fine of £100 for Close, and a fine of £500 for the publisher—put the case in a class by itself. In rejecting his appeal to the Full Court, Judge Fullagar drew a revealing analogy between those objectionable elements in the novel that laid claim to literary realism—a visit to a brothel, for example, and the shouting of 'a drunken man in a public street . . . The general sense of a civilised community', the judge explained, 'condemns both' (p. 55). Judge Gavan Duffy took an even harder line, pronouncing that in a case of obscenity the literary qualities of the book are irrelevant because, at least in Australia, 'Literature is not yet a sanctuary or an Alsatia' (p. 54). His Honour's reference was to the old cant name for the London precinct of Whitefriars, formerly a sanctuary for debtors and law-breakers.[14]

Indeed it was not an Alsatia; and it was becoming less Alsatian by the year.

The most spectacular public exhibition of an embattled literature under attack by the combined forces of the state was undoubtedly the 1950 trial of the communist writer Frank Hardy on the charge of 'criminal libel' arising out of the publication of his novel *Power Without Glory*. (Criminal libel is an antiquated charge, quite distinct from civil libel: it is seen as an offence against public order, and punishable by a long prison term.) The severity of the penalty, in the event of a conviction, helped to give the case a high profile, as did the vigorous national and international pro-Hardy campaign conducted by the Communist Party before and during the trial, and it remains an event of crucial importance in the history of literary institutions in Australia.

As Hardy tells it in *The Hard Way* (1961), his account of the writing, publication and prosecution of the novel, the trial was inseparable from the politics surrounding the passage of the Communist Party Dissolution Bill (1950), and the referendum on the question in 1951. Hardy's novel, researched and written over a period of four years, was an exposé, in the style of Upton Sinclair, of the career of a working-class boy from late nineteenth-century Collingwood, John West, who rises to great wealth and behind-the-scenes power by ruthlessly corrupting the police, the judiciary, and politicians of all parties. The figure of West was largely and obviously based on the real John Wren, a legendary figure in Victorian politics, who was still alive in 1950 and could hardly fail to take action. This he did indirectly, by making his wife Ellen the defamed party; the trial then hinged on the relationship between her and her fictional counterpart Nellie West, who commits adultery, rather than on Wren's nefarious activities.

The case was important firstly because it was not, strictly speaking, about censorship but about personal defamation, which meant that cloudy imponderables about the effects of books on public morality did not need to arise (the judge in the case having ruled, contentiously, that no breach of public order need be proven); nor did the proceedings become mired in sterile and trivial semantics, as usually seemed to happen when obscenity was the issue. Instead the case was able to focus quite sharply on the key issue for defamation purposes, that of whether fictional characters can be assumed to represent real individuals—which also happens to be a key issue in relation to the institutional autonomy of literature.

The second important feature of the case was that Hardy, unlike Close, was *not* convicted. This outcome—as unexpected as the analogous victory in the referendum to ban the Communist Party a year or so later—established a beachhead of literary freedom with considerable symbolic and strategic value for rebuilding institutional autonomy over the next two decades. But the situation was not without its local ironies. One was that Hardy himself, though personally relieved by the verdict, was ambivalent about the tactics his lawyers used to get it, in particular the defence argument that the fictional Nellie West did not resemble the real-life Ellen Wren closely enough to be defamatory. Hardy had wished to emphasise the overall truth of his account and to maintain his right to expose it in the public interest, but more pragmatic counsels had prevailed.[15]

Standing behind that was the further irony that for many years the communists and other writers on the Left had been instrumental, through the FAW, the Writers' League and *Meanjin*, in deliberately dismantling the privileged autonomy of literature to enable writers to become more directly involved, as intellectuals, in the struggles against Fascist oppression. For cultural liberals who believed that literature needed to regain some of its privileged autonomy it must have seemed odd to see Frank Hardy in the vanguard.

As Australia's Cold War intensified through the early 1950s, so the attacks on what remained of an autonomous literary sphere intensified also. The atmosphere was one of heightened fear, anxiety and distrust created on one side by events such as the Chinese Revolution, the Korean War, the Petrov scandal, and the Soviet crackdown in Hungary, and on the other side by the Menzies Government's repeated attempts to outlaw the Communist Party, by the victimisation of public servants, teachers, and academics with suspected communist sympathies, and by the activities of the Industrial Groups in the trade unions.

In such a context it was inevitable that writers, too, especially those on the Left, should have felt the blast from the ideological furnace. In the House of Representatives in 1952 the Catholic Labor MP, Standish Keon, joined with the fiery Liberal Party maverick, W.C. Wentworth, in denouncing the members of the Advisory Board of the Commonwealth Literary Fund (CLF) as communist sympathisers. Their denunciation, useful as it must have been to the Menzies Government, did not lead to the full-scale police investigations and browbeating public interrogations of leftist writers that were happening in McCarthyite America in the late 1940s and early 1950s. There was, however, a long-term program of surveillance conducted by the Australian Security Intelligence Organisation (ASIO) against many writers suspected of having leftist leanings, including Judah Waten, Katharine Susannah Prichard, Kylie Tennant and Alan Marshall. There is also evidence that security dossiers were passed to politicians—including, in some cases, the Prime Minister—and used as a basis for questioning and in some cases vetoing CLF grants to writers previously recommended by the Advisory Board.

POSITIONING THE WRITER IN SOCIETY

That matters were no worse than this was at least partly due to the resilience and adaptability of the literary institution as a whole, and in particular to its ability to reconstitute its threatened autonomy in new ways: internally, on the basis of a new 'national' conception of the writer's role; and externally, by means of new kinds of relations with other institutions—education, journalism and the visual arts.

The image of the writer developed in *Meanjin* in the 1940s was at one stage defined with reference to Jean-Paul Sartre's concept of the committed writer's 'responsibility' to his or her moment in history. The concept was expanded in the editorials of Clem Christesen during and after the war to signify the individual writer's responsibility not just to his or her moment in history, but also to the nation, to ordinary readers, and to the art of literature itself.[16] In that series of secondary responsibilities we can sense not only the renewed strength of literary nationalism, reinforced by a resistance to Modernist 'obscurity' and 'difficulty', but co-existing with it a reluctance to abandon completely the privileged autonomy of the aesthetic.

There were signs of a similar reluctance—of an impulse, that is, to preserve a space for literature as 'high art'—on the nation's periphery, in the revived bohemianism of avant-garde formations such as 'Angry Penguins' in Adelaide and the 'Barjai' Group in Brisbane during and immediately after the war. Of the latter group, a 'strangely anachron-istic literary ganging-up', Peter Porter wrote that they 'believed not only in art but in the calling of the artist' (Porter, though living and writing poetry in Brisbane at the same time, 'preferred to practise art behind a front of bourgeois respectability').[17] But in the centres of national cultural authority, Sydney and Melbourne, social realism reigned, and the writer was a worker—an intellectual or cultural worker, but a worker none the less.

In the more polarised political climate of the early 1950s the notion of the writer as intellectual worker continued to flourish on the Left, in journals such as *Realist Writer, Overland* and the *Communist Review*, through the work of such writers as Katharine Susannah Prichard, Jean Devanny, Frank Dalby Davison and Judah Waten. At the other pole we find, in the course of the same decade, two very different ways of reclaiming a measure of institutional autonomy for literature, both of them somewhat hostile not only to the 'left Australianism' of *Meanjin* and the radical nationalists, but also to Modernism.

The first amounted to a Romantic-idealist assertion of the untrammelled authority and sufficiency of poetry and of the universal imaginative truths it expressed. The early poetry of Judith Wright was a powerful articulation of this tendency, and her later book *Preoccupations in Australian Poetry* (1965) gave it the status of a distinct literary tradition, one in which figures like Hugh McCrae, John Shaw Neilson and R.D. FitzGerald, even Norman Lindsay and William Baylebridge, figured more prominently than they had in earlier histories. Institutionally, this Romantic-idealist tendency has not been a strong presence since the war, but the influence of Douglas Stewart, editor of the *Bulletin* Red Page from 1940 to 1961, should not be underestimated; nor, for that matter, should that of a poet-academic like Val Vallis, a wartime protégé of Stewart and a friend of Wright, who taught aesthetics and Australian literature at the University of Queensland through-out this period, proselytising for an experience of art and literature informed by the aesthetic idealism of Kant, Croce and Suzanne Langer and by the intensities of local landscapes and individual relationships.[18]

In a very different way the journal *Quadrant*, established in 1956, also dramatised the separation of politics from literature on which a rebuilt literary autonomy depended. It did so almost in spite of the abrasive right-wing polemics of its founding editor, the poet and critic James McAuley, for McAuley's extreme anti-liberalism 'prevented even conservative writers from fully endorsing his opinions'.[19] Notwithstanding its connections with the American Central Intelligence Agency (CIA), through the medium of the Congress for Cultural Freedom, *Quadrant* was not as ideologically homogeneous as *Meanjin* and *Overland*, and even writers somewhat to the left of centre politically, such as Judith Wright and Rosemary Dobson, used the new outlet for their work, perhaps 'pleased not to have it wrapped in nationalist clothing'.[20] The literary side of the journal, in other words, exhibited at that time a notable independence from its political side (much as the 'Red Page' of the 1920s and early 1930s seemed largely independent of the *Bulletin*'s reactionary populism at that time).

WRITERS' ORGANISATIONS

Writers' relationships with one another during and after the war were channelled through a variety of formations, from loose 'acquaintance networks' (see, for example, Carole Ferrier's *As Good as a Yarn with You* for the letters of a group of six women writers extending into the 1950s) through 'literary societies' of the older, nineteenth-century sort, to more formally constituted bodies such as the FAW and, later, the Australian Society of Authors (ASA). The latter in particular have been active in arguing the value of literature in general, or of Australian literature in particular, and in promoting the professional interests of writers themselves. All three have functioned, at different moments, as ways of clearing a space for literature.

The FAW, founded in 1928, had operated in the years leading up to the outbreak of war as a strong (and surprisingly effective) lobbyist for government patronage for writers. In the postwar years its central strategy changed from seeking subsidies for writers to seeking market protection for them. The change was clearly signalled in the FAW submission to the Commonwealth Tariff Board Inquiry into Book Publication of 1945 in which the Fellowship proposed a tariff on imported books. This was primarily an 'anti-dumping' move, and its failure led to the formation two years later of the Federation of Australian Literature and Art (FALA) to oppose the dumping of syndicated foreign literary material into the Australian market, a move that received support from a wide array of parents', teachers', artists', and journalists' organisations.[21]

If this represented a moment of unified national purpose, it was one that the FAW was unable or unwilling to sustain for long. Regional and decentralised from its inception, the FAW remained fragmented along state boundaries, and attempts to federate the organisation had little practical purchase, despite the eventual establishment, in 1955, of a federal council and a rotating national presidency. To a degree this fragmentation reflected the politics of the Cold War: in 1950 the South Australian branch withdrew in protest at the 'pro-communist bias' it perceived in the other state branches. But it was also a continuation, or resumption, of the studied political *disinterest* (in both senses of that word) of its first seven or eight years of existence in Sydney and Melbourne; and it may have reflected the literary regionalism evident in some anthologies and literary histories in the less populous states, such as Queensland.

In that sense the FAW, fragmented and politically impotent as it may have been throughout the 1950s, did contribute to a restoration of literature's autonomy precisely by placing literature above or outside politics. This stance has usually been understood as deeply complicit with the 'end-of-ideology' thinking associated with the Right: conservative ideology in aesthetic disguise.[22] There is no doubt some truth in this analysis, but it is also true that the notion of literature as 'above politics' could provide a valuable refuge for writers—usually on the Left—who found themselves under threat of suppression or worse by aggressive anti-communism.

It is one of the ironies of this decade in Australian politics and culture that an organisation like the FAW, so scrupulous in its avoidance of political partisanship, and so attentive to local and regional literary issues, should have been labelled a 'communist front'. Yet, in a fairly weak sense, the old-fashioned 'literariness' of the Fellowship in the 1950s may well have promoted certain expectations of writerly independence among its members. By the end of the 1950s, however, writers had begun to feel that their professional and financial interests might be more effectively advanced by an organisation of a different sort.

In October 1962, at a meeting chaired by the Sydney writer Dal Stivens, with delegates from the Fellowship, PEN, the Poetry Society, the Realist Writers' Groups and others, the ASA was formed. Alan Lawson has insisted that, notwithstanding major differences from the FAW in both administrative structure and policy emphasis, 'the inception of the ASA was less a reaction against the existing bodies (the FAW and PEN) than a specialisation of their activities, an increasing professionalism'.[23]

It may be important, though, to stress both the continuity and the discontinuity in this transition: continuity, inasmuch as the ASA, with its attention to the 'bread and butter' issues of making a living as a writer, sought to secure a measure of *economic* independence for writers complementary to the *literary* autonomy sought by the FAW (and the *political* freedom to which PEN had always given priority). All three bodies, that is, were concerned with the autonomy of literature in one form or another. The discontinuity present in the shift of emphasis from aesthetics to economics (setting aside the political) clearly had the potential, realised on several occasions since 1963, to institutionalise disagreement and conflict about the necessity for government patronage and the definition and importance of literary merit. The drive towards institutional autonomy among writers themselves, in other words, has been a multi-stranded and contradictory progress, but one in which a general direction can fairly be discerned.

State Interventions

Of more importance, probably, than the activities of writers' organisations in shaping the institution of Australian literature since the war has been the role of the government, in both its benign and its more hostile guises. Since the establishment of the CLF as a modest pension scheme for retired and disabled writers in 1908, the federal government has been directly involved in the patronage of literature in Australia. In 1939, as a result of agitation by the FAW and the active support of ex-Labor Prime Minister James Scullin, the CLF was greatly expanded both financially, by a threefold increase in funding, and in the range of its activities which now extended to promoting and assisting the production of literature in Australia. As Lawson puts it, Australian literature became, for the first time, a 'subsidised industry'.[24]

The new measures included the award of fellowships to enable writers to devote themselves to writing, usually for a year; guarantees against loss to publishers of approved Australian literary works; financial assistance to literary magazines such as *Meanjin* and *Southerly*; and the funding of an annual course of lectures on Australian literature to be delivered in universities and country towns around Australia.[25] (The inaugural lecture was inauspiciously prefaced by the appointed lecturer, Professor J.I.M. Stewart of Adelaide University English Department, with the announcement that, having been unable to discover any Australian literature worthy of the name, he had decided to lecture on *Kangaroo* by D.H. Lawrence.[26] Subsequent CLF lecturers had better luck!) The lectures were an ingenious and economical attempt to 'encourage students to study the literature of their own country', thereby widening the readership and knowledge of Australian literature by 'seeding' the academy. By 1964 the Fund had managed to persuade three of the seven universities—those of Sydney, Queensland and Adelaide—as well as the Canberra University College, to incorporate the CLF lectures into their undergraduate courses, and so discontinued funding, considering that the seeds had taken root.

In addition to full fellowships the CLF made some grant funds available to writers for research assistance and typing costs. The committee was enjoined to balance 'excellence and equity' in selecting recipients for funds, and to base its decisions on evidence of 'meritorious work'. The application of a 'merit' criterion was a first for the CLF. Before 1939 the individual writer's financial situation, or that of their dependants, was the only criterion applied; which meant that the always contentious issue of literary worth simply had not arisen in this connection. Ever since the merit criterion came into play, however, the issue of 'standards' has been inescapable and frequently controversial, as questions of who judges literary merit, with what credentials and on what basis, have had to be repeatedly addressed.

Dissatisfaction with the Fund's decisions was not unheard-of in its early years: Professor D.G. McDougall, ex-University of Tasmania, was no doubt dissatisfied at the refusal of his application for a pound a week to pay for the bottle of whisky he was required on medical advice to consume each day.[27] But conflict was virtually guaranteed after 1939, not just because of the merit criterion, but because of the changes to the administrative structure of the Fund. Under the new arrangements the single central committee of the Fund was replaced by a two-tiered structure consisting of a parliamentary committee comprising representatives of the three major political parties, usually the party leaders, and a seven-member Advisory Board made up of creative writers, publishers and academics, with specific representation by the FAW for the first ten years. Frank Wilmot, Vance Palmer and Grenfell Price chaired the Board successively during the period under review, and among the ordinary members were Flora Eldershaw, Geoffrey Dutton, A.D. Hope, Douglas Stewart, Kylie Tennant, the drama critic Harry Kippax and the scholar and literary historian Tom Inglis Moore.[28]

The Board's function was, as its name indicates, advisory to the parliamentary committee, which made the final decisions and allocations. The new structure thus amounted to a rather naked imposition of state control over new writing. The temporary independence some individual writers gained through access to CLF funds thus contrasts markedly with the potentially dependent relationship of writers in general which was created by the new structure. The precise extent to which, in practice, decisions on financial assistance were actually influenced by political considerations is a topic of ongoing investigation as more files are declassified and released. The trend of recent research, however, seems to be in the direction of discovering more rather than fewer politically motivated interventions by the parliamentary committee than was suspected even as recently as ten or fifteen years ago.[29]

Some of the political attacks, of course, were conducted in the public arena. Reference was made earlier to the parliamentary attacks on members of the Advisory Board by Keon and Wentworth in 1952. This was not a new issue for Wentworth, who had denounced the award of a CLF grant to Katharine Susannah Prichard in the 1940s, and in 1955 he was still on the trail of left-ish grant recipients.[30] But the 1952 attack was of particular interest, both because it was the most sustained and damaging—resulting in the resignations of the chairman Vance Palmer and Flora Eldershaw, the two representatives of the FAW, which was itself denounced as a communist front—and because in the parliamentary debate that followed Prime Minister Menzies contrived to appear as something of a champion of liberal tolerance and moderation by arguing that 'the CLF had always been apolitical and only concerned with literary value'.[31] As Fiona Capp and others have shown, however, Menzies had acted very differently earlier in the same year when, on hearing that Judah Waten, a communist, had been awarded a grant, he directed that all CLF applicants thenceforth be vetted by ASIO.[32]

Conservative politicians were not the only critics of the CLF. The much-publicised attacks on the Literature Board in the late 1980s carried on a tradition that began in the mid-1930s, with claims by the press that government assistance to writers would simply protect the mediocre at the expense of the few genuinely talented individuals who could make a living. In the late 1940s and early 1950s Arthur Upfield, best known as the author of the 'Bony' series, launched a similar attack on the CLF, and in 1960 the

Sydney novelist Olaf Ruhen (*Naked Under Capricorn*, 1958), writing in the *Observer*, ridiculed the 'Hand-Out System' of the CLF for its fostering of mediocrity and élitism. He was rebutted a month later by Xavier Herbert, and also, more temperately, by two members of the Advisory Board, Douglas Stewart and Tom Inglis Moore.[33]

PUBLISHING

Central to most critiques of the system of government assistance to writers and subsidisation of a national 'literary industry' is a belief that writers should work to develop a more effective relationship with the commercial market than many of them have bothered to do. But book publishing in Australia since the war has not been quite the story of steady productive growth and efficient marketing that might inspire writers with confidence in their ability to go it alone. For one thing, the growth of the industry during the postwar period was far from steady. In 1940, for example, there were 495 titles published in Australia; in 1961 there were still only 612 books published, an increase of less than 24 per cent in twenty years. After a further twenty years the total had risen to 2790, an increase of 350 per cent. To use a different measure, the *value* of Australian publishing doubled from 1961 to 1965; it had doubled again by 1970, and yet again by 1979.[34]

Paradoxically perhaps, the two relatively sparse postwar decades, the 1940s–1950s, were also those in which there was a significant diversification in local publishing. Several small independent publishers were established, including Jacaranda, F.W. Cheshire, Lansdowne, Rigby, and Sun Books.[35] After 1965 all these independents were taken over by overseas or non-publishing interests, leaving Angus and Robertson almost alone again in the field of Australian publishing.[36] But not quite. The important exception was the Australasian Book Society (ABS), a publishing collective set up under the management of Bill Wannan in 1950, and registered as a corporation in 1952, the year in which it published its first book, *Crown Jewel*, by the West Indies author Ralph De Boissière. It was wound up in 1981.

Perhaps we can see the course of Australian publishing in the 1950s as a brave dash for national economic independence, eventually hauled in by the big international publishing corporations, which then provided the capital needed to boost production to unprecedented levels in the 1960s. The 'brave dash' paralleled other strong but temporary 'breakouts' of cultural nationalism in the same decade, in the work of Left intellectuals like Vance Palmer, Russel Ward, and A.A. Phillips, which were similarly hauled in by the internationalism imposed by Australia's colonial ties and Cold War entanglements.[37]

Of these two forms of imposed internationalism in Australia in the 1950s, that of the British Empire and that of the 'Free World', the latter was certainly the more important in a general political and cultural sense, reflecting the hegemonic power of international anti-communist organisations like the North Atlantic Treaty Organization (NATO), the South-East Asia Treaty Organization (SEATO) and the Congress for Cultural Freedom. But as far as the book trade was concerned, the old colonial connection continued to impose a British-centred international order on Australia, one surprisingly little changed since the Ottawa Empire trade agreement of 1932. This was forcefully re-articulated in 1947 in the notorious British Publishing Traditional Market Agreement instigated by Sir Stanley Unwin, and described thus by Alan Lawson:

> a British publisher buying rights from an American publisher automatically obtained rights to the whole British Empire (except Canada); the U.S. publisher was then obliged to cease supplying the book to Australia and to refuse to sell the rights for an Australian edition to any Australian publisher. The British publisher had two years to exercise the rights (p. 276).

Australian booksellers like Max Harris argued long and hard against the Agreement: the privileged access it gave to British publishers, and the impoverishment of Australian book culture that was its inevitable consequence. It was finally terminated in 1974 by the Whitlam Government.

READERS AND READING FORMATIONS

The other side of the coin of an underdeveloped local publishing industry may sometimes be an abnormally developed local readership, insatiable in its quest for literary nourishment from elsewhere. Since before the war, journalists, publicists and academics had regularly attempted to highlight Australia's underlying 'sophistication' with the claim that it was the largest importer of books per head of population in the world. By the mid-1950s Australia was still the largest export market for British books. In 1962, 23 000 titles were imported from Great Britain, some of which were of course books by Australian authors unable or unwilling to publish locally. They included Patrick White, George Johnston, Morris West, Russell Braddon and Jon Cleary.

Local publishing, though, could claim at least one giant national best-seller, *They're a Weird Mob*, by Nino Culotta (John O'Grady), in 1957. Published by the small Sydney firm of Ure Smith, it outsold all other titles, Australian and foreign, for two years, and stayed on the best-seller lists for longer than any other title, even those other best-sellers of the late 1950s and early 1960s, *Peyton Place* (1956), *Dr Zhivago* (1958) and George Johnston's *My Brother Jack* (1964). The unprecedented success of *They're a Weird Mob*, entirely unpredicted by publishers at the time, and only speculatively explicable even in hindsight, underlines the inadequacy of writing and publishing alone as a means of mapping the institutional contours of Australian literature.

I suggested earlier that the cultural power of the reader, vis à vis that of the writer, increased markedly during the war years, and that in some ways that shift left the literary institution as a whole more vulnerable to external pressure than it had been before the war, and than it could comfortably afford to be in the postwar world of Cold War antagonisms and monopoly capitalism. Many of the developments that took place in those years can be viewed as moves towards re-establishing a degree of institutional autonomy for literature in Australia. This model of analysis can be fairly readily applied to the writing side of the institution, to the various strategies by which writers argued and organised—with varied success and against various forms of resistance—to enhance the moral, political and economic independence and status of their profession. In applying the model to the reading side of the institution I shall be exploring the complementary possibility that reading was systematically divested of some of the potentially disruptive and destabilising power it had so recently acquired.

One symptom of a postwar decline in the power of the reader can be seen in the evolution of that most reader-centred of institutions, the library. The ten or fifteen years after the war appear to coincide with a marked hiatus in library services, between those provided by the libraries of the Mechanics' Institutes, the Schools of Art and the Workers' Education Association (WEA), which were heavily used in the 1930s—supporting the kind of radical reading tradition to which the ABS made its appeal—and the growth of municipal suburban libraries from the 1960s. In the interim, reading was served by little more than the remnants of the older library system (especially in rural areas), the big public libraries in the cities (which did not lend books, in the main), and the private rental lending libraries, which became very popular in the 1930s, and were widespread until as late as the early 1960s. Marc Askew comments,

> These shopfront businesses, charging around threepence per loan transaction, providing the latest thrillers, romances, war stories or westerns, became an institution. They were located close to people's homes, they continually updated their stock, they were open at convenient hours, and located in shopping streets.[38]

What they could not do, catering as they did almost exclusively to the taste for popular light fiction, was to support a broadly political and intellectual reading culture such as existed before and during the war, and which may, in a very different form, have arisen again in the late 1960s—supported partly by the new network of municipal libraries, and partly by the (by then) more widely accessible university libraries.

AUSTRALIAN LITERATURE IN THE UNIVERSITIES

The most comprehensive strategy for regulating the freedom, and hence curtailing the disruptive power, of reading in the postwar period was the establishment of 'Australian Literature' as an object of university study and teaching. To call it a 'strategy' is to imply, wrongly, that those involved in the enterprise were motivated by negative or restrictive aims. Those responsible for planning the first degree-level course in Australian literature, offered at Canberra University College in 1955, Tom Inglis Moore and A.D. Hope, were undoubtedly driven by nothing less exemplary than the CLF's mission: 'to encourage students to study the literature of their own country'; to which we can add the further positive motive that they and others no doubt saw in the systematic study of the national literature a way of adding the weight of academic authority to the often contentious decisions on patronage made by the CLF.

The 'collateral effect' of this move, nonetheless, was to delegitimise and thus disempower what might be termed 'free reading' of Australian literature, and to seek to replace it with the kind of *trained* reading that entertained and encouraged no major departures from an emerging hermeneutic consensus concerning the literature being studied and taught—and which could be depended upon to ignore or devalue the books and authors that were not studied or taught. Looking back at the debate 'Australian Literature in the Universities', initiated by A.D. Hope and hosted by *Meanjin* in several issues through 1954–55, it is easy to be surprised at the reluctance of some academic participants, such as Wesley Milgate, the Challis Professor of English at Sydney University, to countenance the inclusion of Australian literature as a separate course in the BA program. Of the main contributors—Hope, Milgate, A. Norman Jeffares, E. Morris Miller and Vance Palmer—only Palmer, that reliable old nationalist warhorse, was entirely unequivocal and unqualified in his support for the idea; this despite the fact that university teaching of the national literature had been established in the United States and Canada, the obvious comparators, many years earlier.

The usual analysis of this state of affairs is conducted in a vein of left-nationalist indignation; the 'cultural cringe' is invoked and condemned, not without some warrant. But it may be that, all things considered, the caution that was expressed at the prospect of a proliferation of stand-alone courses in Australian literature was well placed. If the larger goal was to secure some sort of independent autonomy for the institution in a political environment that had already shown itself only too ready to withhold it, then perhaps consigning the study and teaching of the literature to an oppositional ghetto on the periphery of the established bastions of cultural authority, the English departments, might not have been a strategically brilliant idea. The kind of integrationist model which was favoured by most contributors to the *Meanjin* debate—a few Australian authors being taught in the same courses with English authors—and which had been practised at the University of Queensland under Professors Stable and Robinson since the 1920s, might well have seemed, and been, the safer and wiser path at the time.

Inclusion in the university curriculum nonetheless proceeded fairly briskly through the remainder of the decade, one crucial step in the process being the appointment of G.A. Wilkes as the Foundation Professor of Australian Literature at the University of Sydney in 1962. The establishment of this Chair was achieved by way of a public appeal for funds (£80 000 was needed, and the Federal Government was unhelpful). The appeal was run by a Committee chaired by Wesley Milgate, which also included Colin Roderick, Gwen Meredith, Gavin Casey and Leslie Rees. During an active campaign of press reports, meetings, lectures and articles, Tom Inglis Moore predicted that there would soon be a Chair of Australian Literature in every Australian university—a prophecy that has never looked like being fulfilled. More alarmingly, Colin Roderick urged that teaching the national literature would 'help to keep undesirable alien influences at bay [and would be] one means of defeating some of the nauseous cults that have attracted some of the juveniles of our own generation'.[39]

As Alan Lawson observes, Roderick's statement was remarkable partly for the fact that it ran counter to the doctrine of the ideological neutrality of criticism, a key tenet of the then-dominant discourse of academic literary studies.[40] That discourse derived in part from a post-Romantic understanding of the 'special' non-scientific and alogical nature of literary language, which had been given a particularly emphatic formulation in the work of the American New Critics, some of whose work—that of Cleanth Brooks and W.K. Wimsatt, for example—was very influential in Australian English departments by the mid-1950s. The roughly contemporaneous advent of 'Leavisism' in Melbourne, of which much—perhaps a little too much—has been made in some recent histories of 'English in Australia', is a more complex, if smaller phenomenon, since in his 'left-liberal' guise (calling for a recognition of the social importance of literature) Leavis was invoked by some early representatives of the New Left in the late 1960s; whereas in his conservative guise he effectively reinforced the essentialist dichotomies of the New Criticism, and provided a parallel rationale for asserting the privileged status of the literary and the ideological neutrality of criticism.

Recent commentary has delighted in 'exposing' such doctrines as conservative wolves in sheep's clothing, but it is worth noting that embattled writers of the Left, such as the communists Katharine Prichard and Frank Hardy, made strategic use of them as a refuge from political persecution. Prichard, for example, called for literature to be reviewed 'on its merits, no matter what the political tendencies of that work may be', while Hardy wrote, in defence of the CLF, that it 'should issue grants on the ground of literary merit only, irrespective of the political standpoint of the writer'.[41]

Critical theories, even critical assumptions and practices, do not have unchanging political functions; the politics change with the historical circumstances. Thus, regardless of the ideological functions performed by New Critical or Leavisite theories about literary language in their places of origin, in Australia in the 1950s and 1960s those same theories seem to have functioned not only as a means of depoliticising literature in a typically conservative denial of the political dimension of social and cultural life, but also as an instrument for defending literature against real threats to its institutional autonomy.

That autonomy was significantly enhanced by the 'professionalisation' of literary research and teaching in the universities, which was facilitated, in turn, by the rigour and sophistication attributed to the method of close textual reading, whether of the New Critical variety, or the very similar 'Practical Criticism' associated with Leavis and 'Cambridge English'. In 1957 the newly professional status of the discipline was affirmed in an important *Meanjin* review by John Barnes of a revised edition of J.K. Ewers's 1945 monograph *Creative Writing in Australia*. Barnes criticised Ewers's work as 'limited and superficial', comparing it unfavourably with the professional rigour and sophistication of A.D. Hope's seminal essay, 'Standards in Australian Literature', which had appeared in the *Current Affairs Bulletin* the previous year (1956).[42]

Hope's literary influence throughout the 1950s was immense, not just because of his published criticism and numerous literary reviews for the *Sydney Morning Herald*, but because of his radio work as the main book reviewer for the ABC, succeeding Vance and Nettie Palmer. His importance reflects the unique cultural function he performed rather than the power or coherence of his critical writing, which at times lacks precision and logical rigour, though it seldom lacks venom. Indeed, the very faults of his criticism reflect the importance of his position: the 'Standards' essay is notably ambivalent, in the end, about the competing claims of 'universal' and 'national' values in literature, as is his earlier contribution to the *Meanjin* debate on the teaching of Australian literature; and that ambivalence both revealed and facilitated the link he was making between the cultural authority of the literary academy, site of 'universal standards', and the literary nationalism of critics like Vance Palmer and John Ewers who were not in a position to access the authority of the universities in the same way.

Hope's apparent functions can be described, half-seriously, as those of a trouble-shooter: setting out from his base in the university to bring rigour and sophistication to the potentially disruptive readers outside the academy, who listen to the radio and buy the daily newspaper. Hope himself made a sharp qualitative distinction between 'review-ing', which he regarded as 'a branch of journalism', and 'assessment', which he regarded as the proper task of the academic literary critic, and as something that went beyond 'parochialism' and 'mere journalism'. Yet he produced both, probably more of the former. Furthermore, what he did not write or broadcast himself he often arranged for others of like mind and style to do: James McAuley, Vincent Buckley and Leonie Kramer all reviewed for the *Herald*, having been recommended to the editor J.D. Pringle by Hope.[43]

Hope, then, was a crucial agent in taming and training the general reader of Aus-tralian literature into university-approved ways of reading and evaluating Australian books. In this respect, even the journal that published his 'Standards' essay, the *Current Affairs Bulletin*, is not without a certain iconic significance. It had been an organ of the Australian Army Education Service through the war, and represented the democratic 'sol-dier-centred' pedagogy the AAES had developed. For a short time in 1945–46 it had seemed that the AAES might be redeployed as a peacetime Adult Education organisation. This did not eventuate; instead, the demobbed troops were shoe-horned into university courses where they encountered, in all probability, much more authoritative and hier-archical prescription and training in the reading of literature than they had experienced in the Army.[44]

One side of Hope's task, and that of the universities, was to disseminate a certain way of reading Australian literature. The other side of it was to establish an agreed con-tent, that is, to establish a canon. Hope was very explicit about this part of the brief in several places, but it was the younger Vincent Buckley whose 1959 essay 'Towards an Australian Literature' put the case for a canon most clearly.[45]

The practical outcome of these impulses was not, of course, a clearly defined and de-fended group of Australian works and authors that commanded anything like universal acceptance as the core and essence of Australian Literature. The outcome, in two words, was 'Patrick White'—though not quite so straightforwardly as that suggests. Hope was himself one of White's most trenchant early critics: his famous characterisation of the prose style of *The Tree of Man* as 'illiterate verbal sludge', however eccentric in its neo-classicism, marks a real division in the ranks of the canonisers, between those like Hope and Buckley, on the one hand, who saw their task mainly in terms of critical discrimi-nation, giving Australian readers the confidence to make unprejudiced judgments, and those like Dorothy Green, Harry Heseltine and Arthur Phillips on the other, who saw their task more in terms of defining and articulating the greatness of certain Australian writers, and of giving readers the confidence to think of such writers as genuine classics.

Whatever the reasons why White, rather than some other writer, became the chosen site of attributed literary greatness in the 1950s and 1960s—and this is a point of some controversy[46]—it is not difficult to trace the *process* by which resistance to his canonis-ation, especially on the Left, was either overcome or excluded by a growing liberal con-sensus that White was indeed a great (if not *the* great) Australian novelist. The initial hostility of critics like Katharine Prichard, Judah Waten and Jack Beasley was soon rejected and displaced by the admiration even of Party intellectuals like Jack Blake and Mona Brand, and of Left academics like John McLaren.[47]

The *effects* of White's canonisation are more difficult to pinpoint. One effect may have been to close off the unwelcome possibility of an all-female canon of modern Australian literature, which is what might have seemed to be emerging in the very early 1950s as the work of writers like Katharine Prichard, Henry Handel Richardson and Eleanor Dark was receiving its share of critical praise and analysis in journals like *Southerly*. What it certainly brought about was an overall sense of Australian literature as a centred totality, controlled and maintained by a university-dominated institution, and well placed to stake a claim to be left alone to its own creative and intellectual devices for the foreseeable future.

INTO THE 1960S

By the early 1960s the institution of Australian literature was emerging from a decade or more of Cold War with its autonomy largely secured: Australian literature was being taught at a growing number of universities; writers were well organised to protect their own professional status and financial interests; CLF grants to writers and projects, if not generous, were slowly increasing; and a number of independent Australian publishers were—for the time being—flourishing. In Patrick White it had a great novelist; in Thomas Keneally a promising and popular one; in A.D. Hope and Judith Wright two arguably great poets; and in *The Summer of the Seventeenth Doll* (first performed 1955) perhaps even a great play. Whether by nationalising it, aestheticising it, studying it, teaching it, or ensuring reasonable sales of Australian books and a reasonable income for a handful of writers, Australians somehow managed to 'rescue' the institution from threats to its autonomy posed by the Right and the Left alike.

By 1962 a consensus of sorts had developed among scholars and critics of Australian literature, and within the institution more broadly. Even the lively debate between Harry Heseltine and Arthur Phillips in that year is noteworthy more for the amicable accommodations made on both sides than for any deep disagreement as to the real character of the 'national literary heritage'.[48]

It was also the eve of Australia's largest commitment of troops to any part of the world since the Korean War, but the silence of Australian writers on that topic is noticeable. By 1965 a military draft had been in place for a year, and a number of soldiers had been sent to Vietnam involuntarily. The 'New Left' took the lead in protest activities in Australian universities; but the New Left was largely uninterested in the study of Australian literature. As an institution, it was unable to offer a creative literary response to a long-term public issue of real substance, that of Australia's involvement in the Vietnam War. The 'clear space' it had expended so much organisational and intellectual energy in staking out for itself had so distanced it from the current concerns of Australian society as to make it politically irrelevant. For a minority of writers and readers, this may have seemed like a good thing, but for the majority it is likely to have seemed a deeply problematical position for a national literature to find itself in.

This chapter began with the example of a single, largely forgotten poem by a twelve-year-old boy, written in 1942. We can end with a roughly parallel instance, a largely forgotten novel by a nineteen-year-old woman, published in 1964. The novel was *Harry's Child*, written by Suzanne Holly Jones, a Melbourne university student; and while there are other, more prominent and weighty landmarks with which it would be possible to mark the end of the period—for example, Peter Coleman's 'symposium' *Australian Civilization* (1962), or Geoffrey Dutton's ground-breaking, multi-authored *The Literature of Australia* (1964)—there is a certain appropriateness in the more modest text. In many ways it too embodies key aspects of the institutional configuration of the moment.

The novel is a sophisticated, self-consciously Modernist internal monologue strongly suggestive of Virginia Woolf. The narrator is initially a little girl who grows, in the course of the novel, to the age of about nineteen. The theme is her developing relationship with her stepfather, who raises her as a single parent, and whom she gradually realises is homosexual. The book was published by the Queensland-based firm of Jacaranda Press, and it was received at the time with considerable national fanfare, featuring enthusiastic testimonials by Judith Wright (one of the readers of the manuscript), press interviews and articles, and confident predictions of a great future for Jones as a writer. These came to very little: Jones published one more novel ten years later, and has been silent ever since.

What *Harry's Child* tells us about the state of the literary institution in 1964 is that it was capable of developing and supporting significant work by a young writer in a more systematic way, at least in the short term, than it had been able to do in 1942. It hints, perhaps, that that capacity has been achieved through a co-ordination of cultural forces and relations: university English departments, independent publishing houses, informal literary mentoring, and sustained press publicity. Few of these were available to Gavin Greenlees in 1942, but he did manage to write about what was happening around him, and to him, in Australia at a particular moment in history; and he was applauded for it. Suzanne Holly Jones was applauded for writing about what was happening to her, but hardly around her, in Australia in 1964—and the institution did little more for her in the longer term than it did for Gavin Greenlees.

10

FICTION IN TRANSITION

Carole Ferrier

'The novel is the organ of becoming, the voice of a world in flux',[1] comments a character in Barnard Eldershaw's *Tomorrow and Tomorrow* (1947). This chapter will look at some of the ways in which this might be the case for fiction in a period of complex and shifting intra-national and international relationships for Australian writers. Leonie Kramer, in her Introduction to the 1981 *Oxford History of Australian Literature*, invoked 'the desire to explain how one arrived where one is, to search the memory for clues to one's sense of identity, and for the moulding and defining conditions that have produced it'.[2] But one doesn't necessarily arrive at the same place as Kramer, or want to lament as she did that this search produced, for most of the writers of the period, a 'sacrifice of artistry to mundane detail', that: 'Other things, such as the relations between workers and bosses, or black and white, or rich and poor, become more important (especially for writers in pursuit of a social and political theory)' (p. 18).

At the end of the 1930s, where I take up my story, let alone at the end of the 1970s, class struggle, racial tension, gender conflict, and capitalist relations of production fracture bourgeois constructions of the universal 'one' that Adrian Mitchell, upon whom Kramer cast the mantle of maintaining Western values for the 1981 'Fiction' section of the *Oxford History*, also sought to sustain, in declaring that 'The "divided loyalty" of the Anglo-Australians is not geographical schizophrenia, but a restless search for the abiding city. The loyalty in question is not to the ancestral past but to the essential self and the truth of humanity' (p. 144). What kind of 'humanity' could be observed by novelists through the 1940s and 1950s in Australia, and how did the 'essential self' interact with that society and with a world in flux? Mitchell, like Kramer not sympathetic to their preoccupation with this question, represents the 1940s and 1950s as 'in fiction emphatically' the 'time of journalistic realism, whose dreary, dun-coloured offspring Patrick White was to complain of' (p. 128). It is in fact White's simultaneous engagement with the 'dun-coloured' and the metaphysical that gives his texts, notably *Riders in the Chariot* (1961) which comes at the end of the period I discuss, their peculiar force.

BETWEEN PLACES

Removal, dis-location, whether briefly or semi-permanently, from their countries of origin and their perceived roots—whether these were in Australia or elsewhere—loom large still in this period for many Australian writers. Indifference towards artists, the lack of a fertile environment for art to develop, and very limited audience and publishing outlets are frequently commented upon. In 1938 Marjorie Barnard and Tom Inglis Moore had approached the Vice-Chancellor of the University of Sydney, Dr Wallace, about founding a Chair of Australian Literature, and encountered 'a sort of professorial impression that there wasn't any'.[3] It has been suggested that this situation produced a particular kind of public sphere:

> the non-institutionalised nature of the field of Australian literature at the time meant that sanction for critical endeavour was granted not by the academy, but by the marketplace, where their status as writers functioned as the single most appropriate qualification for the position of critic or literary intellectual.[4]

Barnard and Eldershaw, like Nettie Palmer, did indeed continue to be publicly and privately influential through this period, even as a more formal sphere of 'criticism' began slowly to emerge in the academy. In 1939 Xavier Herbert wrote to the Palmers—perhaps with a degree of hyperbole, for he hoped to impress them before he met them—telling them that they were 'the potential liberators of Australian Literature from the ignominy in which it is doomed to languish always'.[5]

The Palmers had certainly made a strong commitment to the fostering of Australian literature on their 1915 homecoming, but they were not alone in this at the time. Katharine Susannah Prichard (1883–1969) had spent six years in Europe (with a brief sojourn in the United States) on two visits between 1907 and 1916, but then deliberately returned from Britain. Scots-born Louis Esson, whose travels in 1915–21 had included Ireland, returned to Australia determined to bring with him the lessons learned at the Abbey Theatre. These symptomatic examples suggest a dwindling of the assumption that the way home was the way to England as 'the mother country'. The novels of Martin Boyd (1893–1972), like his life, epitomise the increasingly problematic nature of the notion of England as a longed-for 'home'. *The Cardboard Crown* (1952) in particular, like Henry Handel Richardson's earlier *The Fortunes of Richard Mahony*, suggests that even at the turn of the century (the time of its setting) such longing had become pretty much an upper-class affair, very different to the enticement of 'seeing the world' that sent many young Australians abroad in the 1950s. If England remained the chosen destination for many of those who went away in the 1930s and after World War Two, their search was more for the opportunities offered by difference than for familiarity. Europe also beckoned, and Christina Stead (1902–83) followed the earlier path of Miles Franklin and spent long periods in the United States.

Among those who could be seen as inveterate expatriates, Henry Handel Richardson had remained overseas since 1888. She initially studied music in Leipzig before settling in London, and returned only very briefly to Australia. Stead, similarly, left Australia for London as a young woman in 1928 and resumed residence in Australia only in her old age, in 1974. While *The Man Who Loved Children* (1940) and *For Love Alone* (1944) recreated aspects of her own earlier life in Sydney, the former was transposed to the United States in order, she said, 'to shield the family. I mean it would have been a bit too naked'.[6] An American setting did not, however, prevent her next novel *Letty Fox: Her Luck* (1946) from being banned in Australia (until 1949) because of the exploits of its liberated heroine.

Jean Devanny, when she left New Zealand in 1929, intended to go 'Home', believing England to be a more favourable location for a novelist. Australia was to be merely a transit point but, in the end, she remained in Australia apart from a visit in the early 1930s to the Soviet Union and Europe. Several other members of the Communist Party of Australia (CPA) went to Russia or other centres of Party activity before the Second World War, including Katharine Susannah Prichard in 1933. For Prichard and Devanny, the making of such visits—and the return from them—was part of their double commitment, as activists and writers, to residence in Australia. This was an emphasis encouraged by the postwar CPA, whose members also included Judah Waten, John Manifold, Eric Lambert, Frank Hardy and Dorothy Hewett.

Common to the orientation of almost all the writers of this period is a simultaneous acceptance (even idealisation) of 'natural' Australia, and a discontent with social Australia. In *Waterway* (1938) Eleanor Dark (1901–85) has the young writer, Lesley Channon, meditate on earlier migrants' impressions of the Australian continent their ancestors had attempted to occupy: 'Hostile—no. It had never descended far enough from its majestic aloofness to be hostile. There it was, here it is still, untouched. Not it, she thought, but we, its invaders, have changed'.[7] Franklin returned permanently in the early 1930s, but remained ambivalent about doing so. *My Career Goes Bung*, an earlier work eventually published in a revised form in 1946, still shows, to some extent, 'how impossible the Australian scene was for novel-making',[8] although the artist-heroine's progress in this later work is a little more possible than it was at the end of *My Brilliant Career* (1901), or in *Cockatoos*, another early work late-published (1954). A character in that novel laments that 'they all go away—all the young ones with any promise . . . They stream away like the book of Exodus when they ought to be coming here to the promised land'.[9]

Marjorie Barnard (1897–1987), in discussing Franklin's own earlier departure, quoted (inaccurately) about those who left, 'they could not stay but it was grief to go', the line in *Cockatoos*.[10] She went on to comment that some 'fell by the way like Ignez, the girl who never came back. Miles was nearer to Ignez than to any of her other characters but she did come home again to Australia and to writing' (pp. 79–80). Barnard herself, apart from a relatively short voyage to Europe with her mother, would be for a long time one of those who remained, in Modjeska's phrase, 'exiles at home'. Only much later, when she had stopped writing fiction (apart from the still unpublished *The Gulf Stream*) would she travel extensively through Eastern Europe and parts of Africa, the Middle East and Asia.[11]

The return of Patrick White (1912–90) to Australia in 1948, soon after the end of the Second World War, was not much noticed and his work—along with his unflattering perceptions of the culture of his native land—remained largely unknown until after the 1955 publication of *The Tree of Man*.[12] In 1956 he was interviewed by Kylie Tennant in the *Sydney Morning Herald*,[13] and the first essay on his novels (by Barnard) appeared in *Meanjin*.[14] Martin Boyd had been more peripatetic: he returned in 1947 from one of several European sojourns but lived in Europe from the early 1960s until his death. As with White, recognition in Australia was slow in coming, gradually developing from 1949 till the mid-1960s, when he was judged by some to be one of Australia's finest novelists, and claimed a place with White on the reading lists of emerging university courses in Australian literature. There were similarities in the two men's backgrounds, careers (and, indeed, sexualities) but differences in their sense of sociability are reflected when Boyd notes of White: 'apparently he was cold and unhappy at his school in England while I was warm and full of poetic delight at mine in Australia'.[15] Boyd's representations of class display neither the savage satire that can be found in White nor the latter's ideal-isation of the squattocracy of Rhine Towers in *Voss* (1957), although Boyd's reservations about that novel seem not to have been related to this aspect: 'At first', he said, 'I thought it impressive in spite of [its] rather affected style, but I found it too morbid'.[16]

Boyd's *Lucinda Brayford* (1946) suggests parallels between Australia and Britain in relation to (mildly satirised) class attitudes. Lucinda's parents act as though they believe that the 'relentless acquisition of money, and . . . resolute social activities' in which they engage 'had nothing to do with pleasure, but served some deep if obscure moral purpose, that they were almost a reflection of the Divine Will'.[17] Her husband Hugo's mother, Marian, likewise conveys 'the impression that English gentlepeople did not live in houses with gorgeous ceilings and gilded chairs for pleasure but only from a stern sense of duty to the lower orders' (p. 156). Lucinda's British brother-in-law, Paul, comments on how she must be experiencing 'the excitement of finding yourself in the living stream of cul-ture'. He continues: 'I imagine that Australia is rather out of it. It must be imported, not inherited and continuous' (p. 154). Paul's views on other topics resemble middle period Lawrencean ones: 'The artist and the aristocrat are the only people worthy of consider-ation . . . the rest of mankind should function to make their existence tolerable' (p. 159). Paul has a homosexual relationship with his manservant, Harry (p. 292), and, like Clifford Chatterley, believes: 'Hitler and Mussolini are only the counterpart of Bolshevism . . . We're witnessing the suicide of civilisation' (p. 491). Another Lawrencean parallel is Lucinda's later relationship with Hugo after he has come back wounded from the war. A little earlier, Lucinda has experienced 'the feeling that everywhere was a pervading disintegration' (p. 326).

In discussing why writers who appear to reproduce conservative ideologies might still be worth reading, Engels developed what has come to be known as the 'Balzac paradox'—that writing about the decadent bourgeoisie has value because it must show the inevitable decay of such culture. Boyd's writing from this period can usefully be read in such a way. *The Cardboard Crown*, which he described as 'my one real book',[18] can also be read as postmodernist before its time in its mobilisation of multiple perspectives on the past, including some drawn from the diaries of his grandmother, Emma à Beckett. But there is also much in Boyd that continues an Australian tradition of celebrating landscape. *The Cardboard Crown* records 'that feeling one has in the Australian countryside, that it has known the morning of the world'.[19] Eve Langley's *The Pea-Pickers* (1942) had provoked such a response in Patrick White. Reading it in England, he said, 'I . . . was filled with a longing for Australia, a country I saw through a childhood glow . . . I could still grow drunk on visions of its landscape'.[20] On his return, however, one of his main impressions was of 'the Great Australian Emptiness, in which the mind is the least of possessions' and in which 'the march of material ugliness does not raise a quiver from the average nerves'.[21] A character in *Southern Steel* (1953) similarly perorates, with sentiments characteristic of its author, Dymphna Cusack (1902–81): 'who cares for history and culture in this profit-gluttonous country?'[22] while Elizabeth Harrower's *The Long Prospect* (1958) includes this reflection:

> What the fuss was about Europe few Australians could imagine. Not all of them believed in its existence. To be one of the self-critical minority was to be not so much politically unsound—for there was very little, it seemed, to be political *about*—as thoroughly, disagreeably un-Australian.[23]

There are, then, varieties of expatriate experience: some writers travel abroad meaning to stay away, others are simply visiting; for some to arrive in Australia is to come home, for others it is to arrive into an expatriation in which their migrant voices become heard as a new strain in Australian writing. David Carter has suggested that Vance and Nettie Palmer 'welcomed migrant writers as signs of "national" and democratic or populist cultural activity all over the world even as they welcomed them also as part of the developing project of Australian literature'.[24] Themes of exile and displacement—important in earlier periods but less so during 1919–39—re-emerge in fresh forms and, as articulated in particular by non-Anglo-Celtic migrants, take on different emphases, such as can be heard in the work of Ralph de Boissière (1907–), who moved to Melbourne from Trinidad in 1948 to escape political persecution, or Walter Kaufmann (1924–), who came as a German Jewish refugee in 1942 and wrote of his experiences in Nazi Germany in *Voices in the Storm* (1953).

A major literary figure of this kind was Judah Waten (1911–85). Although he had arrived in Western Australia with his Jewish parents in 1914, and had early ambitions to write, his period of influence began when he abandoned modernist models and wrote of his childhood background in the stories told in *Alien Son* (1952). The Australian experiences of Jewish migrants are also his subject matter in *The Unbending* (1954) and *Distant Land* (1964). The latter opens with a Jewish couple, Joshua and Shoshana, arriving in Melbourne from Poland in 1925, and moves on to the period of the war during which Joshua takes an increasing interest in the position of refugees, having heard firsthand accounts of Dachau. His social concerns are often not matched by other characters in the novel. Shoshana makes wartime profits by buying up stock for their emporium and undercutting other trades, while Jewish leaders are represented in the novel as urging a degree of quietism, agreeing with Joshua's uncle Berel that 'We mustn't lose our heads'.[25] When Joshua goes to see a member of the Jewish Advisory Board he is told that British and American Jewish leaders are of the opinion that 'Once Hitler has dealt with the Communists and other subversive elements and begins to feel secure in his office . . . he will cease his excesses' (p. 87).

As a counterpart to the diversities of Jewish ethnicity raised by Waten and taken up in White's character of Himmelfarb in *Riders in the Chariot* (1964), Jean Devanny's depiction of German Australian characters in *Roll Back the Night* (1945) recalls some of Lesbia Harford's preoccupations in *The Invaluable Mystery*, discussed in Chapter 6. Indeed, for many in Australia, as elsewhere, the recurrence of worldwide warfare produced both an overwhelming sense of *déjà vu* and a deeply anxious desire for some sense of security in the years that followed: much of the literature of 1939–65 bears the imprint of this.

BETWEEN WARS YET AGAIN

The period this chapter covers begins and ends with the dispatch of Australian troops to participate in two wars which demonstrated with an increasing clarity a relative ascendancy of American alliances and influences over those of Britain or Europe. In the Second World War Russia was for most of the time an ally against fascism on the European Front, while American intervention in the Pacific was decisive in ending the war with the detonation of atomic weapons in Japan. In the 1960s conflict the United States, strongly urged on by the Australian government and supported by the Australian army, would engage in an undeclared war against communism in Vietnam, a war from which it would eventually be forced to withdraw.

According to Nettie Palmer, many writers had felt a sense of impending turmoil from the time that the European struggle with fascism took on a military aspect in Spain in July 1936. She reflected in 1939:

> Perhaps a painter or a musician can cut himself off, in his work, from what is going on around him, but a writer can't. I remember thinking, when we came home from Europe [in 1936] that our writers were trying to do just that, but lately all I know have had this sense of the ground quaking beneath them as acutely as I have.[26]

Kylie Tennant's *Ride On Stranger* (1943) moves through the late 1930s to the outbreak of war and the enlistment of many Australians. Among these is the recently married husband of Shannon, the main protagonist, who is left behind on their farm, part of 'the generation between two wars, a generation which was being wiped out'.[27] Shannon meditates: 'Perhaps this war was a desperate gap in the minds of men through which the darkness had pushed its way. The madness she had noticed, the avoidance of children, were both signs of a contest between the will to live and the circumstances which made that living intolerable' (p. 298). It may seem surprising to find a novel quite so resistant to the idea of going to war published in 1943, although the fact that it was 'fiction' (and perhaps the fact that she was a woman) may have offered something of the partial and paradoxical immunity Tennant (1912–88) had discovered in relation to the political censorship of the 1930s: 'I've put my ideas in the form of novels, because back in the Depression you couldn't get the truth published unless it was a lie',[28] she commented in 1962.

The outbreak of war and consequent enlistment decisions and dilemmas feature in many of the novels produced during or just after the Second World War. Prichard's *Winged Seeds* (1950) records the moment when, on 3 September 1939, 'Australia also is at war' was beamed out from radio sets across the country. White's narratorial voice in *The Tree of Man* (1955) recalls it like this:

> It was all very impermanent and inebriating in the Grand Railway Hotel the day the news came, with a train coughing at the platform outside, and the smell of trains, which made men feel that they were going somewhere, that they had been waiting to do so all their lives, and whether it was to be terrible and final, or an exhilarating muscular interlude to the tune of brass bands would depend on the nature of each man.[29]

Sally Gough's family in the second and third volumes of Prichard's goldfields trilogy, *Golden Miles* (1948) and *Winged Seeds* (1950), have much less control over their experience of warfare than is implied in White's concluding phrase; Sally's son, Lal, has been killed in the First World War, another son, Dick, survives only to die later in an industrial accident and her grandson, Bill, is killed in the Second World War.

In the goldfields trilogy and *The Tree of Man* the narration remains behind in Australia with the women, and those who did not go. The same is true of Franklin's *Cockatoos*, in which Ignez reflects on her aunt Rhoda, who has raised her son to be a soldier: 'She thought her darling son looked lovely in uniform, a short-distance intelligence that could not visualise his going far away to kill the lovely darlings of other women'.[30] Eric Lambert's *The Twenty Thousand Thieves* (1951) does visualise the going far away, and follows Australian and other troops to Palestine in 1941. Soon after his arrival, one such soldier, Dick Brett, is 'fiercely aware of being an Australian soldier and for the first time believed whole-heartedly in the legends of the terrible, laughing men in the slouch hats',[31] but the account of the military prison in which Dooley spends some time indicates that not all were eager. The guards make 'military boob so bloody terrible that no one ever wants to go back again. They've got to, otherwise half the army would be getting itself in boob to have a bludge or keep out of the line' (p. 283). There is, none-theless, a certain glamour to some of the representations of fighting. Towards the end of the novel, the Communist Party member, Sullivan, in discussing Dooley's experiences, draws a parallel with their earlier lives during the Depression and the way they were policed as civilians, but still argues for the Party line about the main enemy: 'We're fight-ing to protect what little democracy we've got from fascism' (p. 363). Several other war novels appeared in the 1950s, including T.A.G. Hungerford's *The Ridge and the River* (1952), and David Forrest's *The Last Blue Sea* (1959).

Embedded in Barnard Eldershaw's *Tomorrow* is a historical work that opens in 1924 in 'the antique form of the novel' (p. 44), although by its conclusion at the end of the Second World War it 'seems to have bogged down in world history' (p. 342). Knarf, its 24th-century author, imagines back historically to the soldiers' wartime experience:

> within a generation they were fighting throughout the world, for what they scarcely knew, for brave words and a coloured rag, for things that were only names being already lost. They fought with tenacity and élan, the bravest of the brave. Or was that the incurable romanticism of history? (p. 10)

THE WAR AT HOME

As Cusack's *Southern Steel* reminds us, it was only in the Second World War that 'Bombs on your own country' (pp. 2–3) were experienced by Australians. As in Dark's *The Little Company* (1945), air raid warnings are the context of a married man's affair with a younger woman, and add an extra frisson. *Southern Steel* is set in Newcastle and it is out-side that city that Lance Sweetapple's ships are torpedoed twice. On the second occasion he is fatally wounded, but life goes on with his wife Anne's pregnancy, counterposed to a rather surreal abortion undergone earlier by her friend Mona (p. 202). In Tennant's *Ride On Stranger*, Olly has a botched abortion resulting in death; women like her are, in Shannon's view, 'the broken spears of the revolution against the future, who had said "Stop" to a Juggernaut' (p. 188).[32] At the end of the novel, Shannon takes in an un-married mother and a pregnant cat, as Tennant strives for a positive or, at least, a com-paratively unideological ending.

Come In Spinner, jointly written by Cusack and Florence James (1904–93), gives an even bleaker picture of wartime conditions. When published in 1951, albeit in a censored version, it was attacked by the *Daily Telegraph* critic who, James recalls, 'was not alone in wanting to keep the rackets and the greed and the ugliness of wartime Sydney hidden beneath the good-time surface'.[33] The book focuses on a group of women who work in a beauty salon. There is much drinking, many assignations with American servicemen, and the fiancé of one beautician loses all their savings at baccarat. The young sister of another beautician is saved from a brothel in which she has been naively entrapped. When she goes to court, her family is told by the judge: 'The children who are passing through here now—boys and girl—are as much victims of war as if they'd been hit in an air raid' (p. 551). Later in the novel, the sister of a third beautician dies of an illegal abortion and this event provides something of a touchstone of integrity among the women in that ideologies of respectability are counterposed to working-class solidarity.

The melodramatic wartime world of Xavier Herbert's *Soldiers' Women* (1961) is much more unrelievedly squalid. Rosa stars in a particularly lurid abortion scene: 'What was to be seen was in the bathroom, a narrow cell ablaze with glitter and gleam of china and chromium. The witch knelt crumpled, fainting on the tessellated floor. All bloody at her feet lay the adder-thing, winking its wicked eye'.[34] This bizarrely misogynistic novel also makes some reference (unusual for the time) to lesbian relationships, usually displaced by the ubiquitous American servicemen. Jean Devanny's *The Virtuous Courtesan* (1935) was one of the first texts with an Australian setting to show homosexual and lesbian characters, but it was published in New York and banned in Australia until 1958. Richardson's last novel, *The Young Cosima* (1939) had been, Dorothy Green notes, 'treated with scant sympathy by Australian critics, even by Nettie Palmer' (p. 425). Although this may be partly because one main character is the uncongenial figure of Wagner, it may also have been because of the (albeit discreet) presentation of a homosexual attachment between him and Bulow, Cosima's husband. Richardson commented in a letter in 1939:

> I ought not to have rapped out the word "homosexuality" in my last letter. I'm apt to forget the jar it may give. My excuse is I read Freud and his works so early in life—before his name was even known in England—that his themes have become commonplace to me.[35]

Heterosexual relationships, including adventures less gothic than those of *Soldiers' Women*, are troublesome enough for the characters of Eleanor Dark's *The Little Company*. Some contemporaries perceived this novel as aberrant in appearing relatively unmarked by the effects of the war. Franklin described it as 'a thin dissection of thin people [that] could exist only in this isolation while the world was so upheaved'.[36] Dark's characters, however, are certainly not unaware of upheaval. Her male protagonist, Gilbert, is exasperated by his wife's attempts to provide him with an 'escape' from turmoil in a mountain retreat:

> Could he tell her that he carried the world in his mind, that no matter how profound the silence she provided for him it was still clamorous, that those clamours, that "disturbance" were the ingredients of his craft, that he could not shut them out, and would not if he could?[37]

The several characters who are novelists—and Dark is one of the very few at this period who is brave enough to make her artist figures as close to home as writers—all have a sense of struggling against their times, of experiencing 'creative paralysis' (p. 152). As Gilbert puts it to Elsa Kay, his fellow novelist (and unhappy lover): 'Writers live on their times; they have no material except the life around them . . . So when that life doesn't accept them fully, or recognise them as contributors, it throws the whole burden on them, instead of taking half itself' (p. 152).

Gilbert's fears of 'a dark future . . . the gathering gale of barbarism' (p. 18) may speak for Dark. Modjeska's introduction to the Virago reprint suggests that there were things that could be thought and said in the 1940s but not in the 1950s, arguing for a closing off between these decades: 'Within five years of the publication of *The Little Company* the literary and political climate had changed sufficiently to leave virtually no space for such a novel' (p. xviii). She suggests that Dark stopped writing in the 1950s (publishing only the rather slight *Lantana Lane* in 1959) because the climate was not one in which she could intervene. On the other hand, some things did change for the better for writers between 1940 and 1965, the dates of the first and second publication of Stead's *The Man Who Loved Children*; as Hooton reminds us, 'it sank after its first publication' but was later 'received as a text of international stature'.[38] By contrast, Langley's *The Pea Pickers* (1942), though reprinted three times by 1966, 'made hardly a ripple in the general literary consciousness'.[39]

HISTORY AND NATIONAL CONSCIOUSNESS

Local attempts to produce a convincing picture of Australian cultural identity were reported with cynicism by some writers of this period. One of the targets of Tennant's attack on intellectual pretension in *Ride On Stranger*, for instance, is the patriotic depiction of 'Australianism' attempted by Emma Brewster and her artist colony:

> 'The Growth of Australianism', which Mrs Brewster hoped to present on a series of motor lorries next Eight Hour Day, was her most ambitious effort to date. It included a tableau of the Native Culture, decorated with boomerangs and spears and primitive works of art; and since certain [A]boriginal half castes who had been approached had held out firmly for trade-union hours and pay, the male members of the colony were forced protestingly into the part of [A]boriginals defending their culture in a coat of blacking and a loin-cloth. No one wanted to be the Spirit of Eureka Stockade, because Mrs Brewster had planned her pageant so that the Spirit of Eureka, clad in a flag of the Southern Cross, was held aloft in the brawny arms of several gentlemen who always complained about the weight (p. 99).

Many of the novels of this period, especially the wide-ranging historical sequences, address themselves more seriously to the question of history. Dark opens her Preface to *The Timeless Land* (1941) with the injunction: 'This book has borrowed so much from history that it seems advisable to remind readers that it is fiction'.[40] Humphrey McQueen has suggested that 'the task of writing Australian history had hardly begun in the late 1930s' and, rather than agreeing with those who have construed Dark's novel as 'a comforting tale of nation building', he finds it subversive.[41] Subversiveness could be read in Dark's attempt to reproduce the reactions of Bennilong to the white invaders, and his meditations upon how the history of their arrival (and ambivalently viewed expected departure) might be recorded (pp. 84–5), or in her representation of the convict Andrew Prentice who expects a rebellion of his peers to bring about 'the inevitable downfall of at least one small section of the class he hated' (p. 93). Later, escaped and living in the bush with an Aboriginal woman named Cunnembeillee, Prentice ponders the condition of the Aboriginal people: 'Were they still being taken in by friendly words, beads, looking glasses, smiles?' (pp. 466–7).

Dark's Preface to *Storm of Time* (1948), the second novel in the trilogy, asserts that the story is 'historically as accurate as I could make it, though there are certain incidents the full truth of which will probably never be known'.[42] Governor Hunter's impression is that 'the immemorial layers of the English hierarchy showed a disconcerting tendency to melt into each other like alternating stripes of wet paint' (p. 19). Conor Mannion thinks that 'there were no barriers here: things came close about you—close, clear, demanding, not to be ignored' (p. 127). To Tom Towns, the convict, it seems 'a prison-land in truth, its whole length and breadth a prison where a man needed no shackles on his feet to be a captive . . . that penned him in not with doors and bolts, but with the mazes of its endless forests' (p. 168). With the figure of Johnny Prentice, a white child who has lived since childhood with the Aboriginal second wife of his father, Andrew, away from white settlement, Dark explores a type of hybrid consciousness.

Storm of Time demonstrates the heavy inflection by dominant class interests of patriotic notions like 'rebellion', 'justice' and 'loyalty'. Stephen Mannion, for instance, tells Governor King in 1804: 'I do not regard these miserable savages as a menace by themselves—but taught, inflamed, supported by runaway rogues of our own colour, the matter appears in a different light' (p. 343). King tells his successor, Bligh, that apart from the problem of 'the ordinary felons . . . this place has been deluged with disaffected persons—predominantly Irish—who need careful watching' (p. 430).

The third novel, *No Barrier*, focuses upon Conor and her son Patrick who is involved in a doppelganger relationship with Johnny Prentice, who has survived in the bush since he was a child, and who killed Patrick's father. When Conor gets a letter telling her that Patrick has set off alone to find Johnny, she experiences

> Fear of something huge, implacable and apparently endless. Fear of cruelty which, once released, flowed on like a flood; fear of hatred which bred hatred; fear of injustice which spread like a plague, not halted even by death, proliferating like some malign growth through generations.[43]

If the past was becoming another country, middle-brow readers perhaps preferred a more spectacular tour than that provided by Dark's rather sombre and politically relevant vision. Two writers who tapped into popular interest in Australia's past very successfully were E.V. Timms (1895–1960) and Nancy Cato (1917–). Between 1948 and 1958 the prolific Timms produced ten volumes of a nineteenth-century historical saga with titles like *The Pathway of the Sun* (1949), *The Beckoning Shore* (1950) and *The Valleys Beyond* (1951). Cato's more localised trilogy took as its setting the Murray River in the heyday and decline of the river steamers which were for a time a crucial transport system for pastoral produce. *All the Rivers Run* (1948), *Time, Flow Softly* (1952) and *But Still the Stream* (1962) were combined in the best-selling single volume *All the Rivers Run* in 1978 and made into a television series under that title in 1983. While none of Timms's novels has been a specific television source, there are strong affinities between his chronicling of the Victorian goldfields and the popular television series *Rush*.

Meanwhile, Patrick White had introduced a new metaphysical dimension to the historical novel with *Voss* (1957). The novel is set in the 1840s, with a German hero who considers Australia a country 'of great subtlety'[44] and, as Laura Trevelyan observes, 'does not intend to make a fortune out of this country like other men. He is not all money talk' (p. 28). Notions of belonging emerge in the novel as connected to suffering. Laura writes to Voss: 'Finally, I believe I have begun to understand this great country, which we have been presumptuous enough to call *ours* . . . Do you know that a country does not develop through the prosperity of a few landowners and merchants, but out of the suffering of the humble?' (p. 239). Problems in the notion of history as an accurate factual record are raised when Judd's account of Voss's death confuses it with that of another member of the party; this may be intended to emphasise the view that history matters most as a source of legends. In an ending that recalls Marlow's interview with Kurtz's Intended in *Heart of Darkness*, Colonel Hebden, who has gone on a fruitless search for Voss, is told by Laura:

> 'Mr Voss is already history.'
>
> 'But history is not acceptable until it is sifted for the truth. Sometimes this can never be reached.' . . .
>
> 'No, never,' she agreed, 'It is all lies. While there are men there will always be lies' (p. 413).

Laura predicts, nonetheless, a permanent significance for Voss's story: 'His legend will be written down, eventually, by those who have been troubled by it' (p. 448).

David Carter has suggested that the 1940s and 1950s saw 'a vast amount of signifying activity going into the business of creating something to belong to, a tradition that was always and already there'.[45] The tradition invoked here can be read as a complicated interplay between originally European ideologies and practices, and local inflexions and developments. Rural life offered perhaps, in its frontier conditions—as in the United States earlier and in places like South Africa and New Zealand—more of a local specificity than urban culture, in relation to which many parallels persist with the urban capitalism of Europe.

Much of the fiction of the 1940s, 1950s and early 1960s has been seen as falling away from the militant commitment of the novels of the Depression. Susan McKernan suggests that the novels of the later 1940s 'rarely examined the nature of postwar life in Australia in order to express political commitment; instead they recovered Australian and world history in order to teach readers about the nature of political struggle'.[46] Yet because much of the writing of this time is set in that pre-war period, it involves descriptions of engagement in its struggles and causes them to be relived, frequently with some enthusiasm—even if much postwar fiction *does* show a shift away from the vitality, hope and excitement of the Depression period to the mood of the much harder, longer haul of resistance to capitalist exploitation and oppression through the Menzies period of the 1950s and early 1960s.

Prichard's *Winged Seeds* strives for a positive ending, an Australian reworking of the conclusion of Zola's *Germinal*: the kalgoorluh bursts open and sheds its seeds, this rebirth on the land being metonymically tied to the Aboriginal matriarch Kalgoorla, whom they have just buried. Sally says: 'The seeds we've sown will grow like the wild pears, no matter how hard and stony the ground where they fall',[47] but this cracking hearty lacks conviction after the often traumatic experiences that have gone before. Other texts mobilise similar imagery—dawn at the end of *Tomorrow*, pregnancy at the end of *Southern Steel*, nurturance of pregnant women and animals at the end of *Ride On Stranger*—but the reader often feels a sense of contrivance in closures of any optimism.

Barnard Eldershaw's *Tomorrow* employs a self-conscious realism that takes the form of a futurist novel that writes the present as past and the future as possibility. Completed between 1940 and 1942, its publication was held up by the war and censorship. Knarf's novel within the novel culminates in the complete physical destruction of Sydney by 'the Reds' as a way of creating a new society free of capitalist consciousness. The University, including the Fisher Library and the Medical School, the State Library and the Art Gallery are all sacked and demolished although the books, which proved 'the very devil to burn', are defended ineffectually at the Public Library by 'a few men with no politics but a fanatic love' for them (pp. 394–5).

In Knarf's novel the destruction of the city is 'an act of repudiation of all the city had come to mean, a gesture single in all its complexity, and a solution only in so far as by destroying the accepted mould it forced men to create another' (p. 415). But that other society, as depicted in the framing narrative, has hardly proved a utopian outcome and we are left at the end of *Tomorrow* with the image of Knarf's idealistic son as a young man alone: 'Ben stood on a hillside in the apocryphal night, eating his apple' (p. 415). Notwithstanding the apparent philistinism of 'the Reds', and the negative outcome of their revolution, Barnard defended the novel's politics, telling Devanny, 'it shows what I think may happen, not what I want to happen'.[48]

CPA members were, as has been pointed out, expected to represent desirable revolutionary outcomes. The influence of the CPA and its members in many spheres had been considerable, and only began seriously to decline in the late 1950s. Although their harassment in Australia did not approach the savagery of McCarthy's onslaught on American artists, writer members of the CPA or fellow travellers often found themselves in difficulties. John McLaren's recent *Writing in Hope and Fear*[49] details the state's attempts to control cultural production through the 1950s. In 1952 William Wentworth's parliamentary attacks on the Commonwealth Literary Fund (CLF) particularly targeted Vance Palmer and Flora Eldershaw who, he alleged, had 'done considerable service for the Communist Party'.[50] Thereafter Menzies made sure that names put forward for grants were investigated by Security and in 1954 the granting of CLF funds for Waten's *The Unbending* came under attack.

External events were probably more discouraging for CPA members than local irritants. 1956 saw both Khrushchev's exposure of Stalin's genocide and Russian suppression of Hungarian moves towards an independent regime. Dorothy Hewett recalls the reaction of many communist writers and intellectuals:

> Shaken but determined not to 'throw the baby out with the bath water', we will continue the struggle for socialism, but something has happened to us. Some ultimate innocence has been destroyed for ever . . . Only sometimes we long for the old settled security, the old untainted certainty before the Twentieth Congress and the deposition of the man-God Joseph Stalin, floating in fireworks over Moscow with his moustache ends dripping stars.[51]

From the mid-1950s the literary influence of the Party declined, partly through disaffection of members, partly as it became anathema to literary ALP supporters such as Vincent Buckley.[52] The New Left, which would produce a combative new generation that also understood, in some ways at least, the importance of interventions in Australian cultural production would not begin to have any influence until the early 1970s.

IMAGINED IDENTITIES

Representations of Australian identity in this period are sites of considerable contestation. Literary history has constructed an opposition between what Frank Hardy has called the Patrick White Australia Policy and (socialist) realism. Hardy recalls Frank Dalby Davison saying to him, '"You'll never know what an impact that book of Katharine's, *Working Bullocks*, had on us. Here was a book written by an Australian, written as well as any of the foreign writers, a book with a militant activist as a hero—this book started it all for me and Palmer and all the others"'. He comments further: 'And similarly I read *Working Bullocks* and *Sugar Heaven* and they had the same impact on me and I thought, "These girls are on the right track" '.[53] In the 1940s both women would begin trilogies of an industry, as would Vance Palmer, his being published as *Golconda* (1948), *Seedtime* (1957) and *The Big Fellow* (1959). Prichard's, dealing with the goldfields, consisted of *The Roaring Nineties* (1946) *Golden Miles* (1948), and *Winged Seeds* (1950); of Devanny's planned trilogy, only *Cindie* (1949) was published. The second volume, *You Can't Have Everything*, was the subject of considerable controversy in the Australasian Book Society and the Party, and still remains unpublished.[54]

Most of the socialist realist writing of this time did indeed endeavour to teach about political struggle. Prichard's son, Ric Throssell, recalls her telling him, in relation to *Golden Miles*: 'I'm afraid its straight left won't please some people'.[55] But the boundaries between the socialist realists and the others, in hindsight, are often much less clear cut than they have been drawn. It is perhaps their degree of explicit didacticism, more than anything, that distinguishes many of the novels produced in or around the Communist Party. One of the most powerfully moving accounts of working-class life in Australia, for example, is *Tomorrow*, but this novel was received with hostility or indifference by many on the Left. White was condemned by the *Realist Writer* editorial board as 'one of those privileged intellectuals who is unhappy about the decline in the social status of his class',[56] but Mona Brand's more dialectical view is that not only could 'Mrs Godbold and Amy Parker sit down and enjoy a cup of tea any time with Lawson's Mrs Spicer', but also that if the bourgeoisie 'think White's view is the same as theirs, they are not reading him very thoroughly, and are harbouring a viper in their bosoms'.[57]

In *The Tree of Man* White attempts to 'people a barely inhabited country with a race possessed of understanding', and McKernan suggests that this was 'an understanding which White himself was attempting to gain through writing the novel'.[58] The central characters, Stan and Amy Parker, have intimations of things they cannot fathom. Stan's mother believes that her son 'will teach the words of the poets and God. With her respect for these, she suspected in all twilight and good faith, that they might be interpreted'. But Stan 'was no interpreter' (p. 12). Amy is similarly unable to communicate her glimmerings of understanding (p. 162). She can, however, recognise what is 'wrong with' the artist husband of the local postmistress: 'He knows something' (p. 162). After he has hanged himself, his wife complains, 'I was led to understand I did not understand myself ... nor anything' (p. 281), as she shows Amy and other friends the paintings which are later labelled works of genius when they turn out to be worth *money*. This groping for understanding prefigures White's later *Riders in the Chariot*, in which the four protagonists —Himmelfarb, a Jewish refugee, Miss Hare, a middle-class spinster, Mrs Godbold, a washerwoman, and Alf Dubbo, an Aboriginal painter—all share a mystical concept of the Chariot which stands for a capacity for vision, an important motif in White's developing neo-mysticism.

While, for White, Langley's *The Pea Pickers* conjured up a remembered Australian landscape, it also encapsulates a profound nostalgia for Europe, especially Greece. Robyn Colwill comments of another unpublished novel, *Wild Australia* (submitted to Angus and Robertson in 1953), that Langley was 'blazing trails and exploring and pioneering textual terrains far removed from the safe ubiquities and conventions of those neatly bordered and stone-hedged rationalist, androcentric and monocentric discourses of gender specificity and psychic constructs and representations of the self'.[59] This is also true of White, whose work, with Langley's, can be placed centrally in the rise of the novel of poetic dimensions.

PROBLEMATIC PROTAGONISTS

Women, Aborigines and migrants are usually problematic protagonists by virtue of their marginalisation within dominant cultures. Lucien Goldmann also includes artists—'the creators in every sphere'[60]—in his category of those who consistently pose a challenge to the world around them. Many writers have had difficulty in creating artists in their work, for fear of giving ammunition to those wanting to find autobiographical parallels in personae. Nonetheless, artist figures feature centrally in White's *The Living and the Dead* (1941), as well as the later *The Vivisector* (1970), Eleanor Dark's *The Little Company* and Barnard Eldershaw's *Tomorrow*, while male musicians are central characters in Devanny's *Roll Back the Night* and Richardson's *The Young Cosima*. But the amount of detailed attention given to the figure of the artist, especially the female artist, remains fairly restricted in most works of this period. *My Brilliant Career* and *The Getting of Wisdom* stood almost alone within the female kunstlerroman until Stead's *For Love Alone* (1944), although Barnard Eldershaw's *The Glasshouse* (1936) and *Plaque With Laurel* (1937) evoked a rather restrained world of women writers. Franklin's *Cockatoos* has a plot line similar to that of *My Career Goes Bung*, although Ignez has aspirations to sing as well as to write. A sculptor, Neda, appears in all three volumes of Palmer's Golconda trilogy. Perhaps as punishment for her overreaching artistic aspirations, her son Leo has spent time in a boys' home; when released, he makes her life miserable with emotional bullying and does everything he can to interfere with her affair with Donovan, the Big Fellow of the title of the third volume.

The use of a male artist as the central character in Barnard Eldershaw's *Tomorrow* may have something to do with the duo not singling themselves out as women; that 'in their criticism they appear to construct their authority exclusively on nationalist grounds, with little regard for questions of gender'.[61] This is also true of Nettie Palmer, though it could be argued that all three gave more space and attention to the work of women writers than most male critics. But many women writers of the period—like Betty Roland, Dora Birtles, Stead and Barnard—distance themselves from the supposed excesses of 'feminism'—although it is very much a media construction of it that they invoke.[62] Various women writers' autobiographies written in the 1950s—Franklin's *Childhood at Brindabella*, Prichard's *Child of the Hurricane*, Devanny's *Point of Departure* —are also remarkably reserved about sexual politics, though all were pioneers in this area in their time. Frances de Groen has noted:

> Only rarely was a woman in Australia described as a genius. There were the odd exceptions which proved the rule. Henry Handel Richardson is a case in point. In her fiction, however, she invariably represented the Nietzschean artist as male, while portraying female talent in terms of sensuality (nature) from which the male genius must escape in order to attend to his proper creative business (culture).[63]

As de Groen points out, the supportive situation of Richardson with her husband was unusual, paralleled perhaps only by Stead's with Bill Blake, and in Australia by that of Dark.

In discussing Cusack's short-lived relationship with Xavier Herbert, the subject of her play, *Comets Soon Pass* (1950), de Groen refers to its motif of the 'potato wife', drawn from the practice of taking plant cuttings embedded in potatoes on the sea voyage from England to Australia in early colonial days, and suggests that 'in the Australian community between the wars, "potato" wives and mistresses abounded' (p. 99). P.R. Stephensen had a different view, lamenting in 1938:

> Gone are the robust pioneer days, gone forever, Australia's females are now become vessels, not so much of maternity, as of *modernity*, and the rot has set in—post-war hysteria, post-war boom, post-war emancipation of women, the drift from domesticity, the drift to decadence, to office jobs, to 'equality' with men![64]

Franklin's *My Career Goes Bung* records one of the reactions to its predecessor, *My Brilliant Career*: 'All the girls reckon they ain't going to talk to anyone so unwomanly. Elsie Blinder says her ma says it is indelicate for a girl to write books at all'.[65] Barnard saw *My Career Goes Bung* as 'bristl[ing] with rebellion', and this is particularly true of its comments about gender relations:

> Men strut and blow about themselves all the time without shame. In the matter of women's brain power they organise conditions comparable to a foot race in which they have all the training and the proper shoes and little running pants, while women are taken out of the plough, so to speak, with harness and winkers still on them and are lucky if they are allowed to start at scratch. Then men bellow that they have won the race, that women never could, it would be against *nature* if they did (p. 129).

This dominant ideology did not change appreciably in the 1940s and 1950s. In *Cockatoos*, Ignez insists that she has to go away in order to 'be able to use my talents without being thought mad or unsexed'. In contrast her sister, Blanche, who has some skill as a painter, seems content to have 'won prizes in the domestic arts and needlework sections of the agricultural shows from Cootamundra to Cooma' (p. 187).

While Prichard gives at least a temporary success to the singer Sophie in *Black Opal* (1921), she allows little hope of escape for Violet O'Brien, who is introduced in the first volume of the goldfields trilogy as a waitress for the Giotti family, who, as former opera singers in Italy, encourage her talent (pp. 46, 181, 185–6, 235). Violet goes to Melbourne for training, but is summoned back by her mother and her creative potential is wasted.

The narrator of Dymphna Cusack's *The Sun in Exile* (1955) is a travel writer, Alexandra Pendlebury, and the subject of her observation is a young woman called Vicky who is on her way to England to study art. Vicky's subsequent marriage to a West African means that she becomes effectively exiled from Australia because of the White Australia Policy. But there is no immunity from racism in England either. Mosley's fascist followers attack Olumide, mistaking him for a more prominent African and, in trying to protect him, Vicky has her right hand smashed by a cosh. The ostensibly neutral observer, Pen, recognises Vicky's nostalgia for her homeland and how her art has particular qualities associated with capturing antipodean light; she herself, however, in a contribution to the continuing dialectic of problematised nationalism, is represented as feeling that she has, in many ways, no country.

Stead's *For Love Alone* (1944) is one of the most powerful of Australian novels of women's liberation, and one of the texts that spoke particularly to the second wave of the women's movement from the late 1960s, along with *The Man Who Loved Children*, which Susan Sheridan reads as deconstructing 'the patriarchal family drama'.[66] *For Love Alone* involves a search on the part of Teresa, purportedly for 'love' but in fact for a great deal more: 'strange persons, strange visions, strange destinies'.[67] She finds these to some extent after she has travelled to the other side of the world, but not till she is able to understand the catastrophic nature of the love affair that has been the ostensible motive for her travels, reflecting, 'it's dreadful to think that it will go on being repeated for ever, he—and me! What's there to stop it?' (p. 502). Women writers in Australia did, however, continue to write despite, perhaps in part because of, an unliberated and unliberating environment—and they gained publication in large numbers.

Constructions of female subjectivity at this period share in the increasing inflection of Australian identity by considerations of race and ethnicity. Configurations of pioneer women and race relations, for instance, are central to the historical sagas of Prichard and Devanny, as they look back to the historical antecedents of present power relationships. In Devanny's *Cindie*, the depiction of Cindie offers an instance of the complex historical construction of the figure of the pioneer woman. Like Prichard's Mrs Watt on the West Australian 'frontier' in *Coonardoo* (1929), Cindie may be a benevolent agent of colonialism, but she is inescapably a part of an oppressive process—in her case that of the exploitation of labour on the canefields. The novel spans the period from 1896 to 1907, a time in which fervent debates about indentured labour raged, revealing a conflict of various economic and political interests in the replacement of Kanaka (and Chinese) labour with white. Through Cindie and the character Biddow, Devanny shows how attempts at an egalitarian approach remain paternalistic, and involve exploitation. Cindie and Biddow may attempt a non-racist personal practice, but the economic inequalities bound up with colonial society mean that the blackbirded Kanakas and the Aborigines dispossessed of their land have no real power in relation to their white employers.

Attitudes to Aborigines sometimes divided writers who otherwise had common sympathies. In *The Roaring Nineties* Prichard adopts the motif of Aborigines as benevolent saviours when they save the life of the fever-stricken Sally Gough by transporting her back from the goldfields. This was a narrative motif that persisted from nineteenth-century melodramas such as George Essex Evans's *Loraine* through to twentieth-century films such as *Walkabout*, but it could be seen as open to the kind of charge that Franklin levelled in 1942 against *The Timeless Land*: 'I am unable to judge as I stand so near to it that it is like trying to inspect a wall of pictures when jammed against them. It seems to me like Australian history mixed with the prevailing fashion in sentimentality about the [A]borigines'.[68] Franklin's own historical novels fusing apparent realism and mythology —the family saga originally published under the pseudonym of Brent of Bin Bin—do not escape their own brand of nostalgic sentimentality, although the focus of it is not the Aborigines, who remain almost invisible.

In *Voss*, White gives a somewhat caricatured representation of the Aboriginal people that the expedition encounters, much like that in the later *A Fringe of Leaves* (1976). He does give some space, however, to Jackie, who deserts the expedition to join his own people and eventually kills Voss, cutting his head off in an attempt to 'break the terrible magic that bound him remorselessly, endlessly, to the white men' (p. 394).

More contemporary in its reference is F.B. Vickers's *The Mirage* (1955), the mirage being the prospect of a better life for Aboriginal people, who would for the most part be barred from Australian citizenship until 1967. 'Half castes' like George can apply for citizenship, with its accompanying 'licence' to live outside the legal and social restrictions otherwise imposed on Aborigines, but he rejects this as an irrelevance: 'Are the whitemen going to live alongside you even if you get ten dog licences? Not on your life, they aint'.[69]

Much of the more thoughtful representation of race relations was being done by novelists in or around the Communist Party, whose most prominent critic, Jack Beasley, in lamenting the 'absurdly sentimental' ending of the Western Australian Gavin Casey's *Snowball* (1958), recognised that a representation of 'some ideal struggle of the future with the labour movement leading these people in a united struggle for justice and equality . . . would be unreal at this time. As yet there is no novel that gets to grips with this question'.[70] In Donald Stuart's *Yandy* (1960), however, Beasley saw a vehicle for the fight 'for and with the Aborigines', ranking it with *Coonardoo* and *Capricornia* as one of a mere three 'salient novels of our native people in which outraged social conscience has spoken with artistic power'.[71] Jack Healy would later find the distinguishing feature of Casey's writing to be 'the serious level at which [he] has thought out the issues of race', while saying of Vickers and Stuart: 'Vickers had inherited his image of man and society from the Depression; it was one of police and state against the worker . . . Vickers draws the Aborigine into the shadow of the white man; Stuart draws the white man into the shadow of the Aborigine'.[72]

Christopher Koch's Tasmania in *The Boys in the Island* (1958) appears by comparison oddly removed from history: 'No wars, no disturbances have ever reached the island: no horrors at all, since the last convict transport made the long run from England . . . It lies now like a suburb in the sea, eventless and snug'.[73] The text offers no explanation as to why 'horrors' have nothing to do with the assertion, soon after, that 'The dark stone-age people the colonists found when they came there have all been wiped out; they are a lost race: but they remain a reproachful memory in the island's silence'. Nor does it connect this supposed history with the alienation of a non-Aboriginal population within 'the lonely places of the island which still does not quite belong to them, nor they to it' (p. 6).

In *The Fringe Dwellers* (1961) Nene Gare creates a female figure of black resistance in Trilby, though she tells Giuffré in an interview in the late 1980s: 'I could never have been as brave as she was. I would have been much more like Noonah'. She goes on: 'But I do admire people like Trilby, like Dorothy Hewett. She's a rebel. She's so brave, she doesn't care what anyone thinks, it's just what she thinks of herself'.[74]

Preservation of a sense of oneself becomes a major issue for non-Anglo-Celtic migrants in the kind of society that White evokes in this comment made by a young girl in *Voss*:

> 'My father says that if you cannot be English it is all right to be Scotch. But the Irish and everyone else is awful', said Mary Hayley. 'Although the Dutch are very clean . . . My father says . . . the German was eaten by blacks, and a good thing too, if he was going to find land for a lot of other Germans' (p. 398).

Mona Brand argues that in *Riders in the Chariot* 'Himmelfarb and Alf Dubbo suffer persecution not because they are Jew and Aborigine, but because they are unassimilated Jew and Aborigine'.[75] This view is echoed by David Carter when he describes Judah Waten's writing in the postwar period as being received 'in terms of migration (the passage towards assimilation) rather than ethnicity'.[76]

Against this appropriating tendency, Sneja Gunew and others have developed ways of reading 'minority literatures' that involve 'learning to read differently, in other words, to read via cultural difference'.[77] But migrant writers show migrants as having to contend with both the sympathies and the distrusts generated by their perception of their differences not only from their new environment but also from each other. In Waten's *Distant Land*, Joshua often has occasion in the early years of his work as a travelling salesman to eat at the Greek cafe of Socrates Logus who is 'happy to meet any foreigner no matter where he comes from. We have something in common' (p. 50). The acceptance of common interests is, however, not so easy for Solomon Kochansky, the Russian Jew who arrives with his wife Hannah in Western Australia in 1910 in *The Unbending* (1954). The novel is set around the period of the First World War and several significant characters are members of the Industrial Workers of the World (IWW), persecuted by the state at this period. Kochansky's ambivalence about solidarity with them is explored in some depth. 'It was not only fear, it was not only snobbery, but to come even closer to Feathers and men like him meant to jettison all his dreams, all his aspirations, and this he was not yet prepared to do'.[78]

QUESTIONS OF CLASS

Representations of the class system and class struggle remain important in the fiction of this period. In *The Unbending*, the leader of the IWW in the area meditates on how one of his members has 'a kind of weakness which was common to all Australian rebels':

> He was too soft and easy going and half the time he could not imagine that the boss was as bad as he was painted . . . But could you expect Australian rebels to be any other than what they were? Killeen asked himself. Until recently there had never been a revolutionary movement in Australia and the boss-class did not have to show its real face (p. 216).

A genre of working-class writing that grows in strength, culminating with de Boissière's *No Saddles for Kangaroos*, is industrial fiction. *No Saddles for Kangaroos* was published in

1964, after many years in the writing. It is set in a car factory in Melbourne in a period of reduced struggle, but still manages to include two strikes, and deals with the experiences of Jack Bromley up to his death in an industrial accident. Stephen Knight has suggested that one of the strengths of such working-class industrial fiction has been to 'realise the environmental understructures of urban life'.[79] In Ruth Park's *The Harp in the South* (1948), Knight suggests, 'glamorous Sydney is a different place' (p. 80), as it is when Harry Munster of *Tomorrow* encounters it during the Depression:

> Here he would walk looking for work, here men came in ever greater numbers for ever lessening work. Parched walls, cliff-like shadows, sickly patches of impenetrative light, smell of dust, thin, dry, deserted smell. Life had receded, here were the shards. This was the city, not the bright open spaces where the shops and idle crowds were (p. 100).

A similar picture of the bleaker side of Sydney during the 1930s is offered by John Morrison's *Port of Call* (1950). Its anti-hero, Jim Boyd, attempts to overcome his conditioning as a sailor who 'doesn't belong anywhere'[80] and to achieve a relationship 'that was not to be bought from any harlot ever born' (p. 90). But after a brief rural interlude with a highly eccentric woman (of whom one might have liked to have seen more), back in the city the balance of power shifts from Jim to Susan, a former maid on a station; Jim can only find menial jobs until he finally gets a break on the waterfront, where he discovers 'a quality not to be found anywhere except in communities of men who have much to put up with in common' (pp. 207–8). However, he disgraces himself there as a result of an inadequate understanding of the wharfies' code and his concerns about his personal life with Susan, and eventually goes back to sea on his old ship. In Franklin's *Cockatoos*, the analysis of sexual politics is taken further than it was in *My Brilliant Career*: when Ignez first arrives in Sydney and sees a woman run over by a tram, her Uncle Raymond tells her she cannot be concerned because the woman was 'one of 'em . . . A necessary evil' (pp. 152–3).

The main figure in Ron Tullipan's *March into Morning* (1962) is Arthur Chapman who, at the end of the 1930s, joins the tens of thousands in Queensland living in 'hobohemia'.[81] He meets up with several others who see the system as working 'to keep us young blokes from ganging up, from marching and protesting and demonstrating. Once they got you out on the road they could keep you moving only by allowing you to draw the dole once in each town . . . Just keep 'em moving, round and round in a bloody circle' (p. 37). Chapman contemplates joining up for the war but the invariable question —or answer—when he mentions this is: 'what have you got to fight for?' (pp. 5, 66).

Some critics preferred their industrial fiction undefiled by other issues: both Cusack's *Southern Steel* and Hewett's *Bobbin Up* (1959) provoked debate about the representation of female sexuality. Within the CPA much of the feedback that came to writers was via discussion in meetings. In relation to *Bobbin Up*'s reception in Townsville, Devanny commented that 'the funny thing is: those who object to *Bobbin Up* the most are from the extreme Left! I can't help thinking that Jack Beasley had the right idea when he told me to cut out the sex . . . There is a tendency to snigger among the Left'.[82]

Hewett reported encountering a not dissimilar tendency in Sydney: 'A seaman said I must be a nymphomaniac, and a male Communist maintained "her husband must have written it for her, because no woman could possibly know all that"'.[83] But de Boissière had given Hewett the seal of approval, describing the character of Nell as 'the first time I have come across an unforced, truthful human portrait of a Communist in Australian literature'.[84] And another CPA critic, Paul Mortier, wrote of Hewett's 'courage to tread where none have gone before', asserting: 'Her Nell is the first woman revolutionary hero I have known in Australian literature'.[85] Beasley's view was that 'The creation not only of a typical proletarian but of a woman, with all the difficulties that this involves is a stellar achievement in our literature'.[86]

At the beginning of 1960, however, Devanny was suggesting that Beasley should reconsider *Bobbin Up*. Discussion in her Australasian Book Society (ABS) group had made her realise 'that the capitalist press etc praise that book because they can afford to. The workers' reps in *Bobbin Up* would not inspire terror in the heart of any capitalist'.[87] Great demands indeed were made upon literature by some CPA critics—and by the CPA-dominated ABS, which was an important alternative publisher for Left writing. At the end of the 1950s it 'coldly' rejected Hardy's *The Outcasts of Foolgarah*[88] with one reader describing it as 'a libel on the working class'. J.B. Miles, former Secretary of the Party, considered that 'the characters are dealt with in such a way as to belittle the working class, unionism and the Party'. Hardy later commented 'I don't know what old J.B. would have said if he'd lived to see this final version, the one he saw was far less critical of the left and had what was known in marxist circles as a positive ending'.[89]

A more recent Marxist critic, Stephen Knight, is sympathetic in his discussion of *Bobbin Up*, arguing that, while Hewett is not the first writer to take a female viewpoint in a working-class novel, she nevertheless 'in locating her story among women who are self-aware and interactive workers . . . gives them both autonomous realities and economic power, and she focuses her whole narrative through their response to work as much as the domestic context' (p. 73).

Criena Rohan's *Down By the Dockside* (1963) and Mena Calthorpe's *The Dyehouse* (1961), are two other important working-class texts of the time; Ian Syson's 1993 article discusses further examples of working-class women's writing, its distinctive features and its conditions of production.[90]

INTO THE 1960S

In the early 1960s a shift begins to be apparent to an increasing preoccupation with isolated individuals, and to a world according to the existentialists—despite the fact that White, now a strong influence and literary force, had told Tennant in 1956, 'I find them revolting'.[91] A comparison of the short stories of, say, Prichard or Morrison with those of Barnard and Peter Cowan also shows a shift from bush realism to a more isolated and lonely sensibility.

Elizabeth Harrower (1928–) prefigures later 1960s preoccupations with psychological complexity. In *The Long Prospect* (1958) she pursues some of Stead's concern with young women and sexual repression in the story of Emily and her relationship with Max, a boarder in the house of her domineering and manipulative grandmother Lilian. Emily has not yet reached

> the sad sensation of late youth and middle-age, when what is yearned for is not news of a kind relation or friend, but a word from the past to say that old, lost opportunities are yet to be had; that the old loves, canonised by nostalgia, still remember, are waiting with all the bitter, heavy glamour still intact to take up again, and lead to a happier conclusion, relationships unhappily gone awry (p. 85).

The novel includes frequent authorial asides about sexual politics, including the first of Harrower's powerful critiques of marriage—a theme also found in *Down in the City* (1957) and *The Watch Tower* (1966). Emily's parents are in a situation where 'Dislike, warped passion, non-comprehension—nothing could outweigh the inner, unconscious, fabulously romantic idea of marriage—themselves the hero and heroine'.[92]

Hal Porter's autobiographical *The Watcher on the Cast-Iron Balcony* (1963), Koch's *The Boys in the Island* and Randolph Stow's *The Merry-go-round in the Sea* (1965) all deal with young men growing up, although it could be said that these characters do not grow up a great deal, and their perspectives remain limited. Koch's Francis, for instance, becomes emotionally entangled with a girl from a repressive and domestically violent rural background; when she leaves him for a boy more like her father, his contact with everything feels ruptured: 'For he had loved not just a girl but the country that held her, the land behind the hills'.[93]

Kramer's discussions of Stow unreasonably imply that his project has something of the importance of White's; her comments having much in common, from a very different position, with the *Realist Writer* Board's disdain for White. Neither, dismally but perhaps predictably, can conceive of a more hybrid literary production constrained neither by prescriptive notions of nationalism nor by bourgeois notions of literature. Kramer again: '[Stow's] difficulty arises, as I believe does Patrick White's in *Riders in the Chariot*, from his attempt to fuse the realistic and symbolic levels of his writing; and the problem is situated in his method of presenting characters'.[94] Certainly Stow lacks White's extraordinary ability to reflect dialectical impulses in Australian culture and society, but this is not what bothers Kramer. Vincent Buckley similarly takes Koch far too seriously in terms of his status as *enfant terrible*;[95] neither Koch nor Stow ever gets much beyond a boyish stance, but these critics keep waiting hopefully for them to grow up.

There is, however, a link between Stow and White in that the predilection for the metaphysical (in relation to both landscape and personalities) that manifests itself in Stow's *To the Islands* (1958) and *Tourmaline* (1963) can also be seen increasingly at work in White. *The Solid Mandala* (1966) looks forward to late 1960s preoccupations with mysticism and psychology. McKernan suggests that earlier 'didactic urges' had largely lost energy by then, partly because the writers were not so certain that they had the answers, and partly because writing no longer seemed an effective tool for social reform: 'Even Patrick White found that by the mid-sixties teaching ignorant Australians was less important than an examination of the artistic process itself'.[96]

At the end of 1964 the cold warriors of the Menzies government feared that a reduction of the United States presence in Asia would lead to the dominance of China in the region, and to 'a chain reaction throughout the coloured world in China's favour'.[97] They pushed for escalation of American involvement. In 1965 the first battalion of Australian troops would arrive in Vietnam, the United States air force would begin bombing North Vietnam, and the stage was set for another war that would leave, in its turn, a legacy of liberatory movements that would impact substantially upon the literature of the period that followed.

11

POETRY AND MODERNISM

Chris Wallace-Crabbe

Many writers of ability, many books and plangent moments will be passed over in this chapter which, being a piece of literary history, is concerned above all with change, with those shifts which the optimists and the avant-garde often discern as progress. As F.W. Bateson has written, 'Literary history presupposes by the fact of its existence a process of change. If the writings of one generation did not differ, in one important respect or another, from those of the next generation it could not exist at all'.[1] Whether all the shifts and changes recorded here can be spatially envisaged as movements 'forward' is another matter altogether; after all, the very notion of *progress* in the creative arts is not only a vague, modern idea but a highly debatable one, perhaps already dead.

WAR AND THE MODERN MUSES

The quarter-century which began with the declaration of war against Germany in September 1939 was a period of successive, rapid changes in Australian society. It was being framed by two monstrosities, each of them almost impossible to comprehend: the program of genocide carried out in the Nazi extermination camps and the dropping of atomic bombs on Hiroshima and Nagasaki. It was also a short era in which poetry and poets assumed unusual significance in the mapping of Australian culture.

For Australia, which had been curiously far from the Western Front (although heavily committed to its carnage) in the years 1914–18, it was the years of the Second World War that began to internationalise the terms of our imagination, and also to bring several, clashing kinds of modernity to the fore in the arts. Many of the cultural battles which were fought during this period—first in the visual arts, then in poetry, and a little later in fiction—were struggles between different varieties of modernism: surrealist, expressionist or classicising. Even A.D. Hope (1907–), who teasingly presented himself as anti-modernist, constructed his career and his subversive *oeuvre* in a modernist heritage which had come down to him through Baudelaire, Brennan, Yeats and Joyce; not for nothing did he adopt the impersonal, double-initialled nomenclature of many other classic modernists. And even such communist writers as Judah Waten and Frank Hardy, hostile though they were to the dazzling, difficult stylistic achievements of modernism, saw their own humdrum realism as profoundly modern.

Causal questions are posed for us, as latter-day readers, by the dramatic spectacle of this period. We must wonder how many of the changes in question were engendered by the war itself, especially after the entry of Japan in December 1941; how many by Prime Minister Curtin's turn from Britain to America as a sustaining parent; how many by steadily increasing prosperity after the Depression; and how many by the belated response of the universities to Australian writing.

That there should have been such an efflorescence of powerful, various, dazzling poetry after two decades largely dominated by realist fiction throws up challenging, perhaps insoluble, questions about the cultural influence of war. One negative factor certainly played its part in determining the lineaments of cultural production: the wartime shortage of paper affected the publishing industry so strongly that few novels were published over the years 1941–44; and this in itself may have tipped some emerging writers back towards poetry. Again, for writers in the forces or for people in the emergency services who found themselves on the move, lyric poetry was eminently transportable and could be scribbled down almost anywhere. Not that the forces' magazine, *Salt*, published a great deal of poetry in those war years, but it did use some of the poems of Ian Mudie and of W. Hart-Smith (1911–90), and the former was to edit an anthology, *Poets at War* (1944). In these two poets we also see a significant cross-over: between the nationalism of the Jindyworobak movement, founded in Adelaide by Rex Ingamells in 1938, and that called forth by the war itself.

Alas, the interest in Aboriginal cultures which had been evinced by the Jindyworobak poets was all but extinguished by the national emergency, although it survived in such early Judith Wright (1915–) poems as 'Nigger's Leap, New England' and 'Bora Ring':

> The song is gone; the dance
> is secret with the dancers in the earth,
> the ritual useless, and the tribal story
> lost in an alien tale.

> Only the grass stands up
> to mark the dancing-ring: the apple-gums
> posture and mime a past corroboree,
> murmur a broken chant.

> The hunter is gone: the spear
> is splintered underground; the painted bodies
> a dream the world breathed sleeping and forgot.
> The nomad feet are still.

> Only the rider's heart
> halts at a sightless shadow, an unsaid word
> that fastens in the blood the ancient curse,
> the fear as old as Cain.

The Cold War of the 1950s and early 1960s was also to play its part in Australia's rapid cultural change, now exciting and now dampening. It certainly fuelled the fiercest literary fires of the period, notably those lit by international movements for world peace and for nuclear disarmament. The postwar years were, we should remember, the period in which the Labor Party split into two bitterly opposed political parties, distinguished above all by their attitudes to communism and to particular communist regimes. They were also the age of 'whig history', an influential era when the interpretation of Australia was dominated by the democratic Left, fascinated by labour history, by the unions and by the heroic bush workers of the 1890s. These years swing wildly around that historical fulcrum, 1956, the year of the Western attack on Suez and, more spectacularly, the Soviet invasion of Hungary. The latter event fragmented the Communist Party and generated writing from many positions, notably in the pages of *Overland*. This journal had been founded in Melbourne—so often the home of literary journals—in 1954 by Stephen Murray-Smith (1922–88), and at first incorporated the Marxist publication, *Realist Writer*. After Hungary, it moved to a broad social democrat position, more or less akin to that of *Meanjin*, but more consciously Australian nationalist. It had strong links with the revival and rediscovery of Australian folksongs, crystallised in the musical play, *Reedy River* (1953).

So the generalised conservatism which later writers have so often attributed to the 1950s is in many ways illusory. The country was very far then from the political stagnation and economic complacency which were to mark the 1990s; and a high level of unemployment was unthinkable. And in particular it nourished a new wave of left-of-centre national assertion, epitomised in such hortatory studies as Vance Palmer's *The Legend of the Nineties*, Russel Ward's *The Australian Legend* and A.A. Phillips's *The Australian Tradition*; in the years 1950–55 Manning Clark (1915–91) also published his *Select Documents in Australian History*, two collections which proved to be invaluable tools for the academic study of this country.

A word of caution, or a gesture of complication, is called for at this point. With a smallish population aggregated in widely scattered cities, Australia's 'small country blues' are difficult to yard with a single generalisation. Thus Richard Haese's account of modernism in the visual arts focuses only on Adelaide and Melbourne; and modern impressions of the conservative dullness of the 1950s might be tempered by the present writer's memory that he met only one Melbourne writer in that decade who dared to admit that he supported the Liberal and Country Parties. Again, that social spectrum did not represent the views of the broad suburban public; as Brian Matthews has observed, 'beyond the walls of the increasingly reviled academies, any tendency towards modernist, or worse, surrealist art activated general public, journalistic and some intellectual embargoes'.[2]

But let us now go back a step in time, remembering that the 1950s were, above all, the product of the Second World War, along with the rebirth of cultural nationalism.

Events often choose their occasions: in 1939 W.B. Yeats had died, closing a powerful career, and Australia's only distinctively modern poet, Kenneth Slessor (1901–71), had published 'Five Bells', bringing his poetry to an end, except for a postscript at El Alamein in 1942: an elegiac coda which took the form of a lyric, 'Beach Burial', which remains notable for its formal experimentation with assonance, echo and half-rhyme. Another established poet, R.D. FitzGerald (1902–87), had already turned his back on modernism, seeing 'indiscriminate innovation as merely the technical mask for profounder destructive forces'.[3] The sustained modernist experiments of Bertram Higgins (1901–74) were too remote, too rhetorically intellectual to have much effect on his contemporaries and juniors; he lacked certain notes in the range of feeling, deeper notes which had made the comparably rhetorical Christopher Brennan into both legend and powerful influence, from the 1920s onward. The history of both poetry and scholarship in this country has been remarkably indebted to Brennan.

But destructive forces were manifesting themselves on a worldwide scale at the end of the 1930s, and Australia's assumptions and relations were about to be changed for ever by a highly mobile global war. More pertinently, it was a war in which Australia was under direct threat for the first time since white settlement in 1788; the Battle of Britain, Tobruk and El Alamein, however dramatic, could still be viewed from a spectatorial distance and in a clear relation to the British parent, but when Malaya and the Dutch East Indies fell in rapid succession, this country was itself in the front line. And its reliance upon Britain was no longer central: Professor George Cowling's colonial Australia touching its tousled forelock to Britain (Melbourne *Age*, February 1935) became John Curtin's resolute nation, and the Federal Government reached out for that American support which would defeat the Japanese in the Battle of the Coral Sea, in May 1942— a turning point in the war in the Pacific.

The Second World War was a time of displacement and even of imaginative subversion, as well as of common participation in 'the war effort' and, later, in 'reconstruction'. People were moved from place to place in random ways, not only when on active service, but also in essential industries and in official think-tanks, like the Australian Army Directorate of Research and Civil Affairs, which for years housed James McAuley (1915–76) and Harold Stewart (1916–95), and hence, conceptually at least, the mythical Ern Malley. Surreal images of nightmare, violence and sexual threat were generated at this time not only by painters of the Melbourne school, such as Albert Tucker, but by poets as divergent as Max Harris and Muir Holburn, Mary Bell and the James McAuley of 'Gnostic Prelude' or 'The Incarnation of Sirius'. If Ern Malley can be taken as one voice speaking out of the same dark cities as Tucker's 'Images of Modern Evil', so too can his extreme anti-type, A.D. Hope. As Vivian Smith has written, 'the grotesque and macabre side of Hope's talent has to be considered if one is to see his work steadily and whole'[4] and it was during the war that Hope wrote such violent poems as 'The Massacre of the Innocents', the downright personal 'Ascent into Hell', 'Morning Coffee' and 'Three Romances', as well as bringing to expression the plangently unrelieved despair of that powerful, yet almost scientific lyric, 'X-Ray Photograph':

> For in a last analysis
> The mind has finer rays that show
> The woof of atoms, and below
> The mathematical abyss;
>
> The solid bone dissolving just
> As this dim pulp around the bone;
> And whirling in its void alone
> Yearns a fine interstitial dust.
>
> The ray that melts away my skin
> Pales at that sub-atomic wave:
> This shows my image in the grave
> But that the emptiness within.

In these poems of unresolvable conflict the true voice of modernism came into our poetry, even though Hope, like Yeats before him, disapproved intellectually of a great deal that was modern or avant-garde: his poems knew better than his head what the discursive forms of modern culture understood. It is a matter of significance that more than half the poems which he wrote in the period 1940–45 have sexual intercourse as their theme, their narrative drive or their prime metaphor. Was fucking, perhaps, a primary trope for the extreme conditions of wartime?

The effects of a major war on the production of poetry are complicated and oblique. C.B. Christesen (1911–) set down his speculations about this in a 1942 *Meanjin* editorial, speculating on the possible need for ragged rhythms. In Britain the editors of *Fear No More*, a 1940 Cambridge University Press anthology, saw wartime poetry as confronting man's fate and maintaining spiritual standards: in that country, as in the Antipodes, much of the most striking, expressive and surreal verse was being written by non-combatants, front-line troops often working in a lower key, offering more modest transcriptions of experience, of which David Campbell's ballad, 'Men in Green', would be an Australian example. Among the younger English poets, a movement called the New Apocalypse was taking hold, expressionist, surrealist and even apocalyptic; it was of this movement that Vincent Buckley (1925–88) wrote ruefully that 'The pendulum was swinging rapidly in the direction of a natural religion; and, just as it reached the height of its arc, historical circumstances pressed like an enormous hand to give it a still more violent momentum'.[5]

The Second World War did not generate any body of verse resembling the English trench poetry of Owen, Rosenberg and Sassoon thirty years before; but some outstanding verse did arise from active service. John Manifold (1915–85), both communist and formal stylist, became the only Australian poet with an international reputation; his elegy, 'The Tomb of Lt. John Learmonth A.I.F', has become a classic, and his *Selected Verse,* published in 1949, already contained much of his best poetry, whether lyrical or didactic. Manifold later became a major influence in the revival of folksongs and bush ballads. He is unjustly neglected at present.

The most striking book of poems to arise from war service was Geoffrey Dutton's *Night Flight and Sunrise* (1944). Dutton (1922–) was a young avant-gardist associated with the Angry Penguins group in Adelaide, and his RAAF service provided him with just the cluster of metaphors which his Audenesque, surrealist imagination required. In later years Dutton's writing became more urbane, but it seems no accident that his finest later poem is the backward-yearning 'Abandoned Airstrip, Northern Territory'.

Another poet to serve in the Air Force was Francis Webb (1925–73), in due course to become the admired, adoptive forebear for young poets in the 'Generation of '68', despite his fervent Catholicism. Webb's first book, *A Drum for Ben Boyd,* was full of a Browningesque energy which associated it naturally with the historical vitalism of FitzGerald and Norman Lindsay, but the poems in *Birthday* (1953) and *Leichhardt in Theatre* (1952) were a different matter altogether. They represented a modernism more intense and admirable than anything hitherto seen in Australia. Metaphor was richly dominant; poems like 'For My Grandfather' were at once delicate and obsessive; historical moments could be transformed by an obsessively strong personal music; and the war left its echo, its dynamic illogic on that wonderful poem, 'Dawn Wind on the Islands', which begins,

> The needle of dawn has drugged them, life and death
> Stiff and archaic, mouldering into one,
> Voiceless, having no mission and no path,
> Lolling under a heavy head-dress. When
> The puppet sun jerks up, there will be no
> Convergences: the dead will be the dead,
> Twirled in a yellow eddy, frail and dull.
> These hands of mine that might be stone and snow,
> Half bone, half silent fallen dust, will shed
> Decay, and flower with the first glittering gull.

Webb struggled with recurrent mental illness throughout his career, and some of his most admired poetry was to be written in the very teeth of such disorder and distress; the poems he wrote in Birmingham ('A Death at Winson Green') and in Norfolk during the 1950s are prime examples. His rich tapestry of metaphors and similes has contributed greatly to his popularity among his successors, some of whom might even have taken his mental condition as part of a true poet's inevitable alienation from modern society, or even from all society. 'Five Days Old' represents Webb in an unusually lyrical and publicly open mode.

No generalisation will cover the disparate offerings of poets from the Second World War. Kenneth Mackenzie (1913–55), a full-bloodedly erotic romantic, wrote several strong lyrics of longing out of his service in the army and, in retrospect, a harrowing suite of hospital poems, not collected until 1972. Mackenzie died young, drowning at Goulburn. His poetry, though impressive, was largely forgotten, although it may have left its impress on Judith Wright's early love poetry; and his hospital poems must have touched Webb's imagination. His most terrifying poem, 'Two Trinities' (1952), a moving variation on the traditional motif of dialogue between body and soul, has striking affinities with the early work of Gwen Harwood (1920–95), particularly with her yeasty 'I Am the Captain of My Soul'.

Some poets, stimulated by the war's dislocation of reality, were virtual oncers, stirred to a single expression of strangeness; thus M.B. McCallum, who envisaged in 'The Dream' the weird, anthropomorphic figures of Arm, Leg and Hand, 'Floating in file across a glassy waste of sand', and the journalist Clive Turnbull who gently caught the atmosphere of loss in his plangent 'Do This For Me Then' of 1944. A strong, memorable ballad in a popular idiom was 'Lament for the Gordons', written after the fall of Malaya by David Martin (1915–97), a young Hungarian *émigré* who had not yet made his way to Australia; like Manifold, he had Marxist affiliations. Both were neglected by the conservative Sydney hegemony swanning around the *Bulletin* and Angus and Robertson, as was Laurence Collinson, a younger poet of the Left, whose wryly gay poems might well have been appreciated in a later decade.

ROSTRUMS AND NOSTRUMS

Much else had taken place since the Depression decade which would have lasting effects on literature in this country. The Commonwealth Literary Fund, founded by Alfred Deakin in 1908 and essentially a source of pensions for ill or destitute writers and their families, was greatly expanded in 1939. Under a committee consisting of Menzies, Curtin and Scullin, it now diversified its activities, providing writers' fellowships, support to literary magazines and journals, select guarantees to literary publishers, and a university lecture program on Australian writers and their works. This last was to be strategically important over the next twenty years, generating many of the most influential critical articles of the mid-century period: evaluative studies of our writing by such different figures as A.A. Phillips, Dorothy Green, Vance Palmer, Marjorie Barnard and S.L. Goldberg. Many of these lectures became canonising articles in the new journals, putting Australian writing on the discursive and pedagogical map. In turn, these became the basis of the new books or anthologies of Australian literary criticism which began to appear in the later 1950s, whether nationalist or New Critical or, more often, both; for even the universities were now beginning to interest themselves in the forms of a national culture, and the first Australian Literature courses were to appear before the end of the decade.

Literary magazines of any staying power were a new phenomenon; they may also be a strikingly Australian phenomenon, along with our high level of government subsidies to all the arts and to cultural publishing. Our little magazines do not always stay little: they can often become tough institutions.

The first number of *Southerly* appeared in Sydney in September 1939; the first *Angry Penguins* came from Adelaide in 1940, with an expressly modernist agenda, which would bring it to a gradual end after the Ern Malley hoax of 1944; and Clem Christesen, a Brisbane journalist, issued the first number of *Meanjin Papers* in December 1940. The last-named consisted of work by four poets, but the journal was soon to broaden its generic range. In 1945 *Meanjin* moved to Melbourne, where it was given a home by the University of Melbourne, thus paralleling *Southerly*'s long connection with the University of Sydney. The fact that these two journals have survived to the present day effectively symbolises the modern role of universities as major cultural patrons, with the power to determine literary directions. This is one of the most important single factors in the period under discussion, affecting the character of Australian writing, the scale of book publishing and the nature of criticism.

It is also striking that these two journals, both linked with an array of intellectuals, came visibly to represent two intellectual traditions: a Melbourne line, reformist, socially critical, pro-union and historically nationalist, typified in the writings of Vance Palmer, A.A. Phillips and Geoffrey Serle; and an apolitical Sydney line, deriving both from Christopher Brennan and from John Anderson, aesthetic, libertarian and unashamedly élitist. Various critics have sought to define these opposing schools,[6] to draw clear boundaries around two metropolitan entities, but the emphases of *Meanjin* and *Southerly* do not always enforce these caricatures. Certainly the former published more political writing, and more contributions from overseas writers, some of them prominent figures of the left, while *Southerly* maintained its distance from overt politics; but many leading poets appeared in both. Two *Southerly* editors, Slessor and R.G. Howarth, with John Thompson produced the most elegant, eclectic and attractive of all our anthologies, *The Penguin Book of Australian Verse*, in 1958. On the other hand, it was *Meanjin* which published such overseas writers as Pound, Sartre, Dylan Thomas, Randall Jarrell, Bella Akhmadulina and Nazim Hikmet.

Other literary journals which had their effect on the production and character of verse included *The Austrovert* (1950–53) and *Direction* (1952–55), both of which built bridges between the avant-garde poets of *Barjai* affinities and Melbourne poets with a university base: in both, for instance, Wright and Buckley appeared side by side. For its part, *Barjai* had been a product of Brisbane's intellectually-exciting 1940s, the decade in which Peter Porter, Barrett Reid, Laurie Collinson and their juniors, David Malouf, Judith Green (later Rodriguez) and Rodney Hall, were growing up. Of these, only Reid and Collinson were associated with the journal; nor did it pick up that high-spirited young Brisbanite, Gwen Harwood (1920–95); in this, Brisbane was typical of Australia's extremely fragmented literary non-community. Some of *Barjai*'s bohemian youngsters drifted south (as did most of the Queensland writers mentioned above) and were associated with the short-lived *Ern Malley's Journal* and with the stylish patronage of Melbourne's 'Heide', the artists' colony established by John and Sunday Reed. There was interaction between some of these poets and such leading Aust-expressionist painters as Sidney Nolan, Arthur Boyd, Albert Tucker, John Perceval and Joy Hester; all defined themselves against the academy, although Boyd had historians and philosophers for friends.

A more substantial publication was Adelaide's *Australian Letters* (1957–68) edited by Max Harris (1921–95) and Geoffrey Dutton, with other co-editors; it had the readerly breadth of *Overland*, was catholic in the poetry it published, and reached out into the visual arts. Among other initiatives which emerged from its moderate modernism was a striking series of painter-poet collaborations: also a series of annual anthologies, *Verse in Australia* (1958–61), which varied and augmented the offerings from Angus and Robertson's annual cull, *Australian Poetry* (1941–73). It was through such anthologies that many Australian poets built their reputations, or looked over their shoulders to see who might be galloping close behind them.

Of comparable importance for the development of Australian poetry—and, some would say, for its formal and cultural squareness—is the fact that Douglas Stewart (1915–85), a Lindsayite vitalist from New Zealand, became literary editor of the ultra-conservative *Bulletin* in 1940. Thomas Shapcott has described how this 'dyed-in-the-rural' weekly expanded and diversified its publication of poetry during the 1940s and 1950s.[7] It was in 1941 that Stewart edited the first of Angus and Robertson's annual anthologies, thus setting in train a long poetic alliance between that powerful publishing house and the *Bulletin*.

Stewart's influence was pervasive, but not entirely predictable. An ardent Lindsayite, he was the most powerful conservative force in Australian verse in the 1940s and 1950s, resisting the manifestations of modernism more or less wherever he found them; this conservatism was not merely an attitude to verse-forms and metres, a deep-laid love of the lucid iamb: it was also an attitude to difficult subject-matter, as was seen in his reluctant response to A.D. Hope's sexual and intellectual jacobinism, a response that mellowed in the fullness of time, however, into a favourable review of *The Wandering Islands*. Humphrey McQueen, tracing the uneven spoor of Australian modernism and its discontents, has speculated that 'Hope earned the united disfavour of Lindsay, Slessor, Stewart and FitzGerald by violating their view of Life and of poetry as supra-materialist experiences'.[8] Activated by the pleasure principle, Sydney Vitalism deplored modernist scepticism and the savage barbs of intellectual satire: it did not want to push far beyond a boyish sexiness.

It should be added that Stewart also encouraged the extremely difficult poetry of Francis Webb and the imagist free verse of W. Hart-Smith, along with the poetry of many women, some of them critically neglected by the next generation (Nan McDonald, Nancy Cato and Mary Finnin, for example). Moreover the historical anthologies of *Australian Bush Ballads* (1955) and *Old Bush Songs* (1957) which Stewart edited with

Nancy Keesing were important contributions to a decade which was rediscovering the history of Australian nationalism and the genealogy of un-English voices. His disappearance from recent anthologies of Australian verse is a teasing phenomenon; but the turn of such poems as 'The Silkworms' and 'Brindabella' will come round again.

THE VIVID FLOWERING

Judith Wright (1915–), whose long, excitingly varied career began with *The Moving Image* (1946), was partly at home among the *Bulletin* poets, in that many of her poems dealt with the bush, settlers and kinds of rural epiphany. The descendant of a powerful squatting family, she was from the start aware of earlier modes of culture which her own ancestors had dispossessed, earlier peoples whom the white settlers had murdered, as registered in her strong early poem, 'Niggers' Leap, New England'. As in the United States, it was a peculiar gift to a poet to have been brought up in a region quaintly entitled 'New England', even if it was only a part of New South Wales. In another poem from her first collection, 'South of My Days', Wright exceeds even the cultural confidence of other scions of squatting families, fusing an Australian landscape with her own past *and* with her own body in those often-quoted lines,

> South of my day's circle, part of my blood's country,
> rises that tableland, high delicate outline
> of bony slopes wincing under the winter,
> low trees blue-leaved and olive, outcropping granite—

If Wright exhibited such remarkable confidence, at once regionally traditional and modernist in diction, she also had a recurrent capacity to respond to crisis or to major change: a war, the birth of a daughter, the threat of nuclear warfare, environmental damage, the ghostly echoes of Aboriginal predecessors, all these brought forth differing kinds of poetry from her. The poems can take the form of response or prophecy, plaint or prayer, vision or apotropaic spell.

For Wright, I suggest, philosophical truths have always been immanent in the landscape, waiting there for the patient soul to discover them and to respond appropriately. Thus in *Birds*, her slender 1962 volume, she could simply assume the eloquence of native birds as signs or natural symbols of the Good.

Not all of Wright's poetry in those years exhibited the modesty of her bird lyrics. Some critics have shown impatience with her more prophetic or Blakean poems, while others have found themselves baffled by the zigzag nature of her career, a shifting between tones, forms and thematic concerns. It could, of course, be argued that this instability is a great positive in her career, representing a feminine freedom from what Lawrence had called 'the old stable ego of the character'. Certainly Wright has heralded many approaches in subsequent women's poetry: never more so than in the amazing title poem of her second book, *Woman to Man*. This symbolic lyric—dense, haunting—can be read at the same time as a telling of pregnancy and birth or as a dramatisation of the sexual act.

Very different again was Wright's lofty dialogue, 'The Harp and the King', derived from Arthur Boyd's representation of David playing before Saul but developed as an eschatological drama; different again her compelling lyrics of symbolic landscape, 'Train Journey' and 'The Ancestors'. In subsequent years she has turned away from the grandeur of language in quest of its plainnesses: one reason for this was her belief that language and a worldwide nuclear threat could scarcely exist side by side. But in her early prime she was drawn again and again—like the European modernists—to the yearning hope that older religions and primitive mythologies might point the way toward congeries of truth which had been neglected by the technological civilisations of the West. She builds rhetorical bridges from the Pre-Socratics to the Aborigines, from Blake's Prophetic Books to the later Eliot.

Comparably authoritative and, as I have already suggested, more sensational has been the poetry of A.D. Hope, even from well before the belated publication of his first volume, *The Wandering Islands*, in 1955.

Belated? Yes. But a long life can afford to take on the shapes it needs, as we can also see in the spare, distinguished career of Elizabeth Riddell. Hope's publication had in part been delayed by the fear of publishers that they might be prosecuted for obscenity if they took his poetry on. After several had demurred, the fledgeling left-wing firm of Edwards and Shaw produced a beautiful volume, which arrived on the local scene with considerable éclat.

The Wandering Islands was not only an astonishingly strong, sexual and aggressive collection, remarkable for its leaping wit and for its harsh, Swiftian play of moral logic: full of traps for the human race, for 'the pensive ape who invented civilization/And lived on his wits at the rest of the world's expense'. It also established a vivid Hopean world of the verbal imagination which was to reveal rather little in the way of later development, at least after his wide-ranging *Poems* (1960).

This was not surprising, in the wider perspective, given that he had been forty-eight when that first collection had come off the press. Then and later, his very masculine poems were marked by the play of dualities: the human being as either animal or angel; as sex and spirit; violence and meditation; beauty and possession; art and power; or the story of a being who is driven by both Eros and Thanatos, much as the passionate old Elizabethan pun would have it, or as 'Totentanz: the Coquette' would follow it through. Hope's unusually formal mind also sees one overriding parallel colouring our lives, that between art and love, both of which are capable for their enchanted moment of lifting us beyond grim diurnal knowledge of our condition as temporary beings who will flourish a little, then die, rot and vanish. Poem after poem touches on aspects of this brief glimpse of transcendence or freedom: sometimes it may also take the form of dream, of a dream large enough—like art—to subsume mere self:

Here I come home: in this expected country
They know my name and speak it with delight.
I am the dream and you my gates of entry,
The means by which I waken into light.

This is another reading yet of biblical 'knowledge'. And even nightmares may educate the self into the vastnesses of its lost being, as in that wonderful revenant poem, 'Ascent into Hell'. But again and again love is the key to so much of what life can mean, whether it be artfully shaped (the woman's body in 'The Lamp and the Jar'), backward-looking ('The Return of Persephone') or generating stratagems to conquer time lost, as in the semi-historical narrative of Edward Sackville's yearning for the all-too-seldom seen Venetia Digby. In 'The Judgement' the experience comes to seem more directly personal, even though its fictive frame is controlled by dream.

It has frequently been noted that Hope's chief limitation stands very close to the sources of his greatest strength; that is to say, he inhabits what Malraux called the imaginary museum of the world and its histories. Many of his finest poems draw their strength from the mythical stories which they adapt, play with or satirise. Thus, his most imaginative poem about desire takes the form of a retelling of the biblical legend of Susannah and the elders, told in pretty much the voice of 'the Song of Songs', and saturated by Mallarmé and Valéry; this is the imaginatively redoubling 'Double Looking Glass', his most grandly, glintingly symbolist poem. Here the language is poised on the sill of mere ravishment, but in another medium-large poem, 'The Soledades of the Sun and Moon', Hope goes over the top into the chillier rhetoric of Spanish Gongorism. Too often he draws away from the daily realities Australians read about, and work within, because he is trying to embrace major strands of Western history, religion and science by main force: the gain, of course, is to be found in his huge range of ideas and tropes.

Like so many other writers' aesthetic positions, Hope's aesthetic is deeply inconsistent. On the one hand, he adheres to the principles of poetic impersonality which have descended from Keats and Eliot, and sees poems as free-standing, detached from the mere life of an individual poet; on the other, he tends to envisage the poet as impassioned, rebellious and bold. ('In every age the poet has taken flight/Away from the newer deal, the nobler message'.) Not for nothing did S.L. Goldberg call his fine early essay on Hope 'The Poet as Hero'; and a recent critic, Kevin Hart, has seen Hope's artistic concern with the close bonding of love and death as evidence of his Orphic consciousness.[9] Either art-heroics or Orphism can be a glass in which to read this unusual poetry, which is as amoral as Wright's is moral; indeed, Hope resembles a later generation poet like John Forbes in the way his artefacts stand free of any moral conclusion or consolation. Yet—and here's the rub—Hope's rhythms and diction retain a fullness which sounds as though it could still belong to the lost world of stable values, which may be the cost of his so resolutely standing aside from political conflict or commitment.

In most of these respects, his friend James McAuley was the opposite of Hope. After the expressionist and late-Romantic wildnesses of his first book, *Under Aldebaran* (1946), and after that parallel endeavour, the invention of Ern Malley, McAuley became a Catholic, a political activist and an editor with strongly argued conservative leanings. Indeed, he was the first editor of the country's only literary magazine of the political Right, *Quadrant*. This journal was established by the Congress for Cultural Freedom in 1956, the year of the Soviet invasion of Hungary, and its politics have ever since, whatever their other fluctuations, been resolutely anti-communist. McAuley gave *Quadrant* distinction in his seven years as editor and in his subsequent period (1964–75) as co-editor. Unlike the *Bulletin* conservatives of his time, for instance, his political position was intellectually defined and located in a clear, if sometimes idiosyncratic, history of ideas.

Thus, a stanza like the following one from 'Invocation' springs from a set of cultural attitudes that have been arrived at carefully, even painfully, since his earliest poetry:

> Compose the mingling thoughts that crowd
> Upon me to a lucid line;
> Teach me at last to speak aloud
> In words that are no longer mine;
> For at your touch, discreet, profound,
> Ten thousand years softly resound.

It is remarkable to think that these lines come from the pen of the same poet who, in *Under Aldebaran* had written the gloomily expressionist 'Gnostic Prelude', the black comedy of 'Dialogue' and the jaunty intellectual satire which runs through 'The True Discovery of Australia'. Indeed, Evan Jones has written of the early McAuley's tensions: that '"The Family of Love", for instance, with its brilliant if uncontrolled burlesque of divided views and values in the modern lover, is the most originally and trenchantly "modern" poem of the decade'.[10] McAuley's version of modernity had its origins both in Mallarmé and in Novalis; this diverse pair were among the forebears who helped to light a young poet's descent into the psychic underworld. *A Vision of Ceremony* (1956) turned away from all those soul-struggles to the disappointment of many of McAuley's contemporaries; it sought a broad, well-lighted tradition.

Such determined lucidity as 'Invocation' displays, such an attachment to impersonal tradition, springs from an attempt to empty the ego of its self-assertion and to empty modern history of Romantic diversitarianism. Influenced by the culture of New Guinea, McAuley sought to locate himself in the central traditions of Western Christendom, insulated from their liberal by-products and latter-day heresies. Yet he was also aware of his particular Australian destiny. Not only is this shown in his massively marmoreal Christian epic, *Captain Quiros*, but it was in a more modest way to inform the domestic, personal and suburban poems which he wrote in the mid-1960s, of which 'Because' is the best-known, the most heartbreaking.

McAuley had written about his lineage as a poet in this country, claiming that Brennan was the only strong forebear:

apart from a few lyrics of John Shaw Neilson, it was in this poet, who died in 1932 at the time when my poetic aspirations were beginning to develop, that I found the point of contact which every poet wants and needs with the preceding literature of his own people.[11]

His own course, however, took McAuley steadily away from Brennan's lofty, pure aesthetic, into a poetry where clarity and order bespoke political responsibility. It also took him far away from the expressionism which had revealed itself intermittently in *Under Aldebaran* and playfully in the high-spirited surreal verses which he had concocted, with Harold Stewart, for that fictive bell-wether, Ern Malley: Malley, the garage mechanic genius, was brilliantly fashioned for derisive and divisive effects among the avant-garde.

Never fashionable, nor yet divisive, William Hart-Smith is one of the more attractive poets of the postwar period. Thompson, Slessor and Howarth's eclectic *Penguin Book of Modern Australian Verse* (1958) used three of his poems, among them the haunting 'Black Stockman'. In the following year Hart-Smith published *Poems of Discovery*, in which can be found the most exciting free verse of the mid-century. Some of the lyrics in this collection cohere in the 'Christopher Columbus' sequence; many others distil New Zealand or Australian landscapes. They are like small tunes played with exquisite fingering. 'The Polynesians' and 'Kangaroos' are among the most perfect. His was the final, mature flowering of the Jindyworobak movement, which had come to a formal end with the last of its annual anthologies in 1953, although its later influence may be felt in the poetry of Les Murray and Geoffrey Lehmann.

Rosemary Dobson (1920–) is another poet whose work is marked out by its delicacy. Her early writing was as traditionally iambic/stanzaic as Stewart's, sharing his assumptions about the continuing presence of a Georgian common reader. Typically, her early poems sprang from apprehensions of European painting: later in her career she has turned in the direction of classical Greece, and to the writings of Pausanias. Her nicely turned dubieties are best exemplified by 'The Bystander', with its memorable first line, 'I am the one who looks the other way', and in the title-poem of *Child with a Cockatoo* (1955). Her civilised interests, her concern for verbal grace, these show affinities with the verse of her American contemporaries, Anthony Hecht and Richard Wilbur.

Another of Dobson's contemporaries, but one closer to hand was David Campbell (1915–79), later her collaborator in translating Russian poetry. Cambridge-educated, sportsman, grazier, gentleman, always a colourful personality, Campbell was one of those whom Buckley saw as constituting a new *Bulletin* school, a cluster which would also have to include the gritty, brief densities of bush and coast published by John Blight, notably in *A Beachcomber's Diary* of 1963.[12] I prefer to regard Campbell's poetry, however, as at the heart of a new but traditional genre: Squatter Pastoral.[13] Following in the modest wake of Ethel Anderson, he devised ways of bringing the Elizabethan lyric tradition to bear on Australian conditions, particularly on those of the chill Monaro:

On frosty days, when I was young
I rode out early with the men
And mustered cattle till their long
Blue shadows covered half the plain

And when we turned our horses round
Only the homestead's point of light,
Men's voices, and the bridles' sound
Were left in the enormous night.

And now again the sun has set
All yellow and a greening sky
Sucks up the colour from the wheat—
And here's my horse, my dog and I.
('On Frosty Days')

He had found ways of treating the facts and daily work of south-eastern Australia with a courtly lightness, a wittily haunting ease (as in 'Mothers and Daughters'), which also could chime with the influence of Yeats, as in that lovely lyric, 'Who Points the Swallow'. Here, as elsewhere in his verse, the eloquent lyre is being plucked within cooee of shearing shed and combine harvester. What is more, darker shadows of the *carpe diem* can fall across his lyrics, generating the cruel vision of 'Dear Maurice'.

Nobody better than Campbell sums up a particular historical moment: that of masculine, pastoral, national images, which emerged from the Second World War as emblematic of hope. It is no accident that he was a close friend of Manning Clark.

An old poet who worked on into this period was R.D. FitzGerald, a contemporary of Slessor's, but warier in his response to the flashy *Vision* school of the 1920s. His longstanding interest in Australian explorer and settler history was enriched in its postcolonial alertness by the five early years he had spent as a surveyor in Fiji. His South Pacific knowledge generated the interior dramatic monologue, 'Heemskerck Shoals' (1949) and his epic of heroic Tonga, *Between Two Tides* (1952). His incisive dramatisations of colonial regimes include readings of British India and of the convict system in New South Wales; the latter, 'The Wind at Your Door' was sharpened by the recorded presence of one of his own ancestors at a flogging. The tension between a joy in physical action and his liberal humanist conscience lends real power to FitzGerald's poetry, which has been strangely unfashionable in recent years.

New Impulses and Odd Fish

As suggested earlier in connection with war poetry, interesting poets often resist generalisation or being popped into representative boxes; there will always be some eccentrics and oddballs who refuse to be in the right place, to the discomfort of 'that sly anus of mind, the historian'. One such square peg was Ronald McCuaig (1908–), the quirky Sydney humorist, whose playfulness has not pleased more solemn readers of later generations; another must surely be Lex Banning (1921–65), a long-time invalid, whose astringent lyrics are best seen in his 1956 volume, *Apocalypse in Springtime*. They dance lightly between Eliot and Edith Sitwell.

A poet may be known for a single poem, as Dorothy Hewett (1923–) was for a long time. In her later years Hewett has become a radical bohemian celebrity: poet, 'New Romantic', autobiographer, novelist and the public face of women's poetry. But for many years she was merely the name behind 'Clancy and Dooley and Don MacLeod'. This is a rousing ballad written in response to a political event of radical significance and portent: in 1946 there had been a strike of Aboriginal station hands in the Pilbara district of Western Australia. MacLeod and the two Aboriginal leaders of the strike were gaoled for their militant action, but widespread political lobbying finally led to their release. Hewett did not become prominent as a poet again until the 1970s. Politics and sex have always been her major themes. Andrew Taylor has placed her under the umbrella of 'confessional poetry', suggesting that

> In such poetry, the effect is not so much that reality has been transformed into language, and far less that it is reality signified by language. Rather, it is as though language has been transformed into reality: it has surrendered its linguistic nature as a system of signifiers to become concrete, immediate, the very thing itself, real life.[14]

The effect which is claimed of Hewett's poetry here is very much what Vincent Buckley meant in his posthumously-published *Last Poems* (1991) by 'a poetry without attitudes'.

Another eccentric figure in our map, an imaginative rebel from the traditional squattocracy in which he was reared, is Randolph Stow (1935–), domiciled since 1966 in the England of his ancestors. Stow was also a youthful prodigy in both poetry and prose—and we don't go in for prodigies in Australia, as a rule. In 1958 at the age of twenty-three he had already published three novels and one collection of poems, the fiction having more than a touch of Emily Brontë reborn in Western Australia, the verse gothically shadowed by the Border ballads and mid-Victorian ghosts. His eclecticism was that of a bright young man, still close to the university library.

With *Outrider* (1962) Stow fused his effects and emerged with a truly distinctive voice, one not afraid of extravagant gestures. Beautifully illustrated by Sidney Nolan, this collection is full of richly fantastic or dream-saturated evocations of desert and dry sheep country. He tended to use a longer line than any of his contemporaries and, writing in the cultural isolation of mid-century Western Australia, was not party to the astringencies or wry political discriminations common in poets from the Golden Triangle of the east. Some of the homestead poems here echo early Judith Wright, but Stow is wittier, more nostalgic, even dandyish—if dandies can flourish in the midst of sandhills and mulga. 'Dust' and 'The Utopia of Lord Mayor Howard' are the funniest of his poems, but his rhapsodic weirdness of utterance comes through most strongly in 'Strange Fruit', with its hint of Ern Malley, and in 'The Calenture'. Stow has written little poetry since the 1960s, preferring virtual silence.

It has often been suggested that Stow's contemporaries made up a peculiarly urban/suburban generation, hardly surprising given that so few Australians live in the country or even in small towns. These poets, a number of them from Melbourne and hence closer in spirit to *Meanjin* and *Overland* than to the welcoming *Bulletin*, included the disparate octave who made up the anthology, *Eight by Eight*, in 1963 and that far more popular figure, Bruce Dawe (1930–).

Dawe's background was atypical for his poetic generation. He was a working-class boy in Victoria, picking up a succession of short-term jobs after he left school, and later spending nine years in the RAAF, including service in Malaysia. More typical, however, is the fact that he found a circle of fellow-poets while doing a part-time course at university. Indeed, many of his finest poems were first published in student magazines and papers: their breezy idiom was at once infectious.

It has been widely felt that Dawe was the poet who made common Australian suburbia—so often the object of snobbish literary scorn—into the natural matter of poetry. His grasp of idiom, use of humorous monologues and eye for diurnal detail made him (like Barry Humphries in the world of theatre) Australian in a new, seemingly old-fashioned, way. The critic Peter Kuch has defined Dawe as Homo Suburbiensis, capable of being read as close to the personae of his poems, 'sharp but not censorious, ironic rather than cynical, frank but not outspoken':[15] in short, a decent bloke worrying away at life's problems.

Dawe, Webb and Gwen Harwood are major players in that representative anthology of the 1960s, Shapcott and Hall's *New Impulses in Australian Poetry* (1968), Shapcott himself being a buoyant new lyrical voice. The word 'impulses' is a significant part of this title, for the editors do not claim to be recording any major change: rather, a series of shifts and strengthenings, as well as their regret about 'The insidiousness of the campus environment',[16] in which some of these younger poets were now working—and in which a great many more writers would operate in succeeding decades, replicating a culture which already existed in the United States. Shapcott and Hall do register a sense that these poets have moved away from an insistence on the Bomb as apocalyptic threat, as it had been seen in Wright—and in Edith Sitwell—to an acceptance of it as a fact of life (or death); this is, however, accompanied by some increase in political poetry, particularly evident in Buckley and Dawe. The former is represented in the anthology by his 'Eleven Political Poems', short, tart, anti-communist satires, with particular sardonic scorn reserved for 'Fellow-Traveller'. From a present perspective, the 'new impulses' appear more often matters of townscape and suburban sociology than of politics. However, the anthology is also notable for the appearance of Kath Walker (later Oodgeroo Noonuccal, 1920–95), the first Aboriginal writer to be recognised by the dominant culture, and of David Malouf (1934–), who was to become a major novelist.

The gradual sea-change which this anthology charts is perhaps the same development as that seen in large by Susan McKernan when she writes,

> In the course of the sixties these [political] divisions broke down so that issues such as the
> preservation of the environment, town-planning, educational reform and support for the arts
> were claimed by the left. It was possible to be nationally self-critical, to be interested in
> 'spiritual' or metaphysical values and to vote Labor.[17]

And the change which she sees at this point corresponds with some of the main developments in Judith Wright's immensely authoritative career, with its interweaving of the
spirit and politics, the environmental and the historically critical.

Of the younger post-war generation, the lucid, conservative Vivian Smith, the wry
diplomat J.R. Rowland, and Evan Jones, a recessive figure with a wonderful ear for
rhythm and line, were three who went on with a good deal of consistency. R.A. Simpson
in Melbourne and Bruce Beaver in Sydney are other poets of this generation who arrived
at their main achievement later; both of them, though, remained resolutely urban and
suburban. And the Sydney paediatrician, Grace Perry (1927–87), who had published two
early volumes obscurely in the 1940s, did not bring out a book again until 1963; she
was also the founding editor of the valuably wide-ranging journal, *Poetry Australia*
(1964–*c*. 94).

History confers its meanings in retrospect, and it now seems clear that the two most
proleptically important books of verse published in the first half of the 1960s were Gwen
Harwood's *Poems* (1963) and *The Ilex Tree* (1965), by two young Sydney poets, Les
Murray and Geoffrey Lehmann. Harwood's bold, plangent collection gave the Angus
and Robertson imprimatur to a poet of great significance, one who had emerged from
outside the literary force-fields of Sydney and Melbourne, while the two younger poets
were to go on to very influential careers in the next few decades. By the 1990s Les Murray
(1938–) had probably outstripped Hope and Wright as the best-known Australian poet
across the English-speaking world, and had a reputation comparable to that of Bruce
Dawe inside Australia.

This matter of international and national reputations brings up a cluster of intriguing cultural questions. What, for instance, does an English reputation come to mean
within Australian literary history? Exactly how does our national discourse weight the
fact that ever since his *Poems Ancient and Modern* (1964) the expatriate poet Peter Porter
(1929–) has enjoyed a prestige in Britain unequalled by any other Australian poet, at
least since W.J. Turner? And what, in turn, do our processes of judgment make of the way
in which North American critics or anthologists have found Hope and Murray far more
appealing than Porter? Plainly there are important differences of national assumption—
whether of cultural style, ideology, academic fashion or interest-group formation—
which continue to play their large cognitive part, even in an age of post-nationalism and
of international publishing empires. Porter's lines about England still apply to the

psychological hegemony of most natal or long-adopted nations: 'You cannot leave England, it turns/A planet majestically in the mind'.

As with Porter, most of Gwen Harwood's dazzling achievement lies outside the period under discussion. But she had emerged with quite a fanfare and swirling of cloaks in the mid-1950s. In the early 1960s she was also publishing poems under three pseudonyms: Walter Lehmann, Francis Geyer and Miriam Stone, and later as T.F. Kline. From the start she gained both enjoyment and inspiration from the interplay between the historical self who actually wrote certain poems and the personae deployed therein: again and again her poetry took its way between transcendental belief and game. It was full of the play of light, sexual love, and the otherworld of dreams; Wittgenstein and the great composers made their way through these early poems, as they would to the end of her career. Reflecting on her epiphanies, she has said, 'what is light that we can see it in dreams when our eyes are shut and we are in a room of total darkness? What is it that we can see? What are these nervous impulses?'[18] Her poems inhabit the foreshores of religion and metaphysics, yet finally resist religious belief, crying out instead, 'Remember me'. They are the highly intelligent lyric voices of yearning.

Harwood was to become, within Australia, the central poet for an era of dominantly feminist readings. But all this lay far ahead back in the 1960s, a decade that was to grow far more masculinist as it proceeded: largely under the influence of passionate debate about the war in Vietnam and, perhaps, as a result of male-driven, phallic ideologies of sexual freedom, hippiedom and sexual experimentation. The so-called 'generation of '68' would be aggressively masculine in its interests and groupings, as much so as any generation since the 1890s; but its floruit was paradoxically to coincide with the rise and rise of women's fiction.

From the viewpoint of the very late twentieth century, it is almost impossible to imagine a writer living with that soaring confidence in the imagination as a shaping spirit which Christopher Brennan evinced when he wrote that

> the imaginative act is not, as vulgarly held, the irresponsible creation of unrealities: imagination is a faculty that *perceives* outside of the dusty life of outer weariness, the adequacy of our spirit to those only perfect things, the things of beauty; that unites all hints thereof into a perfect life, the only real one because alone worth being real.[19]

Yet such an inherited belief lingered on after the Second World War in poets as different from one another as Hope, Wright, Webb, Dobson and Harwood.

PART FIVE

SINCE 1965

LITERARY CULTURE SINCE VIETNAM:
A NEW DYNAMIC

Bruce Bennett

The characteristic quality of literary and cultural life in Australia since 1965 has been an 'unsettling' of established values and attitudes, although, as the next century approached, a more cohesive national community was also sought. The idea of 'settling a nation', which had prevailed in much public discourse since Federation in 1901, was replaced from the late 1960s by radical questioning and various revisions of 'the national story' in the face of internal changes and rapid international reorientations. It would be mistaken, however, to call this a period of revolutionary change, since the often rapid shifts in fashion, taste and ideology have been diverse and often contradictory. Furthermore, many of the changes have been driven by technology and have an international rather than a specifically Australian flavour. In this period Australia's changing international relations, influenced by the demands of politics, trade and security, have had a major influence on literary endeavour in the opportunities created (or sometimes denied) for individual creativity and interaction with others.

VIETNAM AND CONSEQUENCES

Chief among the unsettling forces of this period was the Vietnam War. When Prime Minister Menzies announced on 29 April 1965 that Australia would send a battalion of troops to Vietnam, the Australian Labor Party, under Arthur Calwell's leadership, bitterly opposed the decision. From the mid-1960s, too, a residual habit of subservience to and reliance on the former colonial master, Great Britain, was further eroded, prompted in part by British Prime Minister Macmillan's 'winds of change' speech in 1963 and by Britain's protracted entry into the European Community. Menzies's departure as Prime Minister in 1966 was widely regarded as the end of an era, though it was not until the Whitlam Labor government of 1972–75 that Australia's winds of change blew strongly with a new cultural nationalism. During the 1970s and 1980s the always ambivalent relationship with the new cultural master, the USA, strengthened discernibly, along with an enhanced attention to the countries of Asia and the Pacific, especially in the late 1980s and 1990s. All these changes influenced literary and cultural developments, and sometimes, in turn, were influenced by them. Australia thus became a testing ground for intellectual movements, including feminism, post-colonialism and post-modernism.

This book has stressed the significance for Australian literary culture of the two world wars. It is more difficult to assess the impact of the 'regional' Vietnam War on Australian culture and thought. On the one hand, Australia's involvement was restricted in its zone of conflict and in the numbers of Australian troops, which rose to a peak of more than 8000 in 1968.[1] On the other hand, the widespread demonstrations against the war (especially against the drafting of conscripts) and Australia's involvement in it culminated in the second Vietnam moratorium rallies in all capital cities in September 1970, and demonstrated the great symbolic importance of the war in the wider community. The demonstrations focused a public expression of a youthful Australian counter-culture which, even as it expressed its solidarity in strongly anti-authoritarian and anti-American sentiments, paradoxically found itself imitating American modes of expression. For some acute literary observers, such as Frank Moorhouse and Michael Wilding, this complex situation provided the material for both fiction and faction.

The Vietnam War thus provides a convenient introductory locus for considering ways in which literature and history have been intertwined in this period. The first thing to observe is that extended literary works, unlike journalism, do not provide an instantaneous commentary on events. (This point has been made earlier in relation to the writings of the First World War in Chapter 6.) A novel, especially, can take years to write and often benefits from a period of rumination and many revisions. Christopher J. Koch's novel *Highways to a War* (1995), for example, was the fruit of long research and reflection and thus achieved an aesthetic distance from the wars in Indo-China. This novel, which won the Miles Franklin Literary Award in 1996, recounts the search for Mike Langford, a war photographer, explores the psychology of his involvement with people and place in Vietnam in a decade which culminated in the fall (or liberation) of Saigon in 1975, and culminates in his apparent crucifixion in Cambodia after the takeover by the Khmer Rouge. According to conventional critical criteria, *Highways to a War* is a more successful literary work than most of the early fiction of the Vietnam War, which was written by former combatants. Such novels include John Rowe's *Count Your Dead* (1968), Rhys Pollard's *The Cream Machine* (1972), William Nagle's *The Odd Angry Shot* (1975) (from which a film was made), and Michael Frazer's *Nasho* (1984). The anger exhibited by the male Australian characters in such novels has been aptly traced by Peter Pierce to their authors' frustrated sense of a 'reliant, hampered status . . . exaggerated by the legacy of colonial experience' and a consequent tendency to rely for images of their current plight on traditional military and national legends, such as those of the Anzacs, Diggers, Tobruk and Kokoda.[2]

Despite the previous generalisation about experience taking time to bear literary fruit, the first work of fiction by an Australian about Vietnam was Morris West's carefully researched and well-timed novel *The Ambassador* (1965). West anatomised the political, religious and cultural forces at work in Vietnam around his central figure, the American ambassador. Like such previous novels by West as *Children of the Sun* (1957), *The Devil's Advocate* (1959) and *The Shoes of the Fisherman* (1963), *The Ambassador* focuses on moral and political dilemmas and shows the difficulties of decision-making in situations of power and responsibility. West's first-person narrator, Ambassador Amberley, is an unlikeable character; yet West exposes his burden of guilt and responsibility in fictional episodes in which arguments, beliefs and decisions are catechised by a Catholic authorial conscience in the manner of Graham Greene. Despite his international popularity, West has been surprisingly neglected by Australian literary critics. His novels of ideas, although sometimes static and portentous, have continued to attract an international readership through to *Lazarus* (1990), in which West explores the experience of a serious operation and an encounter with death, *The Ringmaster* (1991), *The Lovers* (1993), *Vanishing Point* (1996), and the autobiographical *View from a Ridge* (1996). However, no novel better illustrates West's understanding of complex international situations, and his prescience, than *The Ambassador*. West was a public opponent of Australia's (and America's) military involvement in Vietnam. Having left Australia in 1955 and lived mainly in Europe and North America, he returned in 1980, and further contributed to the public culture through radio, television and university residencies. His acceptance as a significant figure in Australian literary culture indicates a broadening of literary criteria in some universities and other cultural institutions at this time to include popular writing and to applaud international success, although the ambivalent Australian responses to the success (especially in the USA) of Thomas Keneally and Peter Carey revealed a continuing sensitivity about who 'owns' such writers and their work.

The most important social and cultural consequence in Australia of the Vietnam War was the development of a counter-culture in the late 1960s and 1970s. A direct expression of this spirit of protest was an anthology of prose and verse, *We Took Their Orders and are Dead* (1971), edited by Shirley Cass, Ros Cheney, David Malouf and Michael Wilding, which conveys the contributors' opposition to 'the military involvement of the American and other allies in the war in Vietnam'. A spirit of generational protest had been brewing in pre-Vietnam issues such as censorship and the death penalty but ramified during and after the war in Vietnam into issues such as sexual politics, Aboriginal rights and movements to conserve the natural environment. In their book *Seizures of Youth*, Robin Gerster and Jan Bassett agree with Andrew Milner that ' "centrally" the sixties "meant" the Vietnam War and the international protest movement'. But the youthful protesters at universities and in the moratorium marches were rejecting more than the Vietnam War: being ' "against Vietnam" implied a blanket rejection of almost everything associated with the world of their parents'.[3] On the home front, an incipient spirit of generational rebellion had been encapsulated in Alan Seymour's play *The One Day of the Year* (first produced in 1960 and published in 1962). However, the play's protagonist, Hughie, does not extend his protest as far as the counter-culture rebels of the later 1960s and 1970s. With his girlfriend Jan, he criticises Anzac Day and its empty rituals in the student newspaper at his university, but is troubled by a sense of mixed loyalties and affections and decides to remain at home for the present with his father and mother. This muted criticism by a younger generation of the restrictive 'suburban values' of their parents' generation had been insistent in the early 1960s, most notably in George Johnston's novel *My Brother Jack* (1964) and Randolph Stow's *The Merry-go-round in the Sea* (1965). Johnston had lived abroad, mainly in England and Greece from 1951, returning to Australia in 1964 when *My Brother Jack* won the Miles Franklin Award. Seymour moved to England in 1961, as did Stow in 1966. They were part of a much larger group of Australian expatriate writers and artists who saw greater prospects in the 'old world' than in what seemed to many a prematurely middle-aged Australia. To ignore the contribution to Australian culture of Australians who left these shores is, as Ros Pesman remarked, 'to diminish our history'.[4]

AUSTRALIANS ABROAD

The spirit of protest in much writing by Australians in the 1960s and 1970s thus emerged from overseas enclaves. London was a favourite haunt. Germaine Greer, Barry Humphries, Clive James, Peter Porter, Jill Neville and others projected their dramas from this metropolitan vantage point, which remained a powerful publishing stronghold. Richard Neville, joint founder (with Richard Walsh and Martin Sharp) of the Sydney underground magazine *Oz* in 1963, moved to London in 1966 and co-edited a revived *Oz* with Felix Dennis and Jim Anderson. The London *Oz* achieved international notoriety in 1971 when the editors were convicted at the Old Bailey of producing an obscene publication. Neville was sentenced to 15 months imprisonment and ordered to be deported. However, the press and icons of popular culture were rapidly mobilised. The Beatles and the Rolling Stones, who had both toured Australia in the 1960s, offered help, John Lennon reportedly telling the *Evening Standard* that 'Yoko and I have proposed marriage to Richard Neville, so he can't be deported'.[5] In the event, the prison sentence and deportation order were quashed on appeal (with the help of English barrister and author, John Mortimer, and Australian expatriate, Geoffrey Robertson).

Richard Neville's breathless memoir of the 1960s, *Hippie Hippie Shake* (1995), indicates that much of the protest activity of this time was about sexual freedom (of a kind which has been called 'sexist' in the 1990s), censorship, and the use of drugs. But Australians in England, even those who contributed to *Oz*, were far from unanimous about the counter-culture and its activities. Clive James, for example, fundamentally disagreed with the concept of an 'alternative culture' and preferred to contribute to what he called 'civilization'. And like Hughie in *The One Day of the Year* Richard Neville himself apparently could not overcome 'an ingrained respect for my dinkum Aussie Dad and his beliefs' to endorse Germaine Greer's burning of an Australian flag at an anti-Vietnam rally in the Strand on May Day 1969. Self-conscious in their public posturing, these Australian expatriates tended to retain a static view of the 'retarded' country they had left. Neville's joky solution to Australia's problems was 'a charter flight of freaks: a shimmering spectrum of yippies, blacks, situationists, rock icons, the Living Theatre and go-go dancers'.[6] A generation later, the home-grown Gay and Lesbian Mardi Gras in Sydney had stolen this show from the 1960s heterosexuals.

The outstanding literary achievement among the Australian expatriates in London since the 1960s has been that of Peter Porter. After a short stint on the *Courier Mail* in Brisbane, Porter sailed to England in 1951, not returning to his homeland (except briefly in 1954) until 1974. Thereafter, with regular returns for literary festivals and university residencies, Porter has become an important influence on younger poets in Australia, and on the wider literary culture through anthologies, reviews and commentaries.[7] Although criticised for the difficulty of his poetry, and its capacious store of European allusions, Porter has kept alive the sense of an eclectic set of usable poetic traditions, ranging from those of the Elizabethan metaphysicals to modernism. Known in Britain from the early 1960s as a mordant metropolitan satirist of consumerism, war and all forms of tyranny, Porter also developed a personal voice, intelligent, plangent and at times lyrical (in which his memories of Australia figured prominently), which could explore the mysteries of death and love. Porter's poetic achievement is recorded more fully in Chapter 13. It is sufficient to observe here that, with his *Collected Poems* (1983), *A Porter Selected* (1989) and three new volumes in the 1990s, his poetic energy and enterprise showed that Porter could not be written off as one of the 'last of the British Australians'. His influence in Australian literary culture has been to offer a set of alternative poetic visions and possibilities to Les Murray's 'bush baroque', on the one hand, and John Tranter's American-influenced Sydney modernism on the other. Porter's example further illustrates the permeable boundaries of the national literary culture as it became internationalised in the last two decades of the twentieth century.

Other figures have also impacted on Australia from the old metropolis. The influence of cultural critics Clive James and Germaine Greer on Australian thought and opinion has been widely promulgated through the popular media (especially television). James's chief contribution to the literary culture has been through his books of criticism *The Metropolitan Critic* (1974) and *At the Pillars of Hercules* (1979) and his witty and perceptive autobiographical volumes, *Unreliable Memoirs* (1980), *Falling Towards England* (1985) and *May Week Was in June* (1990). James's television reviews and travel writings trace a career based in London but with international dimensions which include reminders of his Sydney suburban upbringing. His emergence as a popular television personality with the BBC in the 1980s led to a diminution of his specifically literary interests but James remained a prolific writer with a strong sense of audience responsiveness. When he appeared at the 1996 Melbourne International Writers' Festival, in conversation with Peter Porter, the audience was reminded of the continuing intellectual brilliance, and range, of this pair.

Germaine Greer has been a more potent catalyst of social change internationally than the other Australians who took up residence in Britain in the 1950s and 1960s. Greer's second book, *The Female Eunuch* (1970), brought her international attention, especially during her American tour in 1971. *The Female Eunuch* is generally regarded as the Australian herald of the women's liberation movement in the 1970s. The scholarly qualities of the book were a product of wide reading and studies in English at the universities of Melbourne, Sydney and Cambridge, but her combination of passion and theatricality of utterance was fostered in writing for newspapers and magazines such as *Suck* (which she co-founded), *Oz, Rolling Stone, Esquire,* and the more sedate *Sunday Times, Listener* and *Spectator.* As a controversialist and promoter of causes Greer has few peers; she has challenged conventional views about birth control (*Sex and Destiny*, 1984) and menopause (*The Change*, 1991); she has researched and resuscitated the reputations of women artists (in *The Obstacle Race*, 1979) and writers (*The Madwoman's Underclothes*, 1986 and, more cantankerously, *Slip-shod Sibyls*, 1995). Like other expatriates, she has made her most significant contribution to the literature of Australia in the genre of autobiography. *Daddy, We Hardly Knew You* (1989), as one reviewer noted, is 'a grippingly told detective story' about the search for the truth about her father;[8] but it is also a moving search for 'home' and her own identity. In an article in the *Guardian Weekly* in 1993, Greer remarked revealingly that 'Australia is, was, and ever shall be someone else's country' and that such a recognition generates 'the ache of exile'.[9]

Barry Humphries's relationship to Australian culture and society has often been perceived as antagonistic, especially during the phase of Australian 'new nationalism' in the 1970s and 1980s. (Playwright Jack Hibberd was one of his strongest critics.)[10] Humphries's satiric fascination with Australian suburbia took up a recurrent motif of Australian intellectuals and writers in the post-Second World War years. But his continuing engagement with the Australian suburbs through his early creations, Edna Everage and Sandy Stone (who were first brought together in the *Wild Life in Suburbia* recordings in 1959) enabled Humphries to show change as well as continuity in the habits and acquisitions of the middle classes which provided his main targets (and his main audience). Humphries's humorous and often devastating evocations of Australian idioms, manners and values have been admired by other writers. His autobiography, *More Please* (1992), offers remarkable insights into a self he describes as 'a dissolute, guilt-ridden, self-obsessed boozer' and who, through the 1970s and 1980s, commuted between England and his homeland 'without ever being quite sure where I really belonged'.[11]

Developments in the technologies of travel and communications since the 1970s have dramatically altered Australians' attitudes to each other and to the landmass itself. These changes were framed by two works of historical diagnosis, Geoffrey Blainey's *The Tyranny of Distance* (1966) and Graeme Davison's *The Unforgiving Minute* (1993). Blainey's book, whose title entered the Australian lexicon, explored the powerful influence of the *idea*, as well as the physical reality, of distance in Australia's history. Australia's 'remoteness' and 'isolation' from the rest of the world as well as the vast distances between places on the continent itself led to Blainey's concluding image, in the mid-1960s, of a country 'adrift'. Graeme Davison's study revealed the massive difference between early concepts of time on this continent, such as the cyclical notions of traditional Aborigines, or convicts 'serving time', and those of contemporary urban businesspeople. Davison observed that between the early 1960s and the early 1990s 'the volume of telephone communications between Australia and the rest of the world . . . increased one thousand-fold, or more than fifteen times faster than the rate of increase of calls within Australia'. This apparent vindication of Marx's prophecy—'the annihilation of space by time'— seems confirmed by the vision of an Australia in the 1990s in which shared time zones (with Japan, China, the Philippines, for example) were more significant than distances and where 'shared time may come gradually to be as important as shared language or shared borders'.[12]

International technological advances were promptly adopted in the affluent areas of urban Australia, with consequential changes to the literary culture. The mobile phone, for example, has changed the nature of 'private' conversation. By the mid-1990s more messages were transmitted worldwide by e-mail than by the often derided 'snail' mail. Enthusiastic advocates of the Internet and World Wide Web claimed a paradigm shift in reading and learning. At the least, the relatively easy instantaneous access to textual information by electronic means threw conventional literary publishing into a new phase. But that is to leap ahead. We should consider first the major changes in Australian literary publishing in the past generation.

LITERARY PUBLISHING

Literary production in Australia has been influenced greatly by the publishing industry and by the educational institutions, magazines and newspapers which developed a reading public for Australian literature. Reflecting on his time with Angus and Robertson in the 1950s, Alec Bolton described the decade as an 'age of innocence'.[13] In relative terms, this seems an apt description of a more leisurely, 'gentlemanly' time before hot metal type gave way to faster electronic publishing techniques and international financial pressures brought about rapid changes of ownership and control. A single firm with a long history of publishing Australian literature, Angus and Robertson had remained a dominant force through the 1950s, publishing around 100 new titles and new editions per year. With George Ferguson as publishing director and Beatrice Davis as literary editor, Angus and Robertson had remained loyal to most of their established authors and had taken on large foundational projects of Australian publishing, including F.T. Macartney's update of Morris Miller's *Bibliography of Australian Literature* (1956), *The Australian Encyclopaedia* (1958), and H.M. Green's *History of Australian Literature* (1961).

The struggles for control of Angus and Robertson in the 1960s reflected larger patterns of destabilisation and reorientation in book publishing. International involvement and takeovers by British, American and New Zealand interests became commonplace. Even as the proponents of Australian literature fought for its independence, the literary culture was tugged towards international waters. However, while UK publishers expanded their interests in Australian subsidiaries through the 1960s and 1970s, it was not until the 1980s that the large American conglomerates moved substantially into Australia.[14] An interesting publishing case study is provided by Penguin's Australian paperback publishing operations, which were set up by Max Harris, Geoffrey Dutton and Brian Stonier in 1961 under an English chief editor, Tony Godwin, and general director, Allen Lane.[15] Donald Horne's book *The Lucky Country* (1964) was an early success, as were Robin Boyd's *The Australian Ugliness* (1960), Robert Hughes's *The Art of Australia* (1966), Patrick White's *Four Plays* (1965) and novels by Randolph Stow and Martin Boyd. However, Harris, Dutton and Stonier became frustrated with the colonialist attitudes of the British-based Penguin publishers, who seemed to them to have little sympathy for an emergent Australian literary culture, and in 1965 left to set up the first independent Australian paperback publishing house, Sun Books, in 1965. In order to keep afloat in the rougher international seas, Sun Books in turn found sanctuary with the large firm Macmillan in 1973[16]—a pattern which would be replicated often in subsequent years.

Despite such apparent threats to an independent Australian literature, a general growth in publishing opportunities for Australian writers occurred from the 1960s. Between 1960 and 1975 membership of the Australian Book Publishers' Association increased from 40 to 91. American-born Frank Thompson, who was publishing manager at the University of Queensland Press from 1961 to 1980, observed a change from publishers who had come from the ranks of writers to publishers whose background was in marketing. Thompson's view of typical Australian publishers metamorphosing from gentlemen to larrikins to entrepreneurs in a single generation is colourful stereotyping,[17] but it does indicate the changing pressures and demands on publishers in the face of technological innovation and market forces. Under Thompson's direction the University of Queensland Press set a lead with their Paperback Poets in 1970 and Paperback Prose in 1972. A later development, in which UQP played a role, was the 'export' to Europe and North America of Australian fiction by writers such as Thea Astley, Peter Carey, Elizabeth Jolley, David Malouf and Thomas Keneally. A major benefit of the Australian Independent Publishers' Association, which was set up in 1975, was its recognition and encouragement of small publishers. Coincidentally, 1975 was also the year when Australia's most successful regional publisher, Fremantle Arts Centre Press, was established under Ian Templeman's direction.[18] At a more scholarly end of the publishing spectrum came the Colonial Texts series and the Academy Editions of Australian Literature which, like the *Oxford Companion to Australian Literature* (1985, 1994), were initiated at University College, Australian Defence Force Academy in Canberra.

Through the 1970s and 1980s many such small publishing groups fanned the flames of creative activity and regional identity. By the 1990s, however, the book publishing industry was again dominated by large foreign-owned publishing groups. As John

Curtain has explained, these groups expanded through amalgamations in London and New York but also by takeovers of indigenous Australian companies: for example, Penguin Australia 'absorbed' the imprints of Lloyd O'Neill, Greenhouse, and McPhee Gribble—previously all leading independents. A series of reports into book publishing by Australian governments 'confirmed the efficacy of economic reality over considerations of cultural nationalism'. Here was an apparent victory for the forces of economic rationalism over those of economic nationalism. Would culture become the handmaid of trade? If such trade-oriented reports were to be believed, Australians since the late 1970s have been more interested in access to books and ideas through London and New York than in fostering an indigenous publishing industry.[19]

In spite of these apparent 'internationalising' tendencies in economics and trade, half the books sold in Australia by the end of the 1980s were published in Australia.[20] The Literature Board of the Australia Council, established by the Whitlam Labor government in 1973 to replace Australia's oldest arts assistance body, the Commonwealth Literary Fund (CLF) (1908–73), contributed greatly to the development of an indigenous literary culture through its programs of assistance to individual writers, to publishers and literary magazines and to the promotion of Australian literature, nationally and internationally.[21] The Literature Board was criticised on various grounds, including its alleged social engineering and adoption of a 'survival of the fittest' approach to literary production; its 'arms length' approach to funding and reliance on peer group assessment methods have also been attacked, especially in the mid-1990s.[22] But the Australia Council's allegedly unwarranted interference with market mechanisms—as certain free market economists portrayed it—contributed strongly to the emergence of many writers, whose time was 'bought' so that they could write. Similarly, programs of subsidy to publishers enabled them to publish the work of Australian writers against the prevailing economic odds. By subsidising publishers of Australian work, and promoting these publications, the Australia Council's intervention had to some extent broken the nexus of colonial domination and allowed a period—a historical breathing space—in which Australian writers and readers could converse more freely and directly with each other. Furthermore, although state subsidy could breed a subservient or 'politically correct' literary culture, there were many counter-examples of writers who were directly or indirectly critical of governments and prevailing attitudes of their time,[23] thus continuing a tradition of writerly independence which had existed during the period of the CLF. Assessments of the general quality of writing in this period have varied, but as the following chapters show, the period since 1965 has been one of vigorous and diverse activity in many literary genres, both within Australia and to a modest extent internationally.

READERS, CRITICS, THEORISTS

The universities have been important institutions in the assessing and valuing of Australian literature since 1965. A report to the Australian government in 1987 contended that Australian studies, including Australian literary studies, were still neglected in the universities.[24] This was in spite of attempts which had been in train since the *Meanjin* debates of the 1950s to introduce Australian literature into the predominantly British-influenced university curricula.[25] By the mid-1970s six of the 18 universities offered full-year courses in Australian literature while most of the others offered part-courses. By the mid-1990s most of the 38 universities included a proportion of Australian literary content, though not always in courses designated as Australian literature—a sign perhaps of the 'naturalisation' of Australian literature in the humanities curriculum. Yet it was significant that, by 1997, there were still only two Australian universities with designated Chairs of Australian literature—the University of Sydney and the James Cook University of North Queensland.

An important landmark in the professionalisation of Australian literary studies was the founding of the Association for the Study of Australian Literature in 1977 and its formal constitution at an inaugural conference at Monash University in 1978. This Association, known as ASAL, developed an international membership which includes writers, editors, teachers and students. Its influence has been considerable in the publications it has sponsored, which include *The Oxford Literary Guide to Australia* (general editor Peter Pierce, 1987, revised 1993) and the *Penguin New Literary History of Australia* (general editor Laurie Hergenhan, 1988). The Association's bulletin, *Notes and Furphies*, published a directory of postgraduate research in Australian literature in 1995 which revealed a remarkable picture. Whereas research in Australian literature in the mid-1970s could be characterised as 'only now beginning to take firm root',[26] the picture in 1995 was of a quite numerous and diverse field of activity: for example, some 267 MA and PhD theses on Australian literary topics had been completed at Australian universities and almost 300 were in progress, including a small number by overseas students working in Australia. Some 30 theses on Australian topics had been completed at universities overseas.[27]

The assessing and valuing of Australian literature has been carried out in a variety of magazines and newspapers as well as on radio and (less frequently) on television. Magazines and journals such as *Southerly* (1939–), *Meanjin* (1940–), *Overland* (1954–), *Quadrant* (1956–), *Westerly* (1956–) and *Australian Literary Studies* (1963–) have operated at the professional end of the spectrum. These magazines have figured prominently in book-length studies of the literary and cultural history of this period including John Docker's *Australian Cultural Elites* (1974), *Cross Currents: Magazines and Newspapers in Australian Literature* (1981), edited by Bruce Bennett, Vincent Buckley's *Cutting Green Hay* (1983), Lynn Strahan's *Just City and the Mirrors* (1984) and John McLaren's *Writing in Hope and Fear* (1996). A joint statement by editors of the literary magazines in 1975 described them as 'moderators in literary life, helping writers to achieve their potential not just by accepting but by rejecting, arguing, criticising, sponsoring and commissioning: each magazine with a different bias and interests'.[28] At the same time, they have served as sources of entertainment, knowledge and understanding at the cutting edges of contemporary literary culture. However, like the nation's most important cultural institution, the Australian Broadcasting Corporation, the major literary magazines became increasingly threatened by reduced government funding in the late 1990s.

Yet the undergrowth was thick with other magazines in the thirty-year period from 1965. Some forty 'mini-magazines' were mentioned in a checklist of new magazines in 1977, many of which had lasted no more than an issue or two.[29] There were many other short-lived experiments. Special interest publications which survived and continued to publish beyond their first few issues included feminist journals such as *Refractory Girl* (1972–) and *Hecate* (1975–); the Aboriginal and Thursday Islander *Identity* (1971–82); regional publications *LINQ* (Townsville, 1971–), *Island Magazine* (Hobart, 1979–) and *Northern Perspectives* (Darwin, 1977–). Literary magazines specialising in a particular genre included *Poetry Australia* (1964–c. 94) and *New Poetry* (1971–82); *Theatre Australia* (1976–82); *Australian Short Stories* (1982–); and *Science Fiction* (1977–). Newer magazines with a literary critical bent included *Meridian* (1982–), *Voices* (1991–1997), *Scripsi* (1981–93), and *Heat* (1996–), the latter two boasting a range of international contributors, especially from Europe. In addition, certain magazines outside Australia published Australian literature and criticism including *Kunapipi* (Aarhus, Denmark, 1979–1996; thereafter Wollongong, NSW, 1996–) and *Antipodes* (Texas, USA, 1987–), the official journal of the American Association for Australian Literary Studies.

Whereas the dedicated literary magazines, committed to providing space for risk-taking experiment and informed commentary and criticism, have generally required government subsidy to survive, a number of commercial magazines have been highly profitable and have developed wide readerships. The king of the 'glossies' in this period has been Australian Consolidated Press's publisher, Richard Walsh, whose Packer-owned organisation published 60 per cent of the magazines sold in Australia in the mid-1990s.[30] Walsh's previous experience as an editor of *Oz* and *Nation Review* revealed a personal interest in satire, politics and ideas which was not usually associated with his ACP publications such as the *Australian Women's Weekly, Cleo, Dolly* or *Cosmopolitan*. Along with other magazine publishers, Walsh has learnt to serve up a mix of populist and more intellectual fare. Some leading Australian writers have contributed to commercial magazines such as *Australian Playboy, Vogue* and *HQ*. Whether at the popular or highbrow end of their spectrum, the commercial magazines have, however, tended towards entertainment (or 'infotainment') rather than the investigation of difficult texts or complex moral, aesthetic or social issues.[31]

Quality literary journalism has increased in major newspapers such as the *Australian*, the *Sydney Morning Herald* and the *Age*, although it has had to compete with business, computer and popular entertainment sections. Significantly, the *Australian*, which included literature and authors in its versions of 'the national story' in general news and features, was increasing its circulation in the 1990s, indicating a growing incorporation of literature into its recurrent narratives of the nation and scrutinies of Australian identity.

Despite a generalised interest in literary topics and literary figures, however, the reviewing of actual books remained as much a 'mixed picture' in the late 1990s as John McLaren had described it in 1981.[32] The Murdoch-owned *Australian* newspaper, which commenced in 1964 as a national daily, had grown in authority and influence under Paul Kelly's editorship as a journal of cultural record and intellectual debate. Its three-page book review section in the *Weekend Australian* became a necessary reference point for literary opinion and judgment, especially during Barry Oakley's literary editorship from 1987 until 1997. Moreover, in keeping with its image of a paper in touch with the national culture, the *Australian* sometimes promoted literary debates to the status of feature articles or, occasionally, to the front pages as news, as we will shortly see. In the generosity of its coverage, the book review section of the *Canberra Times* on Saturdays (under the literary editorship of Robert Hefner since 1988) also set a lead for its larger metropolitan cousins, the *Sydney Morning Herald* and the *Age*. At the same time, the increasing popularity of multi-media entertainment in the 1980s and 1990s influenced book reviewing in all Australian newspapers by privileging interviews and personality pieces on writers, sometimes at the expense of single book reviews. Reviews themselves often drifted towards features, as books were used to highlight contemporary themes or issues (thus reinforcing a tendency towards thematic or 'issues' teaching in the schools and universities). The Australia Council further upset an already volatile situation in 1996 when it decided to subsidise a monthly literary review in the *Australian* newspaper (*The Australian's Review of Books*) while reducing support for the magazine *Meanjin* and eliminating all subsidy for *Australian Literary Studies*, which, under Laurie Hergenhan's editorship, had become the nation's most important scholarly journal in this field. The *Australian Book Review* (1968–74 and 1978–) continued its tradition of reviewing the full range of contemporary Australian books.

In defiance of pronouncements of the 'death of the author' in literary discourse by fashionable French theorists, Roland Barthes and Michel Foucault, interviews and biographical features on Australian writers appeared regularly from the 1970s in colour supplements to the weekend newspapers, as well as in glossy weeklies such as the revamped *Women's Weekly, Vogue, GH, Cleo* and elsewhere. This interest in the 'life stories' of writers, which extended from popular articles to books of literary biography, led to an enhanced curiosity about the relationship of authors' experience to the books they produce. A series of literary controversies and scandals in the mid to late 1990s further stimulated this curiosity. The most sensational scandal followed the publication of a novel, *The Hand that Signed the Paper*, in 1994. This novel, which deals with the complicity of Ukrainians with the Nazis during the Second World War and the question of guilt for their descendants in Australia was widely advertised as having been written by a 22-year-old Ukrainian-Australian Queenslander called Helen Demidenko. The novel won the *Australian*/Vogel award for young writers in 1993 (which award guaranteed publication) and two senior prizes, the 1995 Miles Franklin Prize and the Australian Literature Society's Gold Medal. As the book became more widely read and reviewed, it was criticised vigorously in some quarters for its treatment of historical events and its apparently anti-Semitic tendencies. But the *coup de grâce* was the 'unmasking' of the author when David Bentley, in the Brisbane *Courier Mail* of 19 August 1995, revealed that Helen Demidenko was in fact Helen Darville, the Australian-born daughter of English migrants. While some sympathy was expressed for a young woman 'caught up in her fantasy', other critics accused Darville of concocting a hoax for personal gain. Darville was also accused of plagiarising parts of the novel. Natalie Jane Prior's *The Demidenko Diary* (1996) exploited a popular interest in the personal identity of the author, but Andrew Riemer's *The Demidenko Debate* (1996) and Robert Manne's *The Culture of Forgetting* (1996) examined the book and its reception more closely. Could 'history' and 'literature' be judged in the same way? What were a writer's ethical responsibilities? Was truth-telling more important than inventiveness? The reverberations of the controversy can be observed elsewhere in this history.

The Demidenko-Darville controversy sparked a series of newspaper investigations into other false identities apparently claimed by authors, though few recalled Australian literature's long history of pseudonymous publications with its heyday in the goldfields of the nineteenth century—where many escapees from other situations became 'Smith', or something more imaginative. Paul Radley, who had won the *Australian*/Vogel literary prize in 1980 for the novel *Jack Rivers and Me* (1981), confessed through his psychologist in 1996 that this and two subsequent novels had actually been written by an uncle. The 'authenticity' of Aboriginal literature came under the spotlight in 1996 too, when members of Western Australia's Aboriginal community challenged Mudrooroo (formerly known as Colin Johnson) to authenticate his claim to Aboriginal ancestry following statements by a sister that their grandfather was an American migrant from North Carolina, apparently of Negro or Creole background.[33] In 1997 a white Australian author, Leon Carmen, confessed that he had posed as a female Aboriginal writer, Wanda Koolmatrie, and artist Elizabeth Durack admitted that she had produced paintings by a non-existent Aboriginal artist she named Eddie Burrup. As the new sport of 'spotting the frauds' gathered force, novelist and short story writer Archie Weller's assumption of Aboriginality was also questioned.[34]

From one point of view, these exposés represented a necessary honesty, an insistence, as it were, on correct advertising and fair trading. From another point of view, they may suggest a backlash against a period of 'politically correct' social engineering during which minorities, or apparently silenced groups in the community—the young, migrants, Aborigines, for instance—were emphasised, and subsidised to encourage their work. Yet these events also raise questions about the relationship of artistic merit to biographical identity. Those commentators who espoused the cause of a free-ranging imagination and empathy through these events found themselves under increasing pressure to include biography as a determinant of literary behaviour.

The struggle between journalists and university critics and theorists to influence ways of reading Australian literature has waxed and waned since the 1960s, and has influenced what is published and where. In general, critics from the universities have sought to engage students and readers with the intellectual rigour or moral seriousness of reading literature, but they have done this in contrasting ways. An early approach was to select a cricket team of authors to represent the nation. Vincent Buckley's canon of the 'best' Australian writers numbered twelve: Furphy, Richardson, Herbert, Dark, Palmer, White, Brennan, Slessor, Hope, Wright, Neilson and McAuley.[35] By the mid-1970s, when most universities offered at least part-courses in Australian literature and the pressure towards producing a canon of the 'best' authors and works had eased, a variety of experiments with texts and teaching methods occurred, including a broadening from Anglo-American New Criticism, which had focused on the aesthetic qualities of individual texts, towards the study of social and cultural contexts.[36] Under the influence of Marxist and other socio-literary theories, the earlier interest in the 'Great Australian Novel' (or poem or play) was modified towards an approach to Australian literature which A.D. Hope had himself proposed—the study of the native literature as an entry point to 'the civilization, the way of life and the problems of this country'.[37]

For many in the universities Hope's rationale remained paramount. However, a proliferation of literary theories from the European (mainly French) and American (often Yale) theorists began to affect Australian literary studies in the 1980s. Thus names like Barthes, Baudrillard, Bourdieu, Cixous, Derrida, Deleuze, de Man, Foucault, Guattari, Kristeva, Lacan, Said and others appeared frequently in theses and literary articles. As Veronica Brady has pointed out, the most 'mandarin' were the theories of the deconstructionists, led in Australia from the late 1970s by former Yale professor Howard Felperin at Melbourne University.[38] Based on the work of Jacques Derrida, deconstructionist theory led some students back to the language of texts rather than social contexts, but much tortuous and obfuscatory critical discourse resulted. A conscious cross-over from some of these theoretical interests occurred outside the academy in Helen Daniels's book *Liars* (1988), which presented Australian novelists Peter Mathers, David Foster, David Ireland, Peter Carey, Murray Bail, Nicholas Hasluck, Elizabeth Jolley and Gerald Murnane as sceptical game-players with the idea of 'truth'.

The theories which took firmer root in Australia were those with social and political agendas, especially feminism and postcolonialism. Anne Summers's *Damned Whores and God's Police* (1975; new edition 1994) and Miriam Dixson's *The Real Matilda* (1976) had sown the seeds of later feminist rewritings of Australian literature and society, including those by Ann Curthoys, Marilyn Lake and Carole Ferrier. Helen Garner's book *The First Stone* (1995), about a sexual harassment case in Melbourne and its consequences, stimulated widespread public debate about first- and second-wave feminisms in Australia. The influence of postcolonial theory in Australia became evident with the publication of *The Empire Writes Back* (1989) by three Australians, Bill Ashcroft, Gareth Griffiths and Helen Tiffin, and *Decolonising Fictions* (1993), by Diana Brydon and Helen Tiffin, which introduced a solid comparative dimension into postcolonial studies. No Australian literary text has yet stirred the postcolonial pot as *The First Stone* did for feminism, but

Alex Miller's Miles Franklin Award-winning novel *The Ancestor Game* (1992) incorporated some postcolonial ideas into its exploration of Australian–Chinese relationships.

In spite of these and other significant contributions by Australians to feminist and postcolonial thought, the debates which erupted in the *Australian* from time to time through the 1980s and 1990s about 'common sense' versus 'theory' had an ironic poignancy. In the very period when Australian literature was being 'democratised', and more people had opportunities to read it, the discourses of criticism and commentary in some educational institutions were becoming more esoteric. At its worst, much journalism remained mere sloganising, headline-hunting and sensation-mongering; but as universities opened themselves to ever broader cross-sections of the Australian population and offered wide-ranging liberal arts courses, some university teachers were tempted to create a priestly class of theorists whose name-dropping and brow-clutching abstractions left literary texts far behind. An unfortunate consequence was that the gulf between university theory and journalistic practice militated against the development of a class of writers greatly needed in Australia—literary and cultural journalists.

Responding to the broader base of students now attempting higher education, many institutions introduced courses in popular culture and communications studies. Various studies followed, ranging from the relatively casual to the abstract, systematic and theoretical.[39] Some teachers complained that the close reading of literary texts had been replaced by a tendency towards loose theorising about 'cultural texts'. However, the main effect of this emergent field on Australian literary studies was to place books in a broadly cultural context and especially to bring them into a closer relationship to film and television. Chapter 17 in this *History* explores this important, developing relationship.

Beyond the universities the picture was different. By the early 1990s, according to research carried out for the Australia Council, readers were 'overwhelmingly positive' in their opinions of Australian writers. However, the most popular authors according to surveys conducted in 1994 were Danielle Steele, Catherine Cookson, Paul Jennings and Jeffrey Archer—of whom only Jennings, an author of children's books, was an Australian.[40] Other Australians in the most popular list included Peter Corris, Victor Kelleher, Thomas Keneally, Colleen McCullough and Nevil Shute. Although Keneally and, to a lesser extent, Corris and Kelleher appeared in some literature courses in schools and universities, it was clear that a distinction remained between 'serious' books for study and those that were more popularly consumed 'for entertainment'.

LITERARY GENRES AND HYBRID FORMS

Using the books categorised as 'literature' in the *Annals of Australian Literature* (1992), it can be shown that the total number of books of Australian literature rose from an average of 85 per year in 1965–69 to 122 in 1970–79, and 183 in the decade 1980–89.[41] A further quantum increase occurred during 1990–95, during which over 400 titles appeared each year. It is no exaggeration to say that Australian literature, considered as published literary texts, participated in a general publishing 'explosion' in these years. Whereas it had been possible for a literary editor or keen reader to keep abreast of the broad field of Australian literature in the early 1960s, this was clearly no longer possible by the 1990s. There were other consequences too. Libraries, for example, could not afford to order every publication, as they had once done, and electronic publishing emerged as an alternative means of access. Australian literature teachers and scholars were thus forced to specialise within the broad field of their endeavour according to genres, authors, periods or themes which were considered by cultural authorities to be 'relevant' or 'good', or held special appeal for them or their students.

In a single generation Australian literary studies had been transformed from one with a relative paucity of materials to an abundance, thus raising acute difficulties of selection and specialisation. Would market forces rule? Questions were asked about the readership for literary books.[42] Film and television were radically affecting reading habits and leading to a culture more attuned to visual stimuli (see Chapter 17), while the 'information revolution' seemed to give access through personal computers to a global web of knowledge.

In the midst of such changes, it is interesting to observe what happened to the traditional literary genres. From the 1960s to the 1990s, novels and books of poetry were the most prolific genres, comprising about half the total number of all Australian literary texts published in the period.[43] However, certain variations occurred within this overall pattern. Novels accounted for 28 per cent of all literary genres in the late 1960s but dropped to 20 per cent in the 1970s, rising to the former level in the 1980s and to 34 per cent 1990–95. Books of poetry accounted for 23 per cent of Australian literature publications in the late 1960s but rose dramatically to 39 per cent in the 1970s, dropping to 25 per cent in the 1980s and early 1990s. While an overall predominance of the novel is evident, the rise of poetry publishing in the 1970s probably relates in part to the availability of Australia Council subsidies for a pool of unpublished poets, and the growth of desktop publishing and small presses in that time.[44] Qualitative developments in poetry and the novel are discussed in Chapters 13 and 15.

An examination of other literary genres reveals significant patterns and variations too. Published drama texts, like poetry, increased rapidly in the decade of the 1970s to be the third largest category at 9 per cent. This increase can be attributed largely to the founding by Katharine Brisbane and Philip Parsons of Currency Press in 1971 (as Helen Thomson observes in Chapter 14).

The short story, a genre often neglected by critics and commentators, but not readers, had its publishing heyday in the 1980s, when collections of stories by individual authors or anthologies accounted for some 12 per cent of the total, and held this proportion 1990–95. The rise of the short story in publishers' estimation in the 1980s was built on the popularity of books by Frank Moorhouse, Michael Wilding and others and brought new volumes from Beverley Farmer, Helen Garner, Peter Goldsworthy, Janette Turner Hospital, Elizabeth Jolley, Olga Masters and David Malouf. Writers who had published earlier collections, such as Peter Cowan, John Morrison and Hal Porter, also brought out new volumes of stories in the 1980s. Helen Garner's collection *True Stories* (1996), like so much of her work, explores varieties of narrative form and poses important questions for writers, readers and critics about the disputed boundaries between journalism and fiction. Developments in the short story are discussed further in Chapter 15 as a gauge of changing interests and values in the period.

If any genre can validly claim special prominence since the 1960s it is autobiography. As discussed earlier, controversies and scandals have increased interest in the genre. Although autobiographies have constituted only one in twelve books of Australian literature, their significance has received a fuller recognition than ever before, leading to an acceptance of autobiography in the 1980s as 'a discernible artistic genre'.[45] Joy Hooton's pioneering study of Australian women's autobiographies of childhood, *Stories of Herself When Young* (1990), and David McCooey's study of modern Australian autobiography, *Artful Histories* (1996), have provided critical and theoretical perspectives on the generic qualities of autobiography, or 'life writing'. Some of the autobiographies which have gained literary prominence for the genre since the 1960s include books by Vincent Buckley, Manning Clark, Peter Conrad, Jill Ker Conway, Geoffrey Dutton, A.B. Facey, Germaine Greer, Dorothy Hewett, Barry Humphries, Clive James, Sally Morgan, Hal Porter, Andrew Riemer, Betty Roland, Elsie Roughsey, Bernard Smith, Judah Waten and Patrick White. Most of these books reinforce the view that the special strength of Australian memoirs or autobiography is their evocation of childhood and adolescence, a tendency already noted in Chapter 6. Along with this goes a sense of places 'carried in the heart' and made more poignant by current anxieties of displacement. A subdued but significant element in many contemporary Australian autobiographies is their tracing of a life as part of a national allegory. As part of this 'story of the nation', emphasis on the ethnic dimension has been a relatively recent phenomenon, exemplified in Morgan's popular *My Place* (1987) and Riemer's *Inside Outside* (1992)—thus reflecting a growing imaginative engagement in this period with the figures of the indigene and the migrant.

Nowhere is the mixing of literary modes more evident than in the crossings of history, biography and autobiography. Drusilla Modjeska's writings demonstrate this. Her influential study of women writers between the wars, *Exiles at Home* (1981), was followed in 1990 by *Poppy*, a biography of her mother with a strong autobiographical substructure using diaries, journals, interviews, letters and researched or remembered stories in a fine mixture of fact and fiction. The book won a number of literary awards in the 'non-fiction' category. Beverley Farmer followed up her novel *Alone* (1980) and books of stories *Milk* (1983) and *Home Time* (1985) with a writer's notebook *A Body of Water* (1990), which incorporates narrative, poems, quotations and observations into 13 monthly instalments of a journal representing the author's 'struggle to come to terms with this isolation, this sterility'. Like Modjeska, Farmer deploys the disparate elements of her text in a hybrid form which shows the value of crossing generic boundaries in the service of emotional subtlety and truth-telling capacity.

A significant niche within the genre of autobiography which has received little serious notice to date is political autobiography. Paul Hasluck's engaging autobiography *Mucking About* (1977), written after his retirement from the position of Governor-General in 1974, followed his own adage that 'all autobiographies ought to end about the age of thirty-five' on the grounds that after that age 'a man does not develop much'.[46] Certainly, R.G. Casey's *Australian Foreign Minister* (1972), an expansion of his diaries 1951–60, contains little that is personal or revealing. R.G. Menzies's *Afternoon Light* (1967) and *The Measure of the Years* (1970) are books in which the persona of elder states-man has settled comfortably around the former Prime Minister's memories. A generation later, Australian politics was more 'professionalised' than in the Menzies era and its brief aftermath of Liberal leaders who could not sustain Menzies's powerful appeal. The Whitlam Labor government of 1972–75 and, more particularly, the Hawke and Keating governments of 1983–96 produced memoirs and autobiographies which defied Hasluck's warning and focused on their authors' professional and personal roles in the business of politics. It is in this context that the first-person narratives by Bob Hawke, John Button, Bill Hayden, Graham Richardson and Tom Uren should be seen. Of these, Button's *Flying the Kite* (1994) and Hayden's *Hayden, an Autobiography* (1996) are worthy of men-tion for their ability to place events and personalities with humour and irony, while Richardson's *Whatever it Takes* (1994) displays a deadpan Machiavellianism that is almost disarming. *The Hawke Memoirs* (1994) is notable for its author's personal sense of des-tiny (to which readers had been introduced in Blanche d'Alpuget's biography) and for his pragmatic view of the political process.

Biography also gained stature and authority as a literary genre in this period. In terms of output, biographies matched autobiographies, and between them, they accounted for some 15 per cent of Australian literature in the period. The subjects of bio-graphical studies included explorer Ludwig Leichhardt, military general John Monash, painters Tom Roberts, Noel Counihan and Brett Whiteley, singers Nellie Melba and Joan Sutherland, and politicians Henry Parkes, Malcolm Fraser and (as mentioned) Bob Hawke.

Biographical studies of Australian writers have been especially prominent. Axel Clark's critical biography of Christopher Brennan published in 1980 set a high standard. Many book-length biographical studies of Australian authors have appeared since then, including Dorothy Green's *Henry Handel Richardson and her Fiction* (2nd edition, 1986), Brian Matthews's *Louisa* (1987), Brenda Niall's *Martin Boyd: A Life* (1988), John Barnes's *The Order of Things: A Life of Joseph Furphy* (1990), Brian Kiernan's *David Williamson: A Writer's Career* (1990; 1996), Julie Lewis's *Olga Masters: A Lot of Living* (1991), Bruce Bennett's *Spirit in Exile: Peter Porter and his Poetry* (1991), David Marr's *Patrick White: A Life* (1991), Geoffrey Dutton's *Kenneth Slessor* (1991), Hazel Rowley's *Christina Stead* (1993), Mary Lord's *Hal Porter: A Man of Many Parts* (1993), and Michael Ackland's *Henry Kendall: The Man and the Myths* (1995). The publication of such books, from within and outside the academies, has increased knowledge of the individual writers and their works, and also of the various physical and ideological settings within which they have lived and worked. A further indication of the prominent role played by Australian authors in contemporary culture was their appearance as subjects in Archibald Prize portraits. Archibald winners have included Patrick White by Louis Kahan in 1962, Ray Crooke's portrait of George Johnston in 1969 and Geoffrey Proud's notorious portrait of Dorothy Hewett in 1990.

Although book-length critical studies in the field of Australian literature have never been numerous, their publication has been especially difficult in the 1980s and 1990s. Lacking the general appeal of novels, biographies or autobiographies, literary criticism has found itself caught somewhere between the demands of esoteric specialisation and a more popular appeal. Gallant attempts to defy the sceptics have been made in the UQP Studies in Australian Literature series (general editor Anthony J. Hassall), which has developed an impressive list of single-author and more general studies, and Oxford's Australian Writers series (general editor Chris Wallace-Crabbe). In 1997 the Association for the Study of Australian Literature, recognising the need for more specialist monographs on Australian writing, launched the ASAL Literary Studies series.

Another category of literature which has become especially prominent since the 1980s is writing for children. The Book of the Year Awards for the Children's Book Council have highlighted its importance. Accurate figures are difficult to obtain, but it seems that by the 1990s at least one in ten books of Australian literature were written for children.[47] Since 1987 the Book of the Year Awards have included two categories, one for 'older readers'—those deemed to have the 'maturity to appreciate the topics, themes and scope of emotional involvement'—and the other for 'younger readers'—those categorised as having 'developed independent reading skills but are still developing in literary appreciation'. Winners of the older readers' award have included Lee Harding, Ruth Park, Colin Thiele, Victor Kelleher, Patricia Wrightson, Gillian Rubinstein, Robin Klein, Gary Crew, Isobelle Carmody and Melinda Marchetta. Winners of the Book of the Year Award for Younger Readers have included Christobel Mattingley, Robin Klein, Max Dann, Emily Rodda, Gary Disher and Wendy Orr. The inclusion of courses in children's literature at some universities, together with greater attention to reviewing of these books in weekend newspapers, has led to enhanced understanding and respect for the genre.

The Evidence of Anthologies

In addition to the literary genres mentioned above, a number of other descriptive categories, based on subject matter or themes, emerged with special force between the 1970s and the 1990s. These included regional literature, science fiction, crime/mystery, feminist writings, and gay and lesbian fiction. A good index of these developments may be found in anthologies or miscellanies.

Regional anthologies have been more numerous in contemporary Australia than any other kind. Frequently published in the state or region which provides their focus, these anthologies have often been designed to raise awareness of the landscapes, people and ways of living of the region. Western Australia has been the leading contributor to a regional literary consciousness, but all states and territories, and a number of sub-regions have been represented, especially those from outside the 'golden triangle' of Sydney–Melbourne–Canberra. The titles of some of these anthologies indicate their emphases: *Wide Domain*[48] emphasises the spaciousness of Western Australia and its resources; *North of the Ten Commandments*[49] the lawlessness of the Northern Territory; and *Effects of Light*[50] shifting perspectives on Tasmanian environments and history. An important element in such books, as in regional literary histories, is a sense of place, region and community.[51] Introducing a collection of essays on South Australian writing, Philip Butterss observes that 'the trend towards globalisation is itself, in part, responsible for continuing assertions of the importance of the regional and the local'.[52] In response to the global media networks, internet and pay television, a form of literary environmentalism which values the local and particular was emerging. As Susan Johnson and Mary Roberts remarked in *Latitudes*, an anthology of Queensland writing, 'writing is still a cottage industry' and those who practise it are 'free to choose their environment'.[53] Robert Drewe's two edited anthologies, *The Picador Book of the Beach* (1993) and *The Penguin Book of the City* (1997) are international in scope, but they include writing about Australian places by Australian authors.

Science fiction seems to emerge from a set of creative imperatives almost directly opposed to those of literary regionalism. In his foreword to an anthology of modern science fiction, *Beyond Tomorrow* (1976), Isaac Asimov wrote that Australians' access to American science fiction in the post-1960s period was the key to a new surge of enthusiasm and creativity.[54] Van Ikin's more measured and scholarly survey of the field in *Australian Science Fiction* (1982) claimed a 'renaissance' of the genre from the mid-1970s but linked it with a prior history of speculative fiction in Australia.[55] Writers who had 'established' themselves by the early 1980s were Bertram Chandler, George Turner, Damien Broderick, Lee Harding and David J. Lake. This was an all-male crew, but Yvonne Rousseau, Philippa Maddern, Rosaleen Love and Lucy Sussex also contributed to the genre, as have 'mainstream' writers interested in speculative fiction, such as Peter Carey and Michael Wilding. Van Ikin's anthology *Glass Reptile Breakout* (1990) represented a range of contemporary talent.[56] (Peter Weir's films *The Cars that Ate Paris* (1974) and *The Last Wave* (1977) were related to the literary genre, as were the Mad Max films.) Among the various lines of development in science fiction one can discern a move from the 'hard' technology of big guns and spaceships of the Cold War period towards the 'soft' sciences of anthropology and psychology and environmental studies, and a greater propensity to speculative fantasy.

Crime/mystery stories, too, increased rapidly with encouragement from publishers and editors. When historian Peter Corris turned his hand to stories of crime and detection in early books *The Dying Trade* (1980), *The Empty Beach* (1983) and *Heroin Annie* (1984) he could not have known the extent of the revival in which he would become a leading influence. As anthologies increased, scholars began to assemble an Australian past for the genre. A major figure in the encouragement and promotion of Australian crime fiction in these years was Stephen Knight, whose carefully edited historical anthology *Dead Witness: Best Australian Mystery Stories* (1989) was followed by several volumes of contemporary writings in a Crimes for a Summer Christmas series and by his literary historical study of the genre, *Continent of Mystery* (1997).[57] The predecessors of 1980s crime writers included Arthur Upfield and Carter Brown, who introduced British and American influences respectively. Upfield's popular novels, which featured Napoleon Bonaparte, a part-Aboriginal detective, gave close attention to outback settings and careful plotting. Corris, on the other hand, employed Sydney city settings for his detective, Cliff Hardy, whom Knight describes as 'tough' and 'enduring', and 'the new hero', 'much accepted as an Australian self-projection in the eighties'. Knight has suggested that recent Australian detective figures 'represent the idea of ordinary values raised to a level of transcendence'.[58] Women's detective fiction followed several inventive paths in the hands of writers as varied as Jennifer Rowe, Marele Day, Kerry Greenwood and Janette Turner Hospital. Finola Moorhead's *Still Murder* (1991) and Dorothy Porter's verse narrative *The Monkey's Mask* (1995) showed that feminist ideas and sentiments could be incorporated effectively into this reconstructed genre.

Writing by women (and sometimes specifically addressed to women) came to assume the proportions of a literary genre in the wake of second-wave feminism of the 1970s. One aspect of many anthologies was a rediscovery of earlier writing by women. But new writing was burgeoning, too, in all the traditional literary genres. In her anthology *Room to Move* (1985), editor Suzanne Falkiner claimed that 'it is still easier for a second rate male writer to get into print than it is for a first rate female writer to do the same'.[59] This assertion was more difficult to demonstrate in the 1990s. By 1990, 40 per cent of Australian literary texts were written by women and by 1995 the proportion was 45 per cent.[60] The interest and quality of women's writing in anthologies and other publications over this period varied greatly. Some of these anthologies contributed to the dubious equation of feminist writing and writing by women more generally—a confusion which Susan Lever discusses in Chapter 15. In their anthology of Australian and New Zealand women's short fiction from the 1930s to the 1980s, *Goodbye to Romance* (1989), Elizabeth Webby and Lydia Wevers discerned a departure from the romance form and its variants to a more 'liberatory' mode:

> It is not just a question of bursting out of the frame, rewriting the self in opposition to the past, that is at work in the stories of women writers, but a more general destabilizing of the boundaries which construct the gendered subject, calling into question all the terms which might presuppose identity: wife, mother, daughter, lover, woman, narrative, story.[61]

The titles of anthologies of writing by women in the 1980s indicate the mood and intent of these selections: *Difference, Frictions, Feeling Restless*.[62] A more reassuring tone is evident in *The Babe is Wise* (1987) and *Heroines* (1991).[63] By the 1990s Carole Ferrier could point to a body of work, and associated criticism, which had offered, and continued to offer, 'radical critiques of the situation of women and women writers in Australia'.[64] But the interest remained broader than this: the *Penguin Book of Australian Women Poets* (1986) and other such anthologies have been best-sellers, indicating a broad recognition of the quality and interest of the writing. Helen Garner's *The First Stone* stimulated much debate about feminist doctrines, values and attitudes.

Australian gay and lesbian writing has also been published in magazines and anthologies. Male and female homosexuality was presented as part of 'mainstream' fiction by Frank Moorhouse, Louis Nowra, Elizabeth Jolley and Beverley Farmer in the 1970s and early 1980s, but a more direct approach to sexual orientation has been evident since then. Robert Dessaix's anthology *Australian Gay and Lesbian Writing* (1993) asserted that 'sexuality . . . is *the* leading signifier in anyone's sense of self—anyone, at least, who is culturally aware'.[65] His anthology was published by Oxford University Press and was addressed to a 'mainstream' readership. Dessaix aimed to exemplify 'a homosexual sensibility', though less than half of the writers represented in the anthology would have been expected to identify as 'gay' or 'lesbian'. Many other publications of this time were narrower in their focus and were addressed, through small specialist presses (such as Black Wattle or Wicked Women), to what would have been called, in an earlier period, a 'subculture'.

CHANGING INTERNATIONAL RELATIONS

The earlier part of this chapter drew attention to literary and social consequences of the Vietnam War, and the role of expatriate writers, especially in Britain. Alongside moves by influential elements in Australian society towards an independent sense of nationhood, epitomised by the Republican movement, a variety of international pressures was felt. Chief among these was the influence of North America on Australian education, culture and society. Strangely, few serious analyses of North American influences have been attempted, perhaps because, like the British influences which they in many cases superseded, they were so pervasive. From the 1980s, especially, a new set of cultural influences was also apparent from the so-called Asia-Pacific region, which began to counteract the still dominant Eurocentricity of Australian literary and cultural life.

The moves towards an Australian republic can be characterised in terms of the prominent roles of two literary figures, novelist Thomas Keneally and poet Les Murray. Keneally's *Our Republic* (1993), advocating the republican cause, drew on his Irish background and on a contrast he perceived between America's first Europeans who '*saw* themselves as the redeemed, whereas the first European Australians saw themselves as damned' (p. 52). Keneally's vision of an Australian republic offered a form of redemption through citizenship which would recognise and celebrate these typically difficult and problematic origins. Les Murray's 'vernacular republic' drew on aspects of his Scottish inheritance and was less urgently presented than Keneally's advocacy. In an address delivered in the Senate

Committee Room of the Parliament of Australia in June 1996, Murray seemed attuned to the 'relaxed and comfortable' mood promised by John Howard's Liberal–National Party coalition in the run-up to the March 1996 election, which the conservative coalition won convincingly. Murray's address contained none of the hortatory rhetoric of the previous Labor government under Paul Keating's leadership, and its republican supporters, who had asserted that Australia's national self-respect among Asian nations would be dramatically enhanced if we chose to take the republican path. Murray described himself as a republican in spirit since the Queen's visit to Australia in 1954, when he was 15 and 'the sheer unbridgeability of archaic rank' had struck him. His wish in 1996, however, was that the republic should be produced without division or acrimony, as he considered (with some selectivity in his evidence) the Federation of States had done in 1901. Against the calls to action of Keneally, Donald Horne, Malcolm Turnbull and other leading republicans (including the expatriate writer and art critic Robert Hughes), Murray preferred to indulge a daydream version of the republic: 'We love it better as a field of rosy potential, uncorrupted by the compromises its attainment might bring'. Murray's proposition of an ideal republic was considerably less galvanic than Keneally's, or of those vigorous progenitors of an Australian republic in the nineteenth century such as John Dunmore Lang, Daniel Deniehy and Charles Harpur. Yet it was possible that Murray's casual rhetoric would be more effective in ushering in an Australian republic than the vehement warnings and urgent advocacies of his predecessors.

Literary and cultural interactions between Australia and the USA have tended to be one-way, in spite of the resistance expressed by Les Murray to the symbolism of Sydney's high-rise towers imported from Manhattan, and the metropolitan modernism they epitomised:

> they took eighty years to fly here from Manhattan
> these variant towers. By then, they were arriving everywhere.[66]

However, Murray was less resistant to another set of American influences in Donald Hall's anthology, *Contemporary American Poetry* (1962), from which Louis Simpson's poem 'To the Western World', seems to provide a starting-point for his own poem 'Noonday Axeman' (1985).[67] Another archetypally 'Australian' poet, Bruce Dawe, also found stylistic and imagistic cues in non-metropolitan American verse, which he transferred to the rhythms and images of Australian suburbia. Dawe responded especially to the poetry of Edwin Arlington Robinson and Edgar Lee Masters when he read them in Geoffrey Moore's *The Penguin Book of American Verse*.[68] We can see here a 'quiet' influence of American examples (among others) on two of Australia's greatest modern poets, which enhanced their 'Australian-ness' by encouraging them to incorporate local voices, idioms and rhythms.

Elsewhere, American influences were more pervasive. Thomas Shapcott's anthology, *Contemporary American and Australian Poetry* (1976), revealed an impressive amount of trans-Pacific traffic and used the occasion to criticise Australian poets' tendency to underplay 'flamboyant gesture', against which he proposed American models of greater self-assurance in public performance.[69] John Tranter, a prominent writer in Shapcott's anthology, has shown in his work the importance of imagined encounters with American poets such as Frank O'Hara, Robert Duncan and John Ashbery. An imagined America from popular culture inserted itself in the writings of many other Australians in this period. Poet Robert Adamson recalls such influences in his childhood:

> Australia when I was a boy seemed like
> a far outpost of Hollywood . . .
> I wanted it all to be like Customlines
> Ricky Nelson's guitar
> like Hollywood America
> as limitless as electricity
> as dangerous as the F.B.I.[70]

Like Adamson's poem, Peter Carey's story 'American Dreams', in his first collection *The Fat Man in History* (1974), revealed the powerful ambivalence of an imagined America for young Australians. By the 1990s Carey was working in New York, following in the footsteps of Thomas Keneally.

American influences on Australian film-making, as on poetry and fiction writing generally, have been especially strong in the 1980s and 1990s. Australian film writers and directors such as Peter Weir (who has worked in the US since 1982), Fred Schepisi, Bruce Beresford and others were increasingly drawn into the American (mainly Hollywood-based) cinema industry. The influence was not all one-way, however, and Australian subjects, themes and styles have also made their mark on American and international cinema. Although industrial pressures were less potent for novelists and short story writers than for film-makers, they have also been attracted by American ideas and cultural practice. In his selection of short fiction, *The Most Beautiful Lies* (1977), Brian Kiernan noted how vogueish American fabulists such as Barth, Barthelme, Brautigan and Kerouac were in the 1970s.[71] An acute observer of Australian–American literary interactions, Don Anderson, observed that some Australian writers learnt at this time to employ 'the American cultural narrative par excellence . . . *paranoia*'.[72] Other writers ranged widely. Long-term expatriates in New York, Sumner Locke Elliott and Robert Hughes, maintained strong links with their Australian pasts, which provided emotional loci for their most significant writings. In Glenda Adams's novel, *Dancing on Coral* (1987), New York provides a backdrop to the dissolution of her Australian protagonist's short marriage to a volatile American male; in Robert Drewe's *Fortune* (1986) the legends of America's and Australia's West Coasts are linked; in Rod Jones's *Billy Sunday* (1995) America's legendary 'frontier thesis' is radically reimagined.

The general shake-up of Australian cultural values and attitudes which has been outlined in this chapter has been closely related to the impingement of international influences, increasingly from countries of the Asia-Pacific as well as North America. The very different work of historians Manning Clark and Greg Dening illustrates some of these changes. Clark's reading of recent Australian history in his *Short History of Australia* (1986) is darkly pessimistic. In eloquent Old Testament tones, Clark presents a society twice flawed—once by British philistinism and, since the late 1960s, by American and Japanese materialism. He describes Gough Whitlam's period as prime minister from 1972 to 1975 as 'a moment of hope and promise in the brief history of civilisation in the ancient, uncouth continent'. In the late 1990s Clark's own stature, like Whitlam's, was publicly contested as more conservative social values prevailed. The historical agenda had changed in other ways too. Whereas Clark had shown little interest in countries of the Asia-Pacific and Australia's interaction with them, this preoccupation was the guiding light of Greg Dening's work. Guided by postcolonial theory and his own intensive research into explorations in the Pacific, Dening has contributed to an enhanced awareness of Europe's (and Australia's) long history of engagement in the region through studies such as *Islands and Beaches* (1980).

Although Australia's connections with countries of the Asia-Pacific are still largely driven by commercial and security factors, individual initiatives and links between educational institutions have contributed to enhanced literary and cultural interaction. Australia's literary and cultural engagements with Asia (especially South-East Asia) in the contemporary period have occurred in two 'waves'. The first of these was a spate of novels and films in the late 1970s and 1980s by Australians who had visited countries in Asia either as tourists or in their professional roles as journalists, diplomats or government officials. The novels which started this trend were C.J. Koch's *The Year of Living Dangerously* (1978), Robert Drewe's *A Cry in the Jungle Bar* (1979), and Blanche d'Alpuget's *Monkeys in the Dark* (1980) and *Turtle Beach* (1981). A recurrent figure in these novels is the journalist who travels to Asian 'hotspots' for a story and becomes embroiled emotionally and imaginatively in foreign situations. A second wave of cultural engagement with Asia is marked by the emergence of a group of first-generation Asian-Australian writers. Leading authors in this category are novelists Yasmine Gooneratne (from Sri Lanka), Don 'o Kim (Korea), Dewi Anggraeni (Indonesia), poets Dipti Saravanamuttu (Sri Lanka) and Ee Tiang Hong (Malaysia), and novelists Satendra Nandan (Fiji), Adib Khan (Bangladesh) and Arlene Chai (the Philippines). The highest profile and most prolific Australian writer who draws attention to Australian–Asian relations in his work is Brian Castro. Castro was born in Hong Kong of an English and Chinese mother and a Portuguese father from Shanghai. From his first novel, *Birds of Passage* (1983), to his sixth, *Stepper* (1997), Castro wittily and sceptically engages with questions of personal and national identity; he praises hybridity; and in a published lecture, *Writing Asia* (1995), he interrogated the 'spurious dichotomy . . . Australia/Asia'.[73]

Steering a course between an Australian independent nationalism and the image of Australia 'enmeshed' in Asia, Malaysian-born Australian historian Wang Gungwu has drawn a picture of a hybrid nation as he perceived it from Asia when he was Vice-Chancellor of the University of Hong Kong: 'What may emerge as the basis of Australian national identity is a consensus that Australia is not part of Asia, nor Europe, nor America, but a country with some of the best modern features of those three continents'.[74] Nicholas Jose, writer, teacher and cultural policy adviser, has also engaged with these questions. Jose's third novel, *Avenue of Eternal Peace* (1989), presents an Australian doctor's journey to China in the form of a quest for personal and professional understanding, which involves him in difficult (sometimes comical) cross-cultural encounters, culminating in his temporary apprehension at a demonstration by students in Beijing. In an afterword to the novel, Jose commented on the signs that led to his literary foreshadowing of the demonstrations preceding the massacre of students and members of the public in Tiananmen Square in 1989. Jose's book of essays *Chinese Whispers* (1995) explores many aspects of contemporary Chinese life with a quizzical eye, trying to understand rather than impose his Australian perspective on people and events.[75] His fourth novel, *The Rose Crossing* (1994), extends his imaginative reach from the present backwards to an imagined seventeenth-century 'crossing' between representatives of Chinese and European cultures.

The increased interest in Australian links with Asian and Pacific countries in the 1990s has led to a rediscovery of earlier writers. Robin Gerster's anthology *Hotel Asia* (1995) contains extracts from work by a number of journalistic commentators and literary authors ranging from G.E. ('Chinese') Morrison and Carlton Dawe to recent authors such as Koch and Drewe. A bibliography of Australian literary responses to Asia enlarges the picture.[76] These changing orientations in the literary culture do not eliminate Europe or North America from the map. Australian studies in European and North American universities remain active, and vice versa. However, the map is changing. If Annette Hamilton's theory is accurate—that a combination of fear and desire have characterised Australians' responses to Asia, and stem from a deep historical ambivalence[77]—much remains to be worked out and the prospects for further literary explorations in this theatre seem promising. In this process, the habit of crossing cultures, and comparing them, will become more necessary for Australian writers and readers than it has been to date.

13

POETRY SINCE 1965

Dennis Haskell

The year 1965 is commonly known, thanks to novelist Christopher Koch, as 'the year of living dangerously' in Indonesia. As far as home is concerned, it probably appears to the retrospective Australian gaze as yet another year of living safely—despite the gathering clouds of Vietnam. And yet, for Australian poetry, 1965 was more dynamic than memory might suggest: it can indeed be seen as something of a turning point. Les Murray and Geoffrey Lehmann jointly published their first book, *The Ilex Tree*, while Rosemary Dobson published *Cock Crow* and Bruce Dawe and Peter Porter published their second volumes (*A Need of Similar Name* and *Poems Ancient and Modern* respectively). Donald Horne's ironically titled *The Lucky Country* was published the year before, to an audience on whom the irony was largely lost. The Australia Horne described seems a foreign country to the Australia of the 1990s. 1966 marked the end of the age of Menzies, and the story of Australian poetry is part of the story of that change in the social and political climate of Australia as a whole. The society reflected in the poetry of this period is not—even in the work of Murray, who is inclined to present himself as Jindyworobak-Boeotian[1]—a society of bush frontiers, obsessed with landscape, haunted by solitariness, overwhelmingly male-dominated, and saying what little it had to say with a laconic directness. Rather it is a pluralistic nation, with a diversity of values and beliefs, aware of the proximity not only of Asia but of the whole 'global village' of which it is, sometimes uncertainly, a part.

The closer one gets to the present the more doubtful the application of the term 'history' becomes. The present and near past always make up a bit of bush full of trees and never a forest. In recent Australian poetic history this situation is further complicated by two factors: the sheer volume of publications, and the efflorescence of both modernism and postmodernism. The *Annals of Australian Literature* as revised by Joy Hooton and Harry Heseltine shows that as many books have been published in the last thirty-two years as in the first 180 years of white Australian history. This comparison would certainly hold for poetry, so that any single chapter on this period is bound to be less than comprehensive. What is presented here is an indication of the main poetic movements during the period, a discussion of the most important institutions, and an analysis of the work of some (only some) of the most important individual poets.

It is sometimes claimed that the literary movement of modernism only arrived in the late 1960s; in practice this has constituted a claim that both modernism and post-modernism arrived at the same time. The two are closely related, and in Australian poetry, as opposed to Australian criticism, are not easily distinguishable. Modernism in fact had an early arrival in the 1920s, in the work of Kenneth Slessor and Furnley Maurice, but it then slipped from view, made the muted incursions outlined in Chapter 11 and enjoyed a late propagandising in the 1960s. The movement made up for that lateness by becoming all-pervasive in its influence from the 1970s until the mid-1990s. Partly in reaction to a period in which experiment was difficult to undertake, Australian poetry moved into a period in which experiment was more or less mandatory.

ANTHOLOGIES

Some sense of the changes during the period can be gleaned from the books which purport to be guides through that bush full of trees, the poetry anthologies. Partly thanks to the growth of Australian literary studies in schools and universities, there has certainly been no shortage of them. But apart from educational institutions providing a market—and it has sometimes seemed the only substantial market—for poetry, the number of anthologies and the regularity of their appearance suggest the sheer quantity and diversity of poetic writing during the period, and the wish to characterise it in some way. The anthologies are of all types—the clearly educational, the general interest, the partisan, the regional, the thematic, the generic—and they are often subject to the idiosyncrasies of their particular editors.

A number of these anthologies cover not just the contemporary period but set it in the context of Australian poetry as a whole—anthologies such as Harry Heseltine's *The Penguin Book of Australian Verse* (1972), James McAuley's extremely well-organised *A Map of Australian Verse* (1975), Chris Wallace-Crabbe's Yeatsian titled *The Golden Apples of the Sun* (1980), Rodney Hall's *The Collins Book of Australian Poetry* (1981), *Cross-Country* edited by John Barnes and Brian McFarlane (1984), Les Murray's *The New Oxford Book of Australian Verse* (1986, 3rd edn 1996), and Mark O'Connor's *Two Centuries of Australian Verse* (1988). Understandably, some of these anthologies have space only to gesture towards the contemporary, but this action itself is notable. At the establishment end of the scale is Heseltine's anthology, a largely non-partisan collection which nevertheless has the editor declaring, 'the best of the poetry written in Australia tends to fall after a date somewhere around 1930' (p. 29). This might suggest a strong likelihood of affinity and influence amongst the poets of the modern period but James McAuley (1917–76) notes in the introduction to *A Map of Australian Verse*: 'It is hard to talk of a tradition in Australian poetry because there has been little downward transmission except for some influence of older writers on younger contemporaries. The sense of making a new start recurs' (p. 5).

It is striking to find someone of McAuley's generation making this statement because it is even more applicable to many in the generation after his own, some of whom were in revolt against the influence of Hope and McAuley in particular. Heseltine notes Charles Harpur's view in the mid-nineteenth century that he was 'born into an Australia "unstoried, artless, unenhanced"' (p. 31). It is perhaps a sad reflection that many young poets in the 1960s and early 1970s felt as Harpur did, and had little regard for the touches of experiment already outlined in Chapter 11. McAuley himself noticed 'the conservatism of Australian poetry' in his General Introduction and noted that 'It is mainly through dissatisfaction with this endemic conservatism that some younger poets want to make a fresh start' (p. 5). McAuley aptly notes, 'Whether poetic conservatism is felt to be sound policy or a deplorable fault depends on one's scheme of values' (p. 5), but fresh starts always sound like exciting opportunities and there is no doubt that many young poets in the late 1960s and early 1970s, as well as a few more established poets, wanted just this.

MODERNITY'S BATTLE OF THE BOOKS

That a reaction to conservatism had been pent up for some time provides only one reason for the explosion of activity which occurred, particularly in Sydney and Melbourne. The opportunities provided by university education, the increased spending power of the young, the greater availability of overseas poetry (especially American), an increasing diversity in the Australian population (generated by mass migration since the end of the Second World War), greater awareness of the world through the media and international travel, and Australia's involvement in the Vietnam War all played a part. This attempt at poetic revolution can be seen as intimately related to the social revolution associated with the period in the Western world—so much so that John Tranter (1943–) retrospectively claimed the title 'Generation of '68' for the group of poets he often represented.[2] This attempted, and partly successful, *coup d'état* affected not only the form and content of the poetry published but also the manner of publication. Inexpensive, sometimes just roneoed, magazines with names like *Mok, Our Glass* and *The Great Auk* boomed; Nigel Roberts's *Free Poetry* lived up to its name and was given away, and others followed suit. Through such forms of publication, and through interaction, these young poets encouraged each other. The two national poetry magazines, *Poetry Australia* and *New Poetry* (a new version of the previous *Poetry* magazine) published their work. They found champions in the somewhat older figures, Alexander Craig, Rodney Hall and Tom Shapcott, as well as publishing their own collections, such as Robert Kenny's *Applestealers* (1974). Hall and Shapcott edited the anthology *New Impulses in Australian Poetry* in 1968, the first major anthology to promote this strongly American-influenced work.

Another key form of 'publication' were readings, the most famous being those held at La Mama in Carlton, Melbourne, the Harold Park Hotel in Sydney and at Friendly Street in Adelaide. Readings had never before been an important aspect of Australian literature and they were particularly the province of these new experimentalists. Some of the claims made in these experimental anthologies, populated with many names no longer heard of, make embarrassing reading these days, but it would be a mean spirit that did not think such claims inevitable features of an attempt at wholesale change.

There is no doubt that the most prominent spokesperson for these experimental poets has been John Tranter. With a sense that the whole movement was 'drawing to a close' (p. xxvi) Tranter put together a much publicised anthology, *The New Australian Poetry* in 1979. Tranter's Introduction to the anthology provides the most notable manifesto of these poets, partly because it was prepared with some benefit of hindsight. Despite being written in a moderate tone, the Introduction is, not surprisingly, highly rhetorical and offers some idiosyncratic depictions of literary and philosophical history since the nineteenth century as well as caricatures of the aesthetics of immediately preceding Australian poets. This in itself does not matter much. More important are the principal characteristics which Tranter perceived in the poets he presented: lack of respect for authority as part of a 'wider struggle for freedom', self-conscious experimentation, and an interest in words and literature for their own sake. This third characteristic might well conflict with the first but, writing before the impact of post-Saussurean literary theory had become well known in Australia, Tranter was struggling with important and interesting ideas. Tranter claimed that these poets had set themselves against humanism, were not interested in 'ethics, morality, religion and mythology' or in 'human destiny'; in their work 'words . . . have a reality more solid and intense than the world of objects and sense-perception'. This suggests the dangers of solipsism, irrelevance to anyone other than the poet and narrowness of subject matter. Poems such as Michael Dransfield's 'Poem Beginning with a Line', quoted here in its entirety, succumb completely:

> i sing to my candle
> she sings to me
> ah, bohemia
> you call this living?
> tells me a story, how, once, beset
> &c., but oh, obscure, deep as dim ashbery in her hair

Dransfield, dead in 1973 at the age of twenty-five, was a much-praised poet even outside this movement; 'Poem Beginning with a Line' is about as inconsequential as his work gets but the 1987 publication of his *Collected Poems*, edited by Rodney Hall, only showed how fragile and light his talent was, characterised not so much by Modernist experiment as a limp Romanticism.

Much of the work in *The New Australian Poetry* is self-indulgent and experimental for its own sake, but at their best the poems have a satiric zest, as in some of Tranter's own pseudo-sonnets:

> I'd like to throw an epileptic fit
> at the Sydney Opera House and call it Rodent.
> That's what separates me from the herd.
>
> . . . .
>
> I'm eating my way through my life—
> they said it couldn't be done
>
> but here I am in the Palace of Gastronomes
> crazy about the flavour!

This witty and wonderfully idiotic braggadocio might be seen as equally apt in the anthology as in the jewellery-rattling official cultural centre of the Sydney Opera House. The sense of a guiding intelligence—albeit at a distance—behind the quick, video-clip-style shifts in references is also apparent in the work of John Forbes (1950–98), which Tranter singles out for detailed discussion in the Introduction. Poems such as 'Jacobean', 'Four Heads & How to Do Them', 'The Photograph' and 'Stalin's Holidays' point to a concern with artistic representation or to obviously hypothetical events. These poems are not about life or about art objects but about approaches to situations and events; ultimately their concern is with philosophy and aesthetics. One of the 'Four Heads' is 'The Romantic Head', in which

> The nose while beautiful is like the neck, ignored,
> being merely a prop for the brow that is usually
> well developed & creased in thought—consider the lines
>
> 'the wrinkled sea beneath him crawls' locating the centre
> of the Romantic head above the hairline & between the ears;
> so the artist must see shapes the normal eye is blind to.

Here Wordsworth's claims for the poet as a special being, Blake's assertion that 'To Me This World is all One continued Vision of Fancy or Imagination',[3] Coleridge's honey-dew-fed seer and numerous busts of Byron crumble into verbal dust. Technically, these lines are interesting partly because they move at a carefully gauged pace. A great many of the anthology's poems move fast, conveying a sense of youthful energy, but all too often the poems have to run in order not to stumble. They have to move fast lest the reader notice the triviality of what is being presented. It is always dangerous for poets to ignore the sensual and to throw out a strong association between words and their referents; to the extent—and actually it is far from complete—that the poets do adhere to Tranter's claims, they have thrown away most of the material they might work with. It seems no accident that this is a poetry written by Australia's first television generation. What is most noticeable about Tranter's Introduction and the poems in the anthology is that they only work in reaction: without the targets of moral, intellectual and aesthetic representation to recoil from through satire, parody or (often ironic) allusion there seems to be a gulf of emptiness. The anthology has a hollow centre; the dependence on irony, the interest in the socially unconventional and social misfits, and the wilful obscurity are allied to the poets' sense of superiority over their subjects and over ordinary Australians:

> they speak to a vast audience
> consisting mainly of one another
> all of whom nervously shuffle
> manuscripts and wait their turn
>
> meantime the masses who are
> as usual deaf blind & stupid
> just keep walking to the bus or
> into the office reading newspapers
> and quite obviously don't give a fuck . . .
> (Rae Desmond Jones, 'The Poets')

This kind of raw attitudinising contrasts sharply with the poetry of the more established Bruce Dawe (1930–), renowned for his use of Australian vernacular, deeply respectful of ordinary Australians and their interest in football, television and gardening, and often considered the nation's most popular poet. (Over 100 000 copies of his collected poems have been sold.) Dawe's work since 1965 has not 'developed' in the sense of changing—as modern literary critics often require—but has gained stature through consolidation. In this respect he is a kind of Australian Thomas Hardy, but even more scathing about socially and politically powerful figures.

In the poetry and poetics of Tranter's anthology, despite the experimentalism in technique and the zest that involves, the arguments point to a kind of energetic despair, with the energy seeping away when humour is not present. These are the characteristics of much of Tranter's own work up to this point. Tranter's first book, *Parallax* (1970), featured a brooding back cover photograph of the author in half-darkness, but it has never been recognised that the genuine wit in his work is fed by an underlying pessimism.

Tranter's claim that his anthology encapsulated 'determined and serious attempts to revitalise a moribund poetic culture' was bound to draw a response, and it came in summary form with the publication in 1983 of *The Younger Australian Poets*, edited by Robert Gray (1945–) and Geoffrey Lehmann (1940–). Gray and Lehmann presented poets of the same age who 'were not members of the "generation of '68"' but who 'were aware of the need to renovate and free poetic language in this country'. The sharp difference that they saw between the two groups lay in their poets' valuing of earlier Australian poetry: 'The Australian tradition has been concerned with the experience of a unique place, and such adjustment of awareness as this enforces has often led to a philosophical tough-mindedness'. While the 'generation of '68' had claimed modernism for themselves, Gray and Lehmann saw them as merely uncritical adherents of 'one specific stream of modernism, that from the French symbolists, to the surrealists, to the New York abstractionists'. The alliance of all the 'generation of '68' with the New York poets is dubious, but this statement does point to Gray and Lehmann's interest in concrete representation and communication, and to their strong belief in the potentiality of language to represent objects and experience. While Tranter strongly praised his group for the volume of their work ('No other group of poets in Australia's history has produced such a sheer mass of published writing'), Gray and Lehmann believed that readers had been alienated by 'the newspapers, literary journals and bookshops' being 'flooded with poetry that is semi-literate, pretentious, obscure, silly or vicious'; they sought a 'style of poem which is full of fresh and convincing realistic detail'.[4]

Gray and Lehmann lead off their anthology with Les Murray (1938–) who has always been impatient with deconstructive denial of links between language and the world, seeing in it—as Gray does—an inability 'to step outside ourselves and respect the otherness of things and their quiddity'.[5] Technically the way in which the 'younger Australian poets' reveal that respect is through the use of the image. The way in which this works while maintaining a fascination with language for its own sake is readily apparent in Murray's 'The Broad Bean Sermon':

> Going out to pick beans with the sun high as fence-tops, you find
> plenty, and fetch them. An hour or a cloud later
> you find shirtfulls more. At every hour of daylight
>
> appear more that you missed: ripe, knobbly ones, fleshy-sided,
> thin-straight, thin-crescent, frown-shaped, bird-shouldered, boat-keeled ones,
> beans knuckled and single-bulged, minute green dolphins at suck . . .

With all its shifts in comparison and in rhythm, this is writing which tries to remain accessible to a non-specialist audience through its appeal to the senses and its unifying voice. Open Gray and Lehmann's anthology anywhere at random and you will find vivid images and the urge for clarity:

> A kangaroo is standing up, and dwindling like a plant
> with a single bud.
> > (Robert Gray, 'The Dusk')

> Passengers afloat on many thousand feet
> of air.
> We hiss like a wind pipe,
> tunnel through the night
> sheathed in our grey jet.
> > (Marion Alexopoulos, 'Night Flight')

Murray met the challenges of ranking and élitism among the poets in his own anthology *The New Oxford Book of Australian Verse* by allocating no more than three poems to any poet except 'Anonymous'. Valuing 'what we have come to think of as the fringe domains of poetry'—folk verse, newspaper rhymes, and song lyrics—Murray brings to the anthology populist values and aims. Including nothing in the way of explanatory or bibliographical notes, Murray insisted that the poems stand on their own and cocked his snook at the educational market in doing so. Murray did follow the lead set by Rodney Hall's *The Collins Book of Australian Poetry* (1981) in publishing translations of traditional Aboriginal songs. The anthologies have almost nothing else in common, Hall's being far more selective than Murray's.

In 1991 John Tranter, with Philip Mead, published *The Penguin Book of Modern Australian Poetry* while Gray and Lehmann expanded their previous work to produce *Australian Poetry in the Twentieth Century*. Tranter and Mead included all the poems of Ern Malley, while Gray and Lehmann chose poems to 'appeal to the senses and to affect the emotions'. It is difficult not to regard the inclusion of all the Malley poems as an undergraduate gesture, but it says much about Australian poetry that this action and the almost simultaneous publication of the rival anthologies caused hardly a murmur. The antagonisms of a decade before had died down, the need for experiment had lessened and the differences in concern and technique had diminished. The most notable general anthology since Murray's is neither of these but Peter Porter's *The Oxford Book of Modern Australian Verse*, published in 1996. Porter (1929–), one of the most highly regarded of Australian poets, has lived in London far longer than he has lived in Australia, and thus is outside the various factions that have existed. Porter is an urban and intellectual poet but an eclectic and generous editor. He does not stick to Murray's maximum-of-three-poems rule, but he does give some space to many poets rather than a lot of space to a few. Porter's selections of course reflect his own tastes but his anthology provides probably the best depiction available of Australian poetry during the period. Porter's and Murray's anthologies also point to the dominance of Oxford University Press in the publishing of poetry anthologies in recent years; with the enthusiasm of the poet/publisher Peter Rose behind them, they have played an important role in disseminating Australian poetry to a wider audience.

OTHER ANTHOLOGIES

One feature of the contemporary period has been greater awareness of poetry outside the mainstream, principally because of region, gender or ethnicity. Regional awareness, and a refusal to be swamped by the major population centres, have resulted in the publication of a number of anthologies concerned with a particular area of this large country—including *Effects of Light: The Poetry of Tasmania* (1985), *The Orange Tree: South Australian Poetry to the Present Day* (1986), *North of Capricorn: An Anthology of Verse*

(1988) and *Wordhord: A Critical Selection of Contemporary Western Australian Poetry* (1988). On the whole, the poems in these anthologies exhibit a greater concern with lucidity, plainness and accessibility, and with landscape, than is apparent in contemporary Australian poetry as a whole, as well as little interest in metropolitan 'sophistication'. The publication of these regional anthologies is an important phenomenon of the period, allowing some new voices to emerge, providing a fuller depiction of Australian poetry than that of Sydney–Melbourne based anthologies, and reminding us that in the age of the global village people often gain a sense of identity from communities (plural) smaller than that of the nation.

In an act of defiance Kate Jennings in 1975 published the deliberately unedited feminist anthology *Mother I'm Rooted*. The book was hardly memorable as poetry but was important on social grounds. Despite the growing importance of feminism as a social, intellectual and aesthetic movement, Jennifer Strauss could deliver a paper on recent poetry anthologies to a conference of the Association for the Study of Australian Literature in the late 1980s and point out that women generally numbered less than 20 per cent of the poets represented.[6] The notable exception was Susan Hampton and Kate Llewellyn's 1986 anthology *The Penguin Book of Australian Women Poets*. Hampton and Llewellyn published eighty-nine poets, the overwhelming majority of them contemporary. Their focus was on poetry as well as on politics, and the work is of a high standard, with a particular emphasis, perhaps reflecting the editors' own tastes, on satire. The book includes the wit of Edith Speers' 'Why I Like Men' ('No matter how much you pretend they're ordinary/human beings you don't really believe it') and Jean Kent's 'To the Ironingboard' ('I know you had other plans. Once./You wanted to be a ballerina but/your feet were too big').

Women's writing was more of an established force by the time Susan Lever edited *The Oxford Book of Australian Women's Verse* in 1995. With a stronger historical consciousness, Lever's is a more relaxed anthology, less driven to publish experimental work and covering a wider range of tones. These run from acerbic depictions of the 'battle of the sexes':

> etching a bloody mouth in fluorescent mirrors
> or idly lacquering a hand of claws:
> small weapons for a small war
> (Alison Croggon, 'Songs of a Quiet Woman')

to lyrical observation:

> Waiting for the bus,
> Koori girls bloom like hibiscus
> on the dusty shoulders
> of the road out of town.
> (Deb Westbury, 'Albatross Road')

Also notable are the books *Poetry and Gender*, subtitled *Statements and Essays in Australian Women's Poetry and Poetics* (1989), edited by David Brooks and Brenda Walker, and Jenny Digby's *A Woman's Voice: Conversations with Australian Poets* (1996), a collection of interviews with twelve very different women poets. Brenda Walker in her introduction to *Poetry and Gender* declares: 'The book . . . demonstrates that debates about gender and power blend or align with other inquiries into literary meaning—inquiries which unsettle certain orthodoxies'. This unsettling takes many forms, as the book's subtitle implies, not the least of which is Judith Wright's partial repudiation of the enterprise: 'Christina Stead dismissed some question from an earnest young interviewer on her methods and techniques: "It's boring for a writer, dear. Have another drink"' (p. 71).

Contemporary anthologies include writers with surnames like 'Jaireth', 'Saravanamuttu', 'Sharah', 'Aslanides' and 'Walwicz'. Australian governments' postwar immigration policies have transformed Australian society and this has filtered through into poetry, most often from those who migrated young or the children of migrants, partly fed by educational opportunities greater than their parents had and a greater ease with English. However, not all poetry written in Australia is in English and some of the biggest selling volumes are in languages such as Croatian and Turkish. Untranslated, these works are difficult to judge. There has also been an attempt to bring Australian poetry to other language audiences, especially European ones, through anthologies such as *Made in Australia* (1994), edited by Gisela Triesch and Rudi Krausmann (a collection in English and German), and *Da Slessor a Dransfield* (1977), edited by Bernard Hickey with Giovanni Distefano (a collection in English and Italian). The latter is just one of the books published by Hickey, who has been a longstanding worker for Australian literature in Italy.

Fine work has been produced by poets who migrated to Australia as adults, such as Malaysian-born Ee Tiang Hong, the Fijians Sudesh Mishra and Satendra Nandan, and German-born Beate Josephi, who—strangely—writes poetry in English but prose in German. Of migrant writers the Greeks have been the most prominent—for reasons that are not entirely clear—and Dimitris Tsaloumas and Antigone Kefala, particularly, have made a strong impact. Kefala was actually born in Romania but has been identified with Greece where she lived before coming, first to New Zealand, and then to Australia. She has said that 'The core of the experience I am trying to express is essentially a fatalistic one, my Greekness, I assume',[7] and her cryptic work has a disturbing intensity.

In a sense the other side of the migrant coin is poetry by Aborigines, who have often felt themselves to be treated as exiles in their own country. Their work has attracted an enormous amount of attention in recent years, which has seen the emergence of Jack Davis, Bobbi Sykes, Lionel Fogarty, Graeme Dixon, Janice Herring, Colin Johnson/ Mudrooroo—who is now known not to be Aboriginal but who spent many years believing he was—and others. Their work is included in many of the anthologies discussed above, and was collected by the poet Kevin Gilbert in 1988 as *Inside Black Australia*. Aboriginal poetry is distinguished by its content; social rather than personal, it is a poetry of anger and protest at the treatment of Aboriginal people in white Australia. Little of it is sophisticated in its use of language but sometimes this is the point. Jack Davis (1917–) made a poem about an Aboriginal youth who died in a police cell the title of his third book, *John Pat and Other Poems*:

> The end product
> of Guddia law
> is a viaduct
> for fang and claw,
> and a place to dwell
> like Roeburn's hell
> of a concrete floor
> a cell door
> and John Pat.
>
> ('John Pat')

Lionel Fogarty (1959–) stands out among Aboriginal poets for his attempt to produce a distinctive English, gnarled and contorted. However, most powerful of all Aboriginal poets is the first to publish a collection, under the name 'Kath Walker' (1920–93) in 1964. Changing her name to 'Oodgeroo of the Noonuccal Tribe', she became an almost totemic figure for Aboriginal writing and Aboriginal identity before her death. Much anthologised is the satirical 'No More Boomerang':

> No more boomerang
> No more spear;
> Now all civilized—
> Colour bar and beer
>
> . . .
>
> One time naked,
> Who never knew shame;
> Now we put clothes on
> To hide whatsaname.[8]

The contemporary period has also seen the publication of generic anthologies such as *The Oxford Book of Australian Love Poems* (1993), edited by Jennifer Strauss, and Philip Neilsen's *The Sting in the Wattle: Australian Satirical Verse* (1986, rev. edn 1993). Another anthology worth mentioning, partly because it is a contradiction in terms, is *Off the Record*, edited by ΠO (1985). This is an anthology of performance poetry which came with a record of selected readings. Readings had a renewed boom in the mid-1980s and regular readings have since been held in all the capital cities and many towns. There are now poets who write primarily for performance rather than the page and, whereas good readers were once more scarce than good poets, these people are very much 'performers' rather than just 'readers'. Their work has the limitations of oral poetry: relatively simple statements and straightforward syntax, a reliance on techniques such as repetition (in structure or phrasing or both), the depiction of 'type' characters and situations. Ultimately contemporary performance poetry tends to reveal its origins in the literate pop and folk music of the 1960s and sometimes has its strengths: directness, liveliness and musicality, with large dashes of humour thrown in. Masters of the performance art include Eric Beach, Komninos, Geoff Goodfellow, Ania Walwicz and Steven Herrick. The genre attracts quite a number of migrant writers and ΠO has often attempted to give migrants a voice:

> politz,
>> kech me, plai kartz,
>>> sai
>> : wich yoo nem!
> (eye), giv bodgie nem,
>> : 'Kon'[9]

INSTITUTIONS

The quantity and diversity of poetry in Australia since 1965 would not have been possible without the functioning of many institutions. It is true that poetry remains a marginal art—in the sense that only a few people buy it or read it—and those trying to write it, publish it or promote it can feel like King Canute standing before the waves of indifference. But a stronger infrastructure exists than has probably ever been in place before. It is good to remember that Kenneth Slessor's first book was printed by hand in someone's bathroom; and that any copy found today would be worth a fortune. T.S. Eliot said that 'It matters little whether a poet had a large audience in his own time. What matters is that there should always be at least a small audience for him in every generation';[10] substituting 'him or her' for 'him', the statement holds true today. Poetry survives because for most of those to whom it matters, poetry is the core of their lives and meaning would be unimaginable without it; and because those to whom it does not so directly speak recognise this centrality of value. Virtually everybody approves of the concept of poetry, as newspaper shops full of greeting cards and clichés such as 'poetry in motion' demonstrate.

Perhaps the most important institution is the magazine. This period saw the growth and then the death of the magazines *Poetry Australia* and *New Poetry*. At present the only substantial magazine entirely devoted to poetry is *Salt*, edited by the irrepressible John Kinsella with the help of Tracy Ryan. *Salt* includes Australian and international work, mostly from North America and Britain. As an editor Kinsella is generous and eclectic and his enthusiasm for every aspect of the art shows throughout the magazine.

Poetry is also published in the many literary magazines, small, new and in between, which mark out the nation's literary landscape. These include *Antipodes* (published in the USA), *Kunapipi* (published, until 1995, in Denmark), *Southerly*, *Westerly*, *Overland*, *Meanjin*, *Ulitarra*, *Island*, *Quadrant*, *Voices* and *Heat*, to name a selection. Each of these magazines reflects a regional constituency to some extent, but all are fairly eclectic. The nature of the poems published shifts a little with changes of editors, and each of the magazines is in a perpetual nails-sliding-down-the-cliff-face fight to survive. They are important to writers and a core of interested readers, and long-term Australian culture would take a battering without their capacity to bring new poems and new writers to the surface; however, none has a large print run and none could survive without government grants that are always under threat. Also important are the Poets' Union, whose newsletter *Five Bells* provides information about poetry issues and events throughout Australia, and the Poetry Book Club, administered from Wollongong, which provides cheaper books for subscribers and boosts sales of the poetry books selected.

Government grants come from state government arts bodies and from the Literature Fund (previously Board) of the Australia Council, and the importance of such bodies has increased significantly since the Whitlam Government's invigoration of funding for the arts in 1973. Poetry will always have its devotees and therefore a small niche market. Nevertheless, it would be difficult to overestimate the importance of the Literature Fund in maintaining a continuing publishing culture, in both magazine and book form, of any magnitude. Major publishing houses do publish collections of poetry, partly for prestige purposes, but without Literature Fund subsidies they might never have developed the habit of doing so. The ABC has been a notable supporter of poetry on radio, but less so on television. Programs come and go but the radio program 'Books and Writing' has been going since 1975, under the successive producerships of Jan Garrett, John Tranter, the poet Martin Harrison, the critic and novelist Robert Dessaix and, since 1995, the novelist Ramona Koval. The current offerings, apart from 'Books and Writing', are 'Poetica', 'Arts Today', 'Arts Talk' and 'Book Talk'. These programs provide reviews, features and readings. They supplement print publication activities in the magazines, in newspapers and books. The major newspapers and some of the minor ones customarily publish a poem in their Saturday edition—a gesture towards the genre but not much more—and also publish a small number of reviews of poetry. Poetry does not loom large in newspaper culture but it is not entirely invisible.

In 1969 the University of Queensland Press initiated its 'Paperback Poets' series under the editorship of Roger McDonald and this showed that the publishing of poetry books could succeed. It is in the nature of poetry publishers that they live a dangerous life, but UQP, with Sue Abbey as Poetry Editor, has continued a publishing program until the present day, albeit in more restrained fashion than in the heady days of the 1960s and early 1970s. The traditional great Australian publisher, Angus and Robertson, maintained a distinctive poetry publishing list under the editorship of Les Murray until the late 1980s when Murray took most of his poets to Heinemann and then, in the mid-1990s, to a new publisher, Duffy and Snellgrove. A&R's list has become more mixed in quality, but more varied since Murray's departure. Hale and Iremonger under the editorship of Heather Cam has consistently published a small number of poets, while Five Islands Press, through the determined work of Ron Pretty and others, has made an innovative contribution, workshopping and then bringing to publication a large number of impressive and relatively new names such as Peter Kirkpatrick, Mark Reid and Marcella Polain. Fremantle Arts Centre Press has been a dedicated poetry publisher, with a regional base (it publishes Western Australians); it is not alone in such activities, as a glance at the South Australian Friendly Street Poets and Tasmania's Twelvetrees shows. This is far from a complete list of poetry publishers, as the fact that I have not yet mentioned Penguin makes clear. Penguin is a major publisher with a small but significant interest in poetry from the 1980s to the 1990s. They have published both well-known names such as Anthony Lawrence and J.S. Harry, and first books—the books cover a great variety of styles, showing the willingness to experiment of their editor during that period, Judith Rodriguez. Small presses devoted to poetry and often run by poets come and go under the pressures of time and money but the poetry world would be lost without these largely unnoticed heroes. During the period since 1965 the names include Makar (organised by Martin Duwell); John Tranter's Transit Press; Robert Adamson's Prism and, more recently, Paperbark; Dane Thwaites's Black Lightning Press; Ian Templeman's Molonglo and John Kinsella's Folio Press, as well as the co-operatives Redress, Pariah and Round Table, in which women have been particularly active. Technological improvements have made book publishing easier and easier, and cheaper and cheaper, but the great bugbear of all Australian publishing, in a geographically large and rather remote country with a small population, is distribution. No one has been able to solve this problem but a partial solution looms in the form of the internet—available to anyone who has a computer, and growing by the minute. The growth of this medium, as computers and internet connection become cheaper, may well be its greatest problem. To date most of the input in poetry, as in other areas, comes from the USA, but conducting a heroic job for Australian literature, including poetry, are Peter and Mareya Schmidt; the address is http://www.vicnet.net.au/~ozlit/ and Chapter 6 is the poetry section. In the virtual world of the internet great possibilities exist—but how to sift through page upon page upon page of verse as each mad scribbler taps on a desperate keyboard inside darkened walls? The internet may produce more need for editors than ever known before, but it should also encourage the internationalisation of poetry, especially in the developed world.

The late twentieth century is also the age of the literary prize. Each state has a Premier's Prize, usually for a lesser amount of money than is given for fiction—which also has prominent national prizes such as the Miles Franklin Award, that poetry lacks, although the annual Mattara/Newcastle Poetry Prize is a stand alone prize worth a considerable sum of money—and the Association for the Study of Australian Literature awards the prestigious Mary Gilmore Prize for a first book of poems. There seems little doubt that the money spent on literary prizes could be more equitably and usefully spent on individual grants and contributions towards publishing costs. Prizes are judged by committees; there is a substantial raffle element and many a camel has done well. But prizes capture media attention for literature better than anything except a scandal, and they are consequently loved by politicians.

After publication outlets the most important institution associated with poetry is probably one whose influence has emerged only this century: the university. These days the university, directly or indirectly, may well provide the greater part of the audience for any poet's work—through residencies, through syllabuses, through sponsored readings, through the training (in both senses) of readers' tastes and values, and, not least, through providing employment for many an Australian poet. No one has fully examined the effect of this, in Australia or elsewhere. While poets such as Peter Porter or Chris Wallace-Crabbe seem happy with the idea of a university-based audience, poets as different as John Tranter[11] and Les Murray have railed against it. English Departments tend to value the complex rather than the sensory, the extraordinary rather than the customary, and they tend to intellectualise literature—poetry perhaps most of all. Murray has attacked Pound and Eliot for making poetry appeal 'to a self consciously intellectual audience, with consequent atrophy of its appeal to readers of any other kind'. For this audience 'the question of quality is, finally, irrelevant . . . authors are granted the ultimate accolades for innovation rather than for quality'.[12]

Modernist and postmodernist experiment have found a ready home in the universities, partly because difference is easier to judge than quality. As we near the end of the twentieth century the atmosphere seems to be changing, with some poets, such as Alan Gould, Bruce Beaver, Geoff Page and Rhyll McMaster, returning to the use of rhyme and metre; but we have lived through and are perhaps still living through a period in which experiment has been more or less compulsory. The most radically different way of viewing poetry was put by Robert Gray: 'I want to claim that "the quality of the emotion" should be seen as a natural aesthetic category—in fact, it should be seen as the one by which we ultimately judge a work of art'.[13] Even T.S. Eliot said that 'poetry has primarily to do with the expression of feeling and emotion',[14] but Gray's is a vastly different approach to poetry from that inaugurated by Eliot. It may seem odd that no one has picked up Gray's comment since he made it in 1979, and promulgated or debated it, not even Gray himself in his subsequent writing. The reason is that it is a concept that resists investigation; human emotion is still a 'Cuckooz Contrey'[15] of uncharted, probably unchartable territory. Gray's position is close to that from which non-literary people think about poetry, thereby avoiding élitism, but the link between language and emotion is ultimately mysterious; one cannot track Gray's idea far without falling into the abyss of subjectivity.

INDIVIDUAL POETS

Subjectivity and individualism remain large elements in any consideration of poetry. For all that can be said about social contexts and social movements, the work of poets persists in being stubbornly individual, never explicable solely through social analysis or the analysis of aesthetic tradition, and utterly diverse within the same period—this has never been more true in Australia than in the period since 1965. This chapter has tended to concentrate on writers who came to the fore during the period but many older poets continued to produce significant work—Alec Choate, Bruce Beaver, John Blight, David Campbell, R.F. Brissenden, Vincent Buckley, Bruce Dawe, Rosemary Dobson, Geoffrey Dutton, Gwen Harwood, A.D. Hope, Oodgeroo, David Rowbotham, R.A. Simpson and Judith Wright, to name an incomplete list. Beaver and Campbell have been much admired by some of the younger writers, while Buckley, partly through his teaching and his criticism exercised influence on a number of younger poets, particularly in Melbourne. Buckley (1925–88) is one of those who changed with age, learning a more relaxed voice, learning, as he said 'A poetry without attitudes/that, like a chance at happiness,/arrives too late . . . /turning you slowly into song'.[16] Some poets now in their sixties or older began publishing relatively late and established their reputations post-1965; particularly notable on such a list are Aborigines such as Jack Davis and Kevin Gilbert, and women, whose names could constitute a long list but would have to include Barbara Giles, Dorothy Hewett, Vera Newsom, Elizabeth Riddell, Margaret Scott, Jennifer Strauss, Amy Witting and Fay Zwicky. While Witting is better known as a novelist, the period has also seen some writers who gained a reputation as poets largely turn away from the genre to write fiction, most notably Rodney Hall, Nicholas Hasluck, David Malouf and Randolph Stow. By contrast some Australian poets have attempted to regain a hold on narrative, taking something back from the fiction writers. Alan Wearne's *The Nightmarkets* (1986), Les Murray's *The Boys Who Stole the Funeral* (1980), John A. Scott's *St Clair: Three Narratives* (1986, rev. edn 1990) and Dorothy Porter's *Akhenaten* (1992) have all received attention in this regard. As with all things new, these narrative poems have a link with something that came before, in this case the voyager or explorer poems of Francis Webb, James McAuley and others. Related but different is Laurie Duggan's individualistic employment of poetry as local history in *The Ash Range* (1987), a portrait of Gippsland through collage.

Murray aside, of all these names it is Harwood (1920–95) who has made the greatest impact, achieving enormous respect from almost all camps and being the subject of four critical studies between 1991 and 1994. Largely a traditionalist, Harwood ranges from poems of cool and often mischievous intelligence to poems of poignant elegiac power. To some extent it is her writing consciously from a woman's point of view, with such obvious skill and intelligence, that has brought her to the widespread notice of the age. No few lines could fairly represent her work, but many of her characteristics come together in the poignant 'Mother Who Gave Me Life', whose phrasing, even in its title, recalls hymns:

> Mother who gave me life
> I think of women bearing
> women. Forgive me the wisdom
> I would not learn from you
>
> . . .

At our last meeting I closed
the ward door of heavy glass
between us, and saw your face
crumple, fine threadbare linen . . .[17]

Poets of the generation born around the 1930s have produced a solid body of work which has been known long enough to establish their reputations. Apart from those already mentioned, their number includes Evan Jones, Judith Rodriguez, Tom Shapcott, Philip Martin, Clive James, Vivian Smith, Geoffrey Lehmann, Les Murray, Peter Porter and Chris Wallace-Crabbe. Porter has lived most of his life in England and his poems are replete with references to European literature, music and painting, particularly of the Italian Renaissance. However, there is nothing pretentious about this aspect of Porter's work; this art is genuinely part of his life, and his erudition is lightly worn. He is, famously or notoriously depending on your point of view, the Athenian to Les Murray's Boeotian—urban, sophisticated, intellectual, wry. For all his love of music he is not a very musical poet but he has an important place in a tradition not known for its sophisticated treatment of ideas.

Wallace-Crabbe's *Selected Poems* has an epigraph from Auden, 'Bless what there is for being', and Auden's influence is apparent in his work, which often displays an observant and observing intelligence, somewhat distant from its subjects:

Such words as love, cried Auden bitterly,
Have in our time been soured, debased . . .

. . .

Late nights linger in the backs of pubs
And couples in dark Fords lay bare the heart.
('Every Night About This Time')[18]

However, that Lowellian last line points to another side of Wallace-Crabbe (1934–), who in recent years has shown a greater capacity to lay bare not 'the' heart but his own, as when he wishes 'it were possible to pluck my son/out of dawn's moist air/ . . . /and gather him gasping back into his life'.[19]

In the introduction to his *Oxford Book of Modern Australian Verse* Peter Porter— who is not given to bursts of patriotism—asserts that 'current Australian literature is as impressive overall as that of any of the main countries writing in English'. Given Australia's small population this is remarkable, but one reason for the claim is that 'Australia possesses in Les Murray a poet equal to any in the world'. Murray is a poet who contains multitudes; he may well be the greatest poet Australia has ever produced. Through his poems, essays and pronouncements he has been an extremely controversial figure—his T.S. Eliot Prize-winning book is tauntingly titled *Subhuman Redneck Poems* (1996)—but no one would question his achievement. His most important affinities, it seems to me, are with Hopkins and Wordsworth. Murray, whose books are dedicated 'To the glory of God', is a poet of the natural world and of the egotistical sublime. Like many a major poet before him, Murray feels that his time is out of joint, voicing selfish and 'vehement equities' at odds with the equanimity which is at the heart of things but whose 'equality and justice, to be real,/require the timeless'.[20] His dangers are the dangers of didacticism that Wordsworth also faced and which are intrinsic to the egotistical sublime. At his best Murray is a poet of breathtaking metaphorical virtuosity, evoking in the human and natural worlds an indwelling, Shinto-like holiness 'Of infinite detailed extent/like God's attention. Where nothing is diminished by perspective'.[21]

In 1995 Geoff Page (1940–) published *A Reader's Guide to Contemporary Australian Poetry*,[22] in which he provided brief essays on one hundred contemporary Australian poets plus a list of books by a further one hundred. This is a rough indicator of the richness of Australian poetry since 1965, particularly since poets as good as Syd Harrex, Christine Churches, Anne Lloyd and Philip Neilsen do not feature in either group. It is also a sign that no brief discussion can adequately represent all concerns, styles, aims or prominent techniques of Australian poetry at present. Australian society in the 1990s is a complex, pluralist one, and its diversity of values, interests and beliefs is reflected in the poetry of the period.

Geoff Page himself is a poet of succinct phrasing and clear statement. He has written of his own country upbringing and forebears but never in an intensely personal mode; he is a fine observer, with something like an accessible public voice. His poems tend to have a quiet, measured tone so that they do not call attention to themselves. Page's most characteristic mode is the short line and short stanza form, and the very sense of control and restraint that this form imposes points to a certain sombreness; the poems are often poised on the edge of loss. One feels that 'the stunning/equity of death' is never far away.[23]

One poet of the period who commands attention is Robert Gray. Gray has as sharp an eye as anyone writing in English today and his interest in painting shows in many of his poems, which are often simultaneously delicate and powerful in their descriptions. A late ferry on Sydney Harbour sails

> . . . beyond
> street lights' fluorescence
> over the dark water, a ceaseless
> activity, like chromosomes
>
> uniting and dividing.
> ('Late Ferry')[24]

Such poetry works not just because of acute observation but also because of thought, and Gray's interest in perception is integral to his philosophy. He tends to use simile rather than metaphor out of a respect for things as they are. Gray's deep interest in Zen Buddhism is tied to an aesthetic which refuses belief in essences, and values an ego-free experiencing of nature: 'With the natural object, an artist has all he needs to express him-self . . . Nothing in the mind that isn't first in the senses' (p. 145); 'the less we think we are/the more we can bear; and someone who sees/he is nothing, lightly will bear it all' (p. 169). In one poem about his parents, 'Diptych', Gray depicts his father's manner as 'coolly . . . precise'; this might have seemed true of Gray himself except that his poetry exhibits the quality he attributes to his mother of 'extending Care' (p. 136).

Gray is one of a number of Australian poets who could almost constitute a school of image making—including John Foulcher, Jan Owen, Rhyll McMaster, Andrew Lans-down, Jean Kent and Anthony Lawrence. Foulcher (1952–) is a thoughtful poet who has written particularly well about his mother, seeing her in hospital with 'the drip tapped back to efficiency/. . . / its flat, sucked surfaces/like collapsed lungs'. These lines are quoted from a poem titled, with some irony, 'Living',[25] and in a poem titled 'Conver-sation' Foulcher writes, 'Her telephone is ringing. Thought lies/heavy in the receiver' and recalls 'her worn house/where the telephone cries like a child/for words'.[26]

Jan Owen (1940–) can combine her image making with a wry humour and play with sound patterns; offering 'More on the Dinosaur' Owen reflects, 'No wonder they almost died out,/with one full minute between stubbed tail and ouch,/their logic couldn't connect cause and effect'.[27] Jean Kent's (1951–) feeling for language employs sound pat-terns that evoke the world discussed, untroubled by any poststructuralist sense of lan-guage as self-enclosed system: 'When this storm arrives, trees salaam,/psalms of the sea swamp the mountains'.[28] Desiring a physicality of language, these poems offer an imme-diacy of perception that can be enormously varied in tone. Anthony Lawrence (1957–) recalls how 'Elizabeth sang me to sleep in French'—such lilting gentleness after 'a drink of water/at a monastery, and amoebic dysentery/lowered its hooks the length of my throat'.[29] Lawrence's work has much in common with the poetry of Ted Hughes; both evoke the rawness of nature, red in tooth and claw.

These poets point to a sensory strength in Australian poetry, often present in the con-sideration of landscape, and the perhaps surprising durability of the lyric tradition. Land-scape is the prominent subject of Australian art, including poetry; Australian poets tend to be much more comfortable dealing with the physical world than with relationships—intriguingly enough, except in elegy, which constitutes another strong and largely un-recognised Australian poetic tradition. One poet who does write well about relationships is Paul Hetherington (1958–), often when the past impinges on the present, emphasis-ing 'How deeply caught-up in mistakes/were our loves, our lives, our very thoughts' and yet aware 'how our intimacies remain' with a kind of 'grace'.[30] Others include the often experimental Susan Hampton (1949–), whose first book included an earthy sequence depicting her family, aunts and grandmother in their kitchens;[31] Andrew Burke (1944–), portraying how 'In drear detritus of suburban lives/flags of passion flutter'[32] and with an awareness of the emotional reticence common to Australians, especially men, who don't 'speak enough/of love, tongue tied by emotion'[33] and the younger Tracy Ryan (1964–), whose portraits of relationships are often emotionally harrowing.

All of this represents what is in broad terms the dominant mode of Australian poetry: a poetry of experience. This is not surprising in a country which, outside of Aboriginal culture, has emphasised and extended the philosophy of pragmatism which constitutes a strong part of British heritage. Awareness of that pragmatism is apparent in the work of one of the most prominent younger poets, John Kinsella (1963–) very forcefully declaring, 'There's no salvaging the fruit box,/nails already skeletons when the wood's/decomposition begins', just as 'there's no salvaging a prayer/breached when tides of faith falter/and the homestead collapses'.[34] With his interest in some versions of pastoral, Kinsella's work provides a direct bridge between Australian poetry's present and its past. This might also be said of the poems of Philip Hodgins (1959–95) who wrote of country pursuits in lucid, precisely imaged stanzas, as well as describing, with extraordinary courage, his own suffering from leukaemia. Paradoxically, Hodgins's dramatisations of the 'creature' which 'expands in your guts'[35] suggest psychological good health; these poems are especially powerful when set beside the confessional angst of Bruce Beaver or Andrew Burke, let alone their American predecessors, Lowell, Berryman, Plath and Sexton.

It is a sign of strength that Australian poetry is varied enough to enable an exception to be found for every generalisation. Despite the predominance of an experiential poetry, the work of some writers has a conceptual basis. One is the imaginatively accomplished Kevin Hart (1954–). Hart is a kind of Anglo-Australian Wallace Stevens, for whom 'The landscape is a portrait of the mind'.[36] A studied, meditative poet, his poems take place in a hushed, quiet world and have something of the quality of still life paintings; sometimes even his fine images seem designed to keep the world at bay rather than admit it. Andrew Taylor's (1940–) poetry is characterised by a quiet thoughtfulness, finding 'in the mind/the stirring of words like leaves'.[37] He is not usually thought of as a philosophical poet but there is a strong conceptual element to his work. Philip Salom (1950–) is a poet for whom language and experience do not always readily intersect, so that language can be seen as 'wakefulness/dubbed onto our actions,/ . . . crude, simplistic'.[38] This leaves the poet casting about for possibilities; his poems have a tense intellectual verve, making 'new things, with words, or shapes, or flows/of energy, things never seen' (p. 94) but aware that 'When any possibility is real/you sleep beside the slowly ticking trauma of freedom' (p. 41). Less tense but similarly speculative is the younger Peter Rose (1955–); these are the two Australian poets who most strongly show the influence of Peter Porter. In his most recent volume, *The Rome Air Naked*, Salom has also played with the possibilities offered by the computer, with some poems in fractured fields on the page, some poems surrounded by excerpts from letters, or different poems sharing the one page through the computer's multiple windows. The formats suggest something of Salom's own restless, jagged curiosity. A poet who combines conceptualising skill with enormous wit is John Forbes. Even his titles point to this: 'Ode to Tropical Skiing', 'The Best of All Possible Poems', 'Stalin's Holidays', 'The Stunned Mullet', 'The Sublime According to Quine'.

More straightforwardly comic verse is often neglected in surveys of poetry but this is one area in which Australia has a strong tradition, as a reading of the work of Banjo Paterson, C.J. Dennis, Kenneth Slessor and W.T. Goodge can show. The tradition has been continued since 1965 by poets such as Gwen Harwood, Barry Humphries, John Clarke, the English resident Clive James, and Jim Haynes. Geoffrey Lehmann compiled one collection of comic verse under the title *The Flight of the Emu* in 1990. Much performance poetry relies on humour, and singer-songwriter-sometime poet Jim Haynes is well known in country areas throughout Australia for his clever narratives, many set in a town with the punning name 'Weelabaraback'. Also sometimes worth noticing are popular music song lyrics. Singer-songwriters such as Paul Kelly, Michael Thomas (from the group Weddings, Parties, Anything) and Tim Rodgers (from You Am I) at their best produce evocative work. Rodgers's 'How Much is Enough' begins 'Would it stain if the lights fell down on your name/and each face began to look all the same?', while his 'Soldiers' has the refrain, 'they're digging up the road/And widening it just so you can suffocate at home/All right?'

LOOKING AHEAD

Australian poetry since 1965 suggests a lessening distinction between 'high' and 'low' culture, a more open attitude to literary genres (despite the recent returning interest in metre and rhyme), and an increasingly conversational idiom that has made the more grand manner of, say, Randolph Stow, early Judith Wright or early Vincent Buckley, seem dated. The poetry of the period has been informed by economic highs and lows experienced in Australia during the last three decades, increased education (including a surge in the study of Australian literature and in creative writing courses), an information-laden and media-permeated society that is highly technologised and very much part of the modern world. John Kinsella recently asserted that 'The revolution has been had. Modernism (and postmodernism) has caught up with Australia', and proclaimed the existence of a new internationalism.[39] Ongoing fast-paced developments in technology, amidst other factors, will increase that sense of internationalisation in the future. Contemporary Australian poetry has great diversity—there are enormous differences between, say, the gentle meditations of Judith Beveridge, the dramatisations and dramatic monologues of Geoffrey Lehmann, the combination of Romanticism and irony in the work of Robert Adamson and Dorothy Hewett, and the street-wise attacks of Gig Ryan. That diversity provides the best possible basis for facing internationalism's avid mixture of threat and opportunity. Any attempt to summarise contemporary Australian poetry must note that it fiercely resists summarising, and that that is its greatest single strength.

14

DRAMA SINCE 1965

Helen Thomson

The twenty years that followed the end of the Second World War saw a continuing discouragement of Australian plays, suppressed by the 'circuit' of overseas productions largely controlled by the theatre-owning company, J.C. Williamson, perpetuating the cultural imperialism that had typified nineteenth-century theatre in Australia. There was an ideological problem as well as a commercial one, as the largely Left-wing political impetus that had fuelled Australian drama of the 1930s ran up against the combined forces of the Cold War and Australia's draconian censorship regulations. Few plays from this period have survived to hold a place in historical record; Sumner Locke Elliott's 1948 *Rusty Bugles* is one, as is Douglas Stewart's 1941 verse play for radio, *Fire on the Snow*, as well as the 1942 *Ned Kelly*, the two latter emphasising a romantic version of masculine heroism, with *Ned Kelly* setting it in the Australian bush. Vaudeville and other popular entertainment was gradually incorporated into the new entertainment mediums, cinema, radio and, from 1956, television. Roy ('Mo') Rene's shift from the Tivoli theatre circuit to radio in 1945 was symptomatic,[1] as was Sumner Locke Elliott's permanent move to America in 1948, initially to work in radio, and Dymphna Cusack's abrupt and permanent abandonment of writing for the stage in 1957 after a playwrighting career of more than two decades. In retrospect, it seems as though a single, successful play, Ray Lawler's 1955 *Summer of the Seventeenth Doll*, turned the tide, reflecting images of themselves back to Australian audiences who relished the novelty of this on stage. The play gave them a new, urbanised version of the bush myth, which simultaneously heroicised and interrogated it.

It was rapidly followed by Richard Beynon's *The Shifting Heart* (1956) and Alan Seymour's *The One Day of the Year* (1960), both naturalistic depictions of Australian character and concerns. Earlier generations of playwrights had also written plays Australian in content, style, themes and character. They included Louis Esson, Katharine Susannah Prichard, Vance Palmer, Dymphna Cusack, Sumner Locke Elliott, Mona Brand, Betty Roland and the verse dramatist Douglas Stewart. Some of them wrote for the Pioneer Players in the 1920s and for the New Theatres in the 1930s, part of an international workers' theatre movement which still survives today in Sydney and Melbourne. Their naturalism, which purported to mirror real life, was often distorted by an underlying social realist ideology that minimised aesthetic concerns. The 1950s plays were not only more complex, opening up debates about the 'old' and the 'new' Australia in generational as well as racial terms, reflecting the more complicated postwar and post-immigration notions of national identity; they also deliberately examined universal issues in Australian terms. The development of their naturalism has been described as expressing less a concern to show the differences between Australians and other human beings than with 'conflicts and affinities between human beings who happen to be products of our society'.[2] However, while Australian in content, their naturalistic form, shaped to fit the conventional proscenium-arched theatre, typically proceeding from exposition to complication and a final resolution in three acts, limited them to antipodean versions of the European well-made play. They were deservedly popular, but already old-fashioned by the time of the 1960s, which saw a generational revolt characterised by radical protest. The change was revolutionary because it altered what playwrights had to say, particularly about their fellow Australians. Equally importantly, their politics embraced theatre practice for the first time, radicalising performance and including aesthetic theories of the stage. This strongly differentiated the work of the 1960s from the socialist realist writing of the 1930s and 1940s where political ends had tended to subsume artistic means.

In an era best described by terms prefixed by 'anti'—anti-imperialist, anti-war, anti-capitalist, anti-authoritarian, anti-pretension, anti-bourgeois—the youth culture that set such a political agenda was inevitably iconoclastic. Even plays which were naturalistic and structurally well made, such as Peter Kenna's *The Slaughter of St Teresa's Day* (1959) and his later *A Hard God* (1973), concentrated on Australia's earliest and largest anti-establishment group, the working-class Irish Catholics. Two important playwrights writing in the 1960s and 1970s, Patrick White and Dorothy Hewett, had already broken with stage naturalism and written non-naturalistic plays which owed much to the world-wide movements of expressionism and surrealism. Each in their strongly individualistic way, owing nothing to the communalism or philosophy of the 1960s first wave theatrical innovations, extended Australians' ideas of theatre in their challenging departures from stage naturalism. Each employed poetic speech, dreams, symbols and sometimes music, and their characters expressed a richly imagined inner life that extended the plays well beyond the limits of merely carefully observed realism. White's *The Ham Funeral* (1947, first performed in Australia 1961), *The Season at Sarsaparilla* (1962), *A Cheery Soul* (1963), and Hewett's *The Golden Oldies* (1967), *The Chapel Perilous* (1971), *Bon-bons and Roses for Dolly* (1972) along with nearly all of their other plays, not only differed radically in form, but shifted the dramatic interest away from the particularly masculine concerns of the 1950s plays towards a focus on female experience. The importance of their work lies not in popularity, but in the status of 'classic' Australian plays which their work has acquired, despite, in some cases, originally mixed reactions to it.

A 'NEW WAVE'

The new wave of Australian drama broke with bourgeois forms and preoccupations in a different fashion. The conjunction of alternative venues to the commercial and university theatres such as Melbourne's Union Theatre and a volatile mixture of new young writers, politically committed and rebellious actors, and audiences willing to 'rough it' in converted factories and warehouses, led to the most important of theatrical renaissances in Australia's history. In Melbourne it began at a converted shirt-factory called La Mama, founded in 1967 by Betty Burstall in emulation of New York's off-off-Broadway theatre of the same name; this was followed by the Pram Factory, which in 1970 became the headquarters of the Australian Performing Group (APG). This experimental collective of writers, directors and actors, many of whom were recent graduates of Melbourne and Monash universities, the latter in particular a hotbed of student radicalism and unrest, was dedicated to political action and a radicalism which embraced the process of play-making as much as dramatic form and content. In Sydney, 1966 saw the opening of the Jane Street Theatre, an offshoot of the Old Tote Theatre Company intended for the exclusive production of Australian plays, and the Nimrod Theatre, founded in 1970. All the new groups fitted Peter Brook's definition of 'rough theatre', being anti-authoritarian, anti-traditional, anti-pomp and anti-pretence, but not, for all their apparent egalitarianism, meeting his criterion of being genuinely popular theatre.[3]

In place of traditional theatres demarcated along class lines, the new performing groups, particularly in Melbourne, deliberately democratised the theatre by employing industrial, street and other 'found' spaces, a development that has continued to characterise Melbourne fringe theatre in particular. An emphasis on vernacular speech and the Australian accent, particularly that identified with working-class Australians, was also important. Categories of high and low culture were complicated by the newly upwardly mobile and tertiary educated theatre practitioners for whom the forms and techniques of vaudeville and melodrama signified, paradoxically, both an authentic theatre tradition and an iconoclastic gesture of nonconformity. Traditional, class-tainted aesthetic standards were flouted in favour of political content and newer theories while audience interventions were welcomed as signs of political solidarity. These audiences were small, enthusiastic, mostly university educated, but crucially sharing the theatre groups' political iconoclasm and desire to define themselves in opposition to existing stereotypes. In fact the Australian male was satirised rather than heroicised, defined in terms of his emotional, intellectual and social limitations, and embedded in an inner-suburban subculture where drinking and male bonding continued to be the main preoccupations. The new 'ocker' differed from earlier stereotypes such as the larrikin, in being submitted, in these early plays, to a satiric scrutiny which revealed an unromantic limitation of character, less sentimental than earlier comic treatments. Feminism was in its infancy and had barely impinged on the male playwrights of the 1960s and 1970s, but its influence could be discerned in the weakening of mateship as consolation for socially alienated men.

Earlier representations of Australian character on stage, even when intensely and deliberately differentiated from other national characteristics, were typically rural and largely masculine. Part of Ray Lawler's success with *The Summer of the Seventeenth Doll* was due to his relocating his bush cane-cutter heroes in the living room of a Melbourne suburban house, in Carlton, the same suburb which was to see the Melbourne renaissance of the 1960s and 1970s wave of new plays. The New Wave writing differed from earlier essentially amateur ventures such as the Essons' Pioneer Players and Doris Fitton's Independent Theatre in Sydney, in its opposition to aesthetic as well as political orthodoxies, and its actor-, rather than director- or writer-driven productions. Writers, particularly Jack Hibberd, John Romeril, David Williamson and Barry Oakley in Melbourne, learned their craft in a deliberately democratic and experimental process of collective workshopping. In Sydney the same pattern emerged in slightly different style, most typically characterised by Michael Boddy and Bob Ellis's 1970 *The Legend of King O'Malley*, a musical recontextualising of the larrikin as a conscription protester. Both cities had for the first time genuinely vibrant, creative alternative theatres, engaged in a revolutionary rather than revisionist project of national self-definition. The creative sources were no longer in the bush, but in urban, counter-cultural contestations of social values, for the first time strongly influenced by American writing and political action. The fact that much of the theorising, hotly debated in collective meetings, was drawn from the *Tulane Drama Review*, as well as from European theatrical experimentation by writers such as Bertholt Brecht, and Harold Pinter defined the class and educational level of the APG. Ideologically committed to the political Left and agit-prop street and workplace theatre, they were all members of the first generation to benefit from the postwar expansion of higher education, particularly the new universities such as Monash. There was from the first a degree of idealistic but nevertheless false consciousness in their identification with the working class.

At the beginning of the 1970s the frustration of a generation of young people who had never known anything but conservative political governments, and were facing conscription and military service in Vietnam, fuelled the protest movement which drew Australian youth into international political issues. Self-definition and self-representation, in national terms, seemed to need radical refashioning at the same time as satirical attack became one of the weapons turned against the older generation and its values. These values were represented in traditional theatrical forms, the bourgeois three-act play, the class-marked disjunction between forms of high and low drama and the anglicised accents and preoccupations of characters. Earlier Australian writers such as Louis Esson had employed the Australian vernacular in their plays, and Elliott's *Rusty Bugles* had encountered serious censorship problems for its robust use of it. The incorporation of older, popular theatrical traditions such as vaudeville, burlesque, revue, music hall, stand-up comedy, into satirical depictions of an older generation's icons, also meant that the larrikin tradition could be put to new uses, as it was in the writing of Michael Boddy, Bob Ellis, Jack Hibberd and Alex Buzo. The deadliness of respectable suburban life had been successfully satirised since the first appearance of the Barry Humphries character, Edna Everage, in 1955, followed in 1958 by the dreary but mesmerising Sandy Stone, a pathetic figure of suburbanised and therefore defeated masculinity, in thrall to the essentially feminised constraints of gentility and social conformity. The irreverent vulgarity and employment of an aggressive vernacular speech in theatre productions which drew on vaudeville and used its traditions with political intent was gradually tamed as the political battles of the 1960s were slowly won. One struggle was over censorship. This was dramatically tested in 1968 when Alex Buzo's violent depiction of Australian racism in *Norm and Ahmed* became a test-case for the abolition of existing censorship laws, and when John Romeril's *Whatever Happened to Realism*, performed in 1969 in La Mama's car park, was disrupted by police who arrested the actors for using obscene language in public. More tellingly, obscenity ceased to be a rallying point for resistance and disobedience when commercial productions of plays such as Harry M. Miller's 1969 production of *Hair*, with its nude scene, entered mainstream and popular theatre.

The communitarian ethos of the 1960s served Australian drama well. The collaborative effort which went into productions of the Australian Performing Group meant that new writers had almost unprecedented opportunities to workshop their plays with an ensemble of actors and directors over an extended period of time and a number of productions. They had further opportunities to refashion their work in reaction to audience responses. Audiences were also learning, in the intimacy of small performing spaces, where actors were freed of the constraints and distancing of the conventional theatre's 'fourth wall', of the delights and dangers of intensely physical, often confrontational performances. Actors were completely exposed, their commitment to this kind of theatre tested by audiences within touching distance. Constraints of polite theatrical decorum were simply non-existent, exploded as much by the physical exigencies of converted industrial buildings as by an ideology which identified such decorums with colonial and conservative falsifications of Australian experience.

THE 1970s

Inevitably, some of the directions taken by the early Melbourne and Sydney New Wave playwrights turned out to be dead-ends as political rebellion lost its urgency after 1972 with the coming to power of a reformist Whitlam government. Financial stringencies, however, played a part in the changes, through the limited life cycles of the economic communes which nurtured so many theatre practitioners in this movement, and the need to find funding sources to keep the alternative theatres open. Two significant events in the 1960s were the establishment of Australia's first professional theatre training organisation, the National Institute of Dramatic Art at the University of New South Wales in 1958, which was founded by the Australian Elizabethan Theatre Trust, the first public body for the performing arts (established in 1954), and the setting up in 1968 of the Australian Council for the Arts, which replaced the Trust as a funding body. The combination of professionally trained actors and directors, and the subsidising Council's decision to develop state theatre companies rather than a national company, as well as its financial support for the APG in Melbourne and the Australian Drama Foundation in Sydney's University of New South Wales, fuelled an explosive expansion of theatrical creativity in the 1970s.

The 1970 Festival of Perth included a group of plays from the APG, Jack Hibberd's *White With Wire Wheels*, Alex Buzo's *The Front Room Boys* and John Romeril's *The Man From Chicago* (later *Chicago, Chicago*), effectively establishing a national reputation for the Melbourne collective. This was also the year which saw the landmark production of *The Legend of King O'Malley*, the first in a series of comic, cartoon-like, musical plays which gave Sydney's Jane Street Theatre its distinctive style. Melbourne's alternative theatre was considerably more political in content and emphasis, not only inside the Pram Factory, but outside on the street and at the anti-Vietnam moratorium marches, the first of which was in Melbourne in 1970. John Romeril's and Jack Hibberd's *Marvellous Melbourne*, Brechtian in its episodic structure, songs and epic sweep, reworked Alfred Dampier's nineteenth-century melodrama in a free-wheeling, irreverent satire on 1880s and 1890s Melbourne, with unmistakable contemporary relevance. Barry Oakley's *The Feet of Daniel Mannix* (1971) and *Beware of Imitations* (1973) parodied the two conservative icons of political life, Archbishop Daniel Mannix and Prime Minister Robert Menzies, helping to establish comic actor Max Gillies's acting career. Jack Hibberd's 1969 *Dimboola*, his 1974 *The Les Darcy Show* and *A Toast to Melba* (1976) were in contrast essentially celebratory of Australian character, although also characterised by irony. Hibberd's *A Stretch of the Imagination* (1972) is one of the early APG plays which has survived to enjoy the status of a classic in many subsequent productions. These writers helped build on the already existing reputation for comedy in Australian theatre, and developed what has been called 'the historical pantomime',[4] combining political satire with music-hall techniques and devices.

The first full-length play by David Williamson, *The Coming of Stork*, premiered at La Mama Theatre in 1970, beginning an extraordinary career for one of Australia's most popular playwrights. The following year saw the appearance of two more plays by Williamson, *The Removalists* and *Don's Party*: both were performed around Australia, made into films, taken to London and won a number of awards. Williamson's plays, closer in their essentially naturalistic style to Sydney's Alex Buzo than to his early Melbourne contemporaries such as Jack Hibberd and John Romeril, staked out a particular territory of devastatingly accurate satire of middle-Australia, well educated, well heeled, and well housed. Originally identified with the political Left, the origin of his satires can increasingly be discerned in the morality play rather than any political ideology, and his targets have diversified from the pseudo-radicalism of the Australian middle class, in plays such as *A Handful of Friends* (1976), to fashionable social movements such as feminism in *The Perfectionist* (1982), moral squalor in public life and newspapers in *Sons of Cain* (1985), corruption of the law in *Top Silk* (1989), and in *Dead White Males* (1995) political correctness in universities. His 1996 play *Heretic*, in a break with stage naturalism, contentiously re-staged anthropologists Margaret Mead and Derek Freeman's 'nature versus nurture' debate, ironically attacking Mead, a putative source of the 1960s libertarianism which provided the conditions for Williamson's early success. So prolific and topical is his writing that a reading of Williamson's plays from 1970 to 1996 would provide an extraordinarily accurate picture of Australia's social history, at least that of its middle classes, over the same period.

The dominant preoccupation with Australian masculinity, begun with the bush stereotypes of the 1890s, brought to the city by Lawler's *Summer of the Seventeenth Doll*, held up to ridicule by plays like Buzo's *Norm and Ahmed* (1968) and *The Roy Murphy Show* (1970), Hibberd's *White With Wire Wheels* and, more affectionately, *Stretch of the Imagination* (1972), and also Williamson's *The Coming of Stork*, *The Department* (1975) and *The Club* (1977), in itself indicates the predominantly male authorship of the new wave writing. The essentially negative picture of male bonding rituals in shared houses, football clubs and workplaces, the alienation, arrested emotional development and sheer emptiness of the male lives in these and many other plays, is testimony to the strength of the older Australian stereotypes of masculinity and the need to break out of their constricting parameters. The Australian male character was no longer being heroicised, but it was still dominating the subject matter of these writers' plays, the sheer exuberant energy and excess of the depictions ironically serving to celebrate what was being satirised. In 1972 the Women's Theatre Group separated itself from the APG and produced *Betty Can Jump*, a group-devised show which aimed to break away from the limited range of stereotypical female roles in male-written plays, such as those women deluded by romance in Hibberd's 1974 *Peggy Sue* and his sexually exploited and interchangeable girls in *White With Wire Wheels*. Feminism also made its impact on the 1975 group-devised *The Hills Family Show* which was one of the APG's most popular productions and one out of which Circus Oz developed. Katharine Brisbane records that Sydney's feminist theatre movement had a later beginning: 'A major push came in 1981 when Chris Westwood and others at the Nimrod Theatre organised the Women Directors' Workshop and Women and Theatre Project, to develop playwrights, director and female roles'.[5] Since then, feminist theatre groups have appeared in all states, some performance-based such as Adelaide's Vitalstatistix, established in 1984, others supportive and developmental, such as Sydney's Playworks, begun in 1985, a national organisation committed to nurturing new women writers, encouraging new forms of writing for performance and supporting and developing the work of more experienced women writers.

Of the first wave of writers, David Williamson has had the most success in terms of popularity and remuneration. Jack Hibberd, Bob Ellis, Barry Oakley and Michael Boddy have developed other careers, although all of them continue writing in one form or another. Along with Williamson, only John Romeril and Alex Buzo continued to write plays in 1997. Of these three, only John Romeril has retained the same political commitment to working-class values, the collaborative process of play production, particularly seen in community theatre, and he has moved committedly towards a mapping of Asian-Australian experience. Williamson and Buzo have become recorders, largely in naturalistic form, of Australian middle-class life as it is lived by university-educated men and women in the suburbs of Sydney and Melbourne. Williamson's popularity has a great deal to do with his development as a brilliant comic writer, moving from the satire of his earlier work such as *Don's Party* (1973) towards latter-day morality plays like *Brilliant Lies* (1993). His popularity with audiences is in contrast to mixed and often antagonistic responses he receives from critics, due in part to the blunting of his moral criticism by the plays' abundance of hilarious one-liner jokes. His mid-career move from Melbourne to Sydney fuelled a sense of betrayal in some of his Melbourne peers for whom commercial success could never be reconciled with artistic integrity. Yet Williamson has grown, along with his audiences, his plays changing from undergraduate ockerism to the polished verbal self-examinations of an educated middle class living through numerous social changes. He has also written successfully for film and television, and probably warrants serious analysis in the terms of a tribal myth-maker suggested by Peter Fitzpatrick;[6] not the rural myths, but genuinely new ones born out of the place where most modern Australians live, the suburbs.

John Romeril occupies a completely contrasting position to David Williamson in terms of political commitment and non-commercial orientation.[7] His more outward-looking plays engage with Asia. In particular, his 1975 play, *The Floating World*, about the disastrous re-encounter with Japan of an ex-Japanese prisoner of war and Australian digger, Les Harding, has achieved 'classic' status in the canon of most frequently performed Australian plays, along with Hibberd's *Stretch of the Imagination* and Lawler's *Doll*. The definition of Australian character in an international context links Romeril with the second wave of modern Australian dramatists such as Stephen Sewell and Louis Nowra. Romeril's work with theatre-in-education, youth and community theatre, seen in collaborations with the Melbourne Workers' Theatre, for example, represents one of the few continuing links with the original APG and its anti-establishment, anti-élitist commitment to grass-roots theatre. These two strands of theatre work—Asian oriented and community centred—have become increasingly important aspects of Australian drama. The initial chairmanship of the Community Arts Board of the Australia Council by Jon Hawkes, an original member of the APG and for many years a member of Circus Oz, demonstrates one further link between the counter-cultural 1960s and 1970s and present-day funding mechanisms.

Perhaps the other most significant continuation of this group's work can be seen in the development of circus as a distinctively Australian area of performance excellence. Some early members of the APG helped found and still remain in Circus Oz, which has also benefited from Asian experience in the form of teaching visits from the Nanjing Acrobatic Troupe from 1983 to 1985. Significantly, its national distinctiveness derives from its politicising of circus, from lampooning politicians to making an ideological point about not performing with animals, while the physical skills developed by its human performers had, in part at least, their origins in the intensely physicalised theatre of the APG and its ideological commitment to collective creativity. However, it should be remembered that the apparently radical fusing of serious political theatre with popular entertainment forms was simply putting to new use a long Australian theatrical history. Circus, particularly the large family circuses such as Ashton's, Bullen's, Perry's and Wirth's, had exploited Australian tastes for athletic pursuits, for horsemanship and clowning since the 1840s, while child circus performers were a constant and important attraction.

The Albury-Wodonga children's circus, the Flying Fruit Fly Circus, founded in 1979 as part of the community-based Murray River Performing Group, becoming a separate entity in 1987, tours regularly during school holidays and many of its performers have joined Circus Oz. Adelaide has had a youth circus, Cirkidz, since 1985, and conducts workshops and outreach programs. The Melbourne-based Women's Circus, founded in 1990 from an earlier Wimmin's Circus, is a different community theatre development, originally having a therapeutic and empowering aim for women victims of sexual abuse. It has expanded to a group of more than 100 members, with a long waiting list for its workshops, giving regular public performances in 'found' sites, such as Coburg's abandoned brickworks, and in 1995 performing at the Beijing United Nations Conference on Women. Every State has its circuses: it is claimed that in 1987 there were at least 25 alternative circus groups throughout Australia.[8]

If relatively few direct influences survived from the first wave of the 1960s and early 1970s, at the very least its participants created a cultural confidence in Australian theatre, in audiences as well as actors, writers and directors, which made possible the growth of a theatrical diversity characteristic of the later 1970s. It is entirely fitting, in view of the original ideological aims, that the main influence has been in non-mainstream theatre. Australia Council and State Government funding underpinned experimentation and a steadily increasing proportion of theatre company programs devoted to Australian work. Melbourne's Playbox Theatre Company, founded in 1976 as Hoopla by Carillo Gantner and two ex-APG members, Graeme Blundell and Garrie Hutchinson, developed from predominantly Australian to all-Australian programs. Now affiliated with Monash University, it has played a vital role in the encouragement and development of new dramatic writing. The boldest programming gamble so far has been South Australian Theatre Company Director Chris Westwood's decision to produce only Australian plays for the last five years of the twentieth century. It has not found much support with audiences and, with Westwood's resignation in 1997, is unlikely to be fulfilled. The audience resistance might be interpreted not so much due to Australian work itself, as to the desire, in a city with few mainstream theatre companies, to see new and canonical work from elsewhere in the world as well.

The number of new theatre companies that came into being in the 1970s was another sign of a growth period. Unlike the many small amateur theatrical companies such as Louis and Hilda Esson's Pioneer Players in the 1920s, Wal Cherry's Emerald Hill Theatre Company, 1962–66, and Sydney's Ensemble founded by Hayes Gordon in 1958, these later companies were often affiliated with universities and funded by the Australia Council, and therefore fully professional. They included the Hunter Valley Theatre Company (1976); the Church Theatre (1983–90) and Australian Nouveau Theatre (Anthill) in Melbourne; Nimrod Theatre (1974) and Sidetrack Theatre, founded in 1979, in Sydney; Western Australia's Hole in the Wall Theatre (1965), which like the Nimrod has had several changes of name and management; Brisbane's La Boite (1972) and Adelaide's Troupe Theatre's Red Shed (1976). The availability of theatre venues has continued to shape each capital city's theatrical development. Melbourne's relative abundance of available church halls (utilised, for example, by the Church, St Kilda's Theatreworks, Anthill and Institute for Research into the Art of the Actor, IRAA) has enabled many small groups to develop alternative theatre with the advantage of a permanent home, while Sydney's versatile Performance Space has meant that performance art has burgeoned there. Sydney's lack of large theatres, on the other hand, has meant that the better-endowed Melbourne has been able to house more productions of big musicals such as the profitable Andrew Lloyd Webber spectaculars. The construction of large State Arts Centres in the 1970s has been followed by many imaginative recycling exercises, particularly of industrial buildings, into performance venues, Sydney Theatre Company's two Wharf Theatres being particularly successful examples. Melbourne continues to generate more experimental and fringe theatre groups, not only because there seems to be a number of suitable venues, but because the original first wave culture of experimentation grounded in ideas, aesthetic as well as political, has persisted.

A Second Wave

Some of the first wave dramatists have continued writing for the stage, and very often for film and television as well, frequently incorporating film techniques into plays. David Williamson's plays developed out of a naturalistic, single-set, three unities structure towards plays of many short scenes ranging freely in time and place. This development may well owe something to a 'camera view of life' acquired in film writing.[9] Williamson also has led the trend away from non-textual, physical drama towards plays as essentially dialogue, structures of words, typical of his articulate, middle-class characters. In a category of their own are the prison playwrights, the best known of whom are Jim McNeil, whose *The Chocolate Frog* (1972), *The Old Familiar Juice* (1972) and *How Does Your Garden Grow* (1974) provided vivid pictures of life behind bars, and Ray Mooney, whose plays address the violence endemic to prison life, as in *A Blue Freckle* (1975), *Every Night, Every Night* (1978), and a wider view of social injustice in *Black Rabbit* (1988). The plays of some younger writers such as Hannie Rayson and Joanna Murray-Smith deal with characters who are middle class and verbally fluent like those of Williamson.

This so-called 'text-based' drama has been scathingly attacked by Barrie Kosky, founder of the Jewish Gilgul Theatre Company, in favour of 'poetry, ritual and magic'.[10] Yet there is also considerable experimentalism among the second wave of Australian dramatists, emerging in the late 1970s, including an older generation of Dorothy Hewett, Patrick White, Alma de Groen, as well as the younger Stephen Sewell, Michael Gow and Louis Nowra. They have all taken new and distinctive directions, stretching the parameters of Australian drama. Their plays share an intellectual ambitiousness, raise important issues, and are often large-scale, complex and demanding. They have typically moved away from attempts at defining and dramatising versions of national identity, with all that this implied in terms of limiting, masculine stereotypes such as the battler, the larrikin and the ocker, and instead charted, in many forms, a quest for a myth of Australian-ness. This involves a different order of imagining as well as a more ambitious stagecraft. The mixed critical and audience reception and the paucity of revivals of their plays suggest that even highly educated audiences may prefer to have recognisable images of themselves reinforced in stage representations rather than challenged and questioned. Professional theatre critics tend to applaud ambition, in terms of theme as well as form, without necessarily reflecting those general audience tastes which have made David Williamson a far more popular dramatist than, say, Stephen Sewell.

Sewell's career began with plays panoramic in sweep, internationalist in theme, passionately political (reflecting a Marxism he has gradually abandoned), deeply moral, and employing a wide range of theatrical modes and influences. Peter Fitzpatrick sums them up: 'All the plays are long, passionate, and complicated; the issues they raise, and their density of reference, declare their very serious intellectual ambitions . . . Sewell's work has never had much time for half measures'.[11] *Traitors* (1979), set in Russia, and *Welcome the Bright World* (1982), set in Germany, dealt with revolutionary history. The latter play's dense texture of intellectual debate and historical facts alienated some critics as well as audience members. *Traitors* had its first production at the Pram Factory, providing a link between the first and second wave of writers. *The Father We Loved on a Beach by the Sea* (1978), *The Blind Giant is Dancing* (1983) and *Dreams in an Empty City* (1986) deal with contemporary Australian politics, not as history, but transformed into prophetic and apocalyptic visions embracing, respectively, the resurgence of Fascism among working-class Australians, the collapse of the capitalist system and a critical analysis of the frightening power of multinational companies. They are the antithesis of the 'snapshots' of Australian life, as Sewell describes them, to be found in the bourgeois naturalism of the plays of David Williamson and Alex Buzo. Sewell's plays are not of the suburbs but the city, expanded into an organic symbol of the complex moral instability of contemporary life. Just as passionate, still employing metaphorical structures of myth, classic archetypes and a graphic symbolism, but narrower in focus, are Sewell's more recent family psycho-dramas, *Hate* (1988), *Sisters* (1991) and *The Garden of Granddaughters* (1993).

Louis Nowra's early plays were also internationalist and epic in sweep, *Inner Voices* (1977), *Visions* (1978) and *The Precious Woman* (1981) being set respectively in Russia, Paraguay and revolutionary China, although they can be read metaphorically as post-colonial analyses of present-day Australia. Louis Nowra began his playwrighting career at La Mama Theatre, so he also connects to the first wave of Australian dramatists. He is often linked with Stephen Sewell, partly because both playwrights move beyond realist modes, but where Sewell is passionate, sometimes to excess, Nowra's occasionally Gothic imagination finds cooler expression. Sewell's emotional and imaginative power sometimes risks the criticism that it is melodramatic, a dramatic brinkmanship where '. . . the writer is prepared to follow his vision to the point where it threatens his control over the things he imagines'.[12] Nowra breaks with realism in more formal ways, his frequent use of a play within a play being an example, investing his work with a powerful irony as he draws attention to the artificialities of both the dramatic frame and the acted narrative, each providing a commentary on the other. He also uses music, confesses himself to be heavily influenced by film techniques, and creates imagined worlds dominated by dreams, visions and nightmares.

Nowra's postcolonialism embraces the predicament of Aboriginal Australians, seen in his re-presentation of Xavier Herbert's novel *Capricornia*, significantly appearing in the Bicentennial year 1988, as well as in *Crow* (1994), *Summer of the Aliens* (1992), and, to a degree, in the earlier plays, *Inside the Island* (1981) and *Sunrise* (1983). Aborigines, one group among several in his visions of displacement, exile and alienation, are interestingly also present in his two semi-autobiographical plays, *Summer of the Aliens* and *Cosi* (1992). Two recent plays by Nowra link in subject if not in style with the work of David Williamson: a satiric farce about corporate greed, *The Temple* (1993) and a version of Queensland's recent history, *The Incorruptible* (1995).

Dorothy Hewett's work embodies a different form of radicalism, although her plays, with the exception of the early *This Old Man Comes Rolling Home* (1966), are challengingly anti-naturalistic in their employment of music, pageantry, caricature, ironic comedy and confrontational subjects, particularly female sexuality. Her semi-autobiographical play, *The Chapel Perilous* (1971), and *Bon-Bons and Roses for Dolly* (1972), *The Tatty Hollow Story* (1974) and *The Golden Oldies* (1967) are iconoclastic not only in their uncompromising representation of female lives, but also in their ironic deconstruction of conventional forms of female sexual attractiveness. Harry Garlick suggests that, 'In Hewett's early plays, *Bon-Bons and Roses for Dolly*, *The Tatty Hollow Story*, and *Joan*, she confronts, endorses and interrogates the Hollywood myth of true romance.'[13] Her plays also yoke together aspects of both popular and high culture, a political gesture with its source in Hewett's membership, until 1964, of the Australian Communist Party, and lifelong identification with working-class aspirations. Her later plays, the rock opera *Catspaw* (1974), *Pandora's Cross* (1978), *The Man from Mukinupin* (1979), and the radio play *Susannah's Dreaming* (1981), transform her earlier political interests to embrace environmentalist concerns about the destruction of Australian landscapes, along with poetic evocations of the complex and sometimes threatening character of these landscapes.

The poetic dimension of Dorothy Hewett's plays is matched only by that of Patrick White. His plays have had as controversial a history of audience and critical reception as hers. *The Ham Funeral*, written and set in London in 1947, was rejected, on the grounds of its likely audience unpopularity, for the 1962 Adelaide Festival of Arts, but received high critical praise when produced by the Adelaide University Theatre Guild in 1961, before going on to an Elizabethan Theatre Trust production in Sydney. Both its form and content constituted a challenge to audience expectations, but it signalled what was to become White's characteristic employment of stylised, apparently stereotyped characters, who are developed beyond this by poetic speech, and a powerful symbolism, as well as a persistent preoccupation with the disjunction between the spiritual and the physical lives of its characters. *The Ham Funeral* was followed by *The Season at Sarsaparilla* (1962), *A Cheery Soul* (1963) and *Night on Bald Mountain* (1964), the former two set in the fictional Australian suburb of Sarsaparilla. In these a black satire on conformity and materialism is mixed with a sympathy, not unlike Dorothy Hewett's, for the underdogs and victims of a suburban respectability maintained at the cost of repressing both the sexual and the spiritual sides of the human character. The combination of epic style and unconventional theatrical forms with scathing criticism of Australian philistinism and suburban dullness made all White's plays contentious among audiences who were just learning to enjoy images of themselves on stage.

Nevertheless these early plays of White's received some outstanding productions that confirmed their importance. Director Jim Sharman's production of *The Season at Sarsaparilla* in 1976 (followed by *A Cheery Soul* in 1979) so impressed Patrick White that he wrote his first play for 13 years, *Big Toys*, which was also directed by Sharman in 1977. This play about political corruption could be seen as a precursor to the many plays on similar themes which followed, such as Sewell's *Dreams in an Empty City*, Williamson's *Sons of Cain* and Nowra's *The Temple*. Jim Sharman became Director of the Adelaide Festival of Arts in 1982, and in 1983 Artistic Director of the South Australian Theatre Company which was renamed the Lighthouse Company and operated as an ensemble company. There Neil Armfield also put his distinctive mark on White productions, directing *Signal Driver* (1982), while Sharman directed the later *Netherwood* (1983) and *Shepherd on the Rocks* (1987). While never popular drama, White's plays have attained the status of classics in the repertoires of many Australian theatre companies, and it is certainly true that 'his plays have enlarged the sense of what is possible in Australian theatre'.[14]

Sharing at least an experimentalism with Patrick White's plays are those of Alma de Groen, every one attempting to say something different in a distinctive way. There are more similarities between Dorothy Hewett and de Groen than any other pair of writers; they share an interest in and awareness of the peculiar difficulties of the woman artist in Australia, particularly the playwright struggling for production in an industry largely controlled by male directors, theatre owners and arts administrators. Alma de Groen's plays have moved from an early focus on alienation, male and female, seen in *The Sweatproof Boy* (1968), *The Joss Adams Show* (1970), *Perfectly All Right* (1973) and *The After-Life of Arthur Cravan* (1973), to a deliberate and well-informed feminism that has been contentious because of its insistence that women's problems are inextricably part of men's. Her three latest plays, *Vocations* (1982), *The Rivers of China* (1985) and *The Girl*

Who Saw Everything (1993), all of which have received major productions with state theatre companies in Sydney and Melbourne, have challenged audiences in a number of ways, not least by their interpretations of the world very much in terms of feminist philosophy. *The Rivers of China*, in particular, has a density of reference, both literary and philosophical, matched by a complexity of theatrical modes and symbols. Its dual time-scales and plots parallel 1922, the year which saw writer Katherine Mansfield's death from tuberculosis, and a dystopian 1988, where sex and power roles have been reversed. It raises a challenging argument about gender and art when Mansfield's personality is grafted into the body of a young man. Its density is increased by de Groen's characteristic intertextuality, an invoking of a written culture embracing philosophy as well as literature. It is a play that could be seen as proof of a sophistication in Australian audiences as much as playwrights. De Groen's complex theatricality, her explorations of a variety of non-naturalistic modes, place her firmly among the experimentalist group of playwrights who continue to define a national drama in terms that transcend the national.

THE 1980S AND 1990S

While many of the second wave dramatists are still writing plays, they have not had an obvious influence on younger writers. Possibly this is because they have become identified with notions of high culture, while younger Australians are attracted to popular culture disseminated through the electronic media and music. This is a shared public culture, accessible and affordable. Yet there is not a simple division along generational or class lines, and television and films have brought about an increase in sophistication in audiences, as well as a sense of international community. In the 1990s the difference seems to be that dissolving the barriers between high and low culture is no longer a political issue, as it was for the first wave of 1960s and 1970s dramatists and actors, while ideas of national identity have fractured into hybrid forms. The steady assimilation of American culture has outstripped, to some extent, postcolonial critiques of British imperialism, and the huge popularity of the British-American musical only emphasises the internationalism of popular culture where art and entertainment have unproblematically become the same thing. There are as many different audiences for theatre in Australia as there are different kinds of performance arts to interest them. The main characteristic of 1990s Australian theatre is its diversity, far broader than the older divisions of mainstream and alternative can encompass.

One phenomenon which has helped blur the distinctions both between high and low and local and international culture, has been the growth in arts festivals in all the capital cities, and some of the provincial ones. In most cases a Fringe Festival has attached itself to the main ones, or a strong community theatre component has developed, so that alternative theatre flourishes for a time alongside prestigious, high quality international productions. Perth, the most isolated of Australian capital cities, has the oldest international festival, beginning in 1953 and developing out of its lively university drama activities. The Adelaide Festival of the Arts, originally modelled on the Edinburgh Festival, began in 1960 and has run biennially ever since. Brisbane's Warana Festival, now the Brisbane Festival, has evolved in scope and complexity since its 1962 beginnings, while Melbourne's International Festival of the Arts (originating in 1985 as the Melbourne Spoleto Festival) has, like many of the others, a Writers' Festival attached to it. The Festival of Sydney, which originated in 1977, traditionally begins with a New Year's Eve fireworks display and outdoor concert, while its Mardi Gras with a huge street parade, celebrates gay culture of all kinds. Some of these festivals developed out of street parades—Melbourne's Festival was originally part of Moomba with its parade—but have embraced an enormous diversity of performing arts, music and visual art forms. Successful niche festivals have been developed in towns such as Port Fairy with its Music Festival, Ballarat's Opera Festival, and Tamworth's Country and Western Music Festival. One significant development has been Canberra's National Festival of Australian Theatre, begun in 1990, showcasing theatre performances drawn from all over Australia. The funding sources for all of these festivals are a mixture of government, private and corporate sponsors and ticket sales. They are distinguished by their eclecticism, providing opportunities for Australians to see companies of outstanding quality, and also some of the riskier avant-garde work, both local and international, that would not survive normal commercial exigencies. The festivals provide the most obvious link between culture and tourism, Sydney's Mardi Gras being the most profitable of them all in terms of tourist earnings. The number of overseas visitors attending festival performances makes them a two-way cultural trade, with many non-Australians taking the opportunity to see Australian drama, dance, music and other performance art.

The fact that theatre has become an industry, its performances often described as 'product' by arts administrators, has had some unexpected side-effects. The business world has responded generously in terms of sponsorship, the theatre companies employ large numbers of people, state and federal public service divisions have grown up to service the funding organisations such as the Arts Council, tourist boards assiduously promote the arts, and cornering the market with a glamorous Cameron Mackintosh production, as Melbourne did for some time with *Phantom of the Opera*, which opened there in 1990, can earn millions of dollars for the local economy. Yet overseas tourists often want to see local theatre productions, particularly indigenous dance and drama, as much as koalas and beaches. This has worked to the advantage of Aboriginal arts groups, and the growth in Aboriginal theatre has been one of the most striking developments of the last decade, rivalled only by the growth of community theatre in many forms.

It is not that Aboriginal theatre has fashioned itself in response to commercial, let alone tourist, imperatives. Its sources are far more complex, and it constitutes an important entry point into white culture. The impulse to tell their own stories is of course embedded in Aboriginal culture, but the embracing of white audiences and European traditions of staging signalled an important emergence of pride and self-assertion, claiming a place for themselves in white culture, rewriting white history, asserting the value of their otherness. Jack Davis, a Nyoongah Aborigine from Western Australia, born in 1917, who has lived in both white and black cultures, has been the most important initiator of Aboriginal theatrical enterprise. His plays are wise, robust and humorous, often intensely moving, addressed to both white and black audiences, but their stage production demanded Aboriginal actors, an almost non-existent category of theatre workers at the time his plays were first written. Perth theatre director Andrew Ross, founding artistic director of the Swan River Company in 1982, has encouraged, in many landmark productions of Aboriginal drama, the development of Aboriginal actors, designers, directors and writers since his first production of Jack Davis's *Kullark* in 1979, and is also foundation artistic director, since 1991, of the Black Swan Theatre Company.

Aboriginal drama is invariably political, the urgency of the need for cultural self-definition a stronger imperative in an oppressed people than it has been for white Australians preoccupied with their own national identification. *Kullark*, an Aboriginal version of Western Australian pre and post white contact history, was written in response to the omission of Aborigines from Western Australia's sesquicentenary celebrations in 1979; *Barungin (Smell the Wind)* constituted a protest at white bicentennial celebrations in 1988, and it also movingly dramatises the continuing tragedy of black deaths in custody. While necessarily written in the language of their oppressors, and for the most part traditionally realistic in characterisation and style, Aboriginal theatre nevertheless contains important characteristics which disrupt conventional theatrical forms. Indigenous music is one of these, particularly the use of the haunting didgeridoo and click-sticks; Aboriginal dancing and storytelling is another, as is the employment of untranslated Aboriginal language, in itself a powerful assertion of cultural autonomy. In many plays tribal culture is evoked as a marker of difference and sign of spiritual harmony, even in the midst of realistic pictures of present-day Aboriginal urban squalor and despair.

There have been many Aboriginal representations in white drama, some, like Tony Strahan's *State of Shock* (1986), and the much earlier *Brumby Innes* (1927) by Katharine Susannah Prichard, completely sympathetic, but the growth in Aboriginal writing and performance has made white speaking for black an unacceptable political stance. Black theatre exists primarily to contest white values, even the benign, liberal humanist ones, which have been informed by well-intentioned but damaging ideologies such as assimilation. This can be found in plays like Louis Nowra's *Capricornia*, which problematise the part-Aboriginal, while all white-written plays about Aboriginals tend to propagate a false pan-Aboriginality, failing to provide specific markers of tribal or language groups. Subversive contrasts between white and black cultures, using comedy disruptively—as in the conversion of the hymn 'There is a happy land,/Far, far away./No sugar in our tea,/bread and butter we never see./That's why we're gradually/Fading away', in Davis's *No Sugar*—and depicting white characters as stereotypes in contrast to black individuality, as in Robert Merritt's *The Cake Man* (1975), are recurrent and effective devices. Certain themes recur: the destructiveness of white bureaucracy, however benign, the related phenomenon of 'coconuts', black on the outside but assimilated (often through white adoption) to white values inside; and the disruptive trickster character who outwits white oppressors with cheeky audacity. The growth of Aboriginal plays since Kevin Gilbert's 1965 *The Cherry Pickers* has been matched by the appearance of many Aboriginal companies such as the Aboriginal and Torres Strait Islander Dance Company, the Aboriginal Islander Dance Theatre, Bangarra Dance Company, National Black Theatre, and many others. Both writers and performers have benefited enormously from the National Black Playwrights' Conference, first held in Canberra in 1987. Many Aboriginal companies have toured and performed overseas. Jimmy Chi's Aboriginal musical *Bran Nue Dae* opened at the 1990 Festival of Perth and toured to all states over the following four years, delighting audiences with its engaging celebration of multi-cultural Broome expressed in an eclectic mixture of popular music. Chi's second musical, *Corrugation Road*, directed by Andrew Ross, opened at the 1996 Melbourne Festival to sell-out audiences. The autobiographical monologue of Ningali, telling an extraordinary story of multiple alienation, has had seasons in Edinburgh's Festival and in London. Its sophisticated slippages between cultures, styles, performance modes and musical forms signal the contemporary complexity of Aboriginal performance. In a remarkable act of ironic cultural appropriation, Mudrooroo's 1996 play, *The Aboriginal Protesters Confront the Proclamation of the Australian Republic on 26 January 2001 with a Production of The Commission by Heiner Muller*, signals an Aboriginal contestation of Australian self-congratulation in the event of a Republic. Neil Armfield's 1997 production of John Harding's *Up the Road* emphasised that play's theme of the alienation of successful black bureaucrats from their home communities. Aboriginal drama has from the first, and of necessity, addressed itself to both black and white audiences, and while contemporary writers such as Mudrooroo in his *The Aboriginal Protesters* seem less conciliatory than had Jack Davis, they seem certain to continue to draw audiences, representing one of the most dynamic areas of theatrical innovation and growth at present.

An important shift seems to be under way in Aboriginal theatre, similar to developments in feminism, away from victim representations, towards a more confident self-assertion. Ningali's story is a case in point, and this may have its source in a post-Mabo land-rights optimism as much as in the steady growth of resources, particularly human ones in the shape of Aboriginal writers, directors, administrators and actors. Australian women seem also to have made considerable gains in the theatre over the past thirty years, but they are not really dramatic ones. A few remarkable women have made it to the top in theatre direction and administration: Gale Edwards has become an international director, specialising in Andrew Lloyd Webber musicals and in demand in Britain's Royal Shakespeare Company; Robyn Nevin has extended a distinguished acting career to become the Director of the Queensland Theatre Company; Chris Westwood, co-ordinator of the first Women Directors' Workshop in 1981, and the 1982 Women in Theatre Project, was until 1997 Director of the State Theatre Company of South Australia; while Robyn Archer, another distinguished and popular performer and writer, after directing Canberra's National Festival of Australian Theatre, began in 1998 as Director of the

Adelaide Festival of the Arts. For the majority of women in Australian theatre, however, there is a real sense of struggle to break in to what is still a largely male-controlled hierarchy of power. The Sydney Theatre Company, and its Director Wayne Harrison, have twice been taken to task by the Australia Council over its poor representation of women writers in its seasons, and the very small number of female theatre workers in its company.

Australia's theatre history has seen many remarkable women who founded or ran theatre companies, wrote plays, directed and acted in them, but almost all of them were amateur. Entering the professional ranks has been the problem for women. Equal opportunity and affirmative action programs have meant that women are more likely to be employed in subsidised theatre than in the commercial sector. This is still more likely in alternative theatre groups than in the mainstream, and directors like Liz Jones at La Mama have ensured something like equal representation there. Melbourne's Playbox Theatre Company, producing mainly new Australian work, has a good record of encouraging female dramatists. There are two levels of political action, however, and the second, after equal representation, is the question of feminist content in plays. Mainstream theatre is more likely to produce the work of liberal feminist writers, concentrating on equal rights for women, ensuring a reasonable proportion of women's roles, often engaged in historical revisionism, writing 'herstory', than it is to run the riskier radical feminism that concerns itself almost exclusively with women's issues. This focus is seen as marginal to the concerns of mainstream theatre, where the dominant perspective remains that of the white middle-class male, although the majority of theatre tickets seem to be purchased by white middle-class females. The resistance to women's participation has been much stronger in theatre than in most of the other arts, partly because of the process and structure of productions as opposed to, say, novel publication, and possibly also because a woman dramatist literally gives voice to women in a far more confronting way than more passive forms of literary production. The proportion of women in theatre management is probably crucial, since not only are such women likely to have a good awareness of gender issues, but they have the commissioning power to ensure a reasonable gender balance. The other important measurement of women's success is the proportion of their work in the Australian canon, and there are signs that the historical retrieval of work by writers such as Dymphna Cusack and Oriel Gray (the socialist playwright who shared first prize for her play *The Torrents* in the 1955 Playwrights' Advisory Board competition with Ray Lawler's *Summer of the Seventeenth Doll*), is making an impact on this.

The early 1970s saw the first stirrings of feminism in Australian theatre, predictably at first in the APG and Nimrod groups. Nimrod developed its Women in Theatre group, and at the Pram Factory, in 1972, a group-devised work called *Betty Can Jump* was produced, a play for five women and one deliberately stereotyped, chauvinist male, designed to correct the marginalisation and stereotyping which the women members of the collective thought was happening in the male-written plays. Ultimately it led to an important offshoot of the APG, the Women's Theatre Group. 1972 was also the year of the first production, by the APG, of Katharine Susannah Prichard's powerful play about sexism and racism in rural Western Australia, *Brumby Innes*, which had won a play competition in 1927 but never before had a production. Thérèse Radic's feminist play (written with Leonard Radic) *Some of My Best Friends are Women* appeared in 1976, and the new Hoopla Theatre put on two plays, by Dorothy Hewett and Alma de Groen, in its first, 1976–77 program. Since then there has been a steady growth in women's plays and theatre groups, their writing enormously helped in many cases by Playworks. The ten-year survey, 1985–95, of women and the theatre, produced by Playworks, *Playing With Time*,[15] has identified many issues relevant to women writing for the theatre, from their typically being marginalised in community, alternative and youth theatre work, to the inaccurate perception that their plays do not deal with major ideas and public issues. This book also identifies gains that have been made, not least the fact that since 1985, responding to equal opportunity legislation and formulating a Strategy of Action on women, the Australia Council has directed an equal or near-equal proportion of grants to them. This still leaves a host of problems to do with actually securing commissions from theatre companies and finding suitable and sympathetic directors. Lesbian theatre has so far failed to find a place in mainstream theatre comparable to male gay theatre, particularly in Sydney, although from 1994 the Mardi Gras there has become the Gay and Lesbian Mardi Gras Festival, and more prominence has been given to lesbian issues and theatre.

Such special interest groups as gay and lesbian theatre are often more accurately described as belonging to community theatre, one of the most dynamic and diverse growth areas of Australian theatre over the past 30 years. Defined and shaped by membership of a social group with interests in common, community theatre embraces locality, ethnicity, sex, work or disability in groups which are rarely permanent because often formed to achieve a single, limited aim. The aims of such theatre are social or political rather than aesthetic, and participation in creative activities is considered one of the most important aims. Formal Theatre in Education groups form an important part of community theatre, but much of it is also informally educative as well as empowering for participants, such as Geelong's Back to Back theatre of intellectually impaired young performers, or the Theatre of the Deaf. Such groups challenge limiting preconceptions of disability. Adelaide's Doppio Teatro, in bilingual Italian–English performances, asserts a cultural distinctiveness for one of Australia's many ethnic groups and demonstrates the effectiveness of the multicultural agenda begun by the Whitlam government, replacing earlier assimilationist goals. The same government in 1973 established a Community Arts Committee, which became a Board of the Arts Council in its own right in 1977. The tendency towards broadening the reach of arts funding was strengthened in 1984 when the Theatre Board placed a ceiling on the major theatre companies, recipients of the largest proportion of its funding. There has been a subsequent movement back towards increasing grants to the expensive forms of performance such as ballet and opera, which could hardly survive without subsidy, with the creation in 1994 of the Major Organizations Board. The setting up of a Hybrid Arts Committee in 1995 signals another change of direction in the major funding body for the arts, one that may advantage many non-mainstream groups, women and Aborigines included, as it devises funding strategies for cross-arts, collaborative, non-text based, experimental and ethnic performers and creators. At the moment, political groups of the Left, such as Sydney's Sidetrack and Toe Truck Theatres (the latter now closed), and the Melbourne Workers' Theatre, still enjoy funding assistance, although probably considered of less importance than, say, Youth Theatre, which has many active groups in all capital cities, and in Adelaide, the city with the largest number of youth arts groups, has a biennial Come Out Festival celebrating the work by and for young people.

Community theatre is a highly political arena of debate and activism. The idea of 'cultural democracy' which it represents gives visibility and voice to suppressed, marginalised or oppressed social groups. Its underlying concept of equality and inclusiveness, not requiring particular artistic skills (although many professional facilitators are funded to assist community theatre groups), contests the notion that culture is defined by forms of high art. It has been argued that culture in such a singular sense is the result of a homogenisation of difference, similar to that process which produced an essentially hegemonic idea of Nation.[16] The essential notion of plurality underlying community theatre is therefore an important part of current debates about national identity.

In a similar sense, the hybridity of much contemporary Australian theatre could be read as a contestation of an earlier form of prescriptive, unitary national identity; masculine, Anglo-Saxon and excluding of other such people as women, Aborigines, 'Wogs' and Asians. Barry Humphries is perhaps a key figure here, with his early employment of shock techniques of surrealism subsequently developing into a characteristic comedy which turned Australian parochialism and naive self-congratulatory attitudes savagely against themselves, yet crucially preserved an affection for the objects of his satire. More recently, theatrical phenomena such as *Wogs Out of Work*, and several sequels, drama's equivalent to the success in fiction of Nino Culotta's *They're a Weird Mob* (1957), mark an emergence of ethnic writers. The *Wogs* shows have drawn huge audiences, many of whom have never before attended theatre performances, affirming an ethnic-Australian identity, particularly Greek and Italian, at the same time as they hilariously satirised migrant fashions in dress, hair and housing. The hybridity of theatrical forms has also pushed forward notions of what constitutes theatrical performance. Few playwrights writing in the 1990s are unaffected by techniques and styles drawn from film and television; and criticism of stage plays which merely reproduce familiar formulas such as situation comedy forces a re-assessment of what are live theatre's distinguishing characteristics.

The complexity of the 1990s is also reflected in the variety of politics depicted by contemporary playwrights, very different from the more simply antithetical Right and Left of the 1970s. Melbourne playwright Michael Gurr, for example, has moved from conventionally structured plays about the tensions between the personal and the political

such as his early *A Pair of Claws* (1982) and *Dead to the World* (1986), to his most successful play to date, *Sex Diary of an Infidel* (1992), analysing 'the real congress between
nations',[17] ironic reference to Australia's participation in the sex tour industry in the
Philippines. His later play, *Jerusalem* (1996), is fluid, impressionistic, designed to be performed in the round, and sympathetically examines the new underdogs created by an
economic rationalist political ideology. Sydney's Michael Gow has had a distinguished
career as director and actor as well as playwright. His best known play, *Away* (1986), is
typical of much of his work in its examination of generational conflict, its poetic and
deliberately non-naturalistic language and impressionistic scene changes, and its linking
of Australian contemporary life with the high culture of Shakespeare. His plays have
ranged over a number of modes, from the historical drama *1841* (1988), to explorations
of family fragmentation and the 'coming out' of homosexual children in *The Kid* (1983)
and *Furious* (1991), to the black comedy of *Sweet Phoebe* (1994), which has a completely
unpunctuated script, an attempt to provide the optimum freedom of interpretation for
director and actors. Sydney's Katherine Thomson has maintained, particularly in her
award-winning play *Diving for Pearls* (1991), a persistent political focus on working-class
Australians and their victimisation in an economic rationalist ethos. Also Sydney based,
Nick Enright has written, through the 1980s and 1990s, a variety of successful plays
ranging from musicals such as *On the Wallaby* (1980) to comedies like *Daylight Saving*
(1990), and powerful dramas of political and social commentary like *Mongrels* (1991)
and *Blackrock* (1995). In Melbourne, Joanna Murray-Smith's *Honour* (1995) has not
only won awards but also secured an American production. Hannie Rayson's comedies
have had Australia-wide productions, her 1990 *Hotel Sorrento* also being made into a
film. Tobsha Learner has written many plays with a feminist emphasis, the most successful being *S.N.A.G.(Sensitive New Age Guy)* (1992), *Wolf* (1992) and *The Glass Mermaid*
(1994). Daniel Keene has had a successful writing career, though not always in mainstream theatre, and established connections and a following in the USA, with plays such
as *Cho Cho San* (1984), a variation on *Madame Butterfly* performed partly with puppets,
its first production being with the distinguished Handspan (puppet) Theatre Company;
his most recent play, *All Souls* (1993), typically employs a poetic lyricism to evoke sympathy for the lost souls of its characters.

The political importance of the arts in Australia was perhaps never more obvious
than in the 1993 election campaign when the arts community came out in strong support for the Keating Labor government. The subsequent and important Creative Nation
statement that linked ideas of nationhood with those of creativity confirmed subsidised
arts activities as legitimate investments which were seen to earn profits in terms of
international prestige and local pride. The 1994 creation of the Melbourne-based
Foundation for Australian Cultural Development was one manifestation of this, as had
been the 'Keating' Fellowships for Australian creative artists. Since the change of government in 1996 there is a perception that the arts have declined in political importance.
The 1990s hybridity that characterises theatre as much as any of the other arts forms, like

the vexed question of multiculturalism itself, complicates the crucial funding mechanisms. The number of separate Boards for the Australia Council is evidence of this, as is the linking of new communications technologies with the arts, seen in the creation, in 1996, of two Australia Council residencies for Australian artists to work with digital technology. The arguments for subsidised theatre are rarely questioned, yet the privatisation push, accelerated by the election of Liberal governments in most states, has exacerbated the need for companies to earn profits and compete for sponsorship. Australian theatre and dance companies now annually showcase their wares to international producers in a government-sponsored attempt to earn export dollars. Experimentation such as that which transformed Australian theatre in the 1960s and 1970s is too risky for even smaller subsidised theatres, since financial losses will also lead to loss of funding. Conservative programming is inevitable in such a climate.

Yet the healthy side of hybridisation is the diversity of audiences who help support such a wide variety of writing and performance. Australian theatre owes an incalculable debt to Philip Parsons and Katharine Brisbane, whose Currency Press, founded in 1971, has been the most important publisher of Australian plays. Katharine Brisbane, who was an enthusiastic supporter of the first wave of Australian playwrights, was also the influential national reviewer for the *Australian* newspaper from 1967 to 1974, and a founding member of the Australian National Playwrights' Conference in 1972. Partly because of Currency Press, a canon of Australian plays now exists, is studied in schools and universities and is performed by both large and small theatre companies. That 'Australian' has become a vastly more complex reality since the 1960s is reflected in the enormous diversity of current writing for the stage, an accurate reflection, after all, of the increasingly hybrid audiences for which it is being produced.

15

FICTION: INNOVATION AND IDEOLOGY

Susan Lever

In 1958 Patrick White famously dismissed the work of most of his Australian predecessors as 'the dreary, dun-coloured offspring of journalistic realism'[1] and so announced the beginning of a shift in literary values in Australia—from a concern for the accurate depiction of Australian life to an interest in formal experiment. By the late 1960s White had been joined by a younger generation of Australian prose writers who claimed that they were part of a 'counter-culture' of protest against conventional values. White may be seen as the bearer of a belated novelistic modernism to Australia, in that, in retrospect, international modernism appears to be a pre-war phenomenon, and, by the mid-1960s, the techniques of modernism had been overtaken by the more self-conscious approaches of postmodernism. Yet, in Australia, White's determination to experiment led the way for a widespread interest in formal change; and innovation—whether under the banner of modernism or postmodernism—has been valued as a prime virtue of literary art since the late 1960s.

The major figures of Australian writing to that time were traditionalists, in that they consciously sought to build a national literature which developed the traditions of the past. In the 1940s and 1950s the social realists of the political Left proclaimed themselves to be the inheritors of the Lawson literary tradition, which they were making anew for an urban Australia, while the conservative writers, mostly poets, sought to create Australian forms of European literary traditions.[2] Patrick White, himself, can be read as participating in a traditionalist project in the 1950s, rewriting Lawson's selector characters into *The Tree of Man* (1955) or considering the Australian experience in the light of European philosophical traditions in *Voss* (1957) or *Riders in the Chariot* (1961).

But there have also been political reasons for the demise of traditional realism. The past thirty years have seen the steady undermining, then total collapse, of any practical Marxist politics in Australia. With this has come the loss of a unifying Left culture with a place for writing within its political program. In Australia any cohesive socialist realist program had faded by the early 1960s, at a time when Left nationalism, which had provided a less structured political base for fiction writers, had come under attack as conventional and provincial. That is, by 1965, younger Australian writers could not ally themselves with the Marxist grand narrative of political change, nor could they unselfconsciously undertake the more straightforward nationalist task of speaking of and for their country. At the same time the political energies of the late 1960s, which were directed at opening up Australian society, at removing censorship, increasing education, and lifting the repressive burden of social controls, helped to find a new public place for fiction writing—the expression of the cultural excellence of the nation, and the demonstration of innovation and sophistication as Australia claimed its place among the cultures of the Western world.

The state was revising its attitude to art, too. In 1968 a Liberal Federal government committed itself to an arts policy by setting up an Australian Council for the Arts, expanded as the Australia Council by the Whitlam Labor government in 1975. The Act setting up the Australia Council makes it clear that the government was concerned to promote excellence in the arts, and to make the practice and enjoyment of the arts more accessible to Australian citizens; the aim 'to foster the expression of a national identity by means of the arts' came fifth on its charter.[3] In this way, the Government resisted calling the tune; the arts were to seek 'excellence', to be outward-looking rather than limited to the expression of nationalist attitudes.

This situation might be contrasted with ideas current in the 1950s when novels were often written as a means of educating Australian readers (in 1958 even White referred to his task as teaching), or expressing their distinctive experiences. Indeed, the 1950s legacy may be found in the continuing conditions for the Miles Franklin Award (set down in the 1950s by Franklin herself), which specify that a winning novel 'must present Australian Life in any of its phases'.

Even a cursory comparison of the number of novels published in 1965, 1975, 1985 and 1995 provides evidence of an exponential growth in such writing, particularly in the last decade.[4] Unfortunately, the rise in the readership for serious Australian fiction has not kept pace with publication. Australian readers have much more to choose from than they had forty years ago, not only from Australian, British and American novelists, but from other English-speaking nations, such as Canada and South Africa, as well as an increasing number of translations from Europe and South America. The increasing globalisation of markets for serious fiction—so that readers can access writing from any nation in the world—has created the paradoxical situation where a few Australian writers have international audiences, while others have less chance of being read than they might have had twenty years ago, even in their own country. The notable exceptions to this minimal sales pattern include the Booker prizewinners Thomas Keneally (for *Schindler's Ark/Schindler's List*[5] in 1982) and Peter Carey (for *Oscar and Lucinda* in 1988), together with David Malouf (winner of the first Impac Dublin Literary Award for *Remembering Babylon*, 1995) and more popular writers such as Bryce Courtenay, Colleen McCullough, Di Morrissey, Morris West and—with one novel—the rock musician, Nick Cave. There is also a range of writers such as Sally Morgan, Drusilla Modjeska, Elizabeth Jolley, Helen Garner, Tim Winton, Helen Darville, Mark Henshaw, and Justine Ettler who have sold respectable numbers of at least one book. In the case of most of these high-selling books, it is possible to suggest a particular reason for their success (strong narratives, the creation of some controversy about them in the media, or their capturing of a particular interest of the time, such as postmodernism or feminism). A number of Australian writers also consistently produce novels with the qualities of intelligent entertainment which surely would mean commercial success were they written by British or Americans: I would count Robert Drewe, Blanche d'Alpuget, Peter Goldsworthy, Venero Armanno, Janette Turner Hospital, Marion Halligan and Kate Grenville among these writers, as well as the genre writers such as Shane Maloney and Peter Corris.

In setting up a system of patronage, the Federal Government inevitably incited competition among artists for attention. Without strong readerships to support the careers of writers, the Literature Board of the Australia Council (variously, the Literary Arts Board and from 1996 the Literature Fund) became the arbiter of which writers might be able to make careers from their art, and which must confront, unshielded, the vagaries of the marketplace. Through its publishing program, however, the Board gave publishers the incentive to publish new fiction while leaving in their hands the decisions about which manuscripts might be published. So the way to publication for new writers lay open, while the future after that initial step depended on increasingly ferocious competition.

This process of competition has put a further premium on innovation, as writers seek to demonstrate that they are avant-garde and original, or more avant-garde and original than the next writer. Indeed, innovation is explicitly linked to excellence in the 1996 Australia Council grants handbook, where it states that the Council 'supports contemporary artists whose proposals, in competition with those of other applicants, demonstrate the highest degree of artistic merit and innovation'.[6] In addition, the widespread derision of pre-1960s Australian art as backward, conventional and conservative may have had the long-term effect of overvaluing the apparently new. Australian writers may have been overly conscious of the weakness of a modernist movement in Australia before the war, and they have been inclined to condemn the return to realism in the novel which was a worldwide trend in the 1950s. At any rate, the Australian writer in the 1990s is likely to be acutely aware of an international literary scene, in which Australians must participate as equals, rather than as the favoured patriots or ridiculed provincials of the past.

This emphasis on innovation and internationalism also has ideological implications. Instead of the old ideal of writing as a means of creating community and even nationhood, critical and writing practices have emerged which seek out marginality and difference. In place of unifying political programs in which writers could participate, a series of political interest groups has emerged since the 1960s which at various times has demanded attention for the voices of, for example, women, migrants, Aborigines, gay men or lesbian women. And these different voices have often found the techniques of postmodernism—fragmentation, pastiche, self-conscious irony—to be the most appropriate expressions of the incoherence of contemporary life. As a result, an overview of fiction in Australia for the past thirty years may well find itself incapable of a coherent narrative, but forced merely to identify difference, marginality and fragmentation. Though a little daunted by such a prospect, I will present a historical narrative that offers some unities, and that attempts some logical ordering of what has been called the 'new diversity' of Australian fiction.[7]

PATRICK WHITE AND HIS INFLUENCE

While there have been only a few imitators of White's idiosyncratic style, many younger writers, both men and women, have acclaimed him for his willingness to mix genres and break the rules of conventional writing. In 1973 he became the first Australian writer to win a Nobel Prize, a further mark of his role of establishing an international place for Australian writing. To Australian writers of the next generation White led the way in announcing the preoccupation of the serious contemporary novelist with experiment. The novelists who have dominated Australian fiction since the 1960s—Thea Astley, Peter Carey, David Foster, Helen Garner, David Ireland, Elizabeth Jolley, Thomas Keneally, David Malouf—all display some debt to the fiction of Patrick White. This does not, however, amount to a tradition—though critics may argue about which novelist has earned the coveted mantle of White's greatness.

By 1965 White had completed the first stage of his career, demonstrating how the traditional subjects of Australian fiction and legend—the settler and the explorer—could be rewritten as the focus of contemporary questions about the relationship of the individual to god and society. In *The Aunt's Story* (1948) and *Riders in the Chariot* (1961) he had tried to come to terms with the devastation and destruction of Europe and its meaning for individuals in an ignorant and, apparently, more innocent Australian society. But in the novels published after 1965—*The Solid Mandala* (1966), *The Vivisector* (1970), *The Eye of the Storm* (1973), *A Fringe of Leaves* (1977), *The Twyborn Affair* (1979) and *Memoirs of Many in One* (1986)—White was mainly concerned with contemporary subjects, with an increasing interest in the relationship of the artist to a postwar Australian society. His writing moved to a self-conscious awareness of art as a reconstruction of a fragmented world, with artist figures as unreliable assemblers of the universe.

In the light of Brian McHale's taxonomy of the shift from modernist to postmodernist fiction, White's novels can be seen to participate in an increasing doubt about the art work's ability to structure reality.[8] So, White's novels up to *Riders in the Chariot* might be classified as pre-eminently modernist in their obsession with the individual outsider while his 1960s novels consider the limitations on the knowledge of the artist, and the final works openly declare the provisional and distorted nature of art. By McHale's model, White's novels can be construed as shifting from a predominantly modernist emphasis on the alienated individual and the struggle to know and understand a confusing world, to the loss of confidence in fiction's ability to represent even this condition. So we find an increasing self-reflexivity in White's fiction, with *The Twyborn Affair* questioning the construction of both gender and narrative, and his final *Memoirs of Many in One* adopting an openly postmodern structure with 'Patrick White' reduced to the mere recorder of the many lives of Alex Gray.

Christina Stead's posthumous novel, *I'm Dying Laughing* (1986), invites particular comparison with *The Twyborn Affair* (1979), as it shares both that novel's excessiveness and its focus on the relationship between Europe and the New World in the crisis of the Second World War. Despite recent attacks on White's status,[9] there can be little doubt that, with Stead, he represents one of the major figures of postwar writing in English. Both authors wrote final novels which express a depth of disillusion with modern Western civilisation in terms of grand satires. They move beyond the representational faith of realism, or the seeking of individual difference of modernism, to present a great sweep of disbelief and despair.

To younger novelists in the 1960s White opened up both new subjects and new styles for writing fiction. Thomas Keneally's *Bring Larks and Heroes* (1967), for example, adopted White's strategy in *Voss* of writing over a historical moment with contemporary religious and philosophical concerns; Thea Astley's *The Slow Natives* (1965) exhibited a gallery of characters suffering individual spiritual crises in the manner of White's *Riders in the Chariot*. Clearly, these two writers found White inspirational—Astley wrote *The Acolyte* (1972) in answer to *The Vivisector*, elaborating White's kind of imagistic style to overwhelming proportions. Astley's career, spanning as it does the period from 1958 to 1996, with a novel published almost every two years, provides some markers for change in the possibilities for serious fiction writing in Australia. In the 1960s her writing was associated with that of White, and she was seen as one of the voices casting off the old realism, and adopting a style which dominated its subject matter. I will return to Astley's changing reputation during the course of this chapter.

By 1965 the possibility that the novel could (and even should) do more than grapple with the material conditions of reality had been firmly established. The years since then have also seen the development of the Australian novel, and prose fiction in general, from a base wherein modernism was to be renewed, and where any clear party-political relationship with fiction had ended. This has left fiction writers with the task of finding their own individual directions, often using formal experiment as the testing ground for ideas.

THE INNOVATORS

Literary historians reviewing the Australian novel in 1975 and 1976, such as Harry Heseltine, D.R. Burns or Nancy Keesing, recognised White, Astley and Keneally as the significant figures of the previous decade, but they also pointed to the fiction of David Ireland, Peter Mathers, Barry Oakley and Dal Stivens as a sign of another tradition, which Burns saw as sufficiently Australian to be termed 'larrikin'.[10] Writers usually associated with an earlier period, such as George Johnston, Xavier Herbert and Frank Hardy were publishing after 1965—and some of the 'new writers' of the previous decade (Randolph Stow, Elizabeth Harrower and Christopher Koch) were relatively silent over the next ten years. Any literary history must be skewed by its own chronological position, and we should note that many early reviewers of the period saw the novels of Dal Stivens as offering some alternative to the experiments of White. A contemporary of White, Stivens has produced four novels and several collections of short stories. His comic novel *A Horse of Air* (1970) adopts the strategy of a layered fiction with an unreliable narrative voice and, perhaps, may mark him as the forerunner of some of the innovators of the new generation.

In 1988 when Helen Daniel published her book about the 'new fiction' writers of the 1970s generation, she called them 'Liars' in reference to their various moves away from conventional realism.[11] Thus, she could group together disparate writers—Peter Mathers, Peter Carey, David Ireland, David Foster, Murray Bail, Elizabeth Jolley, Gerald Murnane, Nicholas Hasluck—according to a common tendency to undermine the authority of fiction. The term 'postmodernist' was then not in wide critical use and Daniel defined this new fiction in relation to Latin American writers such as Borges and Marquez, with some reference to French writers (Robbe-Grillet, Sarraute) and Americans (Barth, Pynchon).

In retrospect, the Australian-ness of the novels of writers such as Mathers, Ireland and Foster seems more striking than their signs of international influence. Peter Mathers's *Trap*, published in 1965, may be regarded as one of the signpost novels for a changing mood; and David Ireland's *The Chantic Bird* (completed in 1966, published 1968) confirms that other experiments were in progress. Both novels attacked the complacent orderliness of Australian urban life, using unreliable narrators to observe their anti-authoritarian central figures (in *The Chantic Bird* the central figure narrates his story to an unlikely novelist). Without adopting the clear political stances and conventional realism of earlier writers about working Australia, Mathers and Ireland expressed a satiric anger at the ways in which money and comfort had come to dominate Australian life. In doing so they referred to an older tradition of Australian yarn-spinning, celebrating vernacular language and working-class life. So, in some ways, the new fiction of Mathers and Ireland, at least, can be seen as a development of the old nationalist tradition, without the party-political connections brought to it by the socialist realists of the 1940s and 1950s.

Ireland acknowledged a debt to Laurence Sterne and admitted, under questioning, to encountering Marquez and the nineteenth-century South American writer, Machado de Assis, while writing *The Unknown Industrial Prisoner* (1972).[12] Though this ambitious novel might be said to be experimental in its abandonment of an orderly narrative, and in its fragmented observations of life inside one of the oil refineries on the shores of Botany Bay, it is nevertheless founded on close observation of Australian working life. The power of the novel lies in its detailed account of the demoralising routines and structures of industrial life in Australia. The conditions in which Ireland's working men argue and struggle are recognisably accurate; they convince the reader that they represent an existing situation—the goal of the realist novel. But Ireland cannot solve his workers' problems, as a socialist realist writer would have done; the Great White Father creates a Home Beautiful to provide physical comfort for the workers, but the novel cannot answer the changing problems of work in an age of unstoppable technology. Ireland inserts a belated 'Preface' (six pages before the novel's end) to comment on its fragmentation and lack of resolution. But this, too, constitutes a democratic and anti-authoritarian position—the writer has no greater insight than his characters who, like others (presumably including the reader) 'carry their books inside them'.[13] In Ireland's later *The Glass Canoe* (1976), a powerful satire of Australian male culture and apathy, the writer-researcher, Sibley, is finally sealed inside a beer keg—the writer is an alien figure in the world which Ireland documents.

Despite the novels of Mathers and Ireland (or Barry Oakley and Morris Lurie), Carl Harrison-Ford found in 1977 that the new fiction was essentially confined to the short story genre.[14] While this comment may owe a deal to Harrison-Ford's Sydney perspective, it was nonetheless the case that in the early 1970s a group of short story writers self-consciously promoting change had formed around Frank Moorhouse and Michael Wilding in Sydney.

Indeed, the public acknowledgment of a new kind of fiction might be dated at 1973 when Frank Moorhouse edited a volume of *Coast to Coast*, a short story anthology which had been published annually by Angus and Robertson from 1941 to 1970. Moorhouse's *Coast to Coast* represented a stunning departure from the previous worthy collections of stories from *Meanjin* and *Southerly*. It was published in a larger format, with a hippie drawing on the cover, and contained a range of stories by people that readers had never heard of (and some that were never to be heard of again).[15] In this collection were stories which totally abandoned the realist conventions of the past, or which called on those conventions to present quite different areas of experience to the traditional rural or working-class urban lives familiar to literary readers. Moorhouse himself had already done much to change the ways in which Australian stories were told. With Wilding and others, he deliberately flouted the restrictive censorship laws and conservative attitudes of publishers. In order to find an outlet for new writing, this group created a rogue magazine, *Tabloid Story*, which attached itself to various other newspapers and magazines in order to reach a wider readership.[16]

A fair sampling of this new writing of the late 1960s and early 1970s can be found in Brian Kiernan's collection of short stories *The Most Beautiful Lies* (1977) containing stories by Morris Lurie, Frank Moorhouse, Murray Bail, Peter Carey and Michael Wilding. Kiernan was unwilling to define these writers as a group. Like Daniel ten years later, he grouped the writers as a new generation rather than a new movement—a generation 'not much concerned with the conventions, both literary and social, which had prevailed'.[17] In this way social attitudes and literary experiment were linked. In 1983

Moorhouse edited a second collection called *The State of the Art* which expressed in its title the idea that these stories represented a 'cutting edge' of experiment. When Don Anderson produced his *Transgressions* anthology of stories in 1986 he went so far as to suggest that experimental form and radical politics belonged together, proclaiming: 'To subvert dominant literary stuctures and dominant linguistic and rhetorical patterns is also to subvert dominant ideologies'.[18] This view of the relationship between art and politics has been rarely challenged in the 1980s and 1990s. Indeed, literary critics aligned with political interest groups as diverse as feminists, migrants and Aborigines have all endorsed a form of this doctrine to some degree—though it has often had the effect of reducing criticism to a kind of formal pigeonholing.

One of the attractions of the short story in the 1970s was the possibility for publication through outlets such as *Tabloid Story* and other small magazines which sprang up during the period. Another was that it provided sufficient room for experiments of various kinds—for example, writers could attempt the prose poem without the demand for an elaborate structure, or try their hands at fantasies like Carey's without being required to follow the logic of these in any extended way. But there was a further advantage to the short story: its fragmentary nature denied the writer the possibility of imposing a unifying order on reality. Where the short stories were realist, they offered their visions as partial glimpses rather than new realities. Totalising visions were to be distrusted, the only trustworthy art was aware of its imperfection.

WOMEN'S WRITING AND FEMINISM

The absence of women from this literary revolution was conspicuous. In Australian writing, women have often borne the symbolic burden of respectability and suburban life—a burden evident both in Patrick White's high culture depiction of the housewives in *Riders in the Chariot* and Barry Humphries's popular comic figure, Edna Everage. Certainly, the novels of Ireland and Mathers had little room for the housewife or her children; in Ireland's early work, in particular, the wife was most likely to conspire with the oppressive forces of industry to keep men at their soul-destroying work—and out of the pub (though *The Glass Canoe* is rich with irony on this score). In the more urban writing of the younger writers, women became the objects and sometimes instigators of sexual adventure. But the major political focus for radical activity in the early 1970s, the Vietnam War, became a man's issue because of the threat of conscription for military service; women might protest against the law, but they did not face the imminent risk of finding themselves in the army or in prison. As in the radical political movements, there were women on the margins of the 'new writing', particularly in poetry, but none with a central place until the mid-1970s. By then, however, a reinvigorated feminism could be heard.

During the early 1970s the weekly newspaper of the educated Left was the *Nation Review*, which provided a focus for the social, cultural and political arguments of the time. Like much of the new fiction, the newspaper's iconoclasm retained some of the undergraduate male humour associated with earlier papers such as *Oz* magazine; and Richard Walsh's retrospective collection of items from *Nation Review* contains a letter from Helen Garner written in 1972 asking that the newspaper refrain from using the word 'cunt' as a term of abuse.[19] This short letter might now be seen as a warning that there were women writers waiting their time.

While Germaine Greer's literary critical polemic, *The Female Eunuch* (1970), marks the first Australian contribution to 'second wave' international feminism, a feminist consciousness became evident in Australian fiction with the publication of Helen Garner's *Monkey Grip* in 1977. This account of a young woman's life in an inner-city group house served as a testament to the contradictions being encountered by many women in their efforts to free themselves from the social and sexual inhibitions of the past. On its publication, it was derided by some critics as a loose and simple diary of a sordid existence, devoid of literary quality, while others praised its integrity and lyricism. Regardless of its critical reception, *Monkey Grip* found responsive readers, particularly among women, many of whom saw its negotiation of romantic love, sexual freedom and maternal responsibility as speaking to their own situations, even while it depicted a minority lifestyle.[20]

But *Monkey Grip* is not merely a document of the political place of Australian women in the mid-1970s. By reference to earlier women writers such as Jean Rhys and Doris Lessing, Garner asserted that she was writing within a feminist tradition that examined the sexuality of women, and was interested in finding new formal structures to do so. Far from being a naive diary, her novel consciously explored realist techniques which offered fragmentary glimpses of a woman's intimate life, and it questioned the romance narratives which women often invoke to make their lives meaningful.

Of course, women writers had been publishing fiction throughout the 1960s and 1970s; the work of Astley and Elizabeth Harrower, for example, provides ample evidence that women were developing outside both the social realist/Left nationalist tradition or the popular romance mode. But it was overseas writers—Lessing, Rhys, Virginia Woolf, Sylvia Plath—who provided the first models for radical feminism. The gathering of an Australian women's tradition, which might push the novels of Dorothy Hewett, Dymphna Cusack or M. Barnard Eldershaw into feminist service, was a later development.

Monkey Grip marked a new phase in Australian women's writing in its willingness to address the sexual dilemmas of 'liberation'. In its wake, fiction by women seemed to explode on to the marketplace, supported by a group of women's publishers including McPhee Gribble, Sisters and later Sybylla and Spinifex, as well as mainstream publishers, particularly Penguin. Furthermore, women readers seemed to have an appetite for the new women's fiction, as they discovered that many of their own concerns could be found in writing by other women. Indeed, surveys began to show that, in Australia, women were the book-buyers and, overwhelmingly, readers of fiction.[21] In the 1980s re-issued women's novels from overseas publishers such as Virago filled the bookshops, while Australian publishers such as Pandora and Penguin also re-issued fiction by nineteenth- and early twentieth-century women writers. This phenomenon was mocked or resented by some men writers and critics—Helen Garner noted that Edna Everage had Lessing and Garner on her coffee table in one of Humphries's 1980s shows, and in 1986 Gerard Windsor claimed that women writers received 'special' treatment at the hands of reviewers.[22]

A year after Helen Daniel included only one woman writer in her study of 'Australian New Novelists', Gillian Whitlock called her anthology of women's writing *Eight Voices of the Eighties* (1989), suggesting that the emergence of women writers was the major phenomenon of the decade.[23] Comparing these two books, a reader might conclude that, of the women writers, only Elizabeth Jolley could be called innovative, and that the differences between men and women writers were wide indeed: Whitlock chose Jessica Anderson, Thea Astley (though Astley was also a new voice of the 1950s and 1960s), Beverley Farmer, Helen Garner, Kate Grenville, Barbara Hanrahan, Elizabeth Jolley and Olga Masters as her eight—a choice which overlapped those discussed in Pam Gilbert's 1988 collection of essays, where Jean Bedford replaced Beverley Farmer.[24]

When interviewed, all of these writers recognised the moment of second wave feminism in which they found themselves, but most did not offer any theoretical feminist approach, and some resented being considered as women first, writers second.[25] They were women writers—but feminist critics had already begun to ask whether they were feminist writers. When Kerryn Goldsworthy proposed that Beverley Farmer's writing reacted against a public awareness of feminist issues, Farmer replied that 'feminism may be "a powerful political force" but it's not a dictatorship'.[26] In 1989 Bronwen Levy suggested that by the end of the 1980s women writers like Masters and Jolley were being read as 'mainstream', so that their work no longer offered a challenge to prevailing values.[27]

None of the writers in Whitlock's collection and Gilbert's study appear to have been greatly influenced by the feminist poststructuralist theory sweeping university literature departments in the 1980s. These theories proposed that the Symbolic Order, the very language and structures in which fiction was written, was by definition masculine. Thus, all conventional forms of writing could be regarded as phallogocentric, as inherently masculine, and by participating in them the woman writer submitted to the dominant masculine order. Conventional realist writing, particularly that modelled on nineteenth-century realism, was condemned as the voice of a masculine liberalism enacting all the conventions of late nineteenth-century Western thought—the chronological narrative, the unified subject (usually a principal character whose experiences and viewpoint held the novel together) and a faith in the power of language to represent the actual world. According to such feminist theories, feminist writing belonged with the avant-garde, and writing which worked older traditions of realism might be described as a conservative, middle-class, 'women's' writing. This amounts to a feminist version of Don Anderson's contention that radical form and radical ideology belong together.

The immediate difficulty in applying these theories to Australian fiction lies in Daniel's obvious point—that the avant-garde and experimental initiatives had been taken by men, some of whose work (including the fiction of White, Murnane or Ireland) could be read as misogynistic. On the surface at least, Anderson, Masters, Farmer and Garner appeared to be 'realist' writers, intent on recording or representing women's experience in fairly conventional ways. Certainly Astley, Grenville, Hanrahan and Jolley often wrote more excessive fiction, but even here any alignment with feminist positions might be difficult to pinpoint. Astley's satire, Hanrahan's deceptive naivety, or Grenville and Jolley's Gothic speculations may be seen as experimental—but at some distance from the postmodern projects of Murnane, Wilding, Ireland and others.

For women writers versed in feminist theory, though, the call to experiment and to adapt forms of modernism has been clear. Fictions clearly inspired by feminist theory include Janine Burke's *Speaking* (1984), Marion Campbell's *Lines of Flight* (1985), Mary Fallon's *Working Hot* (1988), Jan McKemmish's *A Gap in the Records* (1985), Finola Moorhead's *Remember the Tarantella* (1987) and Drusilla Modjeska's *Poppy* (1990). Carmel Bird, too, in *The Bluebird Cafe* (1990) and *The White Garden* (1995) has developed for feminist purposes the kind of Nabokovian form favoured by men experimenters.

Lines of Flight is, perhaps, the strongest example of a writer grappling with the problems for the feminist artist of a dominant masculine system and theory. Campbell's protagonist, a young Australian woman studying art in France, negotiates the various post-structural pronouncements on art, each voiced by a male authority of one kind or another. Here, and in her second novel, *Not Being Miriam* (1988), she insists on a political role for art, one which does not concede the creative ground to theory. Campbell's artist must acknowledge her power to order reality, at the same time that she uses that power to challenge more dominant representations of it.

This is the difficulty for the feminist writer who subscribes to the need to challenge not only the central position of masculine experience as the subject for art, but the very formal structures of art which are seen as maintaining masculine authority. The concept of an *écriture féminine* proposes that the woman's body become the guiding metaphor for feminist art, so that writing styles should accordingly mimic the fluid, organic elements in the female body. These theories present some difficult and contradictory elements for negotiation; their emphasis on formal innovation may be seen as rather academic and elitist, and the promotion of the domestic and personal as the appropriate sphere for feminist struggle may inhibit feminists from tackling public political issues. Amanda Lohrey's novel about waterfront politics, *The Morality of Gentlemen* (1984), has been outside the range of feminist criticism, and Sara Dowse's consistently political and historical fictions, such as *West Block* (1983) and *Sapphires* (1994) are rarely included in feminist surveys.

Of the writers who find their way through these feminist formal and political questions, Elizabeth Jolley is outstanding. Her work illuminates many post-structuralist feminist concerns by a process of creative play. Her early novels, *Palomino* (1980) and *Milk and Honey* (1984), developed contemporary Gothic narratives by which she explored dark secrets. The relationships of writing to life become elements of cyclical plots in *Miss Peabody's Inheritance* (1983), *Foxybaby* (1985) and *The Well* (1986). Yet Jolley always explores the darker side, the secret elements in women's lives, and perhaps the driving force behind her work, too, has been autobiographical, in that her masterly trilogy *My Father's Moon* (1989) *Cabin Fever* (1990) and *The Georges' Wife* (1993) seem to be exorcising elements from the writer's own past. Jolley, like Campbell, transforms any autobiographical impulse into a sophisticated, conscious art—nevertheless, her novels speak of women's experiences, and their fears. When reading *The Well, Miss Peabody* or *Foxybaby*, one may enjoy the postmodern layering of narrative, and laugh at Jolley's whimsical or absurdist humour. But the core of such novels always contains a horror—death, incest, loneliness, the use of sex for power—which figures not as an external oppression but as a potentiality within her mildest women characters.

Shortly after Jolley's emergence as a writer in the late 1970s, Olga Masters appeared with a powerful book of short stories, *The Home Girls* (1982). In the years before her death in 1986 she completed two collections of short stories and two novels, with a further book of stories collected posthumously. Masters might be called a realist, of an old-fashioned social kind, in that her work barely subdues a sense of outrage at poverty and injustice. Yet it was also curiously anachronistic in that her subject matter was almost exclusively the country town life of her youth on the far south coast of New South Wales. Through a careful, painstaking devotion to domestic detail Masters re-created Pambula and Cobargo during the Depression in *Loving Daughters* (1984) and *A Long Time Dying* (1987) while urban Sydney during the Second World War is the setting of *Amy's Children* (1987). Like Jolley's women characters, Masters's women were no passive victims but cunning creatures learning to look to material advantage for survival. In retrospect, however, it may be more appropriate to see Masters outside feminist paradigms as a writer prepared, like Eudora Welty and Flannery O'Connor in the USA, to concentrate on a particular place and time, to explore intensely a particular milieu in order to reveal its secrets. As Beverley Farmer has commented: 'No one is like her: sly, garrulous, fussy, with that glow of sensuality, and an alertness, carving a family life to the bare bone like a Sunday joint'.[28]

With the 'arrival' and acclaim of Anderson, Masters and Jolley, Thea Astley's work suddenly appeared to belong to women, rather than to the innovators of the 1960s. Yet her novels up to *An Item from the Late News* (1982) are difficult to recuperate into feminist readings; they often share the disgust for the female body prevalent in the writing of her male contemporaries, and they are inclined to pass judgment on sexually active women—see, for example, the presentation of Iris Levinson in *The Slow Natives* (1965) or the fate of Miss Trumper in *A Boatload of Homefolk*. Astley says that she chose a female narrator for *An Item from the Late News* in response to feminist comments on her consistently masculine viewpoint,[29] and there are conscious (if sometimes anachronistic) declarations of feminist commitment in *It's Raining in Mango* (1987) and *Reaching Tin River* (1990). Nevertheless, Astley's creative impulse appears to be both conservative and sometimes anarchic; she is an individualist and a satirist, and her work resists enlistment to any specific feminist causes.

In so far as feminism is a political movement, attempting to win readers to its cause, the realist (and socially concerned) novel must retain a place among feminist modes. Garner's realism in *Monkey Grip* opened up the publication of feminist fiction in Australia, but some critics of her later work have found it conventional, and even, in *The First Stone* (1995), reactionary. The variation in notions of feminism may be seen in recent critical studies of Jessica Anderson's fiction and Dorothy Hewett's plays: Elaine Barry hails as feminist Anderson's careful efforts to capture women's experience and order it in meaningful ways, while Margaret Williams interprets as feminist Dorothy Hewett's quite opposite interest in the divided individual and disordered fictional structures.[30] That is, feminism may be found in one writer's concern for women's participation in the social order, and in another's refusal of that order.

In Australia, feminist critics, though quick to identify misogyny or sexism, have rarely considered that writing by men might be read as feminist. This remains one of the most obvious gaps in a feminist project which has been intent on promoting the work of women. Ken Gelder discusses the reception by feminists of David Ireland's 'women' novels, *A Woman of the Future* (1979) and *City of Women* (1981) and it may be that Ireland's trespass on feminist territory has been a factor in the diminution of his reputation since the late 1970s.[31] David Foster's *Mates of Mars* (1991), too, tackles the gender divide head on by making fun of both male presumption and feminist idealism, but feminist critics have given little attention to his work.

Feminist fiction, then, cannot be equated with women's fiction, and the critical debate must continue—preferably based on careful readings of individual texts rather than sweeping categorisations according to the most obvious elements of form. While some feminist experiments have explored the 'inner discourse' through fragmentary, speculative fictions, others have begun to blur the distinctions between genres. Drusilla Modjeska's *Poppy* and her later *The Orchard* (1994), mix elements of autobiography and the essay with fiction. Garner's latest books, too, have mixed fictional and journalistic elements—though this has exacerbated the controversy over her decision to write about an actual sexual harassment case in *The First Stone*. Both *The First Stone* and *The Orchard* raise questions about the power of the writer, as these books impose fictional 'ways of seeing' on actual events and living people; the declared autobiographer at least risks self-exposure, but these 'fictions' make free with other people's lives while carefully protecting the author. Beverley Farmer's *A Body of Water* (1990) puts the author/narrator into a more vulnerable position, as she attempts to expose the genesis of her stories and poems in a partially autobiographical narrative.

While the belief that radical feminism lies in radical form may stimulate experiment, autobiographical and realist writing retains a political importance as an avenue for the discussion of race and class issues. These can often be submerged in fiction which operates on the tacit understanding that both writer and reader are *au fait* with the latest French theory discussed in women's studies courses. Sally Morgan's *My Place* (1987) and the autobiographies of other Aboriginal women which followed it, such as Ruby Langford

Ginibi's *Don't Take Your Love to Town* (1988), reasserted the possibilities of autobiographical writing in drawing attention to the social inequalities which have given some women considerable privilege over others in Australian society.

OTHER VOICES

The rise of women's writing in Australia was not so much the emergence of a new force as a reinvigoration of longstanding avenues of female expression. Women writers have taken to the novel from its beginning, finding in its very openness and adaptability a means to express their often more domestic and personal vision of society. Writers of Aboriginal background who came to the novel in the last thirty years could call on no such indigenous tradition. The invention of the novel was entangled in the social, educational and cultural changes in Europe during the Industrial Revolution; it is, in many ways, the archetypal literary genre of modern Western societies.

The use of fiction in the political struggle of Aborigines coincides with their change of legal status in the last thirty years, marked by the granting of federal citizenship in 1967. Through these years the political organisation of Aborigines increased considerably and some began to see a place for writing in the political struggle. Prose fiction, however, has remained a fairly limited mode for Aboriginal writers, representing as it does the conventions of white middle-class liberal attitudes. Poetry and drama have proved more amenable to approximating traditional Aboriginal forms, and have usually found much more immediate responses from Aboriginal audiences. To write novels, particularly high culture novels, is to seek out an educated white audience; Aboriginal writers and activists have found poetry (as in the case of Oodgeroo Noonuccal, Bobbi Sykes, Kevin Gilbert and Lionel Fogarty) to be more widely read or heard, while others have resorted to autobiography as providing a stronger political authority by reference to experience.

In 1965 Mudrooroo (as Colin Johnson) published *Wild Cat Falling* under the patronage of the established writer Mary Durack. It has been accepted as the first novel written by an Aborigine and, despite its author's later reservations and revisions (and recent questions about his ethnic background), justifies continuing attention by readers and critics. For this story about a young Aborigine, living on the edge of white middle-class society, seeking some kind of intellectual explanation for his outsider status, demonstrates in its style the alienating structures of European thought. The unnamed narrator is an aspiring intellectual recognising his own condition in the existentialist ideas of European writers—Kafka, Camus and Beckett. Yet his visits to the university in Perth and discussions with university students make his position outside these intellectual traditions only too clear. The narrator ends as a vagrant and criminal, and Mudrooroo later dismissed the novel's ending, which suggests a fleeting hope of understanding in the eyes of the arresting policeman.

Wild Cat Falling is clearly not so much an account of the 'typical' Aboriginal experience as an attempt to find a way to insert the Aborigine's desire for a voice and an intellectually respected position into the European high culture tradition. It is far more literary and self-conscious than, say, Archie Weller's later fiction about the divided heritage of young urban Aboriginal men, possibly because, true to its time of writing, it looks for a high cultural mode in which to speak rather than identifying with a political movement and the need to provide straightforward information to readers.

It was not until the late 1970s that Mudrooroo published another novel—his *Long Live Sandawara* (1979)—beginning the project of restoring the place of Aborigines in Australian history which culminated in his *Dr Wooreddy's Prescription for Enduring the Ending of the World* (1983). By 1981 Mudrooroo's first novel had inspired Archie Weller to rewrite it for a younger generation in his *The Day of the Dog*, a more openly social realist novel than *Wild Cat*. Weller's *Going Home* (1986), a collection of short stories which questioned the avenues to 'success' for urban and town-dwelling Aborigines, seemed more confident of a sympathetic white audience than Mudrooroo's work—though it was also more popular in its appeal to simple moralities. But *Dr Wooreddy's Prescription* stands as the major achievement by a writer speaking from an Aboriginal viewpoint; Mudrooroo's uncovering of a well-documented genocide—the rounding up and subsequent abandonment of the Aboriginal Tasmanians—conveys both an outrage on the part of an Aboriginal survivor, and an awareness of the ownership of language by Europeans.

The novel is also, of course, the chosen genre of the educated and urbanised. Mudrooroo and Weller are distinguished by their tertiary educations. Neither of them, nor indeed Faith Bandler or Eric Willmot, claimed to speak for tribal Aborigines. Yet, in the late 1970s a writer emerged who invited such an identification—B. Wongar. There was some scandal when it was revealed in 1981 that Wongar was the Yugoslav migrant, Sreten Bozic, and that his books *The Track to Bralgu* (1978), *Karan* (1985) and *Walg: A Novel of Australia* (1986), were less than authentic versions of contemporary tribal Aboriginal stories. Yet the tribal novelist is a contradiction in terms; to write fiction in the Western manner is to participate in a sophisticated English language discourse. Sneja Gunew has argued that the criticism of Bozic represents an attempt to silence his political voice,[32] but Wongar's stories claim to express the political viewpoint of Aborigines, and they adopt a naive pseudo-Aboriginal style which may be seen as simplifying and universalising Aboriginal views.

Two novels which express extremes of approach to contemporary Aboriginal life are Sam Watson's *The Kadaitcha Sung* (1990) and Kim Scott's *True Country* (1993)—the one a fantastic, aggressive narrative of black revenge in Brisbane, the other a sensitive and carefully observed account of Aboriginal life in the Kimberleys. These novels appear to have similar starting points in their desire to understand the meaning of an Aboriginal heritage in contemporary Australia. Watson mixes popular fantasy genres and magic realism with Aboriginal myth and social realism as his hero participates in a violent return of the tribes; Scott prefers a fragmented, seemingly autobiographical, approach to present the complexities of the Aboriginal/white situation on the fringes of society. It is a pity that such novels are most likely to be read in isolation as 'Aboriginal' writing when they engage in the wider discussion raised in novels such as Foster's *Mates of Mars* and Andrew McGahan's *1988* (1995).

While fiction had a brief flourishing in the 1980s as a political medium for Aboriginal writers—particularly men—it has given way to autobiographical writing in the past ten years. Women have been more prominent here, with Sally Morgan, Ruby Langford Ginibi, Glenyse Ward and Mabel Edmonds all writing accounts of their experiences as Aboriginal women. In the case of Aborigines, the autobiography has been particularly important in restoring a history of black lives in Australia, as so much has been omitted from public histories. Autobiographical accounts such as *Raparapa* (1988), a collection of Kimberley stockmen's stories, contribute as much to Australian history as to its literature, bearing in mind that both kinds of writing must face questions about 'authenticity'. Some of these books, particularly Morgan's popularly successful *My Place*, have come under criticism for their failure to acknowledge their white heritage—but these readings seem remarkably literal, failing to see autobiography as a literary as well as a historical genre.

Alongside these autobiographies of Aboriginal experience in modern Australia have come historical studies of the injustices of the past such as those by Henry Reynolds, Roger Milliss and Cassandra Pybus. And evidence presented in government reports such as the inquiry into the forced removal of Aboriginal children from their parents[33] seems bound to influence fiction making. These historical and factual studies, together with the autobiographies, have had a powerful effect on mainstream Australian writing, so that a range of writers, who may have overlooked the Aboriginal presence in their early work, have felt obliged to consider it in their 1980s and 1990s fiction. Once again, Thea Astley provides a significant example. Her 1974 novel, *A Kindness Cup*, broke a virtual silence in postwar fiction by examining the aftermath of a massacre of Aborigines, but it nevertheless concentrated on the moral problems of white liberals; her later novel *It's Raining in Mango* (1987) recognised the ongoing historical struggle of Aborigines in Australian society by creating an Aboriginal family in parallel to her white family.

AUTOBIOGRAPHICAL WRITING

Though the boundaries between fiction and autobiography are currently under dispute it seems appropriate to consider autobiography here, as a rise in autobiographical writing has developed alongside the drive towards experimental fiction, and, in some ways, the autobiography may be seen as the necessary complement to the movement away from realism in fiction. It is curious that Hal Porter—a writer acknowledged as one of the most artificial stylists of the 1950s and early 1960s—should become the leading figure of the modern autobiography. Porter published his first volume of autobiography, *The Watcher on the Cast Iron Balcony* in 1963, and so, according to David McCooey, began the era of modern autobiography in Australia.[34] By this, McCooey suggests that since *The Watcher* autobiography has become a more clearly belle-lettrist genre, one which challenges the novel as a medium for examining the place of the personal in Australian public life. McCooey is one critic who maintains that the boundary between autobiography and fiction is important, while others, such as Gillian Whitlock, see such boundaries as unnecessarily rigid.[35]

It is tempting, however, to see the rise of the autobiography as partially a result of the movement away from realism in the novel, and its accompanying questioning of the authority of the novelist. As the art of the novel demands increasingly imaginative or fantastic powers of its practitioners, so those who believe themselves lacking in inventive power may fall back on the autobiography. The autobiography (as opposed to the memoir) has a kind of democratic appeal in that it provides a means of witnessing for those who have no other claims on our attention. While Whitlock and others insist that fiction and autobiography cannot be separated, it seems clear that the autobiographer and the novelist may be. That is, the successful autobiographer is most often not a novelist; and the successful novelist is most often not a successful autobiographer. So among the most remarkable autobiographies published by Australians in the past thirty years may be counted Graham McInnes's *The Road to Gundagai* (1965), Donald Horne's *The Education of Young Donald* (1967), Clive James's *Unreliable Memoirs* (1980), A.B. Facey's *A Fortunate Life* (1981), Bernard Smith's *The Boy Adeodatus* (1984), Sally Morgan's *My Place*, Ruby Langford Ginibi's *Don't Take Your Love to Town*, Jill Ker Conway's *The Road from Coorain* (1989), and Germaine Greer's *Daddy, We Hardly Knew You* (1989). While James, at least, has also written novels, most of these autobiographers have derived their reputations from critical and historical writing. Of course, there have been autobiographies published by fiction writers—Patrick White's *Flaws in the Glass* (1981) for example—yet such autobiographies seem more like adjuncts to the fiction writing, a kind of commentary on the primary imagination.

The importance of autobiography as a means of witnessing the experiences of particular groups in the community, especially Aborigines and migrants, suggests that this reference to the authority of experience may have radical political uses. But it also may claim the authority of experience over the imagination. Of course, autobiographers may lie, make mistakes, misremember, but it is difficult to argue with those who say they were in the place, at the time. In this way, the autobiography may claim the authority so carefully evaded or recklessly thrown away by experimental novelists.

The autobiography, then, may be a means of returning to the stable individual identities, chronological narratives and authority of the old realist fiction. While several migrants to Australia—Rosa Cappiello, Mary Rose Liverani, and Andrew Riemer—have written brilliant and idiosyncratic autobiographies, non-realist fiction also makes claims to be the most appropriate form to convey the migrant experience. Perhaps the difference may be expressed as follows: autobiography debates the way people believed themselves to experience Australian life, while the novel, based though it may be on experience, speculates about that experience.

It has fallen to the children of migrants, particularly non-British migrants, to adapt the novel to the multiple experience of cultures. Brian Castro's *Birds of Passage* (1983) offers a model of the way in which postmodernist techniques suit the mixed identities of the migrant, particularly the physically different such as Castro's Chinese men. *Birds of Passage* wittily sets a contemporary Chinese-Australian Seamus O'Young against a Chinese goldfields immigrant of the nineteenth century, Lo Yun Shan, placing Seamus in the position of reader of Shan's letters so that the novel operates like a series of boxes, or double mirrors—including a scene where the reader meets the author.

Beth Yahp's novel *The Crocodile Fury* (1992) adapts the mythic storytelling of Malaysia to the contemporary novel, slipping between family history and fairytale, between Christian religion and an older pagan belief system. The chronological or linear narrative so central to the conventional novel is abandoned in favour of cyclic and repetitive structures. Fotini Epanomitis, similarly, tries to replicate the patterns of storytelling in a Greek village in her *The Mule's Foal* (1993); the implied audience is Australian but Epanomitis asks the reader to make what she can of the connections. These writers try to foreground the differences of perspective and ways of structuring experience between, say, an illiterate Greek villager and an educated Australian novel-reader, or a nineteenth-century Chinese scholar and a suburban Australian with Chinese features. In each case, narrative authority is resisted as the first-generation Australian insists on the incompleteness of an individual, singular understanding. Yet, Asia and Europe remain fascinating subjects for non-migrant Australian writers and readers, and more straightforward versions of Asian societies may be found in the writing of Blanche d'Alpuget, Nick Jose, Christopher Koch or Alex Miller. These novels show a continuing confidence in taking foreign countries as 'subjects' for fiction, undaunted by debates about 'orientalism' or 'appropriation'. Much has been made of the question of authenticity in telling stories—whether they be those of Aborigines or migrants, men or women. Where, for example, Wongar's fiction has suffered from critical suspicion that it is fraudulent, it is possible to speculate that he might have been acclaimed for writing an autobiography about a Yugoslav migrant living with Aborigines in the Northern Territory. Perhaps Adib Khan might have received more attention for an autobiography than for his novel, *Seasonal Adjustments* (1994), about a Bangladeshi migrant. Brian Castro, whose sophisticated fiction encompasses rewritings of Freud (*Double Wolf*, 1991) and the continuation of a trilogy by the dead British writer, B.S. Johnson (*Drift*, 1994), cannot be boxed into 'appropriate' subjects for a Chinese-Portuguese-Australian writer. The insistence that a writer must speak for his particular background and culture may prove a way of preventing writers from imaginatively moving across cultures.

This notion that authenticity and authority are held by the author by virtue of an identifiable cultural, racial and sexual identity played its part in the controversy over

Helen 'Demidenko' Darville's *The Hand that Signed the Paper* in 1995. It turned out that the young author, unlike Castro, Epanomitis or Yahp, had no non-British migrant family to authenticate her version of the events she fictionalised—in this case, events in the Ukraine and Poland before and during the Second World War. *The Hand that Signed the Paper* presented itself as a novel—but the blurring between novel and history (and the author's desire to strengthen her autobiographical 'authority') meant that some readers refused the distinction. For them, the novel was 'lies'—and the defence that it was 'Lies' in the sense that Helen Daniel used it in her 1988 book (*Liars*) was unacceptable even to Daniel.[36]

The argument about *The Hand* became an argument about morality and value, though post-structuralist theorists have long denied that criticism has a moral role. So much has been written about what is an interesting, but not brilliant, novel that it would be wasteful to rehearse the arguments here. Among other things, the novel positions itself as an argument against war crimes trials and, in this respect, it is an argument about the relationship between the European past and contemporary (and future) Australia. Such an argument might appear particularly fraught—or topical—at a time when the first war crimes trials in forty years were beginning as a result of more recent events in the former Yugoslavia.

For all its perturbing presumption, *The Hand* is a novel in a long line of Australian novels attempting to connect the comfort of postwar suburban life to the murderous crises elsewhere in the world. In this respect, it follows the tradition of Thomas Keneally's writing; his *A Family Madness* (1985) makes similar connections between the 'dangerous planet' on which we exist and the blind and wilfully innocent approach Australians take towards it. Several of Keneally's novels, including *Confederates* (1979) and *Schindler's Ark* (1982), explore the bloody turmoil in other lands and other times, preferring what Peter Pierce calls 'melodrama' to more reticent or inward approaches to the novel.[37]

One of the complainants about the award of the Miles Franklin prize to Darville was Frank Moorhouse, whose own novel *Grand Days* had been excluded from consideration for the prize in 1994 on the ground that it did not show Australian life in any of its phases. *Grand Days*, though, shares Keneally's and Darville's interest in Europe during a period of crisis—in this case the setting up of the League of Nations in the 1920s and its consequent failure. Yet this novel turns political international events inward to uncover fetishist obsessions (with administrative files!) and the sexually decadent life of the bureaucrats in Geneva. It appears to be part-satire, part-novel of decadence, though the decadence may lie in the prevalent mood of Australian culture in the 1990s.

In *Grand Days* spiritual, moral and political matters are cast aside; only the sexual provides boundaries to test. John Scott's novel, *What I Have Written* (1993) turns the construction of sexual fantasies into the archetypal postmodernist activity. Many other fictions of the 1990s, including the so-called 'dirty realist' writing of Edward Berridge, Justine Ettler, Fiona McGregor, Christos Tsiolkas and Andrew McGahan, appear to abandon politics or the search for any kind of spiritual insight, and turn to sex as a site of increasingly limited 'new' adventures. Furthermore, the sexual in such fiction resists any social dimension—childbirth and family life have no part in them.

The feminist emphasis on 'writing the body', and the interest of gay and lesbian fiction in breaking sexual boundaries has made the sexual to a degree political. But such politics form part of a fragmenting of society rather than looking to any common social and political goals.

THE HISTORICAL PROJECT

Some critics, of course, insist that contemporary art cannot aspire to a unifying vision, as such a vision must erase or override the fragmented and marginal nature of actual experience. Yet in Australia most people are ready to accept that English will remain the community language, and such agreement suggests that communication between disparate groups, however imperfect, may be possible. Recent years have shown that writers, some of whom began their careers as self-styled subversives in the 1970s, have become willing to attempt the kind of national or monumental narratives which once seemed impossible.

The literary accompaniments to the Bicentenary celebrations of 1988 provide some evidence for consideration on this point. Thomas Keneally (*The Playmaker*, 1987), Thea Astley (*It's Raining in Mango*, 1987), Peter Carey (*Oscar and Lucinda*, 1988) Kate Grenville (*Joan Makes History*, 1988), Victor Kelleher (*Wintering*, 1990), David Malouf (*The Great World*, 1990, and *Remembering Babylon*, 1993), Robert Drewe (*Our Sunshine*, 1991), Rodney Hall (*The Yandilli Trilogy*, 1988–93), and David Foster (*Mates of Mars*, 1990) all published 'bicentennial' novels of one kind or other (while Sam Watson's *The Kadaitcha Sung* may be read as an anti-Bicentenary novel). Most focused their attention on Australian history, with Hall writing a trilogy of convictism and crime, Drewe imagining the voice of Ned Kelly, Malouf and Kelleher attempting to place Aboriginal history into a present world-view, and Carey playing with the religiosity and gambling spirit of the late Victorian period. Though Grenville attempted an alternative woman's perspective of Australian history, and Astley wrote a tragi-comic version of a family saga, many of these novels also returned to rather traditional grounds for the discussion of Australian life: the convict, the pioneer, the bushranger, the Australian prisoner of war.

None of these novels is conventionally historical, in that they are not attempts to faithfully reconstruct the past on the basis of the historical record; they are what Peter Pierce has termed 'neo-historical'.[38] They impose contemporary interpretations on the past, finding in it the beginnings of some aspect of present concern. Surprisingly, for all their postmodern playfulness, few of these novels brought any rigorous criticism to bear on contemporary Australian society. Most expressed the tolerant liberal philosophy of the urban middle class, deploring (and often simplifying) the contradictory history of

Australian settlement. A celebratory, if not populist, nationalism emerged despite the postmodern layering of texts. Whatever its dark history, Australia was, it seemed, a fine place to live in 1988.

Peter Carey's career provides a particularly interesting example of a writer whose experimental techniques convey a rather conventional moral and political vision. To compare, for example, *Oscar and Lucinda* with David Foster's earlier novel on a similar subject, *Moonlite* (1981), is to contrast a writer with a remarkable empathy for the attitudes of his own time, to a satirist who sets himself against the accepted wisdoms of the educated Australian liberal. While *Oscar and Lucinda* plays ironically with Victorian religious and social conventions, *Moonlite* unveils the voracious greed at the heart of colonisation. Yet the difference may also lie in the degree to which these novels participate in postmodern attitudes. Carey rewrites the work of Edmund Gosse, Thomas Hardy, Anthony Trollope and George Eliot into an Australian context, openly manipulating his characters for effect. Foster's writing is driven by the passionate contrariness of the satirist; if it is postmodern, it is so by the accident that satire feeds off any material that comes to hand.

There are several thorough critical accounts of the writing of both Carey and David Malouf which provide details of their careers.[39] Carey's development from the writer of fantastic short stories to the creator of the yarn-spinning *Illywhacker* (1985) and the *faux* satirist of *The Unusual Life of Tristan Smith* (1995) shows a remarkable adaptability of technique, but many of his novels give the reader a sense of being one step away from the action as the novelist sets up his effects. Malouf, on the other hand, seems most interested in achieving a kind of epiphany through language. His novels often create lyrical tableaux which gesture towards some mystical apprehension, and, in his hands, Australian history becomes the source of a kind of spiritual quest, reminiscent of early Patrick White novels.

Given the international reputations of these two writers and the way their fiction works through well-established modes, the impatience of younger writers is understandable. Edward Berridge, for example, has recently referred to the older generation as the 'living dead' of Australian writing.[40] The 'grunge' realists prefer to write about the material realities of contemporary city life, rather than to explore Australian history for its visionary moments. Andrew McGahan's second novel, *1988*, however, shows that even a 'grunge' novelist can examine the meaning of Australian history. McGahan's young protagonists leave the city celebrations of 1988 to travel to a remote weather station in the Northern Territory where they must confront the differences between themselves and the local Aborigines, their own failure to live up to the masculine stereotypes of white Australia, the burden of a colonial history, the discomforts and dangers of the natural world, and the seeming irrelevance of their aspirations to be artists. *1988* finds no clear answers to the uncertainty of contemporary Australian life, but it does recognise the disabling nature of a condition where—even after 200 years of settlement—no single person seems able to claim unambivalently to be Australian.

THE STRUGGLE FOR TRANSCENDENCE

The old associations of the realist novel with a political interest in the material conditions of actual life, and the 'fabulist', or more fantastic novel, with some sort of metaphysical understanding have particular significance for the Australian novel. Realism has traditionally been the mode of fiction interested in social problems, and in recording the distinctive features of Australian life. The shifts in realism since the 1950s—the rejection of social realism for more 'experimental' modes, then the move back to a more tentative realism in the work of Moorhouse, Garner and even Tim Winton's first books—have alternated with more consciously 'poetic' writing, such as that by Rodney Hall and David Malouf. While 'magic realism', 'fabulism' or even the broader satires of Ireland and Foster have no obvious spiritual claims in themselves, it cannot be denied that the seeking of transcendence through the novel has remained a strong element in Australian fiction ever since White proposed that god was in a 'gob of spittle'. In a thoroughly secular, firmly materialist society such as Australia, it may be unsurprising that writers continue to seek out the sacred or the spiritual through their art—and that readers want them to do so.

Tim Winton has commented that: 'I reckon anyone who has had a spiritual dimension in their life, whether that's tribal or religious, would find realism leaves huge gaps'.[41] This comment might be applied to the careers of Helen Garner, David Malouf or Beverley Farmer, with each writer beginning with autobiographical realism and gradually moving to speculate about a metaphysical or spiritual dimension beyond the parameters of the observed material world. In Garner's case, though, the move from a fragmented realism to fantasy in *Cosmo Cosmolino* (1992) has produced mixed responses—and her change to feature journalism raises questions about her own satisfaction with this departure from realism. Magical effects such as the flight above the suburban terraces in *Cosmo Cosmolino*, or the swarming of honey bees in *Remembering Babylon*, may strike readers as just as facile as any realist novel about a social problem, and the novelist who takes on the mantle of prophet or visionary runs considerable risks.

The struggle to achieve this 'literary mysticism' has been apparent in a range of Australian writers—and, though Winton sees it as the legacy of a religious upbringing, it may be a result of the lack of religion in contemporary Australian life. While secular readers of the past may have looked to poetry to provide a substitute for religion, they now often seek it in fiction. Unresolvable disputes are likely to develop when writers move beyond the limits of the material and known—does the ending of *Cosmo Cosmolino* represent an abnegation of fictional responsibility or a liberating transcendence of the novel's mundane realities? Yet 'magic realism' has become an almost standard technique in the novelist's repertoire—evident in Australia as early as Ireland's *A Woman of the Future* and Hall's *Just Relations* (1982).

David Foster's *The Glade within the Grove* (1996) published towards the end of the period under review, examines the spiritual state of Australia in the perspective of several millennia. His story of a group of 1968 communards who fall under the spell of the forests mixes 'magic realism', history, satire and farce. Inspired by readings of classical history and Latin poetry, Foster tries to place Australian civilisation (such as it is) against universal time. He laments not so much the decline of Australian civilisation as its failure to become established at all. Foster sees Australia as utterly decadent, and in need of a new form of spirituality. His writing approaches spirituality through a passion for (often obscure) words in all their infinite varieties and rhythms. *The Glade*, with its mix of language and genres, and its bleak satire, engages with most of the literary enthusiasms of our time.

SOME CONCLUSIONS

In a diverse, multicultural, fragmented society there can be no complete and all-encompassing visions. Furthermore, novels no longer form part of the cultural binding of society: they now are marketed to the same variety of consumer groups as other products, so they are not only for children or adults, but for women, feminists, Aborigines, migrants, gays, lesbians, liberals—or, even, for men. These categories divide readers as well as writers, so that the possibility of fiction speaking across groupings has diminished over time. Australian readers rely increasingly on overseas approval (particularly a Booker prize or shortlisting) before committing themselves to buying a new novel.

At the same time, critics have become wary of offering a 'canon' of literary works which might override the diversity of expression and readership operating in a literary community. Alas, a chapter in a literary history, surveying thousands of novels in 12 000 words must represent a contribution to canon-making. I have selected for discussion here novels which seem to exemplify certain trends and developments in Australian fiction as a whole. They do not represent a listing of the 'best' fiction from Australia, though I confess that the novels of David Foster, Elizabeth Jolley, Olga Masters, David Ireland, Marion Campbell, Helen Garner and Andrew McGahan offer me more pleasure than most of the writing discussed in this chapter. Furthermore, when a foreign critic, unfamiliar with the range of Australian publishing, pontificates on which Australian fiction matters,[42] I feel a responsibility to offer some counter-suggestions. In this circumstance, I cannot overlook the publication since 1965 of three novels I believe to be 'great' in the old-fashioned sense of transforming a reader's sense of the possibilities of fiction. These are Patrick White's *The Twyborn Affair*, Christina Stead's *I'm Dying Laughing* and David Foster's *The Glade within the Grove*.

All three novels are excessive, bulging with detail, eccentric and funny. Though they offer quite individual and unrepresentative visions of contemporary society (not confined to Australia), they are all witty satires, conveying bleak visions of Western civilisation. And this common ground provides a kind of conclusion to my narrative of a fragmented culture. For if the contemporary Australian novel functions as an expression of decadence—of taking apart the structures which might hold a society together—then it seems that there can be no great novels, only expressions of difference, marginality, diversity. Yet these satires revel in precisely that difference and diversity, as if the novelists want to record every possible element in the infinite multiplicity of contemporary life. Their irony is not merely a postmodern stylistic tic, but a sense that only a panoramic vision can do justice to the contradictions in the human condition, and that such a vision cannot take itself seriously. These three novels are idiosyncratic histories at the same time that they are prophecies, and they refuse to confine themselves to the small portion of experience granted to the single individual in a compartmentalised society.

Perhaps the literary historian shares some of this encyclopaedic impulse. It is to be hoped that the fragments offered here may be piled upon each other, shaken and re-observed to offer new and illuminating perspectives on the state of Australian literary culture.

16

TRACKING BLACK AUSTRALIAN STORIES: CONTEMPORARY INDIGENOUS LITERATURE

Adam Shoemaker

RECURRENCE

The first chapter of this volume introduced the themes of recurrence and presence in Australian indigenous writing. It reached back in time before conventionally-recorded history and forward to the 1990s and beyond.

Just as this approach casts an eye in many directions, these two chapters link on a practical as well as a theoretical level: the point being emphasised is that Black Australian literature has always been present in this continent. It is not a new phenomenon uncovered since the mid-1960s nor is it the converse, an ancient art of storytelling which only illuminates a frozen past. Rather, indigenous writing is founded upon the notion that Australia has always been—in cultural terms—a full country, not an empty, unoccupied land. To the extent that stories and peoples crisscrossed the continent for thousands of years, verbal art literally brought Australia into being for countless generations of indigenous people.

PETITIONING THE PAST

In this context it is the continuing relevance of various inscriptions which is crucial—none more so than indigenous petitions. Those reflections of Black Australian culture have frequently articulated not only an activist stance but also an appreciation of the power of the word (both spoken and written) on the part of Aboriginal and Islander communities. Many striking examples of such depositions come from South Australia; however, there is none more important than the 1927 submission to federal parliament co-authored by David Unaipon (1872–1967). One year after the Oombulgurri massacre took place at Forrest River in Western Australia, Unaipon and several colleagues mounted one of the least-known and most significant petitions ever submitted to the federal House of Representatives in Canberra.

Its contents were incredibly ambitious, as much in the 1920s as they are today. The deposition consisted of a radical proposal to establish a separate 'Model Aboriginal State' in the Northern Territory, ultimately controlled and administered by Black Australians using a just proportion of federal funding. The key features of the submission were expressed as follows:

Your Petitioners therefore humbly pray that your Honourable House—

1. (a) Will cause to be constituted a model Aboriginal State to be ultimately managed by a native tribunal as far as possible according to their own laws and customs but prohibiting cannibalism and cruel rites. In the meantime such assistance, as may be necessary, to be given, the greatest care being exercised that only those of the highest ability and the very fullest sympathy should be selected for this work. Provision to be made that ultimately the Government may be conducted by aborigines [*sic*], and that it would be possible at some future time that the Administrator himself could be a native.[1]

The document is one of the most remarkable in Aboriginal and Australian history, in large measure because of the assertion of independent indigenous thought and action which it exemplified. Moreover, it was composed at a time when the prevailing anthropological wisdom was that indigenous Australians were inexorably dying out as a race. As a comprehensive rebuttal of that theory, the petition deserves close reading. As a text which is as cogently argued as it is politically revolutionary, the submission is equally fascinating. All the more difficult, then, to explain the critical neglect which has enveloped the document up to this time. This is especially true because it bears the unmistakable imprint of Unaipon's own idiosyncratic (but highly effective) style of writing. In other words, the petition is an ideal introduction to the highly distinctive written world of David Unaipon.

The 'petitioners' write (in a style which is vintage Unaipon):

4. The opinion so generally held that the Australian native is the lowest type of humanity in the world is now found to be quite erroneous. On the contrary he does not belong to any negro race and has been proved to possess great mental powers, ability to quickly learn, and can be taught agriculture, engineering, carpentering, &c., while there are already a number of native Christian clergy.[2]

Of course, the issue arises: How can one justify a discussion of Unaipon in a discussion of contemporary indigenous writing? There are a number of answers to this question, one of the most important being the fact that Unaipon's work is published and discussed more in the 1990s than in any previous decade. In the wake of the Reserve Bank's decision to depict him on the new Australian $50 note released in 1995, his iconic significance has also increased dramatically, a trend further emphasised by the widespread use of Unaipon's face in the print and television advertising for Sydney's *Festival of the Dreaming*, in September 1997.

The entire corpus of Unaipon's written work (including a hitherto unpublished, 300-page manuscript in the Mitchell Library) has now, finally, been recovered and it is so eclectic as to almost defy classification. It combines the deceptive simplicity of the fable with the spiritual depth of religious verse; the apparent realism of anthropological observations with the 'surrealism' of Dreaming narratives. And weaving its way through all of Unaipon's writing is a highly-developed political and national consciousness on behalf of indigenous Australians as well as an extremely clever deployment of humour and insight. One of these most strategic insights is contained in the story 'Naroondarie's Wives':

> He looked around, hoping to see footprints which would lead to him, but there were no footprints and now he was convinced that the strange person was an enemy. A friend will always leave a footprint: this is the teaching of the aborigines. So he thought to himself, like all wise men do, that he would be always upon the alert; and during that day he was not seen.[3]

The interplay here between being seen and 'not seen'—the visible and the invisible—is crucial. Equally, it is a potent comment upon the treatment of indigenous Australians at the time when this was written in the 1920s: seen by some Europeans who specialised in their control or care (missionaries, government officials and so on) but unseen by the vast majority of Australians. At the same time, this apparent paradox, involving as it does elements which are plainly obvious sitting alongside those which are hidden, is a significant, recurring theme in Aboriginal writing. From the deceptive simplicity of the rhymes of Oodgeroo to the multi-levelled dramas of Jack Davis and Eva Johnson; from the life stories of Jackie and Rita Huggins to the radio plays of Lisa Bellear, as much is concealed as is intentionally revealed to the reader or audience-member. This double-sidedness of Black Australian writing says as much about the oral antecedents of the work as it does about ongoing protocols in Aboriginal cultures (for example, the respect accorded to silence and to *not* telling 'the whole story' in certain situations).

It also results in certain paradoxes, such as the presence of the figure of Unaipon on the Australian currency when his life history and achievements are effectively unknown and invisible to the vast majority of Australians. As Ernie Dingo has put it:

> Aboriginal achievement
> Is like the dark side of the moon,
> For it is there
> But so little is known.[4]

Ironically, Unaipon's own literary tracks have been effectively invisible for decades because his entire 1929 manuscript, *Legendary Tales of the Australian Aborigines*, was published under the title *Myths & Legends of the Australian Aboriginals* (1930) by the Scottish-born forensic anthropologist William Ramsay Smith, without any acknowledgment or reference to the real author of the tales. Amazingly, that 1930 volume was reprinted as late as 1996 in London[5] and has been translated into foreign languages such as Japanese. Over the seventy years since the text was first written down, Unaipon, his estate, his descendants and the Raukkan (Point McLeay) community never received any recompense in terms of recognition—let alone royalties—for the sale of the Ramsay Smith volume.[6] Thus, in one sense all of David Unaipon's writing can be seen as petitioning the past for long-delayed recognition of his custodial role as a storyteller. The 1927 submission to federal parliament was as significant in its way as the *Yirrkala* bark petition of 1963 or the Barunga statement of 1988, but it was by no means Unaipon's only foray into the literature of entreaty.

And what of *Yirrkala*? I have already referred in Chapter 1 to the pivotal nature of the *Yirrkala* people's bark petition of 1963. A clear manifesto for rights of self-determination and a plea for custodianship over land, the petition now stands as one of the modern historical treasures of the new Parliament House in Canberra. It is ironic to think that rumours abounded, at the time of the petition's submission to federal parliament, that it was 'ghost written', that is, authored by non-Aboriginal people. At the same time the format of the petition, writing on bark, prefigured the explosion of international interest in bark painting, which reached its zenith internationally in the 1980s and 1990s. Therefore, the petition crystallises key features of all contemporary Black Australian writing: the marriage of art and politics, of the verbal and the visual.

The petition also stands as one of those signposts of change which cannot be ignored in any literary history of Australia. For, as has so often been the case in Black expression, boundaries were being broken through an innovation which was at once textual and activist. In this way the *Yirrkala* people's community expression of their desire (and protest against its suppression) welled up at almost exactly the same time that Oodgeroo (then known as Kath Walker) was publishing her earliest poetry. It was also during the same era in which Mudrooroo (formerly Colin Johnson) was finalising the manuscript of his classic first novel *Wild Cat Falling* (1965).

When Kath Walker's initial volume of poetry, *We Are Going*, was released in 1964, it galvanised a whole segment of Australia's reading public. Rarely in the nation's history has a collection of poetry sold more quickly: it was reprinted seven times in seven months and was published the following year in the United States and Canada. Populist, accessible, impassioned and wry, the poems in *We Are Going* showed the benefits of an oratorical baptism-of-fire. Many (in particular, 'Aboriginal Charter of Rights'—the lead poem in the collection) had already been recited the length and breadth of Australia from 1962 onwards, as Walker campaigned on behalf of the Federal Council for the Advancement of Aborigines and Torres Strait Islanders (FCAATSI). Its passion is undimmed today:

> Give us Christ, not crucifixion.
> Though baptized and blessed and Bibled
> We are still tabooed and libelled
> You devout Salvation Sellers
> Make us neighbours, not fringe dwellers.[7]

The rhyme and rhythm is 'galloping', incantatory, easy to memorise. It is also intensely oral, as if there is an inbuilt imperative to recite the words out loud—and there is. Walker tapped into the twin streams of the Aboriginal verbal art tradition and the 'Western' format of the ballad: an inspiring synthesis which pleased Australian readers as much as it dismayed Australian critics.

As Oodgeroo's long-time friend and publisher, John Collins, has pointed out, even in those early days the detractors were marshalling their forces. Significantly, they fell into two camps, both of whom either implicitly or explicitly tried to disenfranchise the poet. The first was represented by critics such as Andrew Taylor who, writing in *Overland*, attempted to define away Walker's achievement as being 'not poetry in any true sense'.[8] In other words, Walker's identity as a practitioner of her craft was being denied. The second camp constituted a more amorphous, unnamed one but its critique was no less damaging. As Collins wrote many years later, the reception of Walker's second volume of verse, *The Dawn is at Hand* (1966), produced a highly sceptical reaction in some quarters: 'There were other malicious whispers too: "She wasn't a full black so it was the white blood that was writing"; "someone else has ghosted the work if not written it"'.[9] Amazing as it may seem today to those who have the vista of Oodgeroo's entire *oeuvre* of writing to consider, in the mid-1960s there were many readers who felt it was highly unlikely that an Aboriginal woman could, unaided, produce work of such power and passion.

And this was not only typical of the era but was typical of the non-Aboriginal reception of Black literature of all types. What began as rumours concerning the *Yirrkala* petition in 1963 continued in the wake of Walker's *We Are Going* a year later. The pattern continued in 1965 when Colin Johnson was dismissed in some quarters as a creature of the philanthropic concerns of Dame Mary Durack. His *Wild Cat Falling* was seen by some as being (at the least) a co-production by Durack and himself—an impression which Durack's maternalistic foreword to the novel (which has travelled with the text to this day) does little to dispel:

> In the meantime he had sent me his completed M.S. which I showed to my friend, the writer and literary critic, Florence James, then on a visit to Australia. She agreed with me that it was a first novel of unusual promise and significance, but that it was *still in need of some organization* [emphasis mine].[10]

Durack's words continue to establish her sense of superiority over her protégé at the time: 'He . . . seemed to regard *Wild Cat Falling* somewhat in the light of an exercise or a proof of staying power—a deflection, perhaps, of the pointed bone of his Aboriginal heritage'.[11] While we may cringe to read such descriptions today, it is also easy to see how such distancing, dismissive language could establish the belief in the mind of the reading public that Johnson/Mudrooroo could never have written the novel without significant outside assistance.

The same pattern of intrusion continued in the 1970s. While still behind bars in Grafton prison, Kevin Gilbert wrote his first book of poetry and illustrated it with his own original linocuts. Entitled *End of Dreamtime* (1971), the volume was released by Island Press in Sydney, but there was only one drawback: the text of many of the poems had been brazenly rewritten by an unnamed editor without any reference to Gilbert. Not surprisingly, he disowned the production and refused to authorise publication of the original version of his poems until 1978, when *People Are Legends* was released by the University of Queensland Press.

A similar scenario was implied in the case of Robert Merritt, the author of the award-winning play *The Cake Man*, first published in 1978. Merritt wrote the work while incarcerated in Bathurst gaol in 1974 to express—as he put it—'the root causes of Aboriginal despair'.[12] From the earliest days, Merritt had to withstand the round of rumours which suggested that fellow inmate Jim McNeil, the author of *The Chocolate Frog*, *The Old Familiar Juice* (both published 1973) and *How Does Your Garden Grow?* (1974), ghost-wrote *The Cake Man*. Merritt has in fact acknowledged the assistance of McNeil but, as in the case of Mudrooroo's *Wild Cat Falling*, the work is his and his alone: there is a vast difference between writers offering collegial aid and assumptions about the appropriation of text and authorship.

On that note, it is telling that the pattern of recurrent doubt and scepticism settled upon *The Cake Man*. I believe that this was for two main reasons. The first of these was that—like *We Are Going* and *Wild Cat Falling*—*The Cake Man* was clearly a breakthrough text. It was the first published play by a Black Australian, just as the other two titles were anointed by the publishing industry as being 'firsts' for Aborigines in their respective fields of poetry and prose fiction. In all three cases, their novelty may have aided sales but it also meant that their authors had to run the gauntlet of amazement and disbelief; in all three, the question of Black Australian authorship was immediately called into question.

Why is there such an obsession with groundbreaking indigenous achievements of this type? Does the emphasis upon 'firsts' really translate into a desire to know Aboriginal culture or is it an indictment of the social field of the mainstream in that only movements into that field are applauded? The prominent indigenous academic and commentator Marcia Langton has focused on this strange phenomenon in her seminal 1993 essay '*Well, I Heard it on the Radio and I Saw it on the Television . . .*' In Langton's words: 'There is an annoying tendency in the expression of the Australian paternalistic relationship with Aborigines: "The first Aborigine to graduate", to play cricket, to box—and even to make a film'. As she continues:

> But why do whites and blacks get so worked up about the 'first Aborigine to . . .'? It is a kind of declaration of having achieved some kind of equity, as if there were really something to celebrate in finally having overcome all the racism and other obstacles which Aborigines face in gathering the resources to do anything. Indeed, it is actually a denial of the racism against Aborigines. It is a way of saying that we are too backward to do it, not that we are denied the means to do it.[13]

What Langton targets so well here is the strange ambivalence which Aboriginal cultural productions so often encounter in the community. While achievement and 'success' (in this context, publication and book sales) are welcomed and encouraged, there is often an equally strong suspicion that this success is somehow aberrant. From the days of Albert Namatjira, 'Aboriginal achievers' have been feted and promoted, but that very individualised attention has also had the potential to distance the artist from her or his community. At the same time, there are those who always suggest that special treatment or affirmative action is the reason for this prominence; that, somehow, the Black Australian who writes a best-seller or who wins a major award does not do so solely on the basis of merit. At the very least, it is implied that—when it occurs—runaway success is based upon extra-textual factors.

While this is naturally not always so, the attitudinal bias is such that Aboriginal creativity is subjected to scrutiny (and approbation) of a unique sort: what could be termed the curse of authenticity. In brief, a global interest in the so-called 'essence' of Black Australian culture can lead to an almost pathological preoccupation with the 'genuineness' or 'truth' of Aboriginal spirituality. This essentialist preoccupation can be so fervent that, paradoxically, it makes misleading representations of those spiritual beliefs which cater to this popular obsession all the more likely.

REPRESENTATION AND MISREPRESENTATION

It is in this context that Sreten Bozic first broke into print with his collection of short stories, *The Track to Bralgu* (1978). Of course, the book was not published under the name Bozic but under the pseudonym 'B. Wongar' and the twelve stories in the collection —such as 'Jambawal, the Thunder Man' and 'Goarang, the Anteater' all give the impression of an author who is steeped in Aboriginal culture. As South African novelist Alan Paton wrote in the foreword to the volume:

> I do not know enough of the aboriginal contribution to Australian literature to know how far these stories open up a new lode of wealth. But they open up a new world to me, and what is more, the writer who does it is a master of the ancient craft.[14]

At the same time, the critical response to *The Track to Bralgu* was almost uniformly positive, especially in North America. Not only was the collection published in the United States, Canada and the United Kingdom but it received glowing praise from Thomas Keneally in the *New York Times*: 'It is said that among the finest poetry composed on the continent of Australia are the ancient incantatory songs of the Aboriginal peoples. Mr. Wongar's arresting chants do full honour to that tradition'.[15] Even more: in Paris, writing in *Les Temps Modernes*, Simone de Beauvoir enthused that the stories constituted 'Lyrical documents of our time, a time monstrously savage'.[16]

Of course, Bozic/Wongar never actually claimed to be an indigenous Australian— the assumption was left to others and no one was disabused of the notion. Why is this significant? Aside from the fact that these short narratives are often brilliant, Kafkaesque evocations of the entrapment of indigenous culture by a nuclear society, *The Track to Bralgu* highlights the fact that there was such a keen desire, both internationally and domestically, to discover a great new Aboriginal writer of short fiction that one was liter-ally *willed into being* through allusion and suggestion. Once again, the mania to identify 'the first' takes away as much from indigenous culture as it gives to it. In literary and his-torical terms, the Wongar saga is a classic example of misplaced enthusiasm and the heartfelt misappropriation of goodwill. Interestingly, the short volume sold more than 250 000 copies worldwide; far more than any of Wongar's subsequent publications.[17]

The question therefore naturally arises: do some non-Aboriginal authors perceive a need to adopt an indigenous persona and—if so—why? For Wongar it was evidently a matter of profound identification with the plight of Australia's Aboriginal population and a respect for its spiritual and religious beliefs. However, I would still argue that the extra-textual privileging of a Black Australian identity in *The Track to Bralgu* was, on all the evidence, a significant component of its success in commercial terms. This is not to deny the talent of Bozic to evoke the atmosphere and terror of cultures facing genocide. It is to say that the book itself, from its title to its language, from its cover blurbs to its biographical note, draws attention *away* from the text so that the writer becomes the focus of a voyeuristic gaze. Put simply, 'B. Wongar' *becomes* the text, and it is no surprise that the majority of critics have responded accordingly.

Robert Drewe, who in the *Bulletin Literary Supplement* of 21 April 1981 revealed Wongar to be Bozic, is typical of this school of thought. In a 1984 review of *Walg* (1983), the first of Wongar's so-called 'nuclear trilogy' of novels, he wrote: 'Even a genuine belief that one is a reincarnated Arnhem Land Aboriginal inside a Yugoslav body residing in St Kilda, Victoria, doesn't quite diminish the reviewer's unease'.[18]

Yet, in an overwhelmingly positive assessment of Wongar's *oeuvre* Livio Dobrez has pointed out that Wongar's sense of ethnic and migrant isolation, his endurance of racism, his understanding of Aboriginal religion and—above all—his postmodern glimpse of the apocalypse in books such as *Karan* (1985) and *Gabo Djara* (1987) is profoundly moving and persuasive.[19] There is also no doubt that Bozic had every intention of encouraging indigenous writing, however envisaged: in 1985 he proposed the establishment of An Award for Ethno-Fiction in the following terms:

> An international literary award is to be established following the publication of the tribal trilogy *Walg* (c.1983), *Karan* and *Gabo Djara* by B. Wongar. In principle . . . publishers of those novels should hold the author's royalty in trust and award annually an appropriate sum to an indigenous author who in his work successfully manifests the elements of his native culture or struggles for restoration of a cultural environment eroded by outside influences.[20]

As a summary of Bozic's speaking position, this is a fascinating document. Ultimately it is ironic that his focus upon the successful manifestation of 'elements of . . . native cul-ture' is the very issue upon which Wongar's work has been called to task. Implicit in all of this is the overriding question: who becomes the arbiter of this putative authenticity?

This is one of the thorniest issues of the late 1990s in world writing, and centres around theories of voice, representation and authorial positioning. Who speaks for whom? Are there any valid limits to the fictional imagination? In this context, indigenous culture can be many things: an inspiration, a source, a wellspring, a guide. With respect to indigeneity, many are attracted to the notion that the fictional universe should be theoretically unbounded, that anything which can be imagined can be realised on the page. Clearly this is the case in novels such as Patrick White's *Voss* (1957) and *Riders in the Chariot* (1961) as well as Thomas Keneally's *The Chant of Jimmie Blacksmith* (1972); all of which assert the power of the mind to invent, explore and interpret indigenous characters.

Yet we are equally aware that no piece of writing is contextually innocent: the most striking international cases of the 1980s and 1990s include Salman Rushdie's *The Satanic Verses*, Brett Easton Ellis's *American Psycho* and—in Australia—Helen Demidenko (Darville's) *The Hand that Signed the Paper*. It is the friction between freedom and constraint, the way in which political considerations are so thoroughly implicated in the world of writing, that makes the case of indigenous literature such a highly-charged one. Nor is this solely a matter of content. As many theorists have observed, genres are themselves both implicit and explicit productions of cultures and, arguably, of ideologies.

Specific and difficult questions arise. For example, will Aboriginal writers be seen as ambassadors for Australian culture as a whole if they travel or are published overseas? In Black Australian culture every story has an implied audience; therefore, what occurs when there is *no* control over the destination or readership of a published story? And what of the question of intellectual property rights in Aboriginal storytelling—do these exist in a way which is analogous to the case of indigenous visual art? The fact that these are live issues of contemporary debate leads Aboriginal people to throw up their hands in dismay when blatantly exploitative representations of their culture take place.

In the 1990s the most heinous of these misrepresentations have undoubtedly been Marlo Morgan's New Age fable *Mutant Message Down Under* (1993) and Wanda Koolmatrie's 'autobiography', *My Own Sweet Time* (1994). Incredible as it may seem, Morgan, a former chiropractor from Missouri, self-published the first edition of *Mutant Message* in the United States and over 275 000 copies were sold. Why? The book claimed to provide the key to authentic Aboriginal knowledge, a means of saving the decadent West from spiritual impoverishment. Morgan allegedly walked (barefoot and nearly naked) across the centre of Australia for three months, in the company of a lost clan of Aborigines whom she called the Real People. Their knowledge became her knowledge. Their mission to educate the world transformed her into the 'mutant messenger'.

Yet in early 1996 Morgan visited Australia and—in tears—renounced the accuracy of her text and apologised for any damage she had done to Black Australians. This was a direct response to the visit of a delegation of Aborigines who had recently returned from the United States, denouncing the book's falsehoods and misrepresentations. On one side of the Pacific, Morgan had reportedly received $1.7 million from HarperCollins for the rights to her story (which was then released as 'Fiction'); it almost immediately attracted the attention of Hollywood producers. On the other side of the ocean, Aboriginal

Australians, the alleged inspiration for this miraculous travelogue, received nothing but an apology. It is little wonder that emotions ran at a high level in the indigenous community.

But, as false as the Morgan case had been, nothing exceeded the 'Wanda Kool-matrie' hoax for calculated deceit and cynicism. Although *My Own Sweet Time* appeared in 1994, it was not until three years later that it was discovered that the real author of the ostensible autobiography was a 47-year-old white male taxi-driver from North Sydney named Leon Carmen. To make matters worse, the book had been published by Magabala Books—a specialised, Aboriginal-run publishing house based in Broome, Western Australia, and *My Own Sweet Time* had also been awarded the $5000 Dobbie prize for women's writing in 1995. Not only was this an unparalleled example of cross-gender and cross-race deception, but a Black publisher had been specifically targeted for the hoax in the most exploitative fashion possible. Carmen's defence, a mixture of diffidence and illogicality, was that he could not 'break into' print as a white male, implying a pro-Aboriginal (as well as a pro-female) bias in the Australian publishing industry.

As every study of Australian writing (including this one) has demonstrated, this assertion is entirely false. In fact, it is white males who have nearly always been featured in the Australian literary marketplace, from the earliest times of publication to the present day. This is not to imply that females have not made a very significant contribution—they clearly have—but in terms of the senior management of publishing houses, the distribution of literary awards, the membership of funding bodies and the signing of publishing contracts, Australia's industry has almost always been male-dominated. Since the mid-1960s Black Australians have established a significant presence in that industry but—even given the popularity of the work of Oodgeroo and Sally Morgan—there has been no unfair prejudice in favour of indigenous authors. What there *has* been since 1980 is a growing appreciation of Aboriginal talent and storytelling skill.

Seen in its context, the late 1990s debate over authenticity not only disempowers Aboriginal writers; in the most extreme cases it threatens to disempower them from citizenship in the Black Australian literary nation. Here the cases of Mudrooroo and Archie Weller are particularly prominent ones, although the intemperate eye of racial censure has also extended, at times, to Eric Willmot, Sally Morgan and others. The common feature is that the power to define Aboriginality became an issue of *public* debate; far more than a discussion among the literati.[21] Ironically, the seeds of this controversy were sown in the most innocent possible way, with the publication of Sally Morgan's landmark autobiography, *My Place*, in 1987.

MY PLACE AND ITS AFTERMATH

No discussion of contemporary Aboriginal writing can ignore the impact of Morgan's work. Over the past decade Morgan emerged from relative obscurity to become a best-selling author (*My Place* has sold more than 450 000 copies and is still going strong), a renowned artist (whose paintings are held by almost all the major galleries in Australia), and a senior academic at the University of Western Australia (she was appointed Professorial Fellow in Aboriginal Literature and the Arts there in early 1997). Morgan's book has been published worldwide in its original format, although the American edition metamorphoses the text into a detective story, 'complete with clues and solutions', and ranks it alongside the 'American classics' such as *Roots* (1976) and *Gone With the Wind* (1937)![22] One indication of the flexibility of *My Place* is the fact that the book's Australian publishers have also issued it as one of four smaller paperback versions directed at children. In these the various oral narratives contained in the book (such as 'Arthur Corunna's Story' and 'Daisy Corunna's Story') are produced in individually-bound editions. Clearly, the text is a phenomenon: among other things, it is the only book by an Aboriginal author to which an entire critical study has been devoted—Delys Bird and Dennis Haskell's edited collection of essays entitled *Whose Place?* (1992). It is equally clear that, whether in English or in its many translated editions, *My Place* has established a perception of Aboriginal people for thousands of overseas readers. In brief, the book is remarkable: a first work which has become a modern classic.

As a number of commentators have observed, the narrative of *My Place* has a generic relationship with certain other Australian texts such as A.B. Facey's *A Fortunate Life* (1981) which, significantly, has sold at least as well (over 550 000 copies) and was produced by the the same editor, B.R. Coffey, and publisher, the Fremantle Arts Centre Press.[23] The conjunction, timing and popular success of these two books is an intriguing one, and speaks volumes about the burgeoning popular interest in the 'life story' genre in the Australia of the 1980s and 1990s.

Having said that, it is undeniable that, unlike *A Fortunate Life*, *My Place* is a work which divides critics, academics and Aboriginal commentators alike. While it is lauded on the one hand as being, in Judith Brett's memorable phrase in *Australian Book Review*, 'a gift to the reader',[24] commentators such as Mudrooroo have been very harsh in their criticisms of the book. In his 1990 study, *Writing from the Fringe*, he dismissed it as a 'publishing ploy'[25] in the 'battler genre' and derided it scathingly in these now infamous words: 'Sally Morgan's book is a milepost in Aboriginal literature in that it marks a stage when it is considered O.K. to be Aboriginal as long as you are young, gifted and not very black'.[26] Significantly, this sentence disappears in the totally-revised version of *Writing from the Fringe* which was released in mid-1997 under the title *The Indigenous Literature of Australia*, although Mudrooroo still carries the weight of that earlier denunciation. For Mudrooroo's acerbic personal criticism of Morgan was undoubtedly one of the factors which led, ultimately, to his own denunciation by members of the *Nyoongah* community of Western Australia in July 1996.[27]

However, Mudrooroo is not alone in his criticisms of Morgan's work, nor is he the only Black Australian author to take aim at her construction (by the book-reading public as much as by the media) as the archetypal indigenous writer. For one, the prominent Murri researcher and author, Jackie Huggins, expresses her reservations about the ease with which indigenous identity is both discovered and explicated in Morgan's book; as she puts it, 'Precisely what irks me about *My Place* is its proposition that Aboriginality can be understood by all non-Aboriginals . . . To me that is *My Place*'s greatest weakness'.[28] The criticism levelled by Huggins carries particular weight if Morgan's is the only piece of Aboriginal literature which is purchased; if, in this sense, it *becomes* 'Aboriginal literature' for the international reader.

The issue is as much one of the singularity of representation as it is of ideology, for with that singularity comes the risk that readers will, in Huggins's words, 'believe that they are no longer racist because they have read it'.[29] However, the converse is also possible: that *My Place* will in fact be a first taste of indigenous writing for many who would otherwise not be exposed to it at all—and who will be encouraged to read further as a result. According to this interpretation, Morgan's work does not necessarily *have* to become an objective and self-sufficient version of the reconciliation process; it could also be a creative irritant which leads to more critical reflection upon her writing, as well as upon other works by indigenous writers.

THE STAGES OF ABORIGINAL LITERATURE

The challenge is one of seeing seminal works (such as *My Place* or Mudrooroo's *Wild Cat Falling*) as part of an ongoing process of cultural and artistic revolution in the Aboriginal community. Undoubtedly, there are key texts, such as these, which represent turning points, but what is difficult is to determine whether such stages are as relevant to the creators of such works as to those who study them. From this perspective we have to ask, 'Whose interests are served by the establishment of Aboriginal literature as a discrete field of academic enquiry and analysis?' Or, put another way, if all Black Australian writing can be seen on one level as a gesture towards freedom and independence, does the critical industry which now surrounds such work retard or enhance the effectiveness of those aims?

One encouraging response is signalled by the fact that so many Black Australian authors are themselves critics and reviewers as well as producers of original work for criticism and review. With eight novels, four books of poetry, several plays and three published critical studies, Mudrooroo is clearly the most prominent author. His achievements, and those of many other Black Australian writers, signal the fact that Aboriginal literature—like Aboriginality itself—is a field of discussion and debate which cannot be contained (or fully defined) by non-Aboriginal observers. At the same time, many black spokespeople, such as Roberta Sykes, emphasise the crucial role of intercultural understanding which such writing can engender.

Sykes is another who has worked in a wide variety of genres: poetry (*Love Poems and Other Revolutionary Actions*, 1988); interviews and profiles (*Murawina*, 1993); historical and political analysis (*Black Majority*, 1989); biography (*MumShirl*, 1992) and, most recently, the production of the first volume of her three-part autobiography, *Snake Cradle*, (1997–). In fact, it is the multiple talents of indigenous writers which are so noteworthy.

For example, Lisa Bellear publishes as a commentator but is also well known for her poetry (*Dreaming in Urban Areas*, 1996) and radio plays. Ruby Langford Ginibi's three books (*Don't Take Your Love to Town*, 1988, *Real Deadly*, 1992, and *My Bundjalung People*, 1994), have won her a deserved reputation as a storyteller, yet she is also a poet, an essayist and is currently preparing an anthology of Koori humour. Eva Johnson's work also spans several genres, including poetry and drama (*Murras* and *What Do They Call Me?*, 1989) as well as radical political critique. Marcia Langton's cultural assessments (especially '*Well I Heard it on the Radio and I Saw it on the Television . . .*') have changed the way in which both intellectuals and other viewers theorise indigenous films and texts; and Alexis Wright's verse is as impressive as her prose fiction: her *Plains of Promise* (1997) is a remarkable and strikingly spiritual novel.

Some of these authors combine formal lectures on indigenous topics with roles as spokespeople for the indigenous community, as well as the production of original work in their field. Jackie Huggins's political, artistic and social commentary is respected domestically and overseas; however, she is also a dramatist (*Maarkings*, unpublished) and (together with her mother) the author of the award-winning life story, *Auntie Rita* (1994). During 1996–97 the trend towards social critique has extended further, with the publication of Anita Heiss's wide-ranging satire of White Australian society—*Sacred Cows* (1996)—along with the release of Melissa Lucashenko's hard-hitting novel *Steam Pigs* (1997). It is no accident that all of the authors noted above are female for, in the late 1990s, it is Black women who are making many of the most significant inroads into new forms of indigenous literature.

At the same time, this list represents only a small part of the writing talent in the indigenous community. One has to ask then how the rapid expansion and recognition of indigenous writing talent has occurred, and why it has gathered such pace since 1980. For example, if one takes the case of the theatre, the first performance of a play by an Aboriginal author—Kevin Gilbert's *The Cherry Pickers* (published 1988)—only occurred in 1971, yet today, less than three decades later, there are well over thirty Black Australian dramas which have been staged in Australia and overseas. What has happened to change the situation?

There are a number of institutional answers to that question: the policies of the Australia Council and, in particular, the establishment of a strong Aboriginal and Torres Strait Islander Arts Board; the orientation of the Australian National Playwrights' Conference far more towards indigenous perspectives; and, perhaps most important, the inception of independent indigenous companies such as Brisbane's Kooemba Jdarra Indigenous Performing Arts, as well as strongly supportive non-Aboriginal performance houses like Perth's Black Swan Theatre Company. It is also very likely that none of this would have occurred as rapidly without the talents of a dramatist like Jack Davis, whose suite of plays throughout the 1980s and early 1990s revolutionised perceptions of Aboriginal theatre and inspired many other black playwrights to compose their works. Davis's early plays were *Kullark* (Home), *The Dreamers* and *No Sugar*, first performed in

1979, 1981 and 1985 respectively, these plays were published in 1982 (*Kullark* and *The Dreamers*) and 1986 (*No Sugar*). With Merritt's *The Cake Man*, these were 'breakthrough' texts for indigenous theatre in Australia. And, once broken down, that door would never be closed again.

Bob Maza, Eva Johnson, Richard Walley, Sally Morgan, Mudrooroo, Jimmie Chi, Roger Bennett and many others have had theatrical works performed nationally and overseas, with Chi's *Bran Nue Dae* (1990) and *Corrugation Road* (1996) being pivotal productions of black musicals. But the point is that this innovation in indigenous performing arts came about as a result of persistent lobbying by Aboriginal people for ways to enable their cultural voices to be heard. The process was an inescapably political as well as an artistic one, as has been the growth of all indigenous writing in English. In every case, non-Aboriginal collaborators and institutions assisted in vital ways, but without the continuous cultural activism of indigenous Australians the projects would never have begun.

To return to the theme of the stages of Aboriginal writing: in his latest work Mudrooroo has postulated that there are six 'Divisions of Indigenous Literature History', beginning with 'The Time of the Dreaming' and ending with 'The Period of Reconciliation', a post-activist stage of 'sharing cultures'.[30] If this is so (and it appears that Mudrooroo's analysis may be coloured by the now-superseded race relations optimism of the Keating era), one has to ask how this period of *rapprochement* finds its specific literary expression. For example, it is true that stage productions have, since the late 1980s, moved away from what Geoffrey Milne calls the 'more sombre realist portrayals' of earlier works.[31] Yet, at the same time, it is not the case that the most significant recent productions have been 'reconciliatory' in tone; in fact, one of these—Wesley Enoch and Deborah Mailman's *7 Stages of Grieving* (1996)—literally deconstructs the term 'reconciliation' to produce four component anti-words: 'wreck', 'con', 'silly' and 'nation'.

In addition, as Milne points out, shows such as Josie Ningali Lawford's acclaimed solo production *Ningali* (1994) and Maryanne Sam's *Oh My God, I'm Black* (1995) are neither naturalistic nor historical in focus (unlike so much Aboriginal drama of the 1980s). Music and the surreal are prominent features of all of these recent shows, as well as of many productions staged as part of the first of the Olympic Arts Festivals, the *Festival of the Dreaming* in September–October 1997. And that festival, directed by Rhoda Roberts and showcasing hundreds of Aboriginal artists and performers, demonstrated once again the fact that indigenous writing talent is overflowing in the late 1990s; in particular, in works conceived by Black Australian women.

It can be said that if the poetry of Oodgeroo was a bell-wether of political change in the 1960s, it also marked what I would call the first wave of contemporary Aboriginal writing. Together with works by Mudrooroo, Kevin Gilbert and Jack Davis, that stage was marked by the primacy of writing projects as political campaigns: articulate outreaches for justice, freedom and land. Those goals have never been forgotten but, during the 1980s, they became subsumed in a second stage of writing: one in which prose and drama concentrated more upon revisions of the past, the anti-historical. Among these works were Eric Willmot's first novel *Pemulwuy* (1987); Mudrooroo's *Doctor Wooreddy's Prescription for Enduring the Ending of the World* (1983); the plays of Merritt and Davis; the performed work of Oodgeroo in the 'Rainbow Serpent Theatre' at World Expo 88 in Brisbane; and a significant amount of poetry written to protest the 1988 bicentennial.

What I would term the third wave of contemporary Black Australian writing began *circa* 1990 with the national performances of *Bran Nue Dae*. It was marked by eclecticism: an emphasis upon the mysterious, the supernatural, the hyperreal and (frequently) the weirdly humorous. In this phase could be included the films of Tracey Moffatt (especially *BeDevil*, 1993), Sam Watson's *The Kadaitcha Sung* (1990), the 'magic realist' novels of Alexis Wright (*Plains of Promise*, 1997) and Mudrooroo (*Master of the Ghost Dreaming*, 1991); elements of the work of John Muk Muk Burke (*Bridge of Triangles*, 1994) and specific dramatic productions (such as those of Enoch and Mailman, noted above). Of course, these are not hard-and-fast literary delineations; rather, they denote general clusters of interest and significant changes of approach over the past three decades.

At the same time, the third, eclectic stage of Aboriginal writing is marked by the breaking-down of boundaries and of the 'expected' forms of black literature. For example, Philip McLaren enters the realm of crime fiction with his 1994 book, *Scream Black Murder*, and Archie Weller explores the fantasy genre in his novel, *The Land of the Golden Clouds* (1998). Meanwhile, Lionel Fogarty continues to cut across all writing styles with his multi-sourced and highly verbal poetry; and in such works as *Wild Cat Screaming* (1992), and *The Kwinkan* (1993), Mudrooroo defies all categorisation in a display of constantly malleable prose. It must be emphasised that this stage of writing, so marked by experimentation and diversity, never erases the profound sense of political and social engagement which has always characterised Aboriginal literature. Indigenous authors are—almost by definition—political spokespeople. For example, even the prominent Aboriginal lawyer, Noel Pearson, has written a children's book (*Caden Wallah!*, 1994), which is a subtle celebration of Native Title and of the natural beauty of North Queensland. Once again, it is not the case that these three waves of literary production are neat formulations; however, as markers of the general trends in modern indigenous writing in Australia over the past thirty years, they are both suggestive and useful.

PRESENCE

If this chapter began with the theme of recurrence, it ends with the idea of presence, for the one certainty is that Black Australian literature, once an exotic curiosity for the non-Aboriginal reader, is no longer marginal. There has been a sea-change in the field of indigenous writing: from an exploration of the 'fringe' to a consideration of centrality; from an oppositional dialectic to one which supersedes and renounces opposites through what Mudrooroo calls 'maban reality'.[32] This is not to say that indigenous Australians are moving away from an assertion of their cultural independence: quite the contrary.

Instead, it signals the fact that the wider Australian and international community is beginning to recognise and to respect the unique features of Aboriginal culture, in legal, moral and creative terms. Anne Brewster describes this shift in perception extremely well:

> Aboriginal memory is transforming public perceptions of the past in post-invasion Australia. This memory proves to us that Aboriginal people were not simply the passive victims or onlookers of modernisation, but rather the producers and makers of modern Australia through their labour and the knowledge of the country that they shared with the white 'settlers'. Modern Australia thus has a significant Aboriginal heritage.[33]

The next decade will arguably see indigenous authors entering further new territory: perhaps launching a monthly Black Australian arts magazine; writing for cyberspace and multimedia applications; and establishing a truly independent, national Aboriginal and Islander publishing house. In the end, though, it is the written works themselves which will continue to stand up and be counted, both in aesthetic and political terms. And, in the end, the greatest challenge for the non-Aboriginal reader will continue to be one of reading the country through the pages of Black literature. Here, it is appropriate that indigenous authors will always have both the first and the last word.

17

FILM, TELEVISION AND LITERATURE: COMPETING FOR THE NATION

Graeme Turner

If one had set out to test the cultural health of the nation in the mid-1960s, its literature would have certainly been a key site for examination; Australian writing had generated a significant degree of international recognition and national pride. In the 1970s further recognition lay ahead—most notably Patrick White's Nobel Prize for literature in 1973. However, it is also during this decade—at just the point when Australian writing was recognised as the great success story in Australian cultural production—that a serious rival appeared. Over the 1970s, as the result of substantial government support for the revival of the Australian film industry, literature's status as the 'cultural flagship' for the nation was vigorously contested—by film and even, on occasion, by television. As we move towards the end of this account of Australia's literary history, it is useful to look at literature's competitive and complementary relationship with other representational and narrative forms. This will involve some preliminary consideration not only of the cultural placement of the national literature in Australia during the 1990s when the definitions of nation and national identity are subject to vigorous debate, but also of the contemporary state of Australian literary studies as its disciplinary boundaries have shifted and blurred in response to the challenges from other forms, and the acknowledged necessity to deal with the contexts of production and consumption of its objects of study.

CULTURAL DEBATES

The mid-1990s have witnessed an often acrimonious cultural debate between 'the literary community' (variously defined) and the Literature Board of the Australia Council. This debate has had several aspects. One concerned the fate of the small literary magazines, which were threatened with the possibility of a change in policy preferring the establishment of a single well-funded, commercially operated, high profile cultural magazine—a preference which ultimately resulted in Australia Council funding for the *Australian's Review of Books*. A second concerned projected changes in the allocation of writing grants which would radically restrict individual writers' access to Literature Board funding. These debates have been carried on through the literary magazines, the *Australian Book Review* and the newspapers—especially the *Australian* where features writer Luke Slattery has been campaigning against a number of aspects of (his version of) the literary establishment for some time (among them small critical magazines, the role of 'theory', the alleged parochialism of Australian writing). This is only one of several debates around Australian writing which have dominated cultural reporting—often, news reporting—in the period. The media outrage over the Demidenko affair (the awarding of the Miles Franklin award to an author who claimed Ukrainian ethnicity but was later revealed to be Helen Darville, the child of English migrants and the author of a rather elaborate fiction about her own life), and the highly personalised controversy over Helen Garner's *The First Stone* (which dealt with the sexual harassment charges against a former Master of Ormond College at the University of Melbourne) were of a sufficiently high profile to suggest that Australian writing still matters a great deal to its public and to the news media. Nevertheless, I would argue that these contemporary controversies remain significant exceptions—moments when Australian writing, for whatever reason, has been of prominent national interest. Such moments have not been frequent over the last decade. Notwithstanding the success of Australian writing and the enhancement of its visibility here and overseas since the mid-1960s, and despite the popularity of the Writers' Festivals which are now located in most capital cities, it would be wrong to suggest that literature remains, any longer, popularly and securely regarded as the preeminent national art form.

There are some positive consequences of what must be viewed as a slight decline in the perceived importance of the national literature. For instance, individual literary productions are no longer routinely required to achieve the status of the Great Australian Novel (or Poem or Play); that responsibility now belongs to film. There are substantial negative consequences, however. During the first half of the 1990s there were a series of public attacks on the quality of our élite writers. Greg Sheridan and Luke Slattery, both writing for the *Australian*, published feature articles questioning whether the quality of our writers actually supports what they clearly regarded as the triumphalism commonly used to represent our literary achievements since the end of the Second World War. McKenzie Wark, a cultural studies academic and regular columnist in the *Australian*'s Higher Education Supplement, has repeatedly characterised the 'fetishisation' of literature (and the novel in particular) as an outmoded and élitist fashion.[1] In its place, Wark advances the claims of other forms of representation, particularly those carried by the electronic media. Regular instances of media and political criticism of arts grants programs and their outcomes reinforce the impression that such views do attract support.

Certainly it would be true to say that, since the end of the 1970s, the cultural visibility and popular currency of some of the media Wark prefers, film in particular, has outstripped that of literature to a significant degree. With this enhanced cultural visibility comes the assumption of cultural relevance or significance and this is reflected in the level of capital investment, both through private institutions and direct government intervention. More Commonwealth money is being spent on just cleaning up the site for the new Twentieth Century Fox film production studios in Sydney than is contained in the whole budget for the Literature Board. While Australian books do have their market and it continues to grow, it is a market which tends to be invisible to the rest of the culture because of its segmentation from the mainstream entertainment and leisure categories in television programs, magazines and other promotional outlets. Significantly, the controversy around the Demidenko affair had bubbled along privately for nearly a year within sectors of the literary community before finally making it to the general public through the promotional use of the electronic and print media. In addressing this situation, writers have had to accept the necessity of promoting their work through the mass media, even if it does mean appearing on television breakfast programs, as well as writers' festival stages, as 'celebrities'.[2] Today, successful Australian writers circulate through the same promotional system of celebrities and personalities as anyone else if they are to publicise their latest work. Nothwithstanding their acknowledgment of this, and their sometimes grudging willingness to cooperate, most remain much less well known and much less 'marketable' than those celebrities who come from the popular entertainment industries or from sport. (It is 'Ironman' Trevor Hendy who advertises VitaBrits, not Tim Winton.) Consequently, although the literary field has broadened over the 1970s and 1980s—through the extent of its output and the diversification of its genres, sub-genres and modes of writing[3]—this does not seem, in the 1990s, to have much affected its purchase on the national imagination.

This is not surprising, of course. Competition for leisure time, for an audience, for public recognition, let alone for a central place in something as numinous as the 'national imagination', is fierce in the 1990s. Just to maintain its competitiveness against the attractions of the new media technologies must be regarded as quite an achievement for the national literature. Nevertheless, although the film and television industries actually produce a much smaller number of stories and employ a more restricted range of modes of storytelling than the fiction industry, their products are seen by many more people, they occupy a more central place in most Australians' everyday lives, and they also play a significant role in the aesthetic choices and the cultural repertoires of educated Australians.

FILM, LITERATURE AND NATIONALITY

Such a shift has not gone unnoticed, and there are concerns about its meanings and effects. The fact that film and television are entertainment industries before they are cultural industries means that they pursue different cultural, commercial and aesthetic objectives from literature, notwithstanding individual writers' interest in entertaining their readers. The three forms' competition as national expressions is to some extent a competition between incommensurables. Further, while the 'nationality' of Australian literature is rarely at issue (the Miles Franklin award aside), the sense in which our film and television industries might be understood as 'national' is a subject of continued debate.[4] Television drama and feature film production is supported federally through the Film Finance Corporation as well as by state government instrumentalities, but it is also highly dependent upon sales to overseas markets, to multinational cable networks, to video release and so on. The commercial logic of the international film market militates against producing features solely for the Australian audience and thus exerts subtle but powerful pressures towards 'internationalising' local productions. This can affect the financing, casting, and promotion of films as different as *Babe* (1995) and *The Piano* (1993). While the subsidies provided by the Film Finance Corporation would imply some degree of local control, the level of 'pre-sales' commitments required to qualify for subsidy effectively locks Australian producers into a dependent relationship with private investors from overseas.[5] Consequently, while the 'national' audience may have been the primary commercial target of early products of the revival such as *My Brilliant Career* (1979), the success of such projects has paradoxically forced the industry to look beyond this market. The commercial success of the 1980s, *Crocodile Dundee* (1986), targeted both an Australian and an American audience, tailoring the detail of its narrative towards the likely responses from both these markets. Today, most feature films produced in Australia are aimed at a larger market than the nation can provide. Similarly, most television drama (notably current soap operas such as *Neighbours* and *Home and Away*) survives through generating overseas sales. In the television industry as a whole the reduction of local ownership and the gradual erosion of local content regulations have raised serious concerns. In both free-to-air and pay television, the proportion of foreign investment rose steadily over the term of the Hawke–Keating Labor governments from 1983 to 1996 and, despite the elaboration of some provision for local content, pay television seems likely to have an even more attenuated relation to representations of the national culture than broadcast television. Paradoxically, then, although the cultural purchase of the visual media has expanded over the last twenty years, the degree to which they are free to discharge their responsibilities as expressions of the national culture is particularly responsive to commercial and political pressures. The extent and wisdom of this response is debated by those involved in attracting or allocating government funding; it is also a matter of broad social concern for those who wish to reassert the obligations of social and cultural responsibility which implicitly undergird the operations of these sectors of the entertainment industry.

What I have been characterising as the 'competition' between literature and the visual media as 'national' forms is not nearly as direct or explicit as the above account might imply. On a day-to-day basis, it is probably not an issue that exercises the minds of those involved in either form. It may be a competition one sees better from a distance, understood as a shift in the historical conjuncture of cultural formations rather than an explicit or deliberate battle for the Australian mind. Nevertheless, from that distance, one can see that the ground has shifted in favour of the visual media.

Not all of this is due to movements in popular taste, the lure of new technologies, or changes in government cultural policy; indeed, much of the shift in ground can be traced to reorientations within the discipline of literary studies itself. It is useful to review some of these reorientations in order to see how movements within the discipline have helped it deal with other, non-literary, textual forms but, at the same time, have weakened its hold on a specifically national imagination. For instance, an effect of the critique of aesthetics which emerged within literary and cultural theory over the 1970s and 1980s is the partial disabling of one of literature's central legitimating arguments: that its cultural significance is related to its artistic merit. The post-structuralist withdrawal from the certainties of aesthetic value exposed literature to the task of justifying itself in new ways. At the same time, the advocacy of multicultural writing, the new focus on the construction and maintenance of 'difference', the push beyond pluralism into what is now called 'identity politics', effectively ushered in new criteria of critical analysis and judgment: almost all of these criteria rejected such traditional defences of literature as the invocation of 'universal' values and so on. Political interrogations of the literary 'canon' set out to expose the social conservatism and, ultimately, the neo-colonialism of this concept in practice. Such arguments clearly undermined the achievements of what had been the primary constructive activity of Australian literary criticism for most of the twentieth century—arguing the legitimacy of an Australian tradition, a national 'canon'. In a complicated paradox, a group of theories with the general objective of contextualising and demythologising 'the literary', actually undermined a tradition of literary criticism which had dedicated itself precisely to thinking about the relationship between Australian writing and the Australian context.

Even these respectable credentials were challenged when new forms of cultural analysis which foregrounded the context over the text—Australian studies and cultural studies, as two examples—competed with Australian literary studies in the academic marketplace. In contrast to the difficulties such disciplinary shifts posed to advocates of 'the literary', the development of media and cultural studies proved very useful indeed to the visual media. The exploration of theories of 'pleasure',[6] the elaboration of the means of interpreting the productions of film, television and other media, and the interest in the analysis of 'everyday life' which emerged from the 'inter-disciplines' of the new humanities,[7] not only provided film and television with new kinds of formal and institutional analysis but also with new strategies of cultural and social legitimation.

Within Australian literary studies, the last two decades have been periods of radical debate and disciplinary reconstruction; these debates and the process of reconstruction have directly affected the definition of literature, its cultural function, and the centrality of the notion of aesthetics. Two other fundamental and related categories have also been thrown into question. Where once the notion of a national literature was sufficiently secure to enable a campaign of development and justification to establish an Australian tradition, the last twenty years have problematised both the idea of the nation and of the national literature.

Australian literary studies was, of course, founded on the assumption that there is such a thing as a national literature and that talking about Australian literature's formal characteristics, patterns of meanings, and social or political concerns is a worthwhile activity. As practised today, there is nothing idealist about this. As we have seen from earlier in this history, it is widely understood that the construction of the national literature involves a degree of invention. Some of these necessary 'inventions' have come in for close inspection and revision over the last two decades.[8] By the end of the 1980s the dominant construction of the Australian type identified with the radical-nationalist revival of the 1950s (the work of Ward and Palmer in particular) was generally regarded, for varying reasons, as of dubious or limited historical legitimacy. Once this tradition was substantially revised, the relationship between the literature and the nation, hitherto typically autochthonous and relatively unproblematic, became a key site for the elaboration of theory.[9]

The radical nationalist agenda was an intensely patriotic one, grounded in a firm commitment to Australian nationalism. Its effect was both constructive and exclusionary, but it did articulate itself in ways the nation seemed to accept and understand (certainly the longevity of the myths legitimating this agenda suggests it was very securely embedded within the national imaginary). The 1980s revision was harder to sell, and this was exacerbated by its scepticism about nationalism of any kind. Interestingly, many of those working in Australian literary studies over this period were actually quite uncomfortable with the very idea of a national literature. Nationalism is not a popular ideology within the humanities at the end of this century. Nationalism's capacity to override individual differences in order to produce consensus, its capacity to legitimate the most scandalous operations of power, and the graphic lessons of twentieth-century European history combine to make support of the ideal of nationalism appear conservative and backward-looking. Consequently, intellectuals have been prominent in their criticism of large nation-building activities and events in recent years: Patrick White's scorn for the Bicentennial celebrations is a case in point.[10] And so, for some Australian literary critics, their professional interest in a national literary form does involve negotiating contradictions and, often, attempting to explain the fruits of these negotiations to a sceptical and intellectually impatient public.

Given such circumstances, the development of the official policy of multiculturalism was something of a boon—one of the rare occasions when literary theory and government social policy appear to have been more or less in step—as it offered a new way of thinking about nationalism that involved dealing with the articulation and protection of difference rather than its assimilation and erasure. The work of developing a theory of multicultural writing proceeded in tandem with the promotion and analysis of writers from non-English-speaking backgrounds.[11] This work had a professional objective to it, but it was also offered in terms of a critique of prevailing assumptions about the national character and the place of diversity within the national culture. Not only was the idea of a homogeneous national identity rendered problematic, but the basis upon which literary judgments could be made was also called into question (again, the Demidenko affair threw these issues into sharp relief).

Another perspective from which the relation between the nation and its literature could be inspected was provided by postcolonialism. Emerging out of Commonwealth literature or New Literatures in English, postcolonial literary studies have exercised quite a strategic influence by attributing progressive political and cultural potential to the national literatures in postcolonial countries. In its most productive forms, postcolonial criticism has attempted to find ways of thinking about the problems of 'new' literatures that are both transnational—in that they construct historical and political homologies between the various postcolonial literatures—and nationalist, in that they can defend the category of the national as a point of resistance to domination from outside.[12]

Postcolonial criticism, however, is not a nationalist formation in the way that the radical nationalist tradition was. It resists essentialising arguments which see cultural expression emerging organically from territory or ethnicity; rather, cultural expression emerges out of a specific colonial history and articulates itself in languages which have specific political objectives and contexts. What the 'postcolonial' describes, furthermore, is a power relation—a subordinated relation to more powerful, colonising cultures— rather than a set of cultural or ethnic origins. Most importantly, the cultures which post-colonial criticism examines are primarily settler cultures, established through the subordination of their indigenous inhabitants, composed of competing and diverse cultural and ethnic groups, and variously positioned within the global economy to compete for control over their political and social conditions. They are cultures which are deeply and fundamentally divided, within which competing traditions prosper and continue, and where the construction of 'national identity' must be accomplished through the acceptance of the notion of hybridity rather than cultural purity. Within such a tradition, the nation is not produced through the resolution or erasure of difference: rather, the nation is constituted through difference which is itself celebrated as identity. In many cases, this process is the direct product of state cultural policy—such as that which helped establish the fiction industry and the film industry in Australia.

REPRESENTING THE NATION

A common thread through the above account is a focus on the cultural and social, rather than on the aesthetic, function of the literary text. Once the aesthetic 'alibi' is withdrawn from the literary text it is forced to compete on roughly equivalent terms with electronic media forms which have much less trouble popularising themselves as products to be consumed. Importantly, an effect of the focus on representation, perhaps an unintended one, is to assume a level of equivalence between films and novels as texts for cultural analysis. While this extends the cultural purchase of the literary texts to some extent, it has a more dramatic effect on the legitimacy of film texts. Within the wider culture and beyond the boundaries of the academic disciplines, little persuasion was required to encourage audiences to embrace Australian films as central cultural and aesthetic objects.

Film found a place in the centre of cultural nationalist arguments from government, from industry, from all perspectives in Australian life. This factor, combined with film's dramatic impact on Australian audiences during the 1970s, certainly encouraged the discussion of the two media's relation to each other. But there were further, textual, motivations for such a discussion.

John Tulloch's history of early Australian film-making, *Legends on the Screen*, deals with two kinds of screen 'legend'.[13] The first describes the national celebrity which developed around particular screen performers in the period examined—1919–29—a brief golden age before sound arrived and when Australian film stars enjoyed a level of popular celebrity that took 60 years to regain. The second deals with the treatment of the bush legend in Australian film. Tulloch demonstrates the centrality of the bush legend to early Australian films such as *The Breaking of the Drought* (1920), *A Girl of the Bush* (1921), and *The Sentimental Bloke* (1919). Bruce Molloy's *Before the Interval*[14] extends this a little further, examining some of the early Australian 'talkies' in terms of, again, their continuities with the nationalist mythologies customarily located in the writing of the 1890s. The narrative and ideological possibilities for the national film industry, according to these studies, were to some extent already in place before the technology itself had been fully developed as a medium for mass entertainment. Once film-makers discovered the medium's potential for narrative, here and elsewhere, they turned to some of the stories already available to them in their national culture. (The first American narrative feature, for instance, was a western, *The Great Train Robbery*, produced in 1903.) In Australia, the arrival of the feature film occurred less than a decade after Australian writing had finally established itself as a national form with a popular audience. It is not surprising then that there were such close narrative and mythic links between the Australian films of the 1920s and the writing of the 1890s.

Australian film's development of its own stories and narrative style, however, was effectively put on hold for almost forty years by the decline of local film production that was initiated by the introduction of sound and lasted until the government-led revival in the early 1970s. The hiatus in film production in Australia was not the consequence of a single determinant; the decline of the national audience, the corresponding growth in the popularity of Hollywood cinema, and the decline in the number of Australian films which specifically addressed this national audience were the most important factors. Increasingly under the pressure of the competition from Hollywood and to a lesser extent from Britain, Australian films of this period imitated overseas products. The Australian industry produced a diet of light comedies and urban melodramas while investing time and money in the futile venture of establishing a local star system equivalent to that of Hollywood. The generic internationalisation failed, and by the mid-1950s the only significant productions occurring in Australia came as a result of Hollywood's need for a location at 'the end of the world' (*On the Beach*, 1959) or the occasional good fortune of an international best-seller being set here (*The Shiralee*, 1957, *The Sundowners*, 1960). These films promoted Australia as a curiosity, filled with shearers, sheilas, marsupials, and British actors making a mess of the Australian accent. Particularly noticeable in *The*

Sundowners was the inadequacy of Hollywood's conventional film stock and processing: it made Australia look like the American West, evened out the light by either bleaching out the colour in direct light or exaggerating it in the shade. The 'foreignness' of the production to Australian locations could be read off the screen in the failure of the medium to accurately catch the quality of the Australian light.

It is for more complicated reasons than these, of course, that the case for the Australian film industry eventually gained political support at the end of the 1960s.[15] However, the revival of the film industry was a cultural nationalist project, legitimated by the need for cinema to tell Australian stories to Australian audiences. The cultural objective underpinning the re-establishment of the industry through government subsidy clearly influenced the kind of work that was supported by the various funding bodies in the first decade or so, and encouraged producers to work within what became relatively well established narrative frameworks. There was some point in having such frameworks, as it was an industry in great need of guidance and direction in the early days. Without the benefit of even a small-scale local features industry, most of the producers were inexperienced in producing full-length features. Drawn from advertising or documentary backgrounds, they found that developing feature-length narratives was a daunting and unfamiliar task. Understandably, the producers of the 1970s took much the same route as those of the 1920s—they mined the resources of established Australian literary successes. Throughout its first decade (effectively 1971–81), the revival was significantly dependent upon scripts developed from successful novels, both literary and popular (*My Brilliant Career*, 1979, *The Getting of Wisdom*, 1977, *The Chant of Jimmie Blacksmith*, 1978, *Monkey Grip*, 1981, *Age of Consent*, 1969, *Picnic at Hanging Rock*, 1975), biographies (*We of the Never Never*, 1982, *Caddie*, 1976) and plays (*Dimboola*, 1979, *Don's Party*, 1976, *The Removalists*, 1975, *The Club*, 1980). It was also to some extent dependent upon the writers of these sources; both David Williamson and Thomas Keneally worked successfully as scriptwriters on their own texts. Keneally usually appeared as an actor as well.

As Brian McFarlane has suggested, Australian film's reliance upon the literary narrative tradition over this period was pronounced. In his book, *Words and Images: Australian Novels into Film* (1983),[16] McFarlane compares the literary and film texts of *Wake in Fright* (1971), *The Getting of Wisdom*, *The Mango Tree* (1977), *The Night the Prowler* (1978) and *The Chant of Jimmie Blacksmith*, *My Brilliant Career*, *Monkey Grip*, *The Year of Living Dangerously* (1982). While his interest is primarily in the process of adaptation so that he tends not to relate the two versions of each narrative to each other in any other way, McFarlane criticises the closeness of the connection between Australian film and literary texts at the time:

> [In some screenplays] there has been a failure to come to grips with what adaptation means and a consequent growth of a surprisingly literary cinema, characterized by a pervading sense of unadventurous carefulness. What one wants is not a literary cinema which runs the risk of

sounding like an illustrated novel, but, rather, a 'literate' cinema. By this I mean films which sound, whether they are based on novels or not, true to the lives they present and this involves the film-makers, especially director and scriptwriter, in immersing themselves in the creation of a new experience, not in the reheating of one already completed (p. 20).

McFarlane nonetheless understands the reasons for the preferences he criticises, particularly at this point in the industry's development. The film-makers' lack of confidence and experience in making full-length features was responsible for, among other things, a strong preference for certain kinds of narrative (those which eschewed a highly structured, crisis-driven plot, for instance) and for the kind of cultural cachet and formal security that the adaptation of a literary text can provide. These preferences were widely noted[17] and while they may be seen now as retarding influences on the level of script development in the Australian industry over this period they may well have helped significantly in the project of building the audience for Australian films. These were stories, after all, in which many Australians already had an interest. The exploration of literary sources for feature films acknowledged that there must be clear lines of connection between Australian fictions no matter what medium carries them; as narrative forms they are subject to similar processes if they are to establish their cultural significance.

Such a defence did not protect the industry from criticism at the time. Despite the success of such films as *Picnic at Hanging Rock*, the industry was attacked for its conservative subject matter and approach. *Picnic*, while beautiful to look at, offered its audiences a nineteenth-century account of Australian society which implicitly collaborated with the kind of northern hemisphere simplifications which had underpinned the foreign productions of the 1950s and 1960s. *Picnic*'s self-conscious artiness, while proving Australians could make 'quality' films, also rendered it vulnerable to accusations of pretentiousness and irrelevance to contemporary Australia.[18] Similarly, while *Sunday Too Far Away* (1975) was well received overseas and at home, its affectionate celebration of a fading way of life—the anachronistic nature of which was closely tied up with its exclusive masculinity—was especially vulnerable to feminist critique. Having won the position as the cultural flagship, Australian film was, like literature before it, caught in the crossfire created by its contradictory function as both the representative of the nation and an expressive, albeit industrialised, form of representation.

Dermody and Jacka invented a label for the complacent trend they observed in the mainstream of 1970s productions—the AFC (Australian Film Commission) genre:[19]

> The phenomenon of the AFC genre was noted from time to time in the late seventies as a persistent tendency of Australian cinema to fall back on pretty 'period', nostalgia, or 'history' films when it should be addressing the not-so-pretty 'real', contemporary Australian world (p. 32).

These were narratively dull but visually pleasing films which, although not strictly all belonging to the same filmic genre, were the product of a nationalist orthodoxy limiting the kind of project the film bureaucracies would support. They constituted conservative interventions into the process of nation formation, here and abroad. Typically, the AFC genre reclaimed Australian history as worthy of interest, represented it through formal codes and visual styles which would inform foreign viewers that they were watching sophisticated work, and carefully avoided such vulgarities as the melodramatic plotlines preferred by Hollywood.

Like McFarlane, Dermody and Jacka blame the closeness of the relation with literature for the persistence of some of these attributes:

> The films have a literariness that can usually be tracked back to their origins in middle-brow fiction; but even those few not based on novels (*The Picture Show Man, Let the Balloon Go* and *Kitty and the Bagman*) have a literary feeling. This seems to inhere in their gently descriptive and evocative creation of period, and even more plainly in their character—rather than action-based narratives. The stories feel relatively unshaped, motivated by character, interested in 'sensibility' in the tradition of the novel rather than the moral choice and action of the more plotted melodrama. (Compare, for instance, *The Irishman* with *The Man From Snowy River*.) Frequently the literariness is second hand, mediated by the conventions and expectations of originally British 'quality' dramatised literature on television (pp. 32–3).

The issue of 'quality' was crucial. Although Australian audiences took readily to the simple pleasures of *The Adventures of Barry McKenzie* (1972) and the *Alvin Purple* films (1973, 1974), the funding bodies saw their mission as producing 'quality' films which would positively influence foreign audiences' opinion of Australian culture. This further disposed them towards protecting conventional standards of aesthetic quality, standards extrapolated in some cases from literary criticism.

As Dermody and Jacka point out, however, the film industry did not derive its standards of quality only from literature. The visual style of British 'quality' film and television as well as that of European art films of the day (the influence of Bo Widerberg's *Elvira Madigan* on Peter Weir's *Picnic at Hanging Rock*, for instance) also played its part. Further complicating the mix is the local contribution from the Heidelberg school of painters, their works explicitly acknowledged as sources of the visual style in (at least) *Picnic at Hanging Rock, Sunday Too Far Away* and *The Chant of Jimmie Blacksmith*. Interestingly enough, it was the attempt to emulate the Heidelberg School and 'get the light right' which prompted Australian film-makers to experiment with a new Kodak film stock which proved to be the first capable of dealing with the harshness of Australian conditions and reproducing them to local satisfaction on the screen.

An aspect which is underplayed in both McFarlane's and Dermody and Jacka's accounts is the fact that both these narrative forms, novel and film, must inevitably speak as national utterances. Whether they are placed into such a framework by their institutional location or not, they must draw on the available narrative repertoire. It should not be surprising that narratives produced in different forms from within the same culture might share significant formal, structural and ideological attributes. As I have noted elsewhere, film and literary narratives are, in one sense, 'produced by the culture: thus they generate meanings, take on significances and assume forms that are articulations of the values, beliefs, the ideologies of the culture'.[20]

Many of the attributes Dermody and Jacka go on to enumerate as the markers of an excessively literary film culture could also be regarded as markers of Australian narrative in more than these two media. Such markers include the preponderance of loosely structured, episodic stories with a heavy reliance upon the family saga, using history rather than character to drive events; the construction of Australian existence as highly ambiguous, torn between a banal social context and a hostile version of nature; and the repeated nationalist theme of the individual attempting to transcend their location, only to fail either tragically or honourably (*Jimmie Blacksmith*, *Gallipoli*, 1981) or to succeed at some substantial personal cost (*My Brilliant Career*, *Newsfront*, 1978).

This view of film and literature as 'national fictions' proposes key tropes and metaphors as repeated, fundamental, components of Australian narrative.[21] Convictism, for instance, has frequently operated as the ground for analysis of a relationship between the individual and society in which individuals are disaffected from society, alienated from the land, and forced to console themselves through the manner of their accommodation to this situation. While many films have dealt with this explicitly (the several versions of Clarke's *For the Term of His Natural Life*, 1908, 1927, *Breaker Morant*, 1980, *Stir*, 1980), it is also frequently exploited as a metaphor for entrapment (as in *The Chant of Jimmie Blacksmith* and *Wake in Fright*).

Such arguments are easier to make about the beginning of the revival because of the directness of the influences from literature that I have noted above. As the film industry developed over the 1980s, the influence became more subtle and more contested. As film's placement as a cultural project within a general context of policy-driven nation formation declined, and as commercial imperatives became increasingly influential, Australian films have become less likely to explicitly address a national audience in the way that, say, *Newsfront* did. The cultural nationalism that agreed upon the need for a national film industry and which implicitly, if perhaps wrongheadedly, required films to address this need directly through their narratives is no longer as powerful an influence on the industry or its products. The corresponding ascendancy of more commercial, inevitably internationalising, imperatives means that probably the most nationalist film to come out of the second decade of the revival is *Crocodile Dundee* (1986)—itself a sign of the newly contingent function of discourses of the nation, and the strategic nature of its inscription in commercially produced narratives. More positively, where criticism of the AFC genre focused on their nostalgia, their complacent preference for reconstructing the past rather than critically scrutinising the present, the films of the last decade have been much more interested in directing attention to contemporary Australia. The films of the 1970s connected with the radical nationalism mythologised in the 1950s. The films of the 1990s seem much more rooted in the present in their subject matter, their formal characteristics, and in sharing with some of the new developments in Australian writing the capacity to blur the boundaries between the popular and the artistic, the generic and the expressive. Australian film, like Australian writing, has become more generically diverse. A sign of that diversity, acknowledging both the rediscovery of a local audience for commercial Australian productions and the recovery of Australian cinema as a location for political debate, came in November 1992, when *Romper Stomper* and *Strictly Ballroom* occupied first and second place in the Australian box office takings in one week.

The decline of some key nationalist mythologies is visible in other areas. A common complaint about the AFC genre during the 1980s, which echoes contemporary critiques of the dominance of the radical-nationalist strain in Australian literary historiography, referred to its preference for 'male ensemble films'—stories centred around male cultures (workplaces, sporting venues) which effectively reinforced masculine hegemony in discourses of national identity. While this trend was partially countered by a range of strongly woman-centred films over a long period of time (the work of Gillian Armstrong, Anne Turner, and Jane Campion, for instance), its influence is clear in the success of such films as *Sunday Too Far Away*, *Breaker Morant*, the Williamson adaptations, *The Club* and *Don's Party*, and in spawning the much maligned but popular genre of the 'ocker film' (usually, *Stork*, 1971, the *Alvin Purple* films, and *Petersen*, 1974). The influence is no longer so clear or so unequivocal now. The icons of contemporary Australian masculinity are not limited to Jack Thompson or Bryan Brown; included now would be much more equivocal figures—Noah Taylor, Ben Mendelsohn, Alex Dimitriades, and the Sam Neill of *Death in Brunswick* (1991)—coexisting with more traditional Anglo-macho actors such as Gary Sweet. The male ensemble film has had to be radically resituated, it seems, to work in the 1990s. The closest contemporary parallels are *Priscilla, Queen of the Desert* (1993) (admittedly, an ocker film in drag) and *The Sum of Us* (1994) (the casting of Jack Thompson serving to explicitly 'nationalise' gay Australians). Similarly, the discomfort with culturally exclusivist versions of national identity implicated in so much criticism of earlier accounts of the Australian literary tradition is echoed in criticism of Australian films from the beginnings of the revival. Recently, Australian films have begun to reflect the benefits of such criticism: in particular, we are beginning to see the first visible effects of multiculturalism. *Death in Brunswick* and *The Heartbreak Kid* (1993) are two recent films which unselfconsciously construct an Australia made up of multiple and hybridising ethnicities and identities.[22] Popular in their conception of the audience, both films are observant renditions of contemporary Australia which never need to explicitly address themselves to the task of representing the nation. The project for such films and for their audiences is no longer nationalist.

This might be regarded as a sign of the maturity of the industry, and of the success it has achieved in rebuilding an Australian audience for a wide variety of Australian stories. Interestingly, an enabling factor in this disarticulation of the nationalist project from the film industry has been the development of an internationalist commercial outlook. Hence, perhaps, the international success of *Babe*, a film made here with American money, an international cast, but with few visible signs of its cultural origin. While this may be the downside of an industry no longer fixated on the national, it also suggests that film-makers may be becoming a little less constrained by the cultural responsibilities attributed to them. Not to over-emphasise that possibility, it is worth remembering that the industry is still financed under the assumption that it will address the local audience even though its primary objective is to return profits to its investors.

SIGNIFICANT INTERVENTIONS

The patterns of connection and difference I have been raising here have attracted some critical attention since the mid-1980s. In addition to my own *National Fictions*, there have been a number of treatments of Australian narrative in film and fiction. Kay Schaffer's *Women and the Bush: Forces of Desire and the Australian Tradition* (1988) moves between literary forms, film and television as she sets out to rewrite the meaning of the bush tradition from a feminist perspective. This has been an influential contribution, essential now to an understanding of the cultural purchase of the legend of the 1890s. Bob Hodge and Vijay Mishra's *Dark Side of the Dream: Australian Literature and the Postcolonial Mind* (1991) offers a reading of the myths informing Australian narrative but focuses on what they see as 'the domain of repression' within them: 'Australia's colonial history and the relations of domination formed within that history' (p. 204). Importantly, in Hodge and Mishra's account, Aboriginal writing and representations of Aboriginality in film are retrieved as fundamental components of the Australian narrative tradition.

These were significant interventions. Participating in the broad theoretical development of Australian literary studies, these works provided the specific benefit of enabling literary studies to deal with the already established fact that film was now a significant and visible cultural force which shared much of its narrative traditions with literature, but which was set to steal part of its audience. From within the literary studies of the early 1980s such books may have looked like radical departures from established traditions; it would be difficult to regard them in this way now. Both the reorientations internal to literary studies and the blurring of distinctions between it and other disciplinary territories in the humanities have assisted in widening the context of discussion for Australian literature. If the boundaries of literary study appear to have melted under the heat of interdisciplinary enquiry, this has not necessarily weakened the field. One could argue that trade with film has extended literature's purchase, broadened the formulation of its cultural significance and helped to reduce its dependence on the construction of a canon for the discipline's intellectual authority. That said, it is also true that the move towards film was also a move towards another valorised, aesthetic object. It turned out to be much harder to think about other kinds of text, such as those produced for television. Hodge and Mishra, to be sure, find things to say about two television series, *A Country Practice* (1981) (as a representation of the idealised country town), and *Prisoner* (1979) (as another location where criminality, a Foucauldian version of 'delinquency' and an interestingly feminised version of the convict are to be found). But this is rare within Australian literary studies.[23]

Watching television is reputedly the most popular leisure activity in Australia (followed by gardening!) and clearly has eaten into the market for Australian writing. Where film generally has accepted the responsibility of the 'cultural flagship' and endeavoured (from time to time) to produce high-quality films which speak of the national culture in sophisticated ways, it would be harder to establish that television has done this. It is true that when the high-quality period drama was ultimately renounced by the film industry in the mid-1980s, it simply moved into television: the vogue for the historical mini-series revived the parade of worthy costume dramas and literary adaptations which had dominated the early years of the film revival. There were mini-series adaptations of *1915* (1982), *All the Rivers Run* (1983), *The Boy in the Bush* (1984), *A Fortunate Life* (1986), and similar modalities adopted in other period pieces such as *Rush* (1974, 1976) and *Against the Wind* (1978). The earliest attempts at quality Australian television drama in the 1960s were highly 'literate' in McFarlane's terms—the ABC's historical series *The Outcasts* (1961), *The Patriots* (1962) and so on. But during the early 1980s a new kind of mini-series had begun to exploit television's ability to popularise, rather than just faithfully re-create, Australian histories: the Kennedy Miller productions *The Dismissal* (1983), *Vietnam* (1987), and *The Cowra Breakout* (1985), as well as the Burrowes–Dixon mythic rewriting of First World War histories, *Anzacs* (1985). By the 1990s, however, the mini-series and its versions of history had all but disappeared with the remaining claim to quality television residing in such hard-edged police dramas as *Phoenix* (1993). The cultural responsibility so fundamental to the legitimacy of the film industry has sat uncomfortably with the television industry for most of the last decade. Consequently, it has been of much less interest within Australian literary studies. There are no equivalents to *National Fictions* dealing with television. Perhaps, sensibly, the domain of television has been left to media and cultural studies to explore.

From another point of view, it could be argued that television should matter a great deal to Australian literary studies, although not as an aesthetic object or even as a textual form. Television is the most powerful medium through which writers can advertise their wares to their public. Thomas Keneally will appear on *Burke's Backyard* as that week's 'celebrity gardener'; David Malouf will find himself on *Today* explaining the plot of his new novel to Liz Hayes; Peter Goldsworthy will tell stories from his new novel on *The 7.30 Report*. These days, furthermore, the construction of literary reputations is witnessed most vividly on television. Helen Darville's confrontation with Gerard Henderson on *The 7.30 Report* or Jenna Mead's discussion of Helen Garner's *The First Stone* on *Lateline* are important moments in our literary and cultural history. Indeed, it is through appearances on programs such as these—rather than on the various formations of *The Book Show*—that the cultural impact of Australian writing is most extensive. As such, it is probably only a matter of time before it is exposed to greater scrutiny from those who are both its objects and its participants.

The picture I am offering of Australian writing in the 1990s, in a media climate where books must compete for an audience and argue for their continued importance—indeed for their survival—is complicated. Certainly the commercial future of Australian writing is anything but clear. There are threats and challenges other than those presented by film, television and the CD-ROM. Some have to do with the central problem of the production of an Australian culture within an increasingly globalised market for all the cultural industries. This has an effect on the formation of cultural policy as well as on the framing of commercial publishing and marketing decisions. While Australian writing continues to attract critical respect and a transnational readership, it also suffers from a string of commercial and regulatory factors which inhibit its progress. The deregulation of the retail market has increased competition from overseas; the disappearance of all but a few locally owned publishers drastically limits the publishing opportunities for Australian writers; the modification of regulations controlling copyright legislation and photocopying is also eating into sales figures. At the broader, cultural level, there are problems too. The continuing debate over the funding strategies of the Australia Council and the fate of the small magazines has produced uncertainties which must be debilitating. The lack of a comprehensive reviewing policy in most journals and newspapers also drastically limits the ability of Australian writers to reach their audience, and the establishment of the *Australian's Review of Books* has had little effect on this. Many publishers' continuing (frustrating) caution in supporting books of literary criticism at anything but the most rudimentary level is also denying our literature the appropriate critical context for its reception and dissemination. These and other factors all contribute to one's sense that Australian writing will need to negotiate quite a difficult path into the next century.

That said, however, one cannot fail to be impressed by the capacity of Australian writing to survive and prosper despite the difficulties it has encountered. As I review its condition for this final chapter, the picture which emerges most clearly is that of a mature literary culture substantially articulated to other cultural and critical industries, experiencing a range of difficulties: involved in negotiating survival for the local against the pressures of market globalisation; attempting to indigenise international theoretical and critical arguments so as to put them to the best use within a postcolonial context, and negotiating new and hybridised versions of the national through a diversity of textual forms and critical receptions. There seems little more one could ask of it.

Notes

1: White on Black/Black on Black

[1] Marjorie Bil Bil, 'So all these things come together' in *It Just Lies There From the Beginning* (Alice Springs, NT: IAD Press, 1995), 12.

[2] Penny Van Toorn, 'Early Aboriginal Writing', *Meanjin*, 55 (1996), 758.

[3] Stephen Muecke, *Textual Spaces: Aboriginality and Cultural Studies* (Kensington: NSW University Press, 1992), 49.

[4] Mudrooroo, 'Song Twenty-Seven' in *The Song Circle of Jacky and Selected Poems* (Melbourne: Hyland House, 1986), 46.

[5] Mudrooroo, *Doctor Wooreddy's Prescription for Enduring the Ending of the World* (Melbourne: Hyland House, 1983), 163–4.

[6] 'Piruwana' in *Taruru: Aboriginal Song Poetry from the Pilbara*, ed. by C.G. von Brandenstein and A.P. Thomas (Adelaide: Rigby, 1974), 29, 73–4.

[7] *Tom Petrie's Reminiscences of Early Queensland*, ed. by Constance Campbell Petrie (Brisbane: Watson, Ferguson and Co., 1904), 25; reissued by University of Queensland Press, 1992.

[8] Tutama Tjapangarti, 'Wangka Tjukutjuk', *Overland*, 80 (July 1980), 32.

[9] Billy Marshall-Stoneking, *Singing the Snake* (North Ryde, NSW: Angus and Robertson, 1990), 60.

[10] Stephen Muecke and Paddy Roe, *Gularabulu: Stories from the West Kimberley* (Fremantle: Fremantle Arts Centre Press, 1983).

[11] Bill Neidjie, *Story About Feeling* (Broome, WA: Magabala Books, 1989).

[12] *For the Record: 160 Years of Aboriginal Print Journalism*, ed. by Michael Rose (St Leonards, NSW: Allen and Unwin, 1996), 2.

[13] Rose, 2.

[14] Although David Unaipon was being quoted in South Australian newspapers as early as 1910, for example, in 'An Ingenious Aboriginal', *Advertiser*, 10 May 1910, his earliest commissioned newspaper article is 'The Aborigine's Point-of-View', *Advertiser*, 23 November 1936.

[15] Van Toorn, 756.

[16] Quoted in Rose, 5.

[17] Quoted in Rose, 7.

18 Quoted in Rose, 17. Interestingly, Mudrooroo quotes—and edits—this exact passage and re-produces it in *Doctor Wooreddy's Prescription for Enduring the Ending of the World*, 145.

19 Referred to in Jakelin Troy, *Australian Aboriginal Contact with the English Language in New South Wales: 1788–1845* (Canberra: Research School of Pacific Studies, ANU, 1990).

20 'My Father Very Much Hurt' in *North of the Ten Commandments*, ed. by David Headon (Sydney: Hodder and Stoughton, 1991), 95.

21 Quoted in *Paperbark: A Collection of Black Australian Writings*, ed. by Jack Davis et al. (St Lucia: University of Queensland Press, 1990), 53.

22 Rose, 22.

23 'To all Aborigines', *Abo Call*, 1, April 1938, quoted in Rose, 23.

24 One of the best recent treatments of this theme is Simon Ryan's, *The Cartographic Eye* (Cambridge UK; Melbourne: Cambridge University Press, 1996).

25 John Mulvaney, *Encounters in Place* (Melbourne: Cambridge University Press, 1989), 11. Subsequent quotations from Mulvaney are taken from this edition.

26 Mulvaney, 12.

27 Mulvaney, 12.

28 Mulvaney, 13.

29 Thomas Watling, 'Letters from an Exile, 1794', quoted in *Colonial Voices*, ed. by Elizabeth Webby (St Lucia: University of Queensland Press, 1989), 14.

30 Charles Sturt, 'Providential Deliverance from Danger, 1833', quoted in Webby, 61.

31 Quoted in Webby, 64.

32 Thomas Mitchell, 'At the Darling River, 1839', quoted in Webby, 67.

33 Henry Reynolds, *Frontier* (Sydney: Allen and Unwin, 1987), 6.

34 Hale Papers, PRG 275, 130/224, State Library of South Australia, quoted in John Harris, *One Blood—200 Years of Aboriginal Encounter with Christianity: A Story of Hope* (Sutherland, NSW: Albatross Books, 1990), 349.

2: THE 'SETTLING' OF ENGLISH

1 James Cook, *The Explorations of Captain James Cook in the Pacific as told by selections of his own Journals 1768–1779*, ed. by A. Grenfell Price (Sydney: Angus and Robertson, 1969).

2 See Robert Dixon, *The Course of Empire: Neo-Classical Culture in New South Wales, 1788–1860* (Melbourne: Oxford University Press, 1986) for a scholarly discussion of the cultural backgrounds of and intellectual influences on middle and upper class colonists in New South Wales. This reference p. 1.

3 In this chapter I am necessarily writing from a Eurocentric perspective since my concern is with the ways English literary traditions were transformed and 'Australianised' in the experience of colonisation. I must, then, use terms like 'settlement' and 'settler' rather than the now multiple alternatives to describe colonisation and the imperial activities of English, and will refer only briefly to representations of Aboriginality and Aborigines in my discussion, since the previous chapter is devoted to these issues.

4 Homi Bhabha, 'DissemiNation', in *Nation and Narration* (London and New York: Routledge, 1990), 319.

5 Elizabeth Webby's 'Writers, Printers, Readers: The Production of Australian Literature Before 1855', in *The Penguin New Literary History of Australia*, ed. by Laurie Hergenhan (Ringwood,

Vic: Penguin, 1988), is an invaluable source for information about the beginnings of Australian publishing.

[6] Webby, 123.

[7] Quoted in Ross Gibson, *South of the West: Postcolonialism and the Narrative Construction of Australia* (Bloomington and Indianapolis: Indiana University Press, 1992), 37.

[8] H.M. Green, *A History of Australian Literature: Pure and Applied*, rev. edn by Dorothy Green, 2 vols (Sydney: Angus and Robertson, 1984–85; first published 1961), 14.

[9] Elizabeth Perkins, 'Colonial Transformations: Writing and the Dilemma of Colonisation', in *The Penguin New Literary History of Australia*, 148.

[10] In *Colonial Desire: Hybridity in Theory, Culture and Race* (London and New York: Routledge, 1995), 31ff, Robert J.C. Young discusses the significance of the development of European 'culture' in all its meanings and the impact on its colonising processes of those ideas.

[11] Cliff Hanna, 'The Ballads: Eighteenth Century to the Present', in *The Penguin New Literary History of Australia*, 194–5. Hanna provides a comprehensive history of Australian ballads and their literary influence.

[12] All quotations are from the first section of 'British and Irish Broadsides', in *The Penguin Book of Australian Ballads*, ed. by Philip Butterss and Elizabeth Webby, rev. edn (Ringwood, Vic; New York: Penguin, 1993), 7, 11–12, 27.

[13] *Colonial Literary Journal*, vol. I, no. 1, Thursday 27 June 1844, 2–3.

[14] *Colonial Literary Journal*, vol. II, no. 11, Thursday 27 February 1845, 131–2.

[15] Elizabeth Webby (ed.), *Colonial Voices* (St Lucia: University of Queensland Press, 1989), 418.

[16] Examples cited by Webby, *Colonial Voices*, 419, 425.

[17] Margaret Williams, *Australia on the Popular Stage 1829–1929* (Melbourne: Oxford University Press, 1983), 11.

[18] Williams, 12.

[19] Williams, 36–7.

[20] Robert Dixon, 'Public and Private Voices', in *The Penguin New Literary History of Australia*, 131–2.

[21] Ross Gibson, *The Diminishing Paradise: Changing Literary Perceptions of Australia* (Sydney: Angus and Robertson, 1984) and *South of the West: Post-colonialism and the Narrative Construction of Australia* (Bloomington: Indiana University Press, 1992); Paul Carter, *The Road to Botany Bay: an Essay in Spatial History* (London: Faber and Faber, 1987) and *Living in a New Country: History, Travelling and Language* (London: Faber and Faber, 1992); and Simon Ryan, *The Cartographic Eye: How Explorers Saw Australia* (Cambridge; Melbourne: Cambridge University Press, 1996) are among the best known of this kind of work. A group of Australian cultural historians whose work is currently providing illuminating modes of reconstructing the past includes Chris Healy, *From the Ruins of Colonialism* (Cambridge; Melbourne: Cambridge University Press, 1997); Tom Griffiths, *Hunters and Collectors: The Antiquarian Imagination in Australia* (Cambridge; Melbourne: Cambridge University Press, 1996), and Greg Dening's work in historical poetics.

[22] John Oxley, *Journals of Two Expeditions into the Interior of Australia Undertaken by Order of the British Government in the Years 1817–1818* (London: John Murray, 1820) Appendix A, 360–1.

[23] Made enormously successful by Washington Irving, and taken up by Charles Dickens in his *Sketches by Boz*, sketches were popular in contemporary newspapers and magazines.

²⁴ Alexander Harris, *The Emigrant Family or The Story of an Australian Settler*, ed. by W.S. Ramson (Canberra: Australian National University Press, 1967; first published 1849), 19.

²⁵ A recent thesis by Jane Grellier, 'Awe, Disillusionment and Fear: Attitudes to Landscape Among Christian Colonists of Far South-West Australia', The University of Western Australia, 1996, investigates some of these issues.

²⁶ John Ramsden Wollaston, *The Wollaston Journals*, ed. by Geoffrey Bolton and Heather Vose, in progress (Nedlands: University of Western Australia Press, 1991–), vol. II, 21.

²⁷ A. Mitchell, 'No New Thing: the Concept of Novelty and Early Australian Writing', in *Mapped But Not Known: The Australian Landscape of the Imagination*, ed. by P.R. Eaden and F.H. Mares (Netley, SA: Wakefield Press, 1986), 52.

²⁸ In 'A "Complicated Joy": The Aesthetic Theory of Associationism and Its Major Influence on Tasmania's Culture', in *The Flow of Culture*, ed. by Michael Roe (Canberra: Australian Academy of the Humanities, 1987), Robert Dixon defines associationism as 'the theory that material objects appear sublime or beautiful because the spectator endows them with sentiments associated with other scenes and places stored in the memory, or with works of art and literature', 122.

²⁹ Passages from the journal (which is held in the Battye Library, Perth) are reprinted in *No Place for a Nervous Lady: Voices from the Australian Bush*, comp. by Lucy Frost (Melbourne: McPhee Gribble/Penguin, 1984), this reference p. 40.

³⁰ Alexandra Hasluck, *Portrait with Background* (Melbourne: Oxford University Press, 1955), 73.

³¹ *A Faithful Picture: The Letters of Eliza and Thomas Brown at York in the Swan River Colony 1841–1852*, ed. by Peter Cowan (Fremantle: Fremantle Arts Centre Press, 1977), 134.

³² Reprinted as *The Fiction Fields of Australia*, ed. by Cecil Hadgraft (St Lucia: University of Queensland Press, 1966).

Grateful thanks to Jane Grellier for her able research assistance.

3: LITERARY CULTURE 1851–1914

¹ Howard Felperin, *The Uses of the Canon: Elizabethan Literature and Contemporary Theory* (New York: Oxford University Press, 1990), 190.

² Vincent Buckley, 'Towards an Australian Literature', *Meanjin*, 18 (1959), 75.

³ Tom Inglis Moore, 'Draft Plan of Lectures' for the course in Australian Literature, Canberra University College. T.I. Moore Papers, Australian National Library MS 8130. Moore's students also encountered other poets in the generic lectures on folk poetry, bush songs and ballads, and in lectures, for example, on 'Utopianism and the Great Australian Dream', which centred on O'Dowd as the canonical representative.

⁴ A.D. Hope, 'The Australian Scene—Literature and Drama'. Typescript in 'Lectures on General Aspects of Australian Literature', 12. A.D. Hope MSS, Menzies Library, Australian National University.

⁵ Thomas Heney, 'On Some Australian Poems', *Sydney Quarterly Magazine* (September 1888), in *The Writer in Australia*, ed. by John Barnes (Melbourne: Oxford University Press, 1969). Henry Gyles Turner and Alexander Sutherland, *The Development of Australian Literature* (London: George Robertson and Co., 1898). All quotations here and below taken from these editions.

⁶ The *Maitland Mercury*, established in 1843, maintained a regular column for Australian poetry and by 1866 circulated 9000 copies three times a week.

[7] Turner and Sutherland, 23.

[8] See Harpur's 'Discourse on Poetry'. Harpur MSS C386, Mitchell Library, also Harpur's Lecture on Poetry given at the Sydney School of Arts and published in the *Empire*, 2 October 1859.

[9] Harpur was replying to an article published in the *Month* for July 1857 by its editor Frank Fowler on the deficiencies in the 'public censorship' or criticism prevalent in a 'young country' like Australia. Fowler intended 'to set the public right on matters affecting the very vitality of Australian literature'.

[10] All quotations from Frederick Sinnett, *The Fiction Fields of Australia* (1856), ed. by Cecil Hadgraft (St Lucia: Queensland University Press, 1966).

[11] William Walker, *Australian Literature* (1864). Facsimile edited by Victor Crittenden (Canberra: The Mulini Press, 1996). All quotations from this edition.

[12] The title 'laureate' was bestowed on a number of poets in the colonies whose work won no lasting recognition; for example, a reviewer in the *Australasian Chronicle*, 25 January 1848, suggested that Samuel Prout Hill might 'be considered as the "Laureate" of Australia'.

[13] All quotations from G.B. Barton, *The Poets and Prose Writers of New South Wales* (Sydney: Gibbs, Shallard and Co., 1866).

[14] Sladen is the subject of an essay by Chris Tiffin, 'Douglas Sladen as Literary Promoter' in *'And What Books Do You Read?' New Studies in Australian Literature*, ed. by Irmtraud Petersson and Martin Duwell (St Lucia: Queensland University Press, 1996), 38–50. All quotations from *A Century of Australian Song* taken from Douglas B.W. Sladen, *A Century of Australian Song* (London: Walter Scott, 1891).

[15] Brian Elliott, *The Landscape of Australian Poetry* (Melbourne: F.W. Cheshire, 1967), 104.

[16] All quotations from Douglas Sladen, *Australian Poets 1788–1888* (London: Griffith, Farran, Okeden and Walsh, 1888).

[17] All quotations from Desmond Byrne, *Australian Writers* (London: Richard Bentley and Son, 1896).

[18] All quotations from A. Patchett Martin, *The Beginnings of an Australian Literature* (London: Henry Sotheran and Co., 1898).

[19] Compare, for example, Brian Elliott, *The Landscape of Australian Poetry* (Melbourne: F.W. Cheshire, 1967), 184–96, and James McAuley, 'The Rhetoric of Australian Poetry' (1975) in Leonie Kramer ed., *James McAuley. Poetry, Essays and Personal Commentary* (St Lucia: University of Queensland Press, 1988), 110.

[20] See, for example, C.W. Salier's early articles on Harpur and his work in *Southerly*, 4 (1946), 2 (1948), 4 (1948), 1 (1951) and 'The Life and Writings of Charles Harpur', *Journal of the Royal Australian Historical Society*, 32 (1946); Judith Wright, *Charles Harpur* (1963) and *Charles Harpur* (1977); *Charles Harpur* (1973) ed. by Adrian Mitchell; *The Poetical Works of Charles Harpur* (1984) ed. by Elizabeth Perkins; *Charles Harpur: Selected Poetry and Prose* (1986) ed. by Michael Ackland and Ackland's eleven articles on Harpur; see also Michael Ackland, *That Shining Band* (1994). J. Normington Rawling's *Charles Harpur: An Australian* (1962) is a valuable biography.

[21] See, for example, Tom Inglis Moore, *Selected Poems of Henry Kendall* (1957); T.T. Reed, *The Poetical Works of Henry Kendall* (1966); W.H. Wilde, *Henry Kendall* (1976); *Henry Kendall: The Muse of Australia* (1992) ed. by Russell McDougall; Michael Ackland, *Henry Kendall. Poetry, Prose and Selected Correspondence* (1993). Other accounts include Judith Wright in *Preoccupations in Australian Poetry* (1965); Brian Elliott, *The Landscape of Australian Poetry* (1967);

A.D. Hope, *Henry Kendall: A Dialogue with the Past* (1972). *Mapped But Not Known* (1986) ed. by P.R. Eaden and F.H. Mares includes some useful articles on colonial poetry.

22 Frank Maldon Robb, 'Introduction', *Bush Ballads and Galloping Rhymes: Poetical Works of Adam Lindsay Gordon* (orig. *Poems of Adam Lindsay Gordon* ed. with introd., notes and appendices by Frank Maldon Robb (1912). Facsimile edition Rigby (1975) and Seal Book Publication (1995), cxiii. Recent editions include W.H. Wilde, *Adam Lindsay Gordon* (1972) and *Adam Lindsay Gordon* (1973) ed. by Brian Elliott. See also Ian F. McLaren, *Adam Lindsay Gordon: A Comprehensive Bibliography* (1986).

23 Among early accounts of Brennan and his work are A.G. Stephens, *Chris Brennan* (1933); Randolph Hughes, *C.J. Brennan. An Essay in Values* (1934); H.M. Green, *Christopher Brennan* (1939); A.R. Chisholm, *Christopher Brennan: The Man and His Poetry* (1946); and G.A. Wilkes, *New Perspectives on Brennan's Poetry* (1953). Axel Clark published *Christopher Brennan, A Critical Biography* (1980), and numerous critical articles have appeared since 1950, including those by G.A. Wilkes, James McAuley, Judith Wright, Vivian Smith, Annette Stewart, Dennis Douglas, Dorothy Green, Noel Macainsh, and Robert Adamson.

24 See, for example, Laurie Hergenhan, *Unnatural Lives* (1983); Michael Wilding, *Marcus Clarke* (1977); Alan Brissenden, *Rolf Boldrewood* (1972) and Introduction to *Robbery Under Arms* (1968); Bob Hodge and Vijay Mishra, *Dark Side of the Dream* (1990); Robert Dixon, *Writing the Colonial Adventure* (1995).

25 See, for example, Xavier Pons, *Out of Eden: Henry Lawson's Life and Works: A Psychoanalytic View* (1984); Michael Wilding, 'Henry Lawson's Radical Vision', in *Rise of Socialist Fiction 1880–1914* (1987) ed. by G. Klaus; and *The Radical Tradition: Lawson, Furphy and Stead* (1993); Kay Schaffer, 'Henry Lawson: The People's Poet', in *Women and the Bush* (1988) ed. by Susan Sheridan and 'Henry Lawson, the Drover's Wife and the Critics', in *Debutante Nation: Feminism Contests the 1890s* (1993) ed. by Susan Magarey et al.

26 The first issue of *Steele Rudd's Magazine* edited by Rudd appeared in December 1903 and ran until 1907 with revivals under new titles until 1927. A comprehensive study of Rudd's life is found in Richard Fotheringham, *In Search of Steele Rudd* (St Lucia: Queensland University Press, 1995).

27 See, for example, Kay Iseman, 'Barbara Baynton: Woman as "The Chosen Vessel"', *Australian Literary Studies*, 11 (1983), 25–37.

4: LITERATURE AND MELODRAMA

1 Christine Gledhill, 'The Melodramatic Field: An Investigation', in *Home is Where the Heart Is: Studies in Melodrama and the Woman's Film*, ed. by Christine Gledhill (London: British Film Institute, 1987), 5.

2 Michael R. Booth, *English Melodrama* (London: Herbert Jenkins, 1965).

3 *Melodrama: Stage Picture Screen*, ed. by Jacky Bratton et al. (London: British Film Institute, 1994), 8.

4 Ben Singer, cited in Bratton, 4.

5 Peter Brooks, *The Melodramatic Imagination: Balzac, Henry James, Melodrama and the Mode of Excess* (New Haven: Yale University Press, 1976), 5.

6 These articles, beginning with 'In defence of melodrama: towards a libertarian aesthetic',

Australasian Drama Studies, 9 (October 1986), are incorporated in John Docker, *Postmodernism and Popular Culture* (Cambridge: Cambridge University Press, 1994).

[7] John Frow, *Cultural Studies and Cultural Value* (Oxford: Oxford University Press, 1995), 82–7.

[8] Veronica Kelly, 'Female and Juvenile Meanings in Late Nineteenth-Century Australian Popular Theatre', in *The 1890s: Australian Literature and Literary Culture*, ed. by Ken Stewart (St Lucia: University of Queensland Press, 1996), 112–13.

[9] Lawrence W. Levine, *Highbrow/Lowbrow: The Emergence of Cultural Hierarchy in America* (Cambridge, Mass: Harvard University Press, 1988), 184.

[10] Fergus Hume, *Madame Midas* (1888; London: Hogarth Press, 1985), 199.

[11] Richard Waterhouse, 'Popular Culture and Pastimes', in *Under New Heavens: Cultural Transmission and the Making of Australia*, ed. by N.K. Meaney (Melbourne: Heinemann, 1989), 248.

[12] Cited in Levine, 28.

[13] Cited in *The Australian Stage: A Documentary History*, ed. by Harold Love (Kensington: NSW University Press, 1984), 97.

[14] Harold Love, *James Edward Neild: Victorian Virtuoso* (Carlton, Vic: Melbourne University Press, 1989), p. 246.

[15] Cited in Love, *The Australian Stage*, 88–9.

[16] Ken Stewart, 'Theatre, Critics and Society 1850–1890', in *The Australian Stage*, 60. See also Lurline Stuart, *James Smith: The Making of a Colonial Culture* (St Leonards, NSW: Allen and Unwin, 1989).

[17] See David Grimsted, *Melodrama Unveiled: American Theatre and Culture 1800–1850* (Chicago: Chicago University Press, 1968).

[18] Margaret Williams, *Australia on the Popular Stage 1829–1929: An Historical Entertainment in Six Acts* (Melbourne: Oxford University Press, 1983), 266.

[19] *Entertaining Australia: The Performing Arts as Cultural History*, ed. by Katharine Brisbane (Paddington, NSW: Currency Press, 1991), 12.

[20] George Darrell, *The Sunny South*, ed. by Margaret Williams (Paddington, NSW: Currency Press, 1975), Introduction, xii.

[21] *The Sunny South*, 'An Historical Note on the Play', 74.

[22] Cited in Alfred Dampier and Garnet Walch, *Robbery Under Arms*, ed. by Richard Fotheringham (Paddington, NSW: Currency Press, 1985), Introduction, xv.

[23] Citations in Williams, *Australia on the Popular Stage*, 145.

[24] Elizabeth Webby, 'Melodrama', in *The Penguin New Literary History of Australia*, ed. by Laurie Hergenhan (Ringwood, Vic: Penguin, 1988), 213.

[25] See *Editing in Australia*, ed. by Paul Eggert (Canberra: Australian Defence Force Academy, 1990).

[26] Williams, *Australia on the Popular Stage*, 139.

[27] Richard Waterhouse, *From Minstrel Show to Vaudeville: The Australian Popular Stage 1788–1914* (Kensington: NSW University Press, 1990), Introduction.

[28] Kelly, 'Female and Juvenile Meanings', 116.

[29] Typescript, Fryer Library, Brisbane.

[30] Graeme Davison, 'An Urban Context for the Australian Legend', in *Intruders in the Bush: The Australian Quest for Identity*, ed. by John Carroll (Melbourne: Oxford University Press, 1982); and Leigh Astbury, *City Bushmen: The Heidelberg School and the Rural Mythology* (Melbourne: Oxford University Press, 1985).

31 Stewart, *The 1890s*, Introduction, 13.

32 See Richard Fotheringham, *In Search of Steele Rudd* (St Lucia: University of Queensland Press, 1995), 85–6.

33 Bert Bailey, *On Our Selection: A Dramatisation of Steele Rudd's Books*, ed. by Helen Musa (Paddington, NSW: Currency Press, 1984), 95.

34 Elizabeth Morrison, 'Reading Victoria's Newspapers 1838–1901', *Australian Cultural History*, 11 (1992), 128–9.

35 Elizabeth Morrison, 'Cultural Imperialism and Imperial Culture: How the Outreach of British Publishers in the Late Victorian Period Helped Construct an Australian Literary Canon'. Unpublished paper.

36 See Lucy Sussex, ' "Shrouded in Mystery": Waif Wander (Mary Fortune)', in *A Bright and Fiery Troop: Australian Women Writers of the Nineteenth Century*, ed. by Debra Adelaide (Ringwood, Vic: Penguin, 1988), 117–31.

37 Fergus Hume, *The Mystery of a Hansom Cab* (1886; London: Hogarth Press, 1985); and *Madame Midas* (1888; London: Hogarth Press, 1985).

38 Guy Boothby, *A Bid for Fortune: or, Dr Nikola's Vendetta* (1895; Oxford: Oxford University Press, 1996).

39 N. Walter Swan, *Luke Mivers' Harvest*, ed. by Harry Heseltine (Kensington: NSW University Press, 1991), Introduction, xvi.

40 *The Collected Verse of George Essex Evans*, ed. by Firmin McKinnon (Sydney: Angus and Robertson, 1928).

41 See Henry Lawson, *The Bush Undertaker and Other Stories*, ed. by Colin Roderick (Sydney: Angus and Robertson, 1974), 264.

42 C.J. Brennan, *Poems (1913)*, ed. by G.A. Wilkes (1914; Sydney: Sydney University Press, 1972).

43 'Symbolism in Nineteenth-Century Literature', in *The Prose of Christopher Brennan*, ed. by A.R. Chisholm and J.J. Quinn (Sydney: Angus and Robertson, 1962), 288–9.

44 Laura Mulvey, 'Notes on Sirk and Melodrama', in *Home is Where the Heart Is*, ed. Gledhill, 76.

45 Mary Theresa Vidal, *Bengala; Or Some Time Ago*, ed. by Susan McKernan (Kensington: NSW University Press, 1990), Introduction, xx–xxi.

46 *From the Verandah: Stories of Love and Landscape by Nineteenth Century Australian Women*, ed. by Fiona Giles (Fitzroy, Vic: McPhee Gribble/Penguin, 1987).

47 See Susan Sheridan, *Along the Faultlines: Sex, Race and Nation in Australian Women's Writing 1880s–1930s* (St Leonards, NSW: Allen and Unwin, 1995), 41.

48 Tasma, *The Penance of Portia James* (London: Petherick, 1891).

49 Rosa Praed, *The Bond of Wedlock* (1887; London: Pandora, 1987).

50 Cited in Chris Tiffin, *Rosa Praed: A Bibliography 1851–1935* (St Lucia: Department of English, University of Queensland, 1989), 55.

51 See Robert Dixon, *Writing the Colonial Adventure: Gender, Race and Nation in Anglo-Australian Popular Fiction 1875–1914* (Cambridge: Cambridge University Press, 1995), chapter 6.

52 Rosa Praed, *The Brother of the Shadow: A Mystery of To-Day* (1886; New York: Arno Press, 1976).

53 Alex Owen, *The Darkened Room: Women, Power, and Spiritualism in Late Victorian England* (London: Virago, 1989).

54 Tom Gunning, 'The Horror of Opacity: The Melodrama of Sensation in the Plays of Andre de Lorde', in *Melodrama: Stage Picture Screen*, ed. by Bratton et al., 53.

[55] Price Warung (William Astley), *Convict Days* (Sydney: Australasian Book Society, 1960).

[56] Barbara Baynton, *Bush Studies*, ed. by Elizabeth Webby (1902; Pymble, NSW: Angus and Robertson, 1993), 136.

[57] Louis Becke, *By Reef and Palm* and *The Ebbing of the Tide* (1894 and 1896; London: Unwin, 1924), 38.

[58] Norman Lindsay, *The Magic Pudding* (1918; Sydney: Angus and Robertson, 1990).

[59] Cited in Graham Shirley and Brian Adams, *Australian Cinema: the First Eighty Years* (Paddington, NSW: Currency Press, 1989), 12.

[60] Cited in Shirley and Adams, 13.

[61] Cited in Graham Shirley, 'Australian Cinema: 1896 to the renaissance', in *Australian Cinema*, ed. by Scott Murray (St Leonards, NSW: Allen and Unwin, 1994), 6.

[62] Cited in Shirley and Adams, 18.

[63] From the *Bulletin*, 24 July 1913, cited in Shirley and Adams, 32.

[64] Cited in Shirley, 'Australian Cinema: 1896 to the renaissance', 14.

[65] Cited in Shirley and Adams, 57.

[66] Cited in Bert Bailey, *On Our Selection*, Introduction, 63.

5: NATIONAL DRESS OR NATIONAL TROUSERS?

[1] Joseph Furphy, *Such is Life* (1903: Melbourne: Oxford University Press Annotated Edition, 1993), 65. Subsequent quotations are from this edition.

[2] Ellen Augusta Chads (fl. 1880s), 'The Ghost of Wanganilla', in *Tracked by Bushrangers and Other Stories* (Melbourne and Sydney: George Robertson and Co., 1891). Page references are to the version in Fiona Giles, *From the Verandah* (Fitzroy, Vic: McPhee Gribble/Penguin, 1987), 36–43, 38.

[3] Homi K. Bhabha, 'Introduction: Narrating the Nation', in *Nation and Narration*, ed. by Homi K. Bhabha (London and New York: Routledge, 1990), 1.

[4] For example, Anne-Marie Willis, *Illusions of Identity: The Art of Nation* (Sydney: Hale and Iremonger, 1993).

[5] For example, *Debutante Nation: Feminism Contests the 1890s*, ed. by Susan Magarey, Susan Sheridan and Sue Rowley (Sydney: Allen and Unwin, 1993).

[6] Graeme Turner, *Making it National: Nationalism and Australian Popular Culture* (St Leonards, NSW: Allen and Unwin, 1994), 119ff. See also Vijay Mishra and Bob Hodge, *Dark Side of the Dream: Australian Literature and the Postcolonial Mind* (Sydney: Allen and Unwin, 1991).

[7] See Turner, 8; The 'Australian Legend' is a term, and an understanding of Australian nationalism, made famous by Russel Ward in *The Australian Legend* (Melbourne: Oxford University Press, 1958).

[8] Benedict Anderson, *Imagined Communities* (revised edition, NY: Verso, 1991); Turner, 11. See also Patrick Buckridge, 'Nationality and Australian Literature', in *Australian Studies: A Survey* ed. by James Walter (Melbourne: Oxford University Press, 1989), 136–55, and Christopher Lee, 'Man, Work and Country: The Production of Henry Lawson', *Australian Literary Studies*, 15 (May 1992), 110–22.

[9] *Bulletin* (Jan 1880–), initial circulation 3000, rose to about 80 000 during the 1890s: *Bull-Ant* (1890–92), a Melbourne literary weekly, edited by Edward George Dyson; *Worker* (1890–

1974), originated in Brisbane, initially monthly and then weekly—William Lane was its first editor; *Lone Hand* (1907–21), another monthly, initiated by the *Bulletin's* Archibald. Its first edition sold 50 000 in 3 days.

10 Anderson, 24–5.

11 Partha Chatterjee, *Nationalist Thought and the Colonial World: a Derivative Discourse?* (London: Zed, 1986), 5.

12 Elaine Showalter, *Sexual Anarchy: Gender and Culture at the Fin de Siècle* (London: Virago, 1992), 2.

13 Eve Sedgwick, *Epistemology of the Closet* (Berkeley: University of California Press, 1990).

14 For example, *The Rise of Colonial Nationalism*, ed. by D.M. Schreuder, Oliver MacDonagh and J.J. Eddy (Sydney: Allen and Unwin, 1988), 24.

15 See especially Marilyn Lake, 'Toward a Masculinist Context' in *Debutante Nation*, ed. by Magarey et al.; Susan Sheridan, 'Temper Romantic; Bias Offensively Feminist' in *Along the Faultlines: Sex, Race and Nation in Australian Women's Writing—1880s–1930s* (St Leonards, NSW: Allen and Unwin, 1995), 27–35.

16 Lake, 2. Further references to this article are given in the text.

17 See John Docker, *The Nervous Nineties* (Melbourne: Oxford University Press, 1991) and 'Feminist Legend' in Magarey et al.

18 Though much of the 'realism' was also romance as Fiona Giles points out in 'Romance: An Embarrassing Subject', in *Penguin New Literary History of Australia*, ed. by Laurie Hergenhan (Ringwood, Vic: Penguin, 1988), 223.

19 Sheridan, *Along the Faultlines*, 28.

20 Kay Schaffer, *Women and the Bush: Forces of Desire in the Australian Cultural Tradition* (Cambridge: Cambridge University Press, 1988).

21 Docker, 'Feminist Legend', 21; Chris Lee, 'Looking for Mr Backbone: The Politics of Gender in the Work of Henry Lawson', in *The 1890s: Australian Literature and Literary Culture*, ed. by Ken Stewart (St Lucia: University of Queensland Press, 1996), 95–108.

22 Sheridan, *Along the Faultlines*, 29.

23 Leonie Foster, *High Hopes: The Men and Motives of the Australian Round Table* (Melbourne: Melbourne University Press/The Australian Institute of International Affairs, 1986), 4.

24 Where two figures appear in brackets the first refers to serialisation date, and the second to monograph publication.

25 See Richard White, *Inventing Australia: Images and Identity 1688–1980* (Sydney: Allen and Unwin, 1981), 63–84.

26 Serialised *Sydney Mail* 1882–83; appeared in book form 1888; as a one-volume edition 1889; reprinted over 30 times in the next 50 years and staged in the 1890s.

27 See Patrick Brantlinger, 'Nations and Novels: Disraeli, George Eliot, and Orientalism', *Victorian Studies* 35 (Spring 1992), 255–75.

28 White, 73–5; Willis; Schreuder et al.

29 *Henry Lawson: Portable Australian Authors*, ed. by Brian Kiernan (St Lucia: University of Queensland Press, 1976), 111.

30 See, for example, Ross Gibson, *The Diminishing Paradise* (Sydney: Angus and Robertson, 1984); Coral Lansbury, *Arcady in Australia* (Carlton, Vic: Melbourne University Press, 1970); Alan Frost, 'What Created, What Perceived: Early Responses to New South Wales', *Australian*

Literary Studies 7 (1975), 185–205; David Goodman, *Gold Seeking* (St Leonards, NSW: Allen and Unwin, 1995).

[31] Henry Lawson, *Prose Works of Henry Lawson* (Sydney: Angus and Robertson, 1976 [1948]), 6–9.

[32] This has much in common with various other of Lawson's representations of Selection life, as in 'The City Bushman' (1892) and 'Water them Geraniums' from *Joe Wilson and His Mates* (Sydney and Melbourne: Angus and Robertson, 1902).

[33] For example, 'The Heart-Breaking of Anstey's Bess' (1894).

[34] *On Our Selection* (Sydney: Bulletin Co., 1899).

[35] Sally Krimmer and Alan Lawson, 'Introduction' in Barbara Baynton, *Bush Studies, Other Stories, Human Toll, Verse, Essays and Letters*, Australian Authors Series (St Lucia: University of Queensland Press, 1980); A.A. Phillips, *The Australian Tradition* (Melbourne: F.W. Cheshire, 1958).

[36] For example, Schaffer.

[37] A version of 'The Chosen Vessel' was published as 'The Tramp' in the 12 December 1896 edition of the *Bulletin*. Poetry published there is listed in Krimmer and Lawson, 334.

[38] It is notable that even White automatically associates these women writers with an older, more conservative generation—the five years dividing Archibald and Tom Roberts in age from Rosa Praed must have been remarkably important ones (86–7).

[39] See Audrey Tate, *Ada Cambridge: Her Life and Work 1844–1926* (Carlton, Vic: Melbourne University Press, 1991); Margaret Bradstock and Louise Wakeling, *Rattling the Orthodoxies: A Life of Ada Cambridge* (Ringwood, Vic: Penguin, 1991).

[40] 'A Girl's Ideal', serialised *Age* 1881–82, reprinted in *The Penguin Anthology of Australian Women's Writing*, ed. by Dale Spender (Ringwood, Vic: Penguin, 1988), 155–284 (page references are to this edition); *Sisters* (1904; Ringwood, Vic: Penguin, 1989); *The Three Miss Kings*, serialised *Australasian* 1883 (London: Virago, 1987); *A Woman's Friendship*, serialised *Age* 1889 (Kensington: University of New South Wales Press, 1988). 'The Bush Undertaker' was published in the *Antipodean* (1892) and 'The Drover's Wife' in the *Bulletin*, 23 July 1892.

[41] Ada Cambridge, *A Humble Enterprise*, serialised as 'The Charm that Works', *Australasian* 1891 (London: Ward, Lock, 1896); 'A Sweet Day' in *At Midnight and Other Stories* (London, Melbourne: Ward, Lock, 1897), reprinted Giles, *From the Verandah*, 91–104.

[42] See Giles, 'Romance, an Embarrassing Subject', 225.

[43] Henry Lawson, *Joe Wilson and His Mates* (Sydney and Melbourne: Angus and Robertson, 1902); page references are to *Henry Lawson: Portable Australian Authors*, ed. by Brian Kiernan.

[44] 'Homosocial negotiations', in Sedgwick's formulation.

[45] See Christopher Lee's argument in 'Looking for Mr Backbone'.

[46] Henry Lawson, 'Preface' to *My Brilliant Career* (1901; Sydney: Angus and Robertson, 1986), n.p.

[47] See also Giles, 'Romance, an Embarrassing Subject'.

[48] Susan K. Martin, 'Relative Correspondence' in *The Time to Write*, ed. by Kay Ferres (Ringwood, Vic: Penguin, 1993) 54–70.

[49] See, for example, Joy Hooton, 'Mary Fullerton: Pioneering and Feminism' in *The Time to Write*, 38–53, 48.

[50] Furphy's critique of unrealistic female romance writing (which is European rather than Australian in subject matter) was edited out of *Such is Life* and published much later. See Tom Collins [Joseph Furphy], *The Buln-Buln and the Brolga* (Sydney: Angus and Robertson, 1948).

6: Literary Culture 1914–1939

[1] Kylie Tennant, *Foveaux* (London: Victor Gollancz, 1938), chapter VI, 91–2. Further page references within the text are to this edition. First Australian edition, Sydney: Angus and Robertson, 1946; later editions 1969 and 1981.

[2] The original *Book Lover* title becomes 'To God: From the Warring Nations' in Maurice's 1920 collection *The Eyes of Vigilance*.

[3] Written in 1939, 'Australia' was first published in *Meanjin*, 2 (1943), 42.

[4] First published 1981 as *The Bread of Things to Come*.

[5] *The Poems of Lesbia Harford*, ed. by Drusilla Modjeska and Marjorie Pizer (North Ryde: Sirius Books, Angus and Robertson, 1985). Pizer had earlier worked with Nettie Palmer on the latter's selected edition, *The Poems of Lesbia Harford* (Melbourne: Melbourne University Press, 1941).

[6] The finding of the manuscript is described by Richard Nile and Robert Darby in the 'Introduction' to their 1987 McPhee Gribble/Penguin edition.

[7] 'After the Battle', *Bulletin*, 23 January 1919, 3.

[8] Published in the *Bulletin* in 1917 on the anniversary of Gallipoli, 'The Mother' remained uncollected until *Under the Wilgas* (1931), when it was included under the title 'War', the last two lines reading 'Flies in his mouth,/Ants in his eyes'. 'The Woman of Five Fields' was published on Anzac Day (1927) in the *Daily Telegraph*.

[9] T.S. Eliot, *Four Quartets* (London: Faber and Faber, 1944), 21.

[10] See *Ballades of Old Bohemia: An Anthology of Louis Esson*, ed. by Hugh Anderson (Ascot Vale, Vic: Red Rooster Press, 1980), 136.

[11] See, for instance, *Letters of Vance and Nettie Palmer 1915–1963*, sel. and ed. by Vivian Smith (Canberra: National Library of Australia, 1977); *Letters of Mary Gilmore*, sel. and ed. by W.H. Wilde and T. Inglis Moore (Carlton: Melbourne University Press, 1980); *As Good as a Yarn with You: Letters Between Miles Franklin, Katharine Susannah Prichard, Jean Devanny, Marjorie Barnard, Flora Eldershaw and Eleanor Dark*, ed. by Carole Ferrier (Cambridge and Oakleigh, Vic.: Cambridge University Press, 1992); *My Congenials: Miles Franklin and Friends in Letters*, ed. by Jill Roe, 2 vols (Pymble: Collins/Angus and Robertson, 1993).

[12] *Letters of Mary Gilmore*, 138.

[13] On this topic see Patrick Buckridge, ' "Greatness" and Australian Literature in the 1930s and 1940s: Novels by Dark and Barnard Eldershaw', *Australian Literary Studies*, 17 (1995), 29–37.

[14] For further discussion see Carole Ferrier, *Gender, Politics and Fiction: Twentieth Century Australian Women's Novels* (St Lucia: University of Queensland Press, 1985; 2nd edn 1992).

[15] 'The Poor, Poor Country', in *John Shaw Neilson: Poetry, Autobiography and Correspondence*, ed. by Cliff Hanna (St Lucia: University of Queensland Press, 1991), 118–19.

[16] His champions included Gilmore, who published him in the *Worker*; R.H. Croll, editor of *Collected Poems* (1929); James Devaney, editor of *Unpublished Poems* (1947); Vincent Buckley, who included him in his 1950s Commonwealth Literary Fund Lectures; and Judith Wright, editor of *Witnesses of Spring: Unpublished Poems of John Shaw Neilson* (1970).

[17] See, for instance, the verdict of Judith Wright in the *Jindyworobak Review* (1948), 72–3, and W.N. Scott, *Focus on Judith Wright* (St Lucia: University of Queensland Press, 1967), 52. Brian Elliott's *The Jindyworobaks* (1979) provides a critical introduction to a selection of Jindyworobak texts.

[18] In 'The Prodigal Son', *Australian Letters* 1, 3 (1958), 39.

[19] See Vance Palmer, *Louis Esson and the Australian Theatre* (Melbourne: Georgian House, 1948); a more recent and comprehensive account is Peter Fitzpatrick, *Pioneer Players: The Lives of Louis and Hilda Esson* (Cambridge: Cambridge University Press, 1995).

[20] May Gibbs (1877–1969) published with Angus and Robertson. *Snugglepot and Cuddlepie* (1918), *Little Ragged Blossom* (1920), and *Little Obelia* (1921) were combined in *The Complete Adventures of Snugglepot and Cuddlepie* (1942). Ida Rentoul Outhwaite (1888–1960) published numerous books between *Mollie's Bunyip* (1904) and *Nursery Rhymes* (1948), the best-known being *Elves and Fairies* (Melbourne: Lothian House, 1916).

[21] *The Annals of Australian Literature*, 2nd edn, ed. by Joy Hooton and Harry Heseltine (Melbourne: Oxford University Press, 1992); 1st edn ed. by Grahame Johnston, 1970. Further evidence of a growing book trade is in the 1921 initiation of D.W. Thorpe's *Australasian Stationery and Fancy Goods Journal*, which became, after several changed titles, the present *Australian Bookseller and Publisher*.

[22] See Richard Nile and David Walker, 'Marketing the Literary Imagination: Production of Australian Literature, 1915–1965', in *The Penguin New Literary History of Australia*, ed. by Laurie Hergenhan (Ringwood, Vic: Penguin Books, 1988), 286.

[23] Examples of short-lived journals are *Red Ant* (1912), *Birth* (1916–22), *Vision* (1923–24), *The Spinner* (1924–27), *Bohemia* (series one 1939–40).

[24] See, for example, Mary Gilmore in an undated letter to Hugh McCrae: 'Did you know that my only two books of verse (till *Selected Verse*) that I did not have to pay for myself are *Marri'd* and *The Passionate Heart*' (ADFA MS G137 Box 1, Folder 2). *Selected Verse* was subsidised by the CLF.

[25] So called from the title of Craig Munro's *Wild Man of Letters: The Story of P.R. Stephensen* (Carlton: Melbourne University Press, 1984).

[26] Stephensen's work in fact greatly influenced the foundation document of the Jindyworobaks, Rex Ingamells and Ian Tilbrook's *Conditional Culture* (Adelaide: F.W. Preece, 1938).

[27] See Bruce Muirden, *The Puzzled Patriots: The Story of the Australia First Movement*, amended edn (Carlton: Melbourne University Press, 1968).

[28] For details of the FAW, see Len Fox, *Dream at a Graveside: The History of the Fellowship of Australian Writers* (Sydney: Fellowship of Australian Writers, 1989).

[29] For an account of the Palmers and their circle see David Walker, *Dream and Disillusion: A Search for Australian Cultural Identity* (Canberra: Australian National University Press, 1976).

[30] Nettie Palmer's *Henry Handel Richardson: A Study* (Sydney: Angus and Robertson, 1950) is the earliest full-scale discussion of Richardson.

[31] Historical evidence shows rural industries as retaining economic dominance in the 1920s, even though growth in the workforce (hence demographic growth) was taking place in the non-rural sector; in the 1930s manufacturing overtook rural industries as a proportion of Gross Domestic Product (GDP). See Stuart Macintyre, *1901–40: The Succeeding Age*, vol. 4 of *The Oxford History of Australia* (Melbourne: Oxford University Press, 1986), 202–4, 287.

[32] Apart from Franklin's *My Brilliant Career*, see Gilmore's 'Then She Turned and Rode Away', in *Old Days, Old Ways* (Sydney: Angus and Robertson, 1934) or Richard Glover's interview with Judith Wright, 'World Without Words', *Good Weekend: The Age Magazine*, 26 June 1993, 38–9.

[33] Ion L. Idriess, *Flynn of the Inland* (Sydney: Angus and Robertson, 1932), 6.

[34] Xavier Herbert, *Capricornia*, 8th edn (Sydney: Angus and Robertson, 1947), 3.

35 See, for instance, Julie Wells, 'The Writers' League: A Study in Literary and Working-class Politics', *Meanjin*, 4 (1987), 529.

36 For Kisch's own account, see *Australian Landfall*, trans. John Fisher et al. (South Melbourne: Macmillan, 1969).

37 See, for instance, Jack Beasley, *Socialism and the Novel: A Study of Australian Literature* (1957) and *Red Letter Days: Notes from Inside an Era* (1979); Judah Waten, 'Socialist Realism—An Important Trend in Present Day Australian Literature', *Communist Review* (May 1960), 204–7.

38 Cited by Wells, 529.

39 Cited in Drusilla Modjeska, *Exiles at Home: Australian Women Writers 1925–1945* (Sydney: Sirius/Angus and Robertson, 1981), 139.

40 *All That Swagger* (Sydney: Angus and Robertson, 1936). Quotations from the Angus and Robertson Arkon paperback edn, 1979.

41 Edward W. Said, *Culture and Imperialism*, Vintage edn (London: Chatto and Windus, 1994), 84.

42 Nettie Palmer, *Fourteen Years: Extracts from a Private Journal 1925–1939* (Melbourne: The Meanjin Press, 1948), 30–1.

43 Cited in Clive Probyn, 'Succeeding by Letter: Henry Handel Richardson and "this Australia business"', in *From a Distance: Australian Writers and Cultural Displacement*, ed. by Wenche Ommundsen and Hazel Rowley (Geelong: Deakin University Press, 1996), 37.

44 Some examples of the substantial critical discussion accorded Richardson after Palmer's 1950 study are: Dorothy Green, *Ulysses Bound: Henry Handel Richardson and Her Fiction* (Canberra: Australian National University Press, 1973)—revised as *Henry Handel Richardson and Her Fiction* (Sydney: Allen and Unwin, 1986); Dennis Douglas, *Henry Handel Richardson's Maurice Guest* (Port Melbourne: Edward Arnold (Australia), 1978); Axel Clark, *Henry Handel Richardson: Fiction in the Making* (Brookvale, New South Wales: Simon and Schuster Australia, 1990); Michael Ackland, *Henry Handel Richardson* (Melbourne: Oxford University Press, 1996). Monographs on Herbert include Harry Heseltine, *Xavier Herbert* (Melbourne: Oxford University Press, 1973); Laurie Clancy, *Xavier Herbert* (Boston: Twayne, 1981); *Xavier Herbert's Capricornia and Poor Fellow My Country*, ed. by John McLaren (Melbourne: Shillington House, 1981).

7: LITERARY DEMOCRACY AND THE POLITICS OF REPUTATION

1 Ian Turner, 'The Social Setting', in *The Literature of Australia*, ed. by Geoffrey Dutton (Ringwood, Vic: Penguin Books, 1964), 51.

2 W.K. Hancock, *Australia* (1930; Brisbane: Jacaranda, 1961), 262.

3 C. Hartley Grattan, *Australian Literature* (Seattle and Washington: University of Washington Bookstore, 1929), 13.

4 H.M. Green, *Australian Literature* (Sydney: Sydney and Melbourne Publishing Company, 1928), *An Outline of Australian Literature* (Sydney: Whitcombe and Tombs, 1930), *A History of Australian Literature* (Sydney: Angus and Robertson, 1961).

5 Chris Wallace-Crabbe, *Melbourne or the Bush* (Sydney: Angus and Robertson, 1974), 51.

6 George Robertson, evidence to Tariff Board Enquiry, 'Proposal on Books, Magazines and Fashion Plates', Sydney 1930, 37.

[7] Somerset Maugham to A.G. Stephens, cited in *Home*, 1 September 1921, 7.

[8] Nettie Palmer to Vance Palmer, 5 April 1919, Palmer Papers, Australian National Library 1174/1/2100–2.

[9] Vance Palmer, 'Fiction for Export', *Bulletin*, 1 June 1922, 2.

[10] Nettie Palmer, *Modern Australian Literature* (first published 1924) in *Nettie Palmer: Her Private Journal* Fourteen Years, *Poems, Reviews and Literary Essays,* ed. by Vivian Smith (St Lucia: University of Queensland Press, 1988), 330.

[11] *Times Literary Supplement*, 16 December 1926.

[12] Katharine Susannah Prichard to Nettie Palmer, 13 June 1927. In a follow-up letter, 15 September 1928, Prichard claimed that she made less money from *Working Bullocks* than any of her previously published novels. National Library of Australia MSS 1174/1/2669 and /2975–8.

[13] Nettie Palmer to Leslie Rees, 10 March 1934, cited in *Letters of Vance and Nettie Palmer*, ed. by Vivian Smith (Canberra: National Library of Australia, 1977), 104.

[14] Nettie Palmer to Frank Dalby Davison, 31 October 1933, Davison Papers, National Library of Australia, MS 1945.

[15] George Robertson to Louis Esson, 3 September 1928, cited in *Dear Robertson*, ed. by A.W. Barker (Sydney: Angus and Robertson, 1982), 147.

[16] Nettie Palmer to Frank Dalby Davison, 31 October 1933, Davison Papers, National Library of Australia, MS 1945.

[17] A.W. Barker, *One of the First and One of the Finest: Beatrice Davis, Book Editor* (Carlton, Vic: The Society of Editors (Vic), 1991), 10.

[18] Vance Palmer interview, 'Vance Palmer and the Australian Novel', *All About Books*, 19 April 1939, 87–8.

[19] Richard Fotheringham, *In Search of Steele Rudd* (St Lucia: University of Queensland Press, 1994), 137–9.

[20] In this they were aided after 1917 by the ascendancy of bolshevism which actively promoted intellectuals to the vanguard of the revolution as leaders of the masses against capitalism.

[21] Katharine Susannah Prichard to Nettie Palmer, 14 November 1929 (?), Palmer Papers, NLA MS 1174/1/3393.

[22] Katharine Susannah Prichard to Vance Palmer, 4 October 1928, NLA MS 1174/1/2679–80.

[23] Kenneth Slessor, 'Dialect', *Bulletin*, 8 January 1920, 3.

[24] Kenneth Slessor, 'Poetic Licence', *Bulletin*, 24 July 1919, 24.

[25] Letter to the *Bulletin*, 17 July 1919, 3.

[26] Harry C. Douglas, 'Can we write Short Stories?', *Bulletin*, 7 August 1919, 3.

[27] J.A. Hetherington, 'An Attack on Post-War Short Story Writers', *All About Books*, 18 July 1929, 244.

[28] 'Obituary: Playwright', *Bulletin*, 14 April 1921, 25.

[29] See David Walker, *Dream and Disillusion* (Canberra: Australian National University Press, 1976), 139–40.

[30] Beatrice Tildesley, 'The Australian Theatre', *Bulletin*, 7 January 1926, 2.

[31] T. Inglis Moore, submission to the Commonwealth Literary Fund, 5 September 1938, Advisory Board Minutes 1939–1950. Australian Archives CRS A3753, Item 72/2766.

[32] Leslie Rees, *The Making of Australian Drama, A Historical and Critical Survey from the 1830s to the 1970s* (Sydney: Angus and Robertson, 1973). Appendix II: A Selection of Australian Radio

Plays, Written Directly for the Medium and produced by the A.B.C. since 1935. See also K.S. Inglis, *This is the ABC: The Australian Broadcasting Commission 1932–1983* (Carlton, Vic: Melbourne University Press, 1983).

33 A. Thomas, *Broadcast and be Damned: the ABC's First Two Decades* (Carlton, Vic: Melbourne University Press, 1980), 10.

34 *Australian Writers' and Artists' Market* (Melbourne: Australian School of Journalism, nd), 167–8. See also C.F. Ringstat and W.E. Fitzhenry, *The Australian and New Zealand Writers' and Artists' Handbook* (Sydney: W.E. Fitzhenry, 1928) and *The Australian Authors' Handbook*, ed. by W.E. Fitzhenry (Sydney: W.E. Fitzhenry, 1937 and 1938).

35 Reported in *All About Books*, May 1936, 70.

36 J.K. Ewers, *Creative Writing in Australia* (Melbourne: Georgian House, 1945), 78.

37 Nettie Palmer to Leslie Rees, 10 March 1934, cited in *Letters of Vance and Nettie Palmer*, 104.

38 Miles Franklin to W.G. Cousins, 29 December 1933, Angus and Robertson Papers, ML MSS 3269.

39 Beverley Eley, *Ion Idriess* (Potts Point, NSW: Editions Tom Thompson, 1995), 270–1.

40 Diary entry, 9 March 1931, cited in Vivian Smith, *Nettie Palmer: Her Private Journal* Fourteen Years, *Poems and Literary Essays*, 65.

41 George Robertson to Vance Marshall, 6 May 1923, Angus and Robertson Papers, ML MSS 314.

42 Eley, *Ion Idriess*, 289.

43 Idriess figures cited in M.R. Bonnin, 'A Study of Australian Descriptive and Travel Writing', PhD thesis, University of Queensland, 1980, 397–406; Palmer figures in Walker, *Dream and Disillusion*, 217.

44 Tom Inglis Moore to Department of Interior, 5 September 1938, Australian Archives, CRS A344/1/17835.

45 Marjorie Barnard to Nettie Palmer, 8 October 1935, Palmer Papers, NLA MS 1174/1/4793–4.

46 Katharine Susannah Prichard to William Hatfield, 17 August 1932, Angus and Robertson Papers, ML MSS 3269.

47 *Australian Writers' and Artists' Market*, 13.

48 E.V. Timms to W.G. Cousins, 3 June 1930, Angus and Robertson Papers, ML MSS 3269.

49 Reader's Report, 'The Honeymoon Inn', 16 April 1931, Angus and Robertson Papers, ML MSS 3269.

50 Richard Sommerville to Angus and Robertson, 15 July 1931, Angus and Robertson Papers, ML MSS 3269.

51 Unmarked feature article, in Stephensen Papers, Fryer Library, MSS coll 55/12–55/23, Box 2.

52 Lennie Lower, intr. by Cyril Pearl, *Here's Lower* (Sydney: Hale and Iremonger, 1986), 8–9.

53 Quoted in Richard Nile, 'Cartels, Capitalism and the Australian Booktrade', *The Media of Publishing, an Issue of Continuum: An Australian Journal*, 4, 1 (1990), 71–91.

54 Nettie Palmer to Esther Levy, cited in *Letters of Vance and Nettie Palmer*, 40.

55 *All About Books*, 15 February 1932, 27.

56 Reported in *All About Books*, 7 July 1937, 234.

57 Nile, 71–91.

58 Martyn Lyons and Lucy Taksa, *Australian Readers Remember* (Melbourne: Oxford University Press, 1992).

[59] *Argus* competition reported in David Walker, 'Writer and Community', PhD thesis, ANU 1972, 280–2. Sydney Municipal Library, *Annual Report*, 1928. See also R. Munn and E.R. Pitt, *Australian Libraries* (Melbourne: 1935).

[60] F.L. Preece to Davison, undated correspondence, Davison Papers, NLA MS 1945/1/32–5.

[61] *All About Books*, 12 April 1935, 63–4.

[62] ibid., 137, 135.

[63] Cited in Ray. B. Brown, *The Spirit of Australia: the Crime Fiction of Arthur W. Upfield* (Bowling Green, Ohio: Bowling Green State University Popular Press, 1988), 136.

[64] Vance Palmer, *The Legend of the Nineties* (Carlton, Vic: Melbourne University Press, 1954), 167–73.

8: NATIONAL MYTHS OF MANHOOD

[1] Richard White, *Inventing Australia: Images and Identity 1688–1980* (Sydney: George Allen and Unwin, 1981), 125.

[2] Shirley Walker, 'The Boer War: Paterson, Abbott, Brennan, Miles Franklin and Morant', *Australian Literary Studies*, 12 (1985), 207–22.

[3] J.H.M. Abbott, *Tommy Cornstalk* (London: Longmans, Green and Co., 1902), 1–13.

[4] Kay Schaffer, *Women and the Bush* (Cambridge: Cambridge University Press, 1988); Robert Dixon, *Writing the Colonial Adventure* (Melbourne: Cambridge University Press, 1995).

[5] E.M. Andrews, *The Anzac Illusion* (Melbourne: Cambridge University Press, 1993).

[6] I am using the word 'British' here to denote people born within England, Scotland, Wales, and Northern Ireland. In the period with which this chapter deals, however, the words 'British' and 'Briton' were often used to describe white Canadians, Australians and South Africans, thereby linguistically enacting an Imperialism which wished to keep the emerging nations subservient to Great Britain.

[7] Cited in Robin Gerster, *Big-noting: The Heroic Theme in Australian War Writing* (Carlton, Vic: Melbourne University Press, 1987), 25.

[8] Ellis Ashmead-Bartlett, *Despatches from The Dardanelles* (London: Newnes, 1915), 64–5, 70–1, 77.

[9] *Age*, 15 May 1915, 10.

[10] Gerster, 25.

[11] There are no precise sales figures available for these two novelists. It is known that to July 1927 Mary Grant Bruce's total sales were 254 570 and that total sales of all her books are likely to be over the two million mark. Ethel Turner was her competitor at Ward Lock and Co. and certainly her early books were as popular, if not more popular than her rivals. See Brenda Niall, *Seven Little Billabongs: The World of Ethel Turner and Mary Grant Bruce* (Carlton, Vic: Melbourne University Press, 1979), passim.

[12] Dixon, 199.

[13] David Kent, '*The Anzac Book* and the Anzac legend: C.E.W. Bean as Editor and Image-Maker', *Historical Studies*, 21 (1985), 378.

[14] Gerster, 15.

[15] 'Anzac Types', *The Anzac Book* (London: Cassell, 1916; South Melbourne: Sun Books, 1975), 45–8.

[16] G.E. McPhee, 'The Anzac legend: A study of the role of literature in the creation and evolution

of the Anzac legend' (unpublished Honours thesis, University College of NSW, 1995) points out that this text was first published in October 1915 and reprinted four times to January 1916. Since it pre-dates the publication of *The Anzac Book*, McPhee suggests the possibility that this was a more important text in the evolution of the Anzac legend than has previously been recognised.

[17] E.C. Buley, *A Child's History of Anzac* (London: Hodder and Stoughton, 1916), 18.

[18] Mary Grant Bruce, *Captain Jim* (London: Ward, Lock and Co., 1919; Pymble: Angus and Robertson, 1992), 1–11, 182.

[19] Barbara Baynton, 'The Australian Soldier', *The Portable Barbara Baynton*, ed. by S. Krimmer and A. Lawson (St. Lucia: University of Queensland Press, 1980), 323–8.

[20] Gladys Hain, *The Cooee Contingent* (Melbourne: Cassell, 1917), 34–9, 57–62, 63–8, 114–18.

[21] Hain, 119–25.

[22] Oliver Hogue, *Love Letters of an Anzac* (London: Melrose, 1916), 9–13, 42–3, 139, 218.

[23] John Bristow, *Empire Boys* (London: Harper Collins, 1991), 69–70.

[24] Gerster, 63.

[25] Over 104 000 copies of the *Anzac Book* were sold by 1916 (see Andrews, 62). White, 132, remarks that '*The Moods of Ginger Mick* sold twice as well as the *Official History*'. A. Thomson, *Anzac Memories* (Oxford: Oxford University Press, 1994), 153–4, discusses the fluctuating sales of the *Official History* and remarks that by 1942 most volumes had been reprinted many times over and total sales exceeded 150 000 copies.

[26] Andrews, 62.

[27] C.E.W. Bean, *The Story of Anzac* (Sydney: Angus and Robertson, 1921; St Lucia: University of Queensland Press, 1981), 1–17, 46–8, 127, 605–7.

[28] Jane Ross, *The Myth of the Digger* (Sydney: Hale and Iremonger, 1985), 64. Ross provides a very useful discussion of the complex question of 'egalitarianism' within the AIF, 56–71.

[29] See G. Dawson, *Soldier Heroes: British Adventure, Empire and the Imagining of Masculinities* (London: Routledge, 1994).

[30] Bean, 7, 15.

[31] Gerster, 91–3.

[32] E. Morris Miller, *Australian Literature*, vol. I., 1938 (Sydney: Sydney University Press, 1973), 183; Gerster, 93; Brian Elliott, *Singing to the Cattle* (Melbourne: Georgian House, 1947), 129.

[33] The name 'Donald Black' decorates the spine of the book, while J.L. Grey is on the title page. John Lyons Gray is the author's 'proper' name.

[34] D. Black, *Red Dust* (London: Jonathan Cape, 1931), 62–3.

[35] Black, 296–9.

[36] Joseph Maxwell, *Hell's Bells and Mademoiselles* (Sydney: Angus and Robertson, 1932, 1941), 3, 10; Leonard Mann, *Flesh in Armour* (Melbourne: Phaedrus, 1932, 1985), 7.

[37] Maxwell, 1–10, 23, 35–6, 88–9, 131–2, 170, 253.

[38] Black, 164.

[39] Maxwell, 58.

[40] G.D. Mitchell, *Backs to the Wall* (Sydney: Angus and Robertson, 1937), 158.

[41] E.M. Forster, 'A Master of Irony', *Daily Telegraph*, 16 December 1930.

[42] *The Middle Parts of Fortune* was first published privately and anonymously in London in 1929. An expurgated version for general circulation appeared in 1930 under the title *Her Privates We*. Since then unexpurgated editions have appeared under both titles.

[43] I am thinking here of Edmund Blunden, *Undertones of War* (London: Cobden Sanderson, 1928); Robert Graves, *Goodbye to All That* (London: Jonathan Cape, 1929); Richard Aldington, *Death of a Hero* (London: Chatto and Windus, 1929); Siegfried Sassoon, *Memoirs of a Fox-Hunting Man* (London: Faber, 1928) and *Memoirs of an Infantry Officer* (London: Faber, 1930).

[44] Verna Coleman, *The Last Exquisite: A Portrait of Frederic Manning* (Carlton, Vic: Melbourne University Press, 1990), 4, 125 and passim.

[45] Peter Kirkpatrick, *The Sea Coast of Bohemia* (St Lucia: University of Queensland Press, 1992), 85.

[46] Manning Clark, *A Short History of Australia* (London: Heinemann [1964], 1973), 217.

[47] Alistair Thomson, *Anzac Memories* (Oxford: Oxford University Press, 1994), 118–56.

[48] George Blaikie, *Remember Smith's Weekly* (Adelaide: Rigby, 1966).

[49] Beverley Eley, *Ion Idriess* (Potts Point, NSW: Editions Tom Thompson, 1995), 122.

[50] Craig Munro, *Wild Man of Letters: The Story of P.R. Stephensen* (Carlton, Vic: Melbourne University Press, 1984), 172.

[51] Tim Bonyhady, *Burke and Wills: from Melbourne to Myth* (Balmain: David Ell Press, 1991), 273.

[52] Bonyhady, 295.

[53] Eley, 141, 144, 155.

[54] Adam Shoemaker, *Black Words White Page: Aboriginal Literature 1929–1988* (St Lucia: University of Queensland Press, 1989), 54.

[55] Munro, 53, 47.

[56] P.R. Stephensen, *The Foundations of Culture in Australia* (Gordon, NSW: W.J. Miles, 1936), 11. Further references are given after quotations in the text.

[57] Munro, 138–9; Stephensen, 57, 65.

[58] D.H. Lawrence, *Kangaroo* (London: Martin Secker, 1923; Harmondsworth: Penguin, 1972), 87.

[59] Xavier Herbert, *Capricornia* (Sydney: The Publicist, [1938], 1981), 294, 321.

[60] Robert Sellick, 'The Jindyworobaks and Aboriginality', *Southwords: Essays on South Australian Writing*, ed. by Philip Butterss (Adelaide: The Wakefield Press, 1995), 114.

[61] W.B. Spencer and F.J. Gillen, *The Arunta* (London: Macmillan, 1927) is a revised and condensed edition of their *The Native Tribes of Central Australia* (London: Macmillan, 1899).

[62] Brian Elliott (ed.), *The Jindyworobaks* (St Lucia: University of Queensland Press, 1979), xxiii–xxxvii.

[63] Rex Ingamells, *Conditional Culture* (Adelaide: F.W. Preece, 1938) quoted in Elliott, xxvii.

[64] Sellick, 107–14.

[65] Ibid.

[66] A.D. Hope, *Southerly*, 2 (1941), reprinted in Elliott, 248–52.

[67] Written in 1939 and part-published in the *Bulletin* in that year. It was first performed in 1941.

[68] Produced as a radio play in 1942, and published in 1943. It was subsequently staged many times.

9: CLEARING A SPACE FOR AUSTRALIAN LITERATURE

[1] *Daily Telegraph* (Sydney), 15 November 1942, 21. Greenlees did in fact go on to make a name for himself as a poet, but may have been better known for his close association with Rosaleen Norton, 'The Witch of King's Cross', and the scandal surrounding Eugene Goossens some ten years later.

[2] This definition is a convenient amalgam of those given by Peter L. Berger, *Invitation to Sociology: A Humanistic Perspective* (Harmondsworth, Middlesex: Penguin, 1977), 104, and Cora V. Baldock, *Australia and Social Change Theory* (Hunter's Hill, NSW: Ian Novak, 1978), 107.

[3] See Drusilla Modjeska, *Exiles at Home* (North Ryde, NSW: Angus and Robertson, 1981).

[4] Donald Horne, *Confessions of a New Boy* (Ringwood, Vic: Penguin, 1985); Geoffrey Dutton, *Out in the Open: An Autobiography* (St Lucia: University of Queensland Press, 1994).

[5] See Michael Heyward, *The Ern Malley Affair* (St Lucia: University of Queensland Press, 1993).

[6] The books included *Active Service* (1941), published by the Second AIF; *Soldiering On* (1942), *Khaki and Green* (1943) and *Jungle Warfare* (1944), published by the Australian Military Forces; and *On Guard* (1944), by the Volunteer Defence Corps. There were also six companion volumes published by the Royal Australian Navy and the Royal Australian Air Force, 1942–44.

[7] For a fuller discussion of the affair, see Patrick Buckridge, *The Scandalous Penton* (St Lucia: University of Queensland Press, 1994), 295–9.

[8] Buckridge, 240–5.

[9] A.A. Phillips, 'Henry Lawson as Craftsman', in his *The Australian Tradition*, 2nd edn (Melbourne: Longman Cheshire, 1980).

[10] Heyward, 182–212.

[11] Peter Coleman, *Obscenity, Blasphemy, Sedition: 100 Years of Censorship in Australia* (Brisbane: Jacaranda Press, 1962), Prologue. Further references given as page numbers in the text.

[12] Judith Brett, 'Publishing, Censorship, and Writers' Incomes', in *The Penguin New Literary History of Australia*, gen. ed. L.T. Hergenhan (Ringwood, Vic: Penguin, 1988), 456.

[13] Max Harris, 'A Terror of Words', in *Australia's Censorship Crisis*, ed. by Geoffrey Dutton and Max Harris (Melbourne: Sun Books, 1970), 119–20.

[14] *Oxford English Dictionary*, 3rd ed. 1974. See also John McLaren, *Writing in Hope and Fear: Literature as Politics in Postwar Australia* (Melbourne: Cambridge University Press, 1996), Chapter 1.

[15] McLaren, 8.

[16] *Meanjin* 4 (1945), 150.

[17] 'Brisbane Comes Back', *Quadrant* 98 (September 1975), 52–8. Rpt. in *Quadrant Twenty-five Years*, ed. by Peter Coleman, Lee Shrubb and Vivian Smith (St Lucia: University of Queensland Press, 1982), 25–39.

[18] Some of these elements are evident in Vallis's Introduction to *The Queensland Centenary Anthology* (St Lucia: University of Queensland, 1959).

[19] Susan McKernan [Lever], *A Question of Commitment* (Sydney: Allen and Unwin, 1989), 62.

[20] McKernan, 63.

[21] Alan Lawson, 'Australian Literature and Its Institutions', in *And What Books Do You Read: New Studies in Australian Literature*, ed. by Irmtraud Petersson and Martin Duwell (St Lucia: University of Queensland Press, 1996), 212; also Lawson, 'The Recognition of National Literatures: the Canadian and Australian Examples' (unpublished PhD), Department of English, University of Queensland, 1987), 180.

[22] John Docker, *In a Critical Condition: Reading Australian Literature* (Ringwood, Vic: Penguin, 1984), passim.

[23] Petersson and Duwell, 212.

[24] Lawson, 'Recognition of National Literatures', 213.

[25] Barry Andrews, 'The Federal Government as Literary Patron', *Meanjin* 41, 1 (1982), 3–19.

[26] Richard Nile and David Walker, 'Marketing the Literary Imagination', in *The Penguin New Literary History of Australia*, 294.

[27] Andrews, 6.

[28] Andrews, 8.

[29] Fiona Capp, *Writers Defiled: Security Surveillance of Australian Authors and Intellectuals 1920–1960* (Ringwood, Vic: McPhee Gribble, 1993), 117–34; McLaren, 112–14.

[30] Capp, 130.

[31] Andrews, 9.

[32] Capp, 45.

[33] Andrews, 9.

[34] Lawson (1987), 271.

[35] Michael Denholm, *Small Press Publishing in Australia: The Early 1970s* (North Sydney: Second Back Row Press, 1979), 1.

[36] Brett, in Hergenhan (1988), 461.

[37] Lawson (1987), 291–2.

[38] Marc Askew, 'Reading the Australian Reading Public: Some Historical Considerations', in *Books and Reading in Australian Society*, ed. by Jock Macleod and Pat Buckridge (Nathan, Qld: Institute for Cultural Policy Studies, Griffith University, 1992), 138.

[39] T. Inglis Moore, 'Australian Literature in our Universities', *Overland* 6 (Summer 1955–6), 2; and C. Roderick, 'The Chair of Australian Literature: An Appeal', *Biblionews* 9, 5 (May 1956), 14.

[40] Lawson (1987), 234.

[41] K.S. Prichard, 'Critics and Criticism', Address to the FAW, Melbourne, 5 March 1953; Palmer Papers; Frank Hardy, letter to a newspaper, 1954, cited by Capp, 125.

[42] Ewers replied to the criticisms in the same issue: J. Barnes and J.K. Ewers, 'The Question of Standards', *Meanjin*, 16 (1957), 321–3; 434–6.

[43] Cited in Lawson (1987), 234, 130–1.

[44] Darryl Dymock, *A Sweet Use of Adversity: The Australian Army Education Service in World War Two and its Impact on Australian Adult Education* (Armidale, NSW: University of New England Press, 1995), Chapter 6.

[45] Vincent Buckley, 'Towards an Australian Literature', *Meanjin* 18 (1959), 59–68.

[46] See, for example, Simon During, *Patrick White*. Oxford Australian Writers Series (Melbourne: Oxford University Press, 1996), 11.

[47] Patrick Buckridge, 'Intellectual Authority and Critical Traditions in Australian Literature, 1945 to 1975', in *Intellectual Movements and Australian Society*, ed. by Brian Head and James Walker (Melbourne: Oxford University Press, 1988), 205–8.

[48] H.P. Heseltine, 'The Literary Heritage', *Meanjin* 21 (1962), 35–49; A.A. Phillips, 'The Literary Heritage Re-assessed', *Meanjin* 21 (1962), 172–80. For a discussion of the exchange see Buckridge, 195–6.

10: FICTION IN TRANSITION

[1] M. Barnard Eldershaw, *Tomorrow and Tomorrow* (1947; rept. with restoration of some censored passages and originally intended title as *Tomorrow and Tomorrow and Tomorrow*, London: Virago, 1983), 80. References are to the 1983 edn.

[2] *The Oxford History of Australian Literature*, ed. by Leonie Kramer (Melbourne: Oxford University Press, 1981), 18.

[3] Barnard to Vance Palmer, 20 October 1938, NLA MSS 1174/15451. Quoted in Maryanne Dever, '"Conventional Women of Ability": M. Barnard Eldershaw and the Question of Women's Cultural Authority', in *Wallflowers and Witches: Women and Cultural Production in Australia 1910–1945*, ed. by Maryanne Dever (St Lucia: University of Queensland Press, 1994), 136.

[4] Dever, 135.

[5] Xavier Herbert to the Palmers, 10 January 1939, NLA MS1174/1/5483.

[6] Ann Whitehead, 'Christina Stead: An Interview', *Australian Literary Studies*, 6 (May 1974), 242. Notwithstanding Stead's assertion, Joy Hooton has detailed the many ways in which Sam is also identifiably American (*Stories of Herself When Young*, Melbourne: Oxford University Press, 1990, 214–16). See also Hazel Rowley, *Christina Stead: A Biography* (Port Melbourne: William Heinemann, 1993).

[7] Eleanor Dark, *Waterway* (1938; Sydney: F.H. Johnson, 1946), 186.

[8] Miles Franklin, *Laughter, Not for a Cage: Notes on Australian Writing, with Biographical Emphasis on the Struggles, Function and Achievements of the Novel in Three Half-Centuries* (Sydney: Angus and Robertson, 1956), 119.

[9] Miles Franklin, *Cockatoos* (1954; North Ryde, NSW: Eden, 1989), 273.

[10] Marjorie Barnard, *Miles Franklin* (New York: Twayne, 1967), 240. 'She could not stay but, ah, it hurt to go', is the actual line.

[11] Her travels with Vera Murdoch are discussed in Candida Baker, *Yacker 2* (Sydney: Pan 1987), 32.

[12] Patricia Excell, 'Patrick White, *The Tree of Man* and *Meanjin*', *Antipodes* (December 1995), 127–9.

[13] Kylie Tennant, 'Writes in Stained Glass', *Sydney Morning Herald* (22 September 1956), 10.

[14] *Meanjin*, 15 (Winter 1956): 156–70.

[15] Quoted in Brenda Niall, *Martin Boyd* (Carlton, Vic: Melbourne University Press, 1988), 199.

[16] Niall, 199.

[17] Martin Boyd, *Lucinda Brayford* (Melbourne: Lansdowne, 1969), 128.

[18] Niall, 154.

[19] Martin Boyd, *The Cardboard Crown* (London: Cresset Press, 1952), 82.

[20] Patrick White, *Flaws in the Glass: A Self-portrait* (London: Jonathan Cape, 1981), 106.

[21] *Australian Letters* 1, 3 (April 1958); 'Introduction', *Patrick White: Selected Writings*, ed. by Alan Lawson (St Lucia: University of Queensland Press, 1994), 270.

[22] Dymphna Cusack, *Southern Steel* (Richmond, Vic: Marlin, 1977), 21.

[23] Elizabeth Harrower, *The Long Prospect* (London: Cassell, 1958), 109.

[24] David Carter, 'Before the Migrant Writer: Judah Waten and the Shaping of a Literary Career', in *Striking Chords: Multicultural Literary Interpretations*, ed. by Sneja Gunew and Kateryna O. Longley (North Sydney: Allen and Unwin, 1992), 105.

[25] Judah Waten, *Distant Land* (Melbourne: Australasian Book Society, 1964), 86.

[26] Nettie Palmer, *Fourteen Years: Extracts from a Private Journal* (Melbourne: Meanjin Press, 1948), 250.

[27] Kylie Tennant, *Ride On Stranger* (1943; Sydney: Sirius/Angus and Robertson, 1945), 310.

[28] *Forty-two Faces*, ed. by John Hetherington (Melbourne: F.W. Cheshire, 1962), 137.

[29] Patrick White, *The Tree of Man* (1955; Harmondsworth: Penguin, 1977), 187. References are to the Penguin edition.

[30] Franklin, *Cockatoos*, 158.

[31] Eric Lambert, *The Twenty Thousand Thieves* (Melbourne: Newmont, 1951), 27.

[32] Further to this, see Nicole Moore's PhD thesis, English Department, University of Queensland 1997, which examines representations of abortion in women's fiction.

[33] Dymphna Cusack and Florence James, *Come In Spinner* (1951; complete edition, North Ryde, NSW: Angus and Robertson, 1988), Preface, vi.

[34] Xavier Herbert, *Soldiers' Women* (Sydney: Angus and Robertson, 1961), 87.

[35] Dorothy Green, *Henry Handel Richardson and her Fiction* (Sydney: Allen and Unwin, 1986), 450.

[36] Franklin to Cusack, 8 December 1945, ML MS364/30/117.

[37] Eleanor Dark, *The Little Company* (1945; London: Virago, 1985), 158.

[38] Hooton, 199.

[39] Hooton, 345.

[40] Eleanor Dark, *The Timeless Land* (N. Ryde, NSW: Angus and Robertson, 1990), 7.

[41] Humphrey McQueen, *The Timeless Land*, 'Introduction', viii.

[42] Eleanor Dark, *Storm of Time* (Sydney: Collins, 1948), 5.

[43] Eleanor Dark, *No Barrier* (London: Collins, 1953), 167.

[44] Patrick White, *Voss* (Harmondsworth: Penguin, 1983), 11.

[45] Carter in Gunew and Longley, 110.

[46] Susan McKernan, *A Question of Commitment: Australian Literature in the Twenty Years After the War* (Sydney: Allen and Unwin, 1989), 42.

[47] Prichard, *Winged Seeds* (Sydney: Australasian Publishing Company in assoc. with Jonathan Cape, 1950), 381–2.

[48] Barnard to Devanny, 13 March 1947, in *As Good as a Yarn with You: Letters Between Miles Franklin, Katharine Susannah Prichard, Jean Devanny, Marjorie Barnard, Flora Eldershaw and Eleanor Dark*, ed. by Carole Ferrier (Cambridge, UK; Oakleigh, Vic: Cambridge University Press, 1992) 167, 170.

[49] John McLaren, *Writing in Hope and Fear: Literature As Politics in Postwar Australia* (Cambridge, UK; Oakleigh, Vic: Cambridge University Press, 1992) 167, 170.

[50] Hansard, House of Representatives, 28 August 1952: 727. Cited in Maryanne Dever, ' "No Time is Inopportune For a Protest": Aspects of the Political Activities of Marjorie Barnard and Flora Eldershaw', *Hecate*, 17, 2 (1991), 16.

[51] Dorothy Hewett, *Wild Card: An Autobiography, 1923–1958* (Ringwood, Vic: McPhee Gribble/Penguin, 1990), 233.

[52] Vincent Buckley, *Cutting Green Hay* (Ringwood, Vic: Penguin, 1983), 123.

[53] Bruce Molloy, 'An Interview With Frank Hardy (1973)', *Australian Literary Studies*, 7 (1976), 374.

[54] See Jean Devanny, *Point of Departure: The Autobiography of Jean Devanny*, ed. and intro. by Carole Ferrier (St Lucia: University of Queensland Press, 1986); Carole Ferrier, *Jean Devanny and the Romance of the Revolution*, (Carlton, Vic: Melbourne University Press, forthcoming, 1999).

55 *Katharine Susannah Prichard: Straight Left: Articles and Addresses on Politics, Literature and Women's Affairs Over Almost 60 Years, from 1910 to 1968*, ed. by Ric Throssell (Sydney: Wild and Woolley, 1982), 9.

56 Editorial Board, 'The Patrick White Controversy,' *Realist Writer*, 12 (1963), 3.

57 Mona Brand, 'Another Look at Patrick White,' *Realist Writer*, 12 (1963), 21.

58 McKernan, 172.

59 Robyn Colwill, 'Eve Plays Her Wilde Card and Makes the Straight Flush', *Hecate*, 20, 1 (1994), 26.

60 Lucien Goldmann, *Towards a Sociology of the Novel* (Cambridge: Cambridge University Press, 1975), 8.

61 Dever, 143.

62 See examples in Giulia Giuffré, *A Writing Life: Interviews with Australian Women Writers* (Sydney: Allen and Unwin, 1990).

63 Frances de Groen, 'Dymphna Cusack's *Comets Soon Pass*: The Genius and the Potato Wife', in Dever, 91–104. In *The Young Cosima*—though it *is* set in an earlier time—Cosima is a woman of great strength and of literary and musical talent but puts all this at the service of the male musical 'geniuses' around her, being told by her father, Franz Liszt: 'it lies in your power to give what a man stands most in need of, what only a woman *can* give—faith in himself' (Richardson, *The Young Cosima*, London: Heinemann, 1939), 165, while later, her husband, Hans, 'taunted her with being a woman' (184).

64 P.R. Stephensen, *Publicist*, January 1938.

65 Miles Franklin, *My Career Goes Bung* (Melbourne: Georgian House, 1946), 62.

66 Susan Sheridan, '*The Man Who Loved Children* and the Patriarchal Family Drama', in *Gender, Politics and Fiction: Twentieth Century Australian Women's Novels*, ed. by Carole Ferrier (second revised edn, St Lucia: University of Queensland Press, 1992), 136.

67 Christina Stead, *For Love Alone* (Sydney: Pacific Books, 1969), 265.

68 Franklin to the Grattan family, in *My Congenials: Miles Franklin and Friends in Letters*, vol. II, ed. by Jill Roe (Pymble, NSW: Angus and Robertson, 1993), 65–6.

69 F.B. Vickers, *The Mirage* (Melbourne: Australasian Book Society, 1955), 258.

70 'Report to the Fourth Conference of Communist Writers—Abridged,' *Communist Review* (January 1960), 34.

71 Jack Beasley, 'Saga of "McLeod's Mob",' *Communist Review*, 219 (1960), 127.

72 J.J. Healy, *Literature and the Aborigine in Australia* (St Lucia: University of Queensland Press, 1978), 218, 220.

73 Christopher Koch, *The Boys in the Island* (rev. edn., Sydney: Angus and Robertson, 1974), 6.

74 Gare in Giuffré, 21.

75 Brand, 22.

76 Carter in Gunew and Longley, 101.

77 Gunew and Longley, Introduction, xvi.

78 Judah Waten, *The Unbending* (Melbourne: Australasian Book Society, 1954), 157.

79 Stephen Knight, '*Bobbin Up* and Working-Class Fiction', in *Dorothy Hewett: Selected Critical Essays*, ed. by Bruce Bennett (Fremantle, WA: Fremantle Arts Centre Press, 1995), 80.

80 John Morrison, *Port of Call* (London: Cassell, 1950), 83.

81 Ron Tullipan, *March into Morning* (Sydney: Australasian Book Society, 1962), 49.

[82] Devanny to Les Greenfield, 14 October 1959, JD/CORR(P)/212.

[83] Dorothy Hewett, *Bobbin Up* (1959; London: Virago, 1985), xvii.

[84] Ralph de Boissière, 'Factory Novel', *Overland*, 16 (December 1959), 36.

[85] Paul Mortier, *Realist Writer*, 1, 2 (1960), 19–20.

[86] 'Questions of Australian Literature', *Communist Review* (January 1960), 31.

[87] Devanny to Beasley, 5 January 1960, JC JD/CORR(P)/23.

[88] Jack Beasley, *Red Letter Days: Notes from Inside an Era* (Sydney: Australasian Book Society, 1979), 68, 79.

[89] *Sunday Review*, 7 September 1971, clipping in ML MSS 3398.

[90] Ian Syson, '"The Problem Was Finding the Time": Working Class Women's Writing in Australasia', *Hecate*, 19, 2 (1993), 65–84.

[91] Tennant, 'Writes in Stained Glass,' 10.

[92] Harrower, *The Long Prospect*, 41.

[93] Koch, 91.

[94] Leonie Kramer, 'Kramer on Stow', in *Southerly*, 24 (1964), 78–91.

[95] Vincent Buckley, 'In the Shadow of Patrick White,' *Meanjin*, 20 (July 1961), 144–54.

[96] McKernan, 227.

[97] Government documents, quoted *Courier-Mail* (1 January 1996).

II: POETRY AND MODERNISM

[1] F.W. Bateson, *English Poetry and the English Language*, 2nd edn (New York: Russell and Russell, 1961), 4.

[2] Brian Matthews, in *The Penguin New Literary History of Australia*, ed. by Laurie Hergenhan (Ringwood, Vic: Penguin, 1988), 315.

[3] Humphrey McQueen, *The Black Swan of Trespass: The Emergence of Modernist Painting in Australia to 1944* (Sydney: Alternative Publishing Cooperative, 1979), 34.

[4] Vivian Smith, in *The Oxford History of Australian Literature*, ed. by Leonie Kramer (Melbourne: Oxford University Press, 1981), 376.

[5] Vincent Buckley, *Essays in Poetry, Mainly Australian* (Carlton, Vic: Melbourne University Press, 1957), 84.

[6] For instance, John Docker, *Australian Cultural Elites* (Sydney: Angus and Robertson, 1974); *The Sydney–Melbourne Book* ed. by Jim Davidson (Sydney: George Allen and Unwin, 1986); and, obliquely, G.A. Wilkes, *The Stockyard and The Croquet Lawn* (Melbourne: Edward Arnold (Australia), 1981). Bernard Smith's contribution to Davidson is particularly important in the evidence it offers about production in the visual arts. A clear-headed reading of the period which resists easy dichotomies is to be found in Susan McKernan's *A Question of Commitment: Australian Literature in the Twenty Years after the War* (Sydney: Allen and Unwin, 1989).

[7] Shapcott, in *Cross Currents: Magazines and Newspapers in Australian Literature*, ed. by Bruce Bennett (Melbourne: Longman Cheshire, 1981), 148–57.

[8] McQueen, 86.

[9] S.L. Goldberg, 'The Poet as Hero: A.D. Hope's *The Wandering Islands*', *Meanjin*, 16 (1957), 127–39; and Kevin Hart, *A.D. Hope* (Melbourne: Oxford University Press, 1992), 21–7.

[10] Evan Jones, 'Australian Poetry since 1920', in *The Literature of Australia*, ed. by Geoffrey Dutton (Ringwood, Vic: Penguin, 1964), 118.

[11] James McAuley, 'Homage to Chris Brennan', *Southerly*, 18 (1957), 135–42.

[12] Judith Wright offers the best commentary on Blight's empirical cubism and accumulated detail in *Preoccupations in Australian Poetry* (Melbourne: Oxford University Press, 1965), 197–204.

[13] Chris Wallace-Crabbe, 'Squatter Pastoral', in *Falling into Language* (Melbourne: Oxford University Press, 1990), 72–84.

[14] Andrew Taylor, *Reading Australian Poetry* (St Lucia: University of Queensland Press, 1987), 127.

[15] Peter Kuch, *Bruce Dawe* (Melbourne: Oxford University Press, 1995), 34; see also *Bruce Dawe: Essays and Opinions*, ed. by Ken Goodwin (Melbourne: Longman Cheshire, 1990).

[16] *New Impulses in Australian Poetry*, ed. by Rodney Hall and Thomas W. Shapcott (St Lucia: University of Queensland Press, 1968), 10, 6–8. For a detailed analysis of this anthology see Livio Dobrez, *Parnassus Mad Ward: Michael Dransfield and the New Australian Poetry* (St Lucia: University of Queensland Press, 1990), 31–61. A particularly valuable account of the period in question is Alexander Craig's introduction to his *Twelve Poets 1950–1970* (Milton, Qld: Jacaranda, 1971).

[17] McKernan, 216.

[18] Harwood, in Jenny Digby, *A Woman's Voice* (St Lucia: University of Queensland Press, 1996), 55; see also Stephanie Trigg, *Gwen Harwood* (Melbourne: Oxford University Press, 1994), chapter 2, 'Not Confession but Enchantment', 27–45.

[19] Brennan, 'Newer French Poetry', in *The Prose of Christopher Brennan*, ed. by A.R. Chisholm and J.J. Quinn (Sydney: Angus and Robertson, 1962), 314.

12: LITERARY CULTURE SINCE VIETNAM

[1] Graeme Aplin, S.G. Foster and Michael McKernan (eds), *Australians: Events and Places* (Broadway, NSW: Fairfax, Syme and Weldon Associates, 1987), 190.

[2] Peter Pierce, Jeffrey Grey, Jeff Doyle (eds), *Vietnam Days: Australia and the Impact of Vietnam* (Ringwood, Vic: Penguin, 1991), 242, 250.

[3] Robin Gerster and Jan Bassett, *Seizures of Youth: 'The Sixties' and Australia* (South Yarra, Vic: Hyland House, 1991), 121, 46.

[4] Ros Pesman, *Duty Free: Australian Women Abroad* (Melbourne: Oxford University Press, 1996), 222.

[5] Richard Neville, *Hippie Hippie Shake: The Dreams, the Trips, the Trials, the Love-Ins, the Screw-Ups . . . the Sixties* (Port Melbourne: William Heinemann Australia, 1995), 343.

[6] Neville, 140, 195.

[7] See Bruce Bennett, *Spirit in Exile: Peter Porter and his Poetry* (Melbourne and Oxford: Oxford University Press, 1991).

[8] Anthony Clare, 'A Voyage Round her Father: the Truth about Reg Greer', *Sunday Times*, 26 March 1989, G3.

[9] Germaine Greer, 'Home is an Illusion', *Guardian Weekly*, 24 October 1993, 12.

[10] See Jack Hibberd, 'Breakfast at the Windsor', *Meanjin*, 40 (1981), 395–9.

[11] Barry Humphries, *More Please* (Ringwood, Vic: Penguin Australia, 1993), 283, 311.

[12] Graeme Davison, *The Unforgiving Minute: How Australia Learned to Tell the Time* (Melbourne: Oxford University Press, 1993), 146, 154–5.

[13] Alec Bolton, 'Publishing in an Age of Innocence: Angus and Robertson in the 1950s', *Publishing Studies* 1 (Spring 1995), 12–20.

[14] See Craig Munro, 'The A and R War: Profits, Personalities and Paperbacks', *Publishing Studies* 1 (Spring 1995), 21–8.

[15] See Geoffrey Dutton, *Out in the Open: An Autobiography* (St Lucia: University of Queensland Press, 1994), 250–1.

[16] Brian Stonier, 'Local Penguin Learns How to Fly', *Weekend Australian*, 5–6 August 1995, 7.

[17] Frank Thompson, 'Legends in their Own Lunchtimes: Australian Publishing since 1960', *Publishing Studies* 1 (Spring 1995), 32–3, 29–36.

[18] Ian Templeman, 'A Two Book Wonder: A Decade of Publishing—Fremantle Arts Centre Press, 1976–1986', *Westerly*, 31, 1 (March 1986), 78–82.

[19] See John Curtin, 'Distance Makes the Market Fonder: the Development of Book Publishing in Australia', *Media, Culture and Society*, 15 (1993), 24, 233–44.

[20] Curtain, 242.

[21] Thomas Shapcott, *The Literature Board: Brief History* (St Lucia: University of Queensland Press, 1988).

[22] See Stephanie Pribil, 'Biting the Hand that Feeds You: The Connection(s) between Art, State and Marketplace in Australia 1973–1993', BA (Hons) thesis, University of Adelaide, 1993.

[23] For an attack on 'political correctness', see *Double Take: Six Incorrect Essays*, ed. by Peter Coleman (Port Melbourne: Mandarin, 1996). The many books which have received assistance from the Australia Council but which are critical of government, society and prevailing attitudes include David Ireland's *The Unknown Industrial Prisoner*, Alan Wearne's *The Nightmarkets* and Amanda Lohrey's *The Reading Group*.

[24] V.K. Daniels, B.H. Bennett and H. McQueen, *Windows onto Worlds: Studying Australia at Tertiary Level*, The Report of the Committee to Review Australian Studies in Tertiary Education (Canberra: Australian Government Publishing Service, 1987), 63–84.

[25] Bruce Bennett, 'Australian Literature and the Universities', *Melbourne Studies in Education*, ed. by Stephen Murray-Smith (Carlton, Vic: Melbourne University Press, 1976), 106–56. See also Chapter 9 in this book.

[26] Bennett, 135.

[27] 'ASAL Directory of Post-Graduate Research in Australian Literature', *Notes and Furphies*, 35 (October 1995), 25–37.

[28] Quoted in Editorial, *Westerly*, 2 (June 1975), 6.

[29] Michael Dugan, 'Little Magazines 1968–77: A Selective Checklist', *Australian Literary Studies*, 8 (1977), 222–5.

[30] David Leser, 'The Man Who Can't Keep Still', *Good Weekend*, Sydney Morning Herald, 23 March, 1996, 22–30.

[31] See Richard Walsh, 'Magazines', *The Australian Encyclopedia* (Terry Hills, NSW: Australian Geographic Pty Ltd, 1996), V, 1998–2005.

[32] John McLaren, 'Book Reviewing in Newspapers 1948–1978', in *Cross Currents: Magazines and Newspapers in Australian Literature*, ed. by Bruce Bennett (Melbourne: Longman Cheshire, 1981), 240–54.

[33] Victoria Laurie, 'Identity Crisis', *The Australian Magazine*, 20–21 July 1996, 28–32.

[34] By Debra Jopson, *SMH*, 24 March 1997 and Sian Powell, 'Author Chose Aboriginality', *Australian*, 25 March 1997, 3.

[35] Vincent Buckley, 'Towards an Australian Literature', *Meanjin*, 18, 1 (1959), 59–68.

[36] Bruce Bennett, 'Australian Literature and the Universities', 123–32.

[37] A.D. Hope, 'Australian Literature and the Universities', *Meanjin*, 13 (Winter, 1954), 165–9.

[38] Veronica Brady, 'Critical Issues', in *The Penguin New Literary History of Australia*, ed. by Laurie Hergenhan (Ringwood, Vic: Penguin, 1988), 472–3.

[39] For example, from Peter Spearritt and David Walker (eds), *Australian Popular Culture* (Sydney: Allen and Unwin, 1979) to John Docker, *Postmodernism and Popular Culture* (Melbourne: Cambridge University Press, 1994) and John Frow, *Cultural Studies and Cultural Value* (Oxford: Clarendon Press, 1995).

[40] Australian Bureau of Statistics, *Books: Who's Reading Them Now? A Study of Book Buying and Borrowing in Australia* (Redfern, NSW: Australia Council, 1995), 49, 6. The data base used in this survey was the file of Public Lending Rights titles.

[41] Joy Hooton and Harry Heseltine, *Annals of Australian Literature*, 2nd edn (Melbourne: Oxford University Press, 1992). I am indebted to Stephanie Pribil for her analysis of these and subsequent estimates based on the *Annals of Australian Literature*.

[42] *Books: Who's Reading Them Now?* 3–9.

[43] This and other estimates are based on the *Annals of Australian Literature* and additional research carried out by Stephanie Pribil.

[44] See Michael Denholm, *Small Press Publishing in Australia*, 2 vols (Footscray, Vic: Footprint, 1991).

[45] See Chris Wallace-Crabbe, 'Autobiography', in *The Penguin New Literary History of Australia*, 561–3.

[46] Paul Hasluck, *Mucking About: An Autobiography* (Carlton, Vic: Melbourne University Press, 1977), 1.

[47] Based on updated Annals for 1990–95 provided by Stephanie Pribil. It is possible that these figures underestimate the actual numbers of books for children, since this was not an area of concentration in the *Annals*.

[48] Bruce Bennett and William Grono (eds), *Wide Domain: Western Australian Themes and Images* (Sydney: Angus and Robertson, 1979).

[49] David Headon (ed.), *North of the Ten Commandments: A Collection of Northern Territory Literature* (Sydney: Hodder and Stoughton, 1991).

[50] Vivian Smith and Margaret Scott (eds), *Effects of Light: The Poetry of Tasmania* (Sandy Bay, Tas: Twelvetrees, 1985).

[51] See Bruce Bennett, *An Australian Compass: Essays on Place and Direction in Australian Literature* (Fremantle: Fremantle Arts Centre Press, 1991).

[52] Philip Butterss (ed.), *Southwords: Essays on South Australian Writing* (Kent Town, SA: Wakefield Press, 1995), ix.

[53] Susan Johnson and Mary Roberts (eds), *Latitudes: New Writing from the North* (St Lucia: University of Queensland Press, 1986), ix.

[54] Lee Harding (ed.), *Beyond Tomorrow: An Anthology of Modern Science Fiction* (South Melbourne: Wren, 1975), 4.

55 Van Ikin (ed.), *Australian Science Fiction* (St Lucia: University of Queensland Press, 1982), xxxii–xxxvii.

56 Van Ikin (ed.), *Glass Reptile Breakout and Other Australian Speculative Stories* (Nedlands: The Centre for Studies in Australian Literature, University of Western Australia, 1990).

57 See Stephen Knight (ed.), *Crimes for a Summer Christmas* (Sydney: Allen and Unwin, 1990), *More Crimes for a Summer Christmas* (Sydney: Allen and Unwin, 1991), *A Corpse at the Opera House: A Crimes for a Summer Christmas Anthology* (North Sydney: Allen and Unwin, 1992) and Stephen Knight, *Continent of Mystery: A Thematic History of Australian Crime Fiction* (Carlton, Vic: Melbourne University Press, 1997).

58 Stephen Knight (ed.) *Dead Witness: Best Australian Mystery Stories* (Ringwood, Vic: Penguin, 1989), xxiii, xxv.

59 Suzanne Falkiner (ed.), *Room to Move: The Redress Press Anthology of Australian Women's Short Stories* (Sydney: Allen and Unwin, 1985), vii.

60 These figures are based on the updated Annals of Australian Literature compiled by Stephanie Pribil and including all texts in the Aust. Lit. Database in these years.

61 Elizabeth Webby and Lydia Wevers (eds), *Goodbye to Romance: Stories by Australian and New Zealand Women 1930s–1980s* (Wellington and Sydney: Allen and Unwin, 1989), 3.

62 Susan Hawthorne (ed.), *Difference: Writings by Women* (Waterloo, NSW: Waterloo Press, 1985); Anna Gibbs and Alison Tilson (eds), *Frictions: An Anthology of Fiction by Women* (Melbourne: Sybylla, 1982); Connie Burns and Marygai McNamara (eds), *Feeling Restless* (Sydney: Collins, 1989).

63 Lyn Harwood, Bruce Pascoe and Paula White (eds), *The Babe is Wise: Contemporary Stories by Australian Women* (Fairfield: Pascoe, 1987); Dale Spender (ed.), *Heroines* (Ringwood, Vic: Penguin Books Australia, 1991).

64 Carole Ferrier (ed.), *Gender, Politics and Fiction: Twentieth Century Australian Women's Novels*, 2nd edn (St Lucia: University of Queensland Press, 1992).

65 Robert Dessaix (ed.), *Australian Gay and Lesbian Writing* (Melbourne: Oxford University Press, 1993).

66 From 'The Sydney Highrise Variations' in *The Vernacular Republic: Poems 1961–1981* (Sydney: Angus and Robertson, 1982), 199.

67 See Lawrence Bourke, *A Vivid Steady State: Les Murray and Australian Poetry* (Kensington: New South Wales University Press, 1992), 113.

68 See Bruce Dawe, 'Public Voices and Private Feelings', in *The American Model: Influence and Independence in Australian Poetry*, ed. by Joan Kirkby (Sydney: Hale and Iremonger, 1982), 160–72.

69 Thomas Shapcott (ed.), *Contemporary American and Australian Poetry* (St Lucia: University of Queensland Press, 1976), Introduction, xxiii–xxxiii.

70 Robert Adamson, *The Clean Dark* (Sydney: Paperbark Press, 1989), 42–4.

71 Brian Kiernan (ed.), *The Most Beautiful Lies: A Collection of Stories by Five Major Contemporary Fiction Writers: Bail, Carey, Lurie, Moorhouse and Wilding* (Sydney: Angus and Robertson, 1977), xi.

72 Don Anderson, 'I'm Going to America in my Mind', in *Reconnoitres: Essays in Australian Literature in Honour of G.A. Wilkes*, ed. by Margaret Harris and Elizabeth Webby (Melbourne: Oxford University Press, 1992), 195.

[73] Brian Castro, *Writing Asia and Autobiography: Two Lectures* (Canberra: University College, Australian Defence Force Academy, 1995), 1–21.

[74] Wang Gungwu, 'Australia's Identity in Asia', *Australia in the World: Perceptions and Possibilities*, ed. by Don Grant and Graham Seal (Perth: Black Swan, 1994), 240.

[75] Nicholas Jose, *Chinese Whispers: Cultural Essays* (Kent Town, SA: Wakefield Press, 1995).

[76] Lyn Jacobs and Rick Hosking, *A Bibliography of Australian Literary Responses to Asia* (Adelaide: The Library, Flinders University of South Australia, 1995).

[77] See Annette Hamilton, 'Fear and Desire: Aborigines, Asians and the National Imaginary', in *Australian Cultural History (Australian Perceptions of Asia)*, 9 (1990), 14–35.

13: Poetry since 1965

[1] In a celebrated revision of the conflict between city and country in Australian culture, Les Murray contrasted his own rural (Boeotian) values with the metropolitan (Athenian) values of Peter Porter. His commentary on 'On First Looking into Chapman's Hesiod', in *Australian Poems in Perspective*, ed. by Peter Elkin (St Lucia: University of Queensland Press, 1978) is reprinted as 'On Sitting Back and Thinking About Porter's Boeotia' in Les Murray, *The Peasant Mandarin: Prose Pieces* (St Lucia: University of Queensland Press, 1978). Porter responded in an interview with Don Anderson published as 'Country Poetry and Town Poetry: A Debate with Les A. Murray', *Australian Literary Studies*, 9 (May 1979), 39–48.

[2] *The New Australian Poetry*, ed. by John Tranter (St Lucia: Makar Press, 1979), xv.

[3] Letter to Dr Trusler, 23 August 1799, in *Blake: Complete Writings*, ed. by Geoffrey Keynes (London: Oxford University Press, 1966), 793.

[4] All quotations are from the Introduction to *The Younger Australian Poets* ed. by Robert Gray and Geoffrey Lehmann (Sydney: Hale and Iremonger, 1983).

[5] Murray, *The Peasant Mandarin*, 198.

[6] See Jennifer Strauss, 'Anthologies and Orthodoxies', *Australian Literary Studies*, 13 (1987), 87–95.

[7] Antigone Kefala, 'Statement', in *Poetry and Gender: Statements and Essays in Australian Women's Poetry and Poetics*, ed. by David Brooks and Brenda Walker (St Lucia: University of Queensland Press, 1989), 47.

[8] See *The Oxford Book of Australian Women's Verse*, ed. by Susan Lever (Melbourne: Oxford University Press, 1995), 105.

[9] ΠO, 'untitled', in *Off the Record* (Ringwood, Vic: Penguin, 1985).

[10] T.S. Eliot, 'The Social Function of Poetry', in *On Poetry and Poets* (London: Faber, 1957), 21.

[11] See Tranter, Introduction to *The New Australian Poetry*.

[12] Murray, *The Peasant Mandarin*, 75–6.

[13] Robert Gray, *The American Model: Influence and Independence in Australian Poetry*, ed. by Joan Kirby (Sydney: Hale and Iremonger, 1982), 121.

[14] Eliot, 19.

[15] Kenneth Slessor, 'The Atlas', in *Kenneth Slessor: Collected Poems*, ed. by Dennis Haskell and Geoffrey Dutton (Sydney: Angus and Robertson, 1990), 70.

[16] Vincent Buckley, 'A Poetry without Attitudes', in *Last Poems* (Ringwood, Vic: McPhee Gribble, 1991), 147.

[17] Gwen Harwood, 'Mother Who Gave Me Life', in *Selected Poems* (North Ryde, NSW: Angus and Robertson, 1991), 161–2.

[18] Chris Wallace-Crabbe, 'Every Night About This Time', in *Selected Poems* (Oxford, New York, Melbourne: Oxford University Press, 1995), 9.

[19] Wallace-Crabbe, 'An Elegy', in *Selected Poems*, 87.

[20] Murray, 'Suspended Vessels', in *Subhuman Redneck Poems* (Potts Point, NSW: Duffy and Snellgrove, 1996), 24–5.

[21] Murray, 'Equanimity', in *Collected Poems* (North Ryde, NSW: Collins/Angus and Robertson, 1990), 158–60.

[22] Geoff Page, *A Reader's Guide to Contemporary Australian Poetry* (St Lucia: University of Queensland Press, 1995).

[23] Page, 'Grand Remonstrance', in *Selected Poems* (North Ryde: Collins/Angus and Robertson, 1991), 61.

[24] Robert Gray, 'Late Ferry', in *Selected Poems* (Port Melbourne: William Heinemann Australia, 1995), 48. Further page references in text are to this edition.

[25] John Foulcher, 'Living', in *New and Selected Poems* (Pymble, NSW: Collins/Angus and Robertson, 1993), 99–104.

[26] Foulcher, 'Conversation', in *New and Selected Poems*, 145.

[27] Jan Owen, 'More on the Dinosaur', in *Fingerprints on Light* (North Ryde: Collins/Angus and Robertson, 1990), 43.

[28] Jean Kent, 'Storming Home', in *Practising Breathing* (Sydney: Hale and Iremonger, 1991), 84–8.

[29] Anthony Lawrence, 'Incident at Heraklion', in *Three Days Out of Tidal Town* (Sydney: Hale and Iremonger, 1992), 11–12.

[30] Paul Hetherington, 'Grace', in *Acts Themselves Trivial* (Fremantle: Fremantle Arts Centre Press, 1991), 75–6.

[31] Susan Hampton, 'In the Kitchens', in *Costumes* (Chippendale, NSW: Transit Press, 1981), 14.

[32] Andrew Burke, 'Post-Coital Tip', *Pushing at Silence* (Perth: Folio/Salt, 1996), 78.

[33] Burke, 'Walking in Karrakatta Cemetery', *Pushing at Silence*, 46.

[34] John Kinsella, 'The Flightless Nomads', in *The Silo: A Pastoral Symphony* (Fremantle: Fremantle Arts Centre Press, 1995), 64.

[35] Philip Hodgins, 'Cytotoxic Rigor', in *Things Happen* (Pymble, NSW: Collins/Angus and Robertson, 1995), 53.

[36] Kevin Hart, 'Firm Views', in *New and Selected Poems* (Pymble, NSW: Angus and Robertson, 1995), 104–5.

[37] Andrew Taylor, 'Dead Trees', in *Sandstone* (St Lucia: University of Queensland Press, 1995), 34.

[38] Philip Salom, 'The World of Dreams', in *Sky Poems* (Fremantle: Fremantle Arts Centre Press, 1987), 123–4. Further page references in text are to this volume.

[39] Kinsella, 'Towards a New Canon', *The Australian's Review of Books*, April 1997, 23.

14: Drama since 1965

Dates in text refer to first performances unless otherwise indicated.

[1] Philip Parsons, gen. ed., *Companion to Theatre in Australia* (Paddington, NSW: Currency Press in association with Cambridge University Press, 1995), 602.

[2] H.G. Kippax, 'Australian Drama Since *Summer of the Seventeenth Doll'*, in *Contemporary Australian Drama*, ed. by Peter Holloway, rev. edn (Sydney: Currency Press, 1987), 231.

[3] Peter Brook, 'The Rough Theatre', in *The Empty Space* (Harmondsworth: Pelican, 1972), 74.

[4] Brian Kiernan, 'The Development of David Williamson', *Southerly*, 4 (1975), 315; see also Brian Kiernan, *David Williamson: A Writer's Career* (Sydney: Currency Press, 1996).

[5] Katharine Brisbane in *Playing With Time: Women Writers for Performance*, compiled and edited by Colleen Chesterman, with Virginia Baxter, Playworks, 1995, 10.

[6] Peter Fitzpatrick, *Williamson* (North Ryde, NSW: Methuen Australia, 1987), 14.

[7] The contrast between Williamson and Romeril is discussed in Richard Fotheringham's chapter, 'John Romeril: the State Theatre Company Productions 1982–1991' in *John Romeril*, ed. by Gareth Griffiths (Amsterdam: Rodopi, 1993).

[8] Parsons, 144.

[9] Fitzpatrick, *Williamson*, 23.

[10] Barrie Kosky, speech given in Sydney, 10 November 1996, edited and reprinted in the *Age*, 11 November 1996, B7.

[11] Peter Fitzpatrick, *Stephen Sewell: The Playwright as Revolutionary* (Paddington, NSW: Currency Press, 1991), 1.

[12] Fitzpatrick, *Stephen Sewell*, 16.

[13] Harry Garlick, '"Up In The Bio-Box": The Use of Hollywood Myth in Some Early Dorothy Hewett Plays', in *Dorothy Hewett: Selected Critical Essays*, ed. by Bruce Bennett (Fremantle: Fremantle Arts Centre Press, 1995), 218.

[14] Peter Fitzpatrick, *After 'The Doll'* (Melbourne: Edward Arnold, 1979), 68.

[15] *Playing With Time: Women Writing For Performance*, compiled and edited by Colleen Chesterman, with Virginia Baxter (Darlinghurst: Playworks, 1995).

[16] David Watt and Graham Pitts, 'Community Theatre as Political Activism: Some Thoughts on Practice in the Australian Context', in *Community and the Arts: History, Theory Practice*, ed. by Vivienne Binns (Leichhardt, NSW: Pluto Press, 1991).

[17] Michael Gurr, *Sex Diary of an Infidel* (Sydney: Currency Press, 1992), 4.

15: Fiction: Innovation and Ideology

[1] Patrick White, 'The Prodigal Son', *Australian Letters*, 1, 3 (1958), 39, repr. in *The Oxford Anthology of Australian Literature*, ed. by Leonie Kramer and Adrian Mitchell (Melbourne: Oxford University Press, 1985), 338.

[2] For a fuller discussion see my (as Susan McKernan) *A Question of Commitment: Australian Literature in the Twenty Years after the War* (North Sydney: Allen and Unwin, 1989).

[3] Australia Council for the Arts, *Grants Handbook 1996* (Sydney: Australia Council, 1996), 1.

[4] Based on Australian fiction entries in the *Australian National Bibliography* (Canberra: National Library of Australia) for the past 30 years.

[5] Published in Australia and Britain as *Schindler's Ark* (London: Hodder and Stoughton, 1982); in the USA as *Schindler's List* (New York: Simon and Schuster, *c.* 1982).

[6] *Grants Handbook 1996*, 2.

[7] Paul Salzmann and Ken Gelder, *The New Diversity: Australian Fiction 1970–88* (Melbourne: McPhee Gribble, 1989).

[8] Brian McHale, *Postmodernist Fiction* (London: Methuen, 1987).

9 For example, David Tacey's *Patrick White: Fiction and the Unconscious* (Melbourne: Oxford University Press, 1988) uses the fiction as the basis for a Jungian case study to argue that 'White was not equal to the demands of his genius' (224), and Simon During's *Patrick White* (Melbourne: Oxford University Press, 1996) revives the Left nationalist criticism of the 1950s to argue that White was canonised because Australia needed a modernist at the time.

10 Harry Heseltine, 'Australian Fiction Since 1920', in *The Literature of Australia*, ed. by Geoffrey Dutton (Ringwood, Vic: Penguin, 1976), 196–247; *Australian Postwar Novelists: Selected Critical Essays* ed. by Nancy Keesing (Milton, Qld: Jacaranda, 1975); D.R. Burns, *The Directions of Australian Fiction 1920–1974* (North Melbourne: Cassell, 1975).

11 Helen Daniel, *Liars: Australian New Novelists* (Ringwood, Vic: Penguin, 1988).

12 David Ireland, 'Statement', *Australian Literary Studies*, 8, 2 (1977), 192.

13 David Ireland, *The Unknown Industrial Prisoner* (Sydney: Angus and Robertson, 1971), 374.

14 Carl Harrison-Ford, 'Fiction', *Australian Literary Studies*, 8, 2 (1977), 172–8.

15 Frank Moorhouse, *Coast to Coast: Australian Stories 1973* (Sydney: Angus and Robertson, 1973).

16 *Australian Literary Studies*, 8, 2 (October 1977) has several articles which discuss this, including those by Michael Wilding, Carl Harrison-Ford and Frank Moorhouse, See also Michael Wilding, 'The Tabloid Story' in *Cross Currents: Magazines and Newspapers in Australian Literature*, ed. by Bruce Bennett (Melbourne: Longman Cheshire, 1981), 228–39.

17 Brian Kiernan, 'Introduction', *The Most Beautiful Lies* (Sydney: Angus and Robertson, 1977), ix.

18 Don Anderson, 'Introduction', *Transgressions* (Ringwood, Vic: Penguin, 1986), ix.

19 Richard Walsh, *Ferretabilia* (St Lucia: University of Queensland Press, 1993), 136.

20 For a fuller discussion see Kerryn Goldsworthy, *Helen Garner* (Melbourne: Oxford University Press, 1996).

21 Hans Guldberg, *Books—Who Reads Them?* (Sydney: Australia Council, 1990).

22 Gerard Windsor, 'Writers and Reviewers', *Island*, 27 (1986), 15–18.

23 Gillian Whitlock, *Eight Voices of the Eighties* (St Lucia: University of Queensland Press, 1989).

24 Pam Gilbert, *Coming Out From Under: Contemporary Australian Women Writers* (North Sydney: Pandora/Allen and Unwin, 1988).

25 Interviews collected in *Eight Voices*.

26 Kerryn Goldsworthy, 'Feminist Writings, Feminist Readings', *Meanjin* 44 (1985), 514; Beverley Farmer, Letter to the Editor, *Meanjin* 45 (1986), 142.

27 Bronwen Levy, 'Mainstreaming Women Writers', in *Women/Australia/Theory*, special issue of *Hecate*, 17, 1 (1991), 110–15.

28 Beverley Farmer, *A Body of Water* (St Lucia: University of Queensland Press, 1990), 158.

29 Candida Baker, 'Thea Astley', *Yacker: Australian Writers Talk about their Work* (Sydney: Picador, 1986), 29–53.

30 Elaine Barry, *Fabricating the Self: The Fictions of Jessica Anderson* (St Lucia: University of Queensland Press, 1992); Margaret Williams, *Dorothy Hewett: The Feminine as Subversion* (Sydney: Currency Press, 1992).

31 Ken Gelder, *Atomic Fiction: The Novels of David Ireland* (St Lucia: University of Queensland Press, 1993).

32 Sneja Gunew, 'Culture, Gender and the Author-Function: Wongar's *Walg*', in *Australian Cultural Studies: a Reader*, ed. by John Frow and Meaghan Morris (St Leonards, NSW: Allen and Unwin, 1993), 3–14.

33 *Bringing Them Home: Report of the National Inquiry into the Separation of Aboriginal and Torres Strait Islander Children from their Families* (Sydney: Human Rights and Equal Opportunity Commission, 1997).

34 David McCooey, *Artful Histories: Modern Australian Autobiography* (Melbourne: Cambridge University Press, 1996).

35 Gillian Whitlock, 'Introduction', *Autographs* (St Lucia: University of Queensland Press, 1996).

36 As editor of *Australian Book Review*, Daniel orchestrated an ongoing attack on the novel; see *Australian Book Review* (1995–96), editorials, forums and reviews relating to *The Hand that Signed the Paper*.

37 Peter Pierce, *Australian Melodramas: Thomas Keneally's Fiction* (St Lucia: University of Queensland Press, 1995).

38 Peter Pierce, 'Preying on the Past: Contexts of Some Recent Neo-historical Fiction', *Australian Literary Studies*, 15, 4 (1992), 304–12.

39 See, for Carey, Tony Hassall's *Dancing on Hot Macadam* (St Lucia: University of Queensland Press, 1994) and Karen Lamb's *Peter Carey: The Genesis of Fame* (Sydney: HarperCollins/Angus and Robertson, 1992), and for David Malouf, Ivor Indyk's *David Malouf* (Melbourne: Oxford University Press, 1993) and Philip Neilsen's *Imagined Lives: A Study of David Malouf* (St Lucia: University of Queensland Press, 1996).

40 Edward Berridge, 'The Living Dead', *Black and White*, 9 (1994), 27–8, 112.

41 Elizabeth Guy, 'A Conversation with Tim Winton', *Southerly*, 56, 4 (1996–97), 127.

42 See Harold Bloom, *The Western Canon* (New York: Harcourt Brace, 1994).

16: Tracking Black Australian Stories

1 The Parliament of the Commonwealth of Australia, House of Representatives Petition, 'A Model Aboriginal State', Canberra, 20 October 1927, 3–4.

2 The Parliament of the Commonwealth of Australia, 3.

3 David Unaipon, 'Naroondarie's Wives', in *Paperbark: A Collection of Black Australian Writings*, ed. by Jack Davis et al (St Lucia: University of Queensland Press, 1990), 26.

4 Ernie Dingo, 'Aboriginal Achievement', in *Inside Black Australia*, ed. by Kevin Gilbert (Ringwood, Vic: Penguin Books, 1988), 29.

5 William Ramsay Smith, *Myths and Legends of the Australian Aboriginals* (London: George G. Harrap, 1930); rept. as *Aborigine Myths & Legends* (London: Random House, 1996).

6 An authorised, fully-annotated version of Unaipon's *Legendary Tales* is scheduled for publication in late 1998 as part of the author's collected works.

7 Kath Walker [Oodgeroo Noonuccal], *We Are Going* (Milton, Qld: The Jacaranda Press, 1964), 9.

8 Andrew Taylor, 'New Poetry', *Overland*, 36 (May 1967), 44.

9 John Collins, 'A Mate in Publishing', in *Oodgeroo: A Tribute*, ed. by Adam Shoemaker (St Lucia: University of Queensland Press, 1994), 13.

10 Mary Durack, in Colin Johnson, *Wild Cat Falling* (Sydney: Angus and Robertson, 1965), xxv.

11 Johnson, xxv.

12 Robert J. Merritt, *The Cake Man* (Sydney: Currency Press, 1978, 1983), Biographical note.

13 Marcia Langton, *'Well, I Heard it on the Radio and I Saw it on the Television . . .'* (North Sydney: Australian Film Commission, 1993), 55.

[14] Alan Paton, in B. Wongar, *The Track to Bralgu* (London: Picador, 1978), Foreword.

[15] Wongar, back cover.

[16] Wongar, back cover.

[17] Patricia Rolfe, 'The Mystery of the Best-Seller', *Bulletin*, 21 April 1992, 109.

[18] Quoted in Rolfe.

[19] See, for example, Livio Dobrez, 'What Colour is White? A European Experience of Aboriginal Australia', in *Stories of Australian Migration*, ed. by John Hardy (Sydney: New South Wales University Press, 1988) and 'Wongar's Metamorphoses: *The Track to Bralgu*', in *Aspects of Australian Fiction*, ed. by Alan Brissenden (Perth: University of Western Australia Press, 1990), 161–2.

[20] An Award for Ethno-Fiction, Personal submission, undated.

[21] See, for example, Richard Guilliatt's article 'Black, White and Grey All Over', *Sydney Morning Herald*, 11 April 1997, Arts 12–13.

[22] Bain Attwood makes these observations in his article 'Sally Morgan and the Construction of Aboriginality', *Australian Historical Studies* 25 (1992), 317.

[23] See, for example, Stephen Muecke, 'Aboriginal Literature and the Repressive Hypothesis', *Southerly*, 48 (1988), 405–18.

[24] Quoted on the back cover of all current Australian editions of *My Place*, published by the Fremantle Arts Centre Press.

[25] Mudrooroo, *Writing from the Fringe* (South Yarra, Vic: Hyland House, 1990), 162.

[26] Mudrooroo, 149.

[27] For details of this affair, see Victoria Laurie, 'Identity Crisis', in *The Weekend Australian Magazine*, 20 July 1996, 28–32, and subsequent articles in the *West Australian*, such as 'Family Adds Fuel to Literary Fire', *West Australian*, 27 July 1996, 15. Significantly, Mudrooroo refuses to acknowledge the validity of these arguments and continues to identify as an Aboriginal writer (see, for example, the back cover of his *The Indigenous Literature of Australia*, South Melbourne: Hyland House, 1997).

[28] Jackie Huggins, 'Always Was Always Will Be', *Australian Historical Studies*, 25 (1993), 460.

[29] Huggins, 460.

[30] Mudrooroo, *The Indigenous Literature of Australia*, 5.

[31] Geoffrey Milne, 'Much Less Mis-ery en Scène', *Eureka Street*, 6 (July/August 1996), 57.

[32] Mudrooroo, *The Indigenous Literature*, 46.

[33] Anne Brewster, *Reading Aboriginal Women's Autobiography* (Sydney: Sydney University Press, 1996), 6.

17: FILM, TELEVISION AND LITERATURE: COMPETING FOR THE NATION

[1] It is possible also to see the media controversy generated around Simon During's *Patrick White* (Melbourne: Oxford University Press, 1996), particularly During's suggestion that White's achievements were in a sense 'called up' by a nation in need of a literary figure, as an instance of such a position on Australian literature.

2 This trend, and its operation in relation to the reputation of Peter Carey, is covered by Graeme Turner, 'Nationalising the Author: The Celebrity of Peter Carey', *Australian Literary Studies*, 16 (1993), 131–9.

3 See Ken Gelder and Paul Salzman, *The New Diversity: Australian Fiction 1970–88* (Melbourne: McPhee Gribble, 1989).

4 See, for example, Elizabeth Jacka, 'Australian Cinema: An Anachronism in the 1980s', in *Nation, Culture, Text: Australian Cultural and Media Studies*, ed. by Graeme Turner (London: Routledge, 1993), 106–22.

5 For discussion of such issues, see Stuart Cunningham, *Framing Culture: Criticism and Policy in Australia* (North Sydney: Allen and Unwin, 1992).

6 Typical would be John Fiske's argument about television in *Television Culture* (London: Methuen, 1987), but there is a whole genre of criticism of soap opera which foregrounds such audience-oriented modes of criticism. See, for instance, Mary Ellen Brown, *Television and Women's Culture* (Sydney: Currency Press, 1990).

7 See K.K. Ruthven (ed.), *Beyond the Disciplines: The New Humanities* (Canberra: Australian Academy of the Humanities, 1992).

8 Cf. Richard White, *Inventing Australia* (Sydney: Allen and Unwin, 1981); Kay Schaffer, *Women and the Bush: Forces of Desire in the Australian Cultural Tradition* (Melbourne: Cambridge University Press, 1988); Marilyn Lake, 'The Politics of Respectability: Identifying the Masculinist Context', *Australian Historical Studies*, 22 (1986), 116–31; Paul Carter, *The Road to Botany Bay* (London: Faber, 1987); John Docker, *In a Critical Condition* (Ringwood, Vic: Penguin, 1984); Graeme Turner, *National Fictions: Literature, Film and the Construction of Australian Narrative* (Sydney: Allen and Unwin, 1986, rev. edn 1993).

9 In one collection, Susan Magarey, Sue Rowley and Susan Sheridan's *Debutante Nation: Feminism Contests the 1890s* (St Leonards, NSW: Allen and Unwin, 1993), the editors proposed an entirely new construction, with equally sound historical legitimation, that radically reoriented Australian literary history around a feminist critique of conventional histories of the national past.

10 See Graeme Turner, *Making it National: Nationalism and Australian Popular Culture* (St Leonards, NSW: Allen and Unwin, 1994).

11 See Sneja Gunew, 'Denaturalizing Cultural Nationalisms: Multicultural Readings of "Australia"', in *Nation and Narration*, ed. by Homi Bhabha (London: Routledge, 1990), 99–120.

12 See Bill Ashcroft, Gareth Griffiths and Helen Tiffin, *The Empire Writes Back: Theory and Practice in Post-Colonial Literatures* (London: Routledge, 1989); and Bob Hodge and Vijay Mishra, *Dark Side of the Dream: Australian Literature and the Postcolonial Mind* (Sydney: Allen and Unwin, 1991).

13 John Tulloch, *Legends on the Screen: The Narrative Film in Australia 1919–29* (Sydney: Currency Press, 1981).

14 Bruce Molloy, *Before the Interval* (St Lucia: University of Queensland Press, 1990).

15 For an accessible and brief account of the history of the industry, see Albert Moran and Tom O'Regan's *The Australian Screen* (Ringwood, Vic: Penguin, 1989).

16 Brian McFarlane, *Words and Images: Australian Novels into Film* (Richmond, Vic: Heinemann in association with Cinema Papers, 1983).

17 See Turner, *National Fictions*, rev. edn 1993, Chapter 1.

[18] See Ian Hunter's review, 'Corsetway to Heaven: Looking Back to *Hanging Rock*', in *Australian Film Reader*, ed. by Albert Moran and Tom O'Regan (Sydney: Currency Press, 1985), 190–3.

[19] Susan Dermody and Elizabeth Jacka, *The Screening of Australia, Volume 2: The Anatomy of a National Cinema* (Sydney: Currency Press, 1987).

[20] See Turner, *National Fictions*, 1.

[21] See Turner, *National Fictions*, for a detailed elaboration of this position.

[22] See Turner, *Making it National*, for an elaboration of this argument.

[23] An exception is Joy Hooton's 'Laurie and Noelene and *Sylvania Waters*', in *The Abundant Culture: Meaning and Significance in Everyday Australia*, ed. by David Headon, Joy Hooton and Donald Horne (St Leonards, NSW: Allen and Unwin, 1995), 61–70.

A GUIDE TO REFERENCE MATERIAL

This Guide is intended to direct readers to general reference material on Australian literature and to give some idea of the historical development of works of bibliography, history, etc. by a chronological arrangement of items showing the earliest and most recent of significant contributions to each category, along with a selection of important intervening works. The chronological order means that (except in the section of international companions and encyclopaedias) works appear at the time of their first edition, with later and more up-to-date editions noted at that point. While some references dealing with groups of writers are included, it has not been possible to include reference material specifically for individual authors (although some of the works listed below cover individual authors). The Guide is arranged under the following major Headings: General Australian Reference Material; Australian English; Guides to Information Sources for Australian Literature; Bibliographies; Literary History and Criticism, Cultural History; Literary Encyclopaedias, Companions and Guides; Biographical Material; Children's Literature; and Film and Television.

GENERAL AUSTRALIAN REFERENCE MATERIAL

Reference material, including bibliographies, for a number of aspects of Australian history and life can be found in the following:

Australian Dictionary of Biography (Melbourne University Press and Cambridge University Press, 1966–). In progress, published to vol. 14, 1940–80 Di–Kel (1996).

The Oxford History of Australia, gen. ed. Geoffrey Bolton, 5 vols (Melbourne: Oxford University Press, 1986–90).

Australians, A Historical Library, 12 vols (Broadway, NSW: Fairfax, Syme and Weldon, 1987).

The Australian People: An Encyclopedia of the Nation, Its People and Their Origins, gen. ed. James Jupp (North Ryde, NSW: Angus and Robertson, 1988).

Australian English

The development of an Australian English has been a major formative influence in the development of a national literature. The studies listed below show that, while the early interest in the particularities of vocabulary and idioms—especially those due to Aboriginal influence—has persisted, the language of Australian writers is now very much the grown offspring of an English parent with considerable recent affiliations to its American cousin.

James Hardy Vaux, *A Vocabulary of the Flash Language*, included in *The Memoirs of James Hardy Vaux* (1819), ed. by Noel McLachlan (London: Heinemann, 1964).

Cornelius Crowe, *The Australian Slang Dictionary: Containing the Words and Phrases of the Thieving Fraternity, Together With the Unauthorised, Though Popular Expressions Now in Vogue With All Classes in Australia* (Melbourne: n.pub., 1895?).

Edward E. Morris, *Austral English: A Dictionary of Australasian Words Phrases and Usages, With Those Aboriginal-Australian and Maori Words Which Have Become Incorporated Into the Language and the Commoner Scientific Words That Have Had Their Origin in Australasia* (London: Macmillan, 1898; facsimile rpt 1968).

Sidney J. Baker, *The Australian Language* (Sydney: Angus and Robertson, 1945; 2nd edn and rev. 2nd edn, Milson's Point, NSW: Currawong Pub. Co., 1966, 1978).

W.S. Ramson, *Australian English: A Historical Study of the Vocabulary 1788–1898* (Canberra: Australian National University Press, 1966).

G.A. Wilkes, *A Dictionary of Australian Colloquialisms* (Sydney: Sydney University Press, 1978; 4th edn 1996).

A. Delbridge et al., *The Macquarie Dictionary* (Chatswood, NSW: The Macquarie Library, 1981; 2nd rev. edn 1987; 3rd rev. edn 1997).

Nancy Keesing, *Lily on the Dustbin: Slang of Australian Women and Families* (Ringwood, Vic: Penguin, 1982).

Stephen Murray-Smith, *The Dictionary of Australian Quotations* (Richmond, Vic: Heinemann, 1984).

Bruce Moore, *The Australian Concise Oxford Dictionary* (Melbourne: Oxford University Press, 1987; 2nd edn 1992; 3rd edn 1997).

W.S. Ramson, *The Australian National Dictionary: A Dictionary of Australianisms on Historical Principles* (Melbourne: Oxford University Press, 1988).

David Blair and Peter Collins, *Studies in Australian English: The Language of a New Society* (St Lucia: University of Queensland Press, 1989).

Robert M.W. Dixon et al. *Australian Aboriginal Words in English: Their Origin and Meaning* (Melbourne: Oxford University Press, 1990).

A. Delbridge, *Aussie Talk: The Macquarie Dictionary of Australian Colloquialisms,* (Chatswood, NSW: The Macquarie Library, 1994).

Nick Thieberger and W. McGregor, *Macquarie Aboriginal Words: A Dictionary of Words from Australian Aboriginal and Torres Strait Islander Languages* (Chatswood, NSW: The Macquarie Library, 1994).

Lenie Midge Johansen, *The Penguin Book of Australian Slang: A Dinkum Guide to Oz English*, 2nd edn (Ringwood, Vic: Penguin, 1996).

GUIDES TO INFORMATION SOURCES FOR AUSTRALIAN LITERATURE

Fred Lock and Alan Lawson, *Australian Literature: A Reference Guide* (Melbourne: Oxford University Press, 1976; 2nd edn 1980).

Herbert Jaffa, *Modern Australian Poetry, 1920–1970: A Guide to Information Sources* (Detroit, Mich: Gale Research Co., 1979).

Barry Andrews and W.H. Wilde, *Australian Literature to 1900: A Guide to Information Sources* (Detroit, Mich: Gale Research Co., 1980).

A. Grove Day, *Modern Australian Prose, 1901–1975: A Guide to Information Sources* (Detroit, Mich.: Gale Research Co., 1980).

Alan Lawson, David Blair and Marcie Muir, in *Australians: A Guide to Sources* (1987). Volume 9 of *Australians, A Historical Library* (see above).

Manuscript Material

National Library of Australia: *Guide to Collections of Manuscripts Relating to Australia*. 4th series published in microfiche in 1985.

Our Heritage: A Directory to Archives and Manuscript Repositories in Australia, 1983. Contains details of national, state and some university libraries.

Overseas Library Holdings of Australian Literature

Phyllis Mander-Jones, *Manuscripts in the British Isles Relating to Australia, New Zealand and the Pacific* (Canberra: Australian National University Press, 1972).

Gordon R. Elliott, *An Inventory of Australian Writing to 1965* (Ottawa: Humanities Research Council of Canada, 1977). This compilation of literary works by Australian authors provides a selection of background materials and the location of Canadian library holdings of listed works.

Nan Bowman Albinski, *Australian/New Zealand Literature in the Pennsylvania State University Libraries: A Bibliography* (University Park, Pa.: Penn State University, 1989). This revision of Bruce Sutherland's *Australiana in the Pennsylvania State University Libraries* was followed in 1992 by Albinski's *Directory of Resources for Australian Studies in North America*, a joint publication of the Australia-New Zealand Studies Centre of Pennsylvania State University and the National Centre for Australian Studies of Monash University, and by *Australian Literary Manuscripts in North American Libraries: A Guide* (Canberra: Australian Scholarly Editions Centre, Australian Defence Force Academy and the National Library of Australia, 1997).

BIBLIOGRAPHIES

Ongoing Bibliographical Projects

Australian National Bibliography originated in the *Annual Catalogue of Australian Publications*. Commenced in 1936 by the then Commonwealth Library, it is now published by the National Library of Australia, Canberra. By 1950 the *ANB* was regarded as having achieved adequate coverage of all works published in Australia. Since 1972 the listing has been a classified one.

Dictionary Catalogue of Printed Books. Mitchell Library, Sydney, 38 vols plus supplement 1968–70.

Australian Bibliographical Network. This index of holdings in major Australian libraries of Australian books published locally and overseas became an on-line service in 1985, replacing the National Union Catalogue of Australia, a card index catalogue also issued in microform in three series (1974, 1975–80, 1981–84).

Austlit: The Australian Literary Database (1992–). Compiled by the Library of the Australian Defence Force Academy (Canberra) these cumulative CD-ROMs, starting with vol. 1, no. 1, 'Data accumulated to 31 December 1991', provide comprehensive coverage from 1988 of writing by and about Australian writers. There is some pre-1988 coverage, but it is neither comprehensive nor entirely reliable, sometimes incorporating errors from earlier source material.

Bibliography of Australian Literature (BAL) (in progress from the National Centre for Australian Studies, Monash University). This aims to provide full bibliographical and select biographical details on all books by Australian writers from 1788 to the present who have published in the genres of fiction, poetry, drama and children's writing as well as information relating to works published in non-core genres, variant editions, translations, awards received. Location of sighting and of manuscript collections, and sources of further information are also included. A special volume listing Australian literary pseudonyms and variant writing names is due for publication in 1998.

Annotated Bibliography of English Studies (ABES), gen. ed. Robert Clark, University of East Anglia, Norwich, UK. This new electronic publication (available on CD-ROM) claims to provide authoritative guidance on what is most worth reading on all topics in English studies. Bruce Bennett and Catherine Pratt of the Australian Defence Force Academy, Canberra, are advisory editors for the volume, *Australian Literary and Cultural Studies*.

General Bibliographies

The earliest listing of works of colonial literature is George Burnett Barton's *Literature in New South Wales* (Sydney: Thomas Richards, Government Printer, 1866), but major bibliographical work on Australia begins in the 1930s, with the preparation of the still influential work of Morris Miller.

E. Morris Miller, *Australian Literature from its Beginnings to 1935*, 2 vols (Melbourne: Melbourne University Press, 1940). 'A Descriptive and Bibliographical Survey of Books by Australian Authors in Poetry, Drama, Fiction, Criticism and Anthology with subsidiary entries to 1938'. There are general historical introductions to the different sections, including biographical sketches of 'leading authors' and some plot summaries and evaluations of particular works. It also lists critical studies, references etc. after particular works. Generally only first editions are listed. Imprint information is provided. Bibliographies are arranged by years—in chronological order of the first publication by each author.

Revised as *Australian Literature: A Bibliography to 1938 by E. Morris Miller*, extended to 1950; 'edited with a Historical Outline and Descriptive Commentaries by Frederick T. Macartney' (Sydney: Angus and Robertson, 1956). Macartney's single volume amalgamates Morris Miller's separate genre introductions into a single 'Historical Outline', and gives a merged list of authors in alphabetical order, adding biographies, plot summaries, and critical commentaries for a selection of authors.

John Ferguson, *Bibliography of Australia*, 7 vols, covering 1784–1900. Originally published by Angus and Robertson, 1941–1969 (facsimile edn Canberra: National Library of Australia, 1975–77). *Addenda 1784–1850* (Canberra: NLA, 1986), includes literary material *inter alia*.

Grahame Johnston, *Annals of Australian Literature* (Melbourne: Oxford University Press, 1970). Revised and extended by Harry Heseltine and Joy Hooton, in 1992, the *Annals* are useful in showing a range of biographical information and of literary activities in a given year, relating particular publications to other literary events. They lack imprint information.

Martin Duwell and Laurie Hergenhan, *The ALS Guide to Australian Writers: A Bibliography 1963–1990* (St Lucia: University of Queensland Press, 1992; rev. edn *The ALS Guide to Australian Writers: A Bibliography 1963–1995*, 1997). This incorporates annual bibliographies published by *Australian Literary Studies* but with arrangement by authors, omitting the general section of the original bibliographies.

The full bibliographical information in the *ALS Guide* is especially useful for its coverage of **reviews**, although this is selective. No national index of book reviewing has existed since the suspension of the *Index to Australian Book Reviews*, published quarterly from 1965 to June 1981 by the State Libraries Board of South Australia. *The Australian Book Review* (1976–) was re-established under the auspices of the National Book Council with the intention that every book published in Australia should be either reviewed or noticed. While it has been impossible to sustain this policy, its 10 issues per year remain the most extensive resource for reviews. Indexes for October 1978–December 1981 were issued by the Library of the Footscray Institute of Technology (now part of Victoria University of Technology) and the Feb/March issue of *ABR* now carries an annual Index to the previous year. Since 1989 reviews of women's writing have been carried by *The Australian Women's Book Review*.

John Arnold and John Hay (eds), *Bibliography of Australian Literature Project: List of Australian Writers 1788–1992*, 2 vols (Clayton, Vic, Monash University: National Centre for Australian Studies, 1995). The alphabetical list of authors identifies sex, birth and death dates, classification of literary activities, pseudonyms, place(s) of residence, reference sources.

Regional

Paul Depasquale, *A Critical History of South Australian Literature, 1836–1930* (Warradale, SA: Pioneer Books, 1978). Contains 'subjectively annotated bibliographies'.

Bruce Bennett, with Peter Cowan, John Hay and Susan Ashford, *Western Australian Writing: A Bibliography* (Fremantle: Fremantle Arts Centre Press, 1979; rev. edn 1990).

Specialised Bibliographies with Multi-Genre Coverage

These bibliographies are particularly reflective of developing areas of literary activity, hence the prevalence of women's and ethnic writing.

Margaret Bettison and Anne Summers, *Her Story: Australian Women in Print, 1788–1975* (Sydney: Hale and Iremonger, 1980). Lists articles, chapters and books on all issues involving women.

Peter Lumb and Anne Hazell, *Diversity and Diversion: An Annotated Bibliography of Australian Ethnic Minority Literature* (Richmond, Vic: Hodja Educational Resources Cooperative, 1983).

Lolo Houbein, *Ethnic Writings in English from Australia: A Bibliography*, 3rd revised and extended edn (Adelaide: Dept. of English Language and Literature, University of Adelaide, 1984). Includes biographical information on writers of listed works.

Debra Adelaide, *Bibliography of Australian Women's Literature 1795–1990. A Listing of Fiction, Poetry, Drama and Non-fiction* (Port Melbourne: D.W. Thorpe/National Centre for Australian Studies, Monash University, 1991).

Sneja Gunew et al., *A Bibliography of Australian Multicultural Writing* (Geelong: Centre for Studies in Literary Education, Deakin University, 1992).

Lyn Jacobs and Rick Hosking, *A Bibliography of Australian Literary Responses to 'Asia'* (Adelaide: The Library, Flinders University of South Australia, 1995).

Genre-Specific Bibliographies

Drama

S.M. Apted, *Australian Plays in Manuscript: A Checklist of the Campbell Howard Collection Held in the University of New England Library* (Armidale, 1968).

Elizabeth F. Ho, *Australian Drama 1946–1973: A Bibliography of Published Works* (Adelaide: Libraries Board of South Australia, 1974).

Fryer Library, *Hanger Collection: Bibliography of Play Scripts* (St Lucia, 1975).
From Page to Stage: An Annotated Bibliography of Australian Drama 1788–1997 (National Centre for Australian Studies, Monash University, 1998).

Fiction

It is perhaps a sign of the volume of fiction writing that there have been no successors to the first (and not particularly reliable) attempts at a comprehensive bibliography, those of the Western Australian, G.V. Hubble: *Modern Australian Fiction: A Bibliography 1940–1965* (1969) and *The Australian Novel: A Title Checklist 1900–1970* (1970).

More recent bibliographies covering a specific area of fiction are:
Stephen Torre: *The Australian Short Story 1940–1980: A Bibliography* (Sydney: Hale and Iremonger, 1984).
Margaret Murphy, *Women Writers and Australia: A Bibliography of Fiction, Nineteenth Century to 1987* (Parkville: University of Melbourne Library, 1988). Includes identification of pseudonyms.
John Loder, *Australian Crime Fiction: A Bibliography 1857–1993* (Port Melbourne: D.W. Thorpe/National Centre for Australian Studies, Monash University, 1994).

Poetry

Percival Serle, *A Bibliography of Australasian Poetry and Verse: Australia and New Zealand* (Melbourne: Melbourne University Press, 1925).
J.H. Hornibrook, *Bibliography of Queensland Verse, with Biographical Notes* (Brisbane: A.H. Tucker, Government Printer, 1953).
Eleanora I. Cuthbert, *Index of Australian and New Zealand Poetry* (New York: Scarecrow Press, 1963).
Jennifer Strauss, 'An Annotated Bibliography of Contemporary Women Poets of Australia', *World Literature Written in English*, 17 (1978), pp. 63–82.
Elizabeth Webby, *Early Australian Poetry: An Annotated Bibliography of Original Poems Published in Newspapers, Magazines and Almanacks Before 1850* (Sydney: Hale and Iremonger, 1982).
John Fletcher, *Poetry Books and Poetry Broadsheets Published from 1950 to 1980 in New South Wales: A Catalogue* (Sydney: Book Collectors' Society of Australia, 1989).
Sue Murray, *Bibliography of Australian Poetry 1935–1955*, ed. by John Arnold, Sally Batten and Kate Purvis (Port Melbourne: D.W. Thorpe/National Centre for Australian Studies, Monash University, 1991).

Autobiography

Kay Walsh and Joy Hooton, *Australian Autobiographical Narratives: An Annotated Bibliography*: vol. 1 to 1850; vol. 2 1850–1900 (Canberra: Australian Scholarly Editions Centre and National Library, 1993, 1998).

Literary Criticism

Robert L. Ross, *Australian Literary Criticism 1945–1988: An Annotated Bibliography* (New York: Garland, 1989).

Journals and Magazines

John Tregenza, *Australian Little Magazines, 1923–1954: Their Role in Forming and Reflecting Literary Trends* (Adelaide: Libraries Board of South Australia, 1964).

Lurline Stuart, *Nineteenth Century Australian Periodicals: An Annotated Bibliography* (Sydney: Hale and Iremonger, 1979).

Bruce Bennett (ed.), *Cross Currents: Magazines and Newspapers in Australian Literature* (Melbourne: Longman Cheshire, 1981).

Australian Literary Periodicals Database (ALIP) (Canberra: National Library of Australia, 1996). The period covered is 1825–1975.

Publishers

Henry Mayer, *Bibliographical Notes on the Press in Australia and Related Subjects* (Sydney: Department of Government and Public Administration, University of Sydney, 1963).

Geoffrey Farmer, *Private Presses and Australia, with a Check-list* (Melbourne: Hawthorn Press, 1972).

Michael Denholm, *Small Press Publishing in Australia: the Early 1970s* (North Sydney: Second Back Row Press, 1979); *The Late 1970s to the Mid to Late 1980s* (Footscray, Vic: Footprint Press, 1991).

Abe (I.) Wade and Ata and Colin Ryan, *The Ethnic Press in Australia* (Forest Hill, Vic: Academia Press and Footprint Publications, 1989).

LITERARY HISTORY AND CRITICISM, CULTURAL HISTORY

General

Nettie Palmer, *Australian Literature* (Melbourne: Melbourne University Press, 1924).

C. Hartley Grattan, *Australian Literature* (Seattle: University of Washington Book Store, 1929).

H.M. Green, *An Outline of Australian Literature* (Sydney and Melbourne: Whitcombe and Tombs, 1930). A preliminary study for his 2-volume *A History of Australian Literature Pure and Applied* (Sydney: Angus and Robertson, 1961). This 'critical review of all forms of literature produced in Australia from the first books published after the arrival of the First Fleet until 1950' remains an impressive achievement, its continuing usefulness assured by its 1981 revision by Dorothy Green.

Cecil Hadgraft, *Australian Literature: A Critical Account to 1955* (London: Heinemann, 1960).

Geoffrey Dutton (ed.), *The Literature of Australia* (Ringwood, Vic: Penguin, 1964; rev. edn 1976). Bibliographical appendices by Laurie Hergenhan.

John Barnes (ed.), *The Writer in Australia: A Collection of Literary Documents, 1856 to 1964* (Melbourne: Oxford University Press, 1969).

G.A. Wilkes, *Australian Literature: A Conspectus* (Sydney: Angus and Robertson, 1969).

Geoffrey Serle, *From Deserts the Prophets Come: The Creative Spirit in Australia, 1788– 1972* (Melbourne: Heinemann, 1973; rev. edn as *The Creative Spirit in Australia: A Cultural History*, 1987).

Peter Spearritt and David Walker (eds), *Australian Popular Culture* (Sydney: George Allen and Unwin, 1979).

Brian Kiernan, *Criticism* (Melbourne: Oxford University Press, 1974).

Leonie Kramer (ed.), *The Oxford History of Australian Literature* (Melbourne: Oxford University Press, 1981). Bibliography by Joy Hooton.

Richard White, *Inventing Australia: Images and Identity 1688–1980* (Sydney: George Allen and Unwin, 1981).

Ken Goodwin, *A History of Australian Literature* (London: Macmillan, 1986).

Laurie Hergenhan (gen. ed.), *The Penguin New Literary History of Australia* (Ringwood, Vic: Penguin, 1988).

John McLaren, *Australian Literature: An Historical Introduction* (Melbourne: Longman Cheshire, 1989).

James Walter (ed.), *Australian Studies: A Survey* (Melbourne: Oxford University Press, 1989).

Bob Hodge and Vijay Mishra, *Dark Side of the Dream: Australian Literature and the Postcolonial Mind* (Sydney: Allen and Unwin, 1991).

John Frow and Meaghan Morris (eds), *Australian Cultural Studies: A Reader* (St Leonards, NSW: Allen and Unwin, 1993).

Ian Craven et al. (eds), *Australian Popular Culture* (Cambridge, UK and New York: Cambridge University Press, 1994).

Regional

Cecil Hadgraft, *Queensland and its Writers (100 Years—100 Authors)* (Brisbane: University of Queensland Press, 1959).

Bruce Bennett (ed.), *The Literature of Western Australia* (Nedlands: University of Western Australia Press, 1979).

Margaret Giordano and Don Norman, *Tasmanian Literary Landmarks* (Hobart: Shearwater Press, 1984).

Philip Butterss (ed.), *Southwords: Essays on South Australian Writing* (Kent Town, SA: Wakefield Press, 1995).

Drama

Leslie Rees, *Towards an Australian Drama* (Sydney: Angus and Robertson, 1953). Appendices list Australian plays written between 1935 and 1953 and plays broadcast by the ABC in the same period. This was followed by the much more comprehensive *A History of Australian Drama*, vol. 1: *The Making of Australian Drama: A Historical and Critical Survey from the 1830s to the 1970s* (Sydney: Angus and Robertson, 1973); vol. 2: *Australian Drama 1970–1985: A Historical and Critical Survey*, a revised and enlarged edn of *Australian Drama in the 1970s* (London and Sydney: Angus and Robertson, 1987).

Peter Fitzpatrick, *After The Doll: Australian Drama Since 1955* (Melbourne: Edward Arnold (Australia), 1979).

Margaret Williams, *Australia on the Popular Stage, 1829–1929: An Historical Entertainment in Six Acts* (Melbourne: Oxford University Press, 1983).

Harold Love, *The Australian Stage: A Documentary History* (Kensington: New South Wales University Press, 1984).

Other Specialised Histories (Bibliographies included)

J.J. Healy, *Literature and the Aborigine in Australia, 1770–1975* (St Lucia: University of Queensland Press, 1978; 2nd edn 1989).

Carole Ferrier (ed.), *Gender, Politics and Fiction: Twentieth Century Australian Women's Novels* (St Lucia: University of Queensland Press, 1985; 2nd edn 1992).

Adam Shoemaker, *Black Words, White Page: Aboriginal Literature 1929–1988* (St Lucia: University of Queensland Press, 1989; rept 1992).

Histories of Literary Associations, Institutional Bodies

Eve Pownall, *The Children's Book Council in Australia 1945–80* (Curtin, ACT: Reading Time, 1980).

Inglis, K.S. *This is the ABC: the Australian Broadcasting Commission 1932–1983* (Melbourne: Melbourne University Press, 1983).

Thomas Shapcott, *The Literature Board: A Brief History* (St Lucia: University of Queensland Press, 1988).

Len Fox (ed.), *Dream at a Graveside: The History of the Fellowship of Australian Writers 1928–1988* (Sydney: Fellowship of Australian Writers, 1989).

Literary Encyclopaedias, Companions and Guides
International

Australian writers can be seen in an international context in the following:

The Year's Work in English Studies (London: The English Association, 1920–). This has recently included Australian literature in its newly-established section for New Literatures Written in English.

Encyclopedia of Post-Colonial Literatures Written in English, ed. by Eugene Benson and L.W. Conolly, 2 vols (New York and London: Routledge, 1994).

The Oxford Companion to Twentieth-Century Poetry in English, ed. by Ian Hamilton (Oxford and New York: Oxford University Press, 1994).

Reference Guide to Short Fiction, ed. by Noelle Watson (Detroit and London: St James Press, 1994).

Contemporary Novelists, ed. by Susan Windisch Brown, 6th edn (New York: St James Press, 1996).

Contemporary Poets, ed. by Thomas Rigg, 6th edn (New York: St James Press, 1996).

Australian

General

The Oxford Companion to Australian Literature, ed. by W.H. Wilde, Joy Hooton and Barry Andrews (Melbourne: Oxford University Press, 1985; 2nd edn 1994). A comprehensive coverage includes biographical and critical notices of a large number of authors; commentaries on significant individual works; histories of publishers, literary journals, organisations, and prizes; and some discussion of major literary genres and issues.

The Oxford Literary Guide to Australia, gen. ed. Peter Pierce (Melbourne: Oxford University Press, 1987; rev. edn 1993). Compiled under place names (arranged by the States and Territories), this illustrated volume presents a guide to Australian places as they have been represented by, or are associated with, various authors and texts. Provided with maps and an index of authors.

Genre-Specific

Joseph and Johanna Jones, *Australian Fiction*, Twayne's World Author Series (Boston: Twayne Publishers, 1983). Includes bibliography.

Dennis Carroll, *Australian Contemporary Drama* (New York: Peter Lang, 1985; rev. edn Sydney: Currency Press, 1995). Discussion of authors by groups, includes bibliography.

Laurie Clancy, *A Reader's Guide to Australian Fiction* (Melbourne: Oxford University Press, 1992). Authors arranged chronologically by date of birth.

Geoff Page, *A Reader's Guide to Contemporary Australian Poetry* (St Lucia: University of Queensland Press, 1995). For 100 poets, provides brief biographical note, a summary of poet's work and its reception; also listing of names only of further poets and of anthologies published from 1970 to 1992.

Philip Parsons (gen. ed.), *Companion to Theatre in Australia* (Sydney: Currency Press in association with Cambridge University Press, 1995). Invaluable resource for theatrical history as well as for information on plays and playwrights.

William Wilde, *Australian Poets and Their Work: A Reader's Guide* (Melbourne: Oxford University Press, 1996). Alphabetical entries on 556 poets, significant collections and individual poems, critical issues, poetry journals.

BIOGRAPHICAL MATERIAL

Group Biographies, Directories

John Hetherington, *Forty-Two Faces: Profiles of Living Australian Authors* (Melbourne: F.W. Cheshire, 1962).

Graeme Kinross Smith, *Australia's Writers* (West Melbourne: Nelson, 1980). Profiles of some 50 authors.

Drusilla Modjeska, *Exiles at Home: Australian Women Writers 1925–45* (North Ryde: Sirius/Angus and Robertson, 1981). Includes bibliography.

Mary Lord (ed.), *Directory of Australian Authors* (Carlton: National Book Council, 1989).

Who's Who of Australian Writers (Port Melbourne: D.W. Thorpe in assoc. with National Centre for Australian Studies, Monash University, 1991; 2nd edn 1995).

Collections of Interviews

Jim Davidson (ed.), *Sideways from the Page: The Meanjin Interviews* (Sydney: Fontana/Collins, 1983).

Jennifer Ellison, *Rooms of their Own* (Ringwood, Vic: Penguin, 1986).

Candida Baker, *Yacker: Australian Writers Talk About Their Work* (Woollahra, NSW: Pan, 1986); *Yacker 2* (Sydney: Pan, 1987); *Yacker 3* (Sydney: Picador, 1989).

Giulia Giuffré, *A Writing Life: Interviews with Australian Women Writers* (Sydney: Allen and Unwin, 1990).

Jenny Digby, *A Woman's Voice: Conversations with Australian Poets* (St Lucia: University of Queensland Press, 1996). 12 poets, bibliography.

Collections of Letters

Vivian Smith (ed.), *Letters of Vance and Nettie Palmer 1915–1963* (Canberra: National Library of Australia, 1977).

W.H. Wilde and Tom Inglis Moore (eds), *Letters of Mary Gilmore* (Carlton, Vic: Melbourne University Press, 1980).

Carole Ferrier (ed.), *As Good as a Yarn With You: Letters Between Miles Franklin, Katharine Susannah Prichard, Jean Devanny, Marjorie Barnard, Flora Eldershaw and Eleanor Dark* (Cambridge, UK and Oakleigh, Vic: Cambridge University Press, 1992).

Jill Roe (ed.), *My Congenials: Miles Franklin and Friends in Letters*, 2 vols (Pymble, NSW: Angus and Robertson, 1993).

David Marr (ed.), *Patrick White: Letters* (Milson's Point, NSW: Random House Australia, 1994).

Children's Literature

Guides to Information Sources

Lu Rees Archives of Australian Children's Literature: A Guide to the Collections. Ed. Belle Alderman and Margaret Hyland (Canberra: Canberra College of Advanced Education, 1989). Archives established by ACT branch of Children's Book Council in 1974 contain information on authors, illustrators and publishers of children's literature, also awards, foreign translations.

Bibliographies

Marcie Muir, *A Bibliography of Australian Children's Books*, 2 vols (London: Deutsch, 1970, 1976); revised and extended in 2 vols (vol. 2 by Kerry White) as *Australian Children's Books: A Bibliography* (Carlton South, Vic: Melbourne University Press, 1992).

Companions, Guides

Josie Arnold and Tesha Piccinin, *A Practical Guide to Young Australian Fiction* (Sydney: Australian Broadcasting Commission, 1985).

Walter McVitty, *Authors and Illustrators of Australian Children's Books* (Sydney: Hodder and Stoughton, 1989). Biographies and bibliography.

Stella Lees and Pam MacIntyre (eds), *The Oxford Companion to Australian Children's Literature* (Melbourne: Oxford University Press, 1993). Replaces 1984 version edited by Humphrey Carpenter.

Histories and Criticism

H.M. Saxby, *A History of Australian Children's Literature 1841–1941*, 2 vols (Sydney: Wentworth Books, 1969, 1971).

Michael Dugan, *The Early Dreaming: Australian Children's Authors on Childhood* (Milton, Qld: Jacaranda Press, 1980).

Walter McVitty, *Innocence and Experience: Essays on Contemporary Australian Children's Writers* (West Melbourne: Nelson, 1981).

Marcie Muir, *A History of Australian Children's Book Illustration* (Melbourne: Oxford University Press, 1982).

Brenda Niall, *Australia Through the Looking-Glass: Children's Fiction 1830–1980* (Carlton, Vic: Melbourne University Press, 1984).

Biographical Information

Who's Who of Australian Children's Writers (Port Melbourne: D.W. Thorpe in assoc. with National Centre for Australian Studies, Monash University, 1992; 2nd edn 1996).

Film and Television

John Tulloch, *Australian Cinema: Industry, Narrative and Meaning* (Sydney: George Allen and Unwin, 1982).

Brian McFarlane, *Words and Images: Australian Novels into Films* (Richmond, Vic; Heinemann in association with *Cinema Papers*, 1983).

Graeme Turner, *National Fictions: Literature, Film and the Construction of Australian Narrative* (St Leonards, NSW: Allen and Unwin, 1986).

Brian McFarlane, *Australian Cinema, 1970–1985* (London: Secker and Warburg, 1987).

Albert Moran and Tom O'Regan (eds), *The Australian Screen* (Ringwood, Vic: Penguin, 1989).

Scott Murray (ed.), *Australian Film 1978–1992: A Survey of Theatrical Features* (Melbourne: Oxford University Press, 1993).

Wayne Levy, *The Book of the Film and the Film of the Book: A Bibliography of Australian Cinema and TV, 1895–1995* (Melbourne: Academia Press, 1995).

CHRONOLOGY

This Chronology is intended to provide indications of the kind of events that formed the context of Australian literary history and directly or indirectly affected writers, publishers and readers in this country. It is not intended to be historically comprehensive, any more than the citation of particular literary works is intended to duplicate the function of the *Annals of Australian Literature*; rather we have tried to cite a sample of works that are of particular interest in their time and/or representative of the work of significant writers.

Events selected for noting in individual years are arranged in this sequence: international events, national events of general political, economic or social significance, more localised events of the same kind, general cultural events, general literary events, and finally specific publications. While this has meant that the chronological sequence of events within a given year has not necessarily been preserved, we believe that any disadvantage in this is outweighed by the establishment of a regular and easily comprehended pattern of contextualising literary history.

1605	Pedro Fernandez de Quiros, thinking he has discovered the Great South Land, names the New Hebrides Austrialia del Espiritu Santo
1606	Dutch expedition under Willem Jansz explores coast of Cape York Peninsula without recognising it as separate continent
1616	Dirck Hartog makes first recorded European landfall in Australia (on west coast)
1627	Wreck of the *Batavia* on Houtman's Albrolhos leads to mutiny and massacre of crew
1636	Ben Jonson's servant Richard Brome writes play *The Antipodes*
1642	Abel Tasman's expedition on behalf of Dutch East India Company lands at Blackman's Bay, Van Diemen's Land
1688	Dampier's landing on west coast of Australia leads to first English written records of European perception of Aborigines

1694	Tasman's journal of his 1642 voyage to Van Diemen's Land published in England
1703	Dampier publishes *A Voyage to New Holland in the Year 1699*
1760–1820	Reign of George III
1770	Captain James Cook reaches Botany Bay, sails north to Possession Island where he names the east coast of NSW and takes possession of it for Britain
1775–1832	American War of Independence
1776	Adam Smith, *The Wealth of Nations* In Britain the Hulks Act allows the use of ships anchored off shore as prisons
1786	British Government decides to establish a penal colony in NSW
1788	First Fleet under Captain Arthur Phillip arrives at Port Jackson, 26 January; Colony of New South Wales proclaimed; first conflict with Aborigines at Rushcutters Bay Norfolk Island established as prison settlement
1788–1791	Approximately 2100 convicts sent from Britain to Australian colonies, of whom one quarter were women
1789	Mutiny on the *Bounty* George Farquhar's *The Recruiting Officer*, performed by convicts, is first dramatic production in Australia *The Voyage of Governor Phillip to Botany Bay* is first book about Australia to be published in London; Watkin Tench, *A Narrative of the Expedition to Botany Bay*
1789–1795	French Revolution
1790	First official British 'punitive' expedition conducted against Aborigines at Botany Bay
1792	Bennelong, an Aborigine, taken to England by Governor Phillip
1793	*Zoology and Botany of New Holland and the Isles Adjacent* by George Shaw and James Edward Smith (London, 1793–95) is first book to deal only with the natural history of Australia
1796	Colony's first theatre opened by ex-convict Robert Sidaway (closes 1815)
1797–1798	George Bass sails down south-east coast and into Bass Strait
1798	First public clock installed on Church Hill by Governor Hunter
1799–1805	Aboriginal resistance to settlement of Hawkesbury and Parramatta areas
1801	Introduction of ticket-of-leave system allows employment of convicts
1801–1803	Matthew Flinders circumnavigates Australian continent
1802	Flinders meets two ships of Baudin's French cartographic expedition at Encounter Bay off the coast of modern South Australia

George Howe prints first book published in Australia, the *New South Wales General Standing Orders*

1803   Settlement established in Van Diemen's Land on Derwent River, moving to Hobart in 1804
First authorised Catholic mass celebrated in Sydney
Sydney Gazette (1803–42) is first newspaper published in Australia

1803–1804   Attempted settlement on Port Phillip Bay at Sorrento

1804   Coronation of Napoleon I as Emperor of France
Unsuccessful rebellion of 200 Irish convicts leads to suppression of all Catholic worship in the Colony until 1820
First merino sheep brought to New South Wales by John Macarthur
'The Vision of Melancholy' is first poem published locally

1805   Colonial Office grant of land to Blaxland signals policy of encouraging migrants with capital

1807   Law proclaimed barring British subjects from trading in slaves

1808   'Rum Rebellion' against Governor Bligh led by John Macarthur

1810   Michael Massey Robinson appointed Poet Laureate by Governor Macquarie
First formal horse-race meeting in the colony, at Hyde Park
Derwent Star and the Van Diemen's Land Intelligencer appears for 12 issues in Hobart

1810–1821   Macquarie's term as Governor

1811   First mental asylum opens at Castle Hill, Sydney

1813   Blaxland, Lawson and Wentworth cross the Blue Mountains
Norfolk Island prison settlement abandoned

1814   Flinders publishes *A Voyage to Terra Australis* in London

1815   Battle of Waterloo ends reign of Napoleon
School for Aborigines (6 boys, 6 girls) opened at Parramatta
Hostilities between Aborigines and settlers lead to punitive expedition authorised by Macquarie; in December he gives a feast for 179 Aborigines at Parramatta

1816   *Hobart Town Gazette* (1816–25)

1817   Fort Macquarie built to defend Sydney Cove
Bank of New South Wales opens as first Australian bank
First Methodist chapel opens in Castlereagh, near Sydney

1818   Freycinet's French expedition conducts exhaustive exploration and mapping of the north-west coast of Australia
Thomas Wells's *Michael Howe, the Last and the Worst of the Bushrangers of Van Diemen's Land* is first general literary work to be printed in Australia

1819	Beginning of collection of skulls of Aborigines for European educational institutions Barron Field's *First Fruits of Australian Poetry* is first volume of poetry to appear in Australia
1820	Influenza epidemic kills many Aborigines Foundation stone laid for Macquarie's School for Education of Children of the Poor at Hyde Park
1820–1830	Reign of George IV
1821	Female convicts transferred to the female prison-factory at Parramatta Agricultural societies, founded 1821–23 in New South Wales and Van Diemen's Land, begin annual exhibitions First locally produced periodical, *Australian Magazine*, published 1821–22 in Sydney by George Howe
1822–1823	Commissioner Bigge's reports—*The State of the Colony of New South Wales; The Judicial Establishments of New South Wales and Van Diemen's Land* and *The State of Agriculture and Trade in the Colony of New South Wales*—are printed by the House of Commons
1823	First recorded finding of gold in Australia, by government surveyor James McBrien at Bathurst W.C. Wentworth's poem 'Australia' wins Chancellor's Medal at Cambridge University; his *Australasia* becomes the first book of verse published in Britain by an Australian-born author
1824	First issue of *Australian* (Sydney, 1824–48), first privately owned newspaper in the colony Penal settlement opens at Moreton Bay (closes 1839)
1825	Norfolk Island re-opens as prison settlement Sydney Turf Club established Barron Field, *Geographical Memoirs of New South Wales*
1826	Unsuccessful convict mutiny on Norfolk Island Establishment of first subscription library in Sydney, later to develop into Public Library of New South Wales Charles Tompson's *Wild Notes, from the Lyre of a Native Minstrel* (Sydney) is first book of verse by a native-born poet
1827	State Institution established in Van Diemen's Land for convicts suffering from physical or mental disease Mechanics Institute established in Hobart
1828	First NSW census (of white inhabitants only) Masters and Servants Act becomes law in NSW Whooping cough and smallpox arrive with ships transporting, respectively, soldiers and convicts Martial law declared against Aborigines in Van Diemen's Land Charles Sturt explores the Darling and Castlereagh River systems
1829	Swan River Colony proclaimed

	Sturt explores the Murray River system
	Caledonian Theatre, Edinburgh, stages *The Bushrangers*, first play with an Australian theme performed overseas
1830	New South Wales Legislative Council Bushranging Act extends powers of police and general public against suspected bushrangers
	Penal settlement established at Port Arthur
	Assassination of Patrick Logan, Commandant of Moreton Bay
1830–1831	Henry Savery's *Quintus Servinton* is first novel both written and published in book form in Australia (Hobart)
1830–1837	Reign of William IV
1831	Auction of Crown land in NSW to fund assisted immigration; first assisted immigrants arrive in Sydney
	First ball in the Swan River Colony
	In Hobart, convicts Thomas Bock and Daniel Herbert become first known colonials to practise as, respectively, artist and sculptor
	First issue of the *Sydney Herald* (from 1842 *Sydney Morning Herald*)
1832	Port Arthur becomes sole penal settlement of Van Diemen's Land
	First temperance society formed by Quaker missionaries; a field for women's political activities in 1830s and 1840s and during later Suffrage movement
1833	NSW Legislative Council reforms police force on model of London Metropolitan Police Act of 1829; Juries Act allows for jury trials in criminal as well as civil trials
	Edward Henty lands at Portland from Van Diemen's Land, establishing first pastoral settlement in Port Phillip District
	Theatre Royal (Sydney, 1833–38) and Hobart Town Theatre open
	First issue of *Perth Gazette and Western Australian Journal*
1834	Province of South Australia established as non-convict colony
	Punitive expedition under Governor Stirling ambushes and kills Aborigines at Pinjarra, WA
1835	John Batman and John Pascoe Fawkner settle on Port Phillip Bay
	George Augustus Robinson, Protector of Aborigines, arrives at Flinders Island as commandant of a settlement intended for 'remaining' Tasmanian Aborigines, initially 123
	Escaped convict William Buckley found after living with Aborigines for 30 years in Port Phillip region
	John Dunmore Lang publishes first issue of his newspaper the *Chronicle* and opens the Australian College, teaching classics and commercial subjects (closes 1854)
	First colonial performance of a ballet (*The Fair Maid of Perth*) at Sydney's Theatre Royal
	E.H. Thomas's *The Bandit of the Rhine* is first Australian play published in book form
1836	HMS *Beagle*, with Charles Darwin aboard, visits eastern and western Australian colonies

Settlement at Port Phillip (later Melbourne) officially recognised, still as part of Colony of New South Wales

Thomas Mitchell's third expedition proceeds from the Murrumbidgee and Murray rivers southward as far as Portland through territory he names Australia Felix; inquiry held into the episode of his ambush of Aborigines, but no charges laid

Swan River *Guardian* appears in Perth as advocate of rights of workers (1836–38)

Inauguration of *The Aboriginal* or *Flinders Island Chronicle*, the first Aboriginal newspaper produced in the Australian colonies (September 1836–December 1837)

1837	Punitive expedition in response to death of 5 Europeans in northern NSW results in about 300 Aboriginal deaths

First passenger railway opens in Van Diemen's Land; first overland mail runs between Sydney and Port Phillip settlement, newly named Melbourne

Tasmanian Natural History Society founded by Sir John and Lady Franklin

First issue of *South Australian Gazette and Colonial Register*; becomes the *South Australian Register* (1839–1900), then the *Register News-Pictorial* (1929–31)

James Mudie's *The Felonry of New South Wales* published in London

1837–1901   Reign of Queen Victoria

1838   First German Lutheran settlers arrive in SA

Conviction, after re-trial, of those arrested for the Myall Creek massacre of Aborigines

Royal Victoria Theatre opens in Sydney, the Theatre Royal in Adelaide

First issue of *Melbourne Advertiser* (from 1839 the *Port Phillip Patriot and Melbourne Advertiser*)

Anna Maria Bunn's *The Guardian: A Tale, by an Australian* is first novel to be published in Sydney, although it is never offered for sale

1839   Louis Daguerre invents first camera to be in general use

Governor Gipps proclaims Aborigines to have equal rights under the laws of England

Port Darwin named during survey of northern waters by HMS *Beagle*

Berrima Gaol built in NSW

Melbourne Club inaugurated for 'the gentlemen of Port Phillip'

Australasian Chronicle is first Catholic newspaper (*Sydney Chronicle* from 1846)

1840   Transportation to NSW abolished

Edward John Eyre journeys from Adelaide to King George's Sound (1840–41)

Strzelecki climbs and names Mt Kosciusko, highest mountain in Australia

Convict labour used to break strikes in NSW

First issue of *Perth Inquirer*

First parts of Gould's *The Birds of Australia* published in London; completed 1848

Fidelia Hill's *Poems and Recollections of the Past* is first book of verse by a woman published in Australia

| 1841 | Caroline Chisholm establishes Female Immigrants' Home in Sydney
Darlinghurst Gaol receives first prisoners
Gas lighting introduced in Sydney
John Fairfax and Charles Kemp buy *Sydney Herald*
A Mother's Offering to Her Children 'by a Lady Long Resident in New South Wales' (pseudonym for Charlotte Barton) is first children's book |
|---|---|
| 1842 | Australasian Sugar Co. established near Sydney (later Colonial Sugar Refining Co.)
Benjamin Boyd establishes coastal steamship service at Twofold Bay, NSW
Royal Pavilion Saloon opens as Melbourne's first theatre (later the Theatre Royal)
David Burn's *Plays, and Fugitive Pieces, in Verse* is first collection of plays published in Australia
Henry Parkes, *Stolen Moments* |
| 1843 | First land sale in Brisbane
Collapse of Bank of Australia is first of several closures in depression of early 1840s
First Mental Health legislation in NSW (Dangerous Lunatics Act) |
| 1844 | Charles Sturt's expedition fails to discover the supposed inland sea
Ludwig Leichhardt travels from Sydney to Gulf of Carpentaria and then to Arnhem Land (1844–45)
First permanent synagogue opens in Sydney; others in Launceston (1844), Melbourne (1848), Adelaide (1850), Brisbane (1886)
Royal Society of Van Diemen's Land for Horticulture, Botany and the Advancement of Science founded (first Royal Society outside England)
Edward Geoghegan's *The Currency Lass* produced in Sydney
Louisa Meredith, *Notes and Sketches of New South Wales* |
| 1845 | Wreck of migrant ship *Cataraqui* is worst maritime disaster in Australian history with 407 drowned
First major colonial art exhibition is staged in Hobart
Thomas McCombie, *Arabin*; Mary Vidal, *Tales for the Bush*; 'Giacomo de Rosenberg', *Ralph Rashleigh or The Life of an Exile* |
| 1845–1847 | Irish Famine |
| 1846 | Imperial 'Waste Lands (Australia) Act' regulates leasing and alienation of Crown land in NSW
Ludwig Leichhardt leaves from Condamine River, in unsuccessful bid to cross continent; disappears in 1848
First issue of the *Moreton Bay Courier* (*Brisbane Courier-Mail* from 1861)
First issue of the *Argus* (Melbourne, 1846–1957) |
| 1847 | Caroline Chisholm publishes pamphlets in London opposing transportation and urging systematic immigration
T.H. Huxley in Australia 1847–1849
Transfer of survivors of Flinders Island Aboriginal settlement to Oyster Cove
Board of Education formed in South Australia to supervise public education |

Early use of first anaesthetic, ether, for medical and dental work in Sydney, Van Diemen's Land and Melbourne

Art Exhibition of 380 paintings presented by the Australian Subscription Library in Sydney

First opera written, composed and performed in Australia (*Don John of Austria*) is staged at Victoria Theatre, Sydney

First issue of the *Australian Medical Journal*, Sydney

1848   First detachment of native police sent from NSW to the Condamine district for employment against hostile Aborigines; force disbanded 1899

Edmund Kennedy killed by Aborigines during Cape York Peninsula expedition

First iron ore smelted, at Mittagong, NSW

First issue of a foreign-language newspaper, *Die Deutsche Post für die Australischen Kolonien*, in Adelaide

1849   Major gold discovery north-west of Melbourne

Renewed transportation of convicts to Sydney stopped by public protest

Port Phillip Aboriginal Protectorate abolished

Alexander Harris, *The Emigrant Family*

1850   First convict ships arrive in Swan River Colony

Australia League founded to work for universal male suffrage, land reform, and abolition of transportation

University of Sydney becomes first English-speaking university in the Southern Hemisphere; followed by Universities of Melbourne 1853, Adelaide 1874, Tasmania 1890, Queensland 1910, Western Australia 1911

Branches of Young Men's Christian Association established in Adelaide; followed by Melbourne and Sydney (1853) and Hobart (1854)

Henry Parkes becomes founding editor of *Empire* newspaper (1850–58)

1851   Colony of Victoria proclaimed independent of New South Wales

Edward Hargraves discovers gold near Bathurst, NSW

Gold rushes begin at Ballarat and Bendigo in Vic; much immigration follows during 1850s

Massive Victorian bushfires inspire William Strutt's 'Black Thursday' (painted 1862–64)

1852   British government agrees to halt transportation to Van Diemen's Land; last convict ship arrives 1853

First mail steamer arrives in Sydney from England

New South Wales Gold Fields Act formalises licensing system for prospectors

S.T. Gill's sketches of Victorian goldfields published in London

The *Sydney University Magazine* calls for a 'National Literature'

George Robertson arrives in Melbourne; establishes himself as a bookseller and publisher (George Robertson & Co.)

John Dunmore Lang, *Freedom and Independence for the Golden Lands of Australia*

1853   First riverboat steamer on the Murray

Establishment of Melbourne's Public Library

Charles Harpur, *The Bushrangers, a Play in Five Acts, and Other Poems*

1853–1856 Crimean War

1854 Eureka Stockade, unsuccessful rebellion of miners at Ballarat against licensing regulations, follows years of unrest on Australian goldfields; new Victorian gold rushes at Maldon and Ararat
Henry Parkes gains seat on NSW Legislative Council
Cobb & Co. commence coach operations
First Australian electric telegraph line opens between Melbourne and Williamstown
Sydney's Circular Quay, first proposed 1837, completed
First issue of the *Age* (Melbourne)
Catherine Helen Spence's *Clara Morison* is published anonymously; Richard Hengist Horne's *Orion*

1855 NSW and Victorian Constitution Acts proclaimed, with bicameral legislatures
Victoria legislates to restrict Chinese immigration; by 1888 all colonies have discriminatory restrictions on Chinese or non-whites
Lola Montez appears at newly-opened Theatre Royal, Melbourne

1856 South Australian Constitution Act proclaimed; includes manhood suffrage for Lower House of Parliament; Van Diemen's Land officially named Tasmania
Victorian Electoral Act introduces secret ballot, followed by SA (1856), NSW and Tas (1858) and WA (1877)
First May Day march in Victoria to celebrate success of 8-hour day campaign

1856–1858 *Journal of Australasia* publishes first account of Australian literature, *The Fiction Fields of Australia*

1857 Fort on Pinchgut Island, Sydney Cove, erected after Crimean War provoked anxiety about Australia's defences
Telegraphic communication established within Tasmania
Gertrude the Emigrant, by Caroline Atkinson, is first work by an Australian-born woman novelist

1858 Non-Aboriginal population reaches 1 000 000
Gold rush in Qld leads to settlement of Rockhampton
Unsuccessful expedition mounted to search for Ludwig Leichhardt
John McDouall Stuart explores large area in the north of SA (1858–59)
First Australian Rules football match between Scotch College and Melbourne Grammar School
First issue of the *South Australian Advertiser* (from 1899 *Advertiser*)

1859 Charles Darwin, *On the Origin of Species*
Queensland proclaimed as separate colony
Wreck of the SS *Admella* en route between Port Adelaide and Melbourne
Melbourne Trades Hall and Literary Institute opens
James Beaney's *Original Contributions to the Practice of Conservative Surgery* is one of first medical publications in Australia

Henry Kingsley's *The Recollections of Geoffry Hamlyn* published in England
Caroline Leakey's *The Broad Arrow* is rare example of female convict as chief character

1860   McDouall Stuart reaches geographical centre of Australia
Robert O'Hara Burke and William Wills cross the continent from south to north (1860–61), but perish on return journey
Hunter River Coalminers' Mutual Protective Association formed
Basis of National Gallery of Victoria established when Melbourne Public Library authorises fund for purchases in England of visual art collection
James Michael, *John Cumberland*

1861   Troops despatched to quell anti-Chinese riots on Lambing Flats diggings, NSW
Expedition recovers remains of Burke and Wills and rescues John King, sole survivor of their expedition
First Melbourne Cup
First English cricket team visits Australia (1861–62)

1862   McDouall Stuart crosses continent from Adelaide to Indian Ocean
Cobb & Co. extend services into NSW
Gold found at Walhalla, Vic
Victorian Acclimatization Society releases a number of non-native birds in the Botanic Gardens
University of Melbourne establishes first medical school in Australia; Sydney appoints first Dean of Medicine 1883, Adelaide 1884
Henry Kendall, *Poems and Songs*

1863   Northern Territory separated from NSW, placed under jurisdiction of SA
Ben Hall's bushranging gang becomes active
Sydney City Mission founded

1864   First issue of the *Australasian* (1864–1946)
William Walker's lecture 'Australian Literature' is first separate work of Australian criticism; published later in *Miscellanies*, 1884

1865   Bushrangers Dan Morgan and Ben Hall killed in separate incidents
First issue of the *Australian Journal* (1865–1968)
Catherine Helen Spence publishes *Mr Hogarth's Will* under her own name

1866   Mary McKillop founds the order of the Sisters of St Joseph of the Sacred Heart at Penola, SA
Intercolonial Exhibition includes work of newly-arrived Abram-Louis Buvelot
First issue of the *Queenslander* (ends 1939)
G.B. Barton's *Literature in New South Wales* and *The Poets and Prose Writers of New South Wales*, Australian contributions to the Paris Exhibition, are first book-length studies of Australian writing

1867   Gold rushes begin in Qld; riots against Chinese diggers at Crocodile Creek
Copper mining begins at Cloncurry (main activity 1910–20)

NSW Act prohibits supply of liquor to Aborigines
Evening News is first penny newspaper in NSW

1868   Transportation of convicts ends with cessation of transportation to WA
Queensland Polynesian Labourers Act addresses treatment of Pacific islanders
'blackbirded' to work in the sugar industry
Attempted assassination of Prince Alfred by the Fenian Henry O'Farrell leads
to New South Wales Treason Felony Act
The Christian Brothers, a Catholic teaching order, arrive in Melbourne

1869   Matthew Arnold, *Culture and Anarchy*
Qld becomes first colony to provide free elementary education
Australia's largest gold nugget, the 'Welcome Stranger', found near Dunolly,
Vic
Henry Kendall, *Leaves from Australian Forests*

1870   Withdrawal of last British troops from Australia
Construction begins on Adelaide–Darwin overland telegraph, completed
1872
Bushranger 'Captain Thunderbolt' killed near Uralla, NSW
Eugene von Guérard appointed head of painting school at Melbourne's
National School of Art, pupils include Tom Roberts and Frederick McCubbin
First issue of *Town and Country Journal* (closes 1919)
Adam Lindsay Gordon, *Bush Ballads and Galloping Rhymes*; Marcus Clarke's
His Natural Life serialised in the *Australian Journal* (1870–72)

1871   Anthony Trollope's first visit to Australia (1871–72)
First cablegram from overseas to Darwin
Primary education made free and compulsory in WA
Ballarat School of Mines, first institution for technical education, opens
Italian opera being performed in Sydney, Melbourne and Adelaide
The Detective's Album is only novel published by writer of short crime fiction
'Waif Wander' (Mary Fortune)
James Brunton Stephens, *Convict Once*

1872   Gold rush starts at Charters Towers, Qld
Victorian Education Act makes education free, compulsory and secular
Australian Natives' Association formed 'to stimulate patriotism in the native-
born'
First issue of the *Brisbane Telegraph*
David Unaipon, described as the 'true father of Aboriginal literature', is born

1873   Anthony Trollope's *Australia and New Zealand* and *Harry Heathcote of Gangoil*
published in London
Gold rush on Palmer River, Qld
SA government expedition names Ayers Rock (re-named Uluru, 1983)
SA develops Australia's first re-afforestation policy
Alfred Dampier, the new 'King of Melodrama' comes to Australia
First issue of the *Northern Territory Times and Gazette* (1823–1927), thereafter
the *Northern Territory Times* (1927–32)

1874   NSW wool traded with Japan for first time
Maloga mission established as a refuge for the estimated 9000 surviving Aborigines in NSW
Arrival of James Cassius Williamson, American actor who later founds the J.C. Williamson Theatre Company
Book publication of Clarke's *His Natural Life*; from 1882 title becomes *For the Term of His Natural Life*

1875   Havelock Ellis in Australia (1875–79)
Foundation of Presbyterian Ladies College, later the setting for *The Getting of Wisdom*, 1910 (film version 1977)

1876   Escape of Irish republican convicts from Fremantle on the American whaler *Catalpa* organised by John Boyle O'Reilly, author of *Moondyne* (1879)
Truganini, reputedly the last 'full-blood' Tasmanian Aborigine, dies in Hobart, aged 73
Invention of the stump-jump plough
David Syme's *Outline of an Industrial Science* promotes protectionism
First issue of the *Melbourne Review* (1876–85)

1877   Several whites killed by Aborigines on Daintree River, Qld, while occupation by miners of traditional hunting grounds near the Palmer River leads to reported starvation of local Aborigines
Hermannsburg Lutheran mission founded on Finke River, NT
Completion of overland telegraph between Adelaide and Perth connects all colonies
First Australian performance of an opera by Richard Wagner, *Lohengrin*, staged in Melbourne

1878   After dispute with police over horse-stealing, the Kelly bushranging gang becomes active in northern Vic
Australian cricket team plays successful series of matches in England
'Advance Australia Fair' sung in public for first time at a Sydney Scottish concert

1879   Joseph Conrad in Australia; later visits 1880, 1887, 1892, 1893
Australia's first International Exhibition held in Sydney
First Intercolonial Trades Union Congress held in Sydney
SA introduces legislation to end 'baby farming'
First production of a Gilbert and Sullivan opera, *HMS Pinafore*, at Theatre Royal, Melbourne
First issue of Sydney's *Daily Telegraph*
Walter Swan's *Luke Mivers* wins first place in the *Sydney Mail* competition for the best original work of fiction (published as *Luke Mivers' Harvest* in 1899)

1880   Bushranger 'Captain Moonlite' hanged at Darlinghurst Gaol; Ned Kelly captured at Glenrowan and hanged at Melbourne Gaol
Peter Lalor, a leader of Eureka Stockade rebellion, becomes Speaker of Victorian Legislative Assembly

Melbourne International Exhibition opens

First telephone exchange opens in Melbourne; by 1883 exchanges in all capitals except Perth

University of Melbourne admits female students; Sydney follows in 1881

First issue of the *Bulletin*, founded in Sydney by J.F. Archibald and John Haynes

Rosa Praed, *An Australian Heroine*

1881   Intercolonial conference agrees on immigration restrictions

Census declares non-Aboriginal population of 2 250 194

Mt Morgan, near Rockhampton, Qld, becomes Australia's richest gold mine

National Gallery of South Australia opened by Prince Albert Victor

Catherine Helen Spence's *Gathered In* begins serialisation in Adelaide *Observer*

1882   Australian cricket eleven return from triumphant season in the first series of the 'Ashes'

First women's trade union formed after strike of tailoresses in Melbourne

NSW Art Gallery first opens to the public on Sunday

Rolf Boldrewood's *Robbery Under Arms* serialised in *Sydney Mail* (1882–83)

1883   Broken Hill Proprietary Co. formed after discovery of silver and lead in the Barrier Ranges

First coal loaded at Port Kembla, NSW

First regular train service between Sydney and Melbourne; difference in gauges meant passengers must change trains at Albury

Sydney Royal Theatre uses electricity for stage lighting to replace gas lights, which frequently caused fires

Edward Cole's Book Arcade opens in Melbourne

Charles Harpur, *Poems*; George Rusden, *History of Australia* (3 vols)

1884   NSW legislation on Crown lands—providing for purchases and leases by auction, pastoral leases, state forests and reserves—becomes model for all Australian Crown land legislation

Royal Commission calls for investigation of Murray River for irrigation purposes

Massacre at McKinlay River, NT, of Aborigines wrongly identified as responsible for attack on Daly River copper mine

Hugh McKay invents stripper harvester for wheat (Sunshine Harvester)

1885   Death of Gordon at Khartoum; NSW sends 700 volunteer troops to join the British Expeditionary Force in Sudan

Vic Employers' Union formed after successful bootmakers' strike of 1884; Vic Wharf Labourers' Union formed

Royal Commission into use of Pacific islanders ('Kanakas') as labourers finds that of the over 9000 in Qld, many had been kidnapped or intimidated by ships licensed to recruit labourers

Cartoon in Qld *Punch and Figaro* reflects concern at northward incursion of 'furry hordes' of rabbits

Kimberley, WA, goldfield discovered

Sydney's Archbishop Moran becomes Australia's first cardinal of Catholic Church

First issues of the *West Australian*; the *Sunday Times* (first Sunday newspaper in NSW); Melbourne magazine *Table Talk* (closes 1939)

Mary Hannay Foott, *Where the Pelican Builds*

1886   First Australian Antarctic exploration committee formed

Australasian Association for the Advancement of Science founded at University of Sydney

Broken Hill Proprietary Co. opens smelting works at Broken Hill

Vic wharf labourers strike for eight-hour day; Amalgamated Shearers' Union formed at Ballarat, joined in same year by NSW unionists from Bourke and Wagga

WA Aborigines' Protection Board established

Princess Theatre (Melbourne) opens with performance of *The Mikado*

J.F. Archibald editor of *Bulletin* 1886–1902

Fergus Hume, *The Mystery of a Hansom Cab*

1887   Victorian Farmers' Protection Association formed

First issue of the *Radical*, first regular socialist newspaper

William Lane founds and edits the weekly *Boomerang* (1887–92)

Ada Cambridge, *Unspoken Thoughts*

1888   George Eastman invents Kodak camera using paper for film

Brisbane and Sydney connected by rail

Newcastle coalminers' strike disrupts economies of NSW and Vic

Douglas Sladen publishes three anthologies of Australian and New Zealand poetry in London

Louisa Lawson begins publication of *The Dawn: A Journal for Australian Women*

Francis Adams, *Songs of the Army of the Night*

1889   Henry Parkes's Tenterfield oration calls for a national union; first meeting of Premiers takes place in Melbourne in 1890

First annual conference of the New South Wales Free Trade and Liberal Association

Strike of Amalgamated Miners' Union forces Broken Hill Proprietary Co. to agree to compulsory unionism

9 × 5 Impressions Exhibition in Melbourne is condemned by major art critics

1890   Henry George, American advocate of single tax on land, visits Australia

Robert Louis Stevenson in Australia (and 1891)

WA granted self-government

Maritime strike of transport workers, supported by mine and pastoral workers, in conflict with Pastoralists' Union on issue of 'closed shop' versus 'freedom of contract'; breaking of strike involves government recruitment of special constables (250 in Vic)

Murchison goldfields open in WA

William Lane founds New Australia Association and establishes the *Australian Worker* (Brisbane)

First issues of Sydney *Truth*, a Sunday newspaper (from 1958 *Sunday Mirror*, closes 1979) and *The Australasian Critic: a Monthly Review of Literature, Science and Art* (closes 1891)

1891   Rudyard Kipling in Australia; Sarah Bernhardt appears at Her Majesty's Theatre, Sydney
Vessels of the newly established Royal Navy's Australian Auxiliary Squadron arrive in Sydney
First Labor Party members elected to parliament: in SA and NSW
Shearers' strikes in Qld, NSW and Vic are broken by Pastoralists' Union and colonial troops, which forces acceptance of non-union labour; Lawson's 'Freedom on the Wallaby', published in *Worker*, is inspired by shearers' strike
Worker begins fortnightly publication in Brisbane and Sydney; Shearers' Union begins weekly publication of the *Hummer* at Wagga
Ada Cambridge, *The Three Miss Kings*; George Essex Evans, *The Repentance of Magdalene Despar*; Tasma, *The Penance of Portia James*

1892   Qld Elections Act pioneers preferential voting system adopted by Tas (1897), WA (1904), Vic (1911), Federal Parliament (1918), NSW (1926), SA (1929)
Gold rushes begin in eastern WA with discovery of gold at Coolgardie, followed by Kalgoorlie in 1893
Broken Hill miners lose 4-month strike against introduction of piecework rates of pay
William Lane publishes *The Workingman's Paradise* to raise funds for the families of unionists imprisoned during the 1891 shearers' strike
First issue of *New Australia*, journal of the New Australia Association
Price Warung, *Tales of the Convict System*

1893   Some 14 banks fail, affecting thousands of investors
Royal Tar sails for Paraguay with William Lane and about 220 colonists for a planned socialist settlement, New Australia
First public telephone (at the Sydney GPO)
Simpson Newland, *Paving the Way*; Francis Adams, *The Australians*

1894   SA becomes first colony to include women in the franchise (WA follows in 1899, NSW in 1902, Tas in 1903, Qld in 1905, Vic in 1909); women become eligible to vote and to stand for election to federal parliament in 1902
SA Act to Facilitate the Settlement of Industrial Disputes sets the pattern for later arbitration acts in Australia
Second Qld shearers' strike is broken by non-union labour; Australian Workers' Union formed
Differing local times are replaced by fixing of common time zones: one for the eastern colonies, one for SA, and one for WA
Lawrence Hargrave, aviation pioneer, ascends to five metres using four box kites
Women's College opens to provide accommodation for women students of Sydney University
Ethel Turner, *Seven Little Australians*

1895   Mark Twain in Australia

Music School (later the Conservatorium) opens at University of Melbourne; Queensland Art Gallery and Art Gallery of Western Australia are officially opened; Sydney Society of Artists formed with Tom Roberts as first president
'Waltzing Matilda' first sung in public at Winton, Qld
Angus and Robertson begin regular publishing with A.B. Paterson's *The Man From Snowy River*, which sells 10 000 copies in first year of publication
Bulletin publishes first of sketches by Steele Rudd (Arthur Hoey Davis)

1895–1902   Major national drought

1896   Death of Sir Henry Parkes
First film made in Australia (of the Melbourne Cup)
First motion pictures shown in Melbourne and Sydney, where Marius Sestier opens first cinema and shoots earliest Australian films
Bulletin 'Red Page' is set up by A.G. Stephens, who edits it 1896–1906
Henry Lawson, *While the Billy Boils*

1897   Queensland Aboriginals' Protection and Restriction of the Sale of Opium Act provides that Aborigines and 'half-castes', unless lawfully employed or married to white men, must be restricted to reserves under the control of Protectors; this becomes model for legislation in SA, the NT and WA
Australasian Horseless Carriage Syndicate exhibits a motor buggy at Melbourne's Exhibition Building
Inaugural award of Wynne Prize for a landscape in oils or a sculpture goes to Walter Withers for 'The Storm'
First issue of radical weekly *Tocsin*, instigated by Bernard O'Dowd (becomes *Labor Call* 1906–53; *Labor* to its close in 1961)

1898   Federal convention; draft bill for federal constitution fails to obtain necessary majority in referendums held in NSW, Vic, Tas and SA
William Farrer begins experiments to breed suitable Australian wheat strains
Foundation stone laid in Sydney for first Greek Orthodox church in Australia
Exhibition of works of Heidelberg School and Sydney Society of Artists in London
A.C. Rowlandson founds New South Wales Bookstall Company
Barrier Truth appears in Broken Hill as first English-language union-owned paper
'The Beginnings of Australian Literature' delivered in London as a lecture by Arthur Patchett Martin

1899   Commonwealth constitution is approved by all colonies except WA in second round of referendums
Labor governs for six days in Qld as first Labor government in Australia
Electric tramways commence operation in Sydney and Perth
Australian Literature Society founded in Melbourne
First issue of A.G. Stephens's *Bookfellow* (1899–1925)
Steele Rudd, *On Our Selection*; Ethel Pedley, *Dot and the Kangaroo*

1899–1902   Boer War; all colonies send contingents in 1899 to serve in British forces. Federal battalion follows in 1902; total Australian service deaths 1400

1900	British Parliament passes an Act to Constitute the Commonwealth of Australia; amendment retains right to appeal to Privy Council against decisions of Australian courts, except in constitutional matters
	Queen Victoria appoints Earl of Hopetoun as first Governor-General
	Colonies send gunboat and contingent of volunteers to China to support Britain in Boxer Rebellion
	First of series of epidemics of bubonic plague kills 458
	Two Aboriginal brothers, Jimmie and Joe Governor, with Jackie Underwood, kill seven whites in NSW
	Adelaide Conservatorium of Music opens
	First issue of the *Brisbane Truth* (from 1960, *Sunday Sun*)
1901	Proclamation of Federal Constitution and swearing in of the Governor-General in Centennial Park, 1 January, is followed by first federal elections in March
	First parliament of the Commonwealth of Australia opened by the Duke of Cornwall and York (later King George V); Edmund Barton is first Prime Minister
	Census shows (white) population of 3 773 801
	Laying of telegraph cable from SA to Cape of Good Hope begins
	Federal 'White Australia policy' legislation restricts settlement by non-Europeans and empowers immigration officers to require entrants to pass a dictation test in a European language
	Industrial and Arbitration Act of New South Wales constitutes a tribunal presided over by a Supreme Court judge
	Frederick Drake-Brockman explores Kimberley region of WA
	Henry Lawson, *Joe Wilson and His Mates*; Miles Franklin, *My Brilliant Career*
1901–1910	Reign of Edward VII
1902	Federal public service established
	Federal Franchise Act extends franchise to women
	Pacific cable between Australia and Canada opened; first interstate trunk telephone line opened between Mt Gambier, SA, and Nelson, Vic
	First woman to graduate in law (at University of Sydney) is excluded from practice until after the passage of the NSW Women's Legal Status Act of 1918; women first admitted to legal practice in Vic in 1903
	Nellie Melba returns to perform in Australia for the first time
	First issue of *New Idea* as a monthly women's magazine (later weekly)
	Barbara Baynton, *Bush Studies*
1902–1904	NSW Royal Commission on education
1903	Establishment of High Court of Australia; Prime Minister Edmund Barton resigns to serve as a judge; Alfred Deakin succeeds him as Prime Minister
	Coolgardie Water Supply scheme pumps water 560 kilometres to the goldfields
	First issue of Brisbane *Daily Mail* (merges with Brisbane *Courier* 1933)
	First issue of *Steele Rudd's Magazine* (1903–27)
	Joseph Furphy, *Such is Life, being Certain Extracts from the Diary of Tom Collins*; Bernard O'Dowd, *Dawnward?*

1904   Conciliation and Arbitration Act establishes Arbitration Court, NSW
Royal Commission on the Decline of the Birth-rate and the Mortality of
Infants
First Australian Rhodes Scholars chosen
Felton Bequest funds major development of Victorian National Gallery
W.B. Spencer and F.J. Gillen, *The Northern Tribes of Central Australia*

1905   Japan defeats Russia in the Russo-Japanese War
Western Australia Aborigines Act extends controls over Aboriginal reserves
Herbert Hoover (afterwards US President) forms Zinc Corporation (later
Conzinc Riotinto of Australia)
Melbourne to Sydney reliability competition for motor cars
Lothian Publishing Co. founded in Melbourne

1906   British New Guinea becomes a territory of the Commonwealth
Prohibition on daytime surf bathing is removed; Surf Bathers' Lifesaving
Club of Bondi is first in world; seventeen clubs are formed between 1906 and
1912
Sydney's Central Railway Station opened
Melbourne Symphony Orchestra is first Australian permanent orchestra
The Story of the Kelly Gang screened in Melbourne
A.H. Adams becomes editor of *Bulletin* 'Red Page' (1906–09)

1907   Concept of 'basic wage' is formulated in the 'Harvester' judgment delivered
by Mr Justice Higgins in the Conciliation and Arbitration Court
WA completes an 1116-mile (1800-kilometre) rabbit-proof fence, which fails
to keep out rabbits
Carlton and United Breweries established in Melbourne
Australia wins Davis Cup for first time, while Norman Brookes is first
Australian to win at Wimbledon
First film of *Robbery Under Arms* (others 1920, 1957)
First issue of *Lone Hand* (closes 1921)

1908   House of Representatives selects Yass-Canberra area as site of national capital
Deakin government establishes the Commonwealth Literary Fund on the
model of British Royal Literary Fund
Formation of Adelaide Literary Theatre (from 1913 Adelaide Repertory
Theatre)
Mary Gilmore becomes founding editor of the Women's Page of the *Worker*
(resigns 1931)
Film of *For the Term of His Natural Life* (re-made 1927)
Henry Handel Richardson, *Maurice Guest*; Mrs Aeneas Gunn, *We of the Never
Never*; Ernest Favenc; *The Explorers of Australia*; Dorothea Mackellar's 'My
Country' published in the *Spectator* in London

1909   Kitchener invited by federal government to make recommendations on
Australian defence forces (*Memorandum on the Defence of Australia* presented
1910)
Tours of Australia by singers Peter Dawson, Amy Castles and, for third time,
Nellie Melba

1910 First Labor government elected with a majority is formed with Andrew Fisher as Prime Minister
Federal Bills of Exchange Act defines role of banks; Bank Notes Act establishes Australian paper currency
Naval Defence Act provides for an Australian navy which could be placed under British Admiralty in wartime
New South Wales Murrumbidgee Irrigation Area Resumption Act opens up large area of land for settlement
Mitchell Library opens in Sydney
First issue of the Sydney *Sun* as an afternoon daily
Expansion of film industry begins with premiere of *The Life and Adventures of John Vane, the Notorious Australian Bushranger*
C.E.W. Bean, *On the Wooltrack*; Mary Grant Bruce, *A Little Bush Maid*, first of the '*Billabong*' novels; Mary Gilmore, *Marri'd and Other Verses*

1910–1936 Reign of George V

1911 Australian Capital Territory formed by transfer of land from NSW to Commonwealth around Canberra and Jervis Bay; administration of NT transferred from SA to Commonwealth
Commonwealth Electoral Act makes enrolment compulsory but voting is not compulsory until 1924
Mawson Australasian Antarctic expedition leaves Hobart to establish base on Macquarie Island and explore large area of Antarctica, establishing further bases there
The Festival of the Empire (later known as the Commonwealth Games) is held at Crystal Palace in London
Royal Military College established at Duntroon
Melbourne Repertory Theatre founded by Gregan McMahon
Louis Stone, *Jonah*

1911–1914 Approximately 300 000 migrants (mostly British) arrive

1912 Walter Burley Griffin wins competition to design national capital (dismissed as director of design and construction in 1920)
Federal government establishes Commonwealth Bank—'the people's bank'; passes Maternity Allowance Act (Aborigines, Asians and Pacific islanders excluded)
Presbyterian Church sends John Flynn as first director of its mission to NT
The first public children's library in Australia opens in the Sydney Municipal Library
Premiere of *On Our Selection* as stage production
The Golden Treasury of Australian Verse (ed. Bertram Stevens) is released in London and Australia

1913 Foundation stone of Australia House in London laid by George V
The Governor-General, Lord Denman, lays the foundation stone of the federal capital
First Commonwealth penny postage stamp bears map of Australia with kangaroo in centre

1914	First World War begins; Australia follows Britain in declaring war on Germany; War Precautions Act passed
	First Australian shot is fired by Fort Nepean battery against German merchant ship attempting to leave Port Phillip Bay; the first naval victory is the sinking by HMAS *Sydney* of the German cruiser *Emden* in the Indian Ocean
	Australian Naval and Expeditionary Force captures German New Guinea
	First Division of Australian Imperial Force and the New Zealand Expeditionary Force arrive to protect Egypt against Turkey (allied with Germany)
	Australia's first airmail arrives before outbreak of war
	C.J. Brennan, *Poems (1913)*
1915	Under heavy Turkish fire, AIF establishes beachhead at Anzac Cove for Allied landing at Gallipoli (25 April); when evacuated in December, AIF had suffered 7594 dead and 19 500 wounded
	Australian Flying Corps members leave for service in Mesopotamia
	Opening of BHP's steel works in Newcastle
	Establishment of NSW Conservatorium of Music
	C.J. Dennis, *Songs of a Sentimental Bloke*
1916	First Australian troops land in France
	Prime Minister W.M. ('Billy') Hughes's proposals for conscription for overseas service are defeated in a referendum; Federal Labor Party splits on conscription issue, but Hughes remains as Prime Minister with Nationalist support
	Returned Soldiers' and Sailors' Imperial League of Australia (later RSL) founded
	Coalminers' strike settled in conference called under War Precautions Act
	12 members of the suppressed Industrial Workers of the World imprisoned for sedition
	Raymond Longford makes film version of *The Sentimental Bloke* (not screened until 1919, and re-made 1932)
	First issue of *Birth* (closes 1922)
	C.J. Dennis, *The Moods of Ginger Mick*; Furnley Maurice, 'To God: From the Weary Nations'
1917	Bolsheviks seize power in Russia on 17 October; Russia signs separate peace treaty with Germany
	Australians involved on Western Front
	Second referendum rejects conscription; Daniel Mannix, new Catholic Archbishop of Melbourne, is one of most vigorous opponents
	High cost of living provokes major strikes in NSW and Vic; street protests are organised in Melbourne by the Women's Peace Army
	Trans-Australian Railway connects Brisbane to Perth via Sydney, but with changes of gauge at state borders
	Anti-German feeling leads to name changes for over 40 SA towns and districts with names reflecting German settlement (notably in Barossa Valley)
	Henry Handel Richardson, *Australia Felix*
1918	Sir John Monash becomes first Australian to command the Australian

divisions; AIF in action at Amiens, Villers-Bretonneux and in final Allied offensive; First World War ends 11 November

Commonwealth Electoral Act introduces preferential voting for House of Representatives (for Senate in 1919)

First direct wireless message from Britain

May Gibbs, *Snugglepot and Cuddlepie*; Norman Lindsay, *The Magic Pudding*

1919   Paris peace conference creates covenant to form League of Nations

Hughes is a signatory to the Treaty of Versailles, gaining a mandate over German New Guinea

Ireland's right to self-government endorsed by large crowd in rally after Australasian Irish convention in Melbourne

Returning troops bring Spanish flu epidemic: 11 500 deaths

Soldier Settlement schemes set up in all states; War Service Homes Commission stimulates suburban growth

Widespread waterfront and mining strikes

First direct flight from England lands at Darwin

First issue of *Smith's Weekly* (closes 1950)

1920   Prince of Wales tours Australia

Foundation of the Communist Party of Australia (trades union faction affiliates with international body 1922)

Formation of the federal Australian Country Party

Establishment of Queensland and Northern Territory Aerial Services (Qantas); operations commence 1922 between Charleville and Cloncurry

Commonwealth Board formed to control the prickly pear pest; cactoblastus moth imported from Argentina 1928; control achieved 1934

Film releases of Franklyn Barrett's *The Breaking of the Drought*, Beaumont Smith's *The Man from Snowy River* and Raymond Longford's *On Our Selection* (re-made for sound 1932)

1921   First woman elected to an Australian parliament (Edith Cowan in WA); Australian Federation of Women Voters formed

Gladys Moncrieff makes first of more than 3000 appearances in *The Maid of the Mountains*

First Archibald Prize for Portraiture won by William McInnes

C.E.W. Bean's *The Story of Anzac* is first of the 12–volume *Official History of Australia in the War of 1914–18*

The comic strip 'Ginger Meggs', by J.C. Bancks, first appears in the Sydney *Sunday Sun*

1922   Establishment of the Union of Soviet Socialist Republics (USSR)

Empire Settlement Act and legislation for assisted passages leads to some 300 000 immigrants during 1920s

Qld becomes first state to abolish capital punishment (last is Vic in 1975)

State funeral for Henry Lawson

Establishment of Melbourne University Press

First issue of *Sun News-Pictorial* in Melbourne (taken over by *Weekly Times* 1935)

Louis Esson's *The Battler* is first play performed by Melbourne's newly formed Pioneer Players (last performance of Players is 1926)

1923   Establishment of Commonwealth Loan Council increases federal control of economy
Vic police strike inspires militant right-wing group, the White Guard, dedicated to fighting bolshevism
Mt Isa silver-lead field discovered; Mt Isa Mines Ltd begins mining 1925
Kerosene refrigerator, Silent Knight, developed by Edward Hallstrom; Vegemite developed to compete with British yeast extract, Marmite
Opening of first public radio station, 2SB Sydney (later 2BL)
First issue of *Vision* (closes 1924)
D.H. Lawrence's *Kangaroo*, written while he lived at Thirroul, NSW, is published in London

1924   Vic State Electricity Commission begins operating brown coal generator at Yallourn; Shell Co begins refining operations in NSW, the Commonwealth Oil Refineries in Vic
Last run of a Cobb & Co. coach (in Qld)
End of Australia's longest recorded heatwave, 170 consecutive days at or above 100 degrees Fahrenheit at Marble Bar, WA
Radio stations 2FC (Sydney) and 3AR (Melbourne) open
D.H. Lawrence and M.L. Skinner, *The Boy in the Bush* and *A Book of Australasian Verse* (ed. Walter Murdoch) published in London
A Book of Queensland Verse, ed. J.J. Stable and A.E.M. Kirkwood, celebrates Qld centenary with first regional anthology

1925   'Big Brother' movement aims to assist British youths to migrate to Australia as farm workers
John Lang becomes Premier in NSW
'The indigenous art of Australia', article by artist Margaret Preston, pioneers acknowledgment of Aboriginal art
First Australian jazz record made by the group, the Californians
The Australian Encyclopaedia, ed. Arthur Jose, 2 vols (1925–26)

1926   Anna Pavlova tours Australia; Robert Helpmann studies with her company during tour
Creation of the Council for Scientific and Industrial Research, later the CSIRO
Regular electric and underground railway services begin in Sydney
Sydney Contemporary Group of painters holds first exhibition
Formation of Hoyts Theatres Ltd ushers in period of building of 'picture palaces'
First issues of the *Canberra Times* and the *Australian Woman's Mirror*
Katharine Susannah Prichard, *Working Bullocks*

1927   C. Hartley Grattan makes the first of several visits to Australia, leading to 1929 American publication of *Australian Literature*
Parliament House, Canberra, officially opened by the Duke of York
Oombulgurri massacre of Aborigines in WA; Aborigines banned from central Perth (ban lifted 1948)

David Unaipon and other Aborigines petition federal parliament for a separate Aboriginal State

Formation of Australasian Council of Trade Unions (Australian from 1943)

Melbourne underworld figure, 'Squizzy' Taylor, assassinated

SA painter Hans Heysen secures record sales at Sydney exhibition

Royal Commission into film industry finds local film makers being squeezed out by imported films, despite success of locally produced films such as the 1927 adaptation of *For the Term of His Natural Life*

F.J. Gillen and W.B. Spencer, *The Arunta*

1928   Massacre of at least 31 Aborigines follows killing of white man near Coniston; subsequent report by Chief Protector of Aborigines in Qld recommends creation of reserves, special Aboriginal courts, and removal of 'half-caste' children from Aboriginal mothers

During wharf strikes of 1928–29 police fire kills one of striking workers in Melbourne

First solo flight from England, first flights across the Pacific and to New Zealand, and first non-stop flight across Australia; the Flying Doctor Service makes its inaugural flight from its Cloncurry base

Aeroplane Jelly is marketed for first time

Donald Bradman scores 1690 runs in his first season of test cricket during England's 1928–29 tour of Australia

The Jazz Singer introduces 'talking' pictures to Australia

Inaugural meeting of the Fellowship of Australian Writers is held at the Lyceum Club in Sydney

First *Bulletin* novel prize is shared by Katharine Susannah Prichard's *Coonardoo* and M. Barnard Eldershaw's *A House is Built*

1929   New York stock exchange crash; global economic depression begins (the Great Slump)

Severe industrial unrest leads to further strikes and lockouts; right-wing group, Who's for Australia League, forms in reaction to industrial unrest and election of Scullin Labor government; All for Australia League formed 1930

Official report on failures of soldier settlement scheme

Central Australia Railway links Alice Springs to Adelaide via Oodnadatta

Commonwealth censors ban James Joyce's *Ulysses*

London publication of *Ultima Thule* completes Henry Handel Richardson's trilogy (published 1930 as *The Fortunes of Richard Mahony*)

Frederic Manning's *The Middle Parts of Fortune* is published anonymously in London (abridged as *Her Privates We* in 1930)

David Unaipon, *Legendary Tales of the Australian Aborigines*; in 1930 this manuscript is published without acknowledgment as *Myths and Legends of the Australian Aborigines* by William Ramsay Smith

1929–1934   The Great Depression

1930   Harold Lasseter dies during expedition to find the reef of gold he claimed to have discovered years earlier in the NT

Phar Lap wins the Melbourne Cup

Doris Fitton forms the Independent Theatre Company in Sydney
W.K. Hancock, *Australia*; H.M. Green, *An Outline of Australian Literature*;
Norman Lindsay, *Redheap*; Vance Palmer, *The Passage*

1931   Japan invades Manchuria
Isaac Isaacs becomes first Australian-born Governor-General
Newly-formed United Australia Party is elected federally under leadership of
Joseph Lyons
First postwar airmail from England arrives in Sydney
General Motors-Holden formed by merger of General Motors and SA firm
Holden
Cinesound Review begins as first regular Australian-made cinema newsreel.
Ken Hall's sound production of *On Our Selection*, advertised in 1931, is not
shown until 1932
Ion L. Idriess, *Lasseter's Last Ride: an Epic of Central Australian Gold Discovery*;
Kenneth Slessor, 'Five Visions of Captain Cook'

1932   Registered unemployment peaks at 28 per cent; every state establishes
employment councils to provide relief work; townspeople at Cairns attack
travelling unemployed camped in local showgrounds
Australian Broadcasting Commission (ABC) established as national broad-
caster; by 1936 ABC had set up orchestras in all states
Official opening of Sydney Harbour Bridge by John Lang disrupted by inter-
vention of member of right-wing New Guard. Lang later dismissed by NSW
Governor, Sir Philip Game
Phar Lap, record Australian stake winner, dies in USA
'Bodyline' bowling of English test cricket team makes 1932–33 test series
(won 4–1 by England) extremely controversial
Leonard Mann, *Flesh in Armour*

1933   Hitler comes to power in Germany
Australian Antarctic Territory created by British order-in-council (Acceptance
Act ratified in 1936 in Australia)
Third Commonwealth Census shows non-Aboriginal population of
6 629 939
Charles Chauvel's *In the Wake of the Bounty*, starring Australian-born Errol
Flynn, is shown in Sydney
First issue of the *Australian Women's Weekly* (published by Frank Packer) sells
120 000 copies

1934   Czech communist writer Egon Kisch defies government's attempts to prevent
his entry into Australia for anti-war conference; his public appearances
include Sydney FAW's welcome to visiting Poet Laureate John Masefield
Dedication by the Duke of Gloucester of Melbourne's First World War
memorial, the Shrine of Remembrance
Formation of the Book Censorship Abolition League
Adam Lindsay Gordon becomes only poet writing in Australia to be recog-
nised in Poets' Corner, Westminster Abbey
First issue of *Walkabout* published by Australian Travel Association
Christina Stead, *Seven Poor Men of Sydney*; Brian Penton, *The Landtakers*

1935 Italy invades Ethiopia
Greek coup overthrows Republican constitution and restores monarchy
Charles Kingsford-Smith disappears while attempting a record-breaking flight from England to Australia
Giant cane toad is introduced to control beetle destroying sugar-cane crop, but itself becomes a pest
Charles Chauvel wins federal government film competition with *Heritage*, a history of Australia
FAW AGM calls for the abolition of censorship

1936 The Spanish Civil War (1936–39) begins with Franco's invasion of the Republic; some 50 Australians serve in the International Brigade or as volunteer nurses or ambulance drivers
New constitution (the 'Stalin' constitution) for USSR
Abdication of Edward VIII; his brother the Duke of York becomes King George VI
Amendment to WA Aborigines Act allows Aborigines to be taken into custody without trial and to be excluded from prescribed towns without a permit
Formation of the Council for Civil Liberties
New Theatre's production of anti-fascist *Till the Day I Die* is banned after pressure from the German Consul-General
Miles Franklin, *All That Swagger*; Jean Devanny, *Sugar Heaven*; P.R. Stephensen, *Foundations of Culture in Australia*

1937 Japan invades Northern China
Conference of state and federal officials recommends policy of assimilation for part-Aborigines and segregation on reserves for full-blood Aborigines
Severe epidemic of poliomyelitis
The Spirit of Progress, Australia's new air-conditioned train, cannot provide complete service between Melbourne and Sydney because of differences in state rail gauges (line standardised in 1962)
First broadcast of ABC serial *Dad and Dave*; runs until 1953

1938 Germany invades Austria and Czechoslovakia; restricted entry of Jewish refugees until the outbreak of war
Australia's sesquicentenary; celebrations include the first Empire Games in Australia and re-enactment of Phillip's 1788 landing; Aborigines' Progressive Association declares Australia Day a 'day of mourning'
Despite trade union embargo on shipment of iron ore to Japan, R.G. Menzies, as Attorney-General, enforces shipment of pig iron, earning the nickname 'Pig Iron Bob'
Contemporary Art Society formed as protest against conservatism of Australian Academy of Art
First exhibition of Albert Namatjira's paintings held in Melbourne
Cinesound becomes the only remaining Australian film company
Jindyworobak movement founded in Adelaide; Rex Ingamells publishes *Conditional Culture* and first Jindyworobak Anthology appears (last in 1955)
Abo Call, first newspaper written by and for Aborigines, runs for six issues

Xavier Herbert, *Capricornia*; Kylie Tennant, *Foveaux*; Daisy Bates, *The Passing of the Aborigines*

1939   Great Britain and Australia declare war on Germany
Non-aggression pact between Stalin and Hitler
Large number of foreign nationals interned under national security regulations
'Black Friday' bushfires in Victoria
First broadcast of Australia Calling (later Radio Australia)
H.G. Wells, as representative of anti-fascist International Association of Writers for the Defence of Culture, speaks against censorship in Sydney
Expansion of the Commonwealth Literary Fund; first issue of *Southerly*
Brian Fitzpatrick, *British Imperialism and Australia*

1940   France surrenders to Germany; British troops evacuated from Dunkirk; Britain sends contingent of pre-war German refugees on the *Dunera* to Australia, where they are initially interned at Hay, NSW
First contingent of Second AIF embark for service against Italian army in the Middle East; first Royal Australian Air Force contingent departs for training in Canada
Communist Party of Australia is banned
Many writers oppose the National Security legislation which places newspapers, radio and films under control of director-general of information
ABC appoints first woman announcer
Charles Chauvel's *Forty Thousand Horsemen*, starring Chips Rafferty, achieves international release
Inauguration of Commonwealth Literature Fund lectures
Douglas Stewart becomes literary editor of the *Bulletin* (until 1961)
First issues of *Meanjin Papers* (later *Meanjin*), ed. by Clem Christesen, and *Angry Penguins*, ed. by Max Harris (closes 1946)
Christina Stead, *The Man Who Loved Children*

1941   Japan launches Pacific offensive with landings in Thailand and Malaya followed by attack on Pearl Harbor
The Australian Women's Army Service created; men called up for full-time home defence army service
Formation of Labor government under John Curtin
First issues of *Coast to Coast* (1941–73) and *Salt*—the Army Education Service's monthly magazine
First issue of *Poetry: A Quarterly of Australian and New Zealand Verse* (ed. Flexmore Hudson, 1941–47)
Eleanor Dark, *The Timeless Land*; Ernestine Hill, *My Love Must Wait*

1942   Singapore surrenders to Japanese; many thousands of Australians become prisoners-of-war
Japan bombs Darwin; three Japanese midget submarines enter Sydney Harbour; Japan is defeated by Americans in the Battle of the Coral Sea; Australians win control of Kokoda Trail; Hitler invades Russia; ban on CPA is lifted

A Crisis Number of *Meanjin Papers* is produced
C. Hartley Grattan's *Introducing Australia* publicises Australia in America

1943   Japanese defeated in Papua; Japanese suffer losses in battle of Bismarck Sea
Curtin Labor government wins federal election; first two women in federal parliament, Enid Lyons and Dorothy Tangney
First issues of *Australian New Writing* (1943–46) and *Barjai* (1943–47)
Brian Penton, *Advance Australia—Where?*

1944   Japanese prisoners-of-war attempt escape at Cowra; 234 killed
Formation of Liberal Party with R.G. Menzies as leader
Ern Malley hoax perpetrated by James McAuley and Harold Stewart: Ern Malley's poems appear in the Autumn edition of *Angry Penguins* and Max Harris is later prosecuted successfully for obscenity
Christina Stead, *For Love Alone*; Kenneth Slessor, *One Hundred Poems*

1945   German forces surrender in Europe
Atomic bombs dropped on Hiroshima and Nagasaki; Japan surrenders
Establishment of the United Nations
Indonesia claims independence from the Netherlands; period of civil war follows
John Curtin dies; Ben Chifley replaces him as Prime Minister
Strike of Aboriginal stockworkers in the Pilbara region of WA (1945–46)
Howard Florey, co-discoverer of penicillin, is first Australian to be awarded Nobel Prize
The Australian Book Council, later National Book Council, formed in Sydney
Sidney Baker, *The Australian Language*

1946   Australian members of British Commonwealth Occupation Force in Japan include writers T.A.G. Hungerford and Hal Porter
Trans-Australia Airlines established
Assisted migration for English migrants to Australia resumes
Convictions in obscenity trials of Angus and Robertson, as publishers of Lawson Glassop's *We Were the Rats*, and Robert Close, as author of *Love Me, Sailor*; Close case continues through three trials and an appeal to 1948
Film *The Overlanders*, produced in Britain, is released in Sydney
Children's Book of the Year Award begins
Judith Wright, *The Moving Image*; C.E.W. Bean, *Anzac to Amiens*

1947   Independence and partition of India and Pakistan
British Publishing Traditional Market Agreement limits direct access to American books
Postwar European immigration program begins
Census records Australian population at 7 579 358; 'Full-blood' Aborigines, counted separately, are 46 638
Prime Minister Chifley introduces legislation to nationalise banks; later declared unconstitutional

Bob and Dolly Dyer's *Pick-a-box* quiz program commences on radio (transferred to television 1957–71)

T.G.H. Strehlow, *Aranda Traditions*; M. Barnard Eldershaw, *Tomorrow and Tomorrow* (censored; full version published 1984)

1948   Don Bradman retires from test cricket after 21-year career
Sumner Locke Elliott's *Rusty Bugles* banned after 3 performances at Sydney's New Theatre
Rex Ingamells edits *The Jindyworobak Review*; Ruth Park, *The Harp in the South*

1949   Communists come to power in China under Mao Zedong
Chifley government announces plans for Snowy Mountains scheme
The Chifley Labor government is defeated and Robert Menzies becomes Prime Minister
Federal parliament passes the Papua-New Guinea Act merging the two territories
Establishment of the Australian Security Intelligence Organization (ASIO)
Sidney Nolan's 'Ned Kelly' series exhibited in Paris
Gwen Meredith's *Blue Hills* first broadcast by ABC as a sequel to *The Lawsons* (1943–49); last broadcast 1976
Percival Serle, *Dictionary of Australian Biography*

1950   Inauguration of Colombo Plan for technical and educational aid to South and South-East Asia
Menzies introduces the Communist Party Dissolution Bill
Trial of communist writer Frank Hardy on the charge of 'criminal libel' arising from the publication of his novel *Power Without Glory*
Nevil Shute, *A Town Like Alice*

1950–1953   Korean War

1951   Australia, New Zealand and US (ANZUS) defence treaty signed in Washington
Communist Party Dissolution Act is declared invalid by High Court and rejected by subsequent referendum
Eric Lambert, *The Twenty Thousand Thieves*; Kenneth Mackenzie, *Dead Men Rising*

1952   Australia becomes signatory to South-East Asia Treaty Organization (SEATO)
Sir Keith Murdoch dies and son Rupert inherits large holdings in News Ltd of Adelaide
Registration of, and first publication by, Australasian Book Society
Ern Malley's Journal (1952–55)
Martin Boyd, *The Cardboard Crown*; T.A.G. Hungerford, *The Ridge and the River*; Judah Waten, *Alien Son*

1953   Queen Elizabeth's coronation at Westminster Abbey; the *Australian Women's Weekly* sells almost one million copies of coronation issue
First postwar Japanese ambassador to Australia appointed

Atomic testing begins at Woomera, SA
Inauguration of the Festival of Perth
Dymphna Cusack (ed.), *Caddie, the Story of a Barmaid* (filmed as *Caddie*, 1976); Wilfred Burchett, *Their Monstrous War*

1953–1955 Split in Labor Party over attitudes to communism and trade unions leads to formation of Democratic Labor Party

1954 Visit to Australia by Queen Elizabeth II and Prince Philip
Douglas Mawson sets up first permanent Australian station in Antarctica
Defection of Soviet diplomat and spy Vladimir Petrov
The anti-communist Australian Association for Cultural Freedom is established by Richard Krygier
Establishment of Elizabethan Theatre Trust
Overland is begun by Stephen Murray-Smith, incorporating *Realist Writer*, begun in 1952
First issue of *Poetry Magazine* (Sydney, 1954–71; later *New Poetry*)
Vance Palmer, *The Legend of the Nineties*

1955 British and Australian governments announce a new atomic testing ground in SA to be called Maralinga (Aboriginal word for thunder)
First stage of Snowy Mountains scheme declared open
Inauguration of first full-year university course in Australian Literature (at Canberra University College)
First stage appearance of Barry Humphries's character, Dame Edna Everage
Premiere of Ray Lawler's *Summer of the Seventeenth Doll* in Melbourne (filmed in America, 1960)
A.D. Hope, *The Wandering Islands*; Patrick White, *The Tree of Man*; Alan Marshall, *I Can Jump Puddles*

1956 Khrushchev publicly exposes genocide of Stalin regime
Soviet Union invasion of Hungary
British and French attack on Suez Canal
Australian troops participate in 'Emergency' (1956–60) against communist insurgents in Malaya
National Assemblies for Peace held in Melbourne and Sydney, organised by Australian Peace Council
Regular television transmission commences in Australia
Olympic Games held in Melbourne
First issues of *Quadrant* and *Westerly*

1957 Melbourne newspaper the *Argus* (1846–1957) closes
Patrick White's *Voss* is first winner of Miles Franklin Award
First issue of *Australian Letters* (1957–68)
Nino Culotta, *They're a Weird Mob*; Nevil Shute, *On the Beach* (filmed 1959)

1958 Liberal–Country Party coalition wins fifth consecutive election, assisted by Labor 'Split'

Australia's first nuclear reactor becomes operational at Lucas Heights near Sydney

National Institute of Dramatic Art (NIDA) established at University of New South Wales

Founding of Children's Book Council of Australia

First issues of *Nation* (1958–72) and *Melbourne Critical Review* (from 1965 the *Critical Review*)

Vincent Buckley becomes the Foundation Lockie Fellow in Australian Literature

A.A. Phillips, *The Australian Tradition*; Russel Ward, *The Australian Legend*; Randolph Stow, *To the Islands*

1959   Population of Australia reaches 10 million

The Antipodean Group of painters holds its first exhibition in Melbourne

Inauguration of the ABC's annual Boyer Lectures

Recording of Barry Humphries, *Wildlife in Suburbia*

Dorothy Hewett, *Bobbin Up*; Morris West, *The Devil's Advocate*; Judith Wright, *The Generations of Men*; R.D. FitzGerald, *The Wind at Your Door*

1960   Sir Macfarlane Burnet shares Nobel Prize for Medicine

Creation of National Library of Australia, replacing Commonwealth Library

Commonwealth Literature Censorship Board bans Vladimir Nabokov's *Lolita* and Brendan Behan's *Borstal Boy* because of sexual explicitness

Adelaide holds its inaugural Festival of the Arts

Premiere of Alan Seymour's *The One Day of the Year*

Robin Boyd, *The Australian Ugliness*; Bernard Smith, *European Vision and the South Pacific*

1961   Bay of Pigs 'invasion' of Cuba by USA fails

Unemployment reaches highest level since Second World War

Australian Institute of Aboriginal Affairs established in Canberra

Oral contraceptives for women go on sale

Current affairs program *Four Corners* goes to air on ABC television

Australian Book Review, first series (1961–74); second series begins 1978

Premiere of Patrick White's *The Ham Funeral*

H.M. Green, *A History of Australian Literature*

1962   Cuban missile crisis

Australia sends military advisers to Vietnam

Inaugural season of the Australian Ballet in Sydney

First Warana Festival in Brisbane

Barry Humphries tours Australia with *A Nice Night's Entertainment*

First chair of Australian Literature established at University of Sydney, held by G.A. Wilkes

Thea Astley, *The Well Dressed Explorer*; Manning Clark's *History of Australia* (vol. 1)

1963   Assassination of President John F. Kennedy

Richard Walsh and Richard Neville launch satirical weekly magazine, *Oz* (1963–65), with a satire on Queen Elizabeth's tour

Vincent Report of Senate Select Committee criticises the lack of Australian drama on television
Foundation of Australian Society of Authors
First issues of *Australian Literary Studies, Southern Review*, and *Art and Australia*
Hal Porter, *The Watcher on the Cast-Iron Balcony*

1964   Australian troops involved in 'confrontation' of Malaysia by Indonesia (1964–66)
The Beatles tour Australia
Rupert Murdoch establishes the *Australian* as the first national newspaper
First issues of *Poetry Australia* and *Australian Literary Studies*
The Literature of Australia, edited by Geoffrey Dutton
Donald Horne, *The Lucky Country*; George Johnston, *My Brother Jack*; Kath Walker (later Oodgeroo Noonuccal), *We Are Going*

1965   Prime Minister Menzies commits first Australian troops to Vietnam War
Indonesian President Sukarno overthrown by military after abortive communist coup
Unilateral Declaration of Independence by Prime Minister Ian Smith of Rhodesia
Colin Roderick is appointed to the Foundation Chair of Australian Literature at James Cook University
D.H. Lawrence's *Lady Chatterley's Lover* and Vladimir Nabokov's *Lolita* are taken off the Commonwealth's list of banned books
First issue of *Journal of Commonwealth Literature*
Peter Cowan, *The Empty Street*; Colin Johnson (later Mudrooroo), *Wild Cat Falling*; Randolph Stow, *The Merry-go-round in the Sea*

1966   First conscripts leave for Vietnam; battle of Long Tan
General Suharto assumes power in Indonesia
Sir Robert Menzies retires after a record term as Prime Minister
Western Mining Corporation mines nickel ore deposits at Kambalda, WA; 'mineral boom' gathers momentum
Japan becomes Australia's main overseas customer
Introduction of decimal currency
Peter Kocan shoots and wounds Arthur Calwell, leader of the ALP
Jane Street Theatre opens in Sydney, intended for the exclusive production of Australian plays
First volume of *Australian Dictionary of Biography* published
Geoffrey Blainey, *The Tyranny of Distance*; Elizabeth Harrower, *The Watch Tower*

1966–1968   'Cultural Revolution' in China

1967   Execution of Che Guevara in Bolivia
North West Cape Naval Communications Station opened by Prime Minister Harold Holt; first Australian satellite launched from Woomera rocket range
Referendum allows federal parliament concurrent power with states in Aboriginal affairs and decides that Aborigines will be counted in the census

Prime Minister Harold Holt disappears while swimming near Portsea, Vic; John Gorton replaces him as Prime Minister

Ronald Ryan hanged in Pentridge Gaol, Melbourne, the last person to be executed in Australia

La Mama theatre founded in Melbourne by Betty Burstall

Thomas Keneally, *Bring Larks and Heroes*

1968   'Prague Spring'; Soviet invasion of Czechoslovakia

Student riots in Paris and elsewhere in Europe

Discovery of Aboriginal bones at Lake Mungo, NSW, proves Aborigines had inhabited Australia for at least 25 000 years

The woodchip industry begins at Eden, NSW

Establishment of the Australian Council of the Arts

Premiere of Alex Buzo's *Norm and Ahmed*

Rodney Hall and Thomas Shapcott edit *New Impulses in Australian Poetry*

Dorothy Hewett, *Windmill Country*

1969   Race riots in Malaysia

Commonwealth Arbitration Court rules that women should get the same pay as men for work of equal value

Completion of standard-gauge railway line between Sydney and Perth

First Australian performance of rock musical *Hair*; Woodstock popular music festival, New York

First issue of *Australian Author*

Sumner Locke Elliott, *Edens Lost*; Bruce Dawe, *Beyond the Subdivisions*

1970   200th anniversary of Captain Cook's arrival at Botany Bay: visits to Australia by Queen Elizabeth II and Pope Paul VI

The first Vietnam War moratorium marches held in Melbourne and other cities

WA then NSW are first states to lower voting age to 18

The Pram Factory in Melbourne becomes headquarters of the Australian Performing Group (APG); Nimrod Theatre founded in Sydney

Kevin Gilbert's *The Cherry Pickers* becomes the first Aboriginal play to be performed

University of Queensland Press begins extensive publishing of Australian literature

The Annals of Australian Literature (2nd edn 1992)

Germaine Greer, *The Female Eunuch*; Barry Oakley, *A Salute to the Great McCarthy*

1971   Census shows Australian population is 12 755 638, including (for the first time following the referendum of 1967) all Aborigines

Qld government approves sand mining on Fraser Island

Jack Mundey, secretary of NSW Builders' Labourers' Federation, launches first 'green ban'

Conviction in London on obscenity charges of the editors of *Oz* (later overturned)

Penguin Books convicted in Victoria for the publication of Philip Roth's novel *Portnoy's Complaint*
Foundation of Currency Press
Premieres of David Williamson's *Don's Party* and Dorothy Hewett's *The Chapel Perilous*
David Ireland, *The Unknown Industrial Prisoner*; James McAuley, *Collected Poems*

1972   President Nixon visits China
President Ferdinand Marcos declares martial law in the Philippines
Gough Whitlam leads Australian Labor Party to government, withdraws last troops from Vietnam and ends conscription
Aborigines demanding land rights set up tent 'embassy' in front of Parliament House in Canberra
Formation of the Women's Electoral Lobby
Lake Pedder in Tasmania drowned despite a campaign to save it
Premiere of Jack Hibberd's *A Stretch of the Imagination*; first performance of Katharine Susannah Prichard's *Brumby Innes* (written 1927)
First issues of *Tabloid Story*, *Nation Review*, and *Cleo*
Michael Dransfield, *Drug Poems* and *The Inspector of Tides*; Frank Moorhouse, *The Americans, Baby*; Thomas Keneally, *The Chant of Jimmie Blacksmith* (filmed by Fred Schepisi in 1978)

1973   Fascist junta murders Chilean President Salvador Allende
Elizabeth II as Queen of Australia opens the Sydney Opera House
Three-year trade agreement signed between Australia and People's Republic of China; Whitlam becomes the first Australian Prime Minister to visit China
The end of preferential tariff agreements between Australia and the UK follows lengthy negotiations for entry of Britain to European Common Market
The National Gallery of Australia purchases Jackson Pollock's *Blue Poles*
Establishment of Australian Film and Television School
Literature Board replaces the Commonwealth Literary Fund
Patrick White becomes the first Australian to win the Nobel Prize for Literature

1974   Nixon resigns as a result of the Watergate scandal
New immigration policies effectively end 'White Australia' policy
'Advance Australia Fair' becomes the new national anthem ('God Save the Queen' is reinstated 1976)
Cyclone Tracy devastates Darwin
Whitlam government abolishes tuition fees for tertiary education
First issue of *Cinema Papers*
Inauguration of the *Age* Book of the Year, National Book Council and Patrick White literary awards
Premiere of Alex Buzo's *Coralie Lansdowne Says No*
Peter Carey, *The Fat Man in History*; John Docker, *Australian Cultural Elites*

| 1975 | Saigon falls to North Vietnam; Whitlam government accepts a thousand refugees from South Vietnam |

1975 — Saigon falls to North Vietnam; Whitlam government accepts a thousand refugees from South Vietnam
Khmer Rouge under Pol Pot seize power in Cambodia
Papua New Guinea achieves independence
Indonesia invades East Timor; five Australian journalists are killed
Governor-General, Sir John Kerr, dismisses Whitlam Labor government; Malcolm Fraser forms a caretaker government and wins the subsequent election
Australian divorce laws liberalised by Family Law Act
The SA Labor government of Don Dunstan is first to legalise homosexual relations between consenting male adults
First honours under the Order of Australia initiated by Whitlam government
Introduction of colour television
Foundation of the Australia Council, incorporating the Literature Board
Peter Weir's film *Picnic at Hanging Rock*
Premiere of John Romeril's *The Floating World*
First issue of *Hecate: A Women's Interdisciplinary Journal*
David Malouf, *Johnno*; Anne Summers, *Damned Whores and God's Police*; 'B. Wongar', *The Trackers*

1976 — Death of Mao Zedong
Sir Douglas Nicholls becomes first Aboriginal governor (SA)
The bones of Truganini, reputedly the last full-blood Tasmanian Aborigine, are cremated on hundredth anniversary of her death
Foundation of Melbourne's Playbox Theatre
Release of the Australian films *Caddie, Don's Party, The Devil's Playground*
Robert Drewe, *The Savage Crows*; David Walker, *Dream and Disillusion*; Les Murray, *The Vernacular Republic*

1977 — Don Chipp forms the Australian Democrats
Queensland premier Joh Bjelke-Petersen bans street marches
Kerry Packer challenges the cricket establishment by creating World Series Cricket, aimed at television audiences
The *Canberra Times* becomes the first Australian newspaper to introduce complete computer typesetting
Formation of the Association for the Study of Australian Literature (ASAL)
Premiere of Louis Nowra's *Inner Voices*
First issue of *Journal of Australian Studies*
Colleen McCullough, *The Thorn Birds*; Helen Garner, *Monkey Grip*

1978 — First arrival of refugee 'boat people' in Darwin from Vietnam
First Sydney Gay and Lesbian Mardi Gras
Fred Schepisi's film *The Chant of Jimmie Blacksmith* released
The Cake Man by Robert Merritt is first play published by a Black Australian
Jessica Anderson, *Tirra Lirra by the River*; C.J. Koch, *The Year of Living Dangerously*; Peter Porter, *The Cost of Seriousness*; David Malouf, *An Imaginary Life*

1978–1979 — Iranian revolution; the Ayatollah Khomeini returned from exile in 1979

1979 China–Vietnam war
Inauguration of the New South Wales Premier's Literary Awards
First issues of *Island* magazine, and of the journal *Kunapipi*, published in Denmark until 1995
Premiere of Jack Davis's *Kullark* (published 1982)
Patrick White, *The Twyborn Affair*; Gabrielle Carey and Kathy Lette, *Puberty Blues*; John Tranter's controversial anthology, *The New Australian Poetry*

1979–1988 USSR fighting in Afghanistan

1980 Robert Mugabe becomes the first Prime Minister of an independent Zimbabwe (formerly Rhodesia)
Dispute at Noonkanbah, WA, over oil drilling on Aboriginal sacred site
Australia's first 'test tube' baby born in Melbourne
Manning Clark declared Australian of the Year
The Australian–Vogel National Literary Award begins
Clive James, *Unreliable Memoirs*; Shirley Hazzard, *The Transit of Venus*

1980–1988 Iran–Iraq war

1981 *The Oxford History of Australian Literature*
The Macquarie Dictionary
First issue of *Scripsi*
Drusilla Modjeska, *Exiles at Home*; Eric Rolls, *A Million Wild Acres*; Albert Facey, *A Fortunate Life*

1982 British–Argentinian war over Falkland Islands
Labor wins office in Vic after 27 years
Aborigines at Hermannsburg mission, NT, obtain freehold title to their land
Opening of Australian National Gallery in Canberra
Thomas Keneally awarded the Booker Prize for *Schindler's Ark*
Premiere of Alma de Groen's *The Rivers of China*
Peter Weir directs *The Year of Living Dangerously*
Mad Max II becomes greatest financial success of Australian films
First issue of *Australian Short Stories*
Blanche d'Alpuget, *Robert J. Hawke*; Olga Masters, *The Home Girls*

1983 Bob Hawke leads ALP to federal election victory; remains PM until 1991
Ash Wednesday bushfires
Federal government prevents further work on Franklin Dam, Tas
Sex Discrimination Act passed
Alan Bond's yacht *Australia II* wins America's Cup
Elizabeth Jolley, *Mr Scobie's Riddle* and *Miss Peabody's Inheritance*; Brian Castro, *Birds of Passage*

1984 Assassination of Indian Prime Minister Indira Gandhi
'Advance Australia Fair' again becomes national anthem
Geoffrey Blainey criticises rate of Asian migration to Australia
National Film and Sound Archive opens in Canberra
Foundation of multicultural journal *Outrider*

Bernard Smith, *The Boy Adeodatus*; Rosa Cappiello, *Oh Lucky Country* (translated from her 1981 *Paese Fortunato*)

1985   Mikhail Gorbachev elected General Secretary of Soviet Communist Party
Explosive placed by French secret service agents sinks Greenpeace ship *Rainbow Warrior*, Auckland
ANZUS crisis arises from New Zealand's ban on nuclear warships
Rupert Murdoch becomes US citizen, buys majority shares in Twentieth-Century Fox film company and Fox Television Inc.
First Melbourne Spoleto Festival (later the Melbourne International Festival of the Arts)
The Oxford Companion to Australian Literature (second edition 1994)
Judith Wright, *Phantom Dwelling*

1986   'People Power' revolution in Philippines; Corazon Aquino becomes president
US space shuttle *Challenger* explodes shortly after take-off; Soviet *Mir I* space station launched
Queen Elizabeth signs Australia Bill in Canberra, severing remaining legal ties with Britain
Treasurer Paul Keating responds to currency crisis by calling Australia a 'banana republic'
The first 'lap top' computer introduced in USA
Jack Davis, *No Sugar*; Kate Grenville, *Lilian's Story*; Philip Hodgins, *Blood and Bone*

1987   Iran launches missile attack on Baghdad
American (and global) stock exchange crash
Military coups in Fiji
The first national Black Playwrights' Conference and Workshop is held in Canberra
Founding of *Antipodes*—journal of the American Association for Australian Literary Studies
The Oxford Literary Guide to Australia
Sally Morgan, *My Place*; Robert Hughes, *The Fatal Shore*; Paul Carter, *The Road to Botany Bay*; Laurie Duggan, *The Ash Range*; Bruce Chatwin, *Songlines*; Alma de Groen, *The Rivers of China*

1988   Queen Elizabeth opens new Parliament House
Burnum Burnum takes possession of Great Britain on behalf of the Aboriginal people
Bicentenary of the British landing at Botany Bay; in protest Patrick White and Judith Wright refuse to publish in this year
World Expo in Brisbane
Peter Carey's *Oscar and Lucinda* wins the Booker Prize
The Australian National Dictionary
The Penguin New Literary History of Australia
John Forbes, *The Stunned Mullet*; Rodney Hall, *Captivity Captive*; Janette Turner Hospital, *Charades*

1989   Massacre in Tiananmen Square, Beijing

In Iran, Ayatollah Khomeini issues fatwa against Salman Rushdie
Fall of the Berlin Wall
Writer Václav Havel elected President of Czechoslovakia
Gwen Harwood, *Bone Scan*; Robert Adamson, *The Clean Dark*; Rodney Hall, *Kisses of the Enemy*

1990   Nelson Mandela released from prison in South Africa
Australian troops sent to the Gulf War; Iraq defeated in 1991
Formation of the Aboriginal and Torres Strait Islander Commission (ATSIC)
Inauguration of Canberra's National Festival of Australian Theatre
Death of Patrick White
Dame Joan Sutherland gives her final operatic performances in Sydney
First performances of Jimmie Chi's play *Bran Nue Dae* and Hannie Rayson's *Hotel Sorrento* (filmed in 1995)

1991   Assassination of Indian prime minister Rajiv Gandhi
Following collapse of the USSR, Boris Yeltsin becomes President of Russian Federation
Paul Keating replaces Bob Hawke as Prime Minister
Vincent Buckley, *Last Poems*; Tim Winton, *Cloudstreet*; David Marr, *Patrick White: a Life*

1992   Mabo land rights decision of the High Court of Australia
Anglican Church in Australia approves ordination of women
Beth Yahp, *The Crocodile Fury*

1993   Mandawuy Yunupingu of the group Yothu Yindi becomes the first Aborigine to be named Australian of the Year
Fotini Epanomitis, *The Mule's Foal*; John Scott, *What I Have Written* (filmed 1996)

1994   Nelson Mandela becomes first Black President of South Africa
Cultural debate between members of the literary community and the Literature Board of the Australia Council over small magazines and the allocation of writing grants
Dorothy Porter, *The Monkey's Mask*

1995   Resumption of French nuclear testing in the Pacific
Beatification of Mother Mary McKillop
John Kinsella, *The Silo*

1995–1996   Controversies over *The First Stone* by Helen Garner (1995) and *The Hand that Signed the Paper* by Helen Demidenko (Darville) (1994)

1996   John Howard ends thirteen years of Labor rule and becomes Prime Minister
Port Arthur massacre leads to stricter gun laws
Success of Australian film *Shine*: Oscar for Geoffrey Rush
David Malouf wins the Impac Dublin Literary Award for *Remembering Babylon*; Les Murray wins T.S. Eliot Prize for *Subhuman Redneck Poems*
First issue of *Heat*
Robert Dessaix, *Night Letters*; David Foster, *The Glade Within the Grove*; Thea Astley, *The Multiple Effects of Rainshadow*

1997   Death of Diana, Princess of Wales; death of Mother Teresa
        BHP announces that it will close the Newcastle steel works
        Controversial resignation of Robert Manne as editor of *Quadrant*
        Robert Drewe, *The Drowner*; Peter Carey, *Jack Maggs*; Delia Falconer, *The
        Service of Clouds*; Mark Davis, *Gangland*

1998   Economic crisis in some Asian countries; resulting unrest in Indonesia leads
        to resignation of President Suharto
        Constitutional convention on the question of an Australian republic
        Major waterfront dispute is a test case for Industrial Relations Act of Howard
        government
        Oxford Companion to Australian History

Sources used for the compilation of this Chronology include:
The Oxford History of Australia, gen. ed. Geoffrey Bolton, vols 1–5 (Melbourne: Oxford University Press, 1986–90); *Australians: Events and Places*, ed. by Graeme Aplin, S.G. Foster, Michael McKernan, a volume in *Australians: A Historical Library* (Broadway, N.S.W.: Fairfax, Syme and Weldon, 1987); the *Annals of Australian Literature*, 2nd edition, by Joy Hooton and Harry Heseltine (Melbourne: Oxford University Press, 1992); the *Oxford Companion to Australian Literature*, 2nd edition, ed. by William H. Wilde, Joy Hooton and Barry Andrews (Melbourne: Oxford University Press, 1994); the *Companion to Theatre in Australia*, gen. editor Philip Parsons (Sydney: Currency Press, 1995); *A History of Australian Literature* by Ken Goodwin (London: Macmillan, 1986).

Notes on Contributors

Bruce Bennett was born in Subiaco, Western Australia, in 1941. A graduate of the Universities of Western Australia, Oxford and London, he taught at the University of Western Australia from 1968 until 1992 and is now Professor and Head of the School of English at University College, University of New South Wales, at the Australian Defence Force Academy, Canberra. He has travelled widely and held visiting appointments at universities in Europe, North America and Asia. His many publications include a critical biography, *Spirit in Exile: Peter Porter and his Poetry* (1991), and *An Australian Compass: Essays on Place and Direction in Australian Literature* (1991). He is co-editor of *Crossing Cultures: Essays on Literature and Culture of the Asia-Pacific* (1996).

Delys Bird was born in Kalgoorlie, Western Australia. She teaches in the English Department at the University of Western Australia in Australian Studies and Women's Studies, and is Director of the Centre for Women's Studies. She has published on Australian women's writing from the colonial period to the contemporary, and has books on women and detective fiction, *Killing Women* (1993), and an edition of Elizabeth Jolley's radio plays, *Off the Air* (1995). She has also co-edited collections of essays on Elizabeth Jolley's fiction, *New Critical Essays* (1991), and on Sally Morgan's *My Place* (1992).

Patrick Buckridge was born in Brisbane in 1947. He studied English literature at the University of Queensland, graduated in 1968, and spent five years at the University of Pennsylvania, where he completed his doctorate in Renaissance literature and returned to Brisbane in 1975. Since 1981 he has been at Griffith University, teaching mainly Australian literature. His major publication to date is *The Scandalous Penton* (1994), a biography of the Sydney novelist and journalist Brian Penton. He has also published articles and chapters on literary canons and institutions in Australia, and on individual Australian writers.

Adrian Caesar was born near Manchester, UK, in 1955, and was educated at the University of Reading. He subsequently worked as a tutor at the University of New England and is now Senior Lecturer in English at University College, University of New South Wales, at the Australian Defence Force Academy. His publications include three books of literary and cultural criticism and a book of poems: *Dividing Lines: Poetry, Class and Ideology in the 1930s* (1991), *Taking it Like a Man: Suffering, Sexuality and the War Poets* (1993), *Kenneth Slessor* (1995) and *Hunger Games* (1996).

Robert Dixon is Professor of English at the University of Southern Queensland. Born in Sydney and educated at the University of Sydney, he has taught at the University of Sydney, the University of Newcastle, Curtin University and James Cook University. He has published widely on Australian literature, post-colonial literatures, cultural studies and Australian art history, and is the author of *The Course of Empire: Neo-classical Culture in New South Wales 1788–1860* (1986) and *Writing the Colonial Adventure: Race, Gender and Nation in Anglo-Australian Popular Fiction, 1875–1914* (1995).

Carole Ferrier is Associate Professor of English at the University of Queensland where she has been teaching courses on class, gender and race in relation to literature for nearly twenty-five years. She published *Gender, Politics and Fiction* (1982), perhaps the key early anthology of feminist criticism of Australian literature, and a volume of the letters between six Australian women novelists, *As Good as a Yarn with You* (1992). Her biography of Jean Devanny will be published by Melbourne University Press in 1999. She has been editor of *Hecate: A Women's Interdisciplinary Journal* since its inception in 1975.

Dennis Haskell is a poet, critic and editor who has taught at the University of Sydney and is now Associate Professor and Associate Dean of Arts at the University of Western Australia. He has been an editor of the literary magazine *Westerly* since 1985, and has published twelve books of poetry or literary criticism. He has edited *Kenneth Slessor* (1981). His two collections of poems are *Abracadabra* (1993) and *The Ghost Names Sing* (1997).

Susan Lever was born in Sydney, and educated at the Australian National University and the University of Sydney. She teaches mainly Australian literature at University College, University of New South Wales, at the Australian Defence Force Academy. She has published a literary history of Australian writing in the immediate postwar years, *A Question of Commitment* (1989), and edited the *Oxford Book of Australian Women's Verse* (1995). With Catherine Pratt she has edited *Henry Handel Richardson: The Getting of Wisdom, Stories, Selected Prose and Correspondence* for University of Queensland Press (1997).

Susan K. Martin is a Lecturer in the School of English at La Trobe University, Melbourne. Her PhD from Monash University was a study of ideas of the self and the environment in nineteenth-century Australian women's fiction. From 1989 until 1990 she was a Visiting Fulbright Postdoctoral Fellow at Amherst College in Massachusetts. She teaches and researches in the areas of nineteenth- and twentieth-century Australian literature and culture, women's writing and Victorian literature.

Richard Nile was born in Moora, Western Australia, in 1958 and educated at the University of Western Australia and the University of New South Wales. He was the deputy director of the Australian Studies Centre at the University of London (1989–92), during which time he pioneered Australian Studies programs in central and eastern Europe. He is editor of the *Journal of Australian Studies* and Director of the Australian Studies Centre at the University of Queensland. His books include *Cultural Atlas of Australia, New Zealand and the Pacific* (1995), *Australian Civilisation* (1994) and, with Ffion Murphy, *The Gate of Dreams* (1990).

Elizabeth Perkins is Associate Professor of English in the School of Languages, Literature and Communication at James Cook University, Townsville. She has published extensively in Australian literature and has a special interest in comparative contemporary drama. She has edited from manuscript Charles Harpur's *Poems* (Sydney, 1984) and his verse drama *Stalwart the Bush Ranger* (Sydney, 1987).

Adam Shoemaker is a Senior Lecturer in Australian Studies at the Queensland University of Technology and chaired the Brisbane Writers Festival in 1996 and 1997. He first came to Australia from Canada in 1980 as a Commonwealth Scholar and completed a doctorate at the Australian National University. He has worked in a variety of fields, including academia, arts management and public affairs. He is the author of *Black Words, White Page* (1989) and *Mudrooroo: A Critical Study* (1993). He also co-edited (with Jack Davis, Mudrooroo and Stephen Muecke) *Paperbark* (1990), the first national anthology of Black Australian writing. His most recent work is the edited volume *Oodgeroo: A Tribute* (1995).

Jennifer Strauss was born in 1933 at Heywood, Victoria. She is Associate Professor in the Department of English at Monash University. Her most recent publications include *Tierra del Fuego: New and Selected Poems* (1997); critical monographs on Gwen Harwood (2nd edition 1996) and Judith Wright (1995), and she edited *The Oxford Book of Australian Love Poems* (1993) and *Family Ties: Australian Poems of the Family* (1998). She is currently working on an edition of the Collected Poems of Mary Gilmore.

Helen Thomson was born in 1943 in Melbourne. She is Senior Lecturer in the Department of English at Monash University. She has edited several editions of the work of

Catherine Helen Spence, including the University of Queensland Press *Catherine Helen Spence* (1987), and published a number of chapters on Australian women writers. She was the Melbourne theatre reviewer for the *Australian* newspaper from 1979 until 1995, when she became senior theatre reviewer for the *Age* newspaper.

Graeme Turner was born in Sydney, educated in Australia, Canada and the United Kingdom, and is currently Professor of Cultural Studies and Head of the Department of English at the University of Queensland. He is the author of *National Fictions* (1986), *Film as Social Practice* (1988), *British Cultural Studies* (1990), *Making it National* (1994), *Literature, Journalism and the Media* (1996), *Myths of Oz* (1987) (with John Fiske and Bob Hodge), and the editor of a number of collections of Australian cultural and media studies including (with Stuart Cunningham) *The Media in Australia* (1993).

Chris Wallace-Crabbe was born in Richmond, Melbourne, in 1934. He taught in the English Department at the University of Melbourne from 1968 and held a personal chair there from 1987 to 1997. His first book of poems was *The Music of Division* (1959). His *Selected Poems 1956–1994* won the *Age* Book of the Year Prize for 1995, while his most recent critical study is *Falling into Language* (1990). He has travelled widely and held the visiting chair in Australian Studies at Harvard University in 1987–88.

INDEX